W9-BGQ-969

JAPAN'S FOREIGN POLICY
1868–1941

Studies of the
East Asian Institute,
Columbia University

JAPAN'S FOREIGN POLICY

1868–1941

A Research
Guide

EDITED BY

James William Morley

COLUMBIA
University Press
New York and London
1974

Library of Congress
Cataloging in Publication Data

Morley, James William, 1921–
    A guide to Japanese foreign policy.

    1. Japan—Foreign relations—1868–1912.
2. Japan—Foreign relations—1912–1945.   I. Title.
DS881.9.M63   327.52   73–18254
ISBN 0-231-08996-x

Copyright © 1974 Columbia University Press
Printed in the United States of America

to Kurihara Ken

The East Asian Institute
of Columbia University

The East Asian Institute of Columbia University was established in 1949 to prepare graduate students for careers dealing with East Asia, and to aid research and publication on East Asia during the modern period. The faculty of the Institute are grateful to the Ford Foundation and the Rockefeller Foundation for their financial assistance.

The Studies of the East Asian Institute were inaugurated in 1962 to bring to a wider public the results of significant new research on modern and contemporary East Asia.

Contributors

JAMES B. CROWLEY, Associate Professor of History, Yale University, is the author of *Japan's Quest for Autonomy* (1960), and editor of *Modern East Asia: Essays in Interpretation* (1969).

SHINKICHI ETO is Professor of International Relations at the University of Tokyo. His recent works include *Higashi Ajia seijishi kenkyū* (Studies in East Asian political history) (1968); *Sekai no naka no Chūgoku* (China in world politics), with T. Okabe (1969); *Nihon no shinro* (Prospects for Japan) (1970); and "Moderation and Radicalism in the Chinese Revolution," in James B. Crowley, ed., *Modern East Asia: Essays in Interpretation* (1969).

CHIHIRO HOSOYA, Professor of International Relations, Hitotsubashi University, is the author of *Shiberia shuppei no shiteki kenkyū* (A historical study of the Siberian intervention) (1955); coauthor of *Taiheiyō sensō e no michi* (The road to the Pacific War), Vol. V, *Sangoku dōmei: Nisso chūritsu jōyaku* (The Tripartite Pact: The Japanese-Soviet neutrality treaty) (1963); coauthor and coeditor of *Nichi-Bei kankei shi* (A history of Japanese-U.S. relations) (4 vols., 1971); and author of *Roshia kakumei to Nihon* (The Russian revolution and Japan), forthcoming.

FRANK W. IKLÉ is Chairman, Department of History, University of New Mexico. He is the author of *German-Japanese Relations, 1936-1940* (1957); "Japanese-German Peace Negotiations during World War I," *The American Historical Review*, LXXI, No. 1 (October 1965), 62–76; and "The Triple Intervention: Japan's Lesson in the Diplomacy of Imperialism," *Monumenta Nipponica*, XXII (1967), 122–30.

AKIRA IRIYE, Professor of American Diplomatic History at the University of Chicago, is the author of *After Imperialism: The Search for a New Order in the Far East, 1921–1931* (1964); *Across the Pacific: An Inner History of American-East Asian Relations* (1967); and *Pacific Estrangement: Japanese and American Expansion, 1897–1911* (1972).

JAMES WILLIAM MORLEY, Professor of Government at Columbia University, is author of *The Japanese Thrust into Siberia, 1918* (1957); editor with Kuo Ting-yee of *Sino-Japanese Relations, 1862–1927* (1965); editor and contributor to *Dilemmas of Growth in Prewar Japan* (1972) and to *Forecast for Japan: Security in the 1970s* (1972).

IAN NISH is Senior Lecturer in International History at the London School of Economics and Political Science, having taught previously at the University of Sydney. He is the author of *The Anglo-Japanese Alliance: The Diplomacy of Two Island Empires, 1894–1907* (1966); and *Alliance in Decline, 1908–1923* (1971).

SHUMPEI OKAMOTO, Associate Professor of History at Temple University, is the author of *The Japanese Oligarchy and the Russo-Japanese War* (1970); and coeditor with Dorothy Borg of *Pearl Harbor as History: Japanese-American Relations, 1931–1941* (1973).

ROBERT S. SCHWANTES is Vice-President for Programs of The Asia Foundation. He is author of *Japanese and Americans: A Century of Cultural Relations* (1955).

ARTHUR E. TIEDEMANN is Professor of History at the City College of the City University of New York. He is the author of *Modern Japan: A Brief History* (2d rev. ed., 1962); and "Liberalism between the Wars" in *Sources of Japanese Tradition*, compiled by Ryusaku Tsunoda, Wm. Theodore de Bary, and Donald Keene (1958).

Introduction

James William Morley

———◆———

In recent years on both sides of the Pacific, the study of the history of Japan's modern foreign relations has taken a new and promising turn. Before World War II, few official Japanese sources were available. Few memoirs were published—and those that were, were frequently unenlightening. Thus, few Japanese monographs were able to rise above patriotic speculation, legalistic defense, or generalized Marxist criticism, and the little writing done abroad was usually by Western scholars who rarely had the knowledge to do more than to reflect the reports of Western newsmen and diplomats. But since 1945 the situation has changed remarkably.

The War Crimes Trials in 1946–47 began a process of revelation which has not yet stopped. Important ministries of the government have unlocked their files, prestigious personnages have published their memoirs, leading families have opened private papers, until it is possible that, in the amount of documentation available on its foreign relations from the last half of the nineteenth through the first half of the twentieth century, Japan has become second only to the United States. Inevitably this treasure-trove has caught the imagination of Japan's scholars. Some, to be sure, have continued the more or less polemical writing of the past, but an impressive number, particularly of the younger generation, have turned a new corner. Disillusioned by the trauma of defeat and occupation, and also in a sense liberated by it, they have become animated by a spirit of democratic positivism. They are working to break through the cocoon of ideology and the confines of culture to ask simply and directly, what happened and why. They are seeking their answers primarily in Japanese sources never before used, and in addition are searching relevant foreign materials and exploring the use of various Western social science methodologies.

At the same time, a new group of scholars of modern Japanese foreign relations has arisen in the West as well, particularly in the United States and Britain. They have been animated by a similar objective, positivist spirit; and similarly they have been eager to use Japanese sources as fully as may be, to enliven themselves with as intimate an understanding of Japanese society as possible, and to seek the collegial advice of their fellow scholars in Japan. The result over the past twenty years or so has been the publication in Japan and abroad of a large number of source materials and critical monographs.

Partly to take the measure of this new research and partly to give the developing field a sense of direction, a conference was held at Buck Hill Falls, Pennsylvania, on January 28–31, 1963, under the sponsorship of the Japan Foreign Relations Project of the East Asian Institute of Columbia University, with support from the Ford Foundation. An international group of scholars was assembled, including: Ardath Burks, Rutgers—The State University; Robert J. C. Butow, University of Washington; Hilary Conroy, University of Pennsylvania; James B. Crowley, Yale University; Etō Shinkichi, Tokyo University; Hosoya Chihiro, Hitotsubashi University; Akira Iriye, University of Chicago; Marius Jansen, Princeton University; James W. Morley, Columbia University; Ian H. Nish, London School of Economics; Herbert Passin, Columbia University; Hugh Patrick, Yale University; Warner Schilling, Columbia University; Robert Schwantes, Asia Foundation; Arthur E. Tiedemann, City University of New York; George Totten, University of Southern California; Robert Ward, University of Michigan; Herschel Webb, Columbia University; and C. Martin Wilbur, Columbia University. Others who sent papers but were unable to attend included: Peter Berton, University of Southern California; Fujii Shigeru, Kobe University; Horie Yasuzō, Kyoto University; Ohara Keishi, Hitotsubashi University; and Sasaki Seiji, Kobe University. Lewis Austin, Yale University, and Donald Thurston, Union College, served as rapporteurs.

Two general conclusions arose from this conference: the need for a critical guide to the field as it now exists, and the need for the exploration of some new avenues of research. With the assistance of Dale K. A. Finlayson of the East Asian Institute, William F. Morton of York College, City University of New York, and Shumpei Okamoto of Temple University, the present volume was prepared to meet at least partially the need for a guide to the literature. It is divided into two parts: Critical Essays and Bibliography. The essays were drawn from revised versions of several of the papers presented at the Buck Hill Falls conference, to which have been added additional ones by Frank W. Iklé of the University of New Mexico and Arthur E. Tiedemann to round out the volume. The Bibliography is in two parts. The first, entitled "Standard Works," consists of the books and articles mentioned in the Essays. In the Essays they are given in short form only and at points relevant to the topic at hand; in the Bibliography they are all combined into one alphabetically arranged list, with complete bibliographic information. To the "Standard Works" has been appended a second list of "Recent Works," compiled by Shumpei Okamoto and including books published generally in the years from 1963 to 1971.

The original conception of the essays was that each should survey one coherent area of the history of modern Japanese foreign relations, summarizing succinctly the current state of knowledge in that particular area, giving a critical introduction to the sources and monographs relevant to it, and suggesting directions in which future research might profitably be oriented. Since the need at this stage was for a taxonomy, both of subject matters and materials, it was early apparent that a principle of relevance would have to be agreed upon or at least hypothesized. The principle selected was authoritative government policy; that is, subject matters and materials would be adjudged relevant to the study of modern Japanese foreign relations to the extent that they had a discernible bearing on the foreign policy authoritatively formulated and executed by the government.

This conceptual framework has three implications. First of all, it means that the central concern is the actions of the Japanese government. This is not to imply that the foreign relations of private individuals and non-governmental organizations are unimportant. In Japan, as in most modern countries, the political parties, trade unions, business federations, and other unofficial groups have often engaged in foreign relations of their own and recommended their own proposals for policy to the government and the people. But these various activities are here integrated into an overall understanding of the foreign relations process by considering them in their relationship to the same core of concern, namely, government action.

Second, it means that within the government the core concern is with action that is authoritative. One must recognize, of course, particularly in the prewar period, that governmental decisions were frequently formulated at other than authoritative levels and that different government agencies frequently pursued different policies; but again these are made part of the subject depending on their relevance to the action of responsible authorities.

Third, it makes policy the authoritative action to be stressed. Much of the postwar scholarship has probed the sources to find out specifically who made certain foreign policy decisions, by what process, and why. But in only a few cases have attempts been made to interrelate a number of decisions meaningfully over a fairly long period of time. Bricks have been baked, but few walls have been built. It was decided, therefore, to try to relate these various studies to each other by developing a taxonomy of policy.

A policy here is seen as a coherent sequence of related decisions. The supposition is that each such policy can be analyzed in itself. There can be, first of all, the history of the policy: its origin, execution, and termination; and second, its analysis in terms of decision-makers—or over time, policy-makers—their changing definitions of the situation and the determinants of their behavior. In addition, the policies so identified can be analyzed in their relation to other policies, sequentially and contemporaneously. Moreover, it is recognized that policies are of different orders of complexity.

The essay writers were resolved to look for the largest and most comprehensive policies or policy clusters, for what might be termed strategic policies, suggesting then the policies or sub-policies which formed part of this cluster or strategy, and the decisions that were taken within these policies and sub-policies. It was hoped that by drawing up such a policy taxonomy, promising new areas for research would be uncovered and suitable elements for comparison would be identified which, when studied together by others, might be expected to yield tentative hypotheses about the kinds of men who have made policy in Japan as well as the kinds of problems, the kinds of conceptions, the kinds of aims, and the kinds of means which appealed to them. With this approach in mind, the history of Japan's foreign policy was divided into eight subject areas: three functional ones—military, economic, and cultural; and five regional ones— policy toward China, Germany, Great Britain, Russia, and the United States.

It will be apparent to the reader that the conceptual scheme could not be applied equally well in all cases. The fact is that none of the subject areas have been completely researched, so that each writer had to do more than simply survey and classify existing monographic studies. Writers on the functional areas in particular had to start almost from scratch, not because there were no sources available, but because up to now these areas have not usually been treated in Japan as subjects of foreign policy study. Consequently, definitions needed to be worked out, boundaries hypothesized, and preliminary research done by the writers themselves in order to suggest how these subject areas might be developed. Curiously enough, the China area also turned out to be exceedingly difficult to survey in this fashion, the reason in this case being the overwhelming host of materials and interpretations which will require the work of many scholars to synthesize. These special circumstances have naturally affected the closeness with which individual writers have followed the conceptual scheme; and it may be that where they deviate the most, they make most excitingly apparent the fruitfulness of further study in these hitherto neglected areas.

Questions of a different kind also emerged in the course of the work. One of these was the question of what criteria could be developed for telling when a sequence of decisions should be deemed important enough to be called a policy and when policies should be considered so interdependent as to be treated as a policy cluster or strategy. Judgments differed on individual specific cases and no doubt this will always be so. But another question seemed more fundamental: was the Japanese government's authoritative behavior in foreign affairs actually the product of rational, long-range decisions as implied in the policy focus? Were the actions identified by scholars as policies and strategies seen as such by the government officials who performed them? Or do they represent the constructs of scholars who may, in fact, be observing men reacting consistently to the same circumstances, but not consciously from the same policy? Is it not likely that sometimes the Japanese government planned and sometimes it did not, that sometimes it saw its way clearly, sometimes it stumbled badly, and sometimes it muddled through? Indeed, the evidence is overwhelming that this is true, so that this survey of foreign policy points to the same need which so many studies in other areas of policy point to: the need for comparative studies of the varieties of the decision-making process.

In addition, there are many other specific areas of research which are suggested in the essays that follow. Here we may note only a few of the general directions which appear particularly fruitful. One has already been alluded to: the need for more attention to be given particularly to economic and cultural affairs. The importance of economic considerations in Japanese policy has always been stated; but the surprising fact is that there are exceedingly few studies of the history of Japan's foreign economic relations, and almost no attention has been given to the careful, nonideological analysis of the interrelationship of business and politics in Japanese foreign policy. Similarly, Japanese cultural policy has not received the attention it deserves; yet it seems likely that Japan was among the first powers of the world to recognize the importance of such policy and to develop institutions to effectuate it.

The essential relationship of domestic developments to foreign relations needs much greater attention. Too often historians and political scientists alike specialize in one, to which they simply tack on the other adventitiously. A marriage between these two subjects is required. This in turn will require many new techniques drawn from the social sciences and some original thinking as well, for it is a problem not just relating to Japan, but chronic in the disciplines of history, international relations, and comparative politics.

New methods will be essential also if we are to build in a new dimension, namely, the dimension of foreign policy response. Too often the scholar has contented himself with trying to explain the policy of a given country and, at most, its origins. Rarely has he gone beyond to try to measure the effectiveness of that policy in achieving the intended purpose in the other country. If judgments are to be reached, surely this measure is crucial. The difficulty, of course, is that it requires both imaginative social science methodologies and skill and knowledge in studying and interpreting not just the one country, but the other also.

Moreover, the utility of comparison is only now beginning to be recognized. Almost nothing has been done in this area. The scholars of one country's foreign relations—in this case, Japan's—usually analyze only that, with the result that judgments about what are simply universal human reactions to certain types of problems and what are responses conditioned by peculiar circumstances of time, place, culture, or personality are exceedingly difficult to arrive at. Somehow, we must isolate key problems in foreign relations and attempt to make comparative studies of various nations' responses to them. We may then be able to say with at least a little more sureness what is unique and what is universal in a given country's history.

There is then a rich body of materials here awaiting the attention of scholars, materials which, if approached imaginatively, can be expected to form the basis for an improved understanding of Japan and its relations with the world and, beyond that, for new advances in the emerging social science of foreign relations in general. To the extent that this book calls a new generation of scholars to the opportunity, it will have achieved its purpose.

Contents

PART ONE

Critical Essays

I

Japan's Military Foreign Policies

James B. Crowley

❖

DOMESTIC SECURITY, A CONSCRIPT MILITIA, 1868–1879

With the arrival of Perry's gunboats in 1853, Japan's existence as an independent country was immediately jeopardized. The threat was almost absolute because it raised the specter of military defeat and colonization. To a degree unparalleled in western Europe, with the possible exception of Imperial Germany, domestic politics were structured by foreign affairs. This foreign challenge precipitated a political crisis that eventually contributed to the downfall of the Tokugawa system and to the restoration of imperial rule in 1868. Thereafter, the Meiji oligarchy implemented extensive reforms to strengthen the powers of the new government. The intrinsic relationship between foreign policy and the military capabilities of the government was, as Itō Masanori notes, inherent in the dual aims of "establishing diplomatic relations with the powers" and of "building the strength of the country so as not to be despised by the foreign powers."[1] That is, a strong central government was the *sine qua non* for the revocation of the unequal treaties. In turn, this was contingent upon the formation of a military establishment that was completely loyal to the new government and capable of crushing any form of violent resistance to the policies adopted by the imperial government. "First," declared the founder of the

---

[1] Itō Masanori, *Gumbatsu kōbōshi*, I (1957), 26.

modern Japanese army, Ōmura Masujirō, "prepare against civil disturbances; later, of course, prepare against foreign invasion."[2] Consequently, at the beginning of the Meiji era the foreign policies toward the powers were subordinated to the necessity of organizing a stable political government. This task also defined the primary purpose of the military planning and administrative reforms adopted during the initial decade of the Meiji era.

Although Ōmura identified the creation of a national army and the maintenance of domestic order as the two central military objectives of the new government, between 1868 and 1873 there were serious disagreements within the ruling oligarchy on basic diplomatic, fiscal, political, and military policies. In terms of this essay, two questions occasioned major difficulties. Should the new army be based on the principle of universal military conscription or be comprised of the samurai class? Should the government undertake a Korean expedition or concentrate on domestic reforms? Both questions were interrelated, and in 1871, when the Iwakura Embassy embarked on its world tour, neither had been officially resolved. At this time, political power was diffused between two groups: the councilors and the ministers. The former included the chancellor (Sanjō Sanetomi), the senior councilor (Iwakura Tomomi), and the junior councilors (Saigō Takamori, Kido Takayoshi, Itagaki Taisuke, and Ōkuma Shigenobu); the latter included the ministers and vice-ministers of each governmental department (e.g., Ōkubo Toshimichi, Inoue Kaoru, Yamagata Aritomo, Gotō Shōjirō and Etō Shimpei).[3] In principle, the councilors set basic policies and the departmental ministers assumed administrative responsibilities. Despite a verbal agreement that no important new policies would be adopted and that no new appointments as junior councilors would be made in the absence of the Iwakura Embassy, three significant steps were taken in 1873. In January the government promulgated a new conscription system; in May Ministers Etō and Gotō were designated junior councilors; and the councilors then formed an Inner Council entrusting its members with the authority to determine policies for all state affairs.

With the return of the Iwakura Embassy, the last two moves precipitated a heated controversy, one which was waged over the Korean problem.

---

[2]*Ibid.*, p. 27.

[3]Ishii Ryōsuke, *Japanese Legislation in the Meiji Era* (1958), pp. 109–35, is a good description of the government changes in early Meiji.

Saigō Takamori and the recently appointed junior councilors urged a Korean expedition; the members of the Iwakura mission (Ōkubo, Kido, and Itō Hirobumi) stridently opposed the recommendation. The resolution of this controversy was a painful affair. In October 1873, however, the councilors decided in favor of internal reform as the fundamental policy of the government. In protest, Saigō, Gotō, Itagaki, and Etō resigned their posts. To preclude the type of dissension that had emerged during the absence of the Iwakura Embassy, all departmental ministers were then designated as junior councilors. This marked the emergence of the political oligarchy that was to rule the country so successfully over the next decade and a half, i.e., Ōkubo, Itō, Inoue, and Yamagata. Subsequent to this consolidation of political and administrative power, the abandonment of the Korean campaign, and the implementation of the conscription program, the government was confronted by two forms of opposition—open civil disobedience and the popular rights movement. Both were led by the disaffected councilors—Saigō, Etō, and Itagaki. Both posed difficulties which reinforced the decision to stress domestic affairs over foreign affairs. Both were resolved mainly because of the capabilities of the new conscript army. Hence, it would seem helpful to consider briefly the formation of this army.

With the 1868 restoration, Ōmura Masujirō assumed responsibility for quelling the remnants of Tokugawa opposition and for the development of a national army. Mainly because of his studies of French military history, Ōmura was by this time an ardent advocate of a mass conscript army. As the Tokugawa government had employed French advisers, Ōmura also inherited a staff for his War Department, headed by Nishi Amane, which was equally well versed in French language and military history.[4] With this nucleus, he initiated a serious study of possible conscript systems and dispatched his chief assistant, Yamagata Aritomo, to Europe for a firsthand evaluation of the subject. Yamagata returned in the fall of 1870 convinced that Japan should organize an army composed of all subjects rather than attempt to perpetuate in a new form the traditional privileges of the samurai class. Ōmura's untimely assassination in October 1869 temporarily stymied the pursuit of this proposal. However, in 1871, when Yamagata was designated as vice-war minister, he assumed effective control over the War Department.

[4]Umetani Noboru, "Kindai Nihon guntai no seikaku keisei to Nishi Amane" (1954), pp. 19–44.

In that year General Yamada Akiyoshi also returned from a European sojourn and submitted a five-point program for the development of a new army: 1) develop a nucleus of officers that can train recruits drafted by a national conscription system; 2) enlarge in Japan the manufacture of items needed for the new army; 3) establish a public compulsory education system that includes military training as part of the curriculum; 4) after the schools are in operation, enforce a nationwide conscription program; and 5) model the conscription program on that of Switzerland, i.e., three months of active duty for all able-bodied citizens.[5] Underlying this proposal was a dominant loyalty to the emperor and the new governmental leaders, and a denial of the premise that the army belonged to the samurai class. Still, by 1873 the troops at the disposal of the government numbered only 11,600, and all of these hailed from the domains of Satsuma, Chōshū, Hizen, and Tosa. In other words, the army at the service of the new government was still essentially a collection of warriors, many of whom remained loyal to their former lords.

To rectify this potentially dangerous situation, the War Department in 1872 proposed the creation of a regular and a reserve army to be formed by the implementation of universal conscription. Through the support of Saigō, this was approved by the Council of State, and on January 10, 1873, the first conscription law was promulgated.[6] Essentially it called for three years of active service, plus another four years divided between two types of reserve obligations. Under this plan there would be a peacetime force of approximately 31,680 men, with the potential of an immediate mobilization of 46,350 men in case of a national emergency. That this program was designed to create a militia is attested by the fact that, when in full operation, the army consisted of but six battalions, divided among six military districts. Although Yamagata and his staff were oriented in terms of a modest buildup that would preserve domestic tranquillity, it is doubtful whether a similar motivation prompted the junior councilors to approve the conscription system. As mentioned earlier, Itagaki, Etō, and Gotō, like Saigō, had hopes of launching the country on a Korean expedition and were also partisans of a national army to be recruited from the samurai class. Whatever their intentions, the Korean venture was shelved and

[5]Itō, *Gumbatsu kōbōshi*, I, 38.
[6]Izu Kimio and Matsushita Yoshio, *Nihon gunji hattatsushi* (1938), pp. 194–96.

universal conscription was implemented. Moreover, all the conscripts in 1873 were drawn from the Tokyo district; in 1874 they were taken from the Osaka and Nagoya districts. This tactic bypassed the areas of the great domains and automatically altered the Satsuma, Tosa, Hizen, and Chōshū hegemony among the troops at the disposal of the government. As many of the soldiers from these han were, in fact, loyal to Saigō, Gotō, and Etō, one suspects the decision to draw the initial conscripts from other regions was not fortuitous.

Although the adoption of the conscription system and the decision to focus on domestic reform were designed to promote public tranquillity, the implementation of universal conscription, when coupled with the rejection of the Korean campaign, created much public unrest. For example, permeating the uprisings which began first in Saga in 1874 and reached their apex in the Saigō rebellion of 1877 were the slogans "oppose conscription," and "oppose elementary schools," as well as "fight Korea," "restore the daimyō to their rightful place in the government," and "expel the barbarians."[7] These internal forms of armed resistance were tantamount to civil war, and they were put down with great difficulty. It took one year and all of the new conscript soldiers to crush the Saigō rebellion. The victories of the new army were basic to the subsequent stability of the imperial government and to the realization of the sweeping social-economic-political reforms which marked Japan's emergence as a modern state. In terms of foreign policy, they provided the domestic stability that was essential to an orderly conduct of foreign policy and to gaining the confidence and respect of the powers.

PRELUDE TO EMPIRE: A PROFESSIONAL MILITARY ESTABLISHMENT, 1880–1894

From the crushing of the Saigō rebellion to the outbreak of the Sino-Japanese War, the primary mission of the imperial army and navy changed from that of a militia function to that of implementing a basic foreign policy objective of the government: the preservation of the "independence" of Korea. In this interval one witnessed a significant buildup of

---

[7]Matsushita Yoshio, *Meiji gunsei shiron*, I (1956), 438–97.

both services, the enjoining of military personnel from participation in domestic political activities, the creation of two general staffs entrusted with the "right of supreme command," and the fixing of the requirement that the army and navy ministers be drawn from the highest ranks of the two services. Essentially, in these years the army and navy, under the leadership of Ōyama Iwao, Saigō Tsugumichi, Katsura Tarō, and Kawakami Sōroku, acquired the complex administrative and command systems as well as the distinctive ideologies that would subsequently exert a profound influence on the conduct and formulation of foreign policies. Many things contributed to this transformation, among them, the political issues posed by the popular rights movement and the aftermath of the Saigō rebellion, an increasing familiarity with German political and military thinking, a conception of the Korean peninsula as a strategic threat to the security of the nation, the diplomacy of the Ch'ing dynasty vis-a-vis the Hermit Kingdom, and a remarkably talented group of individuals who wished to organize a military establishment equal, if not superior, in professional competence to any in Europe. The following sketch of the 1880–94 period is structured to show why these developments and considerations mark this interval as the genesis of the modern imperial Japanese army and navy.

The opening months of the Saigō rebellion had been hard ones for the new conscript army. As might be expected, the Army Department experienced some difficulty in coordinating the activities of the new battalions and in drafting careful operational plans. In a retrospective analysis of the conduct of this campaign, Katsura Tarō judged these difficulties to be endemic to the French system, which placed operational planning under the command of the army minister.[8] Whether this was a valid conclusion is difficult to say. By this time Katsura was already a convinced exponent of the virtues of the Prussian staff system, a consequence of his six years of study in Germany between 1871 and 1878. Katsura was also the protégé of Yamagata, and apparently he convinced both his patron and Saigō Tsugumichi that operations should be removed from the Army Department. On December 5, 1878, a few years before Helmuth von Moltke was able to effect a comparable legal change in Imperial Germany, an independent general staff, directly responsible to the emperor and charged with the right of supreme command in the conduct of operations, was formally

---

[8]Umetani Noboru, *Meiji zenki seijishi no kenkyū* (1963), pp. 145–48.

created.[9] These powers and responsibilities subsequently were written into the Meiji constitution of 1889 and provided the legal basis for the extensive influence of the general staffs on matters affecting national defense. Because of the profound historic consequences of this right of supreme command, the particular motivations and circumstances leading to its initial adoption merit some attention.

In this regard, one should mention that in 1879 Katsura was a devoted student of Prussian history and had only recently returned to Japan. His desire to organize a general staff and place it directly under the command of the emperor was, in other words, inspired mainly by his conviction that the general staff system was the most effective way to conduct operations, such as those that were necessary in the Saigō rebellion.[10] Of more immediate concern to the ministers of state, especially to Yamagata and Saigō Tsugumichi, was the insulation of the army from further involvement in the mushrooming popular rights movement. Yamagata, for example, justified the request for a separate general staff on the twin grounds that it would promote solidarity within the army by making military officers conscious of their personal obligation to serve the emperor, and that it would help to prevent officers from "bewailing the times," i.e., from becoming involved in domestic politics.[11] Within two years the soundness of Yamagata's fears and advice was recognized by all the ministers of state. On October 11, 1881 the oligarchy decided that, in view of the complex political problems associated with the drafting and implementation of a constitutional government, the services should be the main pillars of imperial rule.[12] In effect, this meant the army and navy were to be regarded as personal servants of the Throne, that they were to serve as the ultimate check against any political movement which might lead in the direction of a republican or constitutional government that would compromise the absolute authority of the emperor.[13] Preferring education and political leadership as the best means to mold a nation under an imperial rule, the

---

[9]Matsushita, *Meiji gunsei shiron*, II (1956), 7–10.

[10]Umetani, *Meiji zenki seijishi*, pp. 146–48.

[11]As cited by Yale Maxon, *Control of Japanese Foreign Policy: A Study of Civil-Military Rivalry, 1930–1945* (1957), p. 24.

[12]Matsushita, *Meiji gunsei shiron*, II, 347.

[13]Umetani, *Meiji zenki seijishi*, pp. 149–54.

oligarchy, as is well known, effectively prepared the way for the promulgation and acceptance of the 1889 Meiji constitution. The substance and results of this political strategy are, of course, beyond our purview, but one intrinsic part of this strategy called for the removal of the armed services from direct involvement in domestic politics. In 1882 an imperial edict was promulgated enjoining all members of the armed services to refrain from any type of political association, movements, and activities.[14] While the original motivations behind this edict were mixed—they included fears that "liberalism" might corrupt the officer corps and weaken its loyalty to the Throne—the principle that members of the services must avoid the realm of domestic politics soon became a standard and unquestioned axiom governing the behavior of all military personnel throughout the Meiji era. For example, in conjunction with the Meiji constitution of 1889, Army Minister Ōyama impressed forcefully upon all divisional commanders that the army must still faithfully adhere to the imperial command that military personnel avoid all political groups, programs, and associations.[15] Whatever the intent behind this framing of the edict, the injunction against politics was soon internalized within the officer corps.

Parallel with this effort to insulate military officers from domestic matters, responsibility for the maintenance of law and order was gradually transferred to the newly created Home Ministry. One should mark, in this regard, the role of military leaders (particularly Yamagata and Saigō Tsugumichi) in organizing the ministry. Whether this should be included as part of a study of the military and foreign policy is difficult to decide. Setting aside the experience and political influence acquired by these men in creating the Home Ministry, the formation of an effective police system relieved the army of its hitherto primary mission, the preservation of domestic order. To this extent, the efficiency of the Home Ministry certainly contributed to the development of a professional army. Equally important to the growth of a professional army were the development of a military educational system capable of producing a professional officer corps, an appreciable increase in the size of the army and navy, and a sense of mission which both defined and justified a strong military establishment in a country

---

[14]*Ibid.*, pp. 163–78; also, Fujiwara Akira, *Gunjishi* (1961), pp. 59–62.
[15]Matsushita, *Meiji gunsei shiron*, II, 345–46.

no longer suffering from serious manifestations of civil unrest. Consequently, one must consider briefly how the new educational system, new strat e ic responsibilities, and new military capabilities which emerged during the 1880s both enabled and contributed to Japan's participation in the scramble for a privileged position on the continent in the closing decade of the nineteenth century.

As suggested, the overriding political issue confronting the Meiji oligarchy in 1880 was the creation of a constitutional government that would preserve the sovereign powers of the emperor and unite the Japanese populace into a nation-state.[16] Within military circles, an enlarged army and an increased conscription program seemed to offer excellent means to promote national solidarity while helping to transform Japan into an independent country. The guiding architects of this scheme were Katsura and Kawakami. Both had studied in Germany in the wake of the Franco-Prussian War and were disciples of Baron Karl von Stein and Count August von Gneisenau—men who previously had outlined similar reforms as a way to unify Prussia and to terminate foreign (Napoleonic) domination over Germany.

Inspired by these nineteenth-century Prussian reformers, Katsura and Kawakami prepared and the government approved in 1882 an expansion of the standing army to six divisions. This provided for a 73,000-man army in time of peace, with a potential mobilization in case of national emergency of 274,000 men. In effect, this represented a 600 percent increase in strength over that originally established with the 1873 conscription program. In addition, serious attention was given for the first time to naval matters. In 1882 the Bureau of Naval Defense recommended an eight-year building program and the creation of a separate Navy Department.[17] The following year the government authorized a program designed to produce a 30,700-ton navy, or some 42 vessels. This was revised to a 54-ship fleet in 1886; and a completely new naval program was adopted in 1892 which envisioned a 120,000-ton fleet.[18] In a moment some of the diplomatic reasons contributing to this sharp upgrading in naval strength

[16]The views of the oligarchy are available in George M. Beckmann, *The Making of the Meiji Constitution* (1957), pp. 126–48.

[17]Matsushita, *Meiji gunsei shiron*, II, 18–20, 33–35, 185–89.

[18]Ono Giichi, *War and Armament Expenditures of Japan* (1922), pp. 44–49.

will be considered. Here one may note that by 1893 Japan possessed 34 warships (63,493 tons) and a standing army of six divisions, plus the Imperial Guard Division. Moreover, by mobilizing the first or active reserve, the army could be doubled to twelve divisions. In other words, by 1893 Japan had a professional army and navy capable of carrying out operations in the Liaotung Peninsula against the forces of the Ch'ing dynasty, if the necessity presented itself.

In conjunction with this naval construction program, the Navy Ministry, which had been in existence since 1886, was reorganized during the cabinet restructuring of 1889. Two years later a Navy General Staff was organized within the Navy Ministry, becoming, in 1893, independent of its parent body with direct access to the Throne on matters of coastal defense operations. At this time, the Army General Staff still retained responsibility for "national defense" and the chief of the Army General Staff was designated as "commander of all imperial military forces."[19]

Parallel with these administrative changes, Kaneko Kentarō undertook a tour to study Anglo-American naval education. On his return a number of reforms were adopted, including the creation of a Navy War College and the principle of drawing cadets for the Naval Academy from the entire country. Comparable developments had already occurred in the army educational system. In March 1884 Acting Army Minister Saigō authorized the patterning of the Army War College after the highly professional Prussian model while keeping the Army Academy patterned after the French system, which placed stress on the morale of the officers.[20] At the same time Ōyama, Katsura, and Kawakami embarked on a personal tour of military educational systems in Europe. During this trip they requested Moltke to select an outstanding staff officer to assist them in the preparation of a suitable curriculum for the proposed War College. The following year Major Jakob Meckel of the Imperial German General Staff arrived in Japan and introduced a new dimension to the planning and policies of the Japanese officer corps. Henceforth, the earlier reform orientations of Stein and Gneisenau were replaced by the staff system and political philosophy associated with the senior Moltke.

As yet, the specific substance of Meckel's teachings and, more crucially,

[19]Matsushita, *Meiji gunsei shiron*, II, 185–95.
[20]*Ibid.*, pp. 210–14, 57–58.

the Japanese interpretation of them remain to be investigated. It seems clear, however, that from this date one witnessed within the elite of the army officer corps a passionate commitment to the axioms that the right of supreme command should be exercised by the emperor and that the conduct of operations should be entrusted to the direction of the General Staff.[21] Also, many of Meckel's judgments quickly permeated the officer corps and influenced governmental policies. On the Korean problem, for example, Meckel's students accepted his conviction that no third power should be allowed to control this peninsula, the "dagger at the heart of Japan."

During the early 1880s Japan and the Western nations had negotiated various agreements with Korea "opening" that country to commercial activities. In 1883, however, the Ch'ing government promulgated a series of trade regulations for Chinese and Koreans which asserted that Korea "having been from ancient times a tributary state of China . . . [these] regulations are to be considered so many concessions on the part of China to her tributary state and are not within the scope of the 'Favored Nations Rule' existing between the several Treaty Powers and China."[22] Two years later, the Ch'ing government appointed Yuan Shih-k'ai as resident of Korea in an effort to reassert Chinese hegemony over the Hermit Kingdom. This ambition conflicted with the basic premise that an "independent" Korea was essential to Japanese national security. Careful logistical estimates, however, convinced the General Staff that it would be inadvisable to try to settle this matter by force of arms. This professional estimate played some part in the governmental decision to negotiate the 1885 Treaty of Tientsin, which "neutralized" Korea by theoretically excluding both Chinese and Japanese influence in the internal affairs of Korea. It also marked a new orientation toward the military expansion program originally authorized in 1882. Prior to this Korean crisis, domestic problems had dictated the enlargement of the services; after 1885, the Korean problem became more pressing and Japan's military and political leaders were always aware that it might be necessary to go to war with China to keep Korea "independent." This is not to imply that they were planning a war, nor that they were willing to go to war over Korea, at least not in 1885. It

---

[21]*Ibid.*, pp. 59–61.
[22]F. Hilary Conroy, *The Japanese Seizure of Korea, 1868–1910* (1960), p. 115.

does signify, in my estimation, a consciousness that the objective of Japan's foreign policy was no longer confined to the revision of the unequal treaties.

By 1890 one also detects within the cabinet and the services a subtle change in the meaning of "national defense." Before this time it meant "building the military strength of the country," i.e., to guarantee domestic tranquillity and convince the powers that Japan had an effective government. With the promulgation of the Meiji constitution in 1889, one senses that this axiom was being supplanted by the "national defense requirements of an empire." The Army General Staff, by this time, deemed control over the Korean peninsula to be absolutely essential to the "defense" of Japan, and the Navy General Staff insisted that a powerful navy was the only way to protect the country from the increasingly dangerous situation caused by the imperialist rivalries of the European nations. Furthermore, the political weakness of China was prompting a rapid extension of European influence in Asia. These three central concerns led Yamagata, in October 1893, to call for a priority on naval expansion. In his estimation, the European nations were working together in a concerted effort to dominate the mainland to the point of excluding Japanese access to the China market: Britain in the Yangtze region, France in Kwangsi, and Russia in Manchuria and Mongolia. If the powers were to act quickly and decisively, Yamagata feared the consequences would be fatal to the long-term welfare of Japan. "Within ten years," he judged, "we shall be at war. At that time our enemy will be neither China nor Korea but Britain, France, and Russia."[23] By 1893 the oligarchy and the military leaders were no longer evaluating an "independent" Japan to mean simply a sovereign state, free from foreign control. Rather, one encounters a growing conviction that an "independent" Japan was one that could and should participate in the quest for imperial rights on the mainland. There were multiple causes behind this atavistic orientation, including Social Darwinism, popular economic theories on the desirability of colonial markets, and the style of European diplomacy prevalent in the closing decades of the nineteenth century. In other words, Korea and the mainland were not only seen through the prism of Meckel's axiom but were complemented by pervasive political and economic considerations.

[23]Matsushita, *Meiji gunsei shiron,* II, 355.

THE WINNING OF AN EMPIRE: WAR WITH
CHINA AND RUSSIA, 1894–1906

Whatever ambitions may have been voiced in the corridors of the General Staffs in 1894, they did not alter the fact that Japan was a minor military power. By 1906, however, Japan had become the dominant power in northeast Asia. This transformation, in turn, defined a new set of diplomatic and strategic responsibilities. In these years the imperial forces had proved their mettle: great battles were fought and won; the nation now claimed a new set of national heroes. Inevitably these triumphs, purchased at the cost of many lives, generated a sense of nationalism and pride throughout every village and in every ward of the cities. Without attempting to deal with the social and political consequences of these wars, the following discussion of the period concentrates on: 1) the expansion of Japanese military capabilities; 2) the outstanding diplomatic-military problems; 3) the policies adopted in response to these problems; 4) the policy-making context of the government during the outbreak and conduct of the Sino- and Russo-Japanese wars; and 5) the degree to which military considerations were involved in the decisions for war, first with China, next with Russia.

As noted previously, by 1893 growing imperial aspirations were discernible in the cabinet and the services. Even so, the problem of treaty revision still constituted the central foreign policy issue. With the Tonghak rebellion of 1894, however, the Korean situation again became the crucial issue. Under the pretext of restoring order in Korea, the Ch'ing government dispatched an army under Yuan Shih-k'ai. This act violated the terms of the Tientsin Treaty and Japan insisted on its right to send troops equal in number to those of the Chinese. This explosive context was the immediate cause of the Sino-Japanese War which, as Hilary Conroy's fine study shows, was precipitated by the policies of the Ch'ing government.[24] To phrase it differently, whatever the ultimate outcome of Japan's Korean policy might have been, the decision for war in 1894 was not part of a calculated plot by the Japanese army or the imperial government. Even so, the Army General Staff was not reluctant to take up the gauntlet.

[24]Conroy, *Japanese Seizure of Korea*, pp. 245–60.

The genrō, on the other hand, were more prone to caution. In particular Yamagata was distressed by Japan's limited naval strength and his fears were not without basis, if only because Admiral Nakamuta Kuranosuke, who was concurrently the navy chief of staff and head of the Navy War College, was advising against a premature conflict.[25] The Army General Staff under Kawakami, however, was fully confident of the army's ability to defeat China. And on July 17, 1894 Admiral Nakamuta was elevated to the sinecure of official adviser to the Privy Council. His successor, Admiral Kabayama Sukenori, voiced none of the worries advanced by his predecessor. Although it is still hard to locate specific information on the degree to which the decision to go to war with China was influenced by the opinions of the General Staffs, it would be difficult to deny that the military buildup over the preceding decade enabled this decision. Nor would it be advisable to discount the relevance of Meckel's staff training to the conduct of operations which brought a smashing and surprising victory over the more numerous Chinese troops. Moreover, it would be extremely worthwhile to ascertain the process by which Meckel's strategic opinion of the value of the Korean peninsula became a guiding axiom, not only of army staff planning, but among the genrō and the cabinet.

While the Army General Staff placed the highest strategic value on the Korean peninsula, prior to the Sino-Japanese War there had been no consciously formulated governmental policy that designated this region as the primary center of Japanese imperial interests. At this time the government was anxious to extend Japanese commercial interests in central and south China, as well as to gain control over the sea approaches to the home islands. Under the terms of the Treaty of Shimonoseki which terminated the Sino-Japanese War, these aspirations were given more substantial foundations. Among other things, China recognized the independence of Korea, ceded Taiwan, the Pescadores, and the Liaotung Peninsula, including Port Arthur, to Japan, and concluded a comprehensive commercial treaty granting Japan most-favored-nation treatment. On April 23, 1895, six days after the signing of this treaty, representatives of France, Germany, and Russia notified the Japanese government that its possession of the Liaotung Peninsula "would be a constant menace to the capital of China, could at the same time render illusory the independence of Korea, and

---

[25]Matsushita, *Meiji gunsei shiron*, II, 197, 426–27.

would henceforth be a perpetual obstacle to the peace of the Far East."[26] Since Japanese military strength precluded any real opposition, the Japanese government, on May 5, capitulated to the Triple Intervention and retroceded its mainland acquisitions.

This deference to the powers was publicly humiliating and a vivid indicator of Japan's military weakness. Moreover, within two years Germany moved into Shantung, an act which precipitated the Russian acquisition of the Liaotung Peninsula and impelled Britain to establish a naval base at Weihaiwei. In several respects these developments were a consequence of Japan's smashing victory over China. In this sense, the Sino-Japanese War may be regarded as having transformed Yamagata's earlier prognosis into a self-fulfilling prophecy. From a different vantage point, as William Langer has noted, this was a new phase of European diplomacy, one which left Britain isolated and at serious odds with both Russia and Germany. Certainly, it signaled the abandonment of "respecting the integrity of China" as the basis of European diplomacy in East Asia. The conflicting imperial policies of the powers after 1898 also made the Far Eastern question extremely serious and complex because "the powers were dealing with the fate of an empire of upward of three hundred million souls and no less than five major states were disputing the spoils."[27] In addition, the dissension among the powers shattered any illusions about collusion among the Western nations and afforded Japan many opportunities to augment its access to the "spoils" of China.

Until the turn of the century, the securing of commercial privileges throughout China and the "independence" of Korea had served as the dual pillars of Japan's continental policy. Before the new surge of imperialism in 1898, neither of these was subject to severe strain by pressures emanating from Europe. This situation was radically altered in the new context of European diplomacy in which British and French spheres were dominant in central and south China and German and Russian spheres in north China. In effect, it posed the fundamental question: should Japan buttress its commercial interest in the region opposite Taiwan or in Korea and Manchuria? The decision would determine whether Japan would seek an alliance with Great Britain or with Russia. In spite of the strategic concern

[26]William L. Langer, *The Diplomacy of Imperialism, 1890–1902* (1951), p. 186.
[27]*Ibid.*, pp. 415–44, 677.

of Korea, neither the civil nor military leaders had been prepared, prior to this time, to establish some sort of priority between north and central China. During the Boxer Rebellion of 1900, for example, influential army officers urged a military expedition into Fukien province. "By this means," ventured Yamagata, "we can in the future build up opposite Taiwan special strength which will serve in time of peace as the focus for trade and industry within China. Thus we can hold in our grip the 'throat of the Far East' and keep in check any intrusion by an enemy." But the clandestine efforts of General Kodama Gentarō, the governor-general of Taiwan, to implement this policy by a series of independent military actions drew the wrath of Navy Minister Yamamoto Gonnohyōe on the grounds that he was improperly "interfering in a zone where the navy was responsible for security."[28] In particular, given Japan's fleet in being, Yamamoto feared any action that might direct the naval power of Britain against Japan. This strategic consideration soon bred a consensus in both General Staffs in favor of an alliance with Great Britain.

Within army circles, an independent Korea had been regarded for more than a decade as being essential to the defense of Japan. As early as June 22, 1903, moreover, the chief of the Army General Staff, General Ōyama, concluded that, "for the long-range welfare of our country," it was necessary to make Korea "part of the Japanese empire."[29] In October 1902 Admiral Yamamoto proposed the adoption of an eleven-year program of naval expansion to develop Japan into a major naval power. To this end, he judged that Japan would require extensive rights in Korea in order to develop Japanese industry to the degree that it could maintain a modern fleet. For different strategic considerations, both services now agreed upon Korea as the paramount national defense issue. But how could Japan best acquire military security and extend its rights in Korea? The alternatives were a Russo-Japanese or an Anglo-Japanese alliance. Without trying to explore the simultaneous negotiations undertaken in London and St. Petersburg in October-December 1901, it may be noted that the genrō were uncertain of the better choice: Itō urged a Russian alliance, Yamagata one with Britain.[30] In this context, the consensus of the General

[28]I.H. Nish, "Japan's Indecision During the Boxer Disturbances" (1961), pp. 450, 455.
[29]Matsushita, *Meiji gunsei shiron*, II, 542.
[30]Ōhata Tokushirō, "Nichi-Ro kaisen gaikō" (1961), pp. 110, 102-7.

Staffs in support of the latter alternative proved of some importance in the final decision to negotiate the 1902 Anglo-Japanese alliance.

Basic to this decision was the awareness that Russia posed the main challenge to Japanese interests in Korea and south Manchuria. Its seizure of Liaotung was a cancerous humiliation and the completion of the Trans-Siberian Railway threatened to preclude the possibility of displacing Russia from the peninsula. Besides, in 1902 Japan possessed sufficient power to undertake a war to oust Russian influence from north Korea. This capability was produced by the ten-year armaments expansion program adopted in 1896 by the Japanese government.[31] Under this plan, the standing army was increased to thirteen divisions (170,000 men), with a potential wartime mobilization of 600,000 soldiers. This more than doubled the army over that authorized in 1882. The imperial navy was augmented by four battleships and six first-class cruisers, giving Japan six battleships, eight first-class cruisers, and a combined fleet tonnage of some 278,000 tons. While this combined strength was adequate for the carrying out of operations in the Liaotung area against the tsarist forces, under no circumstances could Japan contest the power of the British fleet. Fortunately this prospect was diminished because Great Britain wished to reduce its military commitments in the Pacific to concentrate on the Middle East and the sea routes to Australia and New Zealand. In effect, in 1902 both Britain and Japan were distressed by the expansive nature of Russian diplomacy: Britain in terms of India and the Middle East, Japan in regard to Manchuria and Korea. Since Japan rejected any commitment to the defense of British interests outside of East Asia, the Anglo-Japanese alliance focused on the Far Eastern question. In particular, each nation professed a loyalty to the idea of respecting the "independence of China and Korea" while recognizing their mutual special interests in China and allowing that Japan was "interested in a peculiar degree politically as well as commercially and industrially" in Korea.[32] Most crucially, the treaty protected Japan from a possible repetition of the 1895 Triple Intervention. In other words, Japan's ability to wage war against Russia was rooted in the naval security provided by the Anglo-Japanese alliance, as well as in its own intrinsic military prowess.

[31]Ono, *War and Armament Expenditures*, pp. 61–66.
[32]Langer, *Diplomacy of Imperialism*, p. 777.

Granting the paramount interest of the Japanese government in Korea, the diplomatic and military advantages furnished by the alliance with Britain, and the fact that Japanese military leaders were entertaining the notion of incorporating the Hermit Kingdom into the Japanese empire, it is doubtful whether the cabinet or the genrō, at this time, considered the annexation of Korea as the basic objective of the alliance or of Japan's continental policy. Nevertheless, it is evident that the original proposals submitted to the Russian government in the summer of 1903 were decisively structured by strategic considerations. These proposals included, for example, the complete exclusion of Russian influence from Korea; the right to extend the Korean railway up to the Yalu and to link it with the Chinese Eastern Railway and Shanhaikwan-Newchwang line; and "the exclusive right of Japan to give advice and assistance in the interest of good government in Korea, including necessary military assistance."[33] These terms also reflected political and economic considerations. Still, while it made several important concessions during the negotiations between June 1903 and January 1904, especially vis-a-vis Manchuria, the Japanese government adamantly refused to accept Article 5 of the Russian counterproposal of October 3—that Japan would "not use any part of the territory of Korea for strategical purposes or to undertake on the coast of Korea any military works capable of menacing the freedom of navigation in [the] Korean straits." Moreover, as the talks continued, the tsar commented: "Time is Russia's best ally. Every year strengthens us."[34] As indeed it did, a fact which greatly distressed the Japanese General Staffs. Thus, it is reasonable to assume that the strategic importance of the peninsula and the growing military capabilities of the Russian forces in East Asia constituted two pressures in favor of a decision to go to war.

In the quest for empire that commenced in earnest during the closing decade of the nineteenth century, the Meiji oligarchy consistently and brilliantly coordinated the military capabilities of the nation in the conduct of foreign affairs. During these years, moreover, military planning and policies always remained subordinate to political leadership. During the Sino-Japanese War, for example, Prince Itō Hirobumi demanded to parti-

---

[33]Ōhata, "Nichi-Ro kaisen gaikō," pp. 112–15; Andrew Malozemoff, *Russian Far Eastern Policy, 1881–1904* (1958), p. 239.

[34]*Ibid.*, pp. 240, 245.

cipate in the Imperial Headquarters in order to provide political leadership over such issues as the geographical extent of military operations and the appropriate moment to terminate the hostilities.[35] Although the Army General Staff regarded this as a transgression of its imperial prerogatives, Itō was permitted to attend the meetings of this body. Moreover, Yamagata committed the army, in writing, to the principle of overall supervision by the government of the conduct of the war. This precedent of political control over military operations was reinforced during the Russo-Japanese War. At the first meeting of the Imperial Headquarters on February 13, 1904, Prime Minister Katsura, Foreign Minister Komura Jutarō, and the genrō Itō and Yamagata, under a liberal interpretation of Article 2 of the regulations governing this body, attended the session. They emphasized that they would determine the national objectives during the hostilities, including, of course, strategic objectives. Four months later Yamagata personally assumed the post of chief of the Army General Staff. His predecessor, General Ōyama, was transferred to Manchuria, where he became commander-in-chief of the Manchuria army. In this post Ōyama was, in reality, entrusted with complete authority for the conduct of all military operations. Nevertheless, the Imperial Headquarters under Yamagata's leadership always exercised final authority over the army; and both Yamagata and Ōyama, conscious that a clear-cut victory could not be obtained by military means, were always anxious to retain the understanding of the civil officials on whom they felt peacemaking would ultimately depend. For example, when Ōyama sought instructions following the victory at Mukden, Yamagata told him that the emperor had been officially advised that all operations would be conducted in accordance with the political aims of the government.[36]

DEFENSE OF THE EMPIRE: COMPETING STRATEGIC VIEWPOINTS, 1906–1914

With the Portsmouth Treaty, the primary mission of the services centered on the defense of the empire and its recently acquired rights on the mainland, particularly in south Manchuria. At this time there appeared

---

[35]Itō, *Gumbatsu kōbōshi*, I, 145.
[36]Matsushita, *Meiji gunsei shiron*, II, 558–59.

two versions of basic national defense policies, one prepared by the Army, the other by the Navy General Staff. To a significant degree, both were influenced by the changing context of European diplomacy, which greatly reduced the influence and interest of the powers in Manchuria and Korea, and by the rise of the United States as a major naval power with an active desire to preserve the Open Door policy in China. In addition, the American acquisition of the Philippines posed a potential threat to the security of Taiwan. Essentially, Japan now faced two main strategic problems, tsarist Russia and the United States. Despite these concerns, the Japanese government encountered a domestic development which seriously affected military and cabinet policies: the unwillingness of the Diet to sanction any large increase in military expenditures. This soon exacerbated an already existing interservice rivalry and engendered a series of cabinet crises in the 1912–14 interval. The following discussion is presented in terms of the dual national defense policies formulated in 1907 and of their relevance to cabinet politics and foreign policy during the 1906–14 period.

The political control exercised over both military and foreign policies during the Sino-Japanese and Russo-Japanese wars constituted one of the most impressive features of Japanese history during the creation of the empire. After 1906 the success of the previous policies created new strategic concerns which affected the "national defense" estimates of both General Staffs and introduced some new political complexities to the continuance of an effective coordination of the revised versions of national defense. Each service at this time prepared comprehensive estimates of the requirements posed by the termination of the Russo-Japanese War; each was rooted in the premise that Japan should eventually have sufficient military power to permit an independent policy vis-a-vis the mainland. Before considering the substance of each recommendation, it may help to review the basic guidelines proposed by Yamagata in October 1906 in a personal report to the Throne on the national defense policy of the empire and the essential principles underlying this policy.[37] Reviewing the invaluable role of the Anglo-Japanese alliance in the conduct of operations during the Russo-Japanese War, Yamagata stressed that it also revealed the vulnerability of the country's defenses. In effect, Japan's security

---

[37]Imai Seiichi, "Taishōki ni okeru gumbu no seijiteki chii" (1957), Part I, p. 5; Ōyama Azusa, "Yamagata Aritomo teikoku kokubō hōshin an" (1961), pp. 170–77.

was dependent on the goodwill of Great Britain. This dangerous situation could be rectified, reasoned Yamagata, only by a well-coordinated military policy and an effective diplomacy. Specifically, he proposed that some type of rapprochement with Russia be established, if only to keep Russia and China from uniting against Japan, and that a revised treaty with Britain be negotiated that would allow Japan greater access to the regions of central and south China, concede Japanese hegemony in Korea, and neutralize the potential threat inherent in the emergence of the United States as a major actor in the affairs of the Far East. The influence of these suggestions on subsequent policies is attested by the Russo-Japanese entente of 1907 and the Anglo-Japanese alliance of 1911. Yamagata's injunction for a coordinated military and diplomatic policy, however, was not implemented so readily.

In response to Yamagata's memorial, the emperor requested both General Staffs to draft a basic national defense policy and an estimate of the forces necessary for its fulfillment. In February 1907 their official replies to the Throne were submitted, following which they were passed along to Prime Minister Saionji Kimmochi for his opinion. The content of Saionji's evaluation is not available, but after his reply to the Throne, the imperial sanction was affixed to the policies recommended by the two services.

Both national defense plans were based on the premise that Japan eventually should possess sufficient military power to guarantee the security of the empire and to enable the government to pursue whatever continental policy it judged to be in the best interest of the nation. Anticipating a war of revenge by Russia, the army wished to maintain in the field a force adequate to this contingency.[38] To this end, it set a goal of twenty-five divisions in peacetime, with a potential mobilization of fifty divisions in case of war. In effect, this would double the size of the army over that established by the 1896 program. One should note, though, that this was a desired objective. In 1907 the standing army actually totaled nineteen divisions, six more than had been in the field before the outbreak of the Russo-Japanese War. The navy proposed that Japan ultimately should possess two battle fleets headed by 8 capital warships.[39] This was the famous 8–8 plan and technically it called for 8 battleships, 8 heavy cruisers,

---

[38]Itō, *Gumbatsu kōbōshi,* II, 22.
[39]Kawamura Zenjirō, "Hara Takashi naikaku" (1962), p. 39.

27 cruisers, 177 destroyers, and 64 submarines. For the immediate future, however, the 1907 recommendation called for 12 capital warships, the so-called 8–4 plan. Although this naval policy entailed an appreciable outlay of funds, it did not alter Japan's strength vis-a-vis the major powers. In 1905 Lord Fisher designed the *Dreadnought*, the name that became the symbol of the new type of heavy battleship, and the *Invincible*, the first battle cruiser. These two ships outdated the existing fleets of the powers overnight, a fact that was immediately appreciated in Japanese naval circles, as well as in the United States, Germany, and France. To phrase it differently, the expansion of the Japanese navy after 1906 did not alter Japan's naval status. On the contrary, before Fisher's innovation Japan's battleship ratio to the other powers was as follows:[40]

U.K.	Germany	France	U.S.	Japan
39	20	12	11	11

At the outbreak of World War I it was:

39	19	12	10	10

Thus, the 1907 policy of the Japanese navy would be more correctly read as one designed to preserve Japan's existing ratio with the powers.

Given this fact, Japanese naval security was still predicated on an alliance with Great Britain. The 1907 Anglo-Japanese alliance provided this security; in addition, the primary mission of the British Pacific fleet was to safeguard the sea routes to Australia and New Zealand and to protect British interests in Hong Kong and Singapore. The alliance, in effect, entrusted Japan with the preservation of naval security in the northeast Pacific. Without exploring the diplomatic and military reasons behind the revised Anglo-Japanese alliance, one may note that Japanese naval security was as much the product of an Anglo-German naval rivalry and the emerging alliance system in Europe as it was the consequence of Japan's fleet-in-being. With the Anglo-Japanese alliance and in the context of European diplomacy, only the United States presented a potential threat to Japan's empire. In particular, the Open Door policy and the acquisition of the Philippines greatly perplexed the Japanese government. This anxiety was enhanced by the 1906–7 "war scare" which was highlighted by virulent anti-Japanese sentiment in California and by Theodore Roosevelt's dramatic dispatch of the entire American fleet on a world tour that pointedly

[40] *Jane's Fighting Ships, 1914* (1914).

included a sojourn in Japanese home waters. For seemingly good reasons, the "Imperial National Defense Policy" of 1907 designated the United States as "number one hypothetical enemy."[41] In retrospect, after the Russo-Japanese War, each service had construed the requirements of national defense to mean that Japan was obligated to maintain a military establishment capable of defeating both the Russian army and the American navy.

In this context, the key to naval security was the Anglo-Japanese alliance, and the central objective of naval policy was the preservation of its existing superiority in Japanese waters over the American fleet. The army was charged with the protection of the political-economic-military advantages it had won on the field of battle for the emperor. Essentially, this meant hegemony in Korea and south Manchuria. Unlike the navy, which, of necessity, included diplomacy as an integral part of its strategic planning, such concerns seemed quite remote to the leaders of the Japanese army. This fact helps in understanding why Japan's army leaders were prone to regard diplomatic and administrative policies affecting Manchuria as though they fell within the exclusive preserve of the imperial army. This attitude became evident in 1906 when the Army General Staff strongly opposed the decision to make Itō the resident-general of Korea with complete control over all Japanese troops stationed in the peninsula.[42] In south Manchuria, however, units of the imperial army remained under the Kwantung military governor-general. In effect, this region operated under a de facto form of military government. In February 1906 Army Minister Terauchi Masatake aborted Foreign Minister Katō Takaaki's proposal that he should "unify" policy toward Manchuria, if only because of the complexity of relations with Britain and the United States.[43] In particular, Katō felt that the Open Door policy should be recognized, with American and British business concerns participating in the economic development of south Manchuria. The violent opposition of the army to this proposal and the basic policy underlying it soon compelled Katō to resign, only three months after assuming his cabinet portfolio.

Although the army minister was able to shelve this recommendation of Foreign Minister Katō, he was unable to perpetuate the army's complete

[41]Fukudome Shigeru, *Shikan Shinjuwan kōgeki* (1955), pp. 58–59.
[42]Conroy, *Japanese Seizure of Korea*, pp. 334–38.
[43]Shinobu Seizaburō, "Taishō gaikōshi no kihon mondai" (1958), p. 2; Kurihara Ken, "Hayashi Tadasu gaimudaijin no tai-Shin seiryaku kanken" (1957), pp. 196–99.

control of the administration of south Manchuria. With the aid of Prince Itō, Prime Minister Saionji convened a conference on the Manchurian problem on May 22, 1906.[44] Participating were the genrō: Itō, Yamagata, Ōyama, Matsukata Masayoshi, and Inoue; the senior ranking officers on active duty: General Katsura and Admiral Yamamoto; Army Chief of Staff General Kodama Gentarō; and the most important cabinet ministers: Saionji, Foreign Minister Hayashi Tadasu, General Terauchi, Admiral Saitō Makoto, and Finance Minister Sakatani Yoshirō. As a result of this conference, the resident military governor-general in south Manchuria was changed to a governor-general; the South Manchuria Railway Company was organized under the presidency of Gotō Shimpei; and a consulate general was authorized for the Foreign Ministry, a post that made its occupant equal in rank to the highest-ranking army officer in the area. Still, the army continued to regard Manchuria as the crux of the nation's defense. In November 1906, for example, General Ōyama, the governor-general of the Kwantung Leased Territory, proposed that "the foreign policy of south Manchuria should be entrusted completely to the governor-general."[45] This suggestion was not sanctioned by the cabinet, but the premise that military judgment should prevail in fundamental policies affecting this region persisted within military circles. And, as Kurihara Ken has shown, this attitude was a crucial factor in the bitter disputes between the Foreign Ministry and the army during the Taishō era.[46]

Implicit in this approach to Manchuria was the assumption that the army was independent of the cabinet and directly responsible to the emperor for the protection of Japan's position on the continent. This conviction was complemented by two important administrative changes. In 1907 cabinet regulations were revised so as to preclude the necessity for the prime minister to countersign any regulations governing the internal administration of either service.[47] And in 1908 the regulations of the Army General Staff were altered so as to drop the requirement that national defense plans and logistical estimates be channeled through the army minister.[48] These

[44]Japan, Gaimushō (Foreign Ministry), *Nihon gaikō nempyō narabi ni shuyō bunsho, 1840–1945* (1965; first published, 1955), I, 260–69 (hereafter cited as *Nihon gaikō nempyō*).

[45]Imai, "Taishōki ni okeru gumbu," Part I, p. 7.

[46]Kurihara Ken, "Abe Gaimushō seimukyokuchō ansatsu jiken to tai-Chūgoku (Mammō) mondai" (1956), and "Daiichiji dainiji Mammō dokuritsu undō" (1958).

[47]Imai, "Taishōki ni okeru gumbu," Part I, p. 6.

[48]Matsushita, *Meiji gunsei shiron*, II, 609–10.

changes precluded effective cabinet supervision of the internal administration of the services, and they broadened the implications of the independence of the supreme command. In many respects they marked the legal attainment of administrative autonomy. This sense of autonomy, plus particular conceptions about the right of supreme command and the 1907 Imperial National Defense Policy, prompted the army minister in 1912 to shatter the second Saionji cabinet.

The 1907 National Defense Policy had defined one comprehensive objective—a military establishment capable of meeting the strategic threats posed by the Russian army and the American navy. This sanctioned two distinct service missions, both of which were subsumed under the axiom of defending the empire that had been forged between 1894 and 1905. Still, in 1907 neither service actually possessed the goals outlined in this policy: the army stood at nineteen divisions, not twenty-five; and the navy had two new capital warships, not twelve. Previously, in 1873, 1882, and 1896, the government had provided the funds necessary to the implementation of the proposed expansion of the services. After the Russo-Japanese War, however, the Diet failed to approve any major increase in military expenditures. Since the navy was literally building a new fleet, it could function within this limitation and still achieve its immediate goal of twelve new capital ships; but the army could not scuttle one division and replace it with another. Consequently, between 1907 and 1911 the army remained at nineteen divisions.

This frustrating situation was compounded by the belief prevalent in many army circles that the government was morally and legally obligated to fulfill the 1907 national defense plan. When Prince Saionji organized his second cabinet on August 30, 1911, the prospect of increasing the size of the army became more dismal. Adopting a fiscal retrenchment program, Saionji proceeded to reduce the budget of the army from ¥125.6 million to ¥119.6 million, and naval expenditures from ¥108.3 million to ¥95.1 million.[49] Whatever military officers may have thought of this action, the political foundation of his retrenchment policy was beyond dispute: Saionji's party commanded an absolute majority in the Diet. In May 1912, however, on the death of Army Minister Ishimoto Shinroku, the army

[49]Ono, *War and Armament Expenditures*, pp. 296–301.

designated General Uehara Yūsaku as his successor.[50] Moving directly
from his post as chief of the General Staff, Uehara lacked practical experience in the give and take of cabinet politics. This fact helps to explain
Uehara's demand that the cabinet authorize an increase of the army stationed
in Korea by two divisions. Japan at this time had less than a full division
in Korea and the General Staff deemed it imperative that it be augmented
by two divisions. Relying on the 1907 National Defense Policy and the
firm support of Yamagata, Uehara refused to amend or defer his proposal.
Finally, in protest, he resigned. Because the army refused to nominate
another officer for the post of army minister, the Saionji cabinet fell. The
genrō, under Yamagata's sway, then designated General Katsura as the new
prime minister.

At least two cardinal political issues were involved in Uehara's course
of action—the leadership of the prime minister in policy-making, and the
attempt of one service to force its views by means of resignation. The
latter threatened political chaos, if only because the navy possessed the
same degree of power in the cabinet as the army. That interservice rivalry
was an important factor in this crisis is suggested by the fact that the navy
refused to supply a minister for the Katsura cabinet.[51] This was a blunt
warning that it would play the same type of political game as the army.
Unlike Saionji, Katsura invoked the aid of the Throne and obtained an
imperial edict which compelled the appointment of a navy minister. Still,
under the Katsura cabinet the two-division expansion was not authorized.
It is possible to place this clash in the context of a Satsuma-Chōshū rivalry:
the army leaders being composed of officers from the Chōshū region, the
naval officers hailing from Satsuma. This viewpoint, though, is compromised by the fact that Uehara was a Satsuma man and throughout his
career had been a strong critic of Chōshū influence in the Army Ministry.
It can be argued, of course, that his appointment as army minister was
a deliberate effort to undermine the critics who placed the quarrels of
budget priorities in the framework of han rivalry. From this perspective,
it would seem to be more of an interservice struggle over fiscal matters than
a han-rooted conflict.

---

[50]Itō, *Gumbatsu kōbōshi*, II, 27–44.
[51]Robert Scalapino, *Democracy and the Party Movement in Prewar Japan* (1962; first published, 1953), p. 192.

In any case, the popular belief that the downfall of the Saionji cabinet had been caused by a Satsuma-Chōshū type of quarrel united the political parties against the Katsura government and the proposed two-division expansion. In his memorable parliamentary address of February 5, 1913, Ozaki Yukio launched the first dramatic attack on the Sat-Chō oligarchy and its use of the Throne for partisan purposes: "They always mouth 'loyalty' and 'patriotism' but what they are actually doing is to hide themselves behind the Throne, and shoot at their political enemies from their secure ambush. The Throne is their rampart. Rescripts are their missiles." Thus, when Katsura tried to obtain a revocation of a nonconfidence motion by means of an imperial rescript, the majority party, the Seiyūkai, defied the government. The cabinet fell, and from that moment, as Robert Scalapino has noted, "personal intervention by the Throne in political controversies practically ceased."[52]

The next cabinet, under Admiral Yamamoto Gonnohyōe, was ostensibly a Seiyūkai government, but one of distinctive bureaucratic cast. Only Home Minister Hara Takashi and Justice Minister Matsuda Masahisa were active Seiyūkai members before the formation of the cabinet, and both had previously been governmental officials. The remainder of the posts, except for the two service portfolios, went to prominent bureaucrats, who duly enrolled in the Seiyūkai simultaneously with their cabinet appointment. It was, in fact, a government based upon a fragile alliance between the majority political party and the governmental bureaucracies. This situation led to a more conciliatory attitude between the cabinet and the Diet. During the thirtieth session, for example, Prime Minister Yamamoto was confronted by Ozaki Yukio with a famous list of fundamental political questions: Did the government favor cabinets based upon political parties? Were not the regulations restricting the service ministers to generals and admirals on active duty obstructing constitutional government? Should not the civil service system be revised so as to allow more political appointments at high levels? Was the government planning to authorize the two-division increase for the army?[53] To each inquiry, Yamamoto answered in a conciliatory fashion. Specifically, a number of patronage

---

[52]*Ibid.*, pp. 194–95.
[53]*Ibid.*, pp. 202–3.

positions were created; the requirements of the service posts were broadened to include retired high-ranking officers; and the two-division expansion was not sanctioned. These were not radical concessions, but they
marked the first public commitment of the cabinet to the notion of a constitutional form of government which placed great importance on public
opinion and the political parties. In effect, they reflected a rebuke to the
tactics and outlook of Army Minister Uehara and Prime Minister Katsura.

EXPANSION IN THE VORTEX OF THE GREAT WAR, 1914–1921

From 1906 to 1914 the defense of the empire constituted the basis of
Japan's strategic and diplomatic policies. The outbreak of the great European conflagration, however, radically altered the diplomatic and military
context in East Asia and afforded a most opportune moment for the extension of Japanese power over the continent and oceania. In the summer of
1914 the Ōkuma cabinet created the Council on National Defense to
coordinate the budgets and planning of the two services, and in 1915 it
tried to place the determination of foreign policy under the effective control
of the Foreign Ministry by means of the Twenty-One Demands. The adverse diplomatic reactions to the Twenty-One Demands resulted in the
formation of the Advisory Council on Foreign Relations which, in effect,
tried to perform the role played by the genrō during the Sino- and Russo-
Japanese wars. Despite these changes in the policy-making context, the
policies of the Ōkuma cabinet defined a new set of political and military
objectives: the acquisition of the German islands in the Pacific; a political
and economic hegemony over China; and increased control over the areas
adjacent to Taiwan and Korea. Throughout the European war, those objectives served as the guiding axioms of Japanese diplomacy. With the
Russian revolution, the army unsuccessfully tried, during the Siberian
intervention, to broaden this policy to include Japanese control over northern
Manchuria and eastern Siberia. Most of the objectives sought by the
Ōkuma government were realized by a series of wartime treaties and
agreements. During the war, however, the United States greatly expanded
its fleet; and at the Paris Peace Conference, Woodrow Wilson clearly revealed American opposition to Japanese wartime diplomacy. This confrontation between the United States and Japan posed a major problem.

Should Japan attempt, possibly by force, to maintain the advantages it had acquired during the war? Or should it rely on cooperation with the Anglo-American nations as the best means to guarantee national security and its existing rights on the mainland? This issue was resolved in favor of the latter alternative at the Washington Conference. The following discussion of the 1914–21 period is structured to reveal how Japan's wartime diplomacy was formulated and the ways in which the strategic concerns of both services influenced the official policy of the imperial government.

The sudden flowering of the "defend the constitution" movement by attacking the han orientation of the genrō had been occasioned by Uehara's flagrant use of the political power of the army. Underlying this crisis was the inability of the two service ministers to agree upon a common national defense policy which would allocate the available funds according to some type of priority between the plans of the two services. Since the Seiyūkai was against any increase in total military expenditures, Uehara had sought to attain the army's budget request by means of direct action. Although he failed in his primary objective—the two-division enlargement of the Korea forces—the stalemate between the services over the budget issue lasted from 1912 to 1914, when the problem was channeled into a bureaucratic solution which noticeably curtailed the influence of the Diet and the political parties on policy-making. On June 22, 1914 Prime Minister Ōkuma organized the Council on National Defense. Composed of the prime minister as chairman, the foreign, army, navy, and finance ministers, and the chiefs of the Army and Navy General Staffs, the council agreed upon a defense program which sanctioned an increase in the forces stationed in Korea by two divisions and the completion of the 8–4 naval program.[54] Although the Seiyūkai was strong enough to frustrate temporarily the army budget in the Diet, the elections of March 1915 produced a resounding victory for Ōkuma's party, the Rikken Dōshikai (later the Minseitō). The two-division expansion was then promptly passed by the Diet, and for the duration of World War I the political parties endorsed all proposed military expenditures.

The "unified" national defense policy of the Council on National Defense was partly the consequence of the impending European crisis. It was also

[54]Tatsuji Takeuchi, *War and Diplomacy in the Japanese Empire* (1935), p. 182.

the prelude to a rapid expansion of Japanese military power during World War I. As yet, specific information on the role of the military in the major foreign policy decisions taken during the war is lacking. Still, one can trace some of the ways by which the policies and aspirations of the two services combined with the economic and diplomatic objectives of the cabinet to produce the Twenty-One Demands, the secret wartime treaties assigning Japan control over Shantung and the German islands north of the equator, the Siberian intervention of 1918, Japan's policies at the Paris Peace Conference, and the decision to participate in the Washington Conference.

Following the Russo-Japanese War, as noted previously, there existed a continuous rivalry between the Foreign Ministry and the army over which should determine the China policy of the government. This controversy was compounded by the overthrow of the Ch'ing dynasty and the emergence of various warlords in China. The entire problem of military assistance to Chinese revolutionary groups and to the major warlords remains a neglected subject. Kurihara Ken, however, has shown that the Army General Staff was very active during the second Chinese revolution of 1913 in attempts to promote an "independence" movement in Manchuria and Mongolia.[55] And Imai Seiichi notes that Japanese military attachés were urging that Japan give military help to the Peking government in order to promote a central government that would be dependent on Japan.[56] But piecemeal or independent actions by the army raised all sorts of problems vis-a-vis the powers and in terms of cabinet policies. Amidst this internal dissension, the outbreak of the European war afforded a splendid opportunity for the formulation of a coordinated China policy under the leadership of Prime Minister Ōkuma and Foreign Minister Katō Takaaki.

On August 7, 1914 the British government formally requested that Japan furnish naval assistance against the imperial German fleet.[57] While His Majesty's government sought only limited help, the Ōkuma cabinet elected to go to war in order to seize the German base in Shantung and establish control over the German islands in the Pacific. Neither of these objectives was received with enthusiasm in London, but nothing could

[55]Kurihara, "Mammō dokuritsu undō."
[56]Imai, "Taishōki ni okeru gumbu," Part 2, p. 107.
[57]Itō Masanori, ed., *Katō Takaaki* (1929), II, 71–78.

be done to check the scope of Japanese hostilities against Germany. The course of the European war soon gave Japan a relatively free hand in the Pacific. Still, the outcome of the war was far from certain and the genrō were anxious to avoid any moves that might rebound to the future disadvantage of Japan. On September 12, 1914, however, the Peking attaché, Major General Machida Keiu, advanced an outline for a general solution to the China problem;[58] and Foreign Minister Katō, anxious to preserve leadership of Japan's foreign policy, soon absorbed his proposals into a basic policy: the Twenty-One Demands.

The encompassing scope of these demands is well known. Here it is sufficient to note that they sought to extend Japanese influence in Shantung, Kwantung, south Manchuria, Inner Mongolia, and Fukien. In May 1915 the Peking government capitulated and signed a series of treaties incorporating most of the original demands. Thus, for example, it allowed that the German rights in Shantung were to be "completely left to the free disposal of Japan"; Japanese rights in south Manchuria and Port Arthur were extended for ninety-nine years; Japanese subjects were given the right to lease land and to engage in commercial activities in south Manchuria; limited consular jurisdiction over Japanese subjects was granted in Inner Mongolia; and China guaranteed that it would not allow any foreign nation to build any type of naval or military base along the coast of Fukien.[59]

In effect, these treaties strengthened Japan's military position in the environs of Korea and Taiwan and furnished the basis for a rapid extension of Japanese commercial activities on the mainland. For these reasons, they met with strong approval within the services, the cabinet, the Diet, and major industrial concerns. The genrō, though, were opposed to this dramatic policy. Yamagata, in particular, questioned whether it would really promote effective Sino-Japanese relations and feared that it would draw the ire of the great naval powers.[60] This would, in turn, pose some major diplomatic problems after the end of the European war. Katō and Ōkuma ignored this viewpoint. By coordinating the aims and policies

---

[58]James W. Morley, *The Japanese Thrust into Siberia, 1918* (1957), p. 13.

[59]*The Sino-Japanese Negotiations of 1915* (1921), pp. 39–63.

[60]Itō, *Katō Takaaki*, II, 176–80; Obata Yūkichi Denki Kankōkai, ed., *Obata Yūkichi* (1957), pp. 110–65.

of the two services, they thought they could place China policy under the firm control of the cabinet. Thus, the Twenty-One Demands marked the assertion of cabinet autonomy in the formulation of national policy.

Unfortunately for Katō, the Twenty-One Demands and the Sino-Japanese treaties of 1915 engendered a violent anti-Japanese movement in China and obviously met with the disfavor of Britain and the United States. These developments, plus his deliberate dismissal of Yamagata's views, soon compelled Katō to resign the portfolio of foreign minister. And even though his party held an absolute majority in the Diet, when the Ōkuma cabinet resigned in October 1916, the genrō bypassed his nomination in favor of General Terauchi and a "transcendental" cabinet. Under Terauchi the powers of the foreign minister, the political parties, and the cabinet were effectively clipped by the establishment of the Advisory Council on Foreign Relations.[61] Ostensibly this organization was formed to place "foreign affairs" beyond the pale of domestic politics. As it substituted a new technique for resolving dissension within the government, it temporarily checked the tendency of the cabinet to turn to the Diet and the leaders of the parties in settling these conflicts. This fact was appreciated by Katō Takaaki, who refused to join the Advisory Council, insisting that because foreign policy could not be divorced from politics, it should be determined by means of a party cabinet based upon a system of parliamentary responsibility. But the leaders of the two other major parties—Inukai Tsuyoshi and Hara Takashi—elected to participate in the new institution. By so doing, the growth of a more responsible form of parliamentary government was checked. At the same time, as James Morley has shown, it signified the demise of the active leadership of the genrō in policy-making.[62] Thereafter, the cabinet and the Advisory Council on Foreign Relations emerged as the primary locus of decision-making, a development that decisively affected the pattern of civil-military relations in the imperial government in the immediate post-World War I era.

Although Katō's foreign policy had vexed the genrō, it had been his tactics, not his objectives, that were criticized. Consequently, the Terauchi cabinet set out to consolidate the privileges acquired by the Sino-Japanese

[61]Itō, *Katō Takaaki*, II, 260–75.
[62]Scalapino, *Democracy and the Party Movement*, p. 210; Morley, *Japanese Thrust into Siberia*, pp. 25–26.

treaties of 1915. Britain at this time desperately needed Japanese naval assistance in the Mediterranean to combat the deadly submarine campaign of Imperial Germany. Using this situation to its maximum advantage, the Terauchi government agreed to supply this help, provided that Britain would recognize Japan's position in Shantung and its right to the German islands north of the equator. On February 16, 1917, Terauchi was notified:

> His Britannic Majesty's Government accede with pleasure to the request of the Japanese government for an assurance that they will support Japan's claims in regard to the disposal of Germany's rights in Shantung and possessions in the islands north of the equator on the occasion of the Peace Conference; it being understood that the Japanese Government will in the eventual peace settlement treat in the same spirit Great Britain's claim to the German islands south of the equator.[63]

With this secret agreement in hand, Japan readily attained comparable assurance from the Russian, French, and Italian governments.

The only major power remaining uncommitted was the United States. Sensing that the American government would not negotiate an agreement dealing with Shantung or the German islands, the Terauchi government sent Viscount Ishii Kikujirō to Washington in the hope that he might be able to realize some type of detente in terms of Japan's rights in Manchuria. The result was the famous Lansing-Ishii agreement of November 2, in which both countries affirmed the principle of respecting the Open Door and the "integrity" of China. More importantly, it stipulated that "territorial propinquity creates special relations between countries, and consequently, the Government of the United States recognizes that Japan has special interests in China, particularly in the part to which her possessions are contiguous."[64] With this agreement and the secret treaties with the European powers, the Terauchi government had, it thought, laid the diplomatic foundation for the confirmation of Japan's recently acquired rights in Manchuria, Shantung, and the Pacific island possessions of Germany.

The Russian revolution of 1917, however, injected a new and violent element into Japan's wartime diplomacy. Both General Staffs instantly urged a quick move into the Amur basin. Indeed, the army's initial proposal

[63]Russell Fifield, *Woodrow Wilson and the Far East* (1952), p. 54.
[64]*Ibid.*, p. 84.

ventured that the number and disposition of troops should be determined in terms of the convenience of "military operations which may be undertaken later and the desirability of occupying a commanding position in case the Allies jointly send troops." The army also broached the subject of a military alliance with the Peking government. Parallel with these reactions, Foreign Minister Motono Ichirō drafted a policy guide embracing the dual steps of a military alliance with Peking and immediate operations in the Maritime Provinces so that Japan could obtain north Sakhalin, "implant its natural influence in north Manchuria," and establish its "predominant position in the Orient."[65]

Although the services and the cabinet had little difficulty in advancing a solution to the new crisis, the Advisory Council on Foreign Relations preferred to wait until the situation in Russia became clearer and until the views of the powers were known. Consequently, the Siberian policy was to remain unresolved for several months. During this interval, as Morley and Hosoya have shown, the cabinet, especially Foreign Ministers Motono and Gotō Shimpei, and the Army General Staff, favored an independent policy that would secure immediate economic, political, and military advantages in Manchuria and the Maritime Provinces; and the Advisory Council on Foreign Relations, under the influence of Hara Takashi and Makino Nobuaki, insisted that cooperation with the powers, particularly with the United States, should be the basic point of departure for any moves into Siberia.[66] In July 1918 the American government proposed a joint intervention that had the intent of carefully circumscribing the number of Japanese troops and the scope of their activities. Despite the vehement objections of the Army General Staff, the government agreed to accept a joint intervention along the lines outlined by the American government.

The nature of this policy formulation confirmed that the genrō were no longer the ultimate determinant of major policies. It revealed too that the cabinet and the General Staffs were partial to an independent foreign policy. In addition, it demonstrated that, in terms of "national defense" policy, the view of the Army General Staff had become subordinate to the leadership of the army minister, even in strategic matters. For example,

[65]Morley, *Japanese Thrust into Siberia*, pp. 50, 53, 55.
[66]Hosoya Chihiro, *Shiberia shuppei no shiteki kenkyū* (1955).

the government did not create an imperial headquarters during the Siberian intervention. Instead the cabinet assumed responsibility for deciding the limits of military operations. At one point, it set Khabarovsk as the extent of operations and the General Staff, on strategic grounds, opposed the decision. This conflict produced a written agreement between the army minister and the chief of the General Staff which delineated their respective spheres of authority—the determination of objectives at the onset of operations was to be left to the army minister; the conduct of operations was to be entrusted exclusively to the General Staff.[67] Although this was an administrative agreement, it marked the army minister's shift into a position in which his views in the cabinet would prevail over the recommendations of the chief of the General Staff. This development would be of vital importance during the 1920s, the age of Taishō democracy.

On September 29, 1918 Hara Takashi organized the first "party" government in Japanese history. Despite Hara's role in the Siberian intervention and his desire for friendly relations with the United States, his government was strongly committed to the preservation of Japan's new position in East Asia. Thus, at the Paris Peace Conference the Japanese delegation refused to entertain Wilson's proposals that Japan give up its control over Shantung and the Pacific islands of Imperial Germany. In addition to this rigid stand, Hara's domestic platform called for the "fulfillment of national defense," the revamping of the public school curriculum so as to combat dangerous ideas (bolshevism), and the expansion of the industrial capacity of the nation.[68] But the "fulfillment of national defense" posed some difficult problems. Japan's intensive pressure on China during the war had caused widespread apprehension in Britain and the United States. The defeat of Germany had shattered the prewar alliance system and, with it, a major reason for the Anglo-Japanese alliance. The Siberian intervention had demonstrated the limits of aggressive action designed to augment Japan's position in Manchuria, and the almost total involvement of the Soviet government in domestic affairs had curtailed its influence and power in this region. Also, in the course of the war the American navy had become one of the world's most powerful, and at the Paris Peace Conference the opposition of the United States to Japan's continental

[67]Imai, "Taishōki ni okeru gumbu," Part 2, pp. 18–19.
[68]Kawamura, "Hara Takashi naikaku," pp. 36–38.

policy had been clearly demonstrated. More particularly, the failure of the United States to ratify the Versailles Treaty and Wilson's postwar Far Eastern policy had created a host of unresolved diplomatic issues—the Shantung problem, the Yap Island controversy, the Open Door policy, and the question of naval armaments.

All of these issues entailed points of friction with the United States. To phrase it differently, Japan was confronted with the necessity to modify its "national defense" policies so as either to permit an independent course of action in East Asia or to seek some type of accommodation with the Anglo-American nations. In these circumstances, Admiral Tōgō Heihachirō and the Navy General Staff recommended the realization of the famous 8–8 program which called for two battle fleets headed by 8 sixteen-inch capital ships.[69] This would, of course, require a huge expansion of naval armaments; but it would also provide a fleet capable of protecting the home islands, even in the dire circumstance of a war with the United States.

The desire for a great naval force was not caused only by the diplomatic context following World War I. Since 1905 Japanese naval strategy had been rooted in the premise that the United States was the major strategic enemy, and throughout the war the Japanese navy had been expanded to keep its relative strength vis-a-vis the United States. Nevertheless, the policies of the American government at the peace conference and the tremendous wartime growth of the American navy were instrumental in the decision of the Hara cabinet to pursue a major expansion of the imperial navy. The extent of this armament program is revealed by a comparison of the 1914–17 and 1918–21 naval budgets:[70]

1914	¥ 83,260,000	1918	¥215,903,000
1915	84,376,000	1919	316,419,000
1916	116,624,000	1920	403,201,000
1917	162,435,000	1921	483,589,000

By 1921 Japan not only was facing a crushing financial burden in its quest for the "fulfillment of national defense" but was threatening to set off an armaments race with Britain and the United States. Given the unresolved diplomatic issues of the Pacific area and the prospects of an astronomical

---

[69]Arai Tatsuo, *Katō Tomosaburō* (1958), pp. 51–52.
[70]Fujiwara, *Gunjishi*, p. 137.

naval budget if Japan were to become involved in an armaments race, the Takahashi cabinet, including Navy Minister Katō Tomosaburō, readily accepted President Harding's invitation to participate in a conference of the major world powers at Washington to consider the problems of naval disarmament.

THE WASHINGTON TREATY SYSTEM: A NEW STATUS QUO, 1922–1931

The treaties negotiated at the Washington Conference recognized and guaranteed Japanese naval hegemony in the western Pacific, as well as Japan's extensive rights and privileges on the mainland. For this reason it was possible, for the first time, to base Japan's diplomatic and military policies on the principle of cooperation with the Anglo-American nations. Consequently, there emerged in Japan a concept of "national defense" that placed a premium on armament control and adherence to the treaties produced at the Washington Conference. In turn, this strengthened the leadership of the prime minister within the cabinet and of the army and navy ministers within the services. Throughout the 1920s, armament control and the preservation of existing rights via diplomacy characterized the diplomacy of the Japanese government. Still, there were powerful undercurrents working against these policies. In China, the nationalist movement of the Kuomintang raised thorny questions. Should Japan assist this movement and seek to protect its long-term continental interests by friendly relations with a new central government; or should Japan safeguard its privileges by a reliance on military power? In 1927 the Tanaka cabinet formulated a basic policy guide which designated Manchuria as a "special region" in which the government must be ready to resist any encroachments on Japan's position. Following this resolution, especially within the army, one saw an increasing desire for positive actions that would isolate Manchuria from the rest of China. This approach, though, was shelved under the Hamaguchi cabinet decision denying the premise that Manchuria could be divorced from Japan's policies vis-a-vis China and the powers. A second undercurrent which seriously weakened the Washington treaty system was the policy of the American government at the 1930 London Naval Conference. By insisting on a 10:6 ratio in heavy cruisers, the United States challenged the principle of Japanese naval hegemony in the western Pacific. Overriding the objections of the Navy General Staff, the Hamaguchi cabinet committed Japan to the London Naval Treaty. This action unleashed a major domestic crisis over an alleged violation of the right of supreme command and brought on the attack on Hamaguchi by an ardent patriot. The forms of unrest generated by the growth of Chinese nationalism and by the London Naval Treaty were complemented by disenchantment with the government's handling of the economic difficulties engendered by the Great Depression. Some individuals, including a handful of army officers, envisioned a coup d'etat to rectify the deficiencies of the government; others, including the leaders of the minority party, abused the government on the grounds that its weak China policy and the London Treaty had endangered the security of the nation. These manifold expressions of opposition and resentment quickly produced widespread support for the actions of the Kwantung army when, in September 1931, it began the conquest of Manchuria. The move into Manchuria and the responses of the Western nations smashed the principle of cooperation with the powers and launched Japan on an independent continental policy. The following treatment of the 1922–31 period seeks to reveal how the Washington treaty system affected the role of the military in Japan's foreign policy and to outline the genesis of the Manchurian Incident which set a new direction for Japanese strategic and diplomatic policies.

Because the Washington Conference was to be devoted mainly to naval affairs, the Japanese delegation was headed by Navy Minister Katō Tomosaburō. He, along with Secretary of State Hughes and Arthur Balfour, guided the negotiations to their successful conclusion. The achievements of these statesmen were best reflected in the Four, Five, and Nine Power treaties. Under the Five Power Treaty, Japan acknowledged the superiority of the Anglo-American navies by accepting a 5:3 ratio in capital ships with these nations. In addition, the treaty imposed a ten-year moratorium on the construction of capital ships, thereby keeping this ratio without the necessity of further naval expansion. Under the Four Power Treaty, Japan was guaranteed naval superiority in its home waters because it precluded the construction of any new naval bases or fortifications in the western Pacific. Under the Nine Power Treaty, all the contracting powers committed themselves to the somewhat antithetical principles of respecting the "territorial and administrative integrity" of China and of maintaining the "principle of equal opportunity for the commerce and industry of all nations" throughout China.

These treaties marked a successful adjustment of the major problems of the Pacific region. From the Japanese standpoint, they achieved the primary objectives of the imperial government, including those of the Navy General Staff: Japan's home waters were secured from foreign danger; the ability and right of the navy to protect Japanese nationals on the mainland remained unchallenged; and the vexing prospect of an armament race had been avoided. These notable accomplishments, while immensely advantageous to Japan, had not been the consequence of any concessions by the Western powers. Rather they were inherent in the existing strength of the imperial navy and the geographic position of Japan's home islands. Not one of the Pacific island possessions of the United States was fortified in 1922, and there was no chance that Congress would authorize a heavy spending program to change this situation. In effect, the Washington treaty order sanctioned the status quo.

Although the naval aspects of "national defense" were satisfied by the Washington Conference, the army's contention that Japanese control over Manchuria was indispensable to the defense of the empire was not recognized by the powers. On the contrary, as Asada Sadao has shown, the United States interpreted the Nine Power Treaty as canceling the Lansing-Ishii agreement, which had recognized Japan's special interest in Manchuria; but the Japanese government construed the cardinal fourth clause of Article 1—in particular the phrase that "the powers agree to refrain from countenancing action inimical to the security of such states"—to be an implicit recognition of Japan's special interest in Manchuria.[71] To phrase it differently, the status quo to the United States meant the acceptance of the Open Door policy throughout China; to Japan it signified the acceptance of its privileged position in Manchuria. Since the Washington treaties recognized Japanese military supremacy in the western Pacific, the Open Door policy of the United States was literally dependent upon the good intentions of the imperial government. Throughout the 1920s the Japanese government adhered to the letter and the spirit of the treaties

[71]Sadao Asada, "Japan's 'Special Interests' and the Washington Conference, 1921–1922" (1961), pp. 67–68.

negotiated at the Washington Conference, despite the persisting divergence of opinion over the position of Manchuria. Even the most severe
critic of the post-Mukden era, Henry L. Stimson, conceded that Japan
had "for ten years given an exceptional record of good citizenship in the
light of the international world."[72] This decade of good behavior after
1921 reflected a basic change which the Washington Conference had helped
to bring about within the Japanese government. The treaties had confirmed the viewpoint that cooperation with the Western powers, not
unilateral action, was the better method of preserving Japan's leadership
in East Asia. Consequently, it established the priority of foreign affairs
over national defense in the ultimate determination of national policy.
This signified, in turn, the hegemony of civil leadership in foreign policy
matters and thereby contributed directly to the growth of parliamentary
government during the 1920s.

The acceptance of a national defense policy based upon the cabinet's
appraisal of the international scene and the fiscal resources of the government was evident in 1923, when military expenditures were curtailed from
49 percent of the national budget to 30 percent, without apparently endangering either the nation or the empire. This cutback caused appreciable
unrest within military circles, but it was justified, in 1922, by Prime
Minister (Admiral) Katō Tomosaburō on the basis that "national defense"
was not determined simply by military armaments but included agricultural, financial, and industrial capabilities, plus relations with other nations.
This subtle change in the meaning of "national defense" further increased
the authority of the cabinet and service ministers and contributed to
General Ugaki Kazushige's ability to implement the deactivation of the
14th, 15th, 17th, and 18th divisions in 1924 over the objections of the
General Staff.[73] The willingness of the navy and army ministers to accept
and implement a policy of armament control augured well for the development of a responsible type of government.

Without denying the effectiveness or intent of this armament control,
one should observe that Japanese military capabilities were not vitally
affected. On the contrary, because the United States followed a radical
disarmament policy after the Washington Conference, Japan's naval

---

[72]Henry L. Stimson, *The Far Eastern Crisis* (1936), p. 36.
[73]Izu and Matsushita, *Nihon gunji hattatsushi*, p. 200.

program of the 1920s produced by 1930 an absolute superiority over the American fleet in heavy cruisers and submarines.[74] One saw, in other words, the paradox of a disarmament policy which greatly augmented Japanese naval supremacy in the western Pacific. This was, of course, less the consequence of Japan's actions than of an American disarmament policy. Still, Japan's naval hegemony in the western Pacific was not seriously compromised until the American crash naval program of the late 1930s; and this development, as will be indicated, acted as one cause of the decision to strike at Pearl Harbor and undertake the conquest of Southeast Asia. Although Japan's naval power vis-a-vis the United States increased during the 1920s, the reduction of the imperial army was absolute. From 1924 to 1931 the standing army totaled only seventeen divisions, or 250,000 men—a modest force considering the extent of the Japanese empire.[75] Yet even here one must note that the famous 1924 demobilization did not yield a reduction in the total budget for the army. Rather, the savings incurred by this step were channeled into communications and air power.[76] This modernization program enhanced the combat effectiveness of the army and continued Japan's dominant position in south Manchuria. Unlike the navy, which found its relative strength increasing during the 1920s, the army found its primary mission—the protection of Japanese rights in Manchuria—becoming more complex. Indeed, with the growth of Chinese nationalism and the gradual increase of Soviet forces in the Maritime Provinces, the maintenance of Japan's position in Manchuria became a major problem for the Japanese government.

In the public forum of the late 1920s, the foreign policies of the two major political parties, the Seiyūkai and the Minseitō, were conducted in terms of the public statements of Tanaka Giichi and Shidehara Kijūrō. General Tanaka, the head of the Seiyūkai, symbolized the traditional approach of the military to foreign policy, namely, a reliance on military power to preserve Japan's interests in China. Baron Shidehara, a career diplomat who served as the foreign policy spokesman of the Minseitō,

---

[74]U.S., Congress, Senate, *London Naval Treaty of 1930: Hearings before the Committee on Naval Affairs* (1930), and *Treaty on the Limitation of Naval Armaments: Hearings before the Committee on Foreign Relations* (1930), pp. 94, 181–82.

[75]International Military Tribunal for the Far East (hereafter IMTFE), Proceedings, Document 9074.

[76]Mitarai Tatsuo, ed., *Minami Jirō* (1957), p. 183.

represented a more cautious attitude which stressed diplomacy as the best method to protect the empire. The dichotomy between "Tanaka diplomacy" and "Shidehara diplomacy" is well known to readers of Japanese history.[77] Whether they actually represented antithetical approaches to the China problem is currently a lively debate in academic circles. Usui Katsumi, for example, has shown that during the Tsingtao and Shanghai strikes of 1925, Shidehara effectively pressured Chinese officials into suppressing the strikers in a brutal fashion; and Akira Iriye has revealed that Tanaka sought to encourage American interest in Manchuria in the hope that this would promote cooperation between the United States and Japan in the region.[78] Without exploring this problem further, it seems that Shidehara was as fully devoted to preserving Japanese rights in China as General Tanaka and that Tanaka was no less eager for Japanese-American cooperation than Shidehara. Nevertheless, the assassination of Chang Tso-lin and the Tsinan crisis of 1928 enabled the Minseitō to label the Tanaka cabinet as "militaristic" and to assert that this "positive" policy only aroused Chinese hostility and created additional danger to Japanese nationals.

Tactically this was politically astute, and it brought about the downfall of the Tanaka cabinet. In the process, however, "Tanaka diplomacy" was firmly identified with an independent or positive approach to the defense of Japanese rights on the mainland; "Shidehara diplomacy" was labeled as one which relied on diplomacy, economic pressure, and cooperation with the Anglo-American nations. This public posture gave a new dimension to domestic politics. Virtually every articulate segment of Japanese society—the bureaucracies, the zaibatsu, and farm and labor organizations—believed that Japanese rights on the continent were legitimate. In the milieu, Shidehara was particularly vulnerable to the charge of "weak-kneed" diplomacy. Recently Itō Masanori advanced the proposition that Tanaka's dispatch of troops to Tsinan was dictated more by a desire to curry popular favor than by a necessity to protect Japanese lives and property; there is, more-

---

[77]*Shigaku zasshi* (May 1959), p. 98, is a convenient bibliographical review of the controversy.

[78]Usui Katsumi, "Shidehara gaikō oboegaki" (1958), pp. 62–68 and II; Akira Iriye, "Chang Hsüeh-liang and the Japanese" (1960), pp. 37–38.

over, some evidence that the Army General Staff opposed this action.[79] And in his stinging rebuke of the Tanaka cabinet's handling of the Tsinan crisis, Shidehara warned that if domestic considerations were "allowed to dominate and control the conduct of foreign relations, we cannot but be apprehensive of the future of our country and of the peace of the world."[80] Regardless of its veracity, this admonition carried with it a basic reservation, the wish to insulate foreign affairs—the prerogatives of the prime minister and the foreign minister—from the political arena. Thus, after forcing the resignation of Tanaka over the assassination of Chang Tso-lin and the Tsinan crisis, the new Minseitō (Hamaguchi) cabinet refused to divulge any information about either event. It too preferred to contain such affairs of state within the sphere of the cabinet and beyond the scrutiny of the Diet.

By 1930 the destiny of the Minseitō, the standard-bearer of Shidehara diplomacy, was contingent upon proving that it could successfully resolve the complex problems caused by the growth of Chinese nationalism. The ability to perform this task was equally vital to the continuance of the leadership of the prime minister and the foreign minister in the cabinet. Prime Minister Hamaguchi was an unequivocal supporter of Shidehara, but this confidence was not unanimously shared throughout the government. At the famous Eastern Conference of June 27–July 7, 1927, officials of the Foreign, Finance, Army, and Navy ministries plus representatives of the General Staffs and of the Kwantung army adopted a basic guide to the China problem. Although General Tanaka was prime minister at this time, the policy reflected a consensus among military and civilian officials, including those of the Foreign Ministry. Conceding the probability of a "unified" China, the policy guide recommended that Japan, in cooperation with the powers, cooperate with "legitimate" Chinese aspirations; that Japan be prepared to take "decisive" steps whenever Japanese lives or property were placed in jeopardy; and that Japan adopt "vigorous" actions to dissipate anti-Japanese movements on the mainland. Most importantly, it designated Mongolia and Manchuria as absolutely essential to the

---

[79]Itō, *Gumbatsu kōbōshi*, II, 134–36. Opposed to the Shantung expedition were Generals Araki Sadao (chief of the Operations Division), Matsui Iwane (chief of the Intelligence Division), and Minami Jirō (vice-chief of the General Staff). Mitarai, *Minami Jirō*, p. 151.

[80]Takeuchi, *War and Diplomacy*, p. 256.

nation's defense: "If disturbances should spread to Manchuria and Mongolia and menace Japan's special position and interests in this region, the imperial government must be prepared to combat this menace, regardless of where it may originate."[81] The conviction that this region constituted a special zone was widely shared throughout the government. Indeed, the assassination of Chang Tso-lin had been engineered by Japanese army officers for the purpose of frustrating the inroads of the Kuomintang into Manchuria.[82]

Although it failed to specify any direct course of action to be taken in Manchuria and Mongolia, the Eastern Conference reflected a consensus in favor of the use of military force to preserve Japan's position in this region. Equally relevant was the implicit assumption that Manchuria and Mongolia were separate from China, that Japan should have two policies—one for China, another for Manchuria and Mongolia. This notion, however, was not shared by Hamaguchi or Shidehara. There is no evidence to indicate that the Hamaguchi cabinet formally revised the policy adopted at the Eastern Conference, but the stream of criticism directed at Shidehara's moderate China policy by foreign service officers stationed in north China and Manchuria suggests that, in fact, he continued to view the Manchurian problem as an integral part of Japan's China policy.[83] Phrased differently, by 1930 strong dissatisfaction with the basic tenets of Shidehara diplomacy flourished within the Foreign Ministry and the army, and it was becoming increasingly apparent that adherence to the leadership of the prime minister and foreign minister was being corroded by a belief that Shidehara diplomacy was not adequate to the maintenance of Japan's position in Manchuria.

This criticism within the government was supplemented by the accusations leveled by the leaders of the Seiyūkai. In the Diet, charges of a spineless deference to the wishes of the Anglo-American nations and of a supine endurance of Chinese insults and illegal acts were repeatedly hurled at

[81] *Nihon gaikō nempyō*, II, 101–2, is a text of the policy adopted at this conference.

[82] Usui Katsumi, "Chō Sakurin bakushi no shinsō" (1956); Paul A. Dull, "The Assassination of Chang Tso-lin" (1952), pp. 453–63.

[83] Morishima Morito, *Imbō ansatsu guntō: gaikōkan no kaisō* (1950), p. 74; Shigemitsu Mamoru, *Shōwa no dōran* (1952), I, 51; Akira Iriye, "Japan's China Policy in the Twenties," a paper presented at the University Seminar on Modern East Asia: Japan, Columbia University, March 9, 1962.

the Hamaguchi cabinet. This public and private unrest over the China problem was not simply an expression of ultranationalistic sentiments or of irresponsible political opportunism. The difficulties which European nations encountered after World War II with the development of nationalism in colonial regions vividly attests to the deep-rooted political, diplomatic, and military problems confronting Japan in its relations with China, particularly in terms of Manchuria, where Japan had extensive rights and investments. Unfortunately for the Hamaguchi cabinet, the China tangle was compounded by the 1930 London Naval Conference.

In 1930 Japan was the leading military power in East Asia, a position that had been confirmed at the Washington Conference. Each service throughout the 1920s geared its strategic planning to the preservation of this position. In terms of Manchuria, the intensification of the nationalist movement had caused widespread concern in army circles, but this had not yet induced the Hamaguchi cabinet to modify its China policy or to support an expansion of the army in case it should prove necessary to use force in defense of Japan's position in Manchuria. In terms of naval security, the Hamaguchi cabinet had no reason to anticipate any serious problems. Japan's supremacy in the western Pacific had been recognized in 1922, and since that time its shipyards had constructed a fleet of new cruisers, destroyers, and submarines. Because American shipyards had been dormant after the Washington Conference, Japan acquired a commanding superiority over the United States. For example, on October 7, 1929, when Japan received a formal invitation to participate in a conference on naval disarmament in London, it possessed 12 heavy cruisers, the United States but one.[84]

This preponderance, however, was not essential to the national defense policy adopted in 1922, which designated supremacy in the home waters as the primary strategic objective. Consequently, the Navy General Staff judged in 1929 that this goal could be guaranteed by a 10:7 ratio in heavy cruisers with the United States. On October 10 the Japanese government publicly stipulated that this ratio was essential to the nation's defense. With this axiom, the Hamaguchi cabinet was prepared to participate in the London Conference. The 10:7 ratio seemed reasonable: it indicated

[84] Walter Lippmann, "The London Naval Conference: An American View" (1930), p. 509.

the defensive nature of Japanese strategy, and it demonstrated a willingness voluntarily to reduce an existing superiority by allowing the United States to overcome Japanese strength without resort to an armaments race. Or, as Prime Minister Hamaguchi informed the Diet on January 21, 1930: "Our claim to a definite amount of naval strength [10:7 ratio] . . . is based upon the practical necessity of making our defenses secure against foreign invasion. We offer no menace to any nation; we submit to menace from none. On that fundamental principle, it is our desire to secure a naval agreement satisfactory to all parties concerned."[85]

Without recapitulating the negotiations at London in detail, one should note that the American delegation insisted that the 10:6 ratio established for capital warships at the Washington Conference be applied to heavy cruisers. While this demand seemed fair to the American representatives, and to most American historians of the conference, it did challenge the principle of Japan's supremacy in its home waters; every American naval officer, for example, who testified on the London Treaty stipulated that a 10:6 ratio would compromise this possibility.[86] If it were legitimate for the Japanese government and the Navy General Staff to seek confirmation of the principle of naval supremacy in the western Pacific, the insistence on the 10:7 ratio was neither unreasonable nor surprising. But the American delegation's adamant opposition to this ratio led to the so-called Reed-Matsudaira compromise.[87] According to this plan, the 10:6 ratio was established in principle, but the United States agreed not to build up to its full allotted quota in heavy cruisers until the next scheduled conference in 1936. In effect, this would guarantee a de facto 10:7 ratio between the two fleets for the duration of the London Treaty. On this basis, the Hamaguchi cabinet negotiated a new naval disarmament treaty.

The London Treaty soon spawned a major domestic crisis. The chief of the Navy General Staff, Admiral Katō Kanji, claimed that the government had violated the right of supreme command by negotiating a treaty over the objections of his staff; the leaders of the Seiyūkai echoed the char-

[85]Takeuchi, *War and Diplomacy*, pp. 284–85, 289–90.

[86]U.S., Senate, *London Naval Treaty of 1930*; for recent American evaluations, see Robert H. Ferrell, *American Diplomacy in the Great Depression* (1957), pp. 87–106; Elting E. Morison, *Turmoil and Tradition: A Study of the Life and Times of Henry L. Stimson* (1960), pp. 317–38.

[87]Aritake Shūji, *Okada Keisuke* (1956), pp. 32–41, is the most concise treatment of the Reed-Matsudaira agreement.

ges that the treaty compromised national security and that Hamaguchi had violated the Meiji constitution. Hamaguchi frustrated this attack by avoiding any constitutional defense of his actions. Instead he informed the Diet that the chief of the Navy General Staff had participated in planning the logistical aspects of national defense but the responsibility for the final decision rested with the government.[88] This interpretation of the prerogatives of the General Staff prevailed, and the treaty was eventually ratified by the Privy Council. Nevertheless, the authority of the prime minister was effectively compromised by three reactions within the navy. On June 10 and 11 Admirals Yamanashi Katsunoshin and Hori Teikichi of the Navy Ministry were retired; on July 4 Navy Minister Takarabe Takeshi promised to resign in conjunction with the formal approval of the London Treaty.[89] In other words, the senior officers who had deferred to the leadership of the prime minister were cashiered. Second, on July 21 the Navy General Staff drafted a supplemental budget that would enable the navy to build up to the limits established by the London Treaty.[90] Despite his original aim of reducing naval expenditures, Hamaguchi accepted this budget proposal. Third, on July 22 the Supreme War Council presented an official reply to the Throne on the problems raised by the treaty. Without explicitly commenting on the right of supreme command, the councilors judged that: 1) the fundamental policy established in 1922 of supremacy in Japanese waters had been ignored at the London Conference; 2) the treaty created "deficiencies in our naval position"; 3) this necessitated an expansion of the navy to the limits authorized by the agreement; and 4) at the forthcoming conference the national defense policy established in 1922 should be followed rigidly. "For this reason, we believe that the empire should renew its efforts, upon expiration of the treaty, for the completion of its national defense with whatever policy it considers to be best." In other words, regardless of diplomatic considerations, the government should not deviate from the minimum national defense needs established by the Navy General Staff. Hamaguchi did not directly challenge this opinion, but in his memorial attached to that submitted by the

---

[88]Matsushita, *Meiji gunsei shiron*, II, 300.

[89]Aritake, *Okada Keisuke*, pp. 148–52.

[90]This budget called for an expenditure of ¥424 million over a six-year period and was formally authorized on November 11, 1930. U.S., Department of the Army, Office of Military History (hereafter USDAOMH), *Japanese Monograph 145* (1964), p. 6.

Supreme War Council, he tersely noted that the legality of the treaty had not been challenged by the council.[91]

The memorial of the Supreme War Council, the personnel changes within the Navy Ministry, and the adoption of a supplemental budget abridged the power of the prime minister to determine Japan's naval armament policy. This development was buttressed by a popular enthusiasm for the sanctity of the right of supreme command and by a popular conviction that Hamaguchi had compromised the security of the nation.[92] Amidst the furor over the London Naval Treaty, a patriotic youth shot and seriously wounded the prime minister because he thought Hamaguchi had, in fact, violated the Meiji constitution and endangered the country's security. So began the first of a memorable series of violent attacks on Japan's political leaders that would distinguish the early 1930s.

The public and official reactions to the London Treaty also affected the government's approach to the 1932 Geneva Conference on Disarmament. In 1929 Hamaguchi requested Army Minister Ugaki to prepare a policy guide that would enable the government to reduce the size of the imperial army. Ugaki set up the Research Committee on Army Administration under the direction of Colonel Nagata Tetsuzan to draft a policy that would meet the prime minister's desire for a manpower reduction without affecting the combat effectiveness of the army.[93] After the attempted assassination of Hamaguchi, this committee advised: 1) the number of divisions should not be reduced; 2) a manpower cut could be attained by keeping the divisions at less than full strength and by curtailing the length of active duty service for the conscripts; 3) the mechanization program could not be deferred; and 4) all savings realized by the army should be directed toward the development of an army air corps and of technical services. This recommendation conflicted with the prime minister's ambition to implement a manpower reduction and a cutback in the total budget of the army. As another crisis was brewing, the effects of the assassin's

---

[91]Aritake, *Okada Keisuke*, pp. 167–69.

[92]A convenient digest of public opinion is the compilation of newspaper articles and editorials by the Foreign Ministry, cited in Cecil H. Uyehara, *Checklist of Archives in the Japanese Ministry of Foreign Affairs, Tokyo, Japan, 1868–1945, Microfilmed for the Library of Congress, 1949–1951* (1954), p. 58; microfilm S 2.12.0.0–7, pp. 70–367; S 2.12.0.0–8, pp. 1–270.

[93]Mitarai, *Minami Jirō*, pp. 183–85.

bullet and the stringent public abuse of the Seiyūkai forced the resignation of Hamaguchi. His successor, Wakatsuki Reijirō, inherited the task of preparing a basic disarmament policy for the Geneva Conference and a long-term budget program for the army.

Wakatsuki had been the chief Japanese delegate at the London Naval Conference. Consequently, he was conscious of the extent of the controversy engendered in military circles by the naval disarmament treaty. To prevent a similar controversy over the right of supreme command, on June 18 he held a special conference with Foreign Minister Shidehara, Army Minister Minami Jirō, Navy Minister Abo Kiyokazu, and Chiefs of Staff Admiral Taniguchi Naomi and General Kanaya Hanzō. This group agreed that the chief delegate to the Geneva Conference should be a statesman, not a military officer, and that he should possess full authority to act and speak for the imperial government.[94] General Minami, however, insisted that the chief delegate "must adhere to the original instructions and not take into consideration the opinions of delegates from other nations." This style of diplomacy was accepted by Wakatsuki. He, along with Shidehara and Minami, then assumed responsibility for drafting the official policy for the forthcoming Geneva meetings. In view of Wakatsuki's and Shidehara's public advocacy of a reduction in army expenditures, Minami quickly set about to create one policy that would be acceptable to all the important officers in central headquarters. Using the recommendation of the Research Committee on Army Administration as his guide, Minami readily won the agreement of the army chief of staff. On June 1, prior to any cabinet discussion of the instructions for the Geneva delegation, Minami convened the Supreme War Council and obtained its approval of the army's policy. These steps were meant to preclude any internal dissension that might strengthen the power of the prime minister and foreign minister in the formulation of the official government policy.

The army minister planned to supplement this internal pressure by utilizing the reservist organization to arouse public opinion in support of the army's viewpoint. Before this phase was underway, a series of incidents involving Japanese nationals occurred during the summer of 1931 in Korea and Manchuria. The climax was the famous murder of Captain Nakamura

[94]*Ibid.*, pp. 178–79.

Shintarō by troops of Marshal Chang Hsueh-liang's army. By mid-August the Seiyūkai was actively spouting the cause of the ultranationalists: the imperial army was being insulted; Japanese special rights and interests were being jeopardized; the sole cause of these happenings was the "weak-kneed" Shidehara diplomacy. The aggravated situation on the continent as well as the vindictive attacks of the minority party intensified popular and political sentiment against any disarmament move. And on August 4 General Minami addressed the annual conference of divisional commanders. In his talk Minami stressed two themes: disarmament policy and the internal reorganization of the army, and the Manchuria-Mongolia problem. Since it focused on two important foreign policy issues, it marked a manifest intrusion into politics. Accordingly it drew widespread attention in the press, as it was meant to do.[95] Although this address is often identified as concrete evidence that the army was planning to act independently in Manchuria, a closer reading would suggest that it constituted more of an opening phase of a campaign to gain popular support for the army's policy vis-a-vis the budget and the Geneva Conference. One week later, for example, General Kanaya openly criticized the movement for a general armament reduction; and on September 1 the president of the reservist organization, General Suzuki Sōroku, proclaimed the opposition of his organization to any reduction of the army's budget: "If we lack adequate armaments to support our righteous cause, then an international crisis occurs and peace is disturbed."[96] What results this propaganda campaign might have had will never be known. The Manchurian Incident of September 18 shelved the disarmament matter, eventually destroyed the Wakatsuki cabinet, and launched the establishment of Manchukuo.

Although Minami's address was directed more toward disarmament issues, it also represented an indirect attack upon a reliance upon diplomacy to maintain Japanese rights and interests in Manchuria. The growing anti-Japanese sentiment on the mainland, plus the success of the first five-year plan of the Soviet Union, produced a consensus in central headquarters

---

[95]The full text of Minami's talk is reprinted in *ibid.*, pp. 217–18. The *Asahi shimbun* editorial of August 8 commented, "Although disarmament is a worldwide tendency supported by public opinion, there is no doubt that the military is openly disregarding public opinion and defying the government."

[96]*Japan Weekly Chronicle*, September 10, 1931, p. 308.

that a strong policy toward the continent was essential. In August 1931 Colonels Nagata Tetsuzan and Imamura Hitoshi were assigned the task of preparing the army's policy. The result was the "Basic Principles for a Settlement of the Manchurian Problem" which stipulated: 1) anti-Japanese sentiment in Manchuria was creating a serious problem; 2) the General Staff should prepare a plan of operations to govern any contingency requiring the use of force; 3) the army, for the present, should rely upon the efforts of the Foreign Ministry to mitigate the anti-Japanese forces on the mainland; 4) the General Staff, the Army Ministry, and the Foreign Ministry should formulate a fundamental policy for Manchuria; and 5) the Western powers and the Japanese people must be educated as to the true conditions existing in Manchuria. The policy outline concluded: "In bringing about a general understanding within Japan and abroad of the necessity to use force, efforts should be made to obtain practical results at least by the spring of 1932."[97] In effect, it proposed that the military set out to undermine Shidehara diplomacy at two levels—within the government by means of a joint policy between the Army and Foreign ministries, and in the public arena by engaging in an "educational" program that would encourage political and popular opposition to the official policies of the cabinet.

Implicit in this plan, of course, was the assumption that "Shidehara diplomacy" was inadequate to the existing situation and that the army should actively seek to rectify this condition. This lack of commitment to the legally constituted civilian leadership was not confined to the Army Ministry. Between January and March 1931 a number of officers, mostly in the General Staff and members of the Cherry Blossom Society, tried to organize a coup d'etat to bring about the appointment of General Ugaki as prime minister.[98] Behind this plot lurked the conviction that the government was not properly living up to its responsibilities. Although the March Incident failed to materialize, it revealed that, while there was no single conspiracy against the government in army circles, there was a pervasive feeling that the army should not remain passive. Some officers

[97]Mitarai, *Minami Jirō*, pp. 242–43.
[98]On the March 1931 Incident, see Hata Ikuhiko, "Rikugun no habatsu 'Sakurakai,'" (1961), pp. 88–101, and "Sakurakai shuisho" (1958), pp. 65, 81–88; also Ugaki Kazushige, *Ugaki nikki* (1954), pp. 153–59.

urged an "educational" campaign and a new national policy to govern the problems of armament control and Manchuria; others proposed a coup d'etat. Finally, on September 18 the Kwantung army engineered the Manchurian Incident for the purpose of seizing control over Manchuria, a move that proved to be the prelude to a sweeping transformation of Japan's diplomatic and military policies.

MANCHUKUO: BIRTH OF AN INDEPENDENT FOREIGN POLICY, 1931–1933

The hallmarks of Japanese diplomacy during the 1920s—armaments control and cooperation with the Anglo-American nations—were soon obliterated in the wake of the Manchurian Incident. In part, this was the consequence of Japan's move into Manchuria; in part, it was caused by the reactions of the powers, typified by the Stimson Doctrine. Whichever one chooses to stress, the creation of Manchukuo radically altered Japan's relations with China and with the Western powers. Before Manchukuo, the preservation of "Japan's rights and privileges" on the mainland permeated the policies and recommendations of the Army and Foreign ministries. By 1933 the guiding axioms became the "maintenance of peace in East Asia" and "cooperation between Manchukuo and Japan." In this interval, party cabinets and the leadership of the prime minister in determining national policy were replaced by the "national unity cabinet" of Admiral Saitō Makoto and the Five Ministers Conference as the policy-making unit. In terms of strategic planning, the dichotomy that had first occurred in 1907 reemerged—the army designated the Soviet Union as the main problem; the navy judged the United States to be the primary threat. Both services, however, agreed that Japan should strengthen its political and economic influence on the mainland, especially in north China. Essentially, with the formation of Manchukuo and withdrawal from the League of Nations, Japan sought three objectives: the preservation of naval superiority in the western Pacific, the protection of Manchukuo, and the realization of a Japanese hegemony over China. This transformation in military and diplomatic objectives serves as the main theme of the following discussion of the 1931–33 period.

The momentous consequences of the Manchurian Incident on Japan's foreign policy are undeniable, as were its corroding effects on the power of the prime minister in deciding national policy.[99] Without recapitulating the origins of this incident, it is relevant to note that, technically, the Kwantung army carried out its conquest of Manchuria in spite of a cabinet decision of September 19 to localize the matter. On September 19 Army Minister Minami cabled General Honjō Shigeru, the commanding officer of the Kwantung army, that the government had decided on a "non-aggravation" policy; in addition, the chief of the General Staff, General Kanaya, who had ultimate responsibility for operations, sent Honjō a stern order not to advance north of Changchun, not to take over any rail lines other than the South Manchuria Railway, and not to undertake any new military action without instructions from the chief of staff in Tokyo.[100] On the other hand, other members of the General Staff, including Vice-Chief General Ninomiya Harushige, and General Tatekawa Yoshitsugu, chief of the Operations Division, were sympathetic to the Kwantung army's purposes and gave conflicting advice, thus sabotaging the official decisions taken at the center; and on September 22 the Korea army dispatched a regiment across the border into Manchuria. This move violated a cardinal principle of army regulations—the need of an imperial sanction before moving a field army beyond authorized limits. General Kanaya now, however, asked for an emergency cabinet session and through the army minister requested cabinet approval of this act. Although Shidehara and Finance Minister Inoue Junnosuke opposed the request, Wakatsuki noted, "I went immediately to the palace and reported to the Throne that the government thought it should defray the expenses of the Korean troops."[101] To phrase it another way the prime minister was not willing to wage a desperate political battle to maintain civilian control over the General Staff. Toward the end of the year the army minister and the government did try to assert themselves, ordering General Honjō not to participate in the Manchurian independence movement, but they had little effect.[102] The Kwantung army gradually brought all of Manchuria under its control.

---

[99] A popular account is Richard Storry, "The Mukden Incident of September 18–19, 1931" (1957), pp. 1–12.

[100] Mitarai, *Minami Jirō*, pp. 250–51; Hanaya Tadashi, "Manshū jihen wa kōshite keikaku sareta" (1956), p. 48.

[101] Mitarai, *Minami Jirō*, pp. 260–61; Wakatsuki Reijirō, *Kofūan kaikoroku* (1950), p. 377.

[102] Mitarai, *Minami Jirō*, p. 285.

The inability of the cabinet and the senior army officers to halt, even temporarily, the acquisition of Manchuria was compounded by tremendous popular support for the activities of the Kwantung army. The Seiyūkai as well as the major "proletarian parties"—the Dai Nihon Seisantō and the Shakai Minshūtō—abused the governmental leaders as individuals lacking in "national ideals" and called for a strong foreign policy that would secure the resources of Manchuria and Mongolia for the benefit of the Japanese masses. Even Home Minister Adachi Kenzō opposed the prime minister and the foreign minister to the extent of boycotting cabinet meetings.[103] This multiple opposition proved too much. On December 12 Wakatsuki resigned.

The new prime minister, Inukai Tsuyoshi, was immediately pressured by his army minister, Araki Sadao, to sanction the conquest of Manchuria. On December 24 the Supreme War Council formally approved the launching of an "independence" movement and within a week the cabinet authorized the conquest of Chinchow.[104] The seizure of this city, as is well known, prompted the public enunciation of the Stimson Doctrine. Despite the "nonrecognition" policy of the Western nations, the Inukai cabinet on March 12 adopted a basic outline to settle the Manchurian problem along the lines recommended by the army minister and the Supreme War Council.[105] Henceforth, the rift between the imperial government and the Western nations over the Manchurian issue intensified. While the League of Nations investigating committee was preparing its report on the Manchurian Incident, the Japanese government proceeded to organize the state of Manchukuo. And on August 27, 1932 the Saitō cabinet decided to approach the problem of relations with the United States and the League "from the unique standpoint of the imperial government" and to pursue the policy of March 12 regardless of its consequences.[106] This decision had fateful results. On February 24, 1933 the Assembly of the League of Nations, with only Siam abstaining, approved the report of its investigating commission, which called for a new government in Manchuria

[103]Maejima Shōzō, *Nihon fashizumu to gikai* (1956), pp. 290–98; A. Morgan Young, *Imperial Japan, 1926–1938* (1938), pp. 114–15.
[104]IMTFE, Exhibit 188.
[105]*Nihon gaikō nempyō*, II, 205–6.
[106]*Ibid.*, pp. 206–7.

consistent with the territorial and administrative integrity of China. This vote caused the Japanese delegation to stalk out of the Assembly—the imperial government had ventured forth upon the lonely road of an "independent" foreign policy, a move that decisively affected the strategic planning of both services as well as the pattern of civil-military relations within the government.

With the establishment of Manchukuo and the withdrawal from the League of Nations, observed the Navy General Staff on May 6, 1933, "the security of East Asia has come to depend entirely upon the actual power of the Empire." Hence it proposed and was granted a second naval armament replenishment program that would, between 1934 and 1936, require a budget of some ¥477 million.[107] This expansion was justified by the implications of the Stimson Doctrine and the movement into the Pacific of the entire American fleet. It was also complemented by a pervasive conviction in the Foreign Ministry that Japan was destined for a special mission in East Asia. "Japan," reasoned Vice-Foreign Minister Shigemitsu Mamoru in September 1933, "is responsible for guaranteeing peace and security in the Far East. Japan must fulfill this role even if it requires the use of force."[108] This premise led many diplomats to view the national policy as going far beyond the legitimization of Manchukuo. Captivated by the image of a stewardship over Asian affairs, many professional diplomats became steady allies of the Navy Ministry in the vital struggle of cabinet politics and policies. Since each service advanced totally different concepts of the national defense—the navy stressing the South Seas as the essential objective, and the army insisting that Manchukuo and northeast Asia constituted the primary region—this support was crucial in preventing the army's viewpoint from becoming dominant. The realization of either policy would require astute diplomacy, and given Japan's industrial capacity and its military capabilities, simultaneous pursuit of both ambitions would be a dangerous undertaking. Yet, this happened when the inner cabinet, the Five Ministers Conference, attempted to determine one basic national policy in the fall of 1933.

At the first and second meetings of the Five Ministers Conference on

---

[107]USDAOMH, *Japanese Monograph 145*, p. 17.
[108]Top Secret, September 9, 1933, in Japan, Foreign Ministry, "Teikoku no tai-Shi seisaku kankei no ken" (hereafter cited as "Teikoku no tai-Shi seisaku"), Vol. III.

October 16 and 20, the navy minister recommended three fundamental principles to govern national policy.[109] First, Japan should continue to exert pressure on the Chinese government to prevent it from forming an alliance with the United States. Second, Japan must prevent an Anglo-American alliance directed against the imperial government. Third, the only real threat was the United States: "In the next naval conference, Japan must acquire sufficient defensive forces and get rid of the disadvantageous restrictions of the present treaty. In particular, concerning preparations against the United States at this conference, we must adopt an attitude of prudence and take care not to be restricted in our naval policy."[110] In brief, the navy minister believed a rapid expansion of naval power would compel the United States to accept Japanese leadership in Asia. Once this was achieved, China would automatically accept the economic and political help of the imperial government.

The imperial army, usually regarded as the implacable foe of the American government and the Stimson Doctrine, evaluated the situation somewhat differently. The major trouble, suggested the army minister, was the absence of an "inner policy" that would clarify the proper foreign policy. This situation could be rectified if Japan would adhere strictly to an "inner program" for the development of Manchukuo. In line with this policy, the army thought that Japan should strive for good relations with the United States and "participate in a settlement of the disarmament question up to a point where Japan's defensive safety is threatened . . . , without trying to break up the Naval Disarmament Conference." The British government posed no real problem as far as the army could see. "By making use of Britain's desire to dominate the world and the difficult situation in world affairs, Japan can repress any British plans seeking to obstruct the Manchurian policy of the imperial government." As for China, Japan should promote local governments and foster pro-Japanese movements within these regions. But, above all, the real threat to Japan was the communist menace. In particular, the Soviet armament program must be offset and Japan must "reduce the ideological intrigue of the

---

[109]"Go-daijin kaigi no sekijo kaigun daijin no rōdoku seraretaru bun," Top Secret, October 16, 1933, in Japan, Foreign Ministry, "Teikoku no taigai seisaku kankei no ken," Vol. I.

[110]"Kaigun shūsei an," Top Secret, October 20, 1933, in *ibid.*

Third International and bring about the collapse of the Soviet Union."[111] The disagreement between the two services over whether the United States or the Soviet Union constituted the major strategic threat did not carry over to the China problem. The entire conference considered China a fertile field for Japanese political and economic penetration. On October 25 Foreign Minister Hirota Kōki informed his ambassadors in Britain and the United States that the political situation in north China must be improved and that Japan would force China to abandon its anti-Japanese orientation.[112]

While the Army Ministry stressed the importance of the Soviet challenge, the Foreign and Navy ministries fastened their attention on the United States, but disagreed on how to handle it. The naval officers reasoned that a powerful fleet would compel the United States to leave the western Pacific; the diplomats preferred to gain the support of the American government for a recognized sphere of influence for Japan. This would, as Shigemitsu appreciated, justify the expansion of naval strength. Either approach had one objective—to win an economic and political stewardship over China. The assumption that Japan had the moral right, as well as the political-economic-military strength, to act as China's keeper was common to most Japanese. As an unconscious axiom, this sentiment would play a crucial role in the formulation of Japan's China policy, as well as in the strategic planning of the two services throughout the 1930s.

HEGEMONY IN NORTHEAST ASIA: THE NEW POSTURE, 1934–1937

Between 1934 and 1937 Japan extended its political and military influence over the five provinces of north China. In particular, the army launched a series of "independence" movements, culminating in the Ho-Umezu agreement of 1935, which eliminated the Kuomintang from north China and brought about a new organization of local government, the Hopei-Chahar Political Council. In contrast to this forceful approach, the Foreign and Navy ministries preferred to secure Japanese hegemony

---

[111]"Jūgatsu hatsuka goshō kaigi ni okeru rikugun gawa teiji," Top Secret, Parts 3, 4, and 7, in *ibid.*

[112]*Nihon gaikō nempyō*, II, 276.

on the mainland by means of a diplomacy based on the power of the imperial fleet. Reasoning that the Nanking government could resist Japanese leadership only if it received financial and political support from the Western powers, they hoped to cajole Britain and the United States into acceptance of a Japanese Monroe Doctrine. If this should fail, the same result could be attained by means of a preponderant military superiority in the western Pacific. To this end, the Japanese government terminated its obligations under the Washington and London naval treaties and tried to induce the Nanking government to negotiate a comprehensive Sino-Japanese treaty. When this proved futile, the diplomatic talks were ended in January 1936. The inner cabinet then devised a national policy acceptable to both services and the Foreign Ministry, the "Fundamentals of National Policy" of August 7, 1936. In effect, this called for the maintenance of the status quo in north China, the expansion of both services, and the integration of the economic resources of Manchukuo with the industrial complex of the homeland. These aims did not modify those outlined in 1933, but they did breed a new approach to north China. After this August decision, Japan was content to leave north China in limbo, to retain the existing local governments, and to exclude the Kuomintang from the region. The Sian Incident of December 1936, however, caused a resurgence of Chinese nationalism which exerted increased pressure on the Nationalist government to reassert its authority in north China. By 1937 both governments viewed north China through different prisms. Japan wished to keep the status quo and concentrate on the implementation of a five-year economic plan designed to build a powerful military and industrial complex; the Nationalist government was anxious to reestablish its influence in north China and to rely on the economic and political interests of the powers as a check against Japanese pressure. With the Marco Polo Bridge Incident, both governments reacted in terms of these aspirations. Chiang Kai-shek attempted to use the skirmish as a means of reasserting his authority in north China; the Konoe cabinet insisted that the matter be handled by the local government, the Hopei-Chahar Political Council. The subsequent diplomatic maneuvers and military moves of July and August resulted in the China War, a conflict which again transformed the military and diplomatic objectives of the Japanese government. The following account of the 1934–37 period is structured to reveal the genesis, adoption, and consequences of the "Fundamentals of National

Policy" of August 1936, especially as they affected Japan's foreign policy.

The attainment of political hegemony in East Asia would necessitate a complete overhaul of the Washington treaty order, especially the Nine Power Treaty. This task was not without complications. "The path of a rising nation," Foreign Minister Hirota informed the Diet on February 22, 1934, "is always strewn with problems. . . . Japan, serving as only the cornerstone for the edifice of peace in East Asia, bears the entire burden of responsibilities. It is this important position and vast responsibility in which foreign diplomacy and national defense are rooted."[113] In the spring of 1934 Ambassador Saitō Hiroshi tried to convince Secretary of State Cordell Hull that the two governments should issue a joint declaration designating the United States as the stabilizing power in the eastern Pacific and Japan as the dominant nation in the western Pacific.[114] Unfortunately, from the Japanese standpoint, Hull retorted in a quiet tone that the whole idea was inconceivable. Directly after the formation of the Okada cabinet, the navy minister on July 14 pressed the cabinet to approve a policy that would result in the abrogation of the existing naval treaties.[115] Two months later the government formally adopted the "conditions" to be presented at the 1936 naval disarmament conference; but it was clearly understood that the Japanese delegation would not participate in any agreement. For example, when Prince Saionji asked Foreign Minister Hirota whether Japan would still abrogate the treaty even if the powers accepted the Japanese terms, Hirota replied, "We must abrogate it no matter how much the other powers agree to our proposals."[116] Although this attitude was mainly attributable to the new national policy objectives decided upon by the Five Ministers Conference in 1933, it clearly shows that Japan's disarmament policy was being formulated by the navy. Consequently, its strategic planning was actually governing this aspect of foreign policy—a noticeable fact, if one but recalls the context of policy-making during the Hamaguchi cabinet just four years earlier.

[113]U.S., Department of State, *Foreign Relations of the United States, 1934* (1950), III, 13.

[114]*Ibid.*, pp. 654–59.

[115]Aritake, *Okada Keisuke*, p. 259.

[116]Harada Kumao, *Saionji kō to seikyoku* (1951), September 13, 1934, IV, 71; for English translation, see SCAP, Civil Intelligence Section, GHQ, Far Eastern Command, *Saionji-Harada Memoirs* (hereafter cited as *Saionji-Harada Memoirs*), p. 1004.

By this time the concept of "national defense" had also garnered new connotations at the level of public politics. In January 1933 Army Minister Araki explained to the members of the Diet that preparations for national defense belonged to the supreme command. Of course political, economic, and diplomatic matters also had to be considered in determining the national defense policy, and the supreme command should discuss these matters carefully with the government; but the decision should rest with the supreme command and "there should not appear any differences of opinion between the government and the supreme command."[117] And in February 1934 Navy Minister Ōsumi Mineo declared that "naval officers and men are forbidden to submit petitions, hold meetings, or make public their views upon the administration," but added that he believed they could "discuss matters relating to national defense."[118] That is, on these matters naval officers could be active, providing they did not become "addicted" to politics. Most dramatically, in October 1934 the newly organized Press Office of the Army Ministry published "The Essence of National Defense and Proposals to Strengthen It."[119] Claiming that "war is the father of creation and the mother of culture," this tract was deliberately issued to bolster the concept of a "national defense state." In the postwar years most writers have stressed the domestic implications of this publication.[120] At the time, however, the distinguished Minobe Tatsukichi was equally distressed by its consequences for foreign affairs.[121] Pointing out that the pamphlet equated militarism with the imperial governmental system, Minobe then warned of the danger that such an identification would stimulate a virulent nationalism that would erect an artificial dichotomy between the national interest and cooperation with the great powers. In particular, he called attention to its central theme that Japan should have an "autonomous national defense sphere"—a phrase that meant scuttling the Washington and London naval treaties in favor

[117]Matsushita, *Meiji gunsei shiron*, II, 301.

[118]*Japan Weekly Chronicle*, February 1, 1934, p. 136.

[119]IMTFE, Document 3089.

[120]Maruyama Masao, "Nihon fashizumu no shisō to undō" (1965), pp. 29–87; for English translation, see Masao Maruyama, *Thought and Behaviour in Modern Japanese Politics*, edited by Ivan Morris (1963), pp. 25–83.

[121]Minobe Tatsukichi, "Rikugunshō happyō no kokubōron o yomu" (1934). This article was reprinted in a special supplement to the November 1954 issue of *Chūō kōron*, pp. 328–35.

of developing the South Seas and revising the various treaties affecting the mainland. If this policy were followed, thought Minobe, the Western powers would adopt a similar approach to their national defense and Japan would then be confronted with the prospect of war with the Western nations. But the opinions of the venerable law professor were ignored as the basic notion of coordinating national policies under a "national defense state" concept rapidly gained momentum within governmental, business, and military circles.

On July 14, 1934 the Okada Keisuke cabinet established the Cabinet Deliberative Council. This was composed of representatives from the three major political parties, the zaibatsu, and the House of Peers and was headed by Okada and Finance Minister Takahashi Korekiyo. Under this body the Cabinet Research Bureau was created and, within the framework of this group, representatives of the Army and other ministries set out to devise legislative recommendations and common policies for the cabinet. "This may have been a mistake," said Okada later,[122] for here began the effective liaison among military, economic, political, and bureaucratic personnel which produced in 1935 a new administrative arrangement to govern Manchukuo and which, in subsequent years, would produce a series of laws that brought about the growing authoritarianism of the late 1930s. For our purposes, it signifies the bureaucratic implications of the encompassing concept, "national defense state." As yet the specific working procedures of the Cabinet Research Bureau have not been revealed, but it was one way the military indirectly affected foreign policy.

More tangibly, the designation of the Soviet Union and the United States as the two strategic enemies also influenced the China policy of the imperial government. In the fall of 1934 Shigemitsu Mamoru devised a clever strategy which he believed could attain the basic objectives desired by both services without resorting to an open conflict with China, the United States, or the Soviet Union. This feat could be accomplished if Japan gave "direct benefit to China . . . [by] shattering the political power and organizations created by foreign countries." That is, Japan should: 1) eliminate all legal privileges held on the mainland, 2) extend strong support to the Chinese central government, and 3) "deliberately and systematically" destroy the legation rights in north China and Shanghai. These moves would, Shigemitsu reasoned, direct Chinese xenophobia against the Occidental

---

[122]Aritake, *Okada Keisuke*, pp. 302–6.

nations and thereby guarantee effective Japanese leadership in East Asia.
Moreover, added this worthy student of Bismarck, "the withdrawal of
Japanese forces from the northern provinces of China would not bring
any disadvantages to Japan because the imperial army would be stationed
in the Great Wall district and in Manchuria."[123] However, the idea of
withdrawing the army and the navy, albeit a nominal distance in comparison to that required of the Western powers, incurred the relentless
abuse of the Army and Navy ministries. Neither service was anxious to
surrender the tangible tactical and political-economic advantages of the
status quo for the theoretical benefits envisioned by the vice-foreign
minister. Hence, at a fateful December 7, 1934 meeting of the inner cabinet, the ministers decided that "for the time being, it is desirable that
Japan try to reduce to a minimum the influence of the Chinese central
government on the governments in north China."[124] Underlying this
ruling was the political power of the two services and, by definition, the
military responsibilities entrusted to each service to defend existing treaty
rights in general and Manchukuo in particular.

After the creation of Manchukuo, the extension of Japanese influence or,
more accurately, the reduction of the power of the Kuomintang in these
provinces became the dominant feature of Japan's China policy. This was
done by means of the Japanese army. By mid-February 1933 the cabinet
had come to look upon the conquest of Jehol province as desirable.[125]
This campaign brought about the Tangku Truce of May 31, 1933, which
"demilitarized" a zone north and east of Tientsin-Peking in Hopei province.[126] Seeking to erect a buffer zone between Manchukuo and the
Nanking government, the Kwantung army organized the Special Service
Agency, under General Doihara Kenji, for the purpose of launching "local"
Mongolian and Chinese governments throughout north China.[127]

In the spring of 1935, in hopes of checking these intrigues, the Chinese
government proposed the negotiation of a Sino-Japanese friendship treaty.

[123]"Tai-Shi seisaku ni kansuru Shigemitsu jikan no kōju," Top Secret, October 20, 1934,
in "Teikoku no tai-Shi seisaku," III, 7.
[124]"Shina mondai ni kansuru gumbu to no kyōgi no ken," Top Secret, December 12,
1934, in *ibid.*
[125]Harada, *Saionji kō to seikyoku*, February 17, 1933, III, 23; *Saionji-Harada Memoirs*, p. 531.
[126]*Nihon gaikō nempyō*, II, 274.
[127]Mitarai, *Minami Jirō*, pp. 392–93.

While these talks were in process, General Doihara on March 30 drafted the "China Policy of the Kwantung Army." This policy advised that the army should neither support nor oppose the projected "pro-Japanese" policy outlined in the Nanking proposals, insist upon a rigid enforcement of the Tangku Truce agreement, and materially aid the southwestern "warlords" so that they might more effectively resist the Chinese central government.[128] The preceding day the staff of the Tientsin army berated the Chinese officials of the Peiping Branch Military Council and demanded that all Kuomintang officials be removed from Hopei province.[129] Sensing a major incident in the air, the Navy General Staff promptly voiced its "One View of the China Situation." Any new military moves in north China, thought the naval officers, would prompt an Anglo-American intervention because of their mutual interests in north China. More crucially, the navy, given its existing strength, could not deter the anticipated intervention. "If Japan were forced to concede to the powers," worried the Navy General Staff, "just one such instance would produce great disorder in Japan and threaten the peace of the Far East. The situation could never be restored to its former position."[130]

Presumably the considered opinion of the Navy General Staff had some effect. At least, on June 5 the Army Ministry drafted an "Outline of Policy to Deal with the Negotiations Concerning North China" which emphasized the prudence of controlling north China by means of economic penetration and support of the existing governments.[131] Although this policy precluded any direct military action, it did advise the withdrawal of all Kuomintang advisers, as well as all Nationalist troops to a point south of Paoting. Within two weeks the field army negotiated the Ho-Umezu and the Chin-Doihara agreements which realized these objectives.[132] After these military pacts, the primary aim of the Nanking government centered on reestablishing its position in north China, while the Japanese government sought to perpetuate the new status quo.

[128]"Kantōgun tai-Shi seisaku," Top Secret, March 30, 1935, in Japan, Navy General Staff, "Kahoku mondai 'shinsei jiken' keii."

[129]"Peipin hosakan hatsu sambō jichō ate," Cable No. 384, Top Secret, May 29, 1935, in *ibid*.

[130]"Tai-Shi shoken," Top Secret, May 31, 1935, in *ibid*, p. 3.

[131]*Nihon gaikō nempyō*, II, 293.

[132]Hata Ikuhiko, "Umezu Ka Ōkin kyōtei keii" (1957), pp. 65–114; Shimada Toshihiko, "Umezu Ka Ōkin kyōtei no seiritsu" (1959), pp. 50–70.

Another manifestation of military influence was evident in the formulation of Hirota's "Three Principles," the ostensible basis of Japan's China policy between the fall of 1935 and the outbreak of the 1937 China Incident. On September 7 Chiang Kai-shek proposed three principles to serve as the basis of a Sino-Japanese friendship treaty. In effect, they would have restored the status quo ante of 1931 in north China in exchange for de facto recognition of Manchukuo. Foreign Minister Hirota advised his staff that "the enforcement of Chiang's three principles and the abolition of the truce agreements [in north China] are essential for the establishment of good Sino-Japanese relations. . . . But it is necessary first to make some preliminary efforts with the Army and Navy ministries to find a way of resolving these problems."[133] On September 20 the army, navy and foreign ministers ordered their bureau chiefs to prepare a counterproposal to Chiang's principles. One week later the consensus of their subordinates recommended that Nanking 1) exercise a strict control over all anti-Japanese groups in China, 2) sign a cultural-economic agreement with Manchukuo and Japan, and 3) cooperate to suppress the communist menace in East Asia.[134] These recommendations were formally adopted by the cabinet on October 4 and were publicly identified as Hirota's Three Principles.

Most striking about these principles was the ingenuous omission of any reference to previous agreements affecting the situation in north China. In conjunction with its approval of the Three Principles, the cabinet also ruled that the December 7, 1934 policy would remain in effect, i.e., the Kuomintang would be excluded from the region.[135] At a conference in Dairen on October 16–18, the staff of the Kwantung army actually requested public enunciation of an unstated fourth principle: that the centralization of China by the Kuomintang was neither necessary nor desirable. "After all," observed General Okamura Yasuji, "it is predictable that Chiang Kai-shek will persist in his negative attitude until he is driven to the wall . . . [and], for the time being, Japan must maintain its policy based on the spirit of positive force."[136]

---

[133]"Shō taishi dainiji kaidan ni taisuru daijin oshu shian," Top Secret, September 18, 1935, in "Teikoku no tai-Shi seisaku," VI, 15.

[134]Cables No. 687, 689, 716, Top Secret, in *ibid.*, Vol. IV.

[135]"Kankei daijin ryōkai ni taisuru fuzoku bunsho," October 4, 1935, in *ibid.*

[136]"Okamura shōshō raidan yōryō," Top Secret, October 18, 1935, in *ibid.*, p. 6.

Certainly throughout the fall of 1935 the Kwantung army applied tremendous pressure on leading Chinese officials in north China to break away from the Nanking government. However, on November 22 the Five Ministers Conference decided in favor of a situation in north China comparable to that enjoyed by the southwest military clique.[137] The result was the organization of the Hopei-Chahar Political Council on December 12 under General Sung Che-yuan. On November 25 the Kwantung army had established the East Hopei Anti-Communist Autonomous Council headed by Yin Ju-ken in the "demilitarized" zone formed by the Tangku Truce agreement. Both moves appreciably curtailed the prestige and influence of the Kuomintang, shattered any possibility of a Sino-Japanese friendship treaty, and brought about a status quo that seemed adequate for the protection of Manchukuo. Consequently, on January 13, 1936 the Army Ministry adopted an "Outline of Policy to Deal with North China" which defined the ultimate objective as a "stable" north China, headed by local Chinese officials.[138] Within two weeks this policy was quickly seconded by the staff of the Foreign Ministry.

This consensus led Prime Minister Hirota, in the spring of 1936, to organize a secret Committee on the Current Situation for the specific task of devising a coordinated China policy.[139] Composed of officials of the Foreign, Army, Navy, and Finance ministries, it prepared, after four months of negotiations, a guide which listed the following four major objectives: 1) the eventual independence of north China from the Nanking government; 2) the economic development of north China in conjunction with the exploitation of the resources of Manchuria; 3) the promotion of a "Mongolia for Mongolians" movement; and 4) the resumption of talks with the Nationalist government on a "pro-Japanese, anti-Soviet" basis. The Five Ministers Conference approved the recommendations on August 7 and four days later the cabinet adopted them as part of the "Fundamentals of National Policy." Parallel with this national policy decision, the cabinet ruled that the army must avoid any independent activities in China and cooperate with the Foreign Ministry in implementing the new policy.

[137]Cables No. 306, 307, 313, in *ibid.*
[138]*Nihon gaikō nempyō,* II, 322–23.
[139]IMTFE, Document 2446.

This was supplemented by the August 11 "Second Outline of Policy to Deal with North China," which reiterated the cabinet decision.[140]

The willingness of the army to forego additional military pressure in north China was related to an increasing concern over the Soviet problem. In particular, General Ishiwara Kanji of the General Staff, together with Miyazaki Masayoshi, an economic expert of the South Manchuria Railway Company, drafted an ambitious five-year economic program that was designed to integrate the resources of Manchuria and north China into the industrial complex of Japan.[141] In June 1936 a modified version of this five-year plan was accepted by the Army Ministry. Inherent in Ishiwara's program was the premise that the Soviet Union could be defeated only if the industrial and manpower resources of the empire were mobilized through two five-year programs. His planning also gave a priority to army needs—a trait that drew a strong protest from the Navy General Staff. Under the direction of Admiral Fukudome Shigeru, the Navy Staff countered Ishiwara's plan with a "defend the north, advance in the south" policy. These conflicting viewpoints found their way into the "Basic Principles of National Policy" decision reached on June 30 by the army and navy ministers.[142]

In this remarkable policy, both services proposed that the "Imperial Way" be realized by a "consistent policy of overseas expansion." This meant getting "rid of the menace of the Soviet Union, while preparing against Britain and the United States; and bringing about a close collaboration among Japan, Manchukuo, and China." Specifically, the army was to be strengthened so that it could smash the Soviet army with "one blow from the beginning" and the navy was to be enlarged so that it could "maintain the command of the western Pacific against the United States' navy."[143]

Both versions of "national defense" were accommodated by the use of vague language in the "Fundamentals of National Policy" adopted by the Five Ministers Conference on August 7. According to the government's decision, Japan should correct the domineering policies of the Western

[140]IMTFE, Exhibits 216, 979, 213.
[141]Katakura Chū, "Ugaki naikaku ryūzansu" (1956), pp. 161–62; Aritake Shūji, *Ishiwata Sōtarō* (1954), pp. 193–204; IMTFE, Exhibits 842, 715.
[142]IMTFE, Exhibit 977.
[143]IMTFE, Exhibits 1, 2.

powers and substitute a spirit of coexistence and coprosperity based upon the Imperial Way; improve its national defense and become the stabilizing power in East Asia; and develop Manchukuo while preparing against the Soviet Union and the Anglo-American nations. Since these goals were somewhat abstract, the Four Ministers Conference adopted the following day the "Foreign Policy of Imperial Japan," which "clarified" the principles already sanctioned by the Five Ministers Conference. This decision determined that the two fundamental aims of Japan's foreign policy were the frustration "of Russia's aggressive plan in East Asia" and the acquisition of sufficient naval power to guarantee command of the western Pacific. Furthermore, the inner cabinet allowed that "preparations for future advance" into the South Seas were necessitated by the demands of national defense. To allay the fears of the diplomats, the ministers belatedly added that these preparations should be made discreetly so as "not to stimulate the powers concerned but to calm their apprehensions toward our empire."[144] The synthesis of these two decisions, plus the China policy drafted by the Committee on the Current Situation, became the "Fundamentals of National Policy" of August 11.[145]

This national policy failed to give priority to either concept of national defense and likewise failed to outline a specific policy to implement the aspirations included in the decision.[146] Instead, two differing concepts of national defense were sanctioned by the technique of phrasing the objectives in terms vague enough to satisfy the interests of each General Staff. Still, both services were anxious to avoid any military involvement in China. In May 1937 the Army Ministry proposed a "Five-Year Program for the Development of Major Industries" which envisioned the creation of a Japan-Manchukuo-north China economic bloc by 1941. This was supplemented by a "Five-Year Plan for Production of War Matériel."[147] Although north China was included as a long-range goal, the chief of staff of the Kwantung army, General Tōjō Hideki, advised the staff of the Foreign Ministry that, with the exception of east Hopei, the resources

---

[144]*Nihon gaikō nempyō*, II, 344–47.

[145]IMTFE, Exhibit 979.

[146]Another evaluation ruled that it "set out in the utmost clarity the principles which were to guide Japan, both in her relationships with other nations and in completing her internal preparations for war." IMTFE, Judgment, p. 119.

[147]IMTFE, Document 215, Exhibit 842.

of the area were not essential for the realization of current plans for national defense.[148] This preoccupation with a Soviet conflict led the General Staff in June 1937 to rule that the army in north China should avoid any incidents that might complicate the international situation and hinder the effective implementation of the five-year plans.[149]

Despite this policy, on July 7 a small number of Chinese and Japanese troops became involved in a brief skirmish near the Marco Polo Bridge.[150] Since the Konoe cabinet and the General Staff wished to settle the matter promptly, the field army in north China was ordered to dispose of the incident without raising any political demands. On July 11 representatives of the Hopei-Chahar Political Council and the Japanese army negotiated a settlement. At the same moment, however, the Nanking government advised Tokyo that it must approve any agreement and dispatched four divisions to Paoting in southern Hopei. Both actions violated the Ho-Umezu agreement and transformed the fracas at the Marco Polo Bridge into a major diplomatic contest. Prime Minister Konoe, in response, held a press conference in which he notified Nanking that it must refrain from interfering with "local" affairs in north China and announced that Japan was going to mobilize its army to meet any contingency. On July 18 the Nationalist government informed the Japanese Foreign Ministry that it would continue its military preparations and again insisted on its right to approve any settlement of the incident. This was followed by a public appeal to the signatories of the Nine Power Treaty for help in resolving the crisis peacefully, and on July 19 Chiang Kai-shek publicly declared, "If we allow one inch more of our territory to be lost, we shall be guilty of an unpardonable crime against our race."[151] Clearly, the Nationalist government was determined to assume responsibility for any settlement of the incident.

---

[148]"Horinouchi jikan oyobi Ōa Tōa kyokuchō to Tōjō kantōgun sambōchō kaigi yōryō," June 16, 1937, in "Teikoku no tai-Shi seisaku," Vol. VII.

[149]IMTFE, Proceedings, p. 21979. Even the Tokyo Tribunal conceded that the General Staff planning of 1937 "was not directed wholly or principally toward the conquest of China." Judgment, p. 168.

[150]For a more detailed account of this incident, see Kurihara Ken, "Nikka jihen keika gaiyō" (1958), pp. 43–51; Hata Ikuhiko and Shimizu Setsurō, "Rokōkyō jiken" (1956), pp. 2, 80–97; in English, see my article, "A Reconsideration of the Marco Polo Bridge Incident" (1963), pp. 277–91.

[151]*Survey of International Affairs, 1937* (1938), I, 186–87.

While the two governments were adopting contradictory policies, the field army managed on July 19 to work out another solution of the matter. Two days later the Army General Staff canceled its earlier mobilization order, and on July 23 the Army Ministry requested the Foreign Ministry to open formal talks with Nanking to confirm the local agreement. This would have entailed a modification of the official policy of the government, but neither the prime minister nor the foreign minister was willing to follow such a course of action. In effect, both governments were unwilling to modify their initial public posture, a situation that rendered solution of the incident a virtual impossibility. On July 27 the Japanese army forwarded a twenty-four-hour ultimatum calling for implementation of the agreements reached on July 11 and 19. Instead Chinese troops launched an attack. Because they were decisively beaten, General Sung, the head of the Hopei-Chahar Political Council, accepted "free passage" for his troops and withdrew from Peking to the right bank of the Yungting River. The Army General Staff then vetoed further operations in hopes that the government could still settle the matter. At the same time, Prime Minister Konoe publicly called for a "fundamental solution of Sino-Japanese relations."[152] Japan was now willing to open direct talks with Nanking, but on matters far more complex than those raised over the Marco Polo Bridge Incident.

The Five Ministers Conference on August 7 formally decided on the proposals to be submitted to the Nationalist government.[153] Essentially, Japan wished a demilitarized zone in the Peking-Tientsin area, a new political administration in north China to be staffed by Chinese sympathetic to friendly Sino-Japanese relations, and a promise that Nanking would negotiate a general treaty that would grant de facto recognition to Manchukuo and suppress all anti-Japanese groups in China. An impassive observer might have judged acceptance of these terms a remote possibility, in view of Chiang's refusal to recognize a "local" settlement of the Marco Polo Bridge Incident which had not raised any political demands. The Konoe cabinet, though, thought them "beyond the expectations of the Chinese . . . and worthy of winning the respect of the whole world for the fair and disinterested attitude of our Empire."[154] The Chinese response to

[152]IMTFE, Document 617, p. 18.
[153]IMTFE, Document 2146.
[154]IMTFE, Defense Document 2030.

these proposals came on August 14 when Nationalist bombers attacked the Japanese naval installation in Shanghai. The China War had begun.

GENESIS OF JAPAN'S NEW ORDER: THE CHINA WAR, 1937–1940

Following Japan's withdrawal from the League of Nations, the "maintenance of peace in East Asia" had defined the central ambition of the imperial government. This task, in turn, justified the dual concepts of national defense approved by the national policy decision of August 1936. Still, there was an inconsistency between the claim that Japan should be charged with keeping the peace in East Asia and the recognition that its military capabilities were not sufficient to guarantee security vis-a-vis the American fleet and the Soviet army. Because the Army General Staff regarded the Soviet Union as the primary strategic problem, it was throughout the 1937-40 period the source of the strongest and most consistent pressure in favor of terminating the China War. In contrast to this approach, the Konoe cabinet adopted radically new policy orientations to the China War. In the summer of 1937 it proposed to "chastise" the Nationalist government for its mistaken and arrogant ways, and in January 1938, it defined the "establishment of a new order" as the objective of the China War. Each of these policy shifts was adopted over the objections of the Army General Staff. Before November 1937, for example, it refused to sanction operations against Nanking, and before June 1938 it opposed extending operations into south China. The inability of the General Staff to impress its strategic approach on the policies of the Konoe cabinet is particularly striking, because in November 1937 the Imperial Headquarters was activated. The failure can be explained, in large part, by the role of the Navy General Staff in the Imperial Headquarters. Japan's naval leaders did not share the contention that the Soviet Union was the main strategic issue, and the expansion into central and south China directly enhanced Japan's naval strength vis-a-vis the Anglo-American fleets. In effect, the antithetical national defense concepts sanctioned in 1936 now served to prevent the Imperial Headquarters from formulating one guiding strategic policy for the conduct of the China War. This dissension in the Imperial Headquarters enabled the Konoe cabinet to determine the strategy and diplomacy of the China War.

There were several reasons why the cabinet chose not to follow the advice of the Army General Staff, including the popular emotions unleashed by the victories of the army and the casualties incurred in these triumphs, the rapid buildup of two large field armies in China, and the creation of puppet governments in north and central China. Still, in my estimation, a basic cause of the policies of the Konoe cabinet resides in the political visions expressed by the concept of the New Order in East Asia. Once the China War began, the Konoe cabinet constantly enlarged the scope of its declared objectives until it had committed Japan to a goal far more encompassing than the "maintenance of peace in East Asia." Phrased differently, from 1937 to 1940 political and economic considerations were the main determinants of Japan's conduct of the China War. The following discussion of this period is designed to reveal how the interaction of the conflicting strategies of the two General Staffs contributed to the projection of the New Order in East Asia as the basic objective of Japanese foreign policy.

The outbreak of hostilities in Shanghai in August 1937 caught the Japanese government by surprise. The Konoe government had no specific political or military objective for the Shanghai region. On September 5, for example, Foreign Minister Hirota notified the Diet that Japan intended to inflict a decisive defeat on the Nationalist army so that China would "lose its will to fight" and "reflect on the errors of its ways." Prime Minister Konoe warned, however, that, if "China fails to realize its mistakes and persists in its stubborn resistance, our Empire is fully prepared for protracted hostilities."[155] This determination was not shared by the Army General Staff. Desperately anxious to avoid protracted fighting, it pressured the cabinet into accepting the good offices of the German Foreign Office in an effort to negotiate a settlement with the Nanking government.[156]

The Japanese government on November 3 advised the German ambassador, Herbert von Dirksen, of its peace terms: 1) an autonomous government for Inner Mongolia; 2) a demilitarized zone "along the Manchukuo border to a point south of the Peking-Tientsin line"; 3) an enlarged demilitarized zone for Shanghai; 4) the termination of all anti-Japanese activities

---

[155]U.S., Department of State, *Papers Relating to the Foreign Relations of the United States, Japan: 1931–1941* (1943), pp. 392–93, 368.

[156]IMTFE, Document 820.

in China; 5) "a common fight against Bolshevism"; 6) a reduction in duties on Japanese goods; and 7) a guarantee of existing Japanese rights in China. Two days later Chiang Kai-shek insisted that "he could not accept any Japanese demands so long as the Japanese were not prepared to restore the status quo ante." This response posed a vexing problem. By November 13 the Japanese army had complete control over the Shanghai region, yet Nanking refused to come to terms. General Matsui Iwane, the commanding officer in Shanghai, and the cabinet argued that capture of Nanking would induce the Nationalist government to settle the incident. Finally, on December 1 the Army General Staff authorized a campaign against Nanking. Within three days Chiang Kai-shek notified the German Foreign Office that he was now prepared to enter into negotiations on the basis of the terms outlined on November 3. The reaction in Tokyo was ambivalent. The Army General Staff urged a prompt acceptance, but on December 7 Foreign Minister Hirota advised Ambassador Dirksen that the November peace terms were no longer appropriate.[157] Despite this assertion, the Konoe cabinet could not formulate its new terms until December 17, mainly because of the activities of the Army General Staff.

In order to control better the critics of its handling of the conduct of the China War, the Army General Staff in November succeeded in activating the Imperial Headquarters.[158] Unlike the Imperial Headquarters of the Russo-Japanese War,[159] civil officials were specifically excluded. Technically, the cabinet and the Imperial Headquarters were separate institutions, a situation which led to the practice of holding liaison conferences between representatives of the cabinet and of the General Staffs. The first Liaison Conference met on December 14 to determine a coordinated diplomatic and military policy vis-a-vis the China War. General Tada Shun, the vice-chief of the Army General Staff, insisted that there

[157]Dirksen to German Foreign Office, November 3, 1937, Document 514, in U.S., Department of State, *Documents on German Foreign Policy, 1918–1945, from the Archives of the German Foreign Ministry, Series D (1937–1945)* I, (1949), 778–79; Trautman to German Foreign Office, November 5, 1937, Document 516, in *ibid.*, pp. 780–81; Dirksen to German Foreign Office, December 7, 1937, Document 536, in *ibid*, p. 799.

[158]IMTFE, Defense Document 2502, Harada, *Saionji kō to seikyoku*, November 18, 1937, VI, 135; *Saionji-Harada Memoirs*, p. 1925.

[159]Matsushita, *Meiji gunsei shiron*, II, 558–60.

was no need to formulate new peace terms because the government had, the previous month, already informed Chiang Kai-shek of its desires. Home Minister (Admiral) Suetsugu Nobumasa, with the support of the prime minister and the foreign minister, however, judged these terms too mild.[160] This generated an acrimonious exchange between Tada and Suetsugu, one which caused the Liaison Conference to be adjourned without any decision being reached. The Konoe cabinet then proceeded to draft a new set of conditions: 1) China must sign an anti-Comintern pact; 2) special regions and demilitarized zones would be established in areas deemed necessary by the two governments; 3) close economic co-operation between Japan and China must be guaranteed; and 4) China must pay an indemnity.[161] These terms were deliberately vague, in harmony with the desire of Education Minister Marquis Kido Kōichi that they be sufficiently ambiguous as "to cover everything."[162] Konoe convened the second Liaison Conference on December 20 and Foreign Minister Hirota presented the cabinet's new policy.[163] Over the strenuous opposition of General Tada, it was adopted as the official policy of the Konoe government.

Although the prime minister insisted that the government wished to negotiate a settlement with the Nationalist government, the Army General Staff had grave reservations about the sincerity of this position. This apprehension was not unwarranted. In early December, for example, Konoe had confided to Baron Harada Kumao, "After Nanking falls, Chiang Kai-shek's government is going to collapse and Japan is going to issue a statement withdrawing recognition from Chiang's government."[164] To frustrate this plan, General Tada insisted that the government call an Imperial Conference to discuss the China War.

Konoe regarded this maneuver as scandalous—adding that Tada was "such an unreasonable fellow. Sometimes I wonder how he ever got as

[160]Ishii Itarō, *Gaikōkan no isshō* (1950), pp. 299–300; Kazami Akira, *Konoe naikaku* (1951), pp. 88–96.

[161]IMTFE, Defense Document 2502, p. 64.

[162]Harada, *Saionji kō to seikyoku*, December 27, 1937, VI, 193; *Saionji-Harada Memoirs*, p. 1982.

[163]IMTFE, Defense Document 2146, p. 7.

[164]Harada, *Saionji kō to seikyoku*, December 18, 1937, VI, 181; *Saionji-Harada Memoirs*, p. 1969.

far as he did."[165] But the prime minister was not to be outflanked. He structured the Imperial Conference so as to neutralize the opinion of the General Staff. First, he indicated in his request to the Throne that no questions should be raised by the emperor because the cabinet's policy was already decided upon. Second, he added, by special invitation, Baron Hiranuma Kiichirō, the president of the Privy Council and a strong supporter of Admiral Suetsugu. Third, at the Imperial Conference on January 11, 1938 he had Foreign Minister Hirota read the "Fundamental Policy for the Disposition of the China Incident" prepared by the cabinet.[166] Embodying the terms established in December, it added a three-day time limit. If the Nationalist government failed to accept the terms within seventy-two hours, Japan would "annihilate" the central government and promote "new regimes" for a rejuvenated China.

When the third Liaison Conference was convened on January 15, the foreign minister reported that Chiang Kai-shek was stalling and a favorable answer could not be expected. In spite of this, General Tada persisted in his request that the negotiations be continued. As Konoe saw it, the General Staff was "out-and-out in favor of the cessation of hostilities in China . . . and the commencement of preparations against the Soviets." The impasse between the prime minister and the vice-chief of the General Staff was broken by Navy Minister Yonai Mitsumasa, who reminded Tada that the time limit had been set in the presence of the emperor and could not be modified. If Tada continued to oppose Konoe, reasoned Yonai, "either the Army General Staff or the cabinet must resign." The spokesman for the former body accepted defeat and the Liaison Conference decided to terminate all efforts to negotiate with the Nationalist government.[167] The next day Konoe publicly announced that "the Japanese government will cease henceforth to deal with . . . [the Nationalist government] and looks forward to the establishment and growth of a new Chinese regime."[168]

---

[165]Harada, *Saionji kō to seikyoku*, January 19, 1938, VI, 203; *Saionji-Harada Memoirs*, p. 1992.

[166]IMTFE, Document 3090, Appendices 1 and 2. Also, Japan, Foreign Ministry Archives, "Matsumoto Kiroku: Shina jihen," pp. 142–50, cited in Uyehara, *Checklist*, p. 109, Microfilm PVM 42.

[167]Harada, *Saionji kō to seikyoku*, January 19, 1938, VI, 206–7; *Saionji-Harada Memoirs*, pp. 1996–97. Ishii Itarō claims that on January 13 the inner cabinet had already decided to sever all negotiations with Chiang Kai-shek. Ishii, *Gaikōkan no isshō*, p. 302.

[168]*New York Times*, January 16, 1938, p. 33.

This momentous decision was at odds with the aims and aspirations of the Army General Staff. One should not, however, equate the outlook of the General Staff with that of the field armies or of the Army Ministry. Many influential officers in these latter groups favored the expansion of operations and organization of puppet governments in China. I have stressed the viewpoint of the General Staff to bring out the fact that even with the Imperial Headquarters it could not impress its strategic planning as the basic guide to the conduct of operations in China. This inability was due to the existence of two different concepts of national defense which prevented a consensus between the General Staffs; to the extensive administrative liaison between officers in the Army Ministry and the field armies and various political and economic groups actively engaged in the organization of civil governments in areas under the control of the imperial army; and to the cabinet's leadership in the endeavor to crush the Nationalist government and favor individuals who might be more amenable to Japanese influence. This convergence of interest in expanding Japanese power throughout China was evident in the newly established Cabinet Planning Board and in the governments set up in north and central China. Within the limits of this paper, it is not possible to trace the political-economic-military consequences of the China Incident. But it is feasible to indicate how the Army General Staff was consistently overruled in the Liaison Conferences because of the behavior of the Navy General Staff and the Army Ministry.

In February 1938, for example, the government floundered on the issue of what next in China. At the February 14 Liaison Conference the Army General Staff ventured that operations in the Hankow-Canton area were inadvisable because of the increasing Soviet menace. The Navy General Staff, reasoning that Great Britain and the United States constituted the major strategic problem, argued the desirability of air bases in the Hong Kong region. This rift in the Imperial Headquarters prompted the emperor to ask, "Is it possible to put into effect a plan which calls simultaneously for long-term hostilities, military preparations against Russia, and the expansion of the navy?"[169] No one answered the penetrating inquiry, but the army minister promised to look into the matter. Thereafter, the emperor never received another invitation to attend a

---

[169]Harada, *Saionji kō to seikyoku*, March 4, 1938, VI, 248; *Saionji-Harada Memoirs*, p. 2044.

Liaison Conference. Four days later, at the next Liaison Conference meeting, the spokesmen for the two General Staffs again conflicted openly; but on this occasion Navy Minister Yonai also proposed the Hankow operations, and he was seconded by Army Minister Sugiyama Gen.[170] Once more, the Army General Staff was overruled, in part because the two service ministers preferred to try a simultaneous expansion of hostilities rather than tackle the more tedious undertaking of devising a coordinated strategic policy, in part because the cabinet strongly favored the extension of Japanese influence on the continent.

While the two chiefs of staff remained firmly devoted to the dual concepts of national defense sanctioned by the August 1936 national policy, the inner cabinet proceeded to work out a China policy worthy of the new operations. In November 1938 Prime Minister Konoe, in a radio address, proclaimed: "It is the establishment of a new order that will enable us to maintain [the] permanent peace of East Asia that the Empire seeks. This is really the ultimate object of the present expedition."[171] After this pronouncement, the cabinet, on November 25, agreed upon the conditions that would terminate the China Incident.[172] Without reviewing them substantively, it may be fairly noted that they resembled the Twenty-One Demands in scope, they were formulated by the inner cabinet, and they were opposed by the Army General Staff as being too vague. This lone dissenting voice in the highest echelons of the government was silenced by the Imperial Conference of November 31 in which the imperial sanction was affixed to the cabinet's policy.[173] In lieu of opening any new negotiations with Chiang Kai-shek, the government established the Asia Development Board under Generals Yanagawa Heisuke and Suzuki Teiichi to coordinate the activities of the North China Development Company and the Central China Development Company; and it induced Wang Ching-wei to organize a new Chinese government as the legal entity with which it intended to reach a settlement of the China Incident. By these means the Konoe government set out to rejuvenate China as part of the New Order.

[170]IMTFE, Exhibit 357.
[171]IMTFE, Exhibit 268.
[172]IMTFE, Proceedings, pp. 3590–97.
[173]IMTFE, Proceedings, pp. 2400–5.

To approach this in another way, with the China War in progress, the government enthusiastically supported the recommendations of the Cabinet Research Bureau. Consequently it urged the passage of a general mobilization law, and it established the Cabinet Planning Board.[174] The result by 1939 was the existence of a host of new organizations in China and Japan which were linked with this new economic, military, and foreign policy toward China. That is, the China War itself had created many new groups with extensive interests in and commitments to the realization of the New Order. The outlook pervading these organizations, as well as the cabinet and the Army Ministry, differed appreciably from the strategic orientation of the Army General Staff. It also differed from the mentality that had flourished within the Kwantung army during the formation of Manchukuo. In November 1939, for example, Ozaki Hotsumi observed that the Imperial Way type of thinking that had prevailed in Manchukuo had not envisioned a new order for Asia.[175] Rather, the concepts of an "independent" Manchuria and unity among China, Japan, and Manchukuo had characterized the planning of the Kwantung army. Indeed, prior to the outbreak of the China Incident, the Kwantung army, under the leadership of Ishiwara, Itagaki Seishirō, and Hanaya Tadashi, had been anxious to prove the viability of Japanese values and Japanese leadership. By stressing racial pride and the past glories of the Manchus, they proposed to cultivate a "spirit of building a Manchurian nation." The Kwantung army's basic policy guide of July 25, 1936, for example, observed that party politics and a parliamentary system were not appropriate to the immediate needs of "building a nation." Rather, it stressed the value of military leadership plus the political ideas (Imperial Way) of Japan as the way to build a modern national state. On September 18, 1936, in conjunction with the announcement of the promulgation of the Manchurian imperial constitution, General Ueda Kenkichi, the commanding officer of the Kwantung army, declared, "The harmony of the races [of Manchuria] is to be realized through the attainment of the unique Imperial Way political system which reflects the true will of the people."[176] Permeating the mystique of the

[174]IMTFE, Proceedings, pp. 35747–48; Exhibit 453.
[175]Ozaki Hotsumi, "Tōa kyōdōtai no rinen to sono seiritsu no kyakkanteki kiso" (1939), reprinted in November 1954 supplement of *Chūō kōron*, pp. 400–10.
[176]*Ōdachi Shigeo denki* (1956), I, 114–15.

Imperial Way was the conviction that the welfare of East Asia was contingent upon the cooperation of three "independent" states—Japan, China, and Manchukuo.

After the China Incident many individuals enlarged the scope of this ideal to embrace the notion of Sino-Japanese cooperation in the pursuit of a New Order for all Asia. Ironically, many of the army leaders active in building Manchukuo, e.g., Ishiwara Kanji, had little enthusiasm for this new vision.[177] Through the General Staff they pleaded with the government to emulate the actions of Bismarck after the triumph of Sadowa, but to no avail. Too many groups in military, bureaucratic, industrial, and political circles were actively involved in the cause of the New Order. Neutralized by the Navy General Staff in the Imperial Headquarters and by the Army Ministry in the Liaison Conference, the leaders of the Army General Staff were unable to blunt the momentum behind the China policy of the Konoe government. The result, at the highest level of policymaking, was a perpetuation of the conflict between the two General Staffs over the priority issue between the two strategic enemies, plus different approaches to the China Incident put forward by the Army General Staff and the cabinet. This distinctive type of dissension was basic to the overthrow of the Yonai cabinet, the decision of the cabinet to "advance southward," the negotiation of the Tripartite Pact, and the formal recognition of the Wang Ching-wei government. All of these developments occurred between July and November 1940. They constituted a series of interrelated decisions that marked another fundamental policy orientation, one vitally influenced by the conflicting concepts of national defense.

THE COPROSPERITY SPHERE: THE NEW BASIS OF THE EMPIRE, 1940–1941

As long as the Imperial Headquarters could not devise one strategic policy, the cabinet remained the primary policy-making unit. With the German blitzkrieg of 1940, the European empires in the Pacific became acutely vulnerable to Japanese pressure. In this context, the Army Minis-

---

[177]In the postwar era this fact has won a belated popularity for Ishiwara's ideas, especially within those nationalistic circles that earlier had espoused the Greater Coprosperity cause. Ivan Morris, *Nationalism and the Right Wing in Japan* (1960), pp. 46–55, 174–75.

try and the Army General Staff ventured that Japan's security would be greatly enhanced by control of the resources of Southeast Asia, a view that was promptly seconded by the Navy General Staff. By July 1940 both services, at least temporarily, had finally agreed on one strategic policy centering on Southeast Asia. Prime Minister Yonai, however, refused to accept this strategic recommendation as the sole basis of Japan's foreign policy. Although subject to great pressure from the services and from the leaders of the political parties, Yonai remained steadfast. This obstacle was finally removed by the resignation of the army minister, a tactic which brought about the formation of the second Konoe cabinet. This government quickly advanced a new objective for Japan's foreign policy, the Coprosperity Sphere. This was, of course, a euphemism for extending Japanese control over Southeast Asia, but given the context of the European scene, only the United States could possibly frustrate this ambition. Confident that this stumbling block could be removed by means of an Axis pact, the Konoe government believed it could realize the Coprosperity Sphere without having to go to war with the United States. The firm opposition of the American government, however, soon displaced this optimism with a sense of frustration and an increasing concern over the huge expansion of the American fleet. The German invasion of the Soviet Union then confronted the government with another crisis: Should it abandon the Coprosperity Sphere and the southern orientation in favor of opening hostilities against the Soviet Union in order to seize the Maritime Provinces? Or should Japan push into Southeast Asia, even though this would mean war with the United States? Despite the efforts of the Army General Staff and of Foreign Minister Matsuoka Yōsuke, the cabinet chose the latter policy. Matsuoka was dropped from office in July 1941, and on September 6 the third Konoe government adopted a new national policy that committed Japan to acquiring control over Southeast Asia. In conjunction with this policy, the Imperial Headquarters based its strategic planning on the premise that Southeast Asia was the main objective. By October, Konoe was in a quandary—his hopes for a diplomatic rapprochement with the United States had proved illusory and his official policy called for the beginning of hostilities with the United States if Japan could not attain the Coprosperity Sphere by diplomatic means. Unable to face this alternative, Konoe resigned. The burden was then thrust upon General Tōjō Hideki. Accepting the premise that the Coprosperity Sphere was essential to the security of the empire, the Tōjō cabinet made one last diplomatic effort, only to be rebuffed by the American secretary of state. Japan then started the Pacific War with the bombing of Pearl Harbor. The following presentation of the 1940–41 period is designed to indicate how the strategic planning of both services contributed to the adoption of the Coprosperity Sphere as the new policy objective and how this aspiration led to the fatal impasse with the United States.

Between the first and second Konoe cabinets (January 1939-July 1940), the Japanese government was continuously plagued by the demand of the Army General Staff that the government ally with the Axis powers.[178] Favored by the Army General Staff because of its immense value in any Soviet war, the Axis pact project was strongly opposed by the Navy Ministry, as well as by important industrial, political, and diplomatic figures, because of the fear that it might, in fact, precipitate a world war. The blitzkrieg of 1940, however, produced a powerful convergence of opinion within Japan in support of an Axis pact, but for reasons only remotely related to those governing the earlier advocacy of the Army General Staff. In particular, the relatively defenseless state of the European colonial possessions inspired a grandiose vision that Japan could build a powerful political-economic-military bloc by means of new internal political arrangements in Japan and by control over the resources of Southeast Asia. Throughout the spring of 1940 the leaders of the Seiyūkai and the Minseitō, along with Marquis Kido and Prince Konoe, organized a "new political party movement" under the enticing slogans: "strengthen the national defense state," "renovate foreign policy," and "establish a new political system."[179] These political personalities, together with governmental and military figures, pressed the Yonai cabinet for a more positive domestic and foreign policy, one worthy of the rapidly changing world situation caused by the success of Nazi Germany.

Prime Minister Yonai and Foreign Minister Arita Hachirō, however, were apprehensive over the possibility of a war with the United States if Japan were to move directly into Southeast Asia. They preferred to wait

---

[178]Marquis Kido, for example, noted that the Hiranuma cabinet met more than seventy times on the proposed alliance, without success. IMTFE, Exhibit 3340. Also, Maxon, *Control of Japanese Foreign Policy*, pp. 137–41.

[179]Aritake, *Ishiwata Sōtarō*, pp. 371–72.

until the outcome of the European war was actually decided. But Konoe, noted Arita, "saw national policy through domestic politics." He, along with the military-political-bureaucratic-industrial groups active in the new political movement, thought Japan could and should build the New Order with the resources of Southeast Asia. Captivated by the potentialities possible through control over this region, they believed it could be attained, without a war with the United States, by means of an Axis alliance. "The Tripartite Pact was the center of Konoe's world policy," judged his intimate political adviser Kazami Akira.[180] Hence, for reasons divorced from the outlook of the Army General Staff, the leaders of the new political movement actively conspired with governmental and military officials to overthrow the Yonai cabinet.

The degree of harmony among these groups was attested by the first action of the second Konoe cabinet. Meeting in the private Ogikubo residence of Konoe, Army Minister Tōjō, Navy Minister Yoshida Zengo, and Foreign Minister Matsuoka easily resolved that national defense, foreign policy, and internal politics would have to be coordinated.[181] To this end, they affirmed that the cabinet should "renovate" the political parties, strengthen the national defense, and "hasten a solution of the China Incident." The three goals could be achieved, they thought, by means of an Axis alliance. The proposed pact would enable Japan to end the China Incident, neutralize the Soviet Union, promote the "southern policy," prevent the United States from entering the European war, and deter the United States from going to war against Japan in defense of Southeast Asia. Two related aspects of this consensus were the decisions to recognize the Wang Ching-wei government and to strive for a Coprosperity Sphere that would include Southeast Asia as part of Japan's New Order. Within four months the second Konoe cabinet signed the Tripartite Pact, created the Imperial Rule Assistance Association, granted formal recognition to the Wang regime, and in November publicly proclaimed the Coprosperity Sphere the major objective of imperial foreign policy.

Although the Ogikubo conference decided the main outlines of fundamental domestic and foreign policies, the influence of the military in foreign policy-making was greatly augmented in the process of the transfer of the

---

[180]*Ibid.*, pp. 396, 401.
[181]Aoki Tokuzō, *Taiheiyō sensō zenshi* (1953), II, 482.

prime ministership from Admiral Yonai to Prince Konoe. Yonai had maintained cabinet control over foreign policy, a fact that enabled him and Arita to exert effective leadership in policy matters. But under the second Konoe cabinet, the cabinet was primarily absorbed in domestic issues, and the Liaison Conference assumed much greater responsibilities in foreign policy matters. For example, the cabinet decision of July 26 on the "Outline of Fundamental National Policy" dealt almost exclusively with internal political and economic policies. The next day, however, the Liaison Conference decided basic policies vis-a-vis national defense and foreign policy.[182] In particular, it decided on an "advance into Southeast Asia for the purpose of realizing the new political system" and the planned economy outlined in the cabinet's decision of the preceding day. Since this Liaison Conference decision set aside the fundamental policies of the Yonai government, it would seem appropriate to sketch how the two concepts of national defense manifested themselves in military circles so as to contribute to the downfall of the Yonai cabinet and to the decision to give priority to "southern expansion" in conjunction with the decision to negotiate an Axis alliance.

As the European scene became more ominous, the American government authorized, under the Vinson plans, a sizable increase in the strength of the American navy. And in April 1940, following the sudden fall of Holland, Secretary Hull announced publicly that any change in the status of the Dutch East Indies, except by peaceful means, "would be prejudicial to the cause of stability, peace, and security . . . in the entire Pacific area."[183] This policy became more viable with each addition to the American fleet. Without questioning the wisdom or prudence of Hull's declaration, it is undeniable that American foreign policy and strategic planning after this time included the defense of the colonial possessions of the European nations in Southeast Asia.[184] Until the spring of 1940 the Navy General Staff, with the firm support of the Navy Ministry, had consistently opposed the Tripartite Pact, as well as any moves by the army, such as the Nomonhan Incident, that raised the specter of Soviet hostilities. In early July 1940, however, a number of army officers in the General Staff (Colonels Okada Shigeichi, Usui Shigeki, Takatsuki Tamotsu, Takeda

[182]*Nihon gaikō nempyō*, II, 436–38.
[183]Julius W. Pratt, *A History of United States Foreign Policy* (1955), p. 648.
[184]Louis Morton, "Historia Mentem Armet: Lessons of the Past" (1960), pp. 155–64.

Isao, and Kushida Masao), in cooperation with the staff of the Military Affairs Bureau of the Army Ministry, drafted a set of "Main Principles for Coping with the Changing World Situation."[185] They reasoned that a European-African bloc under Germany and Italy was inevitable; Great Britain with American aid would use India and Australia to secure a supply line; in a few years the expansion of the American navy would be completed and a solid Anglo-American strategic-economic bloc would be formed in Southeast Asia; Japan would then be placed in a difficult position unless it took the initiative immediately; and the prerequisites for a successful southern move were security from attack by the Soviet Union, settlement of the China Incident, and a political alliance with Germany and Italy. Consequently, these officers concluded, "Japan must form an economically self-sufficient zone, including the Southern Area, establish a powerful political structure, and institute a planned economy."[186] This policy draft was informally submitted to the Navy General Staff and the Navy Ministry and immediately met with approval, at least in terms of the strategic priority assigned to the southern area and to preparations against the United States. By July 4, and for the first time since the inception of the China Incident, both services had reached a consensus on strategic planning, but with the proviso that the southern expansion be achieved "if at all possible" by peaceful means. Certain instances were allowed, however, that would justify the use of force, such as an embargo by the United States, the use of British territory in the Pacific as American bases, or a significant military buildup in the South Pacific by Britain and the United States.

Although the Imperial Headquarters had informally approved of "southern expansion" as the guiding axiom of strategic planning, the Yonai cabinet refused to accept this as governmental policy, mainly because of its diplomatic implications. On July 12 Prime Minister Yonai advised Army Minister Hata Shunroku at a Four Ministers Conference that preparations were permissible but the actual launching of offensive operations must await a formal cabinet decision.[187] Yonai's attitude, in the face of intensive political and military pressure, constituted an act of great political courage. It

[185]USDAOMH, *Japanese Monograph 146* (1964), pp. 14–18; Tanemura Sakō, *Daihon'ei kimitsu nisshi* (1952), pp. 17–20.
[186]*Ibid.*, pp. 14–15.
[187]Kido Kōichi, *Kido Kōichi nikki* (1966), II, 803–4.

also brought to a climax the various intrigues against his government. In the public realm, Konoe resigned from the Privy Council to participate openly in the formation of the Imperial Rule Assistance Association, and within the government, the chief of the Army General Staff requested General Hata to resign his portfolio. On July 16 Hata resigned and the army refused to nominate another army minister. By this tactic, it brought about the downfall of the Yonai cabinet. Detailed information on this intrigue is still hard to come by. Nevertheless, it was more than simply a question of Yonai's opposition to the Tripartite Pact. Otherwise, the naval authorities would have reacted vehemently, as Admiral Yamamoto Gonnohyōe had done during the crisis unleashed by Uehara Yūsaku's resignation during the second Saionji cabinet. In view of the "Main Principles for Coping with the Changing World Situation" accepted by both services, Yonai's reluctance to sanction a southern expansion was also at odds with the aspirations of the imperial navy. Unquestionably, the driving force behind the intrigue to oust Yonai was the army and the major personalities in the new political movement, but some share of the credit or blame should be traced to the outlook in naval circles which produced a passive reaction to Hata's resignation. "It was felt," commented the then vice-chief of the Navy General Staff, Admiral Kondō Nobutake, in February 1953:

> that if the Navy adhered to its policy of opposition to the alliance, not only would it prove detrimental to the preparation for war in time of national emergency but [it] might, in an extreme case, even result in a serious conflict between the Army and Navy. The Navy felt that the preparations for the defense of Japan might be seriously threatened if she maintained her attitude of opposition.[188]

This feeling, in part dictated by strategic considerations, was an important factor in bringing about the abrupt end of the Yonai cabinet.

Prince Konoe readily assumed office and, as indicated previously, within forty-eight hours his inner cabinet agreed upon the new orientation of Japan's domestic and foreign policies. The ease with which the cabinet reached this consensus at the Ogikubo conference reflects the convergence of disparate groups in favor of southern expansion. Indirectly it also highlights the strength of character displayed by Yonai and his cabinet throughout the spring and summer of 1940. The harmony of the Konoe cabinet

[188]USDAOMH, *Japanese Monograph 146*, Appendix 5, p. 55.

yielded, as mentioned earlier, the "Outline of Fundamental National Policy." According to this policy, the government was to realize the "national defense state" by the establishment of a new political and economic system in Japan and by fulfillment of the new order throughout Asia. Following this, the Liaison Conference on July 27 ruled that the empire would "strive for the immediate settlement of the China Incident by improving internal and external conditions in keeping with changes in the world situation and at the same time will solve the southern area problem by taking advantage of opportunities." These dual aims were to be attained by "political and military strategies" designed to subjugate the Chungking government, including the prevention of any third-power aid to Chiang Kai-shek, and by "political unity with Germany and Italy." Specifically, Japan was to secure control over Indochina, close the Burma Road, and obtain resources from the East Indies, "for the present by diplomatic means" and only to the extent that war with the United States could be avoided. While recognizing that these steps would entail an "inevitable and natural deterioration of relations" with the United States, it was hoped that outright hostilities could be avoided. However, should the general situation turn favorable and the war with China be settled, military force would be used in the south. In that case, it was acknowledged, it might become impossible to avoid a clash with America, and therefore preparations for such an eventuality were to be begun immediately.[189]

Although this crucial policy decision was formulated mainly by military officers, it did not necessarily lack the active support of the prime minister and the cabinet. Yonai, for example, had vetoed this policy, whereas Konoe had embraced the "new political structure" and the Coprosperity Sphere, both of which were rooted in the premise of Japanese control over Southeast Asia. It should be noted, however, that the decision was made by the Liaison Conference. That is, it did not mark the emergence of the Imperial Headquarters as the primary decision-making unit. This distinction is

---

[189] *Nihon gaikō nempyō*, II, 436–38. Robert Butow on this decision judges: "Despite a general implication that diplomacy would take precedence, the essence of the entire proposal was that *if Japan could not get what she wanted through negotiation, she would take what she wanted by force* [italics in original]. The decisions of July 26 and 27, 1940 constituted a pivotal stage in the metamorphosis of the China Incident into the Greater East Asia War." Robert J.C. Butow, *Tojo and the Coming of the War* (1961), p. 153.

important, as will be indicated subsequently. At the moment, one should note that the decisions of July signified a major transformation in national policy. For example, the supplemental comments of the Imperial Headquarters on the meaning of the Liaison Conference decision noted that "the stipulation 'changes in the policy with emphasis placed on measures for the southern area' means changing the policy to one stressing measures for the southern advance from the present policy [which] places emphasis on the China Incident."[190] After this decision, Southeast Asia, not China, constituted the central issue at stake. This fact never emerged clearly in the Japanese-American negotiations, largely because the United States conducted its correspondence with Japan in terms of the China problem and the Axis pact.

The political process by which the second Konoe cabinet organized the Imperial Rule Assistance Association, ratified the Tripartite Pact, recognized the government of Wang Ching-wei, and embarked on the quest for the Coprosperity Sphere is beyond the scope of this presentation. Still, one should recognize that the outstanding victories of Nazi Germany in 1940 had acted as a powerful stimulant which produced at all levels of Japanese society elated visions of Japan's role in Asia. After surveying the European scene, for example, a distinguished panel of academics, businessmen, and former governmental officials judged, in a formal report to the cabinet in the fall of 1940, that the imperial government could and should build an imposing edifice, a New Order, by means of the resources of Southeast Asia. Quoting the most famous early nationalist of the Tokugawa era, Aizawa Seishisai, the panel concluded: "This is a great opportunity such as comes once in a thousand years. It must not be lost."[191] And in defending the proposed Axis alliance before the Privy Council, Prime Minister Konoe affirmed that war between the United States and Japan was not desired. "However, a humble attitude will only prompt the United States to become domineering. Therefore, a demonstration of our strength is necessary."[192] Confident of Germany's victory and possessed by a vaulting imperial ambition, the civil leaders of the government were determined

---

[190]USDAOMH, *Japanese Monograph 146*, Appendix 3, p. 46.

[191]Private papers of Rear Admiral Takagi Sōkichi. Also, for general political orientation during the first four months of the second Konoe cabinet, see Ashida Hitoshi, *Daimiji sekai taisen gaikōshi* (1959), pp. 180–88.

[192]USDAOMH, *Japanese Monograph 146*, pp. 29–30.

to garner a new place in the realm of international politics. Without too much concern about the strategic implications involved in this ambition, they tried to use the Axis pact to gain Japanese hegemony in Southeast Asia. Within military circles, the officers most intimately involved in the quest for the Coprosperity Sphere were located in the Army Ministry. The determination of these officers to achieve control over Southeast Asia would prove to be one of the most decisive influences in the fateful decision taken during the summer of 1941. This can be illustrated by a brief synopsis of military planning and interservice conflicts in the Imperial Headquarters and Liaison Conference.

The impetus toward the adoption of the "southern policy" had started with a consensus among some officers in the Military Affairs Bureau of the Army Ministry and in several sections of the Army General Staff. For reasons that have remained unexplained, the latter group of officers, including Colonels Okada Shigeichi, Tsuchihashi Yūitsu, Takatsuki Tamotsu, and Arao Okikatsu, were transferred out of the General Staff in October 1940.[193] At the same time, General Tanaka Shin'ichi assumed command of the Operations Division. Questioning the feasibility of operations in Southeast Asia, Tanaka proceeded, despite the official governmental policy, to focus the talents of his staff on the Soviet question. He also dispatched, in December 1940, General Yamashita Tomoyuki to Germany to prepare a formal evaluation of the blitzkrieg tactics and their relevance to the imperial army.[194] Yamashita returned in July 1941 convinced that the army needed paratroop divisions, a stronger tactical air force, as well as a thorough revamping of infantry tactics to incorporate an extensive use of medium tanks as the spearhead of infantry attacks. Yamashita's recommendations were endorsed by Tanaka and strongly discounted by Army Minister Tōjō. Still, the General Staff ordered Yamashita to apply his ideas to the Kwantung army, an assignment that inherently would veto any southern operations. The day preceding Yamashita's departure, the strongest partisan of a "northern policy" in the cabinet, Matsuoka Yōsuke, was dropped from the government; and the third Konoe cabinet, at the insistence of Tōjō, forced the revocation of Yamashita's orders. This minor episode reflects a more important fact,

---

[193]Tanemura, *Daihon'ei kimitsu nisshi*, p. 33.
[194]Oki Shūji, *Ningen Yamashita Tomoyuki* (1959), pp. 172–74.

namely, the extreme reluctance of the Army General Staff, or more accurately of the Operations Division, to support the proposed operations
in Southeast Asia. Moreover, available evidence suggests that between
July 1940 and July 1941 the General Staff did not engage in a systematic
study of the logistical and strategic problems raised by the policy of
"southern expansion."

Perhaps because of the attitude of General Tanaka, the Army Ministry
under Tōjō actively endeavored to rectify this deficiency. In January 1941
it created the Taiwan Army Research Division under General Itagaki.
This new group was given the task of working out tactical and strategic
logistical planning for the type of operations necessary in Southeast Asia.
It may seem incredible, in view of the resounding success of the Japanese
army in the initial year of the Pacific War, that prior to the summer of 1941
such plans were lacking in the Army General Staff. But the origins, limitations, and achievements of the Taiwan Army Research Division have
been candidly outlined by Tsuji Masanobu, the architect of the Singapore
campaign.[195] In addition to organizing the Taiwan group, the Army Ministry in March 1941 dispatched Colonel Iwakuro Hideo to Washington to
assist Ambassador Nomura Kichisaburō in his efforts to establish some type
of rapport with the American government. Between the fall of 1940 and
the summer of 1941, as Schroeder indicates, Japanese-American negotiations floundered on the issue of the Axis pact, especially on Japan's
unwillingness to guarantee its neutrality in case of American entry into
the European war.[196] The Army Ministry hoped that if this type of assurance were given, the United States would, in return, indicate a willingness to support Japan's desire to obtain access to the resources of the
Dutch East Indies. To this end, Colonel Iwakuro and Ikawa Tadao of
the Finance Ministry drafted a vague set of proposals which were informally presented to Secretary Hull on April 9.[197] Since the conditions
seemed to offer some basis for discussion, Hull promptly requested that
they be conveyed formally, as an expression of official policy. Without

---

[195]Masanobu Tsuji, *Singapore: The Japanese Version* (1960), pp. 3–23. Tsuji allows that the
lack of staff planning was "one reason for our defeat in the war."

[196]Paul W. Schroeder, *The Axis Alliance and Japanese-American Relations, 1941* (1958), pp.
29–47.

[197]Aritake, *Ishiwata Sōtarō*, pp. 404–7; William L. Langer and S. Everett Gleason, *The
Undeclared War, 1940–1941* (1953), p. 314.

some assurances that the American government would seriously accept a modus vivendi that would open up Southeast Asia to Japanese penetration in return for a free hand to the American government to enter the European war, the Liaison Conference ruled against formally sanctioning the proposal submitted on April 9. In May, Iwakuro advised General Tōjō that Matsuoka's personality and public statements had precluded any rapport with the American government. Hence he recommended a "leaders conference" between Konoe and Roosevelt as the best way to attain a diplomatic settlement.[198] This idea gathered many supporters, and from the beginning of August to mid-October the projected conference constituted the central theme of Japanese-American negotiations.[199] Together the Taiwan Army Research Division and the Iwakuro mission reveal a new dimension to the interests and activities of the Army Ministry. It had ventured into realms normally beyond its purview—diplomacy and strategic planning—in order to realize what it deemed essential for the national defense, that is, control over Southeast Asia.

Parallel with the effort to open serious diplomatic talks with the American government, Japan on April 13 signed a neutrality pact with the Soviet Union. Four days later the Imperial Headquarters adopted another policy for the southern area. In lieu of the optimistic vocabulary of the New Order that had characterized the decisions of the preceding summer, however, this policy advised that Japan should settle the China Incident and "replenish her over-all national defense power *for the purpose of self-preservation and self-defense*" (italics mine). No longer was Southeast Asia being seen only as part of a "Coprosperity Sphere" or of a "New Order"; it had become essential to the defense of the empire. Thus, the decision of April 17 judged that diplomacy should be used to establish "close" economic relations with the Netherlands East Indies, "normal" economic relations with other countries in Southeast Asia, and "intimate and inseparable" relations with French Indochina and Thailand. It also allowed that two circumstances would justify the use of force to guarantee the objectives essential for Japan's "self-existence and defense": an embargo by the United States, Britain, and the Netherlands, or "when the encirclement of Japan by the United States, alone or in alliance with Great

---

[198]Tanemura, *Daihon'ei kimitsu nisshi,* pp. 56–57.
[199]Schroeder, *The Axis Alliance,* pp. 55–56.

Britain, the Netherlands, and China, becomes so restrictive that the situation becomes intolerable from the standpoint of national defense."[200]

This mid-April decision, in my estimation, marks a subtle but crucial change in attitude among many of the most influential officers of the army and navy. What was desired in 1940 as part of a future new order had, by April 1941, become essential to the security of the empire. Whereas the government had ratified the Axis alliance in the fall of 1940 in order to attain the New Order, it had signed a neutrality pact with the Soviet Union in the spring of 1941 and revealed that it would not necessarily invoke the Tripartite agreement in the event that the United States were to become involved in the European war. This change in attitude was related to a fixation on Southeast Asia. As early as February 3, for example, the Liaison Conference confidently declared that "Japan, assuming political leadership in the Greater East Asia Coprosperity Sphere, will assume responsibility for maintaining order therein."[201] Still, the same individuals, four days earlier, in determining the "Outline of Policy toward French Indochina and Thailand," thought the solution to the problems "which confront Japan *on the road to the realization of the Greater East Asia Coprosperity Sphere* lies in the establishment of an intimate military, political, and economic union with French Indochina and Thailand for *Japan's self-preservation and self-defense*" (italics mine).[202] To my knowledge, this latter decision is the first occasion on which the concept of "self-preservation and self-defense" was invoked in policy-making at this level of the imperial government. There is some connection between this new terminology and the effective resistance of Holland to Japanese pressures for access to the East Indies. Since the anticipated results of the Axis pact had not materialized,

[200]"Gist of the Policy of the Army and Navy Sections of Imperial Headquarters in Regard to Measures to the South," in Office of Chief of Military History, Japanese Research Division, United States Army Forces, Far East, and the Eighth United States Army, *Far East History Source File: "Important National Policy Decisions,"* Appendix 8 (hereafter cited as *Far East History Source File*). I am grateful to Stetson Conn for sharing his notes on this policy. Also, *Nihon gaikō nempyō*, II, 495–96.

[201]"Outline for Negotiations with Germany, Italy, and the USSR" (Liaison Conference decision, February 3, 1941), in *ibid.*, II, 481; and *Far East History Source File*, Appendix 5.

[202]"Outline of Policy toward French Indochina and Thailand" (Liaison Conference decision, January 30, 1941), in *Nihon gaikō nempyō*, II, 479–80; and *Far East History Source File*, Appendix II.

the national objectives of July 1940 were clearly being stymied by the policies of the United States. Faced with this situation, the initial motive of extending the principles of the "national polity" throughout Asia by means of a New Order was transformed into a matter of the "existence and defense" of the nation. Thus, the policies of the colonial powers and of the United States became identified as an "encirclement" of imperial Japan. At the moment it is not possible to pinpoint precisely when this change in vocabulary and thought-pattern occurred. Nevertheless, it was basic to the policies adopted by the Imperial Headquarters, the Liaison Conference, and the cabinet throughout 1941, and judging by the available documents, it emerged sometime between January and mid-April. Moreover, it also marked a growing consensus between the Army Ministry and the Navy General Staff that the "southern advance" was the key to the nation's defense.

On February 10, 1941 Captain Ōno Takeji of the Navy General Staff and Colonel Arisue Yadoru of the Army Ministry consulted on a set of guiding principles for potential operations in Southeast Asia. Their recommendation, however, was not presented formally to the Imperial Headquarters until June 6. At this time General Ōshima Hiroshi, the ambassador to Germany, cabled a warning of a probable German invasion of the Soviet Union. Immediately an emergency Liaison Conference was called to decide on a policy in the event of a Nazi-Soviet war. Three tentative choices were discussed: 1) an independent move into Southeast Asia; 2) a compromise with the United States over this region and the beginning of preparations for Soviet operations; and 3) military control over Indochina and the strengthening of the Kwantung army. In other words, the government could decide on "northern expansion," "southern advance," or preparation of the foundations for both with a final decision being reserved for a later date. On June 9 the Army General Staff voted for the third alternative, with priority on strengthening the Kwantung army. The next day, however, in a conference between the chiefs of the Operations sections of the two General Staffs and General Mutō Akira of the Army Ministry, priority was given to the southern problem, that is, General Tanaka Shin'ichi of the Army General Staff was overruled two to one. The issue was discussed in the Liaison Conference on June 11, where Navy Chief of Staff Admiral Nagano Osami demanded priority for preparations against Britain and the United States, and Army Chief of

Staff General Sugiyama Gen remained silent. On June 12 the Liaison Conference agreed to move as diplomatically as possible but adopted Nagano's recommendation.[203]

Despite this ruling, the German invasion of Russia on June 22 precipitated another series of Liaison Conferences. On June 26 Foreign Minister Matsuoka passionately argued that Japan was "morally" obligated to render assistance to its Axis ally. Army Vice-Chief of Staff General Tsukada Osamu, however, opposed precipitate action, arguing that Japan should consider the question from the viewpoint of its own "self-interest." Matsuoka still persisted, but at a meeting of bureau and division chiefs of the services at Tōjō's official residence the next day, with Colonels Arisue Yadoru and Satō Kenryō and Captains Ōno Takeji and Ishikawa Shingo participating, the army and navy reconfirmed their adherence to the policy of giving priority to the southern advance.[204]

On July 2 this decision was officially sanctioned at an Imperial Conference. This "Outline of National Policies in View of the Changing Situation" marked an almost irrevocable step toward war with the United States. "Regardless of whatever changes may occur in the world situation," it ruled, "Japan will adhere to the established policy of creating a Greater East Asia Coprosperity Sphere and thereby contribute to the establishment of world peace." Since the strategic southern area was vital to Japan's "self-preservation and self-defense," all obstacles would be overcome. "To attain this objective, we shall not hesitate to engage in war with Britain and the United States."[205] This decision differed significantly in tone and justification from the decision of the preceding July, which contained no mention of "self-preservation and self-defense" and had placed various conditions on Japan's willingness to enter such a war.[206] Underlying this change were two separate convictions in military planning—the commitment of the Army Ministry to the idea that the Coprosperity Sphere was essential to the nation's defense, and the Navy General Staff's obsession with the huge increase in the American navy authorized by the Stark plan—plus the fact

---

[203]Tanemura, *Daihon'ei kimitsu nisshi*, pp. 46, 49–51.

[204]*Ibid.*, p. 65.

[205]Aoki, *Taiheiyō sensō zenshi*, II, 807–9; *Nihon gaikō nempyō*, II, 531–32. The wording was: "*Teikoku wa hongo mokuteki tassei no tame tai-Ei-Bei sen o jisezu.*"

[206]*Nihon gaikō nempyō* II, 438.

that American policy had consistently revealed an unwillingness to cooperate with the imperial government.

The role of the Navy Ministry, particularly of Navy Minister Oikawa Koshirō, in this decision is difficult to fathom. As will be indicated, in the fall of 1941 Oikawa was anxious to avoid a war with the United States, and his staff did not participate in the special group appointed by Army Minister Tōjō. It is clear, however, that the Army General Staff was divided between General Tsukada, who supported the southern plans, and General Tanaka, who vigorously opposed this policy. In the cabinet, only Matsuoka fought the decisions of the June 28 Liaison Conference and of the July 2 Imperial Conference. Because he continued to urge a reversal of policy in favor of northern operations, the cabinet was reshuffled on July 18, with Admiral Toyoda Teijirō assuming the post of foreign minister. After this change, the advocates of assigning priority to the Soviet matter were effectively controlled. On August 9, while the panzers were sweeping across the Russian plains, the Imperial Headquarters formally decided "to abandon hope for a favorable opportunity to exploit the situation in the north against the Soviet Union, and to concentrate all effort on a southward advance, regardless of any new developments in the German-Soviet War." The same day the Army General Staff issued a general outline of operations that limited the Kwantung army to sixteen divisions and authorized preparations for a "war against the United States and Great Britain that will be started about the end of November in the southern area."[207]

Parallel with the firm commitment of the Army General Staff to the southern operations, the Navy General Staff, following the oil embargo of the United States and the passage of the Stark expansion plan for the American navy, judged mid-October as the date after which successful operations could not be carried out. This deadline was informally agreed upon at an August 29 conference of officers from the two General Staffs and the two service ministries.[208] After this meeting, the Imperial Conference was convened on September 6 to sanction the resulting decision. The session opened with a brief prologue by Prime Minister Konoe. Observing that Britain, the United States, and the Netherlands were "taking every possible

[207]USDAOMH, *Japanese Monograph 77* (1964), pp. 14–15.
[208]Hattori Takushirō, *Dai Tōa sensō zenshi* (1953), I, 178–80.

measure to oppose our Empire," Konoe concluded, "we must complete [our] preparations . . . and at the same time must take all diplomatic means to prevent the outbreak of a disastrous war. Only in case such diplomatic measures fail within a certain period of time should we resort to the last means of self-defense."[209] Specifically, the prime minister then presented the "Essentials for Carrying Out the Policies of the Empire" which had been approved by the Liaison Conference the preceding afternoon.[210] This stipulated that the government was prepared to face a war with the United States, Great Britain, and the Netherlands "for the sake of self-preservation and self-defense," with early October as the deadline for the preparations for war; that it would use "every possible diplomatic means available" to secure acceptance of the empire's minimal demands; and that it would "resolve to wage war" if by the beginning of October there was only a slight possibility of these demands being achieved by diplomatic means.

Essentially, the minimal conditions were as follows: First, the United States and Britain would "refrain from interfering [with] or obstructing" a settlement of the China Incident; that is, they would give no aid to Chiang Kai-shek, close the Burma Road, and support a tripartite pact among Japan, Manchukuo, and China. Second, they would not "jeopardize" the national defense of the empire; that is, they would maintain the status quo in military preparations in the Far East and not build any bases in Thailand, the Netherlands East Indies, or the Soviet Union. Finally, they would "cooperate" with Japan's acquisition of necessary commodities; that is, they would lift the various embargoes and encourage economic cooperation among Thailand, Indochina, and the empire. If these basic terms were met, Japan would not undertake any aggression into adjacent areas, except as dictated by the necessity to end the China Incident; would withdraw from Indochina after a "fair and just" peace with China had been effected; and would respect the "neutrality" of the Philippines. The pervasive influence of strategic considerations in this policy, both in terms of aims and minimal conditions, is undeniable. Furthermore, Chiefs of Staff General Sugiyama and Admiral Nagano contributed supplemental observations. Sugiyama ventured that prolonged diplomatic talks with the United States would mean that:

[209]USDAOMH, *Japanese Monograph 147* (rev. ed. 1964), p. 50.
[210]*Nihon gaikō nempyō*, II, 544–45.

The Empire's national defense strength would gradually decrease, while at the same time the armaments of the United States and Britain would gradually increase. . . . Therefore, we must open hostilities against the United States and Britain while we have confidence in waging war against them. Thus, after considering the meteorological conditions in the anticipated theater of operations, we have decided that the appropriate time for the completion of war preparations is the middle of October.[211]

And after stressing the growing power of the American fleet and the necessity to act promptly, Admiral Nagano advised:

Our Empire has not [the] means by which to subjugate the enemy by invasion operations or to break his will to fight. . . . However, . . . if this first-stage operation should be accomplished promptly, the Empire then will be in a position to secure strategic points in the Southwest Pacific, [and] even if [the] military preparations of the United States develop as scheduled, we shall be able to establish the foundation for a long war by maintaining an invincible position.[212]

Nagano added, with a candor and integrity worthy of the setting, "my explanation herein had been prepared solely on the assumption that war cannot be avoided."[213]

In view of the influence of naval considerations in the policy of September 6, particularly the October deadline and the insistence on a military status quo in the western Pacific, it is legitimate to note that Admiral Nagano's reasoning was determined mainly by the strategic consequences of American naval expansion. Phrased differently, Japan's New Order and the Co-prosperity Sphere did not structure the policy of the Navy General Staff anywhere near the degree to which it had enveloped the cabinet and the Army Ministry. Of course, in terms of its consequences for the Japanese-American negotiations, the minimal demands set by the Navy General Staff, including the time deadline, are of primary importance to a diplomatic historian studying the outbreak of the Pacific War. Setting this issue aside momentarily, the reasoning underlying the viewpoint of the Navy General Staff is of equal significance for those concerned with the way in which military foreign policy manifested itself in the decision of September 6. To a large extent, the attitude of the Army Ministry toward the southern

---

[211]USDAOMH, *Japanese Monograph 147*, Appendix 4, pp. i-ii.
[212]*Ibid.*, Appendix 3, pp. ii-iii.
[213]*Ibid.*, p. iv.

area can be attributed to the pervasive economic and political responsibilities it had acquired during the course of the China War. But Nagano and his staff were less preoccupied with the political and economic aspects of the New Order than they were with the prospects of Japan becoming a second-class naval power. The two-ocean fleet authorized by the Stark plan would have relegated Japan to this status. Rather than accept this development resignedly, the chief of the Navy General Staff preferred the risk of war and possible defeat in order to preserve Japanese naval hegemony in the western Pacific. In conjunction with the Imperial Conference of September 6, for example, Nagano commented to Nakayama Masao: "The government has decided that if there is no war, the fate of the nation is sealed. Even if there is war, the country may be ruined. Nevertheless, a nation which does not fight in this plight has lost its spirit and is already a doomed country. Only if we fight until the last soldier will it be possible to find a way out of this fatal situation."[214]

In many respects this reasoning reflected a type of strategic thinking in which the welfare of the nation was equated with that of the relative position of the imperial navy. Hence, it would seem fair to conclude that the September 6 decision was largely the consequence of a blend of two different forms of military planning—the strategic orientation of the Navy General Staff and the political-economic axioms integrated into the viewpoint of the Army Ministry. And of course one should not discount the importance of the harmony between the policies of the cabinet and the Army Ministry in this decision.

In many ways, the resolution to undertake a war with the United States was the consequence of the expanding national policy objectives engendered first by the China War, later by the European scene. Related factors include the growing naval power of the American fleet, the diplomacy of the United States, and abandonment of the assumption that the Soviet Union constituted a major strategic threat. In a postwar evaluation of the Pacific War, a distinguished group of Japanese army officers observed, "Although the gradual buildup of the army had enabled Japan to enter the Pacific War with an augmented force, the increase in strength had not been planned with this objective."[215] Since 1905 the Army General Staff had

---

[214]Nakayama Masao, *Ichi gunkokushugisha no chokugen* (1956), p. 180.
[215]USDAOMH, *Japanese Monograph 45* (rev. ed., 1964), pp. 14–15.

been obsessed with the Russian problem, and this concern had vitally affected its conduct during the China War. This is another way of saying that the China War itself had redefined Japanese policy and eventually compelled the General Staff to accept a priority for the southern area. The extent of army expansion brought about by the China War is revealed by the following chart:[216]

Number of Japanese Divisions

	1937	1938	1939	1940	1941
In Japan	3	2	7	11	11
In Manchuria	5	8	9	12	13
In China	16	24	25	27	27
Total	24	34	41	50	51

This gave Japan an army which could entertain the hope of conquering Southeast Asia. Still, there is some irony in the fact that it was not the result of the political power or staff planning of the Army General Staff.

In terms of naval planning, the conduct of operations and of diplomacy during the China War had strengthened the contention of the Navy General Staff that the southern area and the United States were the main strategic concerns facing the empire. In 1937 Japan adopted its third naval replenishment program, which called for some 66 ships, including 2 battleships, 2 aircraft carriers, and 14 air units. The second Vinson plan, however, authorized an American expenditure roughly four times that of this program. Hence, in 1939 Japan responded with a fourth replenishment plan calling for 83 vessels. The following year the United States approved the third Vinson plan, and this was followed in 1941 by the Stark plan, which envisioned a 70 percent increase in total United States naval tonnage. To Japan's naval leaders this was an "unlimited and endless armament race." By the fall of 1941 the imperial fleet consisted of 10 battleships, 10 aircraft carriers, 18 heavy cruisers, 20 light cruisers, 112 destroyers, 65 submarines, and 156 vessels in other categories—a total of 391 ships.[217] Compared to the projected American fleet, this was not impressive. Still, in 1941 it was sufficient for the task of an immediate

[216] *Ibid.*
[217] USDAOMH, *Japanese Monograph 160* (1964), pp. 2–3.

conquest of Southeast Asia. This fact, as noted, was basic to the insistence of the Navy General Staff that Japan strike no later than December 1941.

During September and October the Konoe government, in hopes of reaching a detente with the United States, openly allowed that it would not invoke the Tripartite Pact if the United States were to enter the European war.[218] But Secretary Hull's memorandum of October 2 all but smothered any prospect of a diplomatic solution of the conflicting foreign policies of the two nations. About this time, Navy Minister Oikawa appealed to Admiral Nagano to confer with the senior statesmen Admirals Yonai and Okada, in hopes that such a conference would modify the rigid deadline set by the General Staff.[219] Nagano, however, refused to pursue the suggestion. Oikawa then asked Yonai and Okada to request a meeting between the senior statesmen and the cabinet about the September 6 decision; but Okada dryly observed that Konoe had not previously shown any inclination to consult with them on national policy. At a Five Ministers Conference at Konoe's Ogikubo residence on October 12, Oikawa, prior to and during the session, indicated his willingness to alter his position on going to war, if Konoe would take the initiative. In particular, Oikawa proposed that "the determination of the course to be taken should be left to the prime minister." But, he added, "We must make the decision now. It will be embarrassing to the navy . . . after the elapse of two or three months [to] go to war. If we desire to attain success by diplomacy, we must stick to this means to the end." When Foreign Minister (Admiral) Toyoda could not promise success by a reliance on diplomacy because there had to be "two parties" to the negotiations, Army Minister Tōjō insisted that without such assurance Japan must abide by the decision of September 6. Faced with the necessity of a decision, Konoe prevaricated and informed his army minister, "If you insist on waging war, I cannot take the responsibility for it." With impeccable logic, Tōjō retorted that since the prime minister had been present at the Imperial Conference, he

---

[218]Schroeder, *The Axis Alliance*, pp. 59–71.

[219]Aritake, *Okada Keisuke*, pp. 361–68. However, on the occasion of the formation of the third Konoe cabinet (July 1941), Oikawa agreed to serve as navy minister provided that the government would 1) adhere to the July 2 decision of the Imperial Conference; 2) complete the preparations needed in case of war with the United States; and 3) in these preparations, place emphasis on "the fulfillment of naval war preparations." USDAOMH, *Japanese Monograph 147*, p. 34.

could not understand this assertion. Thus, without actively trying to reverse the September 6 policy, Konoe chose to resign his post.[220]

The task of nominating a successor fell to the senior statesmen. At their October 17 meeting, the venerable Wakatsuki proposed General Ugaki Kazushige, but General Abe Nobuyuki opposed the nomination. Hirota then suggested Tōjō, but Admiral Okada dissented. Yonai and Okada expressed strong opposition to selecting any navy officer, and Abe and Hirota again put forth Tōjō's candidacy. In this circumstance, Hara Yoshimichi, president of the Privy Council, ruled that while there was dissatisfaction with Tōjō, the senior statesmen could not agree on anyone else. Hence, they should advise the Throne of their "feeling of negative support" for Tōjō.[221] Thereupon Marquis Kido formally nominated Tōjō as Konoe's successor.

The Tōjō cabinet did not ignore diplomacy. Throughout November it tried in vain to win American interest in a diplomatic settlement of the southern problem, but Secretary Hull continued to demand Japan's withdrawal from China as the price of any Japanese-American detente. Thus, while the formal talks floundered on the China issue, the Liaison Conference and the Imperial Headquarters were preoccupied with Southeast Asia. On October 30 the supreme command informed the cabinet that "initial success" was certain, but that success or failure in the long run would depend upon Japan's "capacity to maintain adequately her naval strength to cope with the United States' expansion of armament."[222] While it thought the neutrality of the Soviet Union could be relied upon, it stressed that a war could not be limited to the Netherlands and Great Britain. In its opinion, the United States would not hesitate to enter the war, as it was doing on the European scene, because the American government believed that it had a voice in the affairs of the southwest Pacific, needed the rubber and tin of this area, would judge the operations a menace to the Philippines, would lose its influence in Chinese affairs if it

[220]On the different versions of this Ogikubo conference, see Butow, *Tojo and the Coming of the War*, pp. 270–71. I have used Tōjō's and Tomita's versions, and only where they both agree on identical points. USDAOMH, *Japanese Monograph 147*, pp. 58–60, and Appendix 6, pp. i–iv.

[221]Aritake, *Ishiwata Sōtarō*, p. 413.

[222]USDAOMH, *Japanese Monograph 150* (1964), Appendix 3, pp. 77–84.

remained neutral, and could not ignore American public opinion which favored a defense of the status quo in the Pacific. The Liaison Conference accepted this "military" estimate and set in motion the final diplomatic overtures and the preparations for the Pearl Harbor, Singapore, and Philippine operations.

Winston Churchill and many other astute observers have regarded the decision to attack Pearl Harbor as an irrational act, "incompatible with prudence or even with sanity."[223] Still, as Louis Morton has shown, the ABD military planning of 1941 virtually committed the United States to the defense of Southeast Asia.[224] In other words, the determination to smash the American fleet at the beginning of the hostilities was logical within the frame of reference established by the decision of September 6; it was just as much a cabinet policy as one of the Imperial Headquarters, and it was not completely faulty in its estimation of American strategic planning as it affected Southeast Asia. In this context, one should stress that the fateful decision to precipitate the Pacific War was not occasioned by the China problem. On November 5 the Tōjō cabinet declared, "Japan, at this juncture, is resolved to wage war against the United States, Great Britain, and the Netherlands in order *to insure self-preservation and to establish a New Order in Greater East Asia*" (italics mine).[225] And as the course of Japanese-American negotiations drifted toward an open rupture, Tōjō called a conference of the senior statesmen on November 29 to advise them of the government's policy and the likelihood of a war with the United States. At this meeting, Admirals Okada and Yonai affirmed that they would, of course, support the government in the event of war.[226] They went on, however, to express their conviction that Japan should refrain from hostilities, even if the negotiations were to fail (an opinion that Konoe had not ventured at the time of his resignation). Most astutely, they openly questioned the fundamental axiom underlying the policy of the Tōjō and Konoe cabinets: "If this war were for self-existence, then we must be prepared to wage war, even if we foresaw eventual defeat; but it might prove dangerous if we resorted to war simply to uphold the

[223]Schroeder, *The Axis Alliance*, p. 200.
[224]Louis Morton, *Strategy and Command: The First Two Years* (1962), pp. 86–103.
[225]USDAOMH, *Japanese Monograph 45*, p. 39.
[226]USDAOMH, *Japanese Monograph 150*, Appendix 4.

Greater East Asia Coprosperity Plan."[227] By November 1941, however, the Tōjō cabinet was not prepared to torpedo the fundamental policy of the government adopted at the inception of the second Konoe cabinet. Hence, the only audible voices for peace at the highest level of the imperial government were politely ignored. Their final inquiry passed unanswered amidst the pervasive conviction that Japan's existence was dependent on the realization of the Coprosperity Sphere. The imperial sanction was given to the operational orders of the Imperial Headquarters, and the three-pronged attack on Pearl Harbor, the Philippines, and Malaya marked the opening of the Pacific War.

A REVIEW OF MATERIALS

I have tried, in this essay, to analyze how the armed services influenced the formation of Japan's basic foreign policies from 1868 to 1941. In particular, emphasis was given to two themes—the changing context of policy-making, and the interaction of the problems, recommendations, and responsibilities of the army and navy leaders in the formulation of foreign policy. With very few exceptions, neither of these concerns has received serious or systematic attention in Japanese writings on Japan's prewar diplomacy or militarism. It is not possible, therefore, to recommend works by Japanese scholars who have pursued these themes in greater detail. Consequently, I should like to review some of the relevant primary sources and then some of the studies in the military and diplomatic fields which best illustrate the approaches being taken by Japanese scholars. For this purpose, the materials relating to two periods are particularly instructive: the Meiji period in the late nineteenth and early twentieth centuries, and the Shōwa era of the 1930s.

Absolutism, Imperialism, and Militarism in the Meiji Period. Unfortunately, scholarly studies of the military in Meiji Japan are few in number. There is, however, an extensive amount of material—biographies, official histories and records, and papers of prominent political and military figures— which can be used to great effect in studying the composition of the

---

[227]*Ibid.*, p. 98. General Tōjō insisted during the Tokyo Tribunal that he had answered all questions at the conference. However, his testimony did not include any answer to this inquiry.

officer corps, the career patterns of outstanding officers, and the basic strategic concepts underlying the policies of both services. For example, the papers of Yamagata, Ōyama, Yamada, and Katsura are now available at the National Diet Library. Valuable official histories include:

Japan, Gunreibu (Navy General Staff), *Meiji sanjūshichi-hachinen kaisenshi* (1909–10).
Japan, Rikugunshō (Army Ministry), *Rikugun enkaku yōran* (1890).
——— *Meiji sanjūshichi-hachinen sen'eki rikugun seishi* (1911).
Japan, Sambō Hombu (Army General Staff), *Sambō enkakushi* (1882).
——— *Meiji nijūshichi-hachinen Nisshin seishi* (1904, 1907).

Fujiwara Akira's *Gunjishi* (1961) includes an unusually complete bibliographic guide to the literature on military affairs during the Meiji period.

What can be done with this type of material is best exemplified by Matsushita Yoshio's *Meiji gunsei shiron* (2 vols., 1956) and Umetani Noboru's *Meiji zenki seijishi no kenkyū* (1963). Matsushita's work is the pioneering and standard history of the institutional framework of both services during the Meiji era. In addition, it etches the basic strategic planning of both services and shows their pertinence to the Sino- and Russo-Japanese wars. Umetani's study is the first detailed investigation of the formation of the new army, beginning in the Bakumatsu period (1850–68). Unlike most of his predecessors in this area of research, he does not believe that the establishment of the new army made the creation of an absolutistic state inevitable. Rather, Umetani feels that during the 1868–80 period Japanese leaders were seeking to "build a modern state," and that it was particular events, especially the Saigō rebellion, the popular rights movement, and the death of Ōmura, which led them to adopt a policy in favor of a Prussian-type constitutional and military system. Since our immediate concern is with foreign policy, one should note the paramount role Umetani assigns to the French military attachés, particularly Albert Charles du Bousquet, in the creation of the imperial army. In his estimation, Ōmura favored the French notion that the army minister should possess control over all aspects of army policy; but with Ōmura's assassination and the initially inept handling of the operations during the Saigō rebellion, this approach, he argues, was supplanted by that of Yamagata, who favored the Prussian system. Without trying to enumerate the wealth of new information and insight provided by Umetani, one may simply note that he has written the best study of the Japanese army in the 1868–

80 period. It should serve as the foundation for a comprehensive reevaluation of the relationships between the formation of the imperial army and the creation of the Meiji state.

The way in which the available sources and studies of Japanese military institutions of early Meiji have been used in the analysis of Japanese foreign relations may be seen in postwar studies of the causes of the Sino-Japanese and Russo-Japanese wars.

In his two-volume *Nihon no gunkokushugi* (1953), Inoue Kiyoshi, a leading Marxist historian, treats the history of Japanese militarism in two stages: the transition from the han armies of the early Meiji to the formation of the army of the emperor system; and the subsequent embodiment within this military system of the imperialistic needs of the Japanese economy. In the first stage, two distinct phases were evident. The creation of the imperial army marked the transformation of the feudalistic warrior-type army into a "bureaucratic-absolutistic" army. This was accomplished with the defeat of the Saigō rebellion. Moreover, this development was not dictated by economic or imperialistic considerations but reflected the internal consolidation of power by the Meiji oligarchy. The second phase came with the acquisition of the independence of the right of supreme command. The army henceforth became the servant of the emperor, not of the government. This privileged position, in turn, created the militaristic cliques of the emperor system. When Inoue moves into the age of empire-building, 1895–1910, his concern with developments within the army blurs in favor of a focus on the domestic consequences of the Sino- and Russo-Japanese wars. One reads, for example, that the Sino-Japanese War was prompted by the oligarchs' (especially Shinagawa Yajirō's and Yamagata's) desire to channel the popular rights movement into support for a policy of overseas expansion. Phrased differently, the Sino-Japanese War aborted the growth of political democracy, stabilized the emperor system, and launched a form of bourgeois imperialism. Although this war was caused by the bureaucratic-militaristic leaders of the government, their policies were linked with the economic aspirations of the capitalist class. After 1898 the power and demands of the capitalists were spurred, so that eventually these served as the fundamental economic cause which hastened the emperor system's aggressive war of 1904–5.[228] In this perspective, both

[228]Inoue Kiyoshi, *Nihon no gunkokushugi* (1953), II, 182–83.

wars were primarily the product of the bureaucratic-militaristic oligarchy, which linked the economic needs of the capitalists to its policies. In a later publication, however, Inoue preferred to see these wars more as the peculiar trait of an underdeveloped nation pursuing imperialism as a means of overcoming the economic contradictions produced by industrialization in a feudal agrarian economy, an approach which credits the bourgeoisie with playing the leading role in the outbreak of these wars.[229]

Without quarreling with this analysis, one may fairly note that it emphasizes general domestic causes for the Sino- and Russo-Japanese wars and the pervasive domestic consequences of these wars. In the process the context of international politics and specific policy decisions is treated in a casual fashion. This approach to the Sino- and Russo-Japanese wars is not unusual in postwar studies of the 1895–1910 period. For example, the prolific communist writer, Kamiyama Shigeo, reasons that one should distinguish between the "feudalistic imperialism" represented by the military and "modern imperialism" represented by Japanese capitalism. Both, he claims, coexisted under the "absolutism of the emperor system," with the former dominant prior to 1905 and both equally influential after the Russo-Japanese War. This dichotomy, in his view, caused the "dual diplomacy" characteristic of the Taishō era.[230] A different variation is expressed by another Marxist scholar, Eguchi Bokurō, who apparently accepts Lenin's theory that in a country ridden with feudal traditions and institutions, the manufacturing class will seek markets in other countries. In his opinion, Japan's leaders aspired to build a capitalistic state and this ambition, irrespective of the actual stage of economic development, constituted the basic cause of these wars. According to another historian of this school, Tōyama Shigeki, the Sino-Japanese War was a transitional war to imperialism, in which the Meiji absolutistic state sought markets for Japan's goods; and the Russo-Japanese War was a true imperialistic war inspired by the objective needs of the capitalistic economy that had matured between 1895 and 1905. Kajinishi Mitsuhaya, however, regards both the Sino-Japanese and Russo-Japanese wars as being of "monopoly capitalistic rank."[231]

---

[229]Fujii Shōichi, "Teikokushugi no seiritsu to Nichi-Ro sensō" (1956).

[230]Kamiyama Shigeo, *Gendai Nihon kakka no shiteki kyūmei* (1953); also, Tōyama Shigeki and Satō Shin'ichi, *Nihonshi kenkyū nyūmon* (1963), I, 309–10.

[231]Eguchi Bokurō, *Teikokushugi to minzoku* (1954), pp. 70–91; Tōyama and Satō, *Nihonshi kenkyū nyūmon*, I, 323–25; Kajinishi Mitsuhaya and others, *Nihon shihonshugi no hatten* (1957), II, 423–60.

In 1955 Shimomura Fujio and Fujimura Michio, who represent a more pragmatic approach to research, launched the first serious criticism of these Marxist explanations of the Russo-Japanese War.[232] Thereafter Shimomura sought to disprove the popular Marxist charges that the Meiji government intended to form a Japan-Manchuria bloc, that the Japanese bourgeoisie had an "ardent desire for monopolies in Manchuria," and that the war was caused by a new stage of Japanese capitalism. Relying on contemporary newspapers and the records of the Japanese Foreign Ministry, Shimomura judged that, in entering the war, the government was primarily concerned with maintaining the "independence of Korea" and the "rights and privileges" gained during the Sino-Japanese War, and that Japan's ambition "to monopolize the Manchurian market" became unimportant after Russian defeats on the battlefield.[233]

As might be anticipated, Shimomura's analysis precipitated a heated academic controversy.[234] Inoue chose to criticize Shimomura's minimizing of the "internal contradictions" caused by the development of capitalism, rather than simply to disregard his impressive array of evidence.[235] The argument stimulated others to offer their own emphases. Furuya Tetsuo suggested that international politics produced the imperialism of 1895–1910.[236] Others around Shinobu Seizaburō insisted that it was the absolutistic bureaucrats who pushed the policy of imperialism in order to augment Meiji absolutism.[237] Hence they reasserted that the internal character of the Meiji state was more decisive than the international situation. Andō Hikotarō offered the compromise: one must include the allure of the "China market," the conflicts among the powers, and the domestic situation to grasp the causes of the Sino- and Russo-Japanese wars.[238] This may seem sensible, but only recently has there been a serious effort by Japanese

---

[232]Shimomura Fujio, "Nichi-Ro sensō to Manshū shijō" (1956); Fujimura Michio, "Nichi-Ro sensō no seikaku ni yosete" (1956), pp. 1–13.

[233]Shimomura Fujio, "Nichi-Ro sensō no seikaku" (1957), pp. 137–52.

[234]Two concise summaries of this debate are in Shinobu Seizaburō and Nakayama Jiichi, *Nichi-Ro sensōshi no kenkyū* (1959), pp. 17–26; Ogiso and others, "Nisshin Nichi-Ro sensō kenkyūshi" (1961), pp. 161–63.

[235]Inoue Kiyoshi, "Nichi-Ro sensō ni tsuite" (1958).

[236]Furuya Tetsuo, "Nihon teikokushugi no seiritsu o megutte" (1956), pp. 40–46.

[237]Nagoya Daigaku Hōgaku Kenkyūshitsu, "Nisshin Nichi-Ro sensō," p. 163.

[238]Andō Hikotarō, "Nichi-Ro sensōshi kenkyū no kadai: shu to shite Nitchū kankeishi no shiten kara" (1960), p. 238.

historians to incorporate the diplomacy of the powers as a central theme
in the origins of these wars.[239] As we begin to learn more about the specific
substance of Japanese foreign policy in the Meiji era, it will become easier to
identify and evaluate the degree to which military considerations were
evident in the decisions for war in 1896 and 1904. Still, this process may be
retarded, if not stymied, by a preoccupation with such enveloping themes
as the "character" of the Russo-Japanese War and the "contradictions"
engendered by the development of Japanese capitalism.

Factionalism, Fascism, and Militarism in the 1930s. There is a similar cluster
of source materials and secondary studies relating to the 1930s and the
origins of the Pacific War. Except for 1941, however, the sources are lean
in terms of official cabinet and military policies and the circumstances under
which they were formulated. Ideally, one should utilize the following: the
records and proceedings of the International Military Tribunal for the Far
East, especially the documents collected but not used at the trial; the
archives of the Japanese Foreign Ministry; the records of the Navy General
Staff collected at the Zaidan Hōjin Shiryō Chōsakai; the records of the
imperial army in the Military History Office of Japan's National Defense
Agency; and the material gathered by biographical associations relating to
distinguished political and military personalities. Only the first are easily
accessible to historians of Japan; many of the documents gathered for the
trials but not formally included in the record, however, have disappeared
into the archives of various governmental ministries, where they remain
unavailable to the historian.

The biographical associations are not open to scholars, but the value of
their materials is attested by three outstanding biographies:

Aritake, *Okada Keisuke* (1956).
Mitarai, *Minami Jirō* (1957).
Suzuki Kantarō den (1960).

Only a few scholars have had limited access to the resources of the Military
History Office. Of the countless published memoirs, the most valuable
are:

Arita, *Bakahachi to hito wa iu: gaikōkan no kaisō* (1959).
Fukudome, *Shikan Shinjuwan kōgeki* (1955).

[239]The reasons for this situation are etched in the opening essays of Nihon Kokusai Seiji
Gakkai, ed., *Kokusai seiji: Nihon gaikōshi kenkyū—Meiji jidai* (1957), and *Kokusai seiji: Nihon
gaikōshi kenkyū—Nisshin Nichi-Ro sensō* (1962).

Ishii, *Gaikōkan no isshō* (1950).
Kido, *Kido nikki* (1947).
Konoe, *Ushinawareshi seiji* (1946).
Morishima, *Imbō ansatsu guntō: gaikōkan no kaisō* (1950).
Shigemitsu, *Shōwa no dōran* (2 vols., 1952).
Tanemura, *Daihon'ei kimitsu nisshi* (1952).
Tōgō, *Jidai no ichimen* (1952).
Ugaki, *Ugaki nikki* (1954).

The most informative histories, in my experience, are:

Aoki, *Taiheiyō sensō zenshi* (3 vols., 1953).
Kurihara, *Tennō: Shōwashi oboegaki* (1955).
Nakamura, *Shōwa seijishi* (1958).
Nihon Kokusai Seiji Gakkai, *Kokusai seiji: Nihon gaikōshi kenkyū—Shōwa jidai* (1960).
Nihon Kokusai Seiji Gakkai Taiheiyō Sensō Gen'in Kenkyūbu, *Taiheiyō sensō e no michi* (8 vols., 1962–63).

The most helpful biographies, apart from those cited, are:

Aoki, *Wakatsuki Reijirō Hamaguchi Osachi* (1958).
Aritake, *Ishiwata Sōtarō* (1954).
Kikkawa, *Arashi to tatakau tesshō Araki* (1955).
Takagi, *Yamamoto Isoroku to Yonai Mitsumasa* (1950).
Yabe, *Konoe Fumimaro* (2 vols., 1952).

On army factionalism and military history, the significant publications are:

Hata, *Nitchū sensōshi* (1961).
Hayashi, *Taiheiyō sensō rikusen gaishi* (1957).
Itō, *Gumbatsu kōbōshi* (3 vols., 1957–58).
Iwabuchi, *Gumbatsu no keifu* (1948).
Majima, *Gumbatsu antō hishi* (1946).
Takagi, *Taiheiyō sensō kaisenshi* (1949).
Takamiya, *Gunkoku taiheiki* (1951).
Tanaka, *Haiin o tsuku* (1946).

In view of the quantity of writings on the 1930s, it is not feasible to indicate how each of these illuminates the influence of the military on Japanese foreign policy during this decade, but a review of the major interpretations will reveal several interesting approaches.

In the closing months of the Pacific War, Prince Konoe penned his memoir, *Ushinawareshi seiji*. According to his recollection, the imperial army had been plagued by a bitter rivalry between an Imperial Way (*kōdō*) and a Control (*tōsei*) faction.[240] The former group favored a war with the Soviet Union, the latter one with China. After the February 26, 1936 Incident, the Control group became dominant within the army, and its actions were instrumental in causing the China War of 1937 and later the outbreak of the Pacific War. Support for this version of the nature and importance of army factionalism was extended by General Tanaka Ryūkichi, a prosecution witness at the Tokyo Tribunal.[241] Tanaka, however, attributed the rivalry to different political attitudes: the Imperial Way faction believed in the mystique of the "national polity" or *kokutai*; the Control faction was entranced by a form of state socialism patterned after the doctrines of Nazi Germany. When the Control group came into ascendancy in 1935 under Army Minister Hayashi Senjūrō, the young officers of the Imperial Way faction resorted to direct action: the assassination of General Nagata Tetsuzan in August 1935 and the abortive rebellion of February 1936. The reaction to the February Incident marked the hegemony of the Control faction in the army. Thereafter the authoritarian nature of the Japanese government increased steadily. The prosecution at the Tribunal naturally accepted the Konoe and Tanaka versions and set out to prove that "militaristic cliques and ultranationalist secret societies resorted to rule by assassination, and thereby exerted great influence in favor of military aggression."[242]

These revelations about army factionalism were skillfully blended by Maruyama Masao into his famous "fascism from above" thesis. Distinguishing the various ultranationalistic societies which mushroomed during the 1930s and the terrorism carried out by youthful military officers as a manifestation of "fascism from below," he equated the outlook and policies of the leaders of the bureaucratic, financial, and military circles with "fascism from above." The crucial turning point of the 1930s was the abortive rebellion of February 26, 1936:

> As a consequence of this uprising, the so-called "Control faction" suppressed the influence of radical fascism in the army by carrying out a thoroughgoing purge, and at the same time attained one by one the military's political demands by using as an excuse against outsiders the menace of radical

[240]Konoe Fumimaro, *Ushinawareshi seiji* (1946), pp. 5–18.
[241]IMTFE, Proceedings, pp. 1945–2177, 14288–422, 15853–951, 22713–55, 22943–68, 29030–64, 29406–18; also Tanaka Ryūkichi, *Haiin o tsuku* (1946).
[242]IMTFE, Proceedings, p. 442.

fascism. . . . Soon after the suppression of radical fascism, a closer alliance of the military, bureaucrats, and zaibatsu was consolidated, bringing about a completed form of a typical fascism.[243]

Another comprehensive interpretation of the development of Japanese fascism and the origins of the Pacific War was advanced by two popular histories:

Rekishigaku Kenkyūkai, *Taiheiyō sensōshi* (5 vols., 1954).
Tōyama and others, *Shōwashi* (2d rev. ed., 1959).

According to these accounts, the Great Depression fostered serious economic and social difficulties throughout the capitalistic world. In turn, this caused the Japanese move into Manchuria, the rise of Hitler to power, and the Ethiopian venture of fascist Italy. One saw, in other words, a worldwide development of fascism and aggression of which Japan was one illustration. In particular, the internal contradictions of Japanese society caused the terrorism of the early 1930s, thereby bringing about a new power alignment among the military, industrial, and landlord groups. This yielded the fascist state, launched Japan into the China War, and eventually brought about a conflict with Britain and the United States over the resources of Southeast Asia.

Each of these interpretations has the merit of placing the military within a complicated political matrix, but neither deals precisely with the formulation of foreign policy. The few Western historians of the period have focused almost exclusively on the role of the military in Japan's foreign policy and the origins of the Pacific War. Richard Storry's *The Double Patriots* (1957) is an unusually lucid extension of Maruyama's "fascism from above" theme. For example, he attributes the expansion into China and then into Southeast Asia to the general influence of the Control faction: "The suppression of the February Mutiny was the last triumph of the *Tōseiha*. The war with China and the Pacific War were, in the final analysis, desperate and, as it turned out, disastrous attempts to consolidate that triumph." More particularly, he suggests that the Marco Polo Bridge Incident was inspired by a conspiracy of field officers comparable to that which had produced the Manchurian Incident.[244] Maxon's *Control of Japanese Foreign Policy* (1957) advanced the concept of *gekokujō*, or rule from

[243]Maruyama, "Nihon fashizumu no shisō to undō."
[244]Richard Storry, *The Double Patriots* (1957), pp. 203, 137–41, 180–91, 216–19.

below, to explain how the army determined foreign policy throughout the 1930s. Using the Mukden and Marco Polo Bridge incidents as prime examples of *gekokujō*, he judges the pattern of policy-making to be as follows: 1) the army in the field provoked an incident; 2) the General Staff supported the deeds of the field army; 3) the army minister compelled the cabinet to defer to the opinion of the General Staff; and 4) the independent actions of the field officers became, in effect, the official policy of the imperial government. Once the China War was in process, the supreme command enabled "anonymous field grade officers" of the army, especially those in the General Staff, to control the direction of Japan's foreign policy.[245]

This theme was greatly refined in Robert J.C. Butow's *Tojo and the Coming of the War* (1961): "Tojo was not so much an initiator of policies as a promoter of them and propagandist for them. . . . It was the chief of staff and his subordinates—particularly the latter—who determined army attitudes and who fostered them, through the war minister and the chief of the military affairs bureau, upon the members of the cabinet."[246] In Butow's skillful hands, this theme has a compelling ring of veracity. Whether one fully accepts his portrait of Tōjō or his evaluation of American foreign policy in 1940–41, he has emphasized the powerful influence of "middle-ranking officers" on Japan's foreign policy so as to place future historians of the decision for war in 1941 in his debt.[247]

The historians cited agree that the imperial army was mainly responsible for the Pacific War; however, this consensus is deceptive. The Japanese writers emphasize domestic considerations, of which the army was one vital element, as the basic cause of Japan's foreign policy; the Western writers prefer to stress the foreign policy of Japan as the fundamental cause of the war and to attribute this policy to the influence of the army. Since the Korean War and the emergence of Communist China, however, the significance of international events has gained increasing attention among Japanese scholars. They lay great stress on the "legalistic-moralistic" basis of American foreign policy which, they say, ignored the power realities in Asia and thereby acted as an important cause of the Pacific War.[248] Follow-

---

[245]Maxon, *Control of Japanese Foreign Policy*, pp. 100, 216.

[246]Butow, *Tojo and the Coming of the War*, pp. 146–47.

[247]For example, James W. Morley's review in *Political Science Quarterly*, LXXXVII, No. 1 (1962), 95–97.

[248]For example, George Kennan, *American Diplomacy, 1900–1950* (1951); Alexander Deconde, ed., *Isolation and Security* (1957).

ing this line of thought, Kaizuma claims that the Pacific War was caused by conflicting approaches to international affairs by the United States and Imperial Japan. In particular, he observes: 1) that the Versailles treaties did not preclude the preservation of existing rights in colonial areas, despite the application of the principle of "national self-determination" to Europe; 2) that the Nine Power Treaty, which ostensibly recognized the "integrity" of China, also confirmed existing privileges; and 3) that the Kellogg-Briand Pact outlawing war specifically allowed all signatories the right to act in self-defense and to decide unilaterally what constituted an act of self-defense. The formation of Manchukuo, he believes, was such an act. But the United States under the Stimson Doctrine advanced an entirely new principle that was not sanctioned under international law. After this step, the course of diplomatic relations deteriorated, and with Secretary Hull's note of November 26, 1941, which was couched in the terminology of the Kellogg-Briand Pact and the Stimson Doctrine, "there was no way that the explosion of the Japanese-American negotiations could be avoided."[249]

This new variation of the "inevitability" theme of the Pacific War is very persuasive and, judging by its popularity, has much merit. Without agreeing with this approach, it is fair to note that it inherently challenges the theses and themes presented in the previously mentioned writings on the origins of the war. In fact, it already has produced a strong reaction in some academic circles. For example, when Ueyama Shumpei in a popular magazine placed the origins of the Pacific War in a context which stressed the interaction of nationalism, power politics, the communist menace, and the tendency of the United States to approach these issues in East Asia through a naive identification with the Nationalist government of China, he drew an acerbic rebuttal from Inoue Kiyoshi. The causes of the Pacific War, Inoue insisted, were located not in the realm of international politics, but in the internal pressures and contradictions of Japanese society, in the realms of Japanese capitalism and militarism.[250] One senses a controversy in the offing comparable to that inspired by Shimomura's evaluation of the Russo-Japanese War and compounded by the active interest of American historians in the origins of the Pacific War.

---

[249]Kaizuma Haruhiko, "Shōwa gaikōshi sōsetsu" (1959), pp. 1–13.
[250]Ueyama Shumpei, "Taiheiyō sensō no shisōshiteki igi" (1961); Inoue Kiyoshi, "Taiheiyō sensō shikan" (1961), pp. 23–35.

Despite these differences in approach and emphasis, over the past few years there has appeared an appreciable amount of new information on army factionalism and its relevance to Japan's continental policy in the 1931–38 period. Kurihara Ken's *Tennō: Shōwashi oboegaki* was the first to call attention to the strong opposition of the Army General Staff to the China War and to the relationship between unrest within the army over the China policy of Army Minister Hayashi and the assassination of General Nagata in the summer of 1935.[251] In a series of publications, Hata Ikuhiko developed these themes in much greater detail. Focusing his analysis on the ambivalent policies in central headquarters and the north China army vis-a-vis the Ho-Umezu agreement of 1935 and the Marco Polo Bridge Incident, he cast the role of the army in a different light than that projected by Konoe and Tanaka.[252] I have reappraised the outbreak of the China War to suggest that it was decisively affected by the diplomacy of Prime Minister Konoe and Foreign Minister Hirota and that the incident was not caused by a conspiracy of army officers.[253] Hata Ikuhiko also has surveyed the origins and activities of the Cherry Blossom Society and the Imperial Way and Control factions, as well as the February 26, 1936 Incident, so as to rectify many of the misconceptions and errors initially circulated at the Tokyo Tribunal. Although retaining the Imperial Way–Control faction format, Hata has advanced the thesis that the Control group represented those officers who subscribed to the principles of "total war" and proposed policies designed to mobilize the economic and manpower resources of the nation, while the Imperial Way faction advocated traditional military concepts, insisting that morale and the aggressive spirit of the troops and officers, not technological warfare or industrial capability, would be the key to victory in war.[254] Elsewhere I have argued that army factionalism in the early 1930s does not readily fall into the Imperial Way–Control dichotomy but was more complex, being rooted in different bureaucratic or administrative and command responsibilities.[255] The opening volume of *Taiheiyō*

[251]Kurihara Ken, *Tennō: Shōwashi oboegaki* (1955), pp. 74–100.

[252]Hata, "Umezu Ka Ōkin kyōtei keii," pp. 2, 65–144; "Nikka jihen" (1959), pp. 71–84; and *Nitchū sensōshi* (1961).

[253]Crowley, "Reconsideration of the Marco Polo Bridge Incident," pp. 277–91.

[254]Hata, "Sakurakai shuisho," pp. 65, 81–88; "Rikugun no habatsu 'Sakurakai,'" pp. 88–101; "Kōdōha to Tōseiha" (1961), pp. 78–90; and "Ni-ni-roku jiken" (1961), pp. 96–108.

[255]James B. Crowley, "Japanese Army Factionalism in the Early 1930's" (1962), pp. 309–26.

sensō e no michi reevaluates the Manchurian Incident, based mainly on the papers of Ishiwara Kanji, to indicate that it was not an independent act of the Kwantung army but had the guidance and approval of central headquarters. Subsequent volumes present abundant new information as well as new interpretations of the origins of the Pacific War, somewhat at variance with those evident in the histories written in the immediate aftermath of the war.

Whether this increasing amount of information on army factionalism, on the policies and activities of the military, and on Japan's foreign policy during the 1930s will occasion some new approaches to the basic problem of how the military influenced foreign policy is difficult to estimate. A preoccupation with the "origins" of the Pacific War or with Japanese "fascism" need not necessarily be conducive to this particular result. That the new information on developments within the army may be confined to the format of past approaches is vividly illustrated in Fujiwara's *Gunjishi*. Fujiwara also sees the absolutism of the Meiji state, the virulent nationalism after the Sino- and Russo-Japanese wars, and the development of fascism after the February 26 Incident as major influences on prewar Japanese history and as the consequences of the deeds and policies of the army. His explanations of these developments, however, differ from those that one finds prior to the writings of Umetani, Kurihara, and Hata. For example, Fujiwara dates the formation of the army of the emperor system to the introduction of Meckel's teachings, and he attributes the emphasis on "patriotism" and an "aggressive combat spirit" within military circles to the "lessons" drawn from the campaigns of the Russo-Japanese War. Phrased differently, Fujiwara believes the autonomous administrative structure of the army and the stress on morale were the products of a rational policy devised by Japan's military leaders. They did not stem from traditional feudalistic and absolutistic values. Nevertheless, they did produce a major contradiction: with the development of Japanese capitalism and of a professional officer corps, emphasis came to be placed on an "abstract love of country" and militarism became fused with nationalism. Thus, parallel with the growth of an urban society, the ideal soldier was fixed in a peasant mold. This idealization of the agrarian sector of Japanese society, he argues, produced another contradiction in the period following World War I. At that time, many staff officers absorbed the "lessons" of this conflict and became proponents of "total war." At the highest levels of the officer corps, this resulted in *semmongunshugi*, the advocacy of highly trained, elite forces rather than mass armies. Among the younger officers and the veterans of the Russo-Japanese War, however, the emphasis on morale, patriotism, and agrarian values continued to flourish. This contradiction produced the terrorism of the young officers who wished to effect a Shōwa restoration and the state fascistic policies of the staff officers who were seeking to coordinate all segments of the nation so that Japan could wage a total war. With the February 26 Incident, the latter view prevailed and Japan became a fascist state. The outbreak of the China War involved Japan in a protracted war, the first in Japanese history. Although the leaders of the army did not desire these hostilities, the necessity to wage extensive operations led to a rapid enlargement of the army, in which the emphasis on morale and the "attack spirit" were again reinforced. This hampered a systematic introduction of new technology, a deficiency that was crucial in the conduct of the Pacific War.[256]

Fujiwara has accomplished a remarkable blend of standard themes in Japanese historiography—absolutism, militarism, and fascism—and of the information revealed in the past six years. He has, so to speak, taken the best of two historical worlds: the army played a deleterious role in the course of modern Japanese history, but at the same time it was one of the most rational aspects of prewar Japanese society. Since he feels no need to deny the positive developments within the army—they were offset by their contradictions—Fujiwara has some unusually ambivalent attitudes about Japan's new Self-Defense Force. It has become a tool of American imperialism and Japanese capitalism but, he acknowledges, if there were "a fundamental social revolution," it could be converted into a "democratic" force.[257] If this were to materialize, one would anticipate some equally revolutionary changes in the historiography of Japanese militarism.

By way of summary, one may note first that there is no good, comprehensive history of the Japanese military establishment covering the entire 1868–1941 period. Second, the themes of militarism and factionalism have been studied mainly in terms of their pertinence to the formation of the Meiji absolutistic state, the creation by the army of the emperor system, the development of a militant nationalism after the Sino- and

---

[256]Fujiwara, *Gunjishi*, pp. 110–11, 131–36, 171–90.
[257]*Ibid.*, p. 241.

Russo-Japanese wars, and the emergence of fascism in the 1930s. These are important subjects, but they have as yet contributed little to an understanding of how particular or important foreign policies were affected by military leaders or strategic considerations. Third, one encounters groups of writings on comprehensive questions: the "character" of the Russo-Japanese War and the "origins" of the Pacific War. Here one detects two distinct approaches. The first emphasizes the domestic causes of these wars; the other stresses the diplomacy of the powers vis-a-vis Japan. At either level, there is slight attention to the substance of Japan's foreign policies, to the aims and aspirations underlying these policies, or to the process by which they were formulated and decided. To state this is inherently to ask for some new approaches to the study of Japanese foreign policy. Hopefully, Japanese historians will rectify this deficiency. Certainly one cannot help contrasting the incisive analysis of Gerhard Ritter's "Staatskunst und Kriegshandwerk: Das Problem des 'Militarismus' in Deutschland" with the somewhat abstract analyses of Japanese militarism. Granting the pervasive influence of militarism in prewar Japan, there remains the task of illuminating the specific ways in which military personnel, acts, and policies affected the formulation and implementation of foreign policies in imperial Japan.

2

Japan's Economic Foreign Policies, 1868–1893

Arthur E. Tiedemann

◆

During the period under review, Japan's economic foreign policies were determined almost entirely by the political objectives of the Meiji leaders. Any discussion of economic foreign policies must begin, therefore, with the Meiji government's political policies. In broad terms, these political policies were as follows: 1) to establish and consolidate the new government's control within Japan; 2) to prevent any further encroachments on Japan's sovereign rights; and 3) to remove the limitations on Japan's judicial and tariff autonomy imposed in the unequal treaties negotiated under the Tokugawa. By the time they achieved power, the Meiji leaders came to see that their aims could best be furthered through the adoption of Western military and administrative techniques. To introduce these techniques required, first, that they be learned by bringing Western instructors to Japan or by sending Japanese abroad; and second, that the equipment necessary for their implementation be secured. Consequently, to the disappointment of their more naive xenophobic followers, the new leaders made no quixotic effort to end foreign contacts but instead committed themselves to a program for the heavy importation of foreign goods and services. Into the country were imported professors, ship's engineers, mechanics, warships, guns, telegraph wire, rails, locomotives, milling machines, and hundreds of other necessary items right down to the woolen cloth and brass buttons of the new bureaucrats' official dress. These imports so vital to the development of military strength and administrative control had, of course, to be paid for, and the acquisition of the required foreign exchange henceforth became a problem of persistent and central concern to the government.

One way to solve such a foreign exchange problem was to seek loans abroad, but prior to the century's end, the Meiji government made little use of foreign borrowings. Only two loans were raised, one for £1 million in April 1870 and the other for £2.4 million in January 1873. Whether there ever was a conscious decision of the government to forego foreign loans and, if so, what the precise reasoning behind the decision might have been are questions which have still not been adequately explored. It may even have been an unexamined, axiomatic premise of the Meiji leaders that foreign loans were politically dangerous and must be avoided. They had undoubtedly observed the "debt collecting" activities of France in Mexico, of Britain in China, and of both countries in the Levant. In their own country they had seen how the powers tried to use the Shimonoseki indemnity negotiations to obtain the opening of Shimonoseki and later to secure the right of free travel throughout Japan. Certainly, the two loans they contracted had been made only when they found themselves in a very tight corner. The 1870 loan was designed to get the Tokyo-Yokohama railroad built quickly and thus end importunate foreign requests for construction rights; the 1873 loan was made because the financial settlement which liquidated the feudal system was pressing too heavily upon the as yet poorly developed money resources of the young government. The harsh terms of these loans may in themselves have been enough to discourage any further foreign borrowing. The interest rates were high and repayment of principal had to begin within a few years. Since payments on these loans averaged about £400,000 a year in the 1870s, those officials concerned with finance (e.g., Ōkubo Toshimichi and Ōkuma Shigenobu) felt keenly the necessity of avoiding any situation which might interfere with repayment. During the Korean debate in the fall of 1873, one of Ōkubo's arguments against war was that it would produce a trade imbalance that would lead to defaulting on foreign debts and thus invite intervention, perhaps even occupation, by Britain. The 1870 loan was, after all, secured by a mortgage on the customs receipts and on the Tokyo-Yokohama railroad's earnings. In the unsettled atmosphere of the 1870s, the exercise of these rights by foreign creditors would have been a political disaster for the new leadership. Indeed, the Meiji government had originally tried to keep the loan and its terms secret in order that the Japanese public might not know of even the existence of such a possibility. Fear of the use that political opponents might make of adverse public reaction to loans was undoubtedly one of the important reasons for the reluctance to use foreign funds.

Even though government loans were avoided, foreign funds could have come into the country through direct investment. But although here again the circumstances of the decision are as yet only meagerly documented, the Meiji government had a fairly definite policy of confining direct foreign investment to the concession areas of the treaty ports. When, as in the case of the Tokyo-Yokohama railroad, the Danish telegraph company, or the Kobe gasworks, foreigners sought permission to expand their activities beyond those limits, they were invariably refused. Where foreigners had already under the Tokugawa made investments outside the concessions— for example, the Takashima Coal Mine or the American shipyard in Kobe— the government hastened to buy them out. The only clearly expressed ground for this policy was the need to keep the field open for future Japanese entrepreneurs. Undoubtedly the government was also aware that its control over economic development would be weakened by the existence of enterprises in which financial interests were held by foreigners enjoying the privileges of extraterritoriality.

One important field in which this loss of control to foreigners appeared imminent was coastal shipping. Foreigners had managed to invade this area by maintaining that the right of their ships to load and unload at the treaty ports was not limited to international traffic but also included purely domestic Japanese goods and passengers moving between those ports. Since the native junk could not compete with the foreign vessel's greater speed, capacity, and economy of operation, the coasting trade between the major ports gravitated toward foreign hands. Fearing this would curtail the nation's economic independence and give the foreigners control over the shipment to the capital of the all-important rice tax, the Meiji government organized a succession of shipping companies for which it purchased modern vessels and to which it gave a monopoly on the transportation of the rice tax. None of these companies was successful, and in 1875 a critical point was reached when the Pacific Mail Steamship Company, the largest of the foreign lines, asked permission to open a coastal service extending to all Japanese ports. To avoid this alternative, the government decided to eliminate the Pacific Mail's competition by purchasing the company's installations in Japan and Shanghai. For a cash settlement another important competitor, the Occidental and Oriental Line, also promised not to enter its ships in the coastal trade or the Yokohama-Shanghai run. As its agent in these matters, the government used the Mitsubishi Steamship Company, the one company that had demonstrated some managerial capability. This company was given the newly acquired foreign properties, the assets of the old government company, and an annual operating subsidy. In addition, it received an annual grant to train Japanese personnel, since for security and financial reasons the government was anxious to reduce its reliance on foreign crew members. Through these measures the Japanese were at least able to establish their dominance in coastal shipping even though 90 percent of the country's overseas trade still moved in foreign ships. However, to buy off foreign competition and to purchase the required modern vessels necessitated heavy expenditures of foreign exchange.

Since these and Japan's other foreign exchange requirements were not, as we have seen, offset by loans or direct investments, the only way left for the Meiji government to cover external payments was the export of goods or specie. Fortunately, Japan did possess some gold and silver deposits and over the centuries there had been a small but steady production. The Tokugawa had from the very beginning of their long rule been greatly concerned both to increase this production and to prevent specie from leaving the country. In 1868 there was, then, a substantial accumulation of specie available to the new government despite the gold drain incurred during the late 1850s by a temporary Japanese overevaluation of silver. The Meiji government inherited whatever gold and silver the Tokugawa had, but probably much the greater part of the country's specie was in private hands. To mobilize this privately held specie for its own purposes, the government in the first instance requisitioned large specie loans from the great merchant houses. Within a few years a more permanent solution was achieved by substituting paper notes for specie in domestic transactions. The gold and silver thus released from duty as a domestic medium of exchange was successfully soaked up by the nation's financial institutions and was used henceforth almost exclusively for reserve or foreign trade purposes. To supplement this existing stock of specie, the Meiji government devoted a considerable portion of its investment funds to raising gold and silver production, which by the 1880s had reached a level of about ¥1.8 million annually. Since this was rather a small sum compared to the average annual import bill in the 1870s of ¥28 million, it was obvious to Japan's leaders that the country's limited supply of specie would soon be exhausted if every effort were not made to earn additional foreign exchange by the export of commodities. Ultimately it was, therefore, to current exports that the Meiji government looked in order to finance the major portion of the imports required by its ambitious modernization program. Consequently, the rate at which modernization could proceed was tied rather closely to the rate at which exports could be expanded.

Luckily, the ten years of foreign trade that preceded the establishment of the new government had already uncovered several Japanese products for which there was a foreign market: silkworm eggs, raw silk, tea, copper, coal, ceramics, sea tangles. Through their agency it was possible to convert Japan's domestic savings into a form that could be used to secure the foreign exchange indispensable to modernization. If these export opportunities had not existed, it is probable that Japan's high rate of domestic savings would have been of somewhat limited value in modernizing the country. Exist they did, however, and the Meiji government moved quickly to take advantage of them. A Commerce Control Office (Shōhōshi, later to become the Trade Control Office, Tsūshōshi) was established in August 1868 and given wide authority over prices, currency, shipping, and foreign trade. Its main function was to encourage the increased production of export commodities and to facilitate their flow to the treaty ports. In many ways the operations of this office were an extension on a national scale of the practices characteristic of the old domain monopolies. Merchants in the treaty ports were organized into foreign trade companies (*shōhō kaisha, tsūshō kaisha, shōsha*) which, though technically voluntary, were actually compulsory. Only merchants belonging to these companies were allowed to engage in foreign trade. From government-controlled exchange companies (*kawase kaisha*) the trading companies received loans in paper currency which were employed as operating funds to organize the supply of export goods from the countryside. When these goods arrived at the treaty ports, they were sold to the foreign merchants for gold or silver and the specie thus obtained was used to repay the original paper currency loan. In this way the specie gained through foreign trade was concentrated in the hands of the government.

The accumulation of specie was not the only objective the government hoped to attain by creating these trading companies. A second motive was to confine the foreigner's activities to the treaty ports and prevent him from encroaching any further into Japan's economic life. The government feared that the foreign merchants would establish direct relations with the native producers and form a kind of "plantation" system that might cause the productive facilities for exports to be developed in separation from the domestic economic structure. Without quite understanding the economic theory of the situation, they were aware that if the export industries were organized by the foreigner, these industries would become primarily part of the foreigner's economic system and the benefits arising from them would accrue more to the foreigner than to the Japanese. It went against the grain to leave to foreigners what the Japanese felt they could do for themselves. Determined that the foreigner's role in managing the export industries should be held to a minimum, the Meiji government adamantly resisted any attempts by foreign merchants, either on their own or through Japanese agents, to penetrate the hinterland and carry on business there. The trading companies were expected to further this policy by interposing themselves between the foreign buyer and the native producer.

Yet a third purpose the trading companies were expected to serve was the inspection of goods offered for export. The Meiji government realized very soon in the game that Japan's markets would be lost if in the rush to expand exports Japanese merchants eager for a quick profit were allowed to ship inferior goods. By restricting the export trade to the trading company members and then subjecting those members to rigorous quality control, the government hoped it could prevent a flood of shoddy merchandise from destroying the foreign markets. As early as 1868, facilities for inspecting silkworm eggs and raw silk had been set up in the treaty ports. The Meiji leaders were also shrewd enough to discern that something more than quality in the traditional sense was needed. They quickly recognized that a place was to be won in Western markets only if Japan turned out standardized exports in the grades and quantities required by the machine technology of the West's mass production industries. The February 1870 decision to establish the famous French-style silk reeling model factory at Tomioka was directly inspired by the news that in London large amounts of Japanese raw silk had had to be discarded as unsuitable for use in Western machines. Through such model factories and through public displays like the 1872 Domestic Enterprise Encouragement Exposition (Naikoku Kangyō Hakurankai), the authorities sought to spread the use of techniques capable of producing exports up to Western standards.

This eagerness to search out and accommodate to the needs of potential markets is one of the important reasons for the rapid expansion that occurred in Japanese exports.

The foreign merchant community was not averse to Japanese efforts to produce quality exports, but they did not like the new machinery for trade control established in 1868–69. To them the new trading companies were monopolies that plainly violated the free trade provisions of the 1858 treaties. Under pressure from the foreign envoys, the Japanese government was obliged to eliminate the monopolistic features of the companies and reduce them to the level of voluntary private enterprises, their former regulatory and development functions being absorbed into the Finance Ministry and the Home Ministry. Since the government did not actually have the trained personnel necessary to put into effect a regulatory system of its own, it still felt constrained to rely upon trade associations for this function. To establish such an association in the raw silk trade and at the same time get around the foreigners' requirement of free enterprise and voluntary action, the Finance Ministry arranged a meeting of the Yokohama silk merchants in the spring of 1873 at which a Raw Silk Improvement Company (Kiito Aratame Kaisha) was "spontaneously" organized. Soon a number of others had sprung up throughout the country, and to these companies was entrusted the enforcement of the government's June 1873 regulations for the control of raw silk manufacture (*kiito seizō torishimari kisoku*).

Inevitably these companies did not limit their activities to improving the quality of raw silk but also sought to regulate the terms of sale in the treaty ports. In addition, quality control easily became a device for limiting production and upholding prices. This comes out quite clearly in the parallel case of the April 1873 regulations for the production of silkworm eggs (*sanshu seizō kisoku*). Under these regulations the producer was allowed to place his eggs only on cards issued by the Finance Ministry, and to each card was affixed a ministry stamp designating whether the eggs were to go into the domestic or the foreign market. By limiting the number of cards and stamps, the Finance Ministry was able to set a ceiling on total national production and determine what proportion would be made available to the foreign merchants. The intention was not simply to support prices by limiting supply, but also to prevent any deterioration in the quality of Japanese raw silk arising from the diversion of large quantities of the better eggs into foreign trade. The government was quite willing to forego the more immediate profits that would come from expanding egg exports in favor of the potentially greater profits to be derived from using these eggs to develop a high quality raw silk industry. The general attitude was that the foreigner should not be allowed to derive a profit from doing something the Japanese themselves could very well do, that as much of the processing as was possible should be done before a product left Japan.

Naturally, these new measures of the Meiji government were regarded by the foreign community as another attempt to interfere with freedom of trade. Faced by the united opposition of the major foreign envoys, the government, despite the reluctance of the Finance Ministry, decided late in 1873 that it had to yield on the issue. The immediate result, in the case of the silkworm cards, was a flooding of the treaty port market in 1874 and a disastrous fall in price. At first the government sought to deal with the problem by supplying the Yokohama dealers sub rosa with funds to buy up and burn about 450,000 cards. However, the following year a more lasting technique was unveiled with the creation, under government regulations, of a system of regional silkworm card manufacturing associations (*sanshu seizō kumiai*). These associations were made responsible for inspecting their members' products and a national council of association presidents was empowered to determine the total number of cards to be produced each year. The new system was enforced through fines and confiscations administered by the local courts and governors. Nevertheless, the foreigners could not legally protest, since the system applied to goods before they entered international trade and therefore did not technically infringe the freedom of trade guaranteed for transactions between Japanese and foreigners in the treaty ports. Several years later this type of organization was made more generally available by the trade association rules (*dōgyō kumiai junsoku*) issued in 1884.

The foreign trade policy of the Meiji government was not confined merely to developing the export lines and the markets which had been opened under the Tokugawa. The new government was not content to rely upon the export opportunities brought to attention by the foreign merchants in the treaty ports. Instead the government itself began to search actively for new overseas markets. From 1872 on a number of consulates were established in the major foreign cities and charged with the mission of gathering commercial intelligence and propagandizing Japanese products. Beginning with the San Francisco International Exhibition of 1871 and the Vienna World Exposition of 1873, Japan participated eagerly in a series of world fairs. Although this was designed to promote Japanese goods, it also gave the Japanese an excellent opportunity to inform themselves of the latest developments in Western technology. For instance, machinery bought at Vienna was placed on display in Osaka in 1874. In that same year the government began the practice of testing the marketability of various Japanese products (e.g., tea, raw silk, rice, wheat, tobacco, camphor, hemp, soy bean sauce) by making trial sale shipments to the more important foreign commercial centers.

Though it pursued an energetic export expansion policy, the Meiji government was plagued almost from its inception with an adverse balance of trade. Exports did expand; in 1875 they were 20 percent higher than in 1868. However, imports rose at an even faster rate; in 1875 they were 180 percent higher than in 1868. A large share of these imports was absorbed, of course, by the various government programs for building a modern administration, creating an economic infrastructure, and developing the armed forces. Military imports in particular became heavy after the institution of the new conscript army in 1873. By 1875 the military were receiving 51 percent of the total central government investment as compared with 6 percent in 1872, the import bill for arms alone coming to ¥632,000. Side by side with this increase of government imports, there was a tremendous expansion in imports of consumer goods for the general public. Partly this resulted from a growing taste for new Western products ranging from lamp oil to celluloid dolls; partly it developed because the West was able in some cases—cotton cloth, cotton yarn, sugar—to offer a product of better quality and cheaper price than the traditional Japanese article. The government would have liked to eliminate what was in its eyes a wasteful and undesirable category of trade, but under the unequal treaties these private imports could not, of course, be controlled by means either of tariff rates or of import quotas. Paradoxically, it may be that this heavy import of consumer goods was part of the price to be paid for the expansion of exports, since the availability of these goods helped provide the incentives necessary to induce the changes in agricultural production required for the development of exports from that sector. In this way the private imports probably made a more immediate contribution to exports than did government imports, many of which were nonproductive or would yield returns only after a substantial elapse of time.

In any event, from 1868 to 1875 Japan had an adverse trade balance totaling over ¥57 million, to which must be added an uncertain amount for the invisible trade deficit. About ¥25 million of this was taken care of by the proceeds of the 1870 loan (only 30 percent of which was actually spent on the railroad) and the 1873 loan. The rest had to be paid for by shipping specie from Japan's own reserves. The bullionist tradition of Tokugawa economic thought made the Meiji leaders especially watchful of and sensitive to specie losses. Consequently, by 1875 they were somewhat in a panic over the huge outflow of specie and resolved that measures had to be taken to end the loss. If the import excess was not ended, wrote Ōkubo, "with a limited national strength we will be meeting an unlimited drain . . . and will face ruin."[1] Action seemed especially imperative at this point since in 1875 payments on the foreign loans would rise to about ¥1.8 million. The government met the immediate problem of specie for the 1875 loan installments by purchasing rice and other agricultural products and shipping them abroad for its own account. But for the more deep-rooted problem of trade imbalance, more long-range solutions had to be sought.

In this situation, attention naturally turned toward the possibility of revising the treaties so as to make possible an increase in tariff rates above the established 5 percent limit. In addition to giving the government some control over imports, this solution would have the extra political advantage of making possible a reduction in the land tax. Ōkuma argued very strongly for this course and suggested that in the meantime the government should institute a "domestic" tax on imported goods or a business tax on transactions involving foreign products. These suggestions were vetoed as transparent subterfuges certain to be considered treaty violations, but it was decided to ask at a suitable time for an upward revision in the conventional tariff. In February 1878 this request was made to the foreign governments, only to be greeted by the most important of them, the British, with a rejection and a patronizing lecture from Foreign Secretary Salisbury on the advantages of free trade. As Inoue Kaoru had commented a few

---

[1] *Ōkubo Toshimichi bunsho* (1927–29), VI, 466.

years earlier, "A country well provided with manufactures demands free trade; a country not yet so provided sets forth the advantages of protection."[2] The Japanese were to try again, notably in 1882 when Inoue disingenuously tried to convince the Tokyo Treaty Revision Conference that tariff autonomy was desired purely for fiscal reasons and would not be used to hinder the import of foreign goods. However, the foreign governments were not persuaded and Japan had to wait for tariff autonomy until 1911, the very end of the Meiji period.

Meanwhile, Ōkubo and Ōkuma, understanding that tariff revision was not likely to materialize in the near future, had in May 1876 proposed a two-pronged attack on the trade imbalance. The basic reason for the problem, they argued, was the failure of production for export to increase at a fast enough rate. This in turn was caused by a lack of sufficient investment funds at low rates of interest. Therefore it was necessary to make more cheap capital available to those producing for export. In line with this argument, the government soon thereafter enlarged its own loan program and revised the national bank regulations so as to increase the amount of paper currency these institutions could issue.

Ōkubo's and Ōkuma's second proposal was that imports be reduced by developing domestic industries that would compete with these foreign goods. Public and private domestic demand should both be filled, they felt, by domestic production. Government agencies should buy abroad only such goods as could absolutely not be produced domestically. The domestic product was to be preferred even if its quality was not up to that of the foreign article. Since this ideal of self-sufficiency seemed almost self-evident to men who had been raised in the autarchic environment of the old domain political economy, this proposed second line of defense was also implemented by the government. Within a few years (1875–79) there were set up the Fukagawa Cement Factory, the Shinagawa Glass Factory, the Senjū Woolen Factory, the Fukagawa White Brick Factory, and the Mita Agricultural Implements Factory. To offset the two largest items of private consumption, cotton yarn and sugar, the government sought to lay the foundations of a modern cotton yarn and a modern sugar industry by importing spinning and refining machinery. In the case of the

---

[2]Quoted in Japan, Tsūshō Sangyōshō (Ministry of International Trade and Industry), ed., *Shōkō seisakushi V: Bōeki (jō)* (1965), p. 210.

spinning machinery, the government in 1876 imported ten 2,000-spindle machines, which it sold to private entrepreneurs on very generous terms (free installation, ten years to pay, no interest charges). It should be noted that the attitude displayed by the government in these activities played a very important role in preventing the conversion of Japan into an agricultural raw materials-exporting country dependent on foreign imports for its manufactures and daily necessities, a fear of which had been expressed by Matsukata Masayoshi as early as 1874. An export boom in primary products, such as Japan was experiencing, gives a country the means of financing industrial development, but frequently the easy profits in the export crops take away the incentive to develop areas of greater risk and less immediate reward, thus diverting investment almost exclusively into what often turns out to be a self-defeating expansion of primary commodity production. The Japanese leaders resisted this temptation and struggled hard to maintain a more structurally balanced economy.

The Japanese leaders also resisted the temptation to relax and allow the foreign merchants to continue their domination of Japan's foreign trade. In the 1860s and early 1870s the import and export of goods was almost entirely in the hands of the foreigner; the Japanese role was limited to buying and selling operations in the treaty ports. In this control of Japan's trade, Ōkubo and other officials such as Maeda Masana saw one of the main reasons for the trade imbalance and the loss of specie. They argued that as long as the Japanese were operating through intermediaries and not coming into direct contact with the foreign consumer, it would be very difficult to learn what the exact needs of the ultimate consumer were, what improvements were required in Japanese products, or how the confidence of the foreign user was to be gained. If the Japanese did not deal directly with the foreign customer, it would not be possible to develop the markets necessary to absorb the enlarged export production the government was encouraging. Moreover, it would be impossible to ascertain the true market value of these exports and thus prevent the foreign treaty port merchants from making huge profits that should be going to the Japanese.

There was a widespread sentiment that the foreign merchants were parasitic interlopers whose activities infringed Japan's national integrity. Behind the drive to eliminate them could be mobilized all the nationalist sentiment of the "rights recovery" movement. "Politically," claimed Asabuki Eiji, a Mitsubishi Shōji official, "Japan is the same as before and has not lost a foot of territory, but in the field of foreign trade . . . our national boundary has been grossly violated. The sole way to recover our commercial sovereignty and widen the nation's foreign trade borders is to have our people themselves go back and forth to foreign countries, themselves export our products, themselves import the foreigner's products. . . . The only real difference [between us and the *jōi* swordsman of yesteryear]," said Asabuki in a blatant appeal to the old exclusionist feeling, "is that we fight them by means of economics and trade."[3] This same type of idea was forcefully expressed in the founding statement of the Maruzen Company:

> The foreigners did not come to our country out of friendship; their real reason for being here is to trade. . . . Their main object is solely to seek profits through trade. When we sit idly by and allow them to monopolize our foreign trade, we are betraying our duty as Japanese. If we once allow them to take over our foreign trade, if we are aided by them, if we rely on them, if we borrow money from them, if we are employed in their companies, if we invite them into our companies, if we respect and admire them, if we run around at their orders, if we fall into that kind of condition, there could not possibly be a greater disaster to our country. A country in that situation is not a country.[4]

There was plenty of patriotic steam behind the desire to displace the foreigner, but as Ōkubo stressed in an 1875 memorandum, Japanese merchants had as yet been unable to offer serious competition because they were lacking both in financial resources and in foreign trade experience. To deal with the problem of educating the exporter, the government created in 1876 a Trade Encouragement Bureau (Kanshō Kyoku). One of the main activities of this Home Ministry bureau was the publication of the *Kanshō shimpō*, a journal devoted to explaining trade opportunities and to arousing a competitive spirit. A few years later the government subsidized the organization of chambers of commerce (*shōhō kaigisho*, 1878; *shōkōkai*, 1883; *shōgyō kaigisho*, 1890) in all the major cities. The functions of these new bodies were to inform businessmen on modern business methods, to disseminate commercial information, and to provide a channel through which the government could solicit facts and opinions from the business community. Of course, they supplied a convenient means for rallying

---

[3] Quoted in Ōnishi Rihei, ed., *Asabuki Eiji kun den* (1928), pp. 87–91.
[4] Yoshino Sakuzō, ed., *Meiji bunka zenshū* (24 vols., 1927–30), IX, *Keizaihen*, 489.

businessmen to the support of governmental policy and assuring some degree of coordination in the nation's economic activities.

The Trade Encouragement Bureau also undertook to give Japanese traders the material support needed to engage in competition with foreigners. Transportation expenses, finding buyers abroad, delays in receiving payments, etc. imposed a very substantial burden upon the working capital of any Japanese who tried to cut out the foreign middleman in the treaty port and ventured the direct export of his goods to the overseas market. A variety of techniques were worked out to subsidize companies which were willing to take such risks. The Trade Encouragement Bureau itself bought up the product of a number of silk mills, which it shipped to the United States in order to establish a kind of yardstick for sales conditions. Government loans to the Mizunuma Silk Mill and three other mills made possible in 1876 the first recorded instances of private direct export. Some firms in foreign trade were assisted by the government's guaranteeing their accounts receivable and their bills of lading. Others were given the exclusive sales rights for the products of government enterprises (e.g., Mitsui Bussan for the Miike coal field). Some received lucrative commissions for acting as the agents for government purchases abroad (e.g., Mitsui Bussan and Ōkura Gumi for buying arms and ships in London). When Mitsui Bussan began the direct export of silk in 1877, it received the right to a government overseas documentary bill account, which meant, in effect, that the government financed the export. This privilege was soon extended to Mitsubishi and several other firms with close government relations. Methods such as these were able to raise the Japanese merchants' share of the foreign trade from less than 1 percent in 1875 to about 15 percent in 1881, but thereafter little progress was made, and right down to 1893 the foreign merchants handled well over four-fifths of the trade.

All in all, the measures taken in the late 1870s by the Meiji government to improve the trade balance did not prove too immediately successful. By 1879 exports were up 80 percent over 1868, but imports had increased by over 200 percent. In the years 1876–79 there was a cumulative trade deficit of ¥12 million and something like ¥23 million in gold and silver was shipped out of the country. Though the specie available to the government was shrinking, the inconvertible paper currency issue rose from ¥100.5 million in 1875 to ¥164.4 million in 1879. This huge currency expansion occurred, of course, as a result of the government's cheap development funds program and because of the expenditures necessary for the suppression of the 1877 Satsuma Rebellion. Its effect was to bring about a fall in the value of the paper yen used in domestic transactions vis-a-vis the silver yen used in international transactions. In 1875 they had exchanged at the rate of ¥1.03 paper to ¥1.00 silver; by 1879 this rate had deteriorated and was ¥1.21 paper to ¥1.00 silver. Associated with the fall in the value of the paper yen was a rise in domestic prices; rice rose from ¥4.09 in 1875 to ¥5.78 in 1879, a 40 percent increase. Government spending and the expansion of exports had enlarged the purchasing power of the Japanese people and had created a growing domestic demand for Western products and for traditional Japanese products. The impact of this demand was felt particularly on domestic products, and their prices, especially that of rice, began a steep climb. Since the increase in the price of rice was greater than the fall in the value of paper currency vis-a-vis silver, Western imports became, in effect, cheaper for the Japanese farm population. On the other hand, the rising domestic prices attracted the Japanese producer, who was finding it difficult in the existing inflationary situation to maintain competitive export prices. The outcome was both an increase in imports and a diversion of production from the more difficult export market to the more familiar and profitable domestic market.

Most subsequent economic analysts have ascribed Japan's balance of payments problem and deteriorating exchange rate in the late 1870s to the inflationary pressures created by the large inconvertible note issue of the government and the national banks. However, this was not the view taken by the key economic official of the time, Ōkuma Shigenobu. Ōkuma argued that the currency in circulation did not exceed the amount required by the country's level of economic activities. Rising prices, he held, were stimulating to production and had a positive effect upon economic development. The exchange deterioration had been brought about not by an excess of paper currency but by a shortage of silver, a shortage caused by the loss of specie due to the import surplus. The real answer to the problem was to increase exports. If exports could be brought into balance with imports, there would be no need to exchange paper yen for silver, which was used strictly for settling international accounts. Consequently, the paper yen could be cut free from silver and its volume of issue determined solely by domestic needs.

In 1879 and through the spring of 1880, therefore, the main thrust of Ōkuma's policy continued to be a liberal extension of loans aimed at increasing production for export. Meanwhile, as a temporary expedient to hold the line until exports had caught up with imports, he instituted certain measures which he thought would relieve the "shortage" of silver. To regularize the specie market and curb speculation he allowed the establishment of a Mexican dollar exchange (February 1879) as well as authorizing the Tokyo, Osaka, and Yokohama exchanges to deal in gold and silver. On two occasions (April-May 1879 and May 1880) he sought to bolster the paper yen by selling silver from the government holdings, a total of ¥8.6 million going for this purpose. However, he had only limited success in this attempt to support the external value of the yen while allowing the domestic inflation to continue unabated. Finally, in February 1880 he set in operation the Yokohama Specie Bank. The capital of this bank was to be subscribed in silver, and Ōkuma regarded it primarily as a device to lure out the silver he believed was being hoarded. In this he was disappointed, since four-fifths of the capital was paid in paper yen. In the meantime the situation continued to grow worse: in 1880 the trade deficit was ¥8.2 million; ¥9.6 million in specie left the country and government holdings were reduced to ¥7.2 million; the paper-silver ratio was 1.48 to 1.00; the price of rice was up to ¥6.28, 54 percent higher than in 1875.

By May 1880 Ōkuma was ready to admit defeat in his efforts to relieve the silver "shortage." The fault lay, he conceded, in the type of currency system Japan had. The solution he now proposed was in one jump to place the note issue on a freely convertible basis. The key element in his new plan was the raising of a ¥50 million foreign loan. Most of Ōkuma's colleagues did not approve of this proposal. Matsukata, then home minister, warned very strongly against the dangers it would entail. Sano Tsunetami, the finance minister, said he could not see the sense of "changing a non-interest-bearing, non-fixed-term internal obligation into an interest-bearing, fixed-term external obligation." He expressed doubts about the loan's repayment and argued that "at this time when there is an increasing clamor for the establishment of a national assembly, we ought not to make any extraordinary change which will give the agitators any opening or pretext."[5] In place of a loan Sano suggested that the government negotiate

[5]Quoted in Meiji Zaiseishi Hensankai, ed., *Meiji zaiseishi* (15 vols., 1904–5), XII, 222.

a ¥15 million prepayment against exports and that taxes be increased sufficiently to retire ¥46 million in paper currency over the following five years. Iwakura Tomomi also ranged himself with the opposition, and in the end there seems to have been an imperial decision placing a foreign loan out of bounds.

Ōkuma's plan had been rejected, yet all the government leaders recognized that something had to be done and done quickly. The rising prices were beginning to threaten the fiscal foundations of the Meiji government. The primary revenue source was, it will be remembered, the land tax. When that tax was instituted it was set at a fixed amount of money for each plot of land. Therefore, increased production or rising agricultural prices did not result in a greater yield from the land tax. Consequently, the government's revenue was rather inflexible. On the other hand, the rising prices and the adverse paper-specie ratio were reducing the amount of goods and services which could be bought with each tax yen. Thus the government's real income from the land tax had been drastically diminished. In addition, given the failure of exports to expand fast enough, the depletion of the specie stocks threatened the government's ability to pay for the imports required by its various projects. This was of particular concern to the government, for Yamagata in 1880 presented a memorial setting forth a vast new program of military expansion which he claimed to be absolutely indispensable to the nation's safety. Since this program would entail heavy imports, it would be impossible to carry out if the balance of payments continued to deteriorate.

In August 1880 Iwakura Tomomi, Kuroda Kiyotaka, and Ōki Takatō jointly offered a plan which they thought would restore the balance of payments. Their point of departure was a report made late in 1879 by the Tokyo and Osaka chambers of commerce which sought to demonstrate that there had been a substantial rise in the farmers' standard of living and that it was the farmers who were the chief market for imported goods. Almost as if relieved to find that the culprit was the old familiar villain of the Tokugawa economic moralists, the trio moved to the attack:

> The principal reason for the imbalance of our foreign trade is the reduction in the land tax and the change in the method of collecting it [i.e., collection in money, not in kind; collection of a fixed sum, not a percentage of the crop].... These changes have brought great happiness only to the farmers and have truly promoted an astonishing wealth [among them].... Farmers

are only paying one-tenth of the old tax; the rest is a windfall for them. . . . Among the farmers, luxurious habits of food and clothing have arisen and their surplus money is being squandered largely in competitive bidding for imported goods. Therefore, imports in recent times can be explained mainly as supplying the demand of the lower order of society, the farmers. . . .

The farmers' unbalanced excesses are spreading their influence to the other three classes—the warriors, the craftsmen, and the merchants. Consequently, the reduction in export goods has not been restricted to sericulture. The profits of entrepreneurs in tea, cotton, and sugar have been reduced by an increase in the value of land, by an increase in the cost of cultivation, and by the stimulation of a rise in the interest rate due to a shortage of financing. In the case of cotton there has been another difficulty. Previously it was more profitable to raise cotton than rice, but now with the rise in the price of rice, many are giving up cotton in favor of rice cultivation. In this way the cotton crop has been greatly reduced and the deficiency in supply must be made up from abroad.[6]

The basic solution to the problem of the import excess would be, they admitted, a protective tariff, but unfortunately Japan did not have the military force to seize its rights. They accepted Ōkuma's theory that the fall in the paper-silver ratio was due not to an over-issue of notes but rather to the trade deficit and the competitive bidding for silver it occasioned. However, they did not see how convertibility would change the import-export balance. They also could not believe that an expansion of exports could be immediately effective since "the tendency for imports to increase is as rapid as the tendency for farmers' wealth to increase. To control the rapid increase in imports by relying on an increase in exports, which is sure to be slow, is like using a buggy to catch a thief escaping by railroad."

Having used an up-to-date simile, the three gentlemen then proceeded to suggest a very traditional solution: reduction of the farmers' income. This could be done, they said, by collecting one-fifth of the land tax in rice and then using government sales of that rice to keep the rice price at a suitably low level. "When the wealth of the farmers is suitably controlled, the import trade will automatically be brought under control." There would not be as much silver needed in the treaty ports, the price of silver would fall, and the paper-silver ratio would be restored. Iwakura

[6]Quoted in Japan, Tsūshō Sangyōshō, *Bōeki (jō)*, pp. 262–63.

and company also saw that there was another very important way in which the government's downward manipulation of the rice price might pay off. "Hitherto," they pointed out, "a rise in the value of specie was linked with a fall in the value of paper notes and an equalizing rise in domestic prices. If controlling the price of rice keeps domestic prices from increasing, a rise in specie will be like a kind of protective tariff . . . domestic products will be cheap like rice but imports will be expensive like silver. Imports will be affected in the same way as they would be by a protective tariff and foreign trade should be improved."

The idea of reverting to collection of taxes in kind met the immediate opposition of Ōkuma, Itō Hirobumi, and Inoue. Inoue, in particular, presented a detailed rebuttal in a memorandum dated August 16, 1880. The rise in the price of rice, he said, was a result of Japan's being brought into the world price structure, not of an increase in consumption by the poorer classes. The term "luxury" meant living beyond one's means; if the farmers' new bright clothes and carriages did not exceed their means, it should be called an improvement in standard of living, not luxury. It was ridiculous to say the farmers were becoming lazy with good living; on the contrary they were bursting with activity. Forcing them back on a non-rice diet would not make them work harder. If they advanced their standard of living, ate rice, dressed well, then they would work even harder to be able to eat, dress, and house themselves even better. The responsibility for the import excess did not rest on the farmers alone. The government itself had imported a great deal in order to modernize the political and military systems as well as to suppress internal disturbances. If government imports were omitted from the accounts, the people's imports and exports would more or less balance.

The Iwakura plan, Inoue contended, should be rejected as both contrary to economic law and stifling to the economic spirit. The only sensible way out of the impasse confronting the government was, according to Inoue, to develop a favorable balance of payments, accumulate specie over time, and then use this specie to make the note issue convertible. The trick, of course, was to reverse the balance of payments. This, Inoue suggested, could be facilitated by four measures: 1) the establishment of a bank which would make export loans; 2) the substitution of native insurance companies for the high-cost foreign insurance companies; 3) the creation of companies for the direct export of Japanese goods; and 4) the sale abroad for specie of rice purchased with paper currency. The financing of the program could be secured by increasing taxes and retrenching government expenditures, two specific ways of accomplishing the latter being the sale of government enterprises and the reduction of the armed forces.

The outcome of what might be called the August debate was the rejection of the Iwakura plan. Instead, it was decided to place the responsibility for formulating economic policy on Ōkuma and Itō, who promptly began to put into effect a number of the measures Inoue had advocated. Mitsui Bussan, Mitsubishi Shōji, and several other major trading firms were persuaded to pool their financial and managerial resources behind a new direct export company, the Nihon Bōeki Shōkai, whose large capital (¥500,000, three-fifths supplied by the Home Ministry) was expected to make it a formidable competitor for the foreign merchants. The Yokohama Specie Bank was converted into an exchange bank and given a ¥3 million low-interest government loan to be used to finance direct exports and "thereby recover our commercial sovereignty in foreign trade and restore the balance of exports and imports."[7] The bank was authorized to give an exporter, at the very low rate of 6 percent, a paper currency loan equivalent to 70 percent of the value of the tea or silk which he had shipped to a foreign market. The bank then acted as the agent for the exporter and collected the sales price of the goods in specie from the foreign buyer. After the collection was made, any difference between the sales price and the loan was adjusted with the exporter in paper currency. In this way the bank was able to convert the proceeds of each transaction into specie held by it at the government's disposal. This system served as a kind of exchange control, since it took the specie out of private hands and enabled the government to exercise great control over the ways in which it was used. It also, of course, diverted resources into the export market by making the recovery of money tied up in production easier and quicker there.

On the domestic economic front, Ōkuma and Itō initiated a policy of retrenchment. The granting of government loans was suspended and steps were taken to speed up the recovery of those still outstanding. The sale of government enterprises was announced, and the civilian departments of the government were ordered to pare their expenses, particularly those

---

[7]Quoted in Higo Kazuo, "Shōwa shoki made no waga kuni seika seisaku to zaisei," X (1960), p. 38.

involving foreign purchases. In an effort to hold foreign payments down to the level of the customs receipts, all agencies were required to prepare a foreign exchange budget as well as their normal yen budget. The government also transferred certain expenses from its own budget to the local governments' budgets, a move certain to result in additional taxes at the local level. At the same time it was reducing the budget, the government raised taxes, largely in the form of increased consumer excises. One aim of this was to decrease the volume of currency by generating a budget surplus that brought into the treasury paper notes that did not go out again in payments. This, of course, would ease the task of establishing convertibility, but it would also serve a larger purpose to which even convertibility itself was merely a means. It was hoped that the contraction of currency, the raising of the value of money by establishing convertibility, the tightening of credit, the curtailment of government spending, and the reduction of disposable income due to increased national and local taxes would bring about a contraction in the domestic market and a fall in prices, and that this in turn would reduce the farmer's income and eliminate him both as an exchange-wasting importer of foreign goods and as an attractive customer who diverted the Japanese producer from his proper task of exporting goods and earning specie. Though Ōkuma and Itō had adopted the modern economic devices of Inoue, their objective was the more traditional one of Iwakura—to insure that the agricultural surplus was used for the government's purposes and not for the private ends of the farmer.

It is true, however, that Ōkuma and Itō were reluctant to push matters to the ultimate. Indeed, in the middle of 1881 they became apprehensive and began to draw back a little. In May they allowed the Yokohama Specie Bank to extend its loan program to producers as well as exporters. A few months later they again brought up the idea of easing the transition to convertibility by means of a huge foreign loan. By September they had fallen back on antiforeignism, and with an interest-free ¥1 million loan they secretly encouraged the Yokohama silk dealers to set up a company called the Federated Raw Silk Warehouse which aimed at nothing less than a monopoly of the trade. In the midst of the resulting uproar, Ōkuma was forced out of the government on the constitutional issue and Matsukata was placed in full charge of economic policy.

Matsukata absolutely rejected the alternative of a foreign loan; to borrow money while subject to the unequal treaties would convert the country into a colony like Egypt or Turkey. He held firmly to the idea that the only way to solve the country's payment problems was a ruthless enforcement of deflationary measures that would strip down the economy for an expansion of exports. Since to him the important thing was to export and earn specie, he did not, at this point, particularly care whether it was a Japanese or a foreigner who handled the transaction. Consequently, within a week of taking office he ended the trade disruption at Yokohama by quietly withdrawing government support from the Federated Raw Silk Warehouse. Shortly thereafter he eliminated the Yokohama Specie Bank's domestic loans and confined its activities strictly to the export trade. When private Japanese exports did not seem to be bringing in enough specie, he had the government itself buy up rice and sea tangles for overseas sales. He also authorized the Yokohama Specie Bank to make export loans to foreigners, telling Sanjō Sanetomi, perhaps with tongue in cheek, that "this was a restoration of foreign exchange rights to Japanese banks."[8] Eventually about 80 percent of the export loans were going to foreigners.

By all measures what came to be known as the Matsukata deflation accomplished its objectives. In five years a revenue surplus of ¥40 million was developed. After 1881 interest rates, wages, and prices all fell. By 1882 imports were down 6 percent and exports up 33 percent compared with 1880; there was an export surplus of ¥8.3 million. The cumulative trade surplus for 1882–85 amounted to ¥28.2 million. By 1885 the paper currency had been reduced to ¥118.5 million and the paper-silver ratio stood at 1.05 to 1.00. The following year, in the midst of the greatest export prosperity Japan had ever enjoyed, the country went on the silver standard.

It is well to note that the success of Matsukata's program had been greatly facilitated by two factors completely unforeseen by him. One was the emergence of a native cotton-yarn industry which was finally able, despite the absence of tariff protection, to compete successfully in the domestic market with foreign yarn. This can be dated from the founding in 1883 of the Osaka Spinning Company, an enterprise that owed nothing to government support and which succeeded through managerial skill and technological competence while the government-sponsored companies floundered in failure. By 1890 over half of Japan's domestic yarn requirement was being supplied by the new industry. The second unforeseen factor

[8]Quoted in Unno Fukuju, "Bōekishijō ni okeru 1880 nendai" (1963), p. 24.

was the gradual decline in the silver-gold ratio which occurred in the 1880s. The result of this change was that although the paper yen was restored to parity with silver, it did not achieve parity with gold. In 1886, for instance, the paper-gold ratio was 1.25. This difference made Japanese products cheaper for gold standard countries and therefore stimulated exports to the United States and Europe. On the other hand, it made gold country products, such as yarn, more expensive for the Japanese and consequently had, as Iwakura predicted in such a situation, much the same effect as a protective tariff.

It is informative to examine the purposes for which the Meiji government used the specie that it accumulated through its direct sales abroad and through its export loan operations. Between 1877 and 1890 something like ¥86 million passed through the government's specie account. Of this amount 40 percent went to buy gold and silver for the currency reserve; 25 percent was devoted to servicing and repaying the foreign debt; and 35 percent was used to pay for government purchases abroad, especially warships, armaments, and communication equipment. This last purpose bulked very large in Matsukata's thinking. In a memorandum of November 1881 he wrote: "At this time when specie is scarce, we still must provide for essential expenditures like those of the army and navy. . . . Therefore our present duty is to increase exports and provide for the accumulation of specie." A few months later, speaking at a prefectural governors conference, he said: "If we wish to expand armaments, we must quickly put our finances in order . . . [for] to expand our armaments, there are still many things . . . for whose supply we must depend upon foreign countries. If we wish to provide ourselves with armaments and not feel ashamed of our independent empire's military system, there must be an increase in imports."[9] This, he pointed out, would have disastrous effects if the objectives of the government's retrenchment program were not achieved.

The retrenchment program, therefore, was never intended to apply to military expenses; rather, it was an indispensable condition to the expansion of the military budget. Under Matsukata, the percentage of central government investment devoted to the military, which had been about 30 to 35 percent, suddenly rose to over 60 percent. In the early 1880s the harvest of

[9] Ōuchi Hyōe and Tsuchiya Takao, eds., *Meiji zenki zaisei keizai shiryō shūsei* (21 vols., 1931–36), I, 339, 572.

specie which the retrenchment program had made possible provided quite handsomely for the needs of the military. However, as the decade wore on, the demands of the military grew larger and Matsukata began to encounter difficulties assembling the foreign exchange their expansion plans entailed. The army budget went from ¥9.5 million in 1882 to ¥15.5 million in 1890. In April 1886 the navy presented a three-year construction program calling for ¥7.4 million in foreign payments; a few years later they came up with a five-year program.

Meanwhile, the happy dreams the Meiji government had entertained of creating counter-import industries which would eliminate the use of foreign consumer goods was turned into a mirage just as the development of the yarn industry seemed to be making it a reality. True, foreign yarn imports were curbed, but then Japanese agriculture proved incapable of supplying the raw cotton needed by the new industry; Japanese sugar refiners were beginning to make headway but only by using materials imported from Taiwan and south China. Eliminating one area of dependence upon foreign imports merely seemed to open another. By the late 1880s raw cotton, raw sugar, rails, and spinning machinery were competing with military imports for foreign exchange and their demands could not be lightly dismissed, for their users were not farmers but the country's leading businessmen. On the surface the trade balance was still favorable, but the overall balance of accounts was beginning to show a deficit. It was clear that the old policies had run their course and that some serious thinking about the economic future of the nation was in order.

General. Japanese:

Furushima, *Sangyōshi* (1966).
Horie, *Meiji ishin to keizai kindaika* (1963).
Inouchi, "Meijiki keizai seisaku shisō no kichō" (1962).
Ishii, *Meiji ishin no kokusaiteki kankyō* (1957; 2d rev. ed., 1966).
Iwakura Tomomi kankei bunsho (8 vols., 1927–35).
Kajinishi and others, *Nihon shihonshugi no seiritsu* (2 vols., 1956).
Kikkawa, *Meiji ishin shakai keizaishi kenkyū* (1943).
Nagata, *Keizai dantai hattenshi* (1956).
Naitō, "Meiji jidai ni okeru Nihon no keizaiteki haikei" (1962).
Nawata, "Fukoku kyōhei" (1955).
Ōkubo Toshimichi bunsho (3 vols., 1927–29).
Ōuchi and Tsuchiya, *Meiji zenki zaisei keizai shiryō shūsei* (21 vols., 1931–36).

Ōuchi, *Nihon keizairon* (2 vols., 1962–63).

Sakatani, *Segai Inoue kō den* (5 vols., 1933–34).

Shōda, "Bakumatsu Meiji shoki no keizai hatten" (1960).

Tokutomi, *Kōshaku Matsukata Masayoshi den* (2 vols., 1935).

Tsuchiya, *Ishin keizaishi* (1942).

—— *Meiji zenki keizaishi kenkyū* (1944).

Waseda Daigaku Shakai Kagaku Kenkyūjo, *Ōkuma bunsho* (5 vols., 1958–62).

Watanabe, *Ōkuma Shigenobu kankei monjo* (6 vols., 1932–35).

Yamaguchi, *Meiji zenki keizai no bunseki* (1956).

—— *Nihon keizaishi kōgi* (1960).

Yokohama Shi Shi Henshūshitsu, *Yokohama shi shi* (5 vols., 1958–63).

Yoshino, *Keizaihen* (1929).

General. English:

Allen, "Factors in Japan's Economic Growth" (1964).

Allen and Donnithorne, *Western Enterprise in Far Eastern Development: China and Japan* (1954).

Brown, "Ōkubo Toshimichi: His Political and Economic Policies in Early Meiji Japan" (1962).

Hirschmeier, *The Origins of Entrepreneurship in Meiji Japan* (1964).

Lockwood, *The Economic Development of Japan: Growth and Structural Change, 1868–1938* (1954).

Rosovsky, "Japan's Transition to Economic Growth" (1966).

Smith, *Political Change and Industrial Development in Japan: Government Enterprise, 1868–1880* (1955).

Foreign trade. Japanese:

Akimoto, "Bōeki shōsha" (1961).

Fujii and Fujii, "1880 nendai no sanshi kin'yū ni tsuite" (1961).

Fujii, "Nihon keizai no hatten to bōeki seisaku" (1964).

Fujimoto, *Kaikō to kiito bōeki* (3 vols., 1939).

Fujita, "Meiji zenki ni okeru shokusan kōgyō seisaku to shōgyōteki nōgyō no hatten" (1961).

Harada, "Shokusan kōgyō seisaku kenkyū no tōmen suru kadai" (1963).

Hattori, "Bōeki no hatten" (1963).

—— "Kaikō to Nihon shihonshugi" (1965).

Higuchi, *Nihon tōgyōshi* (1956).

Hori, *Meiji keizaigakushi: jiyūshugi hogoshugi o chūshin to shite* (1935).

Horie, *Kindai sangyō no seisei* (1958).

Horie, "Meiji shonen no kan'ei sangyō ni tsuite" (1937).

—— "Ishin go no taigai keizai hatten" (1942).

—— "Meiji shonen no kangyō kikan" (1944).

—— "Meiji zenki no bōeki seisaku" (1953).

Irimajiri, "Meiji seifu no shokusan kōgyō seisaku" (1960).

Ishida, "Meiji zenki ni okeru bōsekigyō no hatten to shokuminchiteki kōshinkoku e no yushutsu" (1965).

—— "Meiji zenki ni okeru kindaiteki kōtsū to bōeki oyobi kinu kōgyō" (1965).

Ishii, "Bakumatsu kaikō go ni okeru bōeki dokusen kikō no hōkai" (1942).

—— *Bakumatsu bōekishi no kenkyū* (1944).

—— "Shoki ni okeru bōeki no shinchō" (1959).

—— "Meiji seifu no sanshi bōeki kisoku" (1961).

—— "Chihō jichi no hatten to bōekishō" (1963).

—— "Rengō Kiito Niazukarijo jiken o meguru shomondai" (1966).

—— "Rengō Kiito Niazukarijo jiken sairon" (1967).

Ishizuka, "Ōkubo seiken no seiritsu to kōzō" (1960).

—— "Shokusan kōgyō seisaku no tenkai" (1965).

Itani, "Meiji shonen ni okeru sanshu yushutsu" (1937).

Japan, Gaimushō (Foreign Ministry), *Tsūshō jōyaku to tsūshō seisaku no hensen* (1951).

Japan, Nōshōmushō, Shōmukyoku (Ministry of Agriculture and Commerce, Bureau of Commerce), *Dai Nihon gaikoku bōeki* (1911).

Japan, Tsūshō Sangyōshō (Ministry of International Trade and Industry), *Shōkō seisakushi V: bōeki (jō)* (1965).

Kajinishi, "Shokusan kōgyō seisaku to sangyō shihon no seisei" (1958).

—— "Meiji shonen no sangyō shihon" (1959).

—— "Nihon jūkōgyō no seisei" (1959).

—— "Shihonshugi no ikusei" (1962).

Kajinishi and Kobayashi, "Shokusan kōgyō seisaku to sangyō shihon no seiritsu" (1959).

Kanaya, "Waga kuni taigai tsūshō seisaku to sono konnichi ni itaru made no enkaku" (1934).

Kanno, "Bakumatsu no shōsha" (1930).

—— "Tsūshō kaisha kawase kaisha" (1930).

—— *Bakumatsu ishin keizaishi kenkyū* (1961).

Kawashima, *Hompō tsūshō seisaku jōyaku shi gairon* (1941).

Kikkawa, "Maeda Masana" (1941).

—— "Maeda Masana no shokusan kōgyō undō" (1962).

Kitazaki, "Meijiki ni okeru matchi seizōgyō no hatten" (1960).

Kobayashi, *Meiji ishin ni okeru shōkōgyō no shohenkaku* (1932).

Kodan and Yoshinobu, "Bōeki to shōhin keizai no hattatsu" (1959).

Kokusai Keizai Gakkai, *Nihon bōeki no kōzō to tenkai* (1958).

Maeda, "Iwayuru shōken kaifukusen no ato o kaerimite" (1927).

Mamiya, "Shōhōshi no soshiki to kinō" (1963).

—— "Meiji shoki ni okeru chokuyushutsu kaisha no setsuritsu to tenkai" (1964).

—— "Meiji shonen ni okeru shōhōshi seisaku no tenkai" (1966).

Matsui, *Nihon bōekiron* (1950).

—— "Sangyō shihonshugi to gaikoku bōeki" (1950).

—— "Hōhōron to dankai kubun" (1959).

Matsuzaka, "Nihon keizai no seichō to bōeki kōzō no suii" (1958).

Meiji Shiryō Kenkyū Renrakkai, *Kindai sangyō no seisei* (1960).

Mibe, "Meiji shoki ni okeru waga kuni menka seisan no chōraku" (1937).

Mitsui Bussan gojūnenshi (1935).

Miwa, "1880 nendai no shihonka dantai—Tōkyō Shōkōkai no setsuritsu to sono katsudō" (1964).

Miyamoto, "Meijiki ni okeru bōeki shōsha no seiritsu katei to bōeki shihon no sangyō ikusei (keiei shiteki kōsatsu)" (1963).

Mori and Itabashi, *Kindai tetsusangyō no seiritsu—Kamaishi Seitetsujo zenshi* (1957).

Nagai, "Shokusan kōgyō seisakuron" (1961).

Nagata, "Meiji seifu no kanshō seisaku to shōhō kaigisho" (1963).

—— "Shokusan kōgyō seisaku to shōhō kaigisho" (1963).

Nakai, *Nihon ni okeru bōeki shisō no hensen to sono rekishiteki haikei* (1957).

Nakamura, "Meiji shoki no keizai seisaku—tsūshō kawase ryōkaisha no yakuwari" (1959).

—— "Meiji zenki ni okeru zeiken kaifuku undō" (1966).

Nawa, *Nihon bōsekigyō to gemmen mondai kenkyū* (1937).

—— *Nihon bōsekigyō no shiteki bunseki* (1948).

Nihon Kanzei Kyōkai, *Nihon no kanzei* (1959).

Ōe, "Chūō shūken kokka no seiritsu" (1962).

—— "Ōkubo seikenka no shokusan kōgyō seisaku seiritsu no seiji katei" (1966).

—— "Ōkubo seiken to Nihon shihonshugi" (1966).

Okada, " 'Shōken kaifuku' to Rengō Kiito Niazukarijo" (1960).

Ōnishi, *Asabuki Eiji kun den* (1928).

Ono and Namba, "Nihon tekkōgyō no seiritsu to genryō mondai" (1954).

Ono, *Ishin no gōshō—Ono Gumi shimatsu* (1966).

Onoe, "Kaikō to Nichi-Bei bōeki kankei no hottan" (1959).

Saitō, "Meiji shoki no kangyō to mingyō" (1961–63).

Sakudō, "Bōeki shōsha no hatten to Kansaikei kigyō no keisei" (1963).

Shibusawa Seien Kinen Zaidan Ryūmonsha, *Shibusawa Eiichi denki shiryō*, vol. XV (1957).

Shigefuji, *Nagasaki kyoryūchi bōeki jidai no kenkyū* (1961).

Shima, "Meiji zaisei no gensoku to shite no kōki hōken zaisei" (1941).

Shimbō, "Ishinki no shōgyō kin'yū seisaku—tsūshō kaisha kawase kaisha o megutte" (1962).

Shimoda, "Ishin zengo gaikoku bōekiron" (1937).

Shindō, "Shokusan kōgyō seisaku to kōzangyō—Miike kōzan no kanshū o megutte" (1965).

Shionoya, "Nihon no kōgyōka to gaikoku bōeki" (1966).

Someya, "Shokusan kōgyō seisakka no gairai sangyō to zairai sangyō" (1963).

Suzuki, "Meiji jūnendai ni okeru gaikoku bōeki to burujoajii—Kiito Niazukarijo jiken o megutte" (1958).

Takahashi, "Meiji shoki ni okeru shōsha to shōgyō shihon" (1963).

Takamura, "Kigyō bokkōki ni okeru bōsekigyō no kōzō—Ōsaka Bōseki Kaisha no seiritsu" (1963).

Takeda, "Meiji shonen no shokusan kōgyō seisaku to kaigai tenrankai sandō" (1942).

Tanaka, "Yokohama Kiito Niazukarijo jiken" (1957).

Tanaka, "Seisaku kettei no shiten kara mita Nihon no tetsudō sōsetsu" (1964).

Tanaka, "Meiji zettaishugi to shokusan kōgyō seisaku josetsu" (1963).

Tatemoto, "Meiji shoki ni okeru keizai seichō to shigen haibun" (1965).

Tatemoto and Baba, "Meiji gaikoku bōeki tōkei (Meiji 1–20 nen)" (1966).

Togai, "Meiji ishin zengo no Mitsui" (1964).

Tsuchiya, "Keizai seisakka to shite no Ōkubo Toshimichi" (1935).

—— "Meiji shoki no bōeki seisaku" (1937).

Tsukatani, "Daiikkai Naikoku Kangyō Hakurankai to Meiji shoki tōjiki kōgyō" (1965).

Tsurumi, *Nihon bōeki shikō* (1939).

Umezu, "Meiji shoki no bōeki seisaku to bōeki shisō" (1959).

—— "Keizai hattenki ni okeru bōeki seisaku shisō" (1961).

—— *Nihon no bōeki shisō: Nihon bōeki seisaku shisōshi kenkyū* (1963).

Unno, "Chihō chokuyushutsu kaisha no setsuritsu to tenkai" (1961).

—— "Chokuyushutsu no tenkai" (1961).

—— "Seishi seichagyō no hatten" (1961).

—— "Seishigyō chagyō kumiai no setsuritsu" (1961).

—— "Yokohama bōeki ichiba no kikō" (1961).

—— "Yokohama Rengō Kiito Niazukarijo jiken" (1961).

—— "Bōekishijō ni okeru 1880 nendai" (1963).

—— "Meiji nijūnendai ni okeru 'shōken kaifuku' undō ni tsuite" (1965).

—— "Meiji bōekishi kenkyū to dōkō" (1966).

—— "Yokohama Rengō Kiito Niazukarijo jiken" (1966).

—— *Meiji no bōeki: kyoryūchi bōeki to shōken kaifuku* (1967).

Unno and Morita, "Kaikō igo no shōhin seisan to jinushisei" (1962).

Wazaki, "Fukoku kyōhei—shokusan kōgyō" (1956).

Yamada, "Yokohama Rengō Kiito Niazukarijo jiken to jiyū minken shoshimbun no ronchō" (1965–67).

Yamaguchi, *Bakumatsu bōekishi* (1943).

Yamamoto, "Shokusan kōgyō—sono kenkyū dōkō to mondaiten" (1966).

Foreign trade. English:

Andō, "Development of Heavy Industry" (1958).

—— "Development of Mining Industry" (1958).

Fujii, "The Development of the Japanese Cotton Industry and the Import of American Cotton" (1957).

Hattori, *The Foreign Commerce of Japan since the Restoration* (1904).

Horie, "Foreign Trade Policy in the Early Meiji Era" (1952).

Ishii, "The Opening of the Ports and Early Trade Relations between Japan and the United States" (1957).

Kajinishi, "Development of Light Industry" (1958).

Katō, "Development of Foreign Trade" (1958).

Kojima, "Japanese Foreign Trade and Economic Growth" (1958).

Mori, "Raw Silk Trade with the United States and Our Country's Silk-Reeling Industry" (1957).

Ohara, "General Outline: A Historical Survey of Economic Relations between Japan and the United States" (1957).

Oriental Economist, *The Foreign Trade of Japan* (1935).

Shinohara, "Economic Development and Foreign Trade in Pre-War Japan" (1962).

Takeuchi, "The 'Classical' Theories of International Trade and the Expansion of Foreign Trade in Japan from 1859 to 1892" (1962).

Tsuchiya, "Transition and Development of Economic Policy" (1958).

Yamaguchi, "Manufacture and Export of Tea" (1957).

—— "The Opening of Japan at the End of the Shogunate and Its Effects" (1958).

Financial policy, currency, foreign exchange, and balance of payments. Japanese:

Aoyama, "Ōkuma zaisei to fukoku kōsō" (1963).

Asakura, *Meiji zenki Nihon kin'yū kōzōshi* (1962).

Chō, "Ōkuma Shigenobu no shihei taisaku—sono mujun to shokusan kōgyō to no kanren ni tsuite" (1963).

Egashira, "Takashima Tankō ni okeru Nichi-Ei kyōdō jigyō" (1935).

Endō and others, *Nihon no ōkura daijin* (1964).

Fujimura, "Ōkurakyō Ōkuma Shigenobu no zaisei keizai seisaku kihon kōryō" (1960).

—— "Seinan sensō go no Ōkuma no zaisei seisaku" (1962).

Fukushima, "Meiji shonen no keizai seisaku to shihon chikuseki no mondai—Ōkubo Ōkuma kōsō to Matsukata kōsō" (1952).

Hara, "Meiji shoki kin'yūshi e no ichi kōsatsu—kawase kaisha no setsuritsu o chūshin to shite" (1957).

—— "Daini Kokuritsu Ginkō oboegaki" (1958).

—— "Meiji chūki ni okeru Yokohama Daini Kokuritsu Ginkō no seikaku" (1960).

—— "Shin kin'yū kikō no sōsetsu" (1961).

—— "Meiji shoki Yokohama kin'yūshi oboegaki" (1962).

—— "Daini Daishichijūshi Kokuritsu Ginkō no chokin ginkōka" (1963).

—— "Infurēshonki no ginkō" (1963).

—— "Yokohama Shōkin Ginkō no setsuritsu to sono seikaku" (1963).

—— "Yokohama Shōkin Ginkō shoki no tokushitsu" (1964).

—— *Meiji zenki kin'yūshi* (1965).

Hattori, "Bakumatsu Meiji shoki no gaikoku shihon no katsudō to taiō keitai" (1965–66).

Higo, "Matsukata defure ni kansuru oboegaki" (1958).

—— "Meiji shoki ni okeru enka antei seisaku ni tsuite" (1959).

—— "Jumbikin o meguru Meiji zenki no zaisei kin'yū seisaku" (1960).

—— "Shōwa shoki made no waga kuni seika seisaku to zaisei" (1960).

Hora, "Yōgin sōba to naikoku tsūka" (1954).

—— "Meiji jūnendai no yōgin sōba" (1963).

—— "Meiji shonen no yōgin sōba" (1963).

Horie, "Meiji yonen no heisei kaikaku" (1930).

—— "Meiji zenki no gaishi haijo ni tsuite" (1943).

—— *Gaishi yu'nyū no kaiko to tembō* (1950).

—— "Meiji zenki no kokusai shūshi" (1954).

Ikeda, "Waga kuni kōsai no seiritsu—Meiji shoki kōsai seisaku" (1958).

—— "Chitsuroku shobun no keika to kōsai kōfu—Meiji shoki kōsai seisaku no issetsu" (1960).

—— "Kyūhansai shobun to shinkyū kōsai no kōfu—Meiji shoki kōsai seisaku no issetsu" (1960).

—— "Meiji shoki ni okeru kankin toriatsukai no zaiseiteki igi" (1961).

—— "Kankin suitō no tenkai katei—Meiji shoki ni okeru kankin suitō no kin'yūteki igi" (1962–63).

Ishizaki, "Nihon no shihonshugika to gaishi, 1868–1914" (1966).

Itō, "Tsūshōshi seisaku ni okeru kawase kaisha" (1937).

Kamisaka, "Kaikoku jidai ni okeru bōeki to yōgin to no kōryū kankei" (1954).

Katō, *Hompō ginkō shiron* (1957).

Kikkawa, "Meiji seifu no kashitsuke kin" (1930).
—— "Meiji jidai no seika seisaku" (1953–54).
Kin'yū Keizai Kenkyūjo, *Meiji zenki no ginkō seido* (1965).
—— *Nihon no ginkō seido kakuritsu shi* (1966).
Kobayashi, "Kindai sangyō no keisei to kangyō haraisage" (1965).
Kobayashi and Kitasaki, *Meiji Taishō zaiseishi* (1927).
Kojima, "Meiji shoki no Miike Tankō—tankō kan'ei ni kansuru ichi kōsatsu" (1965).
Mamiya, "Meiji zenki no kin'yūshi ni tsuite" (1966).
Matsuda, *Igirisu shihon to tōyō* (1950).
Matsunari and others, *Nihon ni okeru ginkō no hattatsu* (1959).
Matsuyoshi, *Meiji ishin go ni okeru ryōgaeshō kin'yū* (1937).
—— "Hompō seika seisaku no henkō to jisseki" (1938).
Meiji Zaiseishi Hensankai, *Meiji zaiseishi* (15 vols., 1904–5).
Michida, "Waga kuni bōeki kin'yū no kigen" (1941).
Mitani, *Kokusai shūshi to Nihon no seichō* (1957).
Mitsui Ginkō gojūnenshi (1926).
Mitsui Ginkō Hachijūnenshi Hensan Iinkai, *Mitsui Ginkō hachijūnenshi* (1957).
Mitsuoka, *Yuri Kimimasa den* (1916).
Miyamoto, "Meiji shoki no kawase to Ono Gumi" (1966).
Mizunuma, "Meiji zenki ni okeru Yokohama Shōkin Ginkō no gaikoku kawase kin'yū" (1963).
—— "Meiji zenki Takashima Tankō ni okeru gaishi to sono haijo katei no tokushitsu" (1963).
Nakamura, "Seinansen go no infurēshon to sono taisaku" (1961).
—— "Ōkuma zaisei to jūyonen seihen" (1962).
—— "Ōkuma zaisei tenkaiki no shokusan kōgyō seisaku" (1964).
—— "Meiji jūyonen no seihen" (1965).
—— "Yuri zaisei no taijō" (1965).
Nihon Ginkō Chōsa Kyoku, *Nihon kin'yūshi shiryō: Meiji Taishō* (25 vols., 1954–61).
Nihon Zaisei Keizai Kenkyūjo, *Nihon kin'yū zaiseishi* (1957).
Niwa, *Meiji ishin no tochi henkaku* (1962).
Ōe, *Meiji kokka no seiritsu* (1959).
—— "Nihon shihonshugi no seiritsushi o meguru watashi no hansei" (1961).
—— "Nihon shihonshugi no seiritsu katei—toku ni 1880 nendai o megutte" (1961).
—— "Jōyaku kaisei hōshin no keizaiteki haikei" (1963).
Ōishi, "Ishin seiken to Ōkuma zaisei—Ōe Shinobu shi no shinsetsu o chūshin to shite" (1960).
—— "Ōkuma zaisei to Matsukata zaisei" (1961).

—— "Matsukata zaisei to jiyū minkenka no zaiseiron" (1962).
Okada, "Meiji shoki no yōgin taian" (1952).
—— "Meiji shoki heisei kaikaku ni okeru Ōkuma kō no kōken" (1954).
—— *Bakumatsu ishin no kahei seisaku* (1955).
—— "Nihon bōekigin" (1956).
—— "Nihon engin no kaigai ryūtsūsaku—Honkon o chūshin to shite" (1956).
—— "Meiji shoki ni okeru nigawase kin'yū" (1958).
—— *Meiji zenki no seika seisaku* (1958).
—— "Meijiki ni okeru bōeki kin'yū" (1959).
—— "Kinsatsu kachi ronsō ni tsuite" (1960).
—— *Nihon shihonshugi sōseiki ni okeru kin'yū seisaku* (1960).
—— "Shōhōshi ni yoru dajōkansatsu kashitsuke hōshiki" (1962).
—— "Dajōkansatsu kachi antei hōan ni tsuite" (1963).
—— "Shōhōshi Tsūshōshi ni yoru tsūka kyōkyū seisaku" (1963).
—— "Dajōkansatsu no ryūtsū jōkyō" (1964).
—— "Meiji shoki ni okeru fukuhon'isei no seiritsu" (1964).
—— "Meiji shoki no tsūka kyōkyū seisaku" (1964).
—— "Waga kuni ni okeru daiikki kinhon'isei jidai no tsūka mondai" (1964).
—— "Ōkuma Shigenobu no zaisei keizai seisaku no kichō" (1965).
—— "Ōkuma Shigenobu no kokusai shūshi kinkōron" (1965–66).
Okahashi, "Matsukata zaisei kin'yū seisaku no rekishiteki igi" (1965).
Ono, "Nihon ni okeru Mekishiko doru no ryūnyū to sono kōzai" (1958).
—— "Kindaiteki kahei seido no seiritsu to sono seikaku" (1959).
Osatake, "Yuri zaisei ni tsuite" (1943).
Ōshima, "Meiji shoki no zaisei" (1937).
Ōuchi, *Nihon zaiseiron: kōsaihen* (1932).
—— "Yuri Kimimasa" (1955).
Sakairi, "Meiji shoki ni okeru zaisei" (1956).
Satō, "Matsukata zaisei to gunkaku zaisei no tenkai" (1963).
—— "Kigyō bokkōki ni okeru gunkaku zaisei no tenkai" (1964).
Sawada, "Dajōkansatsu hakkō no shushi to shokusan kōgyō" (1932).
—— *Meiji zaisei no kisoteki kenkyū* (1934).
Sekiyama, "Kyūshohan no gaikoku fusai shobun" (1931).
—— "Eikoku Tōyō Ginkō to waga kuni to no kankei tansho" (1937).
—— *Nihon kahei kin'yūshi kenkyū* (1943).
Shibata, "Shihon chikuseki ni okeru gaishi no yakuwari" (1959).
Shima, *Ōkura daijin* (1949).
Shimbō, "Ishinki no shin'yō seido—Ōsaka Kawase Kaisha o chūshin to shite" (1962).
—— "Tōkyō Kawase Kaisha" (1963).

Shindō, "Meiji shoki no infurēshon" (1954).

Sugii, "Chitsuroku shobun to shichibu ritsuki gaishi boshū" (2 vols., 1959).

Sugiyama, "Kahei kin'yū seido no kakuritsu" (1958).

—— "Kin'yū seido no sōsetsu" (1965).

Suzuki, "Meiji shoki no kōsai seisaku" (1926).

Tabe, "Meiji seifu no kōsai seisaku" (1933).

Takagaki, *Kindai Nihon kin'yūshi* (1955).

—— *Meiji shoki ni okeru zaisei kin'yū seisaku to gaikoku shihon no kankei* (1958).

—— "Kōhon 'shihei shōkyakusetsu' no shuchō—Nihon kindai kin'yūshi kenkyū no issetsu" (1960).

Takahashi, "Meiji zenki ni okeru zaisei seisaku no tenkai" (1954).

—— "Meiji zenki bōeki kin'yū kikō ni kansuru shiron" (1959).

—— " 'Jumbikin' no zaiseiteki igi ni tsuite" (1960).

—— *Meiji zaiseishi kenkyū* (1964).

Tanaka, "Nihon ni okeru tetsudō dō'nyū seisaku no keisei katei" (1962).

—— *Meiji ishin no seikyoku to tetsudō kensetsu* (1963).

—— "Nihon ni okeru tetsudō dō'nyū seisaku no seijiteki haikei" (1963).

Tatemoto, "Meiji 1–34 nen no kokusai shūshi suikei sagyō hōkoku," plus supplement (1966).

Tsuchiya, "Meiji zenki no infurēshon to sono kokufuku" (1958).

Uchida, "Ansei kaikoku to Igirisu shihon—sono kyōdō hōshiki ni kansuru oboegaki" (1958).

Yagisawa, "Meiji shoki no defurēshon to nōgyō kyōkō" (1932).

—— "Seinan sen'eki go no infurēshon" (1932).

Yamaguchi, "Meiji jidai no seishi kin'yū" (1962).

—— *Nihon sangyō kin'yūshi kenkyū—seishi kin'yū hen* (1966).

Yokohama Shōkin Ginkō, *Yokohama Shōkin Ginkō shi* (1920).

Yoshikawa, "Meiji kin'yūshi kanken" (1961).

—— "Meiji ni okeru kyūheika kaikin to heika kirisage" (1961).

Yukizawa, "Ishin seifu to shihon chikuseki" (1959).

Yuri, *Shishaku Yuri Kimimasa den* (1940).

Zaisei Keizai Gakkai, *Meiji Taishō zaiseishi* (20 vols., 1936–40).

Financial policy, currency, foreign exchange, and balance of payments. English:

Emi, *Government Fiscal Activity and Economic Growth in Japan, 1868–1960* (1963).

Fujita, "The Banking System in the Middle Meiji Era (1870–1910)" (1956).

—— "The Development of Overseas Banking System in Japan in the Meiji Era" (1957).

Horie, "Japan's Balance of International Payments in the Early Meiji Period" (1954).

—— "Japanese-American Financial Relations" (1957).

Islam, *Foreign Capital and Economic Development: Japan, India, and Canada* (1960).

Katō, "Development of the Monetary System" (1958).

Kimura, "Fiscal Policy and Industrialization in Japan, 1868–1895" (1955).

McMaster, "Japanese Gold Rush of 1859" (1960).

—— "The Takashima Mine: British Capital and Japanese Industrialization" (1963).

Nakamura, "Ōkuma's Financial Policy and the Political Change of the 14th Year of Meiji" (1962).

Ott, "The Financial Development of Japan, 1878–1958" (1961).

Patrick, "External Equilibrium and Internal Convertibility: Financial Policy in Meiji Japan"(1965).

—— "Japan, 1868–1914" (1967).

Reubens, "Foreign Capital and Domestic Development in Japan" (1955).

Shinjo, *History of the Yen* (1962).

Yamamura, "The Role of the Samurai in the Development of Modern Banking in Japan" (1967).

Maritime transportation. Japanese:

Furuta, *Nihon kaiunshi gaisetsu* (1955).

Inoue, "Meijiki zōsen seisaku no igi to sono kōka" (1966).

Ishii and others, "Meiji shoki ni okeru kaiun kindaika ni kansuru shiryō" (1965–66).

Kudō, "Taguchi Ukichi to kaiungyō hogo mondai" (1963).

Miyamoto, *Meiji un'yushi* (1913).

Nakamura, "Ōkuma zaisei to kaiun—Mitsubishi no seiritsu" (1965).

Sasaki, *Nihon kaiun kyōsōshi josetsu* (1954).

—— *Nihon kaiungyō no kindaika* (1961).

—— "Nihon kaiunshi kenkyū no saikin dōkō" (1965).

Shizuta, *Kaiji rippō no hatten* (1959).

Sugii, "Meiji seifu no kaiun seisaku" (1956).

—— "Jōyaku kaiseishi jō no engan bōeki" (1957–58).

—— "Meiji jidai no kaiun seisaku—seifu no Mitsubishi kan" (1964).

Takase, "Meijiki ni okeru kaiun no kindaika" (1965).

Tominaga, *Kōtsū ni okeru shihonshugi no hatten* (1953).

Yamaguchi, "Meiji shoki no gaikoku kaiun to Mitsubishi Kaisha" (1962).

—— "Meiji shonen Beikoku Taiheiyō Yūsen Kaisha no tai-Nichi shūkōsen"(1963).

Zōsen Kyōkai, *Nihon kinsei zōsenshi* (1911).

Maritime transportation. English:

Kajinishi, "Development of Transportation and Communication Systems" (1958).

Sasaki, "The Maritime Competition in the Early Meiji Era" (1954).

Yamamoto, "Development of the Marine Insurance Industry in Japan" (1958).

Yamamura, "The Founding of Mitsubishi: A Case Study in Japanese Business History" (1967).

3

Japan's Cultural
Foreign Policies

Robert S. Schwantes

Cultural foreign policy should at the outset be distinguished from the wider range of cultural relations. Cultural relations include all the ways in which people in different nations learn about one another. In addition to direct personal contacts through travel, study abroad, business, and so on, cultural relations also include more impersonal communications through the printed word, art forms, the movies, radio, and TV. In this rich and diverse process, the interests and initiatives of countless individuals are the principal motive forces. Except under circumstances in which strong adversary relationships exist, governments usually encourage and facilitate these cultural contacts by private citizens.

Cultural policy refers to the much more limited instances in which officials of the government by conscious decision use one aspect or another of cultural relations for purposes of national policy. Government observation missions can be distinguished from casual travelers, students officially sent abroad from the larger number who go on their own initiative, government information programs from the free flow through commercial channels. Policy is characterized by purpose, decision, and control. In most cases execution of cultural policy requires expenditure of public funds.

Historical study of the cultural policies of the Japanese government involves much the same problems as study of political or economic policies. Ideally, at each point in time one must seek to understand the structure, mechanisms, and personal relationships within the government affecting policy formulation, decision-making, and execution. One must try to reconstruct how the decision-makers defined the situation in which they were acting. The relevant factors may be very broad and diffuse, but the ultimate policy focus should be sharp and precise. Unfortunately, in reconstructing past history, complete and accurate information cannot always be recovered.

If one thinks of various nationalities as having different styles in cultural interaction, it might be said that the Japanese have in modern times been highly inquisitive about and receptive to outside influences and moderately active in projecting their culture abroad. But we seek to identify specific policies rather than to describe tendencies among the whole population.

The general view presented here is that the Japanese government has in modern times made extensive and active use of cultural instruments in pursuit of national purposes. The basic decision to modernize the economy taken at the time of the Meiji Restoration had many consequences in the way of cultural action. The Japanese government's action in employing foreign advisers and technicians, sending out observation missions, and dispatching students abroad now seems quite advanced and sophisticated, remarkably like the techniques used in development programs in many parts of the world today. The initiative and financial support came from the Japanese themselves, without benefit of foreign aid programs. At an early date it became established that it was legitimate for the central government to use public funds for such purposes. Thereafter, Japan could carry out cultural policies more freely and more flexibly than countries with traditions of limited government and greater private initiative.

To survey all of Japan's cultural policies over the past century is manifestly impossible. Discussed here are a few salient topics that seem to have definite prospect of rewarding further research and of illustrating the whole process of decision-making and policy execution in the cultural area. Studies of cultural policy take one into a broad and diverse range of materials; the bibliography cited is meant to be exploratory and illustrative, not complete in any sense. My own personal interest in Japanese-American relations creates an imbalance in that direction that should be corrected by comparable studies of Japanese cultural policy toward other parts of the world.

Japan-United States cultural relations:

Schwantes, *Japanese and Americans: A Century of Cultural Relations* (1955).

Foreign policy decision-making:

Snyder, Bruck, and Sapin, "Decision-Making as an Approach to the Study of International Politics" (1962), pp. 14–185, provides a suggestive conceptual framework for study of the problem, but one that could seldom be fully filled out with concrete historical data.

THE MODERNIZATION POLICY OF THE
MEIJI GOVERNMENT

A study of the basic decision to open the country and modernize the economy would take one into all the intricacies of the closing years of the shogunate and of the restoration movement. Marius Jansen's study of Sakamoto Ryōma, for example, reveals the complex mixture of repulsion and attraction, of "expel the barbarians" and "open the country" sentiments, that resulted from exposure to the outside world. After the Meiji Restoration, however, the decision to accept outside influence for the sake of modernization was quite clear-cut. It was stated explicitly in the fifth article of the so-called Charter Oath promulgated early in 1868: "Knowledge shall be sought throughout the world in order to strengthen the foundation of the imperial polity." These words appeared in Yuri Kimimasa's first draft and survived through several successive revisions of the Charter Oath. The concrete lines of cultural policy stemming from this basic decision offer many opportunities for research.

Employment of Foreign Advisers and Technicians. A contemporary roster entitled *O-yatoi gaikokujin ichiran* lists 214 foreigners employed by organs of the central government in 1871. Their salaries totaled $534,492 (Mexican) per year (equivalent to an approximately equal number of yen at that time), a considerable burden on the new government. Local governments employed 164 additional persons. By 1876–77 expenditures for 484 foreign employees had risen to about ¥1.4 million per annum, representing 2.3 percent of the total budget of the central government.

Case studies in as much depth of detail as possible are now needed to reveal the decision-making processes surrounding the employment of such advisers and technicians. How did Japanese leaders define their needs? How were the foreigners recruited? The "Instructions for the Employment of Foreigners" issued by the Foreign Ministry early in 1870 indicates that the government was fully aware of the problems of getting persons with adequate qualifications and of the various contingencies that might arise during the contract period. What were the working relationships between foreign advisers and Japanese officials? How influential were the views and recommendations of the foreigners in determining policy on substantive matters? What considerations entered into decisions to dispense eventually with their services?

A thorough restudy of the role of Guido F. Verbeck would make an important case study. Through his direct access to leaders like Ōkuma Shigenobu and Soejima Taneomi and as principal of the most important school of Western studies, the School for Foreign Learning, later as adviser to the Senate, this Dutch-American missionary was very influential. He had a key role in recommending and planning the Iwakura Embassy. His recommendations carried great weight in the hiring of other foreigners. Yet we have no study of Verbeck more recent than the biography that William Elliot Griffis published in 1900. David Murray's service as superintendent of educational affairs from 1873 to 1879 should be carefully studied to determine the degree of foreign leadership in the whole educational development in early Meiji. The work of William W. Curgill and his crew of British engineers in building and operating Japan's first railroads would be another obvious subject. To develop comparative data about Japanese handling of advisers, a series of studies should be made covering persons from several different countries.

The Iwakura Embassy of 1871–1873. The Japanese government's decision to send abroad a large mission of officials, headed by persons of the stature of Iwakura Tomomi, Kido Takayoshi, and Itō Hirobumi, to spend almost two years observing and studying the political systems and material culture of Western nations, was for its time a remarkably daring and statesmanlike act. For that reason it deserves at least a fraction of the scholarly attention that has been devoted to the intrinsically far less important 1860 mission to the United States. Marlene J. Mayo's dissertation at Columbia University focused primarily on the relation of the Iwakura Embassy to the revision of existing treaties. But the embassy should also be restudied from the standpoint of cultural policy. A start has been made in Dr. Mayo's other works listed in the bibliography; she also has a manuscript in preparation on this subject.

Lower-ranking officials of the embassy from various departments of the Meiji government made extensive investigations in their specialized fields and compiled copious notes and reports. Tanaka Fujimaro collected material on foreign educational systems, for example, that was published under the title *Riji kōtei*. Kume Kunitake's record of the mission, *Tokumei zenken taishi Bei-Ō kairan jikki*, provides a detailed itinerary and some reactions to the things seen. Certainly it should be possible to assemble much more in the way of diaries and other personal records. Equally important would be a systematic effort to follow the continuing effects of the mission upon determination of government policy along various substantive lines.

The Dispatch of Students Abroad. The outward flow of students from Japan during the period 1865 to 1880 is remarkable both for its large volume and for the degree of official involvement. Since many of the returned students became leaders in the modernization process, there is a wealth of biographical material from which to study the experiences of the individuals concerned. But here we are concerned primarily with the element of government policy-making, a subject on which Ogata Hiroyasu has assembled much of the pertinent documentation.

The pattern of study abroad had already been set before the Restoration. A few individuals like Niishima Jō made their own way semi-surreptitiously, the larger han had sent out small groups, and the shogunate itself dispatched 47 students abroad.

After the Restoration the floodgates were opened. Han lords vied in sending their retainers abroad. The central government encouraged this as a way of unifying the nation and getting the feudal elements to participate in the new modernization policy. In late 1870 both a Council of State decree and an imperial rescript enjoined the nobility to go abroad for study to set an example for the people. Among high officials going abroad became so popular that it was jokingly spoken of as the new "pilgrimage to the Grand Shrine of Ise." The "Rules for Study Overseas" promulgated at that time established a system under which large han (over 400,000 *koku*) were permitted to send three students, medium han (100,000 to 400,000 *koku*) two, and small han (under 100,000 *koku*) one. Five years was projected as the standard period of study, with an allowance of $600–$700 (U.S.) per year. One of the principal reasons for establishing permanent diplomatic representation abroad at this time was to supervise these students.

When the han were abolished in August 1871, the students abroad became a financial burden upon the central government. The Iwakura

Embassy was given instructions "to investigate and determine the fields of study of those students in each country at government expense, to tell those who are delinquent to return, and also to judge the expenses of the students and to approve their allotments." When Itō Hirobumi paid particular attention to this task, he found serious shortcomings. Many who had not had previous study of English were sitting in primary classrooms with very young children. Diplomatic supervision was nominal, and students changed schools and courses of study at will. Relying heavily upon the opinions of one Charles Graham, an Englishman who had taught a number of Japanese, Itō sent back a report that severely criticized the system. Itō's report apparently weighed heavily in a government decision to abolish the existing system of officially supported students. Kuki Ryūichi was sent out in 1873 with the unpleasant task of forcing them to return. At that time there were 373 students abroad, 250 of whom were receiving government support totaling at least ¥250,000 per year.

Although the Meiji government then hesitated for some time before establishing a new system for study abroad, it had not abandoned the idea. In 1875 a system of qualifying examinations given by the School for Foreign Learning (one of the predecessors of Tokyo Imperial University) was set up; but when no one met the requirements, eleven students were chosen from the school itself. Komura Jutarō and Hatoyama Kazuo were in this group. Ten more young men were sent abroad in 1876. Megata Tanetarō was appointed to supervise these students abroad.

Financial stringency at the time of the Satsuma Rebellion of 1877 forced the Ministry of Education to suspend sending new students abroad, but in 1879 the system was resumed again. The number dispatched each year was quite small except in the period 1899–1903, when it reached 40 to 50. In other departments of government, too, a period of study or at least of observation abroad became a standard part of the career patterns of the most promising men. The pattern had been set early in the Meiji period and was never seriously questioned. An extensive study over the years of the persons chosen to go abroad, the countries to which they were sent, and the subjects of their studies or investigation might reveal a great deal about changing purposes and priorities in the Japanese government.

Final years of the Tokugawa shogunate:

Jansen, *Sakamoto Ryōma and the Meiji Restoration* (1961).

The Charter Oath:

Ishii, *Japanese Legislation in the Meiji Era* (1958), pp. 139–46.

Employment of foreigners in Japan:

Griffis, *Verbeck of Japan* (1900).
Honjō, "O-yatoi gaikokujin to waga kuni no keizai oyobi keizaigaku" (1955).
Ogata, *Seiyō kyōiku i'nyū no hōto* (1961), pp. 130–33.
Ōuchi and Tsuchiya, *Meiji zenki zaisei keizai shiryō shūsei* (21 vols., 1931–36), IV, 217–61.
O-yatoi gaikokujin ichiran (1872), reprinted in Yoshino, *Gaikoku bunkahen* (1928), pp. 347–62.
Saigusa, Nozaki, and Sasaki, *Kindai Nihon sangyō gijutsu no seiōka* (1960), includes names and basic information about many of the foreign technicians employed during the Meiji period.
Umetani, *O-yatoi gaikokujin* (1965).

Japanese mission to the United States, 1860:

Nichi-Bei Shūkō Tsūshō Hyakunen Kinen Gyōji Un'eikai, *Man'en gannen kem-Bei shisetsu shiryō shūsei* (7 vols., 1960–61), contains the principal documents concerning the mission together with an exhaustive bibliography.

Iwakura Embassy, 1871–1873:

Altman, "Guido Verbeck and the Iwakura Embassy" (1966).
Japan, Mombushō (Ministry of Education), *Riji kōtei* (15 vols., 1873).
Kume, *Tokumei zenken taishi Bei-Ō kairan jikki* (5 vols., 1878).
Mayo, "The Iwakura Mission to the United States and Europe, 1871–1873" (1959).
——"The Iwakura Embassy and the Unequal Treaties" (1961).
——"Rationality in the Restoration" (1966).

Japanese students abroad:

Hall, "Mori Arinori: The Formative Years" (1965).
Hara, "Tokugawa bakufu no Eikoku ryūgakusei: Bakumatsu ryūgakusei no kenkyū" (1942), is a clear and detailed account of a group of Japanese students in Great Britain in the last years of the shogunate.
Hara, "On Japanese Students Abroad, 1854 to 1873" (1965).
Hayashi, "Bakumatsu no kaigai ryūgakusei" (1963).
—— "Mori Arinori to Tōmasu Rēku Harisu" (1963).
Japan, Mombushō (Ministry of Education), *Mombushō daisan nempō* (1875; reprinted, 1964), p. 10, and Supplement No. 1, pp. 17–19.
Nagai, "Nihon o tazuneru shōgai no tabi: Tsunoda Ryūsaku" (1965).

Ogata, *Seiyō kyōiku i'nyū no hōto* (1961), pp. 15–71.
Shumpō Kō Tsuishōkai, *Itō Hirobumi den* (3 vols., 1940), pp. 675–77.

David Murray:

"D. Marē" (1958).
In Memoriam: David Murray (1915).
Inagaki, "Gakkan Dabiddo Marē no kenkyū" (1955).
Japan, Mombushō (Ministry of Education), *Meiji ikō kyōiku seido hattatsushi* (12 vols., 1938–39). Vol. I reprints the Japanese text of some of Murray's reports.
Tokinoya, "Kyōikurei seitei no rekishiteki haikei" (1952).
Tsuchiya, *Meiji jūnendai no kyōiku seisaku* (1956).

Railroad construction:

Japan, Tetsudōshō (Ministry of Railways), *Nihon tetsudōshi* (3 vols., 1921).
Saigusa, Nozaki, and Sasaki, *Kindai Nihon sangyō gijutsu no seiōka* (1960), pp. 251–58, 264–74.

JAPAN'S PARTICIPATION IN INTERNATIONAL EXPOSITIONS

International expositions provide another focal point for study of Japan's cultural policy. Beginning with the Crystal Palace Exhibition in London in 1851, such expositions were a characteristic phenomenon of the modern age, one manifestation of national aspirations competing through industrial development and commercial rivalry. Japan entered the lists early, by sending Tokugawa Akitake, younger brother of the shogun, to France in 1867 with a suite of twenty-eight officials in response to an invitation from Napoleon III. The new Meiji government sent exhibits to the Vienna Exposition of 1873, accompanied by Japanese craftsmen who studied foreign methods. At the Centennial Exhibition in Philadelphia in 1876, Japan made a special effort to demonstrate its progress in education. At each of the major expositions from that time on—Paris in 1878 and 1900, Chicago in 1893 and 1933, St. Louis in 1904, San Francisco in 1915 and 1939, New York in 1939, right down to Seattle in 1962 and New York in 1964–65—Japan has made a major effort to be well represented. It has made a more than proportionate showing at a host of smaller exhibitions and fairs. Charles P. Bryan remarked in 1912 that "even at the comparatively small city of Charleroi, the industrial centre of Belgium, I observed that the main feature of the exposition last summer was the Japanese section."

Official participation in such expositions requires a deliberate decision of the government, and usually considerable expenditure of public funds. The Japanese Diet authorized ¥630,000 for participation in the Columbian Exposition in 1893, ¥1.3 million for the Paris Exposition of 1900, and ¥1.8 million for the Japan-British Exhibition held in London in 1910. To this must be added large expenditures by prefectural governments and the private firms that provided most of the exhibits. The standard procedure on the part of the Japanese government was to establish a special office within the Ministry of Agriculture and Commerce to coordinate preparations, then to send a sizable party of officials as commissioners.

The government's motivation in participation was stated concisely by Sakata Jūjirō, director of the International Trade Bureau of the Foreign Ministry, in relation to the Panama-Pacific International Exhibition at San Francisco in 1915: "to avail itself of this unique opportunity to see, study, and import the most recent manufactured goods of the highly advanced nations and also to introduce to the American public the latest products of its industrial arts with a view to extending their market, and thereby to strengthen its economic relations with America and to solidify their traditional friendship." Expositions provided a concentrated opportunity for two of modern Japan's principal concerns—to absorb the latest innovations from abroad and to push its own wares.

Exhibition participation often carried overtones of national pride and political motivation. The explanatory publications distributed at European expositions in the nineteenth century were designed to distinguish Japan from China in the minds of foreigners. Japan was eager to make a good showing at Chicago in 1893 to demonstrate that it was modernized enough to deserve revision of the unequal treaties. The Japanese commissioners took particular pride in getting Japanese works admitted for the first time to the fine arts pavilion, instead of only in crafts exhibits. When the onset of the Russo-Japanese War coincided with the Louisiana Purchase Exposition in St. Louis, Russia withdrew from participation and some Japanese favored doing the same. Japanese leaders explicitly decided to continue and afterwards believed that this action played an important part in swinging American public opinion to the Japanese side. The Japan-British Exhibition of 1910 was intended in part to demonstrate the solidarity achieved through the Anglo-Japanese alliance. Participation in the San Francisco exhibition of 1915 can be related to Japan's desire to ameliorate the immigration controversy. Likewise, its part in the New York and San Francisco fairs of 1939 should be studied in the light of Japan's general cultural relations campaign during the 1930s.

One wonders whether Japanese leaders did not begin to have doubts about the constant confusion, effort, and expense involved in participation in the many expositions staged by competing local sponsors around the world. Certainly this was true in other countries, and beginning in France in 1884 organizations began to be formed to regulate and to limit participation. In 1912 Japan joined sixteen European states in signing at Berlin a convention regulating the organization of international expositions, but because of the outbreak of World War I this never came formally into operation. Though Japan used the exposition as a domestic device for stimulating industrial progress, its only attempt to stage an international show came to naught. After the Russo-Japanese War, plans were laid for a Great Japan Exposition to be held in 1912. But in 1908 the opening date was postponed until 1917, and in 1912 the planning office was disbanded entirely. The 1970 Osaka fair was the first full-scale international exposition held by Japan.

Further research could add flesh to the skeleton sketched here. Analysis of changing emphases in exhibits and cultural presentations should be revealing. One difficulty is the diffuse and scattered nature of the materials involved. For study of motivations, biographies of the public figures involved may be helpful, provided they deign to notice what were not necessarily major events in their subjects' careers. Because Tejima Seiichi served as organizer and commissioner for several expositions, his biography is unusually fruitful. But the main reliance will have to be on newspaper articles and on the ad hoc publications that appeared in connection with different expositions. Several examples of the latter class of publications are included below.

Visit to Paris by Tokugawa Akitake, 1867:

> Shibusawa, *Jōi ronsha no to-Ō* (1941).

Participation in international expositions:

> "International Expositions," in *Encyclopedia of the Social Sciences*, VI (1931), 24–26.
> *Tejima Seiichi sensei den* (1929), pp. 216–34.

Vienna Exposition, 1873:

> *Waguneru sensei tsuikaishū* (1938), pp. 413–34.

Philadelphia Centennial Exhibition, 1876:

Japan, Imperial Japanese Commission to the International Exhibition at Philadelphia, *Official Catalogue of the Japanese Section, and Descriptive Notes on the Industry and Agriculture of Japan* (1876).

Japan, Mombushō (Ministry of Education), *An Outline History of Japanese Education, Literature and Arts; Prepared by the Mombushō for the Philadelphia International Exhibition, 1876, Reprinted for the Paris Exposition, 1878* (1877).

Paris Exposition, 1878:

Japan, Commission impériale à l'Exposition universelle de Paris, 1878, *Le Japon à l'Exposition universelle de 1878, publié sous la direction de la Commission impériale Japonaise* (1878).

Japan, Mombushō (Ministry of Education), *An Outline History of Japanese Education, Literature and Arts; Prepared by the Mombushō for the Philadelphia International Exhibition, 1876, Reprinted for the Paris Exposition, 1878* (1877).

World's Columbian Exposition, Chicago, 1893:

Japan, Imperial Japanese Commission to the World's Columbian Exposition, Chicago, U.S.A., 1893, *History of the Empire of Japan* (1893).

Japan, Mombushō, Kambō, Hōkokuka (Ministry of Education, Secretariat, Information Section),*Catalogue of Objects Exhibited at the World's Columbian Exposition, Chicago, U.S.A., 1893.*

Japan, Nōshōmushō (Ministry of Agriculture and Commerce), *A Descriptive Catalogue of the Agricultural Products Exhibited in the World's Columbian Exposition* (1893).

Okakura, *The Hō-ōden* [*Phoenix Hall*]: *An Illustrated Description of the Buildings Erected by the Japanese Government at the World's Columbian Exhibition, Jackson Park, Chicago* (1893).

Paris Exposition, 1900:

Japan, Commission impériale à l'Exposition universelle de Paris, 1900, *Catalogue spécial officiel du Japon* (1900).

—— *Histoire de l'industrie de la pêche maritime et fluviale au Japon* (1900).

—— Empire du Japon, Ministère de l'agriculture et du commerce, Station centrale agronomique, *Notice des objets exposés* (1900).

Louisiana Purchase Exposition, St. Louis, 1904:

Japan, Imperial Japanese Commission to the Louisiana Purchase Exposition, *The Exhibit of the Empire of Japan: Official Catalogue, International Exposition, St. Louis, 1904* (1904).

—— *Japan in the Beginning of the Twentieth Century* (1904).

Starr, *The Ainu Group at the St. Louis Exposition* (1904).

Japan-British Exhibition, 1910:

Japan, Imperial Japanese Government Commission to the Japan-British Exhibition, *An Illustrated Catalogue of Japanese Old Fine Arts Displayed at the Japan-British Exhibition, London, 1910* (1910).

Official Report of the Japan-British Exhibition, 1910, at the Great White City, Shepherd's Bush, London (1911).

Charleroi, Belgium, Exposition, 1911:

Panama Taiheiyō Bankoku Daihakurankai, The Panama Pacific International Exposition (1912), p. 14.

Projected Great Japan Exposition, 1912:

Shibusawa Seien Kinen Zaidan Ryūmonsha, *Shibusawa Eiichi denki shiryō* (1955–65), XXIII, 631.

Panama-Pacific International Exhibition, San Francisco, 1915:

Hakurankai Kyōkai, *Japan and Her Exhibits at the Panama-Pacific International Exhibition, 1915* (1915).

Japan, Imperial Japanese Commission to the Panama-Pacific International Exhibition, San Francisco, 1915, *Japan as It Is* (1915).

Panama Taiheiyō Bankoku Daihakurankai, The Panama Pacific International Exposition (1912).

Golden Gate International Exposition, San Francisco, 1939:

Kokusai Bunka Shinkōkai, *Catalogue of Japanese Art in the Palace of Fine and Decorative Arts at the Golden Gate International Exposition, Treasure Island, San Francisco, California, 1939* (1939).

New York World's Fair, 1939:

Japan, Imperial Japanese Commission to the New York World's Fair, 1939, *Directory and Catalogue of Exhibits at the Japanese Pavilion and Japanese Section of the Hall of Nations.*

New York World's Fair, 1964–1965:

Japan Trade Center, *How to See the Japan Pavilion* (1964).

JAPAN'S CULTURAL ACTIVITIES IN CHINA

Before World War II, Japan's relations with the Asian mainland bulked so large in its national life that the question of how cultural activities relate to changing China policies is one of the most important areas for investigation. The subject is broad and relatively unexplored, and the best that can be done here is to suggest a few leads into further research.

Japan's cultural relationship to China has been ambivalent. On the one hand, Japan has at several periods in its history drawn many cultural elements from China and adapted them into its own civilization. This common cultural heritage and similar, though far from identical, languages provided a basis for a relationship in which Japan had the role of younger brother. On the other hand, Japan stepped out ahead in the modernization process and thereby became a model and guide for China. At the same time, Japan had definite ambitions to extend its political and economic influence in a weak and disordered China.

Japanese Teachers to China, 1895–1911. When defeated by Japan in the war of 1894–95, China decided to follow the example of the victor by moving toward modern education and industrial development. The Ch'ing court abolished the traditional literary examinations and created new graded institutions ranging from primary school to university to provide more practical education. Japanese were numerically preponderant among the foreign teachers employed to help staff these schools. In 1906 there were 500 to 600 Japanese teaching throughout the country. Chinese authorities invited Hattori Unokichi, one of the pioneer sinologists at Tokyo Imperial University, to head the teacher training course at Peking University. Iwaya Magozō of Kyoto Imperial University directed the Shih-hsueh-kuan, a school for Chinese military officers. Japanese specialists helped to establish agricultural schools in nearly every province of China. Most of these teachers had their work cut short by the disorder and financial uncertainty that followed the revolution of 1911. But their work over a decade should be studied for its political as well as its cultural significance.

Chinese Students to Japan. Another consequence of the Ch'ing court's turn toward modernization was a flood of Chinese students into Japan. The flow began with thirteen students brought over by the Chinese legation in 1896, was swelled by many others coming on their own initiative, and reached a peak of 8,000 or more in 1905–6. Waseda, Meiji, and Hosei universities opened special sections for foreign students, and many special schools opened to meet the demand, some of them crassly commercial. To clarify the confused situation, the Ministry of Education in November 1905 issued "Regulations Concerning Public and Private Schools Admitting Chinese Students." The students were affronted by what they interpreted as control and discrimination, and large numbers went back to China. Many returned to Japan the following year, however, and from that time on the Chinese student population in Tokyo fluctuated drastically with each turn in the political situation on the mainland. After the Manchurian Incident of 1931, for example, there was a wholesale exodus, but by 1936 the number had risen again to 5,000 or 6,000. Of Sanetō Keishū's two studies of Chinese students in Japan, the graphs appended to *Chūgokujin Nihon ryūgakushi* give the best estimate of numbers; this book, however, does not supersede his earlier work.

Much further research is needed to define the policy of the Japanese government toward the Chinese students. In the early years the attitude appears to have been primarily a permissive one. In 1908 the Chinese minister to Japan obtained the agreement of the Ministry of Education that the better public institutions—such as the First Higher School, the Tokyo Higher Normal School, and the Chiba Medical School—would accept a definite quota of Chinese students each year. All expenses were to be paid by the Chinese government, however. When students were stranded in Japan at the time of the 1911 revolution, it was Japanese businessmen who raised money to pay their return travel expenses. When the Chinese government repaid this money in 1918, it was placed in the hands of an organization called the Sino-Japanese Association for continued use on behalf of students. A Ministry of Education grant of ¥150,000 to this association in 1921 for the construction of dormitories appears to have been the first Japanese government appropriation for such a purpose. Thereafter, up to 1937 the government supplied over half the funds expended by this organization. Like many other groups of its kind, the Sino-Japanese Association can properly be regarded as semi-official, semi-private in character.

Joint Activities Supported by the Foreign Ministry, 1923– . From 1918 on the "foreign student problem" was discussed from time to time in the Imperial Diet. Concern was expressed over the large numbers of Chinese being trained in Europe and America and in British- and American-sponsored schools in China. These Chinese tended to be oriented favorably toward the West, in contrast to the anti-Japanese attitudes and activities of many who had received their training in Japan. With the example of the American Boxer Indemnity Fund very definitely in mind, in March 1923 the Diet passed a bill creating a special account for cultural activities with China.

Through this special account the remainder of the Boxer Indemnity due to Japan, as well as certain funds due from China under the Shantung settlement of 1922, was to be devoted to joint cultural and educational projects. About ¥2.5 million annually was to be used for a research institute and library in Peking for studies in the humanities and social sciences, an institution in Shanghai for study of the natural sciences, grants to Chinese students in Japan, and subsidies for schools and hospitals run by Japanese in China. An equal amount was to be paid into a sinking fund for permanent support of the same projects. Control of these funds was given to a new Cultural Affairs Division in the Asia Bureau of the Foreign Ministry. Joint cultural consultative committees for the Far East were set up in Peking and Shanghai. The Shanghai committee met in December 1926 and decided on construction of the Shanghai Science Institute, which was completed in the summer of 1931. Its purpose was to train Chinese scholars and to promote the development of medicine and the natural sciences through joint research. In addition to the Peking Humanities Research Institute, the Foreign Ministry eventually also put money into a North China Industrial Research Institute, agricultural research stations at Tientsin and Tsingtao, and modern science libraries in Peking and Shanghai.

Relationship between Government and "Private" Undertakings. Another important problem is to define the exact relationship between the Japanese government and certain nominally private organizations active in China. Foremost among these was the East Asia Common Culture Association, established in 1898 under the leadership of Prince Konoe Atsumaro. The society's primary activity was operation of the East Asia Common Culture Academy, a school in Shanghai which by 1945 had trained over 5,000 Japanese for work in China. In 1921 the academy was given special (technical) school status; in 1939 it became a university. The East Asia Common Culture Academy also did much important research and publication on Chinese subjects, and from 1902 to 1920 the parent society operated a school for Chinese students in the Kanda district of Tokyo. Almost from the beginning the East Asia Common Culture Association received subsidies from the national treasury; from 1924 on it was placed under the supervision of the Cultural Affairs Division of the Foreign Ministry and financed from the Boxer Indemnity Fund. In 1938, for example, the Common Culture Association received grants totaling over ¥450,000. In that same year about ¥1.3 million went to another society called the Universal Benevolence Association, whose aim was to do educational, medical, and social welfare work in China and other countries of Asia.

In general, the Japanese government gave much encouragement and support to academic study of Chinese language, history, archeology, and related subjects. For this the Cultural Affairs Division shared responsibility with the Ministry of Education. The Foreign Ministry provided grants and facilities for research in China and made arrangements for Chinese scholars to teach at Japanese universities. The Far Eastern Cultural Academy in Tokyo and the Far Eastern Cultural Institute in Kyoto, leading institutions in sinological research, in 1938 were each receiving subsidies of about ¥100,000 out of the indemnity fund. The question is who took the initiative in these relationships, the government or the scholars? Was the Japanese government promoting cultural studies primarily for their own sake, or was it using them as instruments of policy in relation to the changing political situation in China?

Miura Horiyuki gives in his book some interesting glimpses of the actual operation of Japanese cultural activities in China. At the end of his career as a specialist in Japanese history at Kyoto Imperial University, Miura was invited by Lingnan University in Canton to lecture on the Meiji Restoration. This invitation was transmitted through, and perhaps stimulated by, the Cultural Affairs Division. Japan's development experience in the Meiji period was a subject of considerable interest in China at the time, so an extensive tour, ranging from Canton to Mukden and involving lectures at many different educational institutions, was arranged for 1930 and early 1931. Miura relied heavily upon the Japanese consulates for arrangements; his social engagements, other than the formal functions with Chinese groups, seem to have been largely in the Japanese community. At Shanghai and Peking arrangements were in the hands of the joint cultural consultative committees for the Far East mentioned above. The active figure in Peking was Segawa Asanoshin, a retired diplomat. At

Canton the Returned Students Association, an organization of Chinese who had studied in Japan, played a part in organizing his program. Miura also mentions several times another group of returned students in Shanghai who published the monthly magazine *Hsueh-i* and were also connected with a special periodical on Japan.

What was the attitude of the Chinese people and the Chinese government to such cultural activities? In general, Miura seems to have been listened to with attention and respect, although some of the lectures planned in the Manchurian area had to be canceled because of anti-Japanese agitation. Miura comments at one point: "There is only one final thing that was extremely regrettable. That was the opposition from the Chinese side to the cultural work of our Foreign Ministry. While I was there, I saw a report that in the central organs of the Nationalist government the policy of abolishing the treaty already concluded between the two governments had been decided upon, and that a committee of three had been sent to Japan to reopen the negotiations."

The extent and nature of Chinese reaction is one of many aspects of this subject that requires further investigation. Another is the relationship between cultural activities directed by the Foreign Ministry and the ambitions and activities of Japanese military forces in China. As Taylor indicates in the section of his book regarding Japanese educational policy in occupied areas of China, this question becomes particularly important after the Japanese occupied parts of north China in 1937 and set up puppet Chinese governments. In August 1938 an East Asia Cultural Council was inaugurated in Peking and a week-long conference was held to discuss ways to promote cultural relations. Did the nature of such cultural activities in China change significantly when they were transferred administratively to the control of the Asia Development Board? The complete story may not be recoverable, but much information about Japanese cultural policies and actions under conditions of war and occupation could probably still be quarried from the surviving records. The following list should be helpful in providing information about Japan's cultural activities regarding China.

General survey of Sino-Japanese relations:

Kuzuu, *Tōa senkaku shishi kiden* (3 vols., 1933–36).
Ueda, *Nikka kōshōshi* (1948).

Japanese teachers in China, 1895–1911:

Hummel, *Eminent Chinese of the Ch'ing Period* (2 vols., 1943–44), II, 871.
Sanetō, *Meiji Nisshi bunka kōshō* (1943), pp. 347–48.
—— *Chūgokujin Nihon ryūgakushi* (1960), pp. 93–104.

Chinese students in Japan:

Sanetō, *Chūgokujin Nihon ryūgaku shikō* (1939).
—— *Chūgokujin Nihon ryūgakushi* (1960).

Policy of the Japanese government toward Chinese students:

Sanetō, *Chūgokujin Nihon ryūgaku shikō* (1939).
—— *Chūgokujin Nihon ryūgakushi* (1960), pp. 117–24.

Joint cultural and educational projects:

Chyne, *Handbook of Cultural Institutions in China* (1936), pp. 240–41.
Japan, Gaimushō (Foreign Ministry), "Tōhō Bunka Jigyōbu kankei kaikei zakken" (1922–41).
—— "Tōhō bunka jigyō kankei zakken" (1922–41). Not examined for this study.
Ueda, *Nikka kōshōshi* (1948), pp. 261–63.
Wright, *China's Customs Revenue since the Revolution of 1911* (3d ed., 1935), pp. 213–14.

Relations of the Japanese government with "private" organizations in China:

Ajia rekishi jiten (1959–62), VII, 14–15.
Japan, Gaimushō (Foreign Ministry), "Tōhō Bunka Jigyōbu kankei kaikei zakken" (1922–41).
Nihon rekishi daijiten (22 vols., 1956–60), XIII, 192.

Japanese government support of sinology:

Japan, Gaimushō (Foreign Ministry), "Tōhō Bunka Jigyōbu kankei kaikei zakken" (1922–41).
Nakamura, *Gendai Nihon ni okeru Shinagaku kenkyū no jitsujō* (1928).

Chinese involvement in Japanese cultural activities in China:

Japan, Gaimushō, Bunka Jigyōbu (Foreign Ministry, Cultural Affairs Division), *Chūka Minkoku kyōiku sono ta no shisetsu gaiyō* (1931).
Japan Times Weekly, September 8, 1938.
Miura, *Meiji ishin to gendai Shina* (1931), pp. 1–30, 197–218.
Taylor, *The Struggle for North China* (1940), pp. 88–96.
Ueda, *Nikka kōshōshi* (1948), p. 261.

JAPANESE-AMERICAN IMMIGRATION QUESTIONS
AND THE "ENLIGHTENMENT MOVEMENT"

Studies of the Japanese immigration question—by which we mean a series of connected but discrete events ranging in time from the San Francisco Board of Education order of 1906 to the passage of federal exclusion legislation in 1924—have focused on the diplomatic exchanges and on events within the state of California. Less attention has been paid to the policies and actions of the Japanese government. One reason has been the relative unavailability of the pertinent documents on the Japanese side. But also involved has been an assumption that Japan was a passive party in the controversy.

Since the primary motivation for American actions lay outside the realm of foreign affairs, in one sense Japanese opinions could not be truly decisive, but it is a mistake to ascribe to Japan complete lack of policy. No one has really tested by historical investigation the charge made at the time, and revived speculatively by Carey McWilliams, that Japan did not particularly want a final settlement of the immigration question. According to this hypothesis, elements favoring military and naval expansion found the California issue a convenient way of rallying Japanese public opinion to their own cause. Charges have even been made that the Japanese government, through its consuls, deliberately manipulated and victimized the Japanese community on the West Coast. The validity of these accusations can be determined only by an extensive examination of Japanese official records. Fortunately, at least part of the documents needed for studying Japanese official policy during the immigration controversy are now available in the microfilms of the Foreign Ministry archives available from the Library of Congress. The principal general files (not examined for this study) are cited in the bibliography that follows this topic under "Official Policy of the Japanese Government."

From the special point of view of cultural policy, it is extremely significant that from about 1913 until at least 1920 the Japanese government supported an extensive campaign to influence American opinion, both in elite circles and more widely, in favor of friendship with Japan and favorable settlement of the immigration question. Japanese documents designate this campaign as the *keihatsu undō* or the *kyōka undō*, either of which can be translated as the "enlightenment movement." The official Japanese files pertinent to this issue are included below under the heading "The Enlightenment Movement."

The Campaign in California. In California the key figure in this movement was Dr. Harvey Guy. After his return from service as a missionary in Japan, Dr. Guy was from 1912 until 1919 a professor at the Pacific School of Religions. He also maintained an office for a lecture bureau on Pine Street, San Francisco.

Dr. Guy's role was essentially that of a public relations man who stimulated and assisted the efforts of other people. In a report to the Japanese consul general dated May 29, 1916, Guy wrote: "You will understand, I am sure, that it has been my special work not only to inspire but to direct the various conferences. . . . I have visited and had personal interviews with all the leaders mentioned before calling them together in a regular meeting. This has required much time and more money, yet the results show that the efforts were well spent." Guy was active in the Japan Society of America (San Francisco) and served one term as its president. He was also closely involved in the activities of the Committee on Japanese Relations of the San Francisco Chamber of Commerce, headed by Wallace M. Alexander. By keeping in touch with Paul Scharrenberg, secretary of the California State Federation of Labor, Guy claimed some measure of success in tempering the hostility of that body on the Japanese question. As a churchman Guy had easy access to churches and religious organizations. Each year he gave a series of public lectures on the immigration question under the auspices of the YWCA of the University of California. He also spoke at meetings of the American Peace Society and the Women's Peace Party. Guy always stood ready to arrange for speakers and other programs on Japanese culture, including the showing of motion picture films, which was not as simple a matter technically then as it is today.

From the available documents, one can glean somewhat indirectly Guy's relationship to the Japanese government. He made written reports to the consul general in San Francisco on roughly a monthly schedule. When these were forwarded to the Foreign Ministry, they were stamped by the chief of the Second Section of the International Trade Bureau, by the bureau chief, and by the vice-foreign minister. On January 6, 1916 Guy wrote to Acting Consul General Numano: "I am placing in your hands certain suggestions for the work of the coming year. You will know what to do with these. I have refrained from enlarging our budget to any great extent except in the matter of the magazine. This you realize is of great importance and should be attended to at an early date." What Guy was proposing was expenditure of from $35,000 to $75,000, either to purchase an existing magazine or to start a new one. This proposal was apparently never carried out, and the sum of money involved was probably far in excess of the amount devoted to regular publicity operations.

A draft paper prepared by Chiba Toyoji, managing director of the California Central Agricultural Association, asking the Japanese Foreign Ministry for a subsidy in support of a campaign against the anti-alien land legislation coming up for an initiative vote in 1920, casts a light on what were probably standing relationships. Chiba asked that extreme care be taken so that no traces remained of the subsidy being paid by the Japanese government. The $25,000 to be used by the Japanese Association of America, he suggested, had best be paid first to Baron Shibusawa Eiichi, as representative of the Japanese-American Relations Committee, and further forwarded by him. An equal amount for use by the Agricultural Association could be paid to Chiba, who was then in Japan. Another $25,000 was to be placed in Consul General Ōta Tamekichi's account, "for activities in which Kawakami Kiyoshi, H.H. Guy, and others play the central part."

In southern California Guy was assisted by Inui Kiyosue, known as the "Japanese silver tongue," and Mrs. Inui. After the Japanese government opened a consulate in Los Angeles in late 1915, the Inuis worked more directly under the guidance of Consul Ōyama Ujirō. Early in 1916 Inui wrote Guy about "the plans formulated by Mr. Ōyama and myself as regards the work here. He thinks I ought to appear as if invited by the Educational Committee of the Japanese Association of Southern California, and I am now in a position so to appear." The Japan Society of Los Angeles, which Guy had helped to establish in 1909, was an important channel for getting the cooperation of community leaders.

The Campaign on the East Coast. The "enlightenment" campaign in the eastern United States was devoted more broadly to presenting in a favorable light the Japanese position on a number of issues connected with participation in World War I and with the Versailles peace settlement. Secondary attention was given to the more general aspects of the immigration question. The East and West News Bureau in New York was the principal instrument. In the work of putting out news releases for American papers, Ienaga Toyokichi was aided by Ōhira Chūgo and an American journalist named Joseph I. C. Clarke. The bureau also systematically collected and transmitted to Japan, through the consul general in New York, clippings from the American press on issues of special interest to Japan. Ienaga, who also held an appointment as professorial lecturer in political science at the University of Chicago, wrote for American magazines and spoke widely before American organizations.

The relationship of the News Bureau to the Japanese government is an ambiguous one that needs clarification through further careful research. In a letter to Viscount Ishii Kikujirō, dated October 8, 1917, Ienaga mentions the bureau's freedom of speech which permitted it to make statements that could be repudiated by diplomatic authorities. "That in giving out to the public these private opinions much discretion and good judgment are needed goes without saying." At a later date Ienaga complained to Ishii that during the Paris peace negotiations he was not kept informed of Japanese plans, and "because of this ignorance, I was constantly swayed by fear, lest the effort I make might be far from hitting the right mark or, worse still, might prove prejudicial to the issue."

Financial support for the bureau is also something of a mystery, perhaps deliberately kept so. In a speech before the Council on Foreign Relations in New York on October 14, 1918, Ienaga contrasted Japanese efforts to the propaganda programs of other nations: "Japan has no such official agency. . . . The present East and West News Bureau had its origins in the deliberations and decisions to contribute the necessary funds of such public-spirited men as Baron Shibusawa [Eiichi], well-known in America; Mr. Nakano [Buei], the then President of the Tokyo Chamber of Commerce; Dr. Takamine [Jōkichi], a scientist of international fame and, withal, a man of good fortune; Mr. Inoue [Junnosuke], the President of the Yokohama Specie Bank; Dr. Ono [Eijirō of the Industrial Bank], and others, who have at heart the welfare of the two nations on the opposite shores of the Pacific." The conjunction of names points toward the Japanese-American Relations Committee established under Shibusawa's leadership in 1916. But the records of the committee as printed in the Shibusawa papers include no record of support or supervision of an enterprise of this magnitude. Ienaga seems to have reported to the Japanese consul general in New York rather than directly to private sponsors in Japan. In fact, too, during this period Takamine Jōkichi and Ichinomiya Reitarō signed some of the reports to the consul general. Kawakami in his study of Takamine, however, makes no mention of the News Bureau, although he notes that Takamine did contribute to support of a "bureau of economic information" in New York from 1908 to 1912.

The Japanese publicity effort was reinforced by many Americans who held similar views on the issues at stake. Ienaga reported with satisfaction that the League to Enforce Peace, headed by ex-President Taft, had distributed 20,000 copies of his leaflet, "The Case of Japan in the Peace Treaty." Dr. Sidney L. Gulick, who had spent a quarter century in Japan as an American Board missionary, was an indefatigable writer and speaker on the immigration question. Gulick was secretary of the Committee on Relations with Japan of the Federal Council of Churches, secretary of a National Committee on American-Japanese Relations headed by George Wickersham, and secretary of the National Committee for Constructive Immigration Legislation. The Japan Society of New York in this period took forthright stands on political questions. Hamilton Wright Mabie, who had gone to Japan in 1912 as an exchange lecturer supported by the Carnegie Endowment for International Peace, opened the pages of *The Outlook* magazine to the Japanese point of view. Hamilton Holt's *The Independent* was also sympathetic. Indeed, it is one of the ironies of history that the immigration question should have turned out so badly for Japan in the exclusion legislation of 1924, despite extensive sympathy and support from highly placed Americans.

Taken as an example of the Japanese government's use of cultural policy, the "enlightenment movement" poses many fascinating questions not yet fully answered. From what quarter did the initiative for the movement come? At what level in the Japanese government was the decision to provide financial support taken? According to what estimate of the situation? What were the objectives, specified or implied, that the government sought to attain through this means? Was the program terminated in 1920, or was there merely a change in handling or filing the records? If terminated, under what circumstances and for what reasons? Is there any connection with the donation to the Japan Society (New York) of $74,000 in securities by large Japanese firms in 1920 to establish a Townsend Harris Permanent Endowment Fund devoted to "educational work along the broadest lines among Americans to disseminate a knowledge of Japan and the Japanese"? Did the Japanese government make any attempt to evaluate the success or failure of the "enlightenment movement"? After the immigration act of 1924, a serious blow to Japanese pride, how was the movement viewed in retrospect? Did experience with this program have any influence upon subsequent Japanese cultural policy? Undoubtedly it would be overly optimistic to expect to find precise answers to all these questions, but the availability of extensive primary records does give promise of a fruitful case study.

Materials on Japanese-American immigration questions and the "enlightenment movement" include:

Bailey, *Theodore Roosevelt and the Japanese-American Crises* (1934).

Buell, "The Development of the Anti-Japanese Agitation in the United States" (1922).

—— *Japanese Immigration* (1924).

Daniels, *The Politics of Prejudice: The Anti-Japanese Movement in California and the Struggle for Japanese Exclusion* (1962).

Flowers, *The Japanese Conquest of American Opinion* (1917).

Ichihashi, *Japanese in the United States: A Critical Study of the Problems of the Japanese Immigrants and Their Children* (1932).

Japan, Gaimushō, Amerika Kyoku (Foreign Ministry, America Bureau), *Hokubei Nikkei shimin gaikyō* (1936).

Japanese Association of America, *The Proposed Land Bills: The Other Side* (1913).

—— *Facts in the Case; They Will Be Carefully Weighed in Considering the Proposed Alien Land Initiative Law* (1920).

—— *Statistics Relative to Japanese Immigration and the Japanese in California* (1921).

Kachi, "Nichi-Bei tsūshō kōkai jōyaku to Kariforunia-shū tochi hō" (1961), a summary of the following work.

—— "The Treaty of 1911 and the Immigration and Alien Land Law Issue between the United States and Japan, 1911–1913" (1957).

Kawashima, *Nichi-Bei gaikōshi* (1934).

McWilliams, *Prejudice—Japanese-Americans: Symbol of Racial Intolerance* (1944).

Thompson, "The Yellow Peril, 1890–1924" (1957).

Zai-Bei Nihonjinkai, *Zai-Bei Nihonjin shi* (1940).

Official policy of the Japanese government:

Japan, Gaimushō (Foreign Ministry), "Hokubei Gasshūkoku ni oite hompōjin tokō seigen oyobi haiseki ikken" (1891–1909).

—— "Beikoku ni okeru hai-Nichi mondai ikken" (1911–14).

Japan, Gaimushō, Tsūshō Kyoku (Foreign Ministry, International Trade Bureau), "Tai-Bei imin mondai ni kansuru Nichi-Bei kōshō keika" (1933).

In addition, the following should be consulted.

Official Japanese files:

Japan, Gaimushō (Foreign Ministry), "Tai-Bei keihatsu undō ikken" (1913–20).
—— "Tai-Bei keihatsu undō jigyō hōkoku" (1914–19).
—— "Tai-Bei keihatsu undō jigyō hōkoku: zai-Nyūyōku sōryōjikan" (1914–19).

Activities of Dr. Harvey Guy:

Japan, Gaimushō (Foreign Ministry), "Tai-Bei keihatsu undō ikken" (1913–20), pp. 47–49, 121, 151.

Activities of the Japanese-American Relations Committee:

Shibusawa Seien Kinen Zaidan Ryūmonsha, *Shibusawa Eiichi denki shiryō* (1955–65), XXXIII, 452–500.

Japan Society of Los Angeles:

Minami Kashū Nikkeijin Shōgyō Kaigisho, *Minami Kashū Nihonjin shichijūnenshi* (1960), pp. 457–58.

Activities of the East and West News Bureau:

Japan, Gaimushō (Foreign Ministry), "Tai-Bei keihatsu undō jigyō hōkoku: zai-Nyūyōku sōryōjikan" (1914–19), pp. 1712–15, 1957, 1959–62.

Study of Takamine Jōkichi:

Kawakami, *Jokichi Takamine: A Record of His American Achievements* (1928).

League to Enforce Peace:

Japan, Gaimushō (Foreign Ministry), "Tai-Bei keihatsu undō jigyō hōkoku: zai-Nyūyōku sōryōjikan" (1914–19), pp. 1980–81.

American magazines:

The Outlook
The Independent

CULTURAL POLICY IN A DECADE OF MILITARISM AND WAR

From the narrow standpoint of Japanese-American cultural relations it is ironic that more time, attention, and funds were probably devoted to cultural exchanges in the years preceding Pearl Harbor than in any previous period.

Expansion of Cultural Relations with America. For the first time a considerable number of Americans went to Japan for serious academic study of Japanese history and culture. The so-called "people's mission," made up of Baron Ōkura Kishichirō, politician Nakano Seigō, and chief editor Takaishi Shingorō of the Mainichi newspaper, which went abroad in 1937–38 was only one of several high-level groups that visited the United States. The Japanese government provided invitations and funds for many Americans to visit Japan, individually and in groups.

Joseph C. Grew, the American ambassador at the time, took a rather skeptical view of these cultural activities:

> So far as I am aware, no constructive work was ever accomplished by such Japanese missions [to the U.S.] and in the case of American missions of editors, teachers, lawyers, businessmen, hotel managers, and other groups frequently brought for propaganda purposes to Japan at the expense of the Japanese Government, the Japanese conception of hospitality is such that more harm than good was frequently done. That hospitality invariably entails an iron-clad program of a tour of spots of historic interest, including always a trip to "Manchukuo," with daily luncheons, receptions, banquets, and formal speeches, and very little opportunity for informal contacts and investigations, with the result that the members of such groups have usually returned to Tokyo in an exhausted condition and not at all sure that their sympathies for Japan and the Japanese had been enhanced by their experiences. I have often told my Japanese friends of the unwisdom of these programs which tend to irk the average American in his dislike of regimentation and formality, but in vain. Habit and custom are too solidly intrenched to adapt Japanese plans to foreign inclinations.

One can easily speculate about the motivation underlying the Japanese cultural effort directed toward the United States. Was it generally assumed within the government that a rational presentation of Japan's position on international issues, buttressed by a picture of Japan as a nation of rich culture, would be persuasive? Was such a view shared by the military leaders? Or was the cultural program perhaps a concession designed to occupy and disarm the internationalist element, on the theory that such activity could do no harm and might do good? What was the relation between government activities and private initiatives? For some Japanese favorably inclined toward America was the emphasis on cultural relations perhaps an evasion of the basic deterioration that was occurring in the relationship between the two countries?

Broadening of World Activities and the K.B.S. Japanese-American exchanges should more properly be viewed as part of an expanded program of cultural relations with all countries. The most important manifestation of this policy was the creation in 1934 of the Society for International Cultural Relations (Kokusai Bunka Shinkōkai). In one sense Japanese withdrawal from the League of Nations made necessary an alternative to Japanese participation in the International Committee on Intellectual Cooperation that was part of the League structure. The announced purpose of the new society was "to introduce and encourage interest in, and study and knowledge of, Japanese culture based upon the ideal of furthering worldwide exchange of cultural relations in the cause of international peace and better understanding."

K.B.S., as the society was popularly called, had an elaborate structure indicative of support from the highest quarters. The Imperial Household made a donation, and Prince Takamatsu Nobuhito became honorary president. For the first five years the chairman of the Board of Directors was Count Kabayama Aisuke, well known as a friend of the United States and Great Britain. Its Advisory Body was made up of nine distinguished representatives from the government and learned institutions, the larger Body of Councillors of over 130 persons drawn from many fields. In June 1935 an informal Foreign Advisory Group was formed from members of the foreign community familiar with the society's work. Essentially, however, the Society for International Cultural Relations was an "outside agency" of the Foreign Ministry and received major financial support from that source. And within the ministry itself a Third Section was added to the Cultural Affairs Division to handle international cultural affairs. It should be noted also that when cultural activities directed to China and Southeast Asia were transferred first to the Asia Development Board and then to the new Greater East Asia Ministry, the cultural work remaining in the Foreign Ministry was shifted to the Fourth Section of the Research Division.

Regarding K.B.S. activities, it must be acknowledged that they were broadly cultural in nature and had only indirect political objectives. The society prepared and published bibliographies and introductory surveys on various aspects of Japanese life. It awarded fellowships to a number of young Westerners for study of Japanese culture. In 1935 it joined with the America-Japan Society in entertaining a large party of visiting ladies representing the Garden Clubs of America. The next year the society arranged for an exhibition of one hundred pieces of Japanese art in connection with the Harvard Tercentenary. In 1938 K.B.S. enlisted the help of the Tokyo Institute of Municipal Research in selecting books for the Japan Institute Library set up in an office in Rockefeller Center. It is significant, however, that when Maeda Tamon and Tanabe Sadayoshi went to the United States to take charge of this library, they did so as "unofficial staff" of the Foreign Ministry.

As Japan drew politically closer to Nazi Germany and fascist Italy, first in the Anti-Comintern Pact of 1936 and then in the Tripartite Pact of 1940, there was a corresponding increase in cultural relations with those countries. On November 25, 1938 Foreign Minister Arita Hachirō and German Ambassador Eugen Ott signed a formal cultural agreement. The agreement itself was couched in the most general terms, but an accompanying press release from the ministry outlined an extensive program of exchanges in many fields. Beneath the fanfare, however, the agreement was, according to Frank Iklé, essentially a compromise measure, designed to please Germany but not to increase political commitment beyond what had been agreed two years before. On March 23, 1939 a similar agreement on cultural cooperation was signed with Italy. In the case of both Italy and Germany, the formal cultural agreements confirmed a tendency toward more extensive exchanges already underway.

Foreign Students. Active efforts to bring foreign students to Japan were another manifestation of broadened cultural policy. The Sino-Japanese Association continued to provide dormitory facilities and other services for Chinese students, who after 1937 were drawn primarily from the areas under Japanese control. In 1935 the Japanese army, especially the Kwantung army, fostered the establishment of a Manchurian Students Scholastic Guidance and Assistance Association to operate hostels for students from Manchukuo. That same year the Foreign Ministry set up an International

Student Institute to deal with students from other areas. A new building in the Shinjuku district of Tokyo provided dormitory, library, and recreational facilities and classrooms for teaching the Japanese language. By 1941 the institute had assisted 280 students from twenty-two countries. The managing director at that time was Yatabe Yasukichi, whose career had been entirely in the diplomatic service.

After the outbreak of the Pacific War, emphasis shifted to students from the "liberated areas" of Southeast Asia. The aim, as Yatabe put it, was to "educate them perfectly in a complete understanding of the Japanese spirit, supply those countries permanently with a fixed number of capable and faithful leaders who could cooperate . . . in the glorious task of establishing the [Greater] East Asia Coprosperity Sphere, and devote themselves to the development of various races." In 1942 student exchange agreements were concluded with Siam and Indochina, and the International Student Institute was shifted to the control of the Greater East Asia Ministry. By the following year the incoming students were primarily those selected and sent by the Japanese army and navy, and a former army officer was put in charge of the language school. By the end of the war in 1945, 246 students had come from Siam, 121 from Indonesia, 64 from Burma, and 73 from the Philippines. Government subsidies to the institute, which had been only ¥50,000 in 1938, reached a peak of ¥1.25 million in 1944.

Cultural policy in a decade of militarism and war:

Grew, *Turbulent Era: A Diplomatic Record of Forty Years, 1904–1945* (2 vols., 1952), II, 948–49.

Kokusai Bunka Shinkōkai (Society for International Cultural Relations), an "outside agency" of the Foreign Ministry:

Japan, Gaimushō (Foreign Ministry), *Nihon gaikō nenkan* (1943), p. 179.
Kabayama Aisuke ō (1955) passes very lightly over Kabayama's connection with K.B.S.
Kokusai Bunka Shinkōkai, *K.B.S. Quarterly*, I, No. 1 (1935), 3, 4–6.
Tōkyō Shisei Chōsakai, *Tōkyō Shisei Chōsakai yonjūnenshi* (1962), p. 274.

Japanese government official cultural relations with Germany and Italy:

Iklé, *German-Japanese Relations, 1936–1940* (1956), p. 86.
Japan Times Weekly, December 1, 1938, pp. 5–6.
Kokusai Bunka Shinkōkai, *Nichi-Doku bunka kyōtei* (1939).

—— *Nichi-I bunka kyōtei* (1939).

Foreign students in Japan:

Supreme Commander for the Allied Powers, Education Research Branch, Civil Information and Education Section, General Headquarters, Far East Command, *Foreign Students in Japan, 1896–1947* (1948).

PROSPECT AND RETROSPECT

The broad outlines of Japan's use of cultural policy could quite easily be brought down to the present. After a hiatus during the years of military occupation, a politically independent and economically resurgent Japan resumed action along familiar lines. Once again Japanese eagerly turned outward to learn what was new, to adapt the most modern ideas and techniques for solution of their own problems. Professors and students again went abroad for academic work; productivity teams were sent out to learn the details of industrial techniques. The Japanese government has cooperated with sponsors abroad in sending out major art exhibitions, troupes of kabuki actors and *gagaku* musicians, and other manifestations of traditional culture. Somewhat hesitantly Japan has begun to reestablish its relationships with Southeast and South Asia and to explore shared elements in Asian cultures.

As one looks back over approximately one hundred years of Japan's modern cultural relations, there is a remarkable degree of continuity. The pervasive Japanese respect for culture as an important aspect of human life has been reflected in government policy. Except possibly at the height of wartime militarism, anti-cultural, anti-intellectual attitudes have not been strong in official circles. The Japanese government has not hesitated to use cultural means for national purposes. Once lines of policy have become embodied in bureaucratic practice, they have been remarkably persistent, despite frequent shifts in personnel.

For cultural policy, as for other aspects of Japanese foreign policy, the actual process of decision-making still requires much research and analysis. Complete historical data are hard to come by for specific cases. One gets the impression that the process is a complex one, with many lines of initiative and interest converging into a consensus that often remains implicit rather than openly defined. The examples and research materials introduced in this brief essay are intended as suggestions for work toward understanding in greater depth decision-making and policy execution in the broad area of Japanese cultural policy.

4

Japan's Policies Toward Britain

Ian H. Nish

❖

TOWARD FRIENDSHIP WITH BRITAIN, 1868–1907

In describing the major turning points in Japan's relations with Britain, it must first be established how Japan regarded Britain at the time of the Meiji Restoration. This can be deduced from remarks made in October 1873 when the Imperial Council was debating whether to send an expeditionary force to Korea. Ōkubo Toshimichi as a member of the council set out his views in a lengthy memorandum, in which he argued that there were two countries of vital importance to Japan—Russia and Britain—with both of whom relations were unsettled. "Throughout Asia Britain is especially strong . . . watching the scene avariciously and suddenly stepping in at a moment of crisis. Many of our foreign loans at present derive from Britain. If Japan now gets involved in trouble [over Korea], our godowns will become empty, our people will become poor, and we may not be able to honor our debts. Britain will certainly use this as a pretext to interfere in our internal affairs. . . . It was in this way that India became a British possession."[1] Ōkubo therefore urged that Japan should not implicate itself in an adventure in Korea, for fear of predatory actions by Britain and other European powers, and was successful in winning over the council. His statement is probably representative of the thinking toward Britain of those who acted as the leaders of the new Japan in the 1870s and 1880s.

Ōkubo's statement also throws light on several aspects of the world view of the Meiji leaders. First, it suggests that there were genuine fears of

---

[1] Katsuta Magoya, *Ōkubo Toshimichi den*, III (1911), 124–25.

foreign ambitions and a large measure of antiforeign feeling after the Restoration. The older *jōi* doctrines calling on the Japanese to "repel the barbarian" had generally disappeared, and the government was taking steps to prevent assaults on foreigners and their property. Nevertheless there was a deep-rooted fear of foreign expansion into Japan. Second, this suspicion was directed at European powers rather than at the United States. America, which had "opened" Japan and concluded the first commercial treaties, had lost some of its interest there because of the more pressing concerns of its own Civil War. As Ōkubo saw it, the main danger came from Britain, Russia, and France. Third, among those three powers, the main danger was thought to come from Britain, which held a major share of Japan's foreign trade and was its leading creditor. This was all the more surprising, as Britain had been the ally of the new leaders in the pre-Restoration struggles. It had thrown in its lot with the daimyō of Satsuma and Chōshū in their opposition to the shogun. Despite this, the new leaders of the Sat-Chō coalition seem to have regarded Britain not as a former ally, but as a power capable of invading their islands or of acting as it had done in India or China. Japan's worst suspicions seemed to be confirmed by the tough policy Britain had been pursuing under Sir Harry Parkes, its minister from 1865 to 1882.

The Meiji leaders adopted Ōkubo's proposal that Japan should not become involved in Korea but should instead work toward the revision of the treaties imposed during the late Tokugawa period. As Ōkubo wrote: "Japan's treaties with the various countries of Europe and America are unequal and contain many things which injure our standing as an independent power. Thus Britain and France, on the ground that Japan's internal situation is insecure and inadequate to protect their nationals, have built barracks and posted troops here as though our country was one of their dependencies." The revision of the treaties was urgently taken up by early Meiji governments.

Treaty Revision and Britain, 1868–1894. Negotiations for treaty revision dominated Anglo-Japanese relations for the first twenty-five years of the Meiji period to the virtual exclusion of other matters. Approaches were made to other powers; but Britain, as the country having the most trade with Japan, was the focus of the negotiations. When achievement of its wishes was delayed, Japan placed the blame on Britain. This was a serious accusation, because treaty revision was a part of Japan's struggle for independence and international recognition, and the repeated failures, although they could often be attributed to the maneuvering of politicians in Japan, were among the most emotionally charged subjects of the time. It is therefore important to give a brief sketch of Japan's approach to treaty revision and Britain's role in it.

The Meiji leaders sought to free Japan from two main features of the unequal treaties: extraterritorial jurisdiction and fixed tariffs. The Anglo-Japanese treaties of 1854 and 1858 gave Britain the privileges of appointing consuls and enjoying extraterritorial rights, while a memorandum on trade fixed the tariff on British exports and imports at 5 percent. After 1868 official approaches were made to Britain, and Iwakura Tomomi on his visit there discussed the possibility of revision at three conferences he had with the foreign secretary, Lord Granville. Terajima Munenori, foreign minister from 1873 to 1879, succeeded in concluding the Washington treaty of July 1878 whereby Japan would recover its tariff autonomy if other trading powers agreed. Britain, however, was not prepared to grant Japan the right to fix tariffs unilaterally, though it agreed to discuss an increase in the tariff rate.[2] On the broader issue of extraterritorial privileges, the most Britain would concede was that its treaties with Japan would be modified when Japanese laws attained the standards of Western countries. This gave rise to the widespread feeling in Japan that Britain was the main obstacle to the achievement of treaty revision.

From 1880 to 1889 Japan persevered in conducting negotiations by assembling representatives of the trading powers at conferences in Tokyo. In July 1880 a draft treaty was circulated among the powers. Britain expressed disapproval on the ground that the draft represented a complete overhauling of the treaties themselves rather than merely a revision of existing provisions. At a conference in January 1882, a majority of the treaty powers approved the Japanese proposals, except for Britain and France. The conference continued for six months without reaching any solution. When Britain showed itself to be the spearhead of the opposition, the Japanese foreign minister laid fresh proposals before the British minister

---

[2]Salisbury to Ueno, February 11, 1878, in Japan, Gaimushō (Foreign Ministry), *Nihon gaikō nempyō narabi ni shuyō bunsho* (1965; first published, 1955), I, 73–74 (hereafter cited as *Nihon gaikō nempyō*; page references, unless otherwise noted, are to the section of documents).

in Tokyo in August 1884.[3] The British government, however, joined with Germany two years later to suggest a basis for settlement containing constructive ideas of their own, and at a conference in April 1887, it was agreed to adopt their formula with substantial amendments. This decision met with a storm of opposition within Japan and prevented the agreement from being adopted.[4]

Foreign Minister Ōkuma Shigenobu (1888–89) persuaded the cabinet that collective conferences should be dropped in favor of parallel discussions with separate countries simultaneously. This bore immediate fruit in a treaty signed with Mexico (1888) and agreements reached with the United States, Germany, and Russia (1889). Britain, however, wanted consultation with the other powers and offered so many amendments that the agreements had to be deferred. The terms of the draft leaked through to the London *Times*, and opinion in Japan was roused by the nature of the Japanese proposals, which were thought to be humiliating to national dignity. An Imperial Conference in October opposed a settlement on this basis and the Kuroda Kiyotaka cabinet resigned.[5]

Starting on a fresh basis, the new cabinet headed by Yamagata Aritomo decided in February 1890 to open negotiations first with Britain. The justification for this was that Britain had the largest stake in Japan's foreign trade and had been the most demanding of the powers in earlier negotiations. The proposals met with a "generous response" from the British government, although it sought numerous changes.[6] Indeed, a workable settlement seemed in sight when the foreign minister was forced to resign in May 1891 because of the Ōtsu Incident involving an attempt on the life of the visiting Russian crown prince.

Mutsu Munemitsu (foreign minister from 1892 to 1896) also proceeded on the assumption that once Britain was satisfied, the other powers would follow suit. The cabinet accepted his plea that the new proposal should be for a completely bilateral treaty, that is, one which conferred equal benefits on both parties.[7] After a few initial parleys, the negotiations were opened

[3]Inoue to Plunkett, August 4, 1884, in *ibid.*, pp. 97–100.

[4]Anglo-German proposals, June 15, 1886, in *ibid.*, pp. 107–11.

[5]December 10, 1889, in *ibid.*, pp. 129–32.

[6]F.C. Jones, *Extraterritoriality in Japan and the Diplomatic Relations Resulting in Its Abolition, 1853–1899* (1931), p. 140.

[7]Japan, Gaimushō (Foreign Ministry), *Jōyaku kaisei kankei Nihon gaikō bunsho*, IV (1960), 1–2, Document 1.

in London in April 1894, and the treaty was concluded on July 16. It consisted of a new tariff which was to be introduced from the date of signature and a treaty on extraterritoriality to take effect after the Japanese legal codes had been fully amended and introduced. This was accomplished in 1899 when consular jurisdiction for Britain and other countries that had concluded separate treaties on the lines of the Anglo-Japanese treaty ceased.

For various reasons the treaty of 1894 cannot be treated as an important turning point in Anglo-Japanese relations. Negotiations had been opened with Britain not because Britain had in the past been sympathetic but because it had been obstructionist. The treaty entailed benefits which mainly came into effect after five years. Its announcement was followed within a fortnight by the outbreak of war with China and was lost in the excitement of that event. Thus, Britain's conciliatory policy could hardly be expected to make much immediate difference in relations with Japan.

On the other hand, it was important that treaty revision had at last been accomplished after a long succession of failures had made revision a psychological problem for all politically minded Japanese.[8] Did the Japanese feel some gratitude to Britain because it took the first step? Or were they resentful of Britain as the main obstacle in the past to treaty revision? The authorities are divided. The view that Britain was the main obstacle is taken by Conroy, Yanaga, and Kamikawa (among others).

Conroy, *The Japanese Seizure of Korea, 1868–1910* (1960).
Kamikawa, *Japan-American Diplomatic Relations in the Meiji-Taisho Era* (1958), pp. 137–55.
Yanaga, *Japan since Perry* (1949), pp. 191–97.

But the author of the only specialized study, F.C. Jones, is inclined to defend Britain for delaying the abolition of extraterritoriality until the new Japanese legal system had proved itself.

Jones, *Extraterritoriality in Japan and the Diplomatic Relations Resulting in Its Abolition, 1853–1899* (1931).

Perhaps it is true that Britain in the period from 1890 onward may have redeemed some of the bad reputation it had acquired during the previous two decades. In the earlier period it was certainly Britain's voice that was decisive in preventing treaty revision. But it may be that even then Britain

[8]Memorandum by Aoki, London, July 19, 1894, in *Nihon gaikō nempyō*, I, 152–54.

was blamed too much: it was not really possible to reach a consensus among the powers since they were commercial rivals and were jockeying for position in the Japanese market. After 1890 some credit was due Britain for recognizing Japan as the first country in the world where extraterritorial arrangements could be removed.

Rapprochement, 1894–1898. Japan's leaders found it hard to gauge Britain's likely reaction to war with China, which was in the offing. Would Britain intervene, as in the past, to prevent hostilities in the Far East? Would Britain support China and in an emergency join the war on the Chinese side? Britain was traditionally more friendly to China than to Japan. Aoki Shūzō, the Japanese minister in London, suggested that it was necessary for Japan to keep Britain and China apart and was confident that this could be done since Britain was becoming disillusioned with Li Hung-chang and the Peking government.[9] On the other hand, the dispute which was looming ahead concerned Korea, where Russia had already shown itself to be an interested party. That Britain took Russian interference there seriously was shown in its occupation of Port Hamilton between 1885 and 1887. It was therefore feasible, in Aoki's view, for Japan to appeal to Britain on the ground that Russia should not be allowed to gain anything from the disturbed condition of Korea. He was confident, he told Japan's foreign minister, that Britain would look favorably on Japan's actions in Korea provided they did not injure British interests and were effective in preventing Russian aggression there.[10]

The nearest Japan came to a declaration of policy toward Britain was in a message from the foreign minister on July 18, 1894, which read: "England has been very friendly to us in connection with treaty revision, and since the Russian intervention she has shown us goodwill in every way. Moreover our object is to contend against China and Korea, and it is deemed highly important that we should maintain good terms as far as possible with other powers."[11] Japan would try not to alienate Britain or any other power. From June onward, however, when Britain was busily

[9]*Ibid.*

[10]Aoki to Mutsu, June 12, 1894, in Japan, Gaimushō (Foreign Ministry), *Nihon gaikō bunsho*, XXVII/2 (1953), 268–69, Document 612 (hereafter cited as *Nihon gaikō bunsho*).

[11]F. Hilary Conroy, *The Japanese Seizure of Korea, 1868–1910: A Study of Realism and Idealism in International Relations* (1960), p. 257.

occupied in mediating between Japan and China, the Japanese did not go out of their way to accept British suggestions. For a while Japan showed itself interested; but from July 11, when it decided on war, Japan turned down British overtures and began to take preparatory steps against China.

At the start of the war, the Japanese made two important gestures toward Britain. They promised that "no warlike operations shall be undertaken against Shanghai or its approaches," where British commercial interests were mainly at stake.[12] They further offered compensation if Japan was found to be responsible for the sinking of the British-owned merchant vessel, *Kowshing*. The Japanese government, however, became distinctly less conciliatory to Britain after the latter declared its strict neutrality and thereby showed that the suspected alliance with China did not exist.

For the rest of the war there was an underlying hostility toward Britain, whose offers of mediation were rejected. There seems to be ample support for the view that "during the war with China, feelings in Japan were by no means friendly to England. Her arbitrary limitation of the area of hostilities was strongly felt by our military men."[13] As the Japanese armies advanced, their commanders found that their plan of attack on China was frustrated by the guarantees given to Britain and threatened to withdraw them. Prime Minister Itō Hirobumi wrote in a private letter in October that Britain was "rousing foreign powers against Japan."[14] So suspicious did Itō become of Britain that he wanted to entrust Russia with an advance indication of Japan's peace terms. If the powers did intervene in the struggle as most Japanese statesmen expected, it looked as though Britain, and not Russia, would be their leader.

It was only with the coming of the peace that the chance of intervention by the powers materialized. On April 4 Japan informed the powers of its peace terms in the hope of winning their approval. John W. Kimberley, the British foreign secretary, was asked for his support, but he seemed to be indifferent to Far Eastern problems. Then the Chinese government invited the powers to intervene on its behalf. While Russia, France, and Germany were inclined to accept, Britain showed little interest. On April 23 the three

[12]Mutsu to Paget, July 23, 1894, in *Nihon gaikō bunsho*, XXVII/2, 400–2, Documents 734–35.

[13]A.M. Pooley, ed., *The Secret Memoirs of Count Tadasu Hayashi* (1915), p. 113.

[14]Itō to Mutsu, October 16, 1894, in *Nihon gaikō bunsho*, XXVII/2, 478–79, Document 799.

ministers handed over notes in Tokyo recommending the return of the Liaotung Peninsula. By a clear change in policy, Japan tried to enlist the practical support of Britain together with the United States and Italy in an attempt to neutralize the effect of the Triple Intervention. Britain was sympathetic enough but declined to interfere; it was opposed to using force where it had so little at stake. On April 26 Japan appealed again, inquiring how much help Japan could expect from Britain, and received the reply that "Britain previously decided to observe strict neutrality and wishes to maintain the same attitude now. Although it holds Japan in very warm regard . . . it cannot help her over the proposed concessions." Authorities agree that it was Britain's refusal that put an end to Mutsu's scheme for standing up to the three powers. That day it was decided at an Imperial Conference to accept the advice of the three powers, and the cabinet proceeded to arrange for permanent withdrawal from Liaotung.[15]

What were Japan's relations with Britain at this stage? Is there evidence of the later Anglo-Japanese alliance developing in 1894–95? Certainly Britain twice abstained from action which could have been damaging to Japan. First, Britain could have used the signing of the Anglo-Japanese treaty of 1894 as a lever to prevent Japan from going to war but, after some hesitancy, the foreign secretary did sign it and let Japan follow its own plans. Second, Britain could have joined the Triple Intervention but refused the invitation. In these negative ways, Britain identified itself as the power most favorable to Japan's objectives. But Britain never thought seriously of positive intervention on Japan's behalf. In any case, it was too early yet to speak of Japan's approaching Britain for an alliance. Japan had asked Britain in 1895 for help on an ad hoc basis, although it was not too sanguine of Britain's response. Britain was not yet looked on as a source of long-term friendship.

Finding itself during the crisis of 1895 without supporters, Japan took the difficult decision to lie low for a while to build up its strength. That is why Japan played little or no part during the 1898 crisis in the Far East—it was for the most part an observer. By reason of earlier experiences Japan was drawn to Britain rather than the other powers, but that alignment was not a close one and did not result in effective action. Japan's diffidence may best be illustrated by the way in which it consented to the transfer

[15] *Nihon gaikō nempyō*, I, 171.

of Weihaiwei to Britain. This was done in such a two-edged way that the goodwill of the gesture was largely lost. In February 1898 China offered Britain the lease of Weihaiwei after the Liaotung indemnity was paid and Japanese troops were evacuated. Britain consulted Japan and received the reply that it had been Japan's desire that China should take over Weihaiwei but that "from the moment it is unable to do so, Japan has no objection to its possession by a power disposed to assist in maintaining the independence of China." The British cabinet was disappointed by Japan's lukewarm response and sought clarification. Japan would offer "concurrence" in Britain's intention but not the "approval and support" for which Britain asked.[16] Unaccountably, the Japanese went on to ask Britain for "support" if Japan should find it necessary to take similar measures; these were unspecified but may have referred to a lease in Fukien, which did not materialize.[17]

Japan tempered its policy toward Britain with caution because its main overseas concern was with Korea, where Britain had few interests. It was even then negotiating an understanding with Russia over Korea, which was finally concluded as the Nishi-Rosen agreement of April 25, 1898.

There was no clear-cut Japanese policy toward Britain in this period. Some have detected evidence of a rapprochement after the Triple Intervention of 1895, and there were specific incidents where both stood on the same side; however, there was little sign of practical cooperation. Indeed, Japan's policy at this time may best be described as nonalignment, not identifying itself automatically with any power grouping but pursuing its own interests cautiously and inconspicuously. Not that the Japanese leaders were opposed to alignments. They thought it necessary to prepare for them by diplomatic means. In their approach to Britain, they sent as minister to London in 1894 a person of extremely pro-British sympathies, Katō Takaaki. Meanwhile, in the military field, as Mutsu Munemitsu wrote in his political testament, it was felt that Japan should look to its strength and, as its army and navy increased, should woo Britain as its ally.[18]

---

[16]Komura to Satō, April 2, 1898, in *Nihon gaikō bunsho*, XXXI/1 (1954), 423–24, Document 371.

[17]April 22–24, 1898, in *Nihon gaikō nempyō*, I, 185–86.

[18]Mutsu Munemitsu, *Kenkenroku* (1939), written shortly before Mutsu's death in August 1897.

The First Alliance with Britain, 1899–1902. Over the next two decades the keynote of Japan's foreign policy was the Anglo-Japanese alliance, which was first signed on January 30, 1902. Japan's decision in favor of the agreement, which involved an overall appraisal of its foreign policy, was made at meetings of the cabinet and genrō in December 1901. The issues at stake, which had been under discussion for some six months, are generally presented in their simplest form: would Japan align itself with Britain or Russia? But the choice was not really such a straightforward alternative.

On November 28 the cabinet of General Katsura Tarō accepted, with amendments, a draft treaty it had received from the British government and thus committed itself in principle to alliance with Britain. But the emperor refused to accept the decision without consulting the elder statesmen, who were divided into two camps, one group favoring arrangements with Russia and the other, with Britain. The first included Inoue Kaoru and Itō Hirobumi, who was then in St. Petersburg and on December 4 was to present the Russian foreign minister with the draft of a Russo-Japanese agreement of his own devising. The emperor insisted that Itō be consulted, even when he was so far away. The remainder of the genrō were called to a meeting in Tokyo on December 7.

In preparation for the meeting, Foreign Minister Komura Jutarō wrote a memorandum on behalf of the British agreement and in opposition to an agreement with Russia, which might or might not be available. His main argument was that an agreement with Britain, which he felt was a sated power, was more likely to be enduring than one with Russia, which was still pursuing its ambitions. Without necessarily accepting Komura's arguments, the genrō (including Inoue) favored concluding the agreement with Britain. When Itō's hostile comments arrived from Europe next day, they were referred by the emperor to the cabinet, which turned them down "since it was not possible to foresee a Russo-Japanese agreement materializing and further delay would only induce Britain to withdraw its proposals."[19]

This was not really a decision in favor of Britain rather than Russia. It implied that Japan would conclude an agreement with Britain in order to strengthen itself for later bargaining with Russia over Korea rather than

---

[19]Memorandum by Komura, December 7, 1901, in *Nihon gaikō nempyō*, I, 201–3.

trying to settle with the Russians while diplomatically isolated. The leaders had to decide upon priorities rather than among alternatives.

These were the crucial decisions that clinched the policy of alliance with Britain and opened the way for the final stage of negotiations. They also represented the culmination of a period of Anglo-Japanese cooperation. There had been earlier instances in which Japan had been aligned with Britain against Russia. But because of the indecision of the Japanese leaders and especially the known desires of the Itō group for a "reinsurance treaty" with Russia, these had not resulted in overtures being made. When did Anglo-Japanese relations reach a stage where the alliance became a possibility? This is a subject of some controversy.

It is doubtful whether the alliance became a practical proposition before the Boxer troubles in China and the siege of Peking. It was at this time that Japan gave up the policy of isolation or noninvolvement it seemed to have been following since 1895. When Japan considered sending troops to China to join the international force, it first consulted and got the approval of Britain. Britain had sufficient confidence in Japan to urge it on three occasions to send a strong force to China. On June 23, 1900 Britain appealed to Japan on account "of the critical condition of the legations and also of the force which has been sent to relieve them" and asked it "to send a further force to their succour." But the Japanese found Russia, France, and Germany reluctant to agree to a large Japanese force being sent to Peking. So Britain, which was the prime advocate of a Japanese expedition, had to intercede for Japan with the powers. Britain got undertakings that no objection would be raised and renewed its appeal to Japan. On July 6 the Japanese decided to send the Fifth Division, thus bringing their force in China to 22,000 men, and to mobilize further troops. A week later Britain offered Japan financial aid up to £1 million if it agreed to send 20,000 troops in addition to its existing promises.[20] But the Japanese government, on the advice of army leaders, declined the offer.

This episode is evidence of a special relationship developing between Japan and Britain. Japan went far toward accommodating Britain even though it knew that such action was unwelcome to the other powers. Britain found itself arguing on Japan's behalf with the powers that had

[20]*Ibid.*, p. 194.

brought about the crisis in 1895. Japan was not yet aligned but was veering toward Britain over problems in China. On the other hand, where Britain had only minor interests and Japan was seriously involved, as in Korea and Manchuria, Japan had to look circumspectly to the other three powers. Thus, in July 1900 Foreign Minister Aoki Shūzō sent Russia a draft treaty offering recognition of Russian interests in Manchuria in return for recognition of Japan's interests in Korea. Russia declined, and Japan asked Germany whether it would "raise any objection to Japan placing Korea under [Japan's] sphere of influence." Germany replied noncommittally and Japan decided not to proceed. This illustrates how Japan came to see that mere recognition by Britain would not improve its position in Korea and that it was indispensable to negotiate with Russia directly to that end.[21]

After the relief of the Peking legations, Russia withdrew its large forces to Manchuria, from where they menaced Japan's interests in Korea. The Japanese reacted much less timidly than their attitude in 1900 suggested. Indeed, at one stage in March 1901, war seemed likely between Japan and Russia, but the Russians dropped their demands about China for the time being. Tension persisted throughout 1901, and most Japanese leaders (apart from exceptions like Itō) preferred to avoid negotiations with Russia and to resort instead to talks with Britain. This was probably a victory within Japan for the bureaucrats of the Army and Foreign ministries, both of which were traditionally anti-Russian. In this atmosphere, negotiations between Britain and Japan proceeded slowly from July 1901 to the signing of the alliance in January 1902.

The Second Alliance with Britain, 1902–1905. One of the common misapprehensions about the first alliance was that it prevented Japan from seeking a peaceful solution of mutual problems with Russia and thus contributed to the outbreak of the Russo-Japanese War in 1904. On the contrary, Japan took the precaution of securing assurances from Britain that it might negotiate separately with Russia to relieve tension in the Far East. The British foreign secretary, in conversation with Itō in January 1902, for example, confirmed that there could be no objection to such negotiations provided their objects were not incompatible with the

---

[21]I. H. Nish, "Japan's Indecision during the Boxer Disturbances" (1961).

alliance.[22] It is probable that, whether Britain agreed or not, Japan intended to undertake such talks. Thus, in January 1902 the Japanese cabinet confirmed that it "desired to come to an arrangement with Russia over Korea," although it did not for the present intend to give final orders for the conclusion of an agreement with Russia.[23] This implies that the Anglo-Japanese agreement of 1902 was not an exclusive one that prevented a peaceful solution of Russo-Japanese differences.

It was not surprising, therefore, that Japan, on August 12, 1903, handed to Russia a *note verbale* protesting Russia's continued occupation of Manchuria but offering a settlement on the basis of the exchange of Russian predominance in Manchuria for Japanese predominance in Korea—the so-called "Manchuria-Korea exchange" plan. Japan did not consult Britain, and Britain thought it unwise to mediate lest it be held responsible either for urging Japan to go to war or for restraining Japan from a "just war." Thus, when Japan asked for financial aid on January 1, 1904, Britain declined on the ground that a loan would only encourage Japan to declare war and would to that extent be provocative.[24] Nonetheless, Britain had earlier shown that its sympathies were with Japan when it purchased two Chilean battleships for its own navy to prevent their being sold to the Russians.

At the outbreak of war in February 1904, Japan made it plain that it had no intention of invoking Britain's intervention under the alliance unless special circumstances arose. The Japanese never had occasion to call for British assistance even in the face of the Russian Baltic fleet. Britain therefore maintained a policy of strict neutrality during the war, although it sympathized with the Japanese cause.

These aspects of the war are emphasized to dispel two common notions. Japan's overture to Russia in 1903 was not a shift in policy from its alliance with Britain but was perfectly consistent with that alliance; and secondly, Japan was not pushed into war with Russia by Britain nor did the Anglo-

[22]Great Britain, Foreign Office, *British Documents on the Origins of the War, 1898–1914*, Vol. II, *The Anglo-Japanese Alliance and the Franco-British Entente* (1927), pp. 108–11, Document 120.

[23]Kurino to Itō, January 20, 1902, in Hiratsuka Atsushi, ed., *Itō Hirobumi hiroku* (1929), Supplement, p. 58, Document 71.

[24]Komura to Hayashi, December 31, 1903, in *Nihon gaikō nempyō*, I, 220.

Japanese alliance precipitate the war. Japan entered the war of its own volition, without pressure or restraint from Britain.

It was in the later stages of the war, when things were going in its favor, that Japan decided to enter into the second Anglo-Japanese agreement, a decision which was much less of a turning point than that of 1902. The Japanese cabinet first decided on April 8, 1905 to suggest to Britain that the 1902 treaty should merely be renewed for an extended period. Britain, however, did not agree to a simple renewal on the existing terms and asked for it to be expanded to cover the obligations of an offensive-defensive alliance and for its scope to be extended to take in India. On May 24, a few days before the crucial naval battle of Tsushima took place, the Japanese cabinet agreed to revise the alliance on these terms, which certainly seemed to favor Britain.[25]

The cabinet wanted the alliance to be continued, if one may judge from its resolution, because of a double fear of Russia and of isolation after the war. Even if Japan were successful in the war, it could not destroy Russia's great potential to make trouble in the future. "Since Russia will increase its armaments in the Far East significantly in order to take revenge some day, it is necessary for us to take increased precautions. . . . If Japan concludes an offensive-defensive alliance with Britain and builds up its armaments to the same extent as Russia's in the Far East, there is less likelihood of Russia contemplating revenge."[26] Equally strong was Japan's fear of isolation from the rest of the world. The more successful Japan was in the war, the more the powers would turn against it. For Japan to accept a radical revision of the alliance was therefore not a shortsighted decision based on anxiety that it might not defeat the Russians in the forthcoming naval battle, but one based on the recognition that even if Japan won the war decisively, it would need friends in the postwar period. With these motives, the revised Anglo-Japanese agreement was signed in London on August 12, 1905.

In 1905 there was not the opposition to the treaty that had been generated in 1901 by Itō and Inoue in their capacity as genrō. Until the start of the Russo-Japanese War, Itō still clung to his pro-Russian views and his desire to negotiate a settlement with Russia before all else. As war approached, he could no longer claim that the alternative of a Russo-

[25]*Nihon gaikō bunsho*, XXXVIII/1 (1958), 7–8, Document 10.
[26]*Ibid.*, pp. 15–17, Document 18.

Japanese agreement existed. The alliance of 1905 was therefore concluded with general approval, including the cordial agreement of Itō and without the delaying tactics he had used earlier. Negotiation of the alliance of 1905 was not completed until the military and naval aspects, which had been left for later discussion by experts, were ironed out. This could not be arranged until May 1907, when Admiral Yamamoto Gonnohyōe and General Nishi Kanjirō visited Britain to conduct discussions.[27] The Japanese had found that part of the 1902 agreement committing Britain to maintain a Far Eastern squadron equal to that of Russia to be the greatest advantage which they derived from the alliance. In 1905 they again tried to commit Britain to keep a large Far Eastern squadron even after the defeat of the Russian fleet. Britain refused and Japan did not pursue the demand. From 1905 onward Britain withdrew its battleships from the Far East. The naval-military discussions of 1907 did not alter its position and were unquestionably a disappointment to the Japanese. Nonetheless, Japan became the dominant naval power in the Far East and the Pacific.

Paradoxically, the second alliance increased the scope and extended the obligations imposed on the signatories but was less effective than the first alliance. By 1907 Japan learned that it had less common ground with Britain than before Russia's defeat. While there were still some who tried to restore the alliance, it never regained the standing it had had for both parties between 1902 and 1905.

Government documents:

France, Ministère des affaires étrangères, *Documents diplomatiques français, 1871–1914* (1929–59).

Germany, Auswärtiges Amt, *Die grosse Politik der europäischen Kabinette, 1871–1914* (40 vols., 1922–27).

Great Britain, Foreign Office, *British Documents on the Origins of the War, 1898–1914* (11 vols., 1926–38). Vol. II, *The Anglo-Japanese Alliance and the Franco-British Entente* (1927), Vol. IV, *The Anglo-Russian Rapprochement, 1903–1907* (1929), and Vol. VIII, *Arbitration, Neutrality and Security* (1932), are most relevant to this theme. British published material on Far Eastern affairs, however, is small. To compensate for this there are abundant blue books. The archives of the British Foreign Office for Japan and China are open to researchers in accordance with a thirty-year rule.

[27] *Nihon gaikō bunsho*, XL/1 (1960), sec. 3, 27–46.

Japan, Gaimushō (Foreign Ministry), *Nihon gaikō bunsho* (1936–   ).

—— *Jōyaku kaisei kankei Nihon gaikō bunsho* (4 vols., 1941–50). Material on the Anglo-Japanese commercial treaty of 1894 is contained in IV (1950), 1–25.

—— *Nihon gaikō nempyō narabi ni shuyō bunsho* (2 vols., 1965; first published, 1955).

Biographies and memoirs. English:

Allen, *The Rt. Hon. Sir Ernest Satow: A Memoir* (1933).

Dickins and Poole, *The Life of Sir Harry Parkes* (1894), II, is relevant to the period under discussion.

Pooley, *The Secret Memoirs of Count Tadasu Hayashi* (1915), is a vital work which contains a detailed account of the alliance of 1902 but nothing on 1905. It is also interesting for Hayashi's first period as foreign minister, 1906–8. The opening of the British archives and the publication of Japanese documents have not altered the fundamentals of the account it gives of the negotiations of 1901, although Itō's unconstructive role in them was in any case widely known throughout the Far East long before the publication of Pooley's work. The authenticity of these memoirs is often called into question, since there is no Japanese counterpart for them. But the account of events which they give is recognizably similar to Hayashi's official writings. Naturally, Hayashi is inclined to play up his own role in events. A textual comparison of Pooley's book with relevant documents in *Nihon gaikō bunsho* would be useful for future research.

Rich and Fisher, *The Holstein Papers*, Vol. IV (1963).

Satow, *A Diplomat in Japan* (1921), describes his experiences during a formative period in Anglo-Japanese relations, 1862–69.

Siebold, *Japan's Accession to the Comity of Nations* (1901).

Biographies and memoirs. Japanese:

Aoki, *Aoki Shūzō jiden* (1970).

—— *Jōyaku kaisei kiji* (1891).

Inoue Kaoru Kō Denki Hensankai, *Segai Inoue kō den* (5 vols., 1933–34), is informative on major issues of policy.

Ishii, *Gaikō yoroku* (1930), throws some light on the alliance negotiations.

Itō, *Katō Takaaki* (1929), Vol. I, is the most detailed biography of a diplomat. Katō was minister to London, 1895–99, and ambassador to London, 1909–13.

Japan, Gaimushō (Foreign Ministry), *Komura gaikōshi* (1953), Vol. II, an official diplomatic biography of Komura Jutarō, is useful for the late Meiji period, when Komura consistently held high office.

Shumpō Kō Tsuishōkai, *Itō Hirobumi den* (3 vols., 1940), is informative on major issues of policy until Itō's death in 1909.

Tokutomi, *Kōshaku Katsura Tarō den* (2 vols., 1917), also is valuable on major policy issues.

—— *Kōshaku Yamagata Aritomo den* (3 vols., 1933), is of similar importance.

Anglo-Japanese relations:

Japan, Gaimushō (Foreign Ministry), "Nichi-Ei gaikōshi" (2 vols., 1937, printed for private circulation).

Kajima, *Nichi-Ei gaikōshi* (1957), is the most valuable study of Anglo-Japanese relations for this period. The work begins with Will Adams and ends with the Washington Conference. Written too early to make use of published Japanese documents beyond the year 1900, it covers the same ground as the earlier Foreign Ministry work cited above, for whose publication Kajima was partially responsible in the Foreign Ministry.

Standard works on the unequal treaties and treaty revision:

Jones, *Extraterritoriality in Japan and the Diplomatic Relations Resulting in Its Abolition, 1853–1899* (1931).
Yamamoto, *Jōyaku kaiseishi* (1943).

Crisis of 1894–95. Both of the following books take up aspects of Anglo-Japanese relations as part of larger studies:

Conroy, *The Japanese Seizure of Korea, 1868–1910* (1960).
Tabohashi, *Nisshin sen'eki gaikōshi no kenkyū* (1951).

Triple Intervention, 1895:

Rich and Fisher, *The Holstein Papers*, Vol. III (1961), has much to say about the motives of Germany and the European powers toward the intervention and about the reactions of Japan as seen from the viewpoint of the German Foreign Office.

First and second Anglo-Japanese alliances:

Chang, *The Anglo-Japanese Alliance* (1931), is a sound work based on the English and German published documents then available; emphasis is placed on the impact of the alliance on Korea and China.

Dennis, *The Anglo-Japanese Alliance* (1923), is in the nature of a tract against pre-1914 entente diplomacy.

Gal'perin, *Anglo-Iaponskii soiuz, 1902–1921 gg* (1947), offers the most comprehensive treatment of the subject, using a wide range of sources in Japanese, German, French, English, and Russian.

Imai, "Nichi-Ei dōmei kōshō ni okeru Nihon no shuchō" (1957), examines the diplomacy of Japan from the Manchurian crisis of March 1901 to the conclusion of the alliance.

Langer, *The Diplomacy of Imperialism, 1890–1902* (2d ed., 1951), links the alliance to European diplomacy in Asia, treating the whole range of European imperialist ventures from 1890 to 1902.

Nish, *The Anglo-Japanese Alliance* (1966).

Shinobu and Nakayama, *Nichi-Ro sensōshi no kenkyū* (1959), is perhaps the best extended treatment of Japan's activities in Korea and Manchuria and offers a valuable description of the setting in which the Anglo-Japanese alliance took root. The work of several hands, it is a comprehensive study of the period down to 1905.

Japan's policy toward Great Britain during the Russo-Japanese War:

Suematsu, *The Risen Sun* (1905), is a book of articles written mainly for the European press. Suematsu, who was Itō's son-in-law, was sent to Britain for the period of the war to publish information that would show Japan in a favorable light in Britain and on the continent. The material contained in this volume is therefore important for an understanding of Japan's foreign policy. It was only one part of a large apologetic literature appearing in English at this time.

Takahashi, *Takahashi Korekiyo jiden* (1936), provides a detailed account of Takahashi's experiences as Japan's financial commissioner during the Russo-Japanese War, when he was responsible for negotiating war loans in Europe and America.

Japan's policy toward Britain before 1898 has not attracted many researchers; in a number of bibliographies consulted, there is no mention of any monographic study. Such a field may not offer many subjects of the highest significance before Japan became a leading power. Nonetheless, there is some scope for research into the subjects discussed earlier, which are all to some extent disputed and controversial. One such subject would be Britain's image in Japan after the Restoration, apparently a combination of suspicion and respect, which can be illustrated from the Iwakura Embassy of 1871–73 and the Itō mission of 1882–83. There is also room for a reassessment of the revision of the Anglo-Japanese commercial treaties in the light of the archives of both countries. It might be hoped that the records of business houses and chambers of commerce and the English-language newspapers of the Japanese treaty ports would supply useful information on the economic background to treaty revision. Third, there is a group of research topics connected with Britain's role during the 1894–95 crisis. Was there any substance to Japan's fear of Britain's entering the war on China's side? Was there any prospect of Britain supporting Japan during the Triple Intervention?

There are many issues connected with Anglo-Japanese relations in the period from 1898 to 1907 which are ripe for further research. There is not the dearth of publications of diplomatic interest that is a handicap for the earlier period. Material is abundant in the *Nihon gaikō bunsho* series, which becomes much more detailed in its coverage from 1900 onward and includes supplementary volumes on special topics.

In addition to the main course of Anglo-Japanese relations, there are a number of peripheral topics toward which research could usefully be directed. One such subject is Japan's policy toward Korea and Manchuria and its effect on Britain. What influence did Japan's policies there have on the growth of anti-alliance feeling in Britain during these years? Did the Japanese modify their policies at all for fear of British opposition?

Another topic is Japanese emigration to the British dominions and its effect on the alliance. What did the Japanese think of their virtual exclusion from Australia, Canada, and other parts of the British empire? Did it result in opposition to the alliance itself? A detailed study of these countries, either together or separately, would be invaluable; and there are plenty of published documents in *Nihon gaikō bunsho* for Canada and Australia. One of the puzzles is that there is not much evidence of the thinking in Tokyo. This suggests two possible interpretations: either that the Japanese felt so deep a sense of grievance they kept silent about it, or that it was not a matter of high policy which would have been allowed to supersede superior aspects of policy like the alliance. On the surface the second seems the more plausible explanation.

THE ALLIANCE WEAKENED AND ENDED, 1907–1930

The Third Alliance with Britain, 1907–1912. Relations between Britain and Japan after the Russo-Japanese War were ruffled by Japan's activities in Manchuria and Korea. As early as March 1906, Britain and the United States had protested to Japan that it was not observing the doctrine of the Open Door in Manchuria and was using its political control to benefit its own nationals.[28] Even after this was settled there were persistent disputes

---

[28] *Nihon gaikō nempyō*, I, 258–59.

over railways. Japan's activities in Korea excited Britain's suspicion, although this was less marked than over Manchuria. As against this, there was a cluster of new agreements—the Franco-Japanese agreement (June 10, 1907), the Russo-Japanese agreement (July 30, 1907), and the Anglo-Russian entente (August 31, 1907)—that certainly lessened the tensions out of which the Anglo-Japanese partnership had originally arisen.

There was evidently an important reassessment of Japan's foreign relations in the years 1907–8 which throws light on its relations with Britain. This may have been touched off by Yamagata's plan for national defense which was presented to the Throne in October 1906. In it Russia was identified as the major enemy, and the main defense obligations were directed against Russia in accordance with the Anglo-Japanese alliance.[29] A year later, in 1907, when Itō as resident-general in Korea presented his views on "the attitude of Britain, Germany, and the United States toward Japan," he was inclined to doubt whether the alliance was still so decisive. Itō thought that, with the recent conclusion of the various treaties with Russia, Britain felt the main source of trouble for the future had disappeared and the value of the Japanese alliance was no longer so great. Germany was suspicious of Japan because of the "yellow peril." If Japan was to avoid being isolated, Itō thought it must pay more attention to the needs of other powers.[30]

Foreign Minister Hayashi Tadasu, in placing Itō's views before the cabinet and the genrō, stressed that Japan should make the British alliance the vital instrument of its foreign policy and should follow in the commercial sphere the principles of equal opportunity and the Open Door.[31] Itō and Hayashi were both convinced that Britain was being alienated by Japan's commercial aggressiveness in Manchuria and China. The policy of the Open Door was probably honored by Hayashi and his successor, Komura Jutarō, although it was often difficult to get officials on the spot to accept the rulings of Tokyo.

Despite the striving of governments, the tendency was for Britain and Japan to drift apart. There was the deterioration in relations between Japan and the United States over immigration and Manchuria, which Britain

---

[29]Ōyama Azusa, "Yamagata Aritomo teikoku kokubō hōshin an" (1961).

[30]Itō to Hayashi, November 6, 1907, in *Nihon gaikō bunsho*, XL/3 (1961), 789–91, Document 2199.

[31]Hayashi to Cabinet, November 29, 1907, in *ibid.*, pp. 791–803, Document 2200.

could not overlook. There was the Russo-Japanese agreement of 1910 which showed that the two powers were ready to cooperate over railways and railway finance in Manchuria. There was the annexation of Korea in August 1910, to which Britain raised no official objection but which naturally caused some apprehension. In practice the most damaging to Japan's reputation in Britain itself may have been the negotiation of the Anglo-Japanese commercial treaty of 1911, in which Japan's attitude seemed to be unconciliatory and certainly antagonized mercantile opinion at first.

Since the governments were acting in the face of some opposition, it is not surprising that the third Anglo-Japanese agreement of July 13, 1911, should be a weaker treaty than those that preceded it. The occasion of the renewal was the negotiation of an arbitration treaty between Britain and the United States, which had by this time become very suspicious of Japan. It was felt that the forthcoming arbitration treaty would be weakened if Britain had obligations to support its ally in certain circumstances against the United States. A modified Anglo-Japanese treaty was thus concluded in order to exclude the United States from the purview of the alliance, but the arbitration treaty was not ratified by the United States.

The Japanese decision was taken at a cabinet meeting on April 5, 1911, just two days after the commercial treaty was signed. The cabinet resolution, as proposed by Komura, stated significantly that it was unnecessary to reaffirm that the alliance was the "backbone" of Japanese foreign policy. Japan conceded that America should be excluded from the scope of the alliance but sought to expand it to take in Japan's continental frontier. Japan should try to get Britain to recognize Japan's special rights on its border in Manchuria, though this might not be acceptable to Britain. "Since the main object behind the present revision of the alliance is to extend its duration, it would be better for us not to press this point if it becomes clear that Britain cannot agree to it."[32] This meant that the main object of policy was to replace the 1905 treaty, which was due to last until 1915, with one that would run to 1921 for the added security that this would give Japan. It is doubtful whether any adequate explanation of Japan's ultimate objectives has been offered. At any rate, Britain, while agreeing to the extension of time, would not consent to extending its scope to Manchuria's borders. The 1911 treaty was necessarily watered

[32]*Ibid.*, XLIV/1 (1962), 341–45, Document 80.

down, because relations between the two countries had been strained since 1906.

`By 1912 Japan had surmounted the two international problems that were most unsettling in 1898: humiliation at the hands of the three powers in 1895 and isolation. In place of isolation, Japan found itself allied with the strongest European power, Britain. Its position was "reinsured" by treaties with Russia, which removed many areas of tension, and an agreement with the United States, which may, however, only have papered over the cracks left by disagreements between them. In place of earlier humiliation, Japan was the strongest power on land in East Asia and by sea in the Pacific. It is doubtful whether the British alliance added much to Japan's strength. An emergency did not arise to test it.

The Alliance, China, and the Pacific, 1912–1915. Sir John Jordan, the British minister in Peking, reporting to the Foreign Office in 1918, wrote: "The Far Eastern problem may now be defined as the problem of Japan's position in China."[33] This was probably true throughout the Taishō period. From 1905 Japan had progressively been establishing its position on the Asian continent, and with the annexation of Korea in 1910, the focus of its attention moved to China and especially Manchuria. During the Chinese revolution of 1911, the Japanese were involved in a number of intrigues to improve Japan's interests. Japan first was anxious to see the Ch'ing dynasty continue or some form of constitutional monarchy established; but when it approached Britain for support, it was urged not to interfere in the domestic affairs of China. In due course Britain and Japan mutually agreed to recognize Yuan Shih-k'ai as the president of the new republic.[34]

Japan's main continental interests lay in Manchuria, which it wanted to reserve for itself or, if necessary, to share with the other interested power, Russia. When these two powers found that they were being squeezed out of consortium loans to China, they discovered a common bond that led to the conclusion of a series of treaties. These stemmed from the Russo-Japanese entente of 1907. The second agreement of 1910 defined the spheres of Japanese and Russian interest in Manchuria and provided for mutual

---

[33]Jordan to Balfour, December 23, 1918, in Great Britain, Foreign Office, *Documents on British Foreign Policy, 1919–1939*, First Series, VI, *1919* (1956), 566 (hereafter cited as *Documents on British Foreign Policy*).

[34]*Nihon gaikō nempyō*, I, 357–59.

respect for their rights. The third secret agreement of July 1912 defined their spheres of special interest in Inner Mongolia. Some have seen in these treaties a challenge to the policy of the British alliance from those who favored an alliance between Russia and Japan. There is some evidence that this was not so. The Japanese thought these agreements applied to an area not covered by the alliance and did not consider them irreconcilable with it. Certainly Japan consulted Britain during the negotiations for the 1907 and 1910 treaties.

In some ways this was a period in which Japan tried to strengthen the alliance. One of the strongest foreign ministers of this time, Katō Takaaki (1913, 1914–15), was a stout advocate of the alliance and made it his avowed policy to remove the causes of disagreement between the two powers, e.g., by settling railway disputes in south and central China. If it sometimes appeared to Britain that Katō was merely manipulating the alliance for Japan's own aggrandizement, it must nonetheless be admitted that he was a convinced supporter of the British link and that his actions often served Britain's interests also.

Indeed Katō had definite views on how the alliance should be maintained. When the war in Europe started, Japan was asked by France and Russia whether they might join the alliance. But Katō was opposed to extending the British alliance to include other powers and wrote: "Both Russia and France are in practice our allies since they are at present engaged in a war alongside us. But to add these countries to the Anglo-Japanese alliance would deprive it of its special character as a defensive-offensive alliance and turn it into an entente of some kind. I am opposed to an entente because it will weaken the force of the alliance and lessen its value."[35] Katō tried to avoid watering down the alliance as he conceived it, but the alliance was subjected to two tests during the early months of the war that served to weaken it.

One test followed Britain's declaration of war on Germany on August 4. By an imperial rescript on August 23, Japan too declared war and then attacked and occupied the German-leased territory of Kiaochow. This might seem to indicate that Japan was acting in line with the allies and Britain in particular. This was only partially true. Britain did not want Japan to enter the war beyond the China seas and tried to confine the

[35]Itō Masanori, *Katō Takaaki* (2 vols., 1929), II, 113.

sphere of Japan's operations, and Japan decided on its course of action in full knowledge of Britain's disapproval. This disagreement was the first major dispute between the allies and is worth looking at in more detail.

On August 4 the Japanese government announced its intention of observing strict neutrality toward the war but added that, in the event of an attack upon Hong Kong or Weihaiwei, Japan would support Britain, if called upon to do so. This was a straightforward obligation under the alliance, since these were British territories in the Far East and an attack upon them would bring the alliance into force.

Two days later Britain told the Japanese that if they "would employ some of their warships [to locate and destroy German warships in Chinese waters], it would be of very greatest assistance to us. It means, of course, an act of war against Germany but we do not see how this is to be avoided." On August 7 and 8 cabinet meetings were held to hear the foreign minister's recommendations. Japan, he said, was not required to enter the war as an obligation under the present alliance; the circumstances in which that would be necessary had not yet arisen. Katō nonetheless recommended intervention on two grounds: to keep friendly with Britain who had made the request [*sic*], and to raise the status of Japan in the international sphere by expelling Germany from bases throughout the East. The cabinet and genrō agreed to enter the war on Britain's side, but the decision was much more far-reaching than Britain's request, whereby Japan was asked only for help in destroying German armed vessels.[36]

Britain was suspicious of Japan's intentions. It asked Japan to postpone its declaration of war and later canceled its request for help in dealing with German shipping. On August 11 Britain agreed to accept Japan's participation provided the sphere of Japanese operations was restricted. Japan claimed that a promise of limitation was premature until the declaration of war was issued and forthwith handed Germany an "advice" or ultimatum that showed Japan intended to back Britain and the allies. It contained no guarantee about limiting war operations.[37]

That this ultimatum came as a surprise to Britain can be seen from the memorandum that was passed to Katō on the same day. It was desirable, it stated, that Japan should make it clear that it would not occupy German

[36]*Ibid.*, pp. 78–79.
[37]*Nihon gaikō nempyō*, I, 379–81.

islands in the South Pacific which were of importance to British dominions, intervene on the western seaboard of the American continent, or take possession of the Netherlands East Indies. Such suspicions did exist, the memorandum added, laughable as they might appear.[38] When Japan showed no keenness to deny having such intentions, Britain on August 17 made a remarkable public statement without warning Japan: "It is understood that the action of Japan will not extend to the Pacific Ocean beyond the China seas except insofar as it may be necessary to protect Japanese shipping lines in the Pacific, nor beyond Asiatic territory in German occupation on the continent of Eastern Asia."[39] This was a serious unilateral action on Britain's part. But when the Japanese declared war on August 23, they gave no definite undertaking that they would confine their activities to the spheres laid down by Britain.

What is significant is not Japan's entry into the war but its avoidance of any limitation on its sphere of operations. It was not that Britain was opposed to Japan's entering the war. Indeed Britain's special request for assistance against the German raiders implied that Japan could probably not avoid war. What was objectionable to Britain and to its dominions was Japan's decision not to confine itself to Chinese waters, however unreasonable the British expectation may now seem. Japan circumvented Britain's wishes and took its own decision in its own interest in full knowledge of British opposition.

This was the first time that a disagreement with Japan had closely affected Britain's own interests and objectives. One consequence of Japan's decision was that it took over the German Pacific islands north of the equator to the chagrin of Australia. Japan's entry into the war also was a fillip to Japanese naval development, a move that was viewed with mistrust in that quarter which Britain least wanted to offend, the United States. There had previously been cases when Japan had seemed to be acting in China in a spirit of rivalry toward Britain, but it had generally been China which had suffered most. This, however, affected Britain, and the differences between the two allies were aired in public.

Added significance was given to this issue by Japan's actions toward neutral China during the war. By the end of 1914 Japan had taken over

[38] Itō, *Katō Takaaki*, II, 93–94.
[39] *Ibid.*, pp. 96–99.

most of the German interests in Shantung. In January 1915 it placed before Yuan Shih-k'ai a set of demands and aspirations intended as a basis for negotiations—the so-called Twenty-One Demands. Katō claimed that while he had been ambassador in London, he had received assurances that Britain would not object to Japan's taking up outstanding problems with China.[40] When the demands leaked out, however, they were universally condemned in the United States and Britain, and both governments made strong formal protests. Britain criticized group five, the most far-reaching of the Japanese demands, and urged Japan five times to avoid breakdown of negotiations on that account.[41] This served to remind Katō that if he thought Britain's consent had been given in advance, he was mistaken. But, in practice, Britain could not afford in 1915 to have a dispute with Japan over China. The Twenty-One Demands were opposed to the principles of Chinese independence and of the Open Door contained in the preamble of the alliance. Moreover, some provisions, e.g. those helping Japanese capitalists to control the Han Yeh P'ing Company, seemed to be calculated to infringe Britain's interests in the Yangtze valley. For the rest of the war and during the Paris Peace Conference, Japan continued to be deeply involved in the affairs of China, territorially, politically, and financially, and Britain remained a tacit observer.

The Ending of the Alliance, 1916–1923. During the war, it was not unnatural that a new relationship between Britain and Japan should develop. New levels of prosperity and power made Japan less restrained. Where formerly it had been inclined to consult Britain, it was now ready to act on its own and in the face of British policy and the British alliance. Where formerly Japan had fought shy of antagonizing Britain, it was now prepared to oppose Britain's interests directly and, in the case of China trade, openly. To some extent this had been true of its decision to take part in the war and to transmit the Twenty-One Demands. It may also be illustrated by three incidents from the close of the war.

Though Japan's contribution to the war sometimes disappointed Britain, it did try to identify itself conscientiously with the allied cause. In October

---

[40]*Ibid.*, pp. 132–40.

[41]Memorandum by Bryan, March 13, 1915, and note by Grey, May 4, 1915, in *Nihon gaikō nempyō*, I, 385–401.

1915, after some opposition within the country, Japan gained admission to the Convention of London. It therefore engaged not to conclude peace separately during the war and was given the status of a full ally.[42] In February 1917 it turned this to good account when it secured from Britain, France, Russia, and Italy guarantees of support at the peace conference for Japan's claims to German rights and possessions that Japan had taken over during the war.[43] Having laid its plans well, it was able to secure its major demands at the Paris Peace Conference.

Second, the racial equality clause. At the insistence of Prime Minister Hara Takashi, the Japanese tried to insert within the covenant of the League of Nations, then being drafted, some provision for the principle of racial equality. In February 1919 Japan proposed that a phrase be included in the preamble of the covenant preventing "discriminatory treatment either at law or in fact in respect of nationals of any other state which is a member of the League on grounds of race or nationality." This proposal can only have been made in the knowledge of the embarrassing consequences it would have for Britain. Britain was keen to preserve the Japanese alliance, but it knew that a racial equality clause, if written into the League charter, would be opposed by Australia and (possibly) Canada because of their immigration problems. When the issue was pressed to a vote by Japan, Britain had to choose between its ally and its dominions and supported the dominion opposition. The matter was dropped, but not without giving public demonstration of a split between the allies.[44]

Third, the intervention in Siberia. The Siberian intervention is generally treated as an aspect of American-Japanese and Soviet-Japanese relations, since it was mainly among those powers that tension arose. But it deserves mention in the context of Anglo-Japanese relations if it is accepted that "Allied policy toward Russia in these years so largely originated in London."[45] The idea of a large-scale intervention probably took root in Britain and was for official purposes first communicated to Japan in June 1918. Then the United States came round to agreeing to a joint expedition but with an upper limit of 12,000 Japanese troops. In August the Japanese

[42]*Ibid.*, p. 418.
[43]*Documents on British Foreign Policy*, First Series, VI, *1919*, 562–63.
[44]Shidehara Heiwa Zaidan, ed., *Shidehara Kijūrō* (1955), pp. 143–44.
[45]Richard H. Ullman, *Intervention and the War* (1961), p. vi.

cabinet decided to send troops to Vladivostok but issued a public statement making no commitment over objectives or numbers. Britain had conceived the objective to be to reopen an eastern front in European Russia but, as Ullman writes, "The idea that British interests in a restored Eastern Front were to any real degree shared by Japan was thus another of the false assumptions underlying British policy. . . . The assumption was to be proved wrong only in September 1918 when 70,000 Japanese troops flooded into Eastern Siberia and made no attempt to move west."[46] The two powers were out of line. It could have been Britain's failure to communicate its views; more probably it was Japan's desire to serve its own interests first. When Britain pressed in October for troops to be sent to western Siberia, the Japanese cabinet decided that its expeditionary forces were not to go west of Lake Baikal.[47] By pouring in troops in such large numbers, the Japanese converted the allied expedition into a Japanese one, as it remained until the Japanese withdrawal in October 1922. In the Siberian intervention, the Japanese seem to have cooperated with the allies to a degree but in the long run sought their own advantage.

The mainstream of Japanese policy toward Britain was concerned with the question whether the Anglo-Japanese alliance, which was liable to lapse in 1921, would be renewed. As before World War I, the alliance stood between Japan and isolation. Its erstwhile alliance with tsarist Russia had not survived the Russian revolution. The subject was first broached on May 19, 1920, by the newly arrived British ambassador, Sir Charles Eliot. The Japanese cabinet was consulted and the foreign minister replied: "The Japanese Government is also in favor of its renewal. As to the seat and time of negotiations, it is a matter of no serious concern to the Japanese Government whether it be in London or in Tokyo. We shall naturally make preparations for drawing up a draft of the revised text of the Treaty."[48] The Japanese government was evidently enthusiastic, but no negotiations resulted.

There were certain considerations that stood in the way of the renewal of the alliance. Both allies, as founder members of the League of Nations,

---

[46]*Ibid.*, p. 332.

[47]Cabinet decision, October 15, 1918, in *Nihon gaikō nempyō*, I, 471.

[48]Uchida to Eliot, May 22, 1920, as cited in Cecil H. Uyehara, *Checklist of Archives in the Japanese Ministry of Foreign Affairs, Tokyo, Japan, 1868–1945, Microfilmed for the Library of Congress, 1949–1951* (1954), p. 80, microfilm UD 40.

were keen that the alliance should conform to the ideas of that body, which was trying to make alliances between nations illegal except when sanctioned by the League. So far as Japan was concerned, it was vulnerable to criticism from China. From June 1920 on, the Chinese declared their opposition to the alliance, on the ground that Japan was abusing it in China, and promoted a movement to oppose its renewal. Britain was open to complaint from two quarters. Among the dominions, Canada was an outright opponent of the alliance, being supported by South Africa. In this Canada was largely reflecting the hostility of the United States, on whose goodwill Britain was greatly dependent. The Americans still doubted whether, in the event of war between the United States and Japan, Britain might not have an obligation to go to Japan's support. However far-reaching the assurances by Britain and Japan, the United States was not satisfied and seems to have wanted to exploit the uncertainty in order to demolish the alliance.

To meet at least part of this opposition, the two powers agreed to issue on July 8, 1920, a joint declaration informing the League that "they recognize the principle that if the said Agreement be continued after July 1921, it must be in a form which is not inconsistent with that covenant."[49] It is clearly implied that continuation of the alliance was contemplated. Japan was ready to open negotiations at any time, but Britain claimed that it could not agree to the continuation without consulting its dominions and the imperial conference could not be held until June 1921.

To prevent the alliance from lapsing automatically in July 1921, Britain asked Japan to join in a further declaration prolonging the alliance by three months.[50] Within this period Britain hoped to convene a conference confined to Japan, the United States, and Britain to discuss the alliance and the Pacific situation. But the United States wanted to link the issue with disarmament and convened instead a conference of all Pacific powers, which opened at Washington in November 1921.

Japan's policy was to collaborate in the Washington Conference in the hope of salvaging as much of the alliance as possible. In the instructions to its delegates, Japan stated:

In considering the continuation or otherwise of the Anglo-Japanese

---

[49]*Nihon gaikō nempyō*, I, 515.
[50]*Ibid.*, p. 528.

alliance in relation to the [proposed] treaty for the limitation of armaments or a three-power convention (United States, Britain, and Japan), Japan has no objection either to the Anglo-Japanese treaty being brought into line with the above treaty or convention or to its continuing as it stands. If Britain wishes to substitute the above treaty or convention for the alliance, there can be no question to our agreeing to it.[51]

Japan was prepared to leave the solution to Britain, not because it did not value the alliance, but because Britain could deal more effectively with the American opposition. Shidehara Kijūrō, who was one of the Japanese delegates, wrote that for Japan "to plead strongly for the continuation of the alliance would only cause Britain embarrassment and therefore be purposeless and undignified."[52] On the whole, the Japanese showed much restraint and understanding on this delicate issue. In place of the three-power alliance proposed by Britain, there was signed a Four Power Convention to which France also became a party. With the exchange of ratifications on August 17, 1923, the Anglo-Japanese alliance came to an end.

The passing of the alliance was not something of Japan's choosing and most Japanese viewed it with regret. If Japan had had an influential voice, it would have called for its renewal. There is some disagreement as to whether Japan blamed Britain for allowing the alliance to be terminated. Some have so alleged, but there is no evidence that the Japanese government allowed it to cloud relations with Britain. Britain continued to be the power with which Japan had the closest relationship, and this was necessary if it were to avoid isolation. The policy speeches of Shidehara as foreign minister show that, while there were many prickly issues in relations with China, Russia, and the United States, relations with Britain were never critical.[53] In a sense this was to be expected. The British alliance was never a very intimate one: it was never so binding that the policies of the signatories were invariably in alignment. Thus, even when it came to an official end, there was no marked change in relations.[54]

Relations in China after the End of the Alliance, 1924–1930. After the Washington Conference, the Anglo-Japanese alliance was in effect replaced by

[51]*Ibid.*
[52]Shidehara Heiwa Zaidan, *Shidehara Kijūrō*, pp. 228–29.
[53]*Nihon gaikō nempyō,* II, 72–75, 83–92.
[54]Charles N. Spinks, "Behind Japan's Anglophobia" (1938), presents an alternative view.

a network of treaties. The security of the Far East now rested in theory with the United States, Britain, and Japan jointly. But there was not much evidence of cooperation between the three major Washington powers in the face of their main problem, rising Chinese nationalism.

For most of the 1920s, Japan's foreign policy was directed by Shidehara Kijūrō, foreign minister under Katō Takaaki (1924–26), Wakatsuki Reijirō (1926–27 and April–December 1931), and Hamaguchi Osachi (1929–31). Shidehara generally acted in line with the League of Nations and thus with Britain, which found itself in a position of leadership in that body. If Japan and Britain were united in emphasizing the need for peace and disarmament in the world at large, they were often at cross-purposes in China. This was not something new to the 1920s or brought about by a deliberate change of policy: it had developed gradually because of the differing needs of the two powers. This was recognized in a British Foreign Office memorandum: "Japan's interests in China are so different from those of Great Britain that her policy is bound to take a somewhat different turn from our own . . . . We can never count upon the support of Japan, though it may sometimes suit her convenience to work with us."[55] Important disagreements did arise over the findings of the Peking Tariff Conference of 1926, and it was generally admitted that there was not much scope for long-term cooperation.

An opportunity for Anglo-Japanese cooperation presented itself in 1927 when the Kuomintang armies violated foreign rights in Nanking and Hankow. Shidehara agreed to join in a five-power protest to China, but in an important policy statement on April 6, he announced that Japan would confine itself to diplomatic means.[56] Accordingly, when Britain proposed that Japan send two divisions, Shidehara opposed it, the formal rejection being given on April 26, shortly after the Wakatsuki cabinet had been forced to resign.[57] Despite this, Britain sent its own forces to Shanghai. It is probable that Shidehara tried where possible to act in an accommodating spirit toward Britain but felt on this occasion that an independent diplomatic settlement would suit Japan's interests better.

His successor, General Tanaka Giichi, who combined the office with the

[55]*Documents on British Foreign Policy*, Second Series, VIII, *Chinese Questions, 1929–1931* (1960), 25.

[56]*Nihon gaikō nempyō*, II, 95–96.

[57]Shidehara Heiwa Zaidan, *Shidehara Kijūrō*, p. 284.

prime ministership (1927–29), decided in 1927 and again in 1928 to send an expeditionary force to Shantung, even if it meant incurring the bitter hostility of the Chinese.[58] Japan deployed about 2,000 troops in Shantung in 1927 but withdrew them by early September. In April–June 1928 Japan dispatched more than two divisions to the same area; fighting, which broke out in May between these troops and soldiers of the Chinese Nationalist army, came to be known as the Tsinan Incident. In May 1928 it was suggested that some understanding over policy toward China might be reached between Britain and Japan. Japanese sources mention the approach as coming from Britain, but a British source attributes the overture to Japan.[59] The Tanaka cabinet decided in August that this could best be pursued when Count Uchida Yasuya, a former foreign minister, was at a conference in Paris to sign the Kellogg-Briand Pact on the repudiation of war. His mandate was to explain the aims and objectives of Japan's policy in China and to discuss ways and means of cooperation. His brief was contained in a memorandum explaining Japan's actions concerning the old and new marshals of Manchuria, Chang Tso-lin and Chang Hsueh-liang respectively, and the Tsinan Incident of 1928.[60] Uchida first discussed the matter with Lord Cushendun, Britain's delegate at Paris. Later he proceeded to London, where Lord Birkenhead, who was acting for the foreign secretary, spoke at a banquet in Uchida's honor of the need for Anglo-Japanese cooperation in order to safeguard the various treaty rights the two powers had in China. He admitted that Japan had wide interests in Manchuria and suggested that, although the Anglo-Japanese alliance had ended, its spirit still continued. Uchida replied that Anglo-Japanese understanding was necessary for peace and order in the Far East. In his report to his government on September 28, Uchida observed that the atmosphere of understanding in British cabinet circles was very strong but that Foreign Office officials expressed themselves much more cautiously and observed that an understanding would not necessarily be easy to attain in view of the many practical problems.[61]

[58]*Nihon gaikō nempyō*, II, Chronology, p. 35, and Documents, p. 96 (1927 expeditions); Chronology, p. 40 (1920 expeditions).
[59]*Documents on British Foreign Policy*, Second Series, VIII, *Chinese Questions, 1929–1931*, 25.
[60]*Nihon gaikō nempyō*, II, 117–19.
[61]*Ibid.*, pp. 121–22.

Just how persuasively Uchida put the case for an understanding with Britain is difficult to assess. An official British account records that Uchida's "tentative project did not lead to any very practical result. The ministers of the two countries in Peking were, however, instructed to keep in particularly close touch with one another. . . . Such has been the basis of British and Japanese policy in China since that date [1928] and it has worked to the satisfaction and advantage of both parties."[62] If the practical results of this cooperation were limited, Japan was given some assurances which must have been encouraging, even if they were noncommittal. The British prime minister said, at the lord mayor of London's banquet in November, that "the spirit of the historic Anglo-Japanese Alliance still flourishes and constitutes one of the strongest guarantees of peace in the Far East."[63] Nonetheless, this fell short of the contemplated understanding over China, which proved more and more difficult to achieve as the years went by.

Over naval policy, too, the Japanese civilian ministries were trying to minimize growing differences with the foreign powers. At the Geneva Naval Conference of 1927 Japan had played a mediating role between Britain and the United States. By the succeeding conference in London in 1930, these two had sorted out their differences and stood together against Japan's demands. It is probable that Britain thought Japan less of a naval menace than did the United States and was able to use its good offices to gain acceptance for a compromise formula. In the period down to 1936, it was the United States rather than Britain which stood out as the main hindrance to Japan's naval expansion.

Japan may have seen the ending of the alliance with regret and sought to maintain some of its substance in practice. But basic differences in policy toward China were arising in the 1920s that made this more difficult. The crux was that, by December 1928, Britain decided to recognize the new Nanking government and to offer it complete tariff autonomy, whereas Japan was resisting the Kuomintang and trying to circumscribe its growth. It cannot be said that such divisions were unknown in the alliance period, for the allies often pursued dissimilar policies. But the differences were by 1930 more radical and a rift was developing.

Government documents: Since the British Foreign Office archives are open

---

[62] *Documents on British Foreign Policy*, Second Series, VIII, *Chinese Questions, 1929–1931*, 25.
[63] *Survey of International Affairs, 1928* (1929), pp. 431–32.

for this period, the researcher can use them to supplement printed collections such as:

Great Britain, Foreign Office, *Documents on British Foreign Policy, 1919–1939* (1947–   ). First Series, Vol. VI (1956), pp. 562–1074, contains a long section on the attitude of Britain to "Japanese policy towards China and adjacent territories and . . . the continuation of the Anglo-Japanese Alliance, June 28, 1919—April 1, 1920." First Series, Vol. XIV, *Far Eastern Affairs, April 1920 —February 1922* (1966), continues the story to the end of the Washington Conference in 1922. Materials on the Siberian intervention are included in a section regarding Russia in First Series, Vol. III (1949), pp. 308–827.

Japan, Gaimushō (Foreign Ministry), *Nihon gaikō bunsho*. The series at the time of writing covers the period to 1919.

—— *Sekai taisen kankei Nihon gaikō bunsho* (1939), with the subtitle "Documents diplomatiques japonais relatifs à la guerre mondiale de 1914–1918," covers Japan's entry into World War I. This vital handbook of the Foreign Ministry contains documents on Japanese wartime diplomacy from Sarajevo to January 1918. It includes materials about the negotiations on extending the alliance to cover the European allies and on China's entry into the war.

—— *Tsūshō jōyaku kankei Nihon gaikō bunsho* (1954), I, Part 1 (1910–11), 441–1139, is a special series which contains material on the Anglo-Japanese Treaty of Commerce and Navigation of 1911.

Biographies and memoirs. British:

Dugdale, *Arthur James Balfour, First Earl of Balfour* (2 vols., 1936), and the following book view Anglo-Japanese relations from London. Vol. II of the Dugdale work is relevant to this period.

Grey, *Twenty-five Years, 1892–1916* (2 vols., 1925).

Parlett, "In Piam Memoriam" (1959), is a brief memoir of Sir Charles Eliot, ambassador to Tokyo, 1920–26.

Tilley, *London to Tokyo* (1944), is another account of a British ambassador to Japan.

Biographies and memoirs. Japanese:

Ishii, *Gaikō yoroku* (1930).

Itō, *Katō Takaaki* (2 vols., 1929), II.

Shidehara Heiwa Zaidan, *Shidehara Kijūrō* (1955), has some information about the negotiations for the commercial treaty of 1911.

Shidehara, *Gaikō gojūnen* (1951).

Of lesser interest from a policy standpoint are:

Hayashi, *Waga shichijūnen o kataru* (1935).

Suma, *Gaikō hiroku* (1956).

Accounts by British journalists in the Far East:

> Bland, *Recent Events and Present Policies in China* (1912).
> Pooley, *Japan's Foreign Policies* (1920).
> Young, *Japan under Taisho Tenno, 1912–1926* (1928).

Other writings by these authors together with those by Malcolm D. Kennedy, B. L. Simpson (Putnam Weale), and H. G. W. Woodhead are also helpful.

World War I:

> Great Britain, Foreign Office, *British Documents on the Origins of the War, 1898–1914*, Second Series, X–XI, deal sketchily with the start of the war in its Far Eastern aspect.
> La Fargue, *China and the World War* (1937).
> Lowe, *Great Britain and Japan, 1911–1915* (1969).
> Nagaoka, "Ōshū taisen sanka mondai" (1958).

Washington Conference:

> Iriye, *After Imperialism: The Search for a New Order in the Far East, 1921–1931* (1965).
> Kajima, *Nichi-Ei gaikōshi* (1957), describes Anglo-Japanese relations to 1921.
> —— *Nichi-Bei gaikōshi* (1958), with detailed references to the Washington Conference, ends with the rejection of the Lansing-Ishii agreement in 1923.
> Nish, "Japan and the Ending of the Anglo-Japanese Alliance" (1967).

Anglo-Japanese alliance:

> Chang, *The Anglo-Japanese Alliance* (1931), and the following two works, also referred to above, continue the account through the period under discussion here.
> Dennis, *The Anglo-Japanese Alliance* (1923).
> Gal'perin, *Anglo-Iaponskii soiuz, 1902–1921 gg* (1947).
> Nish, *Alliance in Decline* (1972), contains a full bibliography on this topic.
> Wood, *China, the United States and the Anglo-Japanese Alliance* (1921), is especially interesting for the period after 1911, to which more than half the book is devoted. It contains some important appendices for the years 1920–21.

There is plenty of scope for research on a wide range of subjects relating to Anglo-Japanese affairs in the later Taishō period. With the Foreign Office archives open for the whole period, a complete reassessment of Anglo-Japanese relations should be possible.

On a more specialized level, there is need for research on Japan's policy toward Britain in China and Manchuria. One subject where, despite the preparatory work of Ikei Masaru, there is scope for study is the degree of Anglo-Japanese cooperation over the 1911 revolution in China. There is a special volume in the *Nihon gaikō bunsho* series, the British Foreign Office archives for Japan and China are accessible, and the papers of Sir John Jordan, the British minister in Peking, are open to inspection at the Public Record Office, London. The same sources throw light also on Japan's part in consortium loans to China and in railway finance.

Another field of research is that of dominion influence on British policy toward Japan. This would cover a number of unexplored themes: Australian feeling toward Japan during World War I; Australian opinion on the racial equality clause in 1919; Canadian attitudes toward the renewal of the alliance; and India's worries about Japanese assistance to the independence movement in British India and to Indian political exiles in Japan, for example. One of the few relevant studies is the following:

Ohsawa, *Two Great Indians in Japan: Rashbehari Bose and Subhas Chandra Bose* (1954), Vol. I.

While these would be matters of prime concern in the elucidation of British policy, they are also of considerable interest for Japan, which by then had trade and consular relations with all these countries.

THE DRIFT APART, 1931–1941

Japan, Britain, and China, 1931–1936. The first major split between Britain and Japan was associated with Japan's renewed activity in China in 1931–32. The Japanese government's decision to uphold the actions of its armies in Manchuria did not bring about a decisive change in relations with Britain because Britain had long admitted that it was not primarily interested in Manchuria and that Japan had certain rights there. But the clash between the Japanese and Kuomintang armies near Shanghai early in 1932 was much closer to Britain's real interests. On February 2 the powers most affected were led by Britain to call for a reduction in Japanese forces there and their withdrawal from contact with the Kuomintang forces. Britain later requested Japan, both directly and through the Assembly of the League, to cease warlike acts at Shanghai. It was largely through British mediation that a settlement between Japan and China was locally negotiated on May 5, 1932.[64]

In March 1932 an independent Manchukuo government was set up with the assistance and protection of the Japanese army in Manchuria. Six months later Japan recognized the new regime. The League of Nations Assembly, on February 24, 1933, overwhelmingly approved a recommendation that the regime in Manchuria was not to be recognized by members of the League, either de facto or de jure. In these circumstances, Japan after some heart-searching withdrew from the League.[65]

Throughout the crisis, Britain worked for a negotiated settlement of the Manchurian Incident and frequently asked Japan to make concessions in order to break the deadlock. In March 1933 Britain appealed to Japan not to take the drastic action of leaving the League. But in vain. There can be little doubt that Japan's decision to withdraw from the League, whose continuance was a basic objective of British policy, was taken in the knowledge that it must cause some estrangement between Britain and Japan.

But the Japanese did not consider that all hope of Anglo-Japanese cooperation in China had disappeared. Uchida, who was foreign minister (1932–33), was evidently angling for some sort of accommodation with Britain as well as with France. In a resolution passed on August 27, 1932, the cabinet approved a plan for dealing with the international situation, which included the statement:

> The restoration of Anglo-Japanese understanding in China is very desirable considering that Britain's interests and influence are still strong in China today. . . . At the end of 1926 the British government became extremely tolerant toward China and adopted the so-called New Policy that made it difficult for us to reach an understanding there. A trend toward some change in the New Policy has lately become noticeable. By encouraging this trend, we may take the first steps toward restoring Anglo-Japanese understanding. To promote an understanding by respecting Britain's position in China proper, especially in Shanghai, Kwantung, the Yangtze valley, and south China, to which Britain attaches special importance, would react favorably on our standing in Manchuria.[66]

[64] *Nihon gaikō nempyō* II, 196–97.
[65] *Ibid.*, pp. 268–70.
[66] *Ibid.*, pp. 206–10.

There is no evidence that this was more than an aspiration or that negotiations were opened on this basis. But even as an aspiration, it is significant.

The next aspect of Japanese policy was in response to a new British initiative in China. Britain tried to extricate the Kuomintang government from its financial problems by circulating among the powers certain proposals for international assistance. Japan, which had been pursuing an independent course of action in China in the 1920s, did not favor a return to the days of the international consortium. The so-called "Amō declaration" (April 1934) defined what Japan considered to be its rights there; the British reply by way of warning defined British and Chinese rights and Japan readily gave assurances.[67] In February 1935 Britain proposed an exchange of views with Japan and the United States over financial help to China. Japan, however, refused to participate in international economic assistance to China. Foreign Minister Hirota Kōki privately expressed his suspicion that "Britain in the name of friendship is now trying to increase restrictions on Japan's special position in East Asia."[68] So Britain turned to unilateral action.

In the summer of 1935 Sir Frederick Leith-Ross, an adviser to the British Treasury, led a mission to China. On his way there, he had discussions with Japanese ministers in the hope that Japan, together with the United States and France, might accept an invitation to collaborate with the mission. Despite the cordial atmosphere in which the discussions were held, there was an underlying suspicion. On September 17 Japan declined to cooperate in an international loan for China's currency reform, alleging that the time was premature. Japan announced in November its "unofficial opposition" to the activities of the British mission, and this distrust persisted through to Leith-Ross' meeting with Foreign Minister Arita Hachirō in June 1936.[69]

The Leith-Ross mission was a symbol of the rift between Japanese and British views on China proper. The British object was to bolster the Nationalist government, whereas Japan probably wanted to keep it weak. The mission and the actions that stemmed from it seemed to be examples of an anti-Japanese policy on Britain's part. This at least was the Japanese

[67]Irving S. Friedman, *British Relations with China, 1931–1939* (1940), pp. 45–46.
[68]*Ibid.;* and *Nihon gaikō nempyō*, II, 290–93.
[69]*Ibid.*, pp. 298–303, 334–40.

assumption, and they would not agree to Leith-Ross' overtures. Britain's intent is not clear and is in need of research. Sir John Pratt insists it was not anti-Japanese.[70] Certainly, after China's currency system had been reformed, its dependence on Britain and the United States, both economically and politically, increased in a way that seemed to the Japanese to be to their detriment.

At this time Japan also took a crucial decision to free itself from the restrictive naval agreements of the Washington and London conferences. On December 3, 1934, the Japanese cabinet finally decided, after many threats in previous months, to give notice of withdrawal from the Washington naval treaty, effective from the end of 1936.[71] The powers convened a further naval disarmament conference in London, but the Japanese delegates left the discussions on January 15, 1936. Once Japan had withdrawn from the League, it may not have seemed such a big step to break with the naval settlement. It had, however, more serious implications: both Britain and the United States were more directly affected by naval issues in the Pacific than by happenings in Manchuria and north China; it was natural that relations should become further strained. Japan had "severed one more link with the nations seeking the peaceful solution of international problems."[72]

Japan, Britain, and Germany, 1936–1939. For most of the period after 1870, Britain had probably been the most important Western power in Japan's foreign affairs. After 1936 steps were taken to make Germany, first, Japan's collaborator and, later, its ally.

That Britain continued to be a major consideration in Japan's policy-making can be gleaned from the resolution passed by the Hirota cabinet on August 7, 1936. An inner cabinet, consisting of the prime minister and the ministers of foreign affairs, finance, the army, and the navy, met to formulate a positive national policy that is elaborated in two memoranda. They laid down as the basis of Japanese policy the need for building up a three-nation coalition of Japan, Manchukuo, and China that would eliminate the threat of the Soviet Union in the north and "make provision

[70]John T. Pratt, *War and Politics in China* (1943), pp. 234–36.
[71]*Nihon gaikō nempyō*, II, 287–88.
[72]Robert L. Craigie, *Behind the Japanese Mask* (1945), p. 17.

for" Britain and the United States. The idea of a coalition with Germany to check the activities of the Soviet Union was also approved.[73]

The inner cabinet further considered that Japan should keep on friendly terms with Britain and persuade it to take a favorable attitude toward Japan in its disputes with the Soviet Union. Since it was highly desirable for Japan's continental policy to try to break the deadlock in Anglo-Japanese relations, it was resolved that Japan must try to persuade Britain to respect Japan's essential interests in China and, in return, would agree to respect British interests there. Moreover, the Japanese should strive to improve overall relations; there was a fear that otherwise Britain, with the support of the United States, the Soviet Union, and China, would pursue a policy hostile to Japan.[74]

The mainstream of Japan's policy seemed to be moving in the direction of an understanding with the Axis powers. The Anti-Comintern Pact with Germany was signed in November 1936, and Italy joined the treaty in November 1937. The pact might seem to have been anti-British in intention, but this was not necessarily so. While the negotiations were going on with Germany, the Foreign Ministry, with the reluctant approval of the army, was making similar approaches to Britain and Holland. These powers were sounded as to whether they would join an anti-Soviet front.[75] The approach to Britain was unofficial and was made by Yoshida Shigeru, who took over as ambassador to London in June 1936. In Holland the approach was made by the Japanese charge d'affaires, Yamaguchi Iwao, on October 12. Neither power was attracted to the idea of joining such an agreement.

The Japanese motive in making these approaches is not known for certain. It may have been the Japanese hunch that Britain and Holland were anxious about the spread of communism to their colonial territories and to Asia generally. The indications were that the Soviet Union was no longer inhibited by its five-year plan from infiltrating overseas, especially in colonial territories like India and the Dutch East Indies. Thus the two powers might be willing to conclude anti-Comintern agreements. Another suggestion is that in a period of intense trade difficulty for the Japanese,

---

[73]*Nihon gaikō nempyō*, II, 344–45; also Hata Ikuhiko, "Futsu-In shinchū to gun no nanshin seisaku (1940–1941)" (1963), pp. 148, 150, 168.

[74]*Nihon gaikō nempyō*, II, 345–47.

[75]Harada Kumao, *Saionji kō to seikyoku*, V (1951), 114–15.

the leaders saw the communist bogey as a convenient tool to get the tariff walls in British India and the Dutch East Indies lowered against Japanese goods and mercantile expansion.

The idea of an Anglo-Japanese understanding was not lost sight of in 1937, although the Japanese approach was on a different basis. Foreign Minister Satō Naotake (March–June 1937) felt that Japan's policy in China could not succeed without some agreement with Britain. He proposed such an agreement, covering economic and financial questions. It was publicly announced that Yoshida was engaged in general conversations with Britain as a preliminary to more formal negotiations. But Satō's resignation, which was forced on him by the military, and the Marco Polo Bridge Incident brought these talks to a standstill.[76]

After the Japanese armies became involved in China, hopes of an understanding disappeared, but the need for Anglo-Japanese liaison was as great as ever. True, Prime Minister Konoe Fumimaro turned down the British offer of mediation to settle the China question.[77] But Japan showed itself ready, in conversations in July 1938 between Foreign Minister Ugaki Kazushige and Ambassador Robert Craigie, to iron out the major causes of dispute between the two powers. Later, in July-August 1939, discussions were held between Foreign Minister Arita Hachirō and Craigie to overcome problems connected with the Japanese blockade of the British settlement in Tientsin. It was at the insistence of Britain that the talks were suspended on August 21, 1939.[78] It seems to emerge from this that, despite the highhandedness of the army in China and the undoubted strength of its position, the Japanese Foreign Ministry was ready to negotiate limited settlements with Britain.

Another factor that has to be taken into account in assessing Japan's policy toward Britain is the tremendous pressure successive governments faced from Germany to expand the Anti-Comintern Pact into an alliance against Britain and France. At meetings of the inner cabinet, the foreign ministers consistently opposed the army suggestion that Japan should

[76] *The Annual Register: A Review of Public Events at Home and Abroad for the Year 1937* (1938), p. 167; Friedman, *British Relations with China*, pp. 89–90.

[77] Harada, *Saionji kō to seikyoku*, November 1, 1938, Supplement (1956), pp. 360–62.

[78] *Documents on British Foreign Policy*, Third Series, VIII-IX, *1938–1939* (1955); and *Nihon gaikō nempyō*, II, 416–17.

contract to give Germany support against its European enemies. It was not until 1940 that the Foreign Ministry gave way on this point.[79]

During the period from 1936 to 1939, the mainstream of Japanese foreign policy was moving toward a greater understanding with Germany. Until the outbreak of the European war, this policy was not essentially anti-British. The Foreign Ministry as a whole was anxious to avoid undue commitment to Germany, either in Europe or in Asia. It felt that Britain, as the leading foreign power in China, should be humored rather than alienated. If this line of policy was sometimes blurred, it was because the ministry did not have exclusive grasp of the reins: there was a tussle for power with the military, which was trying to have the major say in the diplomatic sphere, especially in the making of China policy.

Even within the Foreign Ministry itself, there was a Sūjikuha or "Axis faction," but it did not come into ascendancy until 1940. Its members tried to strengthen the three-power pact and later to add the Soviet Union. Their policy was avowedly anti-British. The other wing in the Foreign Ministry, the Ei-Beiha or "Anglo-American faction," advocated a line of compromise with Britain. It did not oppose the Anti-Comintern Pact and wanted Britain to join, even in 1938 and 1939. This is part of the explanation for the ambivalence in Japan's foreign policy that was so baffling to Britain.

Japan, Britain, and Southeast Asia, 1939–1941. Japan's policy toward Britain was influenced by two circumstances that coincided with the outbreak of the war in Europe. The first was that the United States began to assume a major role in the Far East. Throughout the 1930s Britain had been the power most active in supporting the Kuomintang and, as the Japanese saw it, most hostile to Japan's interests. There is probably substance in the British ambassador's comment that from 1937 to 1940 "Britain played the unenviable role of public enemy No. 1."[80] But as the United States intervened there more actively after 1939, largely because of its concern for Britain's inevitable withdrawal, it was American-Japanese relations that displaced Anglo-Japanese relations as the axis of Far Eastern diplomacy. The second circumstance was that Japan's ally, Germany,

[79]For Arita's and Ōshima's views, see *ibid.*, pp. 408–12.
[80]Craigie, *Behind the Japanese Mask*, p. 99.

concluded a nonaggression pact with the Soviet Union in August 1939. This temporarily discredited those in the Japanese Army and Foreign ministries who were calling on Japan to enter into an alliance with Germany and helped to improve relations with Britain. The Hiranuma cabinet was forced to resign.

British Ambassador Craigie described the succeeding cabinets of General Abe Nobuyuki (August 1939–January 1940) and Admiral Yonai Mitsumasa (January–July 1940) as "two moderate governments." The Abe cabinet adopted a policy of noninvolvement in the European war, which was as much as Britain could expect from a power that had treaties with Germany and Italy Japan's eyes were focused on China. On September 5, 1939, Craigie was given a note of "friendly advice" that belligerents should withdraw their ships and military forces from those parts of China occupied by the Japanese. But it was not until August 1940 that British troops were finally withdrawn from north China.

At the end of 1939 Abe's three senior ministers prepared an instructive statement on foreign policy that showed how even a cabinet which was comparatively well-disposed toward Britain could not fail to take advantage of Britain's involvement in war with Germany.[81] The memorandum stated that Japan had various methods of control over Britain. "As Britain becomes progressively more involved in Europe, we may gradually get it to concede various practical points, including the adjustment of Japan's rights in China. This may form the basis for a fundamental understanding which may help in resolving the present incident or in establishing our New Order in East Asia." In resolving the China Incident, the Japanese tried to benefit from the discomfiture of Britain, which was regarded as the main external cause of the failure of Japanese arms. Britain was, therefore, asked to withdraw recognition of Chungking, check anti-Japanese activities in British settlements, stop financial aid to the Kuomintang, and close the Burma Road. To the construction of its New Order in East Asia, Japan also considered Britain to be the obstacle. It became Japan's objective to exploit the European situation in order to "remove the barriers to Japanese trade with the various parts of the British empire and to make possible our progress, especially in Southeast Asia." In the face

---

[81]Memorandum by Nomura (Foreign), Hata (Army), and Yoshida (Navy), December 28, 1939, in *Nihon gaikō nempyō*, II, 421–24.

of these demands, Britain's policy was to stall, to make minor concessions, and to dissuade Japan by diplomatic means from interfering in Southeast Asia. For the time being, Britain could still employ these stalling tactics without serious repercussions.

On occasion it was Britain that took a firm line and found Japan prepared to be moderate. Early in 1940 the British navy boarded the Japanese liner *Asama Maru* and arrested twenty-one Germans making their way home for enlistment. Japan protested strongly and demanded the return of the Germans. Eventually a joint statement was drawn up in which Britain agreed to return some of the Germans and Japan agreed not to carry belligerent nationals on its vessels. The question of blockade came up again when Britain sought in March to limit war supplies traveling to the Soviet Union and Germany via Siberia. The talks, which were held with Ambassador Shigemitsu Mamoru in London, continued hopefully until the end of June. Britain's approach has been described as a "policy of cautious stubbornness."[82] For present purposes, it is sufficient to observe that the Tokyo government was remarkably moderate, considering the strength of its position.

It was natural that Japanese pressure should increase as the tide turned against Britain in the European war. In June 1940 Japan again demanded that Britain cease assisting Chiang Kai-shek and that the Burma Road and the transit route through Hong Kong should be closed. There were rumors that Japan might soon enter the war on Germany's side. Britain therefore agreed to the temporary closing of the road. It is often forgotten that this agreement was the result of negotiations and that Japan agreed— though it naturally tried to prevent the fact being made public—to the closure being limited initially to three months.

The reasons Japan's policy toward Britain was reserved and cautious were probably two. First, Japan could not afford to alienate Britain, which was vital to it as a source of raw materials such as oil, tin, and rubber. Much of Japan's foreign trade was with the British Commonwealth, the United States (which was becoming Britain's partner), and the Dutch East Indies (which also was working with Britain). Too aggressive an attitude toward Britain might leave Japan without essential supplies. Second, Japanese leaders were undecided about the direction of Japan's

---

[82]W. Norton Medlicott, *The Economic Blockade*, I (1952), 428.

expanding interests. Some favored consolidation in China, some a move against the Soviet Union, some a campaign against Southeast Asia. As a result, many civil and military leaders were content to watch developments.

The decisive turning point in Japan's relations with Britain was the Japanese government's decision to proceed with an attack on Southeast Asia. Japan's ambitions in China and Siberia did not injure Britain directly, but a decision to attack Malaya meant an infringement of British territory and a fundamental change in Japanese policy toward Britain. One of the first decisions of the Konoe government (July 1940–July 1941) was to make Southeast Asia rather than China the long-term objective of its strategy. The new attitude is shown in the statement on national policy published on August 1, 1940. The relevant section states that British and other European colonies in East Asia and contiguous islands should be incorporated into Japan's New Order, that positive steps should be taken to this end, and that any proposal to discuss it at a conference of the powers should be resisted. Even if the China Incident were not settled, the Japanese should use force to resolve the southern question but should try to confine the opposition to Britain alone. It might not be easy to avoid war with the United States, and Japan should be prepared for such an eventuality.[83] To fulfill this policy statement, the Konoe cabinet attempted to settle the China Incident, entered into an alliance with the Axis powers (September 1940), and from February 1941 sought an accommodation with the United States.

War against the British territories in Southeast Asia was only a matter of time. This was certainly the deduction of Anthony Eden that underlay his statement of warning early in February to Shigemitsu, then Japanese ambassador in London. It was still the theme of the slightly dilettantish letter from Churchill handed to Foreign Minister Matsuoka Yōsuke on April 12.[84] The main brake on Japan's action was probably its uncertainty as to whether United States intervention would follow inevitably upon the invasion of British and other territories. In August 1940 Shigemitsu

---

[83] *Nihon gaikō nempyō*, II, 435–36.

[84] W.S. Churchill, *The Grand Alliance* (1950), Vol. III of *The Second World War*, pp. 189–90. The Churchill letter is dated April 2, 1941. See also Eden to Shigemitsu, February 7, 1941, in *Nihon gaikō nempyō*, II, 482–85; and Churchill to Matsuoka, April 12, 1941, in *ibid.*, pp. 489–90.

reminded his government that British and American policies were not joint but parallel and were not completely united in objectives or in their application.[85] It therefore became the prime object of the Japanese to see if the United States could be persuaded to keep out of a war in Southeast Asia. In this they failed, for the Americans insisted on identifying themselves with the European powers in any negotiations. Japan's failure to detach the United States became clear in the parallel economic actions of all the Pacific powers against Japan in July 1941 and in the Churchill-Roosevelt policy statements of the following month.[86]

There was some fluctuation in Japan's attitude toward Britain during the summer of 1941. But any evidence of an accommodating spirit on the part of Foreign Minister Admiral Toyoda Teijirō was short-lived and ended with the coming to power of the Tōjō cabinet in October 1941. The first unqualified statement that Japan was intending to declare war on the British empire was made at a Liaison Conference on November 2.[87] An imperial rescript declaring war jointly on the United States and Britain (in that order) was issued on December 8 and diplomatic relations ceased. The order may not be insignificant: Britain was in the shadow of the United States, even though the war was to be waged primarily against British and other European-held territories in Southeast Asia. By 1941 it would appear that Japan considered its relations with Britain secondary to those with the United States, the Soviet Union, and possibly the Axis powers.

In the previous decade relations between Japan and Britain had deteriorated gradually. This deterioration was never focused on any one event until the final attack on British possessions in Southeast Asia. The major events of the period—the Manchurian Incident, the Anti-Comintern Pact, the war against China—were not primarily aimed against Britain, though their cumulative effect was to alienate it. It is difficult to decide how far this deterioration was the deliberate intention of Japan's policy objectives. After 1936 the Foreign Ministry was often divided within itself, and one wing was prepared to follow a policy toward China and Germany which was anti-British in conception. As against this, a majority in the ministry sought to avoid measures that were overtly anti-British and, presumably on the theory that diplomacy is "the application of common sense and tact

[85] *Ibid.*, p. 540.
[86] *Ibid.*
[87] *Ibid.*, p. 554.

to the conduct of official relations," tried time and again to prevent a rupture developing and to maintain the traditional courtesies. As the decade wore on, the Axis faction gained the upper hand, but even then several parallel policies were followed, so that it is difficult to describe with assurance what authoritative policy was. Unquestionably the consequence of these divisions was that relations with Britain in practice deteriorated.

Anglo-Japanese relations in the recent period have been less well served than German-Japanese and American-Japanese relations. There is no monograph devoted exclusively, or even mainly, to Japan's relations with Britain, such as Kajima's study of the period down to 1921. This fact seems to confirm the observation that Anglo-Japanese relations in the late 1930s formed only a secondary theme in Japanese policy-making.

General studies of the period in which Japan's policy toward Britain is considered incidentally:

Aoki, *Taiheiyō sensō zenshi* (3 vols., 1953).
Clifford, *Retreat from China: British Policy in the Far East, 1937–1941* (1967).
Friedman, *British Relations with China, 1931–1939* (1940).
Jones, *Japan's New Order in East Asia: Its Rise and Fall, 1937–1945* (1954).
Louis, *British Strategy in the Far East, 1919–1939* (1971).
Nihon Kokusai Seiji Gakkai Taiheiyō Sensō Gen'in Kenkyūbu, *Taiheiyō sensō e no michi* (8 vols., 1962–63).

Government documents. Great Britain (the British Foreign Office archives are open to 1945 at present):

Great Britain, Foreign Office, *Documents on British Foreign Policy, 1919–1939* (1947–   ). Second Series, Vol. I, 1929–1931 (1946), pp. 3–311, includes materials on the London naval treaty; Vols. VIII–XI (1960–70) include materials on the Manchurian crisis to June 1933. Third Series, Vols. VIII–IX (1955), are devoted entirely to the Far Eastern crisis of 1938–39.

These volumes provide abundant material on British attitudes but seem to be inadequate for any reappraisal of Japanese policy. The volumes for 1938–39 deal with the minutiae of Japanese actions against British subjects in China and the conference over Tientsin. It is doubtful whether they add much of significance to what is already known from:

Craigie, *Behind the Japanese Mask* (1945).

It is a matter of regret for students of the Far East that the terminal date for the third series of British documents was fixed at the start of the European war in 1939 instead of 1941. Japan's relations with Britain after 1939 are, however, dealt with in:

U.S., Department of State, *Documents on German Foreign Policy, 1918–1945* (16 vols., 1949–57).
Woodward, *British Foreign Policy in the Second World War* (1962).

Another source of information on the immediate prewar period is the series of war histories published by Britain, Australia, New Zealand, Canada, India, and other governments. While these are unequal in their historical value, they were often written with access to special archives.

Government documents. Japan:

Japanese archives are accessible through the microfilm reproductions, made by the Library of Congress, of historical materials in the Foreign, Army, and Navy ministries.
Japan, Gaimushō (Foreign Ministry), *Nihon gaikō nempyō narabi ni shuyō bunsho* (2 vols., 1965; first published, 1955), remains the only printed source of Japanese diplomatic documents for the period after 1919 until the appropriate volumes in the *Nihon gaikō bunsho* series are published.
—— *Shūsen shiroku* (1952), in the early chapters treats the diplomacy of the 1930s and 1940s.

International Military Tribunal for the Far East:

Asahi Shimbun Chōsa Kenkyū Shitsu, *Kyokutō kokusai gunji saiban kiroku mokuroku oyobi sakuin* (1953).
Asahi Shimbunsha, *Tōkyō saiban* (3 vols., 1962).
Dull and Umemura, *The Tokyo Trials* (1957).
Kyokutō Kokusai Gunji Saiban Kōhan Kiroku Kankōkai, *Kyokutō kokusai gunji saiban kōhan kiroku* (2 vols., 1948).

Biographies and memoirs. British:

Craigie, *Behind the Japanese Mask* (1945).
Sansom, *Sir George Sansom and Japan* (1972).

The following comment on Japan's activities in the 1930s but are mainly devoted to the Chinese scene:

Knatchbull-Hugessen, *Diplomat in Peace and War* (1949).
Pratt, *War and Politics in China* (1943).
Teichman, *Affairs of China* (1938).

British reaction to Japan's policies:

Churchill, *The Gathering Storm* (1948), Vol. I of *The Second World War* (6 vols., 1948–53), contains much information of value.

Eden, *The Memoirs of Anthony Eden, Earl of Avon: Facing the Dictators* (1962). Chap. II of Book Two is devoted to the early phases of the war with China but concentrates on Eden's "pursuit of closer Anglo-American cooperation as the only effective deterrent to Japan in the Pacific."

Among contemporary writings, there is the suggestive article by an American scholar who was resident in Japan:

Spinks, "Behind Japan's Anglophobia" (1938).

Biographies and memoirs. Japanese:

Harada, *Saionji kō to seikyoku* (9 vols., 1950–52, 1956).
Kamimura, *Gaikō gojūnen* (1960).
Kase, *Mizurī gō e no dōtei* (1951); translated as *Journey to the Missouri* (1950).
Shidehara Heiwa Zaidan, *Shidehara Kijūrō* (1955).
Shidehara, *Gaikō gojūnen* (1951).
Shigemitsu, *Gaikō kaisōroku* (1953).
—— *Shōwa no dōran* (2 vols., 1952); translated in part as *Japan and Her Destiny* (1958).
Yoshida, *Kaisō jūnen* (4 vols., 1957); translated in part as *The Yoshida Memoirs: The Story of Japan in Crisis* (1962).
Yoshizawa, *Gaikō rokujūnen* (1958).

The Shigemitsu and Yoshida works have special value because of the authors' residence in Britain. Vols. I and IV of the Yoshida memoir are of greatest interest, but there is unfortunately no detailed treatment of his ambassadorship in London (1936–38).

Nihon Kokusai Seiji Gakkai, *Kokusai seiji: Nihon gaikōshi kenkyū—Shōwa jidai* (1960), deserves special attention for its bibliography and articles.

There is no shortage of historical problems to be taken up. Little British research on policy in the Far East has yet been published for the modern period, and the same seems to be true for Japanese research on relations with Britain. On the British side there is no parallel to the wide interest shown by American historians in the years immediately before the Pacific War. It may be that Britain's role in the period 1939–41 was not as important as that of the United States, and British policy may to that extent be less significant. But this consideration does not apply to

Anglo-Japanese relations in the 1920s and 1930s when Britain was the leading external power in China. For these years especially Japan's policy toward Britain is still an important field for research.

CONCLUDING COMMENTS

Japan's relations with Britain over the entire period under review (1868–1941) might be described as a gradual growth of good relations followed by their slow deterioration. Japan's rights as an independent state were acknowledged by Britain in 1894; there was a peak of friendship reached at the time of the first alliance (1902–5); the alliance continued without serious incident but declined in effectiveness year by year until its end in 1923; even then there was no abrupt deterioration of relations, and it was not until the crises of the 1930s that Japan and Britain gradually parted ways. Thus the course of Japan's relations with Britain from 1907 onward seems to have been unspectacular, without major incident, and downhill most of the way.

These characteristics may well be peculiar to Japan's relations with Britain. Russo-Japanese relations seem to be different in kind: a phase of hostility or war is followed by a phase of rapprochement, and relations fall into well-defined segments. In Anglo-Japanese relations this oscillation is much less marked. Why should this be so? Possibly the reason is that Japan and Russia for long periods shared a common frontier in Korea and Manchuria, and this immediate confrontation of interests served to heighten the tension caused by even minor disagreements. But Japan was never strong enough to break Russia's power in the Far East completely, and so hostility had to be followed by some form of compromise if unending tension was to be avoided. By contrast, Britain never had a contiguous frontier with Japan. Down to the late 1930s Britain was most concerned with the effect of Japan's expansion on British trade with China or with the effects of Japan's occupation of the Pacific islands on Britain's imperial interests. These never caused the extreme tension that direct contact brings. In short, Japan's relationship with Britain tended to be a fairly remote one, even in the alliance period. Unlike the oscillating quality of Russo-Japanese relations, Japan's relations with Britain in the twentieth century were not punctuated by serious recurrent crises and were notable rather for the gradual attrition of goodwill.

What were the enduring determinants of Japan's policy toward Britain? Policy toward Britain is only part of overall Japanese foreign policy. That overall policy is best defined as the desire for "national growth," which many Japanese considered to be synonymous with "national expansion." Throughout this period Japan was pushing ahead the twin aspects of this national expansion—on the continent of Asia and in the world at large.

The basic policy toward Britain was to use British friendship as long as possible for the attainment of these objectives. Britain's friendship was required before the unequal treaties were removed. Then Japan entered into the alliance. By this it achieved some of the objectives of its continental policy by obtaining recognition of its rights in Korea. With Britain's blessing, it was accepted as an Open Door power in China. Similarly, in the fulfillment of its worldwide objectives it sought Britain's naval help. Japan was dependent on Britain for naval shipbuilding and naval technology. Moreover, Japan required the help of Britain's Far Eastern squadron if it was to maintain command of the seas and move its troops to any battleground in continental Asia without hindrance from the Russian squadron. This was no longer necessary after 1905; British battleships were withdrawn from the Far East. Japan was therefore left as the supreme naval power in the western Pacific and by that token a world power.

There came a time when Britain was no longer prepared to be used as an accessory in developments that were becoming increasingly hostile to its interests. Though portents were noticeable as early as 1907, this turning point in Britain's attitude occurred about 1914. On the continent of Asia, Japan confronted Britain's trading position in China with its sphere of interest in the Yangtze valley. This could not remain unaffected by the landing at Tsingtao, the best harbor on the China coast, the penetration into Shantung, and the presentation of the Twenty-One Demands. Though these measures might be represented as anti-German, they were still not likely to commend themselves to Britain. In the world at large, Japan attempted to occupy the German Pacific islands as a means of extending the range of its naval power and partly succeeded. But Britain insisted on occupying the southernmost islands as being vital to the security of Australia and New Zealand. This was an example of Britain trying to check Japanese expansion while the alliance lasted.

After the end of World War I, and more particularly after 1931, Japan's continental and world objectives could be achieved only at some sacrifice to Britain. Though Japan was anxious to keep the friendship of Britain, it had to treat Britain's actions in practice as a restraint upon the fulfill-ment of its policies. In China, Britain upheld its own interests and to some extent those of China against Japan, while Japan could never be sure that British naval power would not be diverted from Singapore to Hong Kong and Far Eastern waters. It was the threat of British naval power that helped to discourage any attempted invasion of Southeast Asia until 1941.

Underlying this account of Japan's actions, there are certain elements which may be described as determinants of Japanese policy toward Britain. First, Japan was clearly influenced by its concern for British naval power, initially for the contribution it could make to Japan, later for its potential threat to Japan's expansion. Second, its policy was conditioned by the competition it faced from Britain's established position in China and the Pacific.

It is sometimes argued that Japan's policy toward Britain was determined by its concern for British trade and capital. It is debatable how far this is so. Thus, while the Anglo-Japanese alliance was being negotiated in 1901, there is no evidence that Japan was influenced by a need for trade or foreign capital, although the conclusion of the alliance may have resulted in an improvement in both these sectors. On the contrary, the alliance was concluded despite the existence at the time of several bitter commercial disputes that suggested to foreigners that Japan was not a safe ground for investment. It is possible that the position changed by the time Japan became a fully industrialized country depending largely on imported materials. By the late 1930s Japan was certainly indignant toward Britain because the British empire was an important market for its goods and raw materials and in both cases hampered the Japanese by protectionist trade policies.

The tentative nature of these generalizations underlines the need for a more intensive study of nearly every aspect of Japan's relations with Brit-ain than has yet been made.

5

Japan's Policies
Toward China

Etō Shinkichi

◆

The study of Japan's policies toward China has been undertaken primarily by diplomatic historians using, especially in the postwar period, the official documents of the Foreign Ministry and to some extent relevant military and private archives. The result has been an impressive number of monographs on particular incidents and periods, some of the more important of which are listed below. It should be recognized that little consensus on periodization, to say nothing of interpretation, has yet emerged, so that the division offered here, on the basis of what are presumed to be major policies, is personal and tentative. Many more monographic studies of a historical type are needed before a satisfactory overall explanation of Japan's China policies can be attempted. In addition, the resources of the behavioral sciences need to be brought to bear on problems of a new type: those relating to the dynamics of policy and to the formulators and the executors of policy, their purposes, and their relations with one another. Some suggestions for the methodology of conducting such a study, together with relevant sources, are also offered below.

THE ADJUSTMENT OF NATIONAL BOUNDARIES
AND FOREIGN RELATIONS, 1868–1895

Fervent nationalism supported the Meiji government from its inception. This national feeling consisted on the one hand of a mixture of "premodern ethnocentrism" with modern state consciousness, and on the other of crisis consciousness in international politics. Furthermore, the men who established the new government did so at great personal risk, and they emerged from a civil war with deep insight about the workings of power politics. It was rather natural, therefore, that they sought to promote measures calculated to enrich and strengthen Japan and to raise the country's national prestige through the expansion of Japanese influence over weaker adjacent areas. The immediate motives that prompted this policy, however, are more difficult to discover, although there is no doubt that one was to redirect the repressed energies of the samurai class, which was disgruntled by the loss of its former special privileges.

The first basic aim of the Meiji government's continental policy, therefore, was the adjustment of the country's boundaries and its relations with its neighbors. To define national boundaries in the north, Japan had to solve problems involving Sakhalin and the Kuril Islands, and in the south it had to cope with issues involving the Bonin and Ryukyu islands. With regard to neighboring areas the Meiji government had to establish new arrangements relating to Korea and Taiwan.

Before embarking on full-scale relations with the continent, the leaders of the Meiji government in 1871 concluded a treaty of friendship and commerce with the Ch'ing dynasty in China. The Western powers had subjected both Japan and China to unequal treaties. In the treaty of 1871 the two countries accordingly recognized each other's right to consular jurisdiction. In reality, however, Japan attempted to get China to submit to an unequal treaty similar to the treaties the Ch'ing government had concluded with the Western powers. Japan withdrew its demand only because of strong Chinese opposition. Little study has been made of this Sino-Japanese treaty. Only one work, Wang Yun-sheng's *Liu-shih-nien lai Chung-kuo yü Jih-pen*, refers to this subject in some detail.

Having secured a treaty with China, Japan's leaders turned to problems involving Korea, the Ryukyu Islands, and Taiwan. In 1873 they divided over a proposed military expedition against Korea. They held in common a strong sense of nationalism involving a desire to enhance the world prestige of the Japanese empire. Moderates, however, felt that a premature international adventure would endanger the country. The moderates finally prevailed and the government canceled the projected expedition. On the other hand, Japanese leaders did use military force to settle both the Ryukyu (1872–81) and Taiwan (1874) questions. This was particularly true in the case of Taiwan. Ōkubo Toshimichi, who had opposed the policy of the Korean expedition the year before, strongly advocated the use of military power on this occasion, and the Japanese government followed Ōkubo at the risk of war with China.

Since World War II many Japanese scholars have bitterly criticized the leaders of the Meiji government for being subordinate to the West and for adopting aggressive policies toward other Asian countries. These criticisms contribute to an understanding of factual developments, but they do not analyze the fundamental reasons behind the aggressive policies of the Meiji government, nor do they give adequate explanations for the fervor of Japanese public opinion since the early Meiji period concerning China and Korea.

We must therefore reexamine Japanese policy toward China in order to try to answer these basic questions. On the Ryukyu question several essays are available, but almost no studies exist on the Taiwan question. Every student of the history of Taiwan should read the books by Inō and Yanaihara. A monthly magazine, *Taiwan seinen*, also known as *Taiwan chinglian*, published by the United Formosans for Independence, a group advocating independence for Taiwan, often provides useful historical essays. Mukōyama Hiroo, a professor at Kokugakuin University in Tokyo, has written a comprehensive history of Taiwan under Japanese rule with an excellent bibliography, but it has not yet been published.

Whether the motivation for Japanese policy toward Korea was a desire for territorial aggrandizement or a wish to assist Korea in becoming a modern independent nation is another much-debated question. Most Korean scholars and Marxist scholars in Japan support the former view. Hilary Conroy and Tabohashi Kiyoshi argue the latter. Whatever the outcome of this debate, it is certain that until the outbreak of the Russo-Japanese War in 1904, Korea had the "alternative" of maintaining its independence through positive internal reforms. If Korea had taken this alternative course, there is no doubt that Japan would have had no justification for or intention of dispatching troops there.

Scholars have explored the Korean question and the Sino-Japanese War of 1894–95 with comparative thoroughness. Some Marxists, including Shinobu, tend to make economic ambition the major cause of the war. Minami and Oka play down the economic cause and pay more attention to psychological motives. The works of Ueda and Yano furnish a guide to source materials on international problems surrounding the war.

Checklists of government archives:

Kuo and Morley, *Sino-Japanese Relations, 1862–1927: A Checklist of the Chinese Foreign Ministry Archives* (1965).

Uyehara, *Checklist of the Archives in the Japanese Ministry of Foreign Affairs, Tokyo, Japan, 1868–1945, Microfilmed for the Library of Congress, 1949–1951* (1954).

Young, *Checklist of Microfilm Reproductions of Selected Archives of the Japanese Army, Navy, and Other Government Agencies, 1868–1945* (1959).

Sino-Japanese cultural relations at the close of the Tokugawa period:

Kimiya, *Nikka bunka kōryūshi* (1955).

The Sino-Japanese Treaty of Friendship and Commerce, 1871:

Wang, *Liu-shih-nien lai Chung-kuo yü Jih-pen* (7 vols., 1932–34).

The Ryukyu problem:

Hanabusa, "Okinawa kizoku no enkaku" (1955).
Miura, "Meiji jidai ni okeru Ryūkyū shozoku mondai" (1931).
Tomimura, "Ryūkyū ōchō no chōkō bōeki saku" (1960).
Ueda, "Ryūkyū no kizoku o meguru Nisshin kōshō" (1951).
Yasuoka, "Ryūkyū shozoku o meguru Nisshin kōshō no shomondai" (1957).

The Taiwan problem:

Inō, *Taiwan bunkashi* (3 vols., 1928).
Mukōyama, "Nihon tōchika ni okeru Taiwan minzoku undō shi" (1961).
Ong, *Taiwan: Kumon suru sono rekishi* (1964, rev. ed. 1970).
Shi, *Taiwanjin yonhyakunenshi* (1962).
Tabohashi, "Ryūkyū hammin bangai jiken ni kansuru kōsatsu" (1933).
Taiwan seinen; also known as *Taiwan chinglian.*
Yanaihara, *Teikoku shugika no Taiwan* (1929).

The Korean problem and the Sino-Japanese War of 1894–95:

Conroy, *The Japanese Seizure of Korea, 1868–1910* (1960).
Harada, "Chōsen heigō to shoki no shokuminchi keiei" (1963).
Hatada, *Chōsen shi* (1951).
—— "Meijiki no Nihon to Chōsen" (1962).
Hatano, "Shimonoseki jōyaku dairokujō daiyonkō no seiritsu shita haikei ni tsuite" (1958).
Hō, "Shin-Futsu sensōki ni okeru Nihon no tai-Kan seisaku" (1960).
—— "Shimonoseki jōyaku ni tsuite" (1961).
—— "Chōsen mondai o meguru Jiyūtō to Furansu: shu to shite Yamabe shi setsu ni taisuru hihan" (1962).

—— "Kōshin jihen o meguru Inoue gaimukyō to Furansu kōshi to no kōshō" (1963).

Maejima, "Kanjō seihen: Hokushin jihen ni itaru Nihon 'teikoku' gaikō no ichi sokumen" (1959).

Minami, "Nisshin sensō to Chōsen bōeki" (1951).

Nakatsuka, "Nisshin sensō" (1962).

—— "Nisshin sensō to Chōsen mondai" (1963).

Oka, "Nisshin sensō to tōji ni okeru taigai ishiki" (1954–55).

Okudaira, *Chōsen kaikoku kōshō shimatsu* (1935).

Sakurai, "Chōsen no kindaika to Nisshin sensō" (1962).

—— "Kindai Nikkan kankei shiryō kaidai" (1962).

Shin, "Kankoku no kaikoku: Unyō gō jiken o megutte" (1960).

—— "Kōka jōki chokugo no Kan-Nichi gaikō" (1962).

Shinobu, *Mutsu gaikō: Nisshin sensō no gaikō shiteki kenkyū* (1935).

Tabohashi, *Kindai Nissen kankei no kenkyū* (2 vols., 1929).

—— "Kindai Nis-Shi-Sen kankei no kenkyū" (1930).

—— "Kindai Chōsen ni okeru kaikō no kenkyū" (1934).

—— *Nisshin sen'eki gaikōshi no kenkyū* (1951).

Tanaka, "Nissen kankei no ichi dammen: Keijō jingo no hen" (1957).

Usui, "Jōyaku kaisei to Chōsen mondai" (1962).

Yamabe, "Chōsen kaikaku undō to Kin Gyokukin: Kōshin jihen ni kanren shite" (1960).

—— "Kōshin jihen ni tsuite: toku ni 'Jiyūtō shi' no ayamari ni kanren shite" (1960).

—— "Kōshin nichiroku no kenkyū" (1960).

—— "Nisshin Tenshin jōyaku ni tsuite" (1960).

—— "Jingo gunran ni tsuite" (1961).

—— "Kōshin jihen to Tōgaku no ran" (1961).

—— "Itsubi no hen ni tsuite" (1962).

—— "Nihon teikokushugi to shokuminchi" (1963).

Yamawaki, "Mazampo jiken" (1959–63).

Yuasa, "Kindai Nitchō kankei no ichi kōsatsu: burujoajii no tai-Chōsen seisaku o chūshin to shite" (1962).

International aspects of the Sino-Japanese War:

Ueda, "Nisshin sen'eki to kokusaihō" (1962).

Yano, *Nisshin eki go Shina gaikōshi* (1937).

ADDITION OF KOREA TO THE JAPANESE
SPHERE, 1895–1904

After the Sino-Japanese War of 1894–95, the Japanese government set about immediately to attain a position of national equality with the Western powers. Examples of the implementation of this policy include the successful efforts for treaty revision and the maintenance of tight military discipline among Japanese soldiers at the time of the Boxer Rebellion.

Furthermore, the Japanese people, enraged by the Triple Intervention (1895), determined with vengeance to resist further Russian expansion in the Far East. Accordingly, when Japan was confronted with Russian infiltration in Korea, the government's objective became the maintenance of the territorial integrity of that country.

This is a much-debated point. Many Marxist scholars emphasize that a goal of the Russo-Japanese War of 1904–5 was the acquisition of the Manchurian market. Shimomura asserts, however, that the Japanese government did not intend to go beyond the maintenance of Korea's territorial integrity. Fujii and Inoue advocate the market theory. It is undeniable that there were Japanese decision-makers, like Foreign Minister Komura Jutarō, who promoted the expansion of Japanese rights and interests into Manchuria after the war with Russia. But as far as the Japanese government's objective immediately before the war is concerned, Shimomura seems to have the better of the argument. As long as Russian influence was restricted to Manchuria, regardless of the uneasiness it might have caused Japan, the Japanese government would have taken no steps toward war. Furthermore, the Anglo-Japanese alliance, which was based on the antagonism between Britain and Russia, maintained at least temporarily the balance of power in the Far East. The period 1894–1904, then, is best seen as one when Japan's primary continental purpose was to keep Korea within Japan's sphere of influence.

Japanese policy prior to the Russo-Japanese War:

Abe, "Nisshin kōwa to sangoku kanshō" (1961).
Imai, "Nichi-Ro sensō zengo Manshū zairyū Nihonjin no bumpu jōtai" (1960).
Maejima, "Ro-Shin mitsuyaku to Katō gaikō" (1960).
Mori, "Meiji nijūkyūnen Nisshin tsūshō jōyaku to shihon yushutsu" (1961).
Satō, "Kōakai ni kansuru ichi kōsatsu" (1951).

—— "Meiji sanjūsannen no Amoi jiken ni kansuru kōsatsu: kindai Nitchū kōshō shijō no hitokoma to shite" (1963).

The Boxer Rebellion:

Eguchi, "Giwadan jiken no igi ni tsuite" (1951).
Ichiko, "Giwaken no seikaku" (1948).
Inō, "Giwadan jihen to Nihon no shuppei gaikō: daigo shidan shutsudō ni itaru made no keii" (1952).
Kawamura, "Hokushin jihen to Nihon" (1957).

Japanese policy toward Manchuria:

Baba, "Nichi-Ro sensō go no tairiku seisaku" (1961).
Fujii, "Teikokushugi no seiritsu to Nichi-Ro sensō" (1956).
Imai, "Nichi-Ro sensō to tai-Shin seisaku no tenkai" (1960).
Inoue, "Nichi-Ro sensō ni tsuite" (1958).
Kurihara, "Nichi-Ro sensō go ni okeru Manshū zengo sochi mondai no ippan" (1961).
Ōhata, "Nichi-Ro sensō to Man-Kan mondai" (1958).
Shimomura, "Nichi-Ro sensō ni tsuite: Manshū shijō" (1956).
—— "Nichi-Ro sensō to Manshū shijō" (1956).

THE CONSOLIDATION OF RIGHTS AND INTERESTS, 1905–1915

With the outbreak of the Russo-Japanese War, Korea lost the "alternative" of maintaining its independence. Since an independent Korea would block the flow of communication between Japan proper and its new rights and interests in Manchuria, the Japanese government decided from geopolitical considerations to place Korea under Japanese control by military force. Consequently, in February 1904 Japan forced Korea to accede to the Japan-Korea Protocol, which gave Japan the right to interfere in Korea's internal affairs. And through successive treaties of protection and amalgamation, in 1910 Korea became a Japanese colony.

The acquisition by Japan of rights and interests in Manchuria terminated the short period of amicable relations between Japan and China that had emerged after the war of 1894–95, and a period of unending friction commenced between the two nations. Since Japan merely succeeded to the rights and interests that Russia had held in China, many of them had early terminal dates or were insecure. Therefore, after the Russo-Japanese War, consolidation of the newly acquired rights and interests became the objective of the Japanese government. For this purpose Japan first resorted to alliance and entente with the Western powers. By recognizing the powers' spheres of influence in China south of the Wall, Japan succeeded in having the powers recognize its rights and interests in southern Manchuria.

Japan further consolidated its rights and interests by dispatching two ultimatums to the Chinese government: one concerned the policy question related to the Mukden-Antung rail line, and the other included the Twenty-One Demands. Japan also showed signs during the 1911 revolution of taking advantage of China's internal turmoil; from this time on both the revolutionaries and the Yuan Shih-k'ai regime were suspicious of Japanese intentions.

Sino-Japanese friction following the Russo-Japanese War:

Baba, "Nichi-Ro sensō go no tairiku seisaku" (1961).
Imai, "Nichi-Ro sensō to tai-Shin seisaku no tenkai" (1960).
Kikuchi, "Daini Tatsu Maru jiken no tai-Nichi boikotto" (1957).
Kurihara, "Nichi-Ro sensō go ni okeru Manshū zengo sochi mondai no ippan" (1961).
Ōhata, "Nichi-Ro sensō to Man-Kan mondai" (1958).
Tamashima, *Chūgoku no me* (1959).

Japanese objectives following the Russo-Japanese War:

Hayashi, "Kantō mondai ni kansuru Nisshin kōshō no keii" (1960).
Nakayama, "Saionji shushō no Manshū ryokō ni tsuite: Nichi-Ro sen go no Manshū mondai, sono ni" (1962).

The Mukden-Antung line question:

Kikuchi, "Ampō tetsudō kōchiku mondai to tai-Nichi boikotto ni tsuite" (1960).

The Twenty-One Demands:

Horikawa, *Kyokutō kokusai seijishi josetsu: nijūikkajō yōkyū no kenkyū* (1958).
Ishida, "Ōkuma rōkō to tai-Shi gaikō: iwayuru nijūikkajō mondai o megurite toku ni daigokō kibō jōkō ni tsuite" (1954–56).
—— "Nijūikkajō mondai o terasu kokusai kaigi: Parī kaigi, Washinton kaigi o tsūjite" (1958).
—— "Tai-Ka nijūikkajō mondai to rekkoku no teikō" (1958).
Matsumoto, *Nisshi shin kōshō ni yoru teikoku no riken* (1915).
—— *Taishō yonen Nisshi kōshōroku* (1921).

Yim, "Yüan Shih-k'ai and the Japanese" (1964).

The Chinese revolution of 1911 and Japan:

Hatano, "Shingai kakumei to Nihon" (1954).
Igarashi, "Shingai kakumei to Nihon oyobi Nihonjin: namboku dakyō e no katei ni okeru Nihon no taiō" (1961).
Ikei, "Nihon no tai-En gaikō: shingai kakumeiki" (1962).
Irie, "Shingai kakumei to shinseifu no shōnin" (1956).
Kurihara, "Abe Gaimushō seimukyokuchō ansatsu jiken to tai-Chūgoku (Mammō) mondai" (1956).
―― "Daiichiji dainiji Mammō dokuritsu undō" (1958).
Kuroba, "Iwayuru Nunobiki Maru jiken ni tsuite" (1962).
Nozawa, "Shingai kakumei to Taishō seihen" (1960).
Somura, "Shingai kakumei to Nihon" (1960).
Usui, "Nihon to shingai kakumei: sono ichi sokumen" (1957).

THE MAINTENANCE OF RIGHTS AND INTERESTS, 1915–1931

After Japan legally consolidated its rights and interests in China through treaties related to the Twenty-One Demands and World War I, the maintenance and full realization of those rights and interests became the central aim of its China policy. The Terauchi cabinet assisted Tuan Ch'i-jui because Terauchi thought that Japan's vested interests in China would be more secure if a unified pro-Japanese regime could be set up under Tuan's leadership.

The Hara cabinet which succeeded Terauchi's, on the other hand, promoted a policy of nonintervention in Chinese internal affairs. Until 1931 succeeding cabinets more or less faithfully carried out this policy, except during the years under the Tanaka cabinet, 1927–29. Some writers, such as Eguchi, assert, however, that Japan in these years actually wanted to interfere in Chinese internal affairs.

The Tanaka cabinet, however, found it could not completely renounce the policy of nonintervention. In 1927 and 1928 Tanaka dispatched troops to Shantung with the stated purpose of protecting Japanese residents in that area. These unnecessary expeditions originated in fact in Seiyūkai considerations for "face." Leaders of the party had actively criticized former Foreign Minister Shidehara Kijūrō for his nonintervention policy toward

China and when in power felt compelled to adopt a "positive policy." Moreover, the Seiyūkai at that time had many members like Mori Kaku, then parliamentary vice-minister of foreign affairs, who strongly advocated an even more aggressive policy toward China. Therefore, when troops of the Chinese Nationalists marched into north China, the Tanaka cabinet twice sent troops to Shantung. One result was the Tsinan Incident of May 1928. Shortly afterwards, staff officers of the Kwantung army assassinated Chang Tso-lin. Chinese nationalism, more and more infuriated by these actions, now turned its force against Japan.

The Kuomintang government's success in unifying China strengthened the nationalist movement throughout the country. Before long, the anti-Japanese movement in Manchuria became so strong that it posed a threat to Japan's rights and interests there; in September 1931, in defense of these interests, the Kwantung army fabricated the Manchurian Incident.

World War I and Japanese policy:

Mitani, " 'Tenkanki' (1918–1921) no gaikō shidō" (1965).
Uchiyama, "Nichi-Doku sensō to Santō mondai" (1960).
Ueda, "Daiichiji taisen ni okeru Nihon no sansen gaikō" (1948).
Usui, "Chūgoku no taisen sanka to Nihon no tachiba" (1960).
—— "Ōshū taisen to Nihon no tai-Man seisaku: Namman Tōmō jōyaku no seiritsu zengo" (1962).

Tuan Ch'i-jui supported by Japan:

Kitamura, "Kōtsū Ginkō shakkan no seiritsu jijō" (1961).
Nishihara, *Yume no shichijūyonen* (1949).
Saitō, *Saikin Shina kokusai kankei* (1931).
Shōda, *Kiku no newake: Nisshi keizaijō no shisetsu ni tsuite* (1918).

The Tanaka cabinet:

Eguchi, "Kaku Shōrei jiken to Nihon teikokushugi" (1962).
Etō, "Nankin jiken to Nichi-Bei" (1959).
—— "Shidehara gaikō kara Tanaka gaikō e: gaikō mondai o midari ni tōsō no gu ni suru to dō naru ka" (1963).
—— "Keihōsen shadan mondai no gaikō katei" (1965).
Fujii, "Sen-kyūhyaku-nijūnen An-Choku sensō o meguru Nitchū kankei no ichi kōsatsu: Hembōgun mondai o chūshin to shite" (1960).
Hanabusa, "Santō mondai no kaiketsu ni kansuru Nikka kōshō" (1960).
Ikei, "Daiichiji Hō-Choku sensō to Nihon" (1962).
—— "Dainiji Hō-Choku sensō to Nihon" (1964).

Nakamura, "Go-sanjū jiken to zaikabō" (1964).

Saitō, *Shina kokusai kankei gaikan* (1924).

Somura, "Washinton kaigi no ichi kōsatsu: Ozaki Yukio no gumbi seigen ron o chūshin ni shite" (1958).

Takakura, *Tanaka Giichi denki* (2 vols., 1958–60).

Tanaka Giichi kankei bunsho mokuroku (1961).

Usui, "Go-sanjū jiken to Nihon" (1957).

—— "Tanaka gaikō ni tsuite no oboegaki" (1959).

Yamamoto, "Washinton kaigi ni okeru Chūgoku mondai: kaigi ni taisuru Nihon no taido o chūshin to shite" (1961).

The Tsinan Incident:

Japan, Sambō Hombu (Army General Staff), *Shōwa sannen Shina jihen shuppei shi* (1930).

Morton, "Sainan jihen, 1928–1929" (1960).

The assassination of Chang Tso-lin:

Hirano, *Manshū no imbōsha: Kōmoto Daisaku no unmeiteki na ashiato* (1959).

Saitō, "Chō Sakurin bakushi no zengo, sono 1" (1955).

—— "Chō Sakurin no shi" (1955).

Chinese nationalism turns against Japan:

Inō, "'Tanaka jōsōbun' o meguru ni san no mondai" (1963).

Nakamura, "Go-sanjū jiken to zaikabō" (1964).

Saitō, "Chō Sakurin bakushi no zengo, sono 1" (1955).

—— "Chō Sakurin no shi" (1955).

Tamashima, *Chūgoku no me* (1959).

Usui, "Go-sanjū jiken to Nihon" (1957).

—— "Chōsa jiken" (1961).

Manchurian problems:

Fuse, *Mammō ken'eki yōroku* (1932).

Nomura, "Manshū jihen chokuzen no Tōsanshō mondai" (1960).

Satō, *Mammō mondai o chūshin to suru Nisshi kankei* (1931).

Shinobu, *Mammō tokushu ken'eki ron* (1932).

Sonoda, *Tōsanshō no seiji to gaikō* (1925).

Yanaihara, *Manshū mondai* (1934).

THE ESTABLISHMENT OF MANCHUKUO AND THE SEPARATION OF NORTH CHINA, 1931–1937

The tendency of the Japanese army in the Kwantung Leased Territory to take positive action in defiance of orders from the central government came into the open in 1928. The murder of Chang Tso-lin in June of that year made the phenomenon clear to all knowledgeable observers. Matters reached a climax on September 18, 1931, in Mukden. The Tokyo government was indecisive and failed to take strong action. The frustrated Japanese people, however, rejoiced over developments, and the army's use of force was a kind of catharsis. As a result, even some responsible officials began to support the army's decisive action, and the government became more and more impotent. After the incident, the Kwantung army's plan to establish Manchukuo succeeded. Next, activists carried out operations in rapid succession to separate north China and Suiyuan; and in 1936 the official policy of the Japanese government decreed that the five provinces of north China should be made "autonomous."

Besides the books on the Manchurian Incident by Maxon, Ogata, and Yoshihashi, Kimura Yoshito's dissertation manuscript is on deposit at Tokyo University. Hata's book is a compilation of several essays based mainly on military records; it also includes a list of publications concerning the era. An outstanding work edited by the Manshikai clarifies problems related to the economic development of Manchuria, but many other subjects, such as Japanese investments in Manchuria or the activities of the South Manchuria Railway Company, remain unexplored. Seki and Shimada have used basic materials to write a bird's-eye view of the topics noted below.

Pre-Manchurian Incident:

Seki, "Manshū jihen zenshi" (1963).
—— "Tairiku gaikō no kiki to sangatsu jiken" (1965).

Manchurian Incident:

Kimura, "Manshū jihen to Ishiwara Kanji" (1962).
Maxon, *Control of Japanese Foreign Policy* (1957).
Ogata, *Defiance in Manchuria: The Making of Japanese Foreign Policy, 1931–1932* (1964).
Yoshihashi, *Conspiracy at Mukden: The Rise of the Japanese Military* (1963).

Post-Manchurian Incident:

Shimada, "Manshū jihen no tenkai" (1962).

The Shanghai Incident:

Shimada, "Shanhai teisen kyōtei shimpan mondai" (1955).

—— "Shiryō: Shōwa shichinen Shanhai teisen kyōtei seiritsu no keii" (1955).
Suzuki, "Shanhai jihen no suii ni tsuite: toku ni seifu to gumbu no dōkō" (1961).

Economic development of Manchuria:

Manshikai, *Manshū kaihatsu yonjūnenshi* (1964).
Young, *The Research Activities of the South Manchurian Railway Company, 1907–1945* (1966).

Aspects of Japanese continental policy:

Hata, *Nitchū sensōshi* (1961).
Shimada, "Kawagoe-Chō Gun kaidan no butai ura," Part 1 (1963).
Tamashima, *Chūgoku no me* (1959).
Usui, " 'Shina jihen' zen no Chū-Nichi kōshō" (1960).
Yamashita, "Manshū jihen no hassei" (1962).
Yazawa, "Sen-kyūhyaku-sanjūgo-rokunen ni okeru Kokumintō no tai-Nichi seisaku to shimbun no kō-Nichi ronchō" (1961).

THE ATTEMPT TO SUBJUGATE CHIANG KAI-SHEK, 1937–1945

After the Marco Polo Bridge Incident of July 7, 1937, the army gradually usurped the powers of the Foreign Ministry until the ministry came to be called the "foreign affairs bureau of the army." Throughout these years the Japanese government aimed at the subjugation or dissolution of the Chiang Kai-shek regime, except during the short period in 1940 when the Army General Staff proposed to withdraw troops from China voluntarily; this proposal, however, suddenly died with the success of the German blitzkrieg in Europe.

Studies of the period:

Etō, "Chūgoku ni taisuru sensō shūketsu kōsaku" (1958).
Horiba, *Shina jihen sensō shidō shi* (2 vols., 1962).
Inada, "Senryakumen kara mita Shina jihen no sensō shidō" (1960).
Lu, *From the Marco Polo Bridge to Pearl Harbor: Japan's Entry into World War II* (1961).
Nakamura, "Nikka jihen no gen'in to hatten no yurai" (1960).
—— "Rokōkyō jiken no boppatsu to hatten" (1960).
Nihon Kokusai Seiji Gakkai Taiheiyō Sensō Gen'in Kenkyūbu, *Taiheiyō sensō e no michi* (8 vols., 1962–63), vols. 3–4.

Okada, "Nitchū sensō ni tsuite" (1961).
Tamashima, *Chūgoku no me* (1959).

Japanese repatriation after the war:

Hikiage Engo Chō, *Hikiage engo no kiroku* (1950).

CONCEPTS AND SOURCES FOR DYNAMIC ANALYSIS

In the future, if the study of Japan's China policies is to yield more than descriptive knowledge, it must be based on a more explicit understanding of the processes by which policy was formed. The following analytical concepts may prove useful.

Initial Response. The immediate response of an individual or group to an external stimulus is a kind of conditioned reflex. Take, for example, the immediate reaction of the average Japanese to the news of the Triple Intervention. It was probably an outraged, "How could we have given up our Liaotung Peninsula?" As he underwent a process of rational judgment, however, he finally realized, "It would be tough to fight Germany, France, and Russia." The average Japanese upon hearing the report of the Manchurian Incident in 1931 shouted in exultation, "We did it!" He had not the slightest doubt about the deceptive announcement of the Kwantung army that the explosion on the tracks of the South Manchuria Railway had been detonated by Chinese soldiers. For the time being, such an immediate response, which has not yet undergone a process of rationalization, can be called an initial response. Different people have different initial responses; the majority of Japanese, however, show a more or less common response, due to a similar environment. The bureaucrat, politician, and all those who have an important role in decision-making are not exceptions in their initial responses; nor are their initial responses much different from those of the masses.

Responsible Officials. The group of government officials responsible for policy-making included cabinet members, high-ranking officials of the Foreign Ministry, middle-ranking officials in the Asia Bureau of the ministry, and responsible officers in the Army Ministry and the Army General Staff. In a government that maintains a huge bureaucratic system, unless the leadership of cabinet members is very strong, the basic draft of a policy is usually formulated among middle-ranking bureaucrats. It becomes a policy of the government after undergoing a process of successive adjustments at the hands of higher bureaucrats. In most cases the draft is not amended except for certain detailed points. In Japan this tendency was strengthened as the bureaucratic system became consolidated and the number of political leaders who had personally participated in the Meiji Restoration gradually decreased.

As we have observed, the initial response of responsible officials to an outside stimulus is basically no different from that of other Japanese. The only difference is that they, being in positions of authority where accurate information is most accessible, tend to reach the most "practical" and therefore "conventional" conclusion.

Interested Agencies. Included were politicians, bureaucrats, local "subleaders," and others not directly responsible for the management of foreign affairs. They were not experts on China affairs, but they applied great pressure and influence on actual decision-making through their organizations and by use of their political positions. In Japan there have been many instances in which the bureaucrat played the same role as that of the pressure group in America. After the Meiji Restoration, Japan concentrated all its efforts on rapidly catching up with the West's achievements of the previous three hundred years, and therefore the establishment of nongovernmental organizations was considerably behind that of the state organization. Consequently, units within the governmental organization often took over roles usually performed in other countries by civil organizations. For instance, throughout the Meiji and Taishō eras, the bureaucrats of the Ministry of Agriculture and Commerce (reorganized in 1925) were the staunchest advocates of a modern labor relations law, and the Agricultural Policy Bureau of the Ministry of Agriculture and Forestry (established in 1925) stressed the necessity of land reform in prewar Japan. In addition, there have been many examples of organizations set up as civil bodies which actually were mere auxiliary organs of the state and thus subject to the strong leadership of the bureaucrats. The Imperial Reservists Association and the Imperial Education Association were examples of this type of "civil" organization. Membership in these organizations, which came in direct contact with the public, included such people as local politicians, small businessmen, small- and medium-scale landlords, and schoolteachers.

Interested Private Sector. This is a category for those who had a special interest in China affairs, having reached their own opinions by attentively following current developments in Sino-Japanese relations. Journalists specializing in China affairs, some scholars on China, and military men who were commonly called *shinaya* or "China hands" were outstanding examples of members of this group. Associations of China activists, who devoted themselves to China affairs with a great sense of mission and ambition, such as the members of the China Affairs League and the Dark Ocean Society, also were included. Other organizations of the interested private sector were the associations of Japanese residents in China, the League of the Japanese Textile Industry in China, and the Society of Japanese Businessmen in China, each of which clearly had a special interest in China.

These organizations were generally nationalistic and seldom went so far in their activities as to defy the framework of *kokutai* or the national polity of Japan. Within this framework, they frequently championed policies contrary to those of the government, as during the Hibiya Riot at the time of the Portsmouth Treaty (1905) and in the behind-the-scenes maneuvering of the China activists who assisted the Chinese revolution of 1911, when the official policy of the Japanese government was to support the Yuan Shih-k'ai regime. In contrast to the responsible officials who were apt to resort to makeshift policies, these organizations were generally more radical and, in a sense, irresponsible. At times they displayed great power to move the masses by utilizing the masses' emotional initial response.

The growth of an interested private sector on the China question, which in some cases included people who were against the established system of the state, was considerably delayed in Japan. It finally sprouted after World War I and reached its climax in the movement of the Alliance for Nonintervention in China at the time of the Tanaka cabinet and in the activities of the Proletarian Science Research Center. This interested private sector, however, gradually declined after the Manchurian Incident in 1931 because it failed to mobilize the masses against the existing system.

The research problem, then, is two-fold: first, to describe accurately the above-mentioned elements, i.e., the initial response, responsible officials, interested agencies, and interested private sectors; and, second, to investigate the relationships among them. For the former purpose, recourse should be had to a great variety of sources which until now have been little consulted by researchers. A discussion of some of the more important of these sources, together with the few analytical studies so far attempted, follows.

The Japanese Image of China. As suggested above, an "initial response" occurs when an individual reacts to an outside stimulus according to a preconceived notion gained from his own experience. When information on China affairs is transmitted to an individual, his intial response depends upon his preconceived image of China. Therefore, to estimate the nature of the initial response, it is necessary for us to grasp clearly not only the structure of various organizations but also the nature of the image of China held by Japanese.

In postwar Japan, extensive field surveys and questionnaires have enabled social scientists to analyze Japanese national character, racial and nationality distances, and national images in the minds of the people. Four books are suggestive:

Nihon Jimbun Gakkai, *Shakaiteki kinchō no kenkyū* (1953).
Ningen Kankei Sōgō Kenkyūdan, *Nihonjin: bunka to pāsonariti no jisshōteki kenkyū* (1962).
Tōkei Sūri Kenkyūsho Kokuminsei Chōsa Iinkai, *Nihonjin no kokuminsei* (1961).
Wagatsuma and Yoneyama, *Henken no kōzō: Nihonjin no jinshukan* (1967).

With respect to prewar Japan, two general works are listed below along with several prewar books specifically on the Japanese image of China. Most of them are simple and impressionistic compared with some of the postwar works. No student has ever undertaken a serious study of the long-held Japanese dream of the emancipation of Asian peoples. The books by Takeuchi and Kamei and the article by Hanzawa are useful introductions to further study. Mushakōji's note is an attempt to make a brief sketch of Japanese images of the external world from the standpoint of behavioral science.

There seem to be three approaches to the study of Japanese views of China. The first is the use of biographies, diaries, and written works of the officials responsible for Japanese policy. There were several responsible officials in the field of Chinese affairs who left materials to be analyzed. These are listed below.

A second approach is through the images of China held by middle-ranking military officers, entrepreneurs, and journalists who lived in China. These included such men as Colonel Tōmiya Kaneo, the journalist Kikuchi Teiji, and an active member of the Amur River Society and the Dark Ocean Society, Uchida Ryōhei.

A third approach is to extract Japanese views on China from a survey of literary or popular writings and school textbooks. For instance, Natsume Sōseki's *Botchan* and *Man-Kan tokoro-dokoro* will give us a glimpse of his views on China. Karasawa Tomitarō made an extensive survey of Japanese school textbooks in his *Kyōkasho no rekishi*. Would it not be possible to draw Japanese images of foreign countries from textbooks? It might also be useful to analyze the writings of such men as Takezoe Shin'ichirō, a poet and Japanese minister to Korea, 1882–87.

Karasawa, *Kyōkasho no rekishi: kyōkasho to Nihonjin no keisei* (1956).

Natsume, *Botchan* (1907; reprinted, 1942).

——*Man-Kan tokoro-dokoro* (1910).

Takezoe, *Gen. Isan monzen* (1883).

—— *Dokuhōrō shibun kō: fu Sen'unkyō'u nikki* (1912).

Prewar Japan:

Aya and Furuichi, "Nichi-Man jidō no rekkoku kan" (1934).

Japan, Mombushō, Shakai Kyōikukyoku (Ministry of Education, Bureau of Social Education), *Sōtei shisō chōsa gaiyō* (1931).

Japanese images of China (prewar studies):

Hamano, *Shinajin katagi* (1926).

Kasai, *Ura kara mita Shina minzokusei* (1935).

Kikuchi, *Chōkyōrō mampitsu* (1936).

Matsunaga, *Shina gakan* (1919).

Takigawa, *Hōritsu kara mita Shina kokuminsei* (1941).

Watanabe, *Shina kokuminsei ron* (1922).

Japanese images of China (postwar studies):

Banno, "Nihonjin no Chūgoku kan: Oda Yorozu hakushi no 'Shinkoku gyōseihō' o megutte" (1962).

Etō, "Nihonjin no Chūgoku kan: Suzue Gen'ichi o megutte" (1961).

Sekai no naka no Nihon (1961).

Somura, "Uchida Ryōhei no Chūgoku kan" (1957).

—— "Tairiku seisaku ni okeru imēji no tenkan" (1965).
Takeuchi, "Kangakusha no Chūgoku kikō: Nihonjin no Chūgoku zō, nōto 1" (1959).
—— "Sōseki no 'Man-Kan tokoro-dokoro': Nihonjin no Chūgoku zō, nōto 2" (1959).

Japanese images of Asia and the world:

Hanzawa, " 'Manshūkoku' no isan wa nani ka" (1964).
Kamei, *Dai Tōa minzoku no michi* (1941).
Mushakōji, "Nihonjin no taigai ishiki: apurōchi settei no tame no nōto" (1961).
—— "From Fear of Dependence to Fear of Independence" (1964).
Takeuchi, *Ajiashugi* (1963).

Writings of responsible officials on China:

Hara, *Yamamoto Jōtarō ronsaku* (2 vols., 1939).
Katsura Tarō kankei bunsho mokuroku (1965).
Katsura Tarō Papers in the Kensei Shiryō Shitsu, National Diet Library.
Koiso Kuniaki Jijoden Kankōkai, *Katsuzan Kōsō* (1963).
Matsuoka Yōsuke, *Tōa zenkyoku no dōyō* (1931).
—— *Ugoku Mammō* (1931).
—— *Mantetsu o kataru* (1937).
Mutsu Munemitsu papers in the Kensei Shiryō Shitsu, National Diet Library.
Obata Yūkichi Denki Kankōkai, *Obata Yūkichi* (1957).
Ōkuma Shigenobu papers in the Shakai Kagaku Kenkyūjo, Waseda University.
Tanaka Giichi kankei bunsho mokuroku (1961).
Tanaka Giichi papers in the Yamaguchi Kenritsu Monjokan, Yamaguchi; microfilms are available in the Kensei Shiryō Shitsu, National Diet Library.
Ugaki, *Ugaki nikki* (1954).
Yoshizawa, *Gaikō rokujūnen* (1958).
Zai-Ka Nihon Bōseki Dōgyōkai, *Funatsu Shin'ichirō* (1958).

Views of the interested private sector:

Banno, "Nihonjin no Chūgoku kan: Oda Yorozu hakushi no 'Shinkoku gyōseihō' o megutte" (1962).
Etō, "Nihonjin no Chūgoku kan: Suzue Gen'ichi o megutte" (1961).
Kikuchi and Nakajima, *Hōten nijūnenshi* (1926).
Kikuchi, *Chōkyōrō mampitsu* (1936).
Takeuchi, "Kangakusha no Chūgoku kikō: Nihonjin no Chūgoku zō, nōto 1" (1959).
Tōmiya Taisa Kinen Jigyō Iinkai, *Tōmiya Kaneo den* (1940).

Uchida, *Shina kaizō ron* (1911).
—— *Nihon no san dai kyūmu* (1912).
—— *Zen Mammō tetsudō tōitsu ikensho* (1930).

The Role of Organizations. Except for a descriptive official history of the Foreign Ministry, there is not at present available a complete history of the Japanese armed forces or their ministries. Therefore, the structural framework within which the "responsible officials" acted is difficult to ascertain.

On the other hand, there are a number of institutional histories and chronological compilations of facts and documents relating to the activities and functions of various interested agencies and private organizations. These refer to official bodies, such as the Kwantung Government-General and the Deposits Division in the Ministry of Finance; to semi-private organizations, such as the South Manchuria Railway Company, the Bank of Korea, the Tientsin Residents Association, and the Imperial Reservists Association; and to various private bodies, including business firms, such as the League of the Japanese Textile Industry in China, and residents associations. Few of these bodies have been studied; and those which have, such as the Dark Ocean Society studied by Herbert Norman, need to be looked at again objectively. The following are among the most significant sources.

Bank of Korea:

Chōsen Ginkō, *Chōsen Ginkō nijūgonenshi* (1934).
Chōsen Ginkō Shi Hensan Iinkai, *Chōsen Ginkō ryakushi* (1960).

Bank of Taiwan:

Taiwan Ginkō, *Taiwan Ginkō jūnenshi* (1910).
—— *Taiwan Ginkō jūnen kōshi* (1916).
—— *Taiwan Ginkō nijūnenshi* (1919).
—— *Taiwan Ginkō yonjūnenshi* (1939).

Dark Ocean Society:

Norman, "The Genyōsha: A Study in the Origins of Japanese Imperialism" (1944).

East Asia Common Culture Association:

Koyūkai, *Tōa Dōbun Shoin Daigaku shi* (1955).
Tōa Dōbunkai, *Tōa Dōbunkai kiyō* (1937).

Tōa Dōbun Shoin (Shanghai), *Sōritsu sanjisshūnen kinen Tōa Dōbun Shoin shi* (1930).

East Asia Research Institute:

Tōa Kenkyūsho, *Tōken seika tekiyō* (1943).

Finance Ministry, Deposits Division:

Nakatsumi, *Yokimbu hishi* (1928).

Foreign Ministry:

Gaimushō Hyakunenshi Hensan Iinkai, *Gaimushō no hyakunen* (2 vols., 1969).
Mikami, "Gaimushō setchi no keii" (1963).

Imperial Reservists Association:

Teikoku Zaigō Gunjinkai, *Teikoku Zaigō Gunjinkai sanjūnenshi* (1944).

Kwantung Government-General:

Kantōchō, *Kantōchō shisei nijūnenshi* (1926).
—— *Kantōchō shisei sanjūnenshi* (1936).
Kantōchō, Chōkan Kambō, Bunshoka, *Kantōchō yōran* (1925, 1927, 1928, 1934).

Mukden Chamber of Commerce and Industry:

Hōten Shōkō Kaigisho, *Hōten keizai sanjūnenshi* (1940).

Naigaimen Company:

Motoki, *Naigaimen Kabushiki Kaisha gojūnenshi* (1937).

North China Development Company:

Kita Shina Kaihatsu Kabushiki Kaisha, *Kita Shina Kaihatsu Kabushiki Kaisha oyobi kankei kaisha gaiyō* (1940–44).

Oriental Development Company:

Tōyō Takushoku Kabushiki Kaisha, *Tōyō Takushoku Kabushiki Kaisha sanjūnenshi* (1939).

Shanghai Residents Association:

Shanhai Kyoryū Mindan, *Mindan sōritsu sanjūgoshūnen kinenshi* (1942).

In addition, on the Japanese in Shanghai:

Yonezawa, "Shanhai hōjin hattenshi" (1938–39).

Sino-Japanese Business Company:

Noguchi, *Chū-Nichi Jitsugyō Kabushiki Kaisha sanjūnenshi* (1943).

Sino-Japanese Steamship Company:

Asai, *Nisshin Kisen Kabushiki Kaisha sanjūnenshi oyobi tsuiho* (1941).

South Manchuria Railway Company:

Andō, *Mantetsu: Nihon teikokushugi to Chūgoku* (1965).
Andō and Yamada, "Kindai Chūgoku kenkyū to Mantetsu Chōsabu" (1962).
Andō, "Mantetsu Kaisha no sōritsu ni tsuite" (1960).
Mantetsu Sōsaishitsu Chihōbu Zammu Seiri Iinkai, *Mantetsu fuzokuchi keiei enkaku zenshi* (3 vols., 1939).
Minami Manshū Tetsudō and Mantetsu Sangyōbu, *Mantetsu chōsa kikan yōran* (1936).
Minami Manshū Tetsudō Kabushiki Kaisha, *Minami Manshū Tetsudō Kabushiki Kaisha jūnenshi* (1919).
—— *Minami Manshū Tetsudō Kabushiki Kaisha nijūnen ryakushi* (1927).
—— *Minami Manshū Tetsudō Kabushiki Kaisha dainiji jūnenshi* (1928).
—— *Minami Manshū Tetsudō Kabushiki Kaisha sanjūnen ryakushi* (1937).
Young, *The Research Activities of the South Manchurian Railway Company, 1907–1945* (1966).

Tientsin Residents Association:

Tenshin Kyoryū Mindan, *Tenshin Kyoryū Mindan nijisshūnen kinenshi* (1930).
Usui, *Tenshin Kyoryū Mindan sanjisshūnen kinenshi* (1941).

Universal Benevolence Association:

Hosaka, *Dōjinkai yonjūnenshi* (1943).
Ono, *Dōjinkai sanjūnenshi* (1932).

The Role of Individuals. Policy is made by men; that is, the process from the "initial response" down through various rational judgments to the concrete decision of a policy is work done by men. Therefore, biographical studies of important politicians and major "opinion leaders" are as important as studies of organizations. To be useful, however, biographies should not tell "a story of a great man," but rather should focus on the process by which a given man responds initially to certain information, constructs his rationalizations, and finally reaches his conclusions.

The following are useful bibliographies of biographies of prominent Japanese of the past century.

Ikeda, "Ningen kiroku shomoku" (mimeographed and privately circulated).
Nihon Gakujutsu Kaigi Daiichibu, *Bunkakei bunken mokuroku 14: Nihon kindaishi*

—denki hen (1963).

Tōyō Bunko, *Tōyō Bunko shozō kindai Nihon kankei bunken bunri mokuroku* (1961–63).

There are many biographies and memoirs of responsible officials who played important roles in Sino-Japanese relations. These include works on two Japanese ministers at Peking and one at Nanking; Japanese consuls at Mukden, Kirin, and major Chinese cities; four foreign ministers; and other Japanese diplomats.

Some of those who were either in interested agencies or in the private sector and were also appointed responsible officials for certain periods have memoirs or biographies. They were primarily politicians or military officers. Besides the responsible officials, a number of persons in interested agencies have biographies or memoirs. Some of the key figures listed below include: Ishiwara Kanji, the planner of the Mukden Incident; Aoki Norizumi, a long-term army officer in China; Sasaki Tōichi, the army officer who first appreciated the prospects of Chiang Kai-shek; Tōmiya Kaneo, the commander on the spot when Chang Tso-lin was killed; and Kōmoto Daisaku, the planner of Chang's assassination. In addition, Naitō Konan, a professor of Oriental history at Kyoto Imperial University, influenced thinking about China during the late Meiji and Taishō eras. His writings are described in the Masubuchi and Ikeda articles. Nishihara Kamezō, the famous promoter of Japanese loans to Tuan Ch'i-jui, is represented by his autobiography and articles by Kitamura and Hatano.

There are also important sources on certain entrepreneurs, particularly in the cotton industry, and on a number of China activists. As shown in Marius Jansen's *The Japanese and Sun Yat-sen*, many Japanese took part in the Chinese revolution of 1911–14. Tanaka's biography of Yoshino Sakuzō describes the attention paid to the democratization of China and Japan during the Taishō period, while later, more radical pro-Chinese figures include Suzue Gen'ichi, Aoyama Kazuo, and Kaji Wataru.

In addition, there are biographies of Chinese leaders written by Japanese, especially about Sun Yat-sen. A list of writings on Sun is available in the compilation by Nozawa.

One must realize, however, that many of these biographies and memoirs were written simply to praise their subjects. Only a few are worthwhile analytically. Among these latter are Suzue's biography of Sun Yat-sen, books by Watanabe and Shinobu on Mutsu Munemitsu's diplomacy, and

Tanaka's works on Kita Ikki. To these should be added certain critical shorter studies: Hatano's and Uno's articles on Li Hung-chang, Nomura's on Sun's nationalism, Terahiro's two essays on Miyazaki Tōten, and Ishizaka's article on Kita. Although the bulk of the remaining biographies and memoirs are neither analytical nor critical, they have little purposely planned distortion; the Japanese prefer silence in this respect.

Foreign ministers:

Arita, *Hito no me no chiri o miru: gaikō mondai kaikoroku* (1948).
—— *Bakahachi to hito wa iu: gaikōkan no kaisō* (1959).
Shidehara Heiwa Zaidan, *Shidehara Kijūrō* (1955).
Shidehara, *Gaikō gojūnen* (1951).
Shigemitsu, *Shōwa no dōran* (2 vols., 1952).
—— *Gaikō kaisōroku* (1953).
Takakura, *Tanaka Giichi denki* (2 vols., 1958–60).

Ministers, consuls, and other diplomats:

Hayashi, *Waga shichijūnen o kataru* (1935).
Horiuchi, *Chūgoku no arashi no naka de: Nikka gaikō sanjūnen yawa* (1950).
Ikei, "Funatsu Shin'ichirō zen Hōten sōryōji yori Debuchi gaimujikan ate Manshū Chūgoku shutchō genchi hōkoku shokan" (1963).
Ishii, *Gaikōkan no isshō* (1950).
Morishima, *Imbō ansatsu guntō: gaikokan no kaisō* (1950).
Obata Yūkichi Denki Kankōkai, *Obata Yūkichi* (1957).
Yoshizawa Kenkichi, *Gaikō rokujūnen* (1958).
Zai-Ka Nihon Bōseki Dōgyōkai, *Funatsu Shin'ichirō* (1958).

Diet members:

Hara, *Yamamoto Jōtarō ronsaku* (2 vols., 1939).
—— *Yamamoto Jōtarō denki* (1942).
Matsuoka, *Tōa zenkyoku no dōyō* (1931).
—— *Ugoku Mammō* (1931).
—— *Mantetsu o kataru* (1937).
Yamaura, *Mori Kaku* (1940).

Military officers:

Fujimoto, *Ningen Ishiwara Kanji* (1959).
Hirano, *Manshū no imbōsha: Kōmoto Daisaku no unmeiteki na ashiato* (1959).
Koiso Kuniaki Jijoden Kankōkai, *Katsuzan Kōsō* (1963).
Saigō, *Itagaki Seishirō* (1938).
Sasaki, *Aru gunjin no jiden* (1963).

Satō, *Bōryaku shōgun Aoki Norizumi* (1943).
Tōmiya Taisa Kinen Jigyō Iinkai, *Tōmiya Kaneo den* (1940).
Yamaguchi, *Higeki no shōgun Ishiwara Kanji* (1952).
Yokoyama, *Matsui taishō den* (1938).

Intellectuals:

Aichi Daigaku Kokusai Mondai Kenkyūjo, *Ko Naitō Konan sensei chojutsu mokuroku* (1954).
Ikeda, "Naitō Konan no En Seigai ron" (1963).
Masubuchi, "Nihon no kindai shigakushi ni okeru Chūgoku to Nihon, II" (1963).

Entrepreneurs:

Fujisaki, *Manshū to Aioi Yoshitarō* (1932).
Kita, *Wada Toyoji den* (1926).
Nakajima, *Fūunji Sogō Shinji den* (1955).
Ōoka, *Kita Matazō kun den* (1933).
Takasaki, *Manshū no shūen* (1953).
Taniguchi Ō Denki Hensan Iinkai, *Taniguchi Fusazō den* (1934).
Uchiyama, *Heikin yūsen: Chūgoku no konjaku* (1955).
—— *Kakō roku* (1960).

Japanese activists in China. Compilations of biographies:

Kuzuu, *Tōa senkaku shishi kiden* (3 vols., 1933–36; reprinted, 1966).
Tai-Shi Kōrōsha Denki Hensankai, *Tai-Shi kaikoroku* (2 vols., 1936).
—— *Zoku tai-Shi kaikoroku* (2 vols., 1941–42).

Japanese activists in China:

Aida, *Kawashima Naniwa ō* (1936).
Haji, *Ginkō sobyō* (1959).
Hanawa, *Ura Keiichi* (1924).
Inoue, *Kyojin Arao Sei* (1910).
Itō, *Kōryū to tōfū* (1964).
Jansen, *The Japanese and Sun Yat-sen* (1954).
Kawashima, "Hokushi no jōsei ni nagaruru kihon seishin" (1937).
—— "Tai-Shi narabi ni tai-Mammō no komponteki keirin" (1926).
Kazankai, *Konoe Kazan kō* (1924).
"Kishida Ginkō" (1958).
Koyama, *Tōa senkaku Arao Sei* (1938).
Kudō, *Konoe Atsumaro kō* (1938).
Matsumura, *Nagai Ryūtarō* (1959).
Munakata, *Tōa no senkakusha Sanshū Nezu sensei narabi ni fujin* (1943).

Nashimoto, *Chūgoku no naka no Nihonjin* (1958).
Shanhai Zasshisha, *Hakusen Nishimoto kun den* (1934).
Shirayanagi, *Konoe ke oyobi Konoe kō* (1941).
Shiroiwa, *Konoe Kazan kō no dai-Ajia keirin* (1933).
Sugiyama, *Senkusha Kishida Ginkō* (1952).
Tōa Dōbunkai, *Konoe Kazan kō kinenshi* (1934).
Tōa Dōbun Shoin Koyū Dōsōkai, *Sanshū Nezu sensei den* (1930).
Uchida, *Shina kaizō ron* (1911).
—— *Nihon no san dai kyūmu* (1912).
—— *Zen Mammō tetsudō tōitsu ikensho* (1930).

Japanese participants in the Chinese revolution, 1911–14:

Ike, *Shina kakumei jikkenki* (1911).
Kayano, *Chūka minkoku kakumei hikyū* (1941).
Kita, *Shina kakumei gaishi* (1921).
—— *Zōho Shina kakumei gaishi* (1937).
Miyazaki, *Sanjūsannen no yume* (1902).
Yamanaka, *Jitsuroku: Ajia no akebono daisan kakumei no shinsō* (2 vols., 1961–62).

Liberal and pro-Chinese activitists:

Aoyama, *Bōryaku jukurenkō* (1957).
Etō, "Nihonjin no Chūgoku kan: Suzue Gen'ichi o megutte" (1961).
Kaji, *Dasshutsu* (1948).
—— *Hansen shiryō* (1964).
—— *Nihon jimmin hansen dōmei* (9 vols., 1961).
Suzue, *Chūgoku kaihō tōsōshi* (1953).
Tanaka, *Yoshino Sakuzō* (1958).
Yoshino, *Nikka kokkō ron* (1948).
—— *Nisshi kōshō ron* (1915).

Biographies of Chinese:

Andō, *Ō Chōmei jijoden* (1940).
Asano, *Daigensui Chō Sakurin* (1928).
Fuse, *Shina kokumin kakumei to Hyō Gyokushō* (1929).
Naitō, *Seiden En Seigai* (1913).
Nozawa, "Nihon ni okeru Son Bun kankei bunken mokuroku" (1957).
Okano, *Go Haifu* (1939).
Sawada, *Joden Ō Chōmei* (1939).
Sekiya, *Kaiketsu En Seigai* (1913).
Sonoda, *Chō Sakurin* (1923).

Miscellaneous biographies:

Aishingyōro Kō, *Ruten no ōhi: Manshū kyūtei no higeki* (1959).
Hatano, "Nishihara shakkan no kihonteki kōsō" (1959).
Inukai, *Tōsukō wa ima mo nagarete iru* (1960).
Kikuchi, *Chōkyōrō mampitsu* (1936).
Kitamura, "Kōtsū Ginkō shakkan no seiritsu jijō" (1961).
Komai, *Dai Manshūkoku kensetsu roku* (1933).
—— *Tairiku e no higan* (1952).
Nishihara, *Yume no shichijūyonen* (1949).

Recommended analytical biographies and articles:

Hatano, "Ri Kōshō sen-happyaku-hachijūnendai ni okeru tai-Nichi seisaku ni tsuite" (1961).
Ishizaka, "Kita Ikki kenkyūshi josetsu" (1963).
Nomura, "Son Bun no minzokushugi to tairiku rōnin: sekaishugi minzokushugi dai-Ajiashugi no kanren ni tsuite" (1957).
Shinobu, *Mutsu gaikō: Nisshin sensō no gaikō shiteki kenkyū* (1935).
Suzue, *Son Bun den* (1950).
Takeda and Takeuchi, *Mō Takutō: sono shi to jinsei* (1965).
Tanaka, *Nihon fashizumu no genryū: Kita Ikki no shisō to shōgai* (1949).
—— *Kita Ikki* (1959).
Terahiro, "Chūgoku kakumei to Miyazaki Tōten" (1953).
—— "Chūgoku kakumei ni okeru Chū-Nichi kōshō no ichi kōsatsu: Miyazaki Tōten o chūshin ni shite" (1954).
Watanabe, *Mutsu Munemitsu den* (1934).

Some Remaining Questions. These include national character, the nature of the emperor system, and the motivation for Japanese expansion.

By national character is meant those characteristics which are common to all or nearly all members of the nation because of a common historical, social, and cultural background. This, of course, cannot be ascertained by analyzing one individual; it must be sought in those characteristics of an individual that resound among other individuals of the same nation. Japan's national character definitely expressed itself in this way with respect to China policy. For instance, the Japanese have an excessive respect for the pure; they tend to reject compromise or reconciliation in politics and to agree with the "extremist" who maintains a high degree of purity. Because of this tendency, radical opinions often tend to prevail, and actions tend to suffer from a lack of flexibility. This national characteristic can be seen, for example, in Japan's policy during the League of Nations debate on the Manchurian question and in Japan's insistence in 1937 on excessively severe terms at the peace negotiations with China promoted through the mediation of Dr. Oskar Trautmann, the German ambassador to China.

Another Japanese trait is that of excessive sensitivity to shame, symptomatic of a "shame culture." This trait induced a strong sense of army prestige among military men, leading eventually to an attitude whereby no sacrifice was too great if it would maintain the prestige of the army. The Tsinan Incident, referred to above, is an example of how the Japanese army used force merely to save "face." As a result, the basic aim of dispatching troops—the protection of the Japanese residents in the area—was forgotten and many Japanese residents were killed. The military men on the spot did not show any sense of guilt, nor was there any reprimand from higher officials for this mistake. Such national character traits might well be included in the study of Japanese policies toward China.

It is interesting to note in connection with the Japanese national character that the outpourings of mass emotion, which often occurred during the Tokugawa regime in such forms as the *okage mairi* (a mass pilgrimage to the Grand Shrine of Ise) and the *"ee ja nai ka"* ("Why shouldn't I?") frenzy, suddenly disappeared with the Meiji period. During the feudal regime, the masses, who were oppressed, engaged in these outbursts as a kind of catharsis. Does this mean that in post-Meiji Japan the oppression of the masses was mitigated? Or did war come to take the place of mass frenzy?

The emperor system also presents problems for students of Japan's China policy, for it oppressed not only politics but also every aspect of social activity in prewar Japan. On the one hand, it functioned as the strongest element uniting the state, but on the other, it stood as an obstacle to the development of rational thinking. Did Japanese leaders really believe in the ideology of the emperor system when they had to deal with the bitter realities of international politics? Ishiwara Kanji's writing, for example, is filled with emperor-worship. On the other hand, in 1931, in defiance of an order from the central government, the emperor's executive organ, Ishiwara advocated Japan's further advance into Manchuria. Ultimately he went so far as to declare that had the central government continued its "interference" with the Kwantung army's action, the army would have solved the Manchurian question independently, even if it had necessitated the severance of the Kwantung army from Japan proper. Thus, whenever Ishiwara encountered the reality of international politics, he seems to have ignored the emperor, whom he professed to worship.

Sugiyama Gen is another case in point. In his capacity as minister of the army, he once told the emperor that the China Incident would be solved within one month. It did not bother him at all that his prediction turned out to be inaccurate. Again, in September 1941 the emperor asked him, as chief of the General Staff, the possible outcome of a war in the Pacific. Sugiyama answered, "It will be over in three months." This drew an angry retort from the emperor. "If you can say that China's great size is the cause of the protracted war, isn't the Pacific Ocean even greater? Then how can you say that a war in the Pacific will be over in three months?" Sugiyama could only lower his head and make no reply. The incident, however, did not change Sugiyama's policy, and Japan rushed into the Pacific War. Obviously, Sugiyama did not consider the emperor inviolate. Then can we say that the emperor was regarded seriously? This old and yet not fully analyzed question has always haunted the researcher.

Another important question is: Why, from the waning days of the Tokugawa regime on, were the Japanese so interested in overseas expansion? England launched its overseas expansion after losing its territory in Brittany. In contrast, Japan sought a foothold on the Asian continent but in the end lost everything because it clung to its rights and interests on the continent. Was the expansion of its commercial market the basic "incentive" for Japan's overseas adventure? Oka Yoshitake and Minami Tokuko do not believe so. Long before Japanese industrial products started flooding the China market, many Japanese, such as Kishida Ginkō, Arao Sei, and Nezu Hajime, entered China, still under the Ch'ing dynasty, with the dream of emancipating the mainland. These people appear to have been motivated by a sense of Pan-Asianism rather than dreams of economic expansion. More research is needed on this desire to emancipate Asia, for it constituted the reverse side of fervent Japanese nationalism.

6

Japan's Policies Toward Germany

Frank W. Iklé

THE ESTABLISHMENT OF DIPLOMATIC RELATIONS, 1855–1861

Germany's initial policy toward Japan was primarily conditioned by German trade interests in the Far East. These were large enough by the 1860s to warrant the sending of a German diplomatic mission, which concluded a most-favored-nation treaty with Japan by Prussia on behalf of the Zollverein in 1861, and which established the first German diplomatic mission in Tokyo by order of the king of Prussia. For several decades thereafter, Germany's rapidly growing trade, especially after Prussia's victory over France, the unification of Germany at Versailles in 1871, and the impact of the industrial revolution, led Germany to pursue interests in the Far East which were predominantly commercial. Until the accession of William II, there existed no such thing as a definite German policy toward Japan beyond the protection of its commercial interests, for as long as Bismarck remained the pilot of the German ship of state, he opposed the acquisition of territories in the Far East.

Japan's initial policy toward the new Germany, on the other hand, was essentially conditioned by the unequal treaty structure. Germany was seen primarily as merely one of the Western nations benefiting from the unequal treaties that had been imposed upon Japan ever since Perry's arrival. Treaty revision therefore occupied considerable space in the realm of early Japanese-German relations. Nevertheless, it was not long before German contributions in law, politics, the sciences, medicine, education, and the arts of war came to be appreciated by Japan. Eager to be modern and Westernized, Japan began to seek the services of Germany, believing it to be not only advanced, but ideologically congenial. Moreover, it appeared to be sufficiently remote and disinterested so as not to represent an immediate threat.

The first contact between Germany and Japan in modern times took place when August Ludorf, the supercargo of the brig *Greta*, chartered to take one hundred tons of coal to the Perry expedition, petitioned the Tokugawa shogunate from Shimoda on July 4, 1855, for a treaty with Prussia extending it the same privileges as the treaties Japan had just concluded with the United States, Russia, and Britain. His request was denied in October of that year, but this did not prevent a number of German merchants from settling in Japan, primarily in Yokohama and Nagasaki. Growing German commercial interests in Japan, together with Prussia's rise in power, then led to the first official German mission, that of Count Fritz Eulenburg.

The Eulenburg mission was a well organized and sizable undertaking. Besides Eulenburg himself as ambassador of the king of Prussia, it included Ferdinand von Richthofen, the famous German geologist who was later to distinguish himself in China, and Max von Brandt, a very able diplomat who was to become Germany's first expert on Far Eastern political questions. The Eulenburg mission arrived in Tokyo in September 1860 aboard the *Arcona*, the accompanying vessel having been lost in a violent storm en route. Negotiations between the shogunate and Eulenburg eventually resulted in a treaty between Japan and Prussia, on behalf of the entire German Zollverein, which was signed on January 24, 1861. These negotiations were greatly aided by the support of Townsend Harris, who made available the services of his Dutch interpreter, Hendrick Heusken. Three years later, in January 1864, the treaty was formally ratified aboard the German naval vessel *Gazelle*. It was this unequal treaty, embodying most-favored-nation clauses, which was to govern the relations between Germany and Japan until 1899. The year 1861 marks also the beginning of Max von Brandt's service as the first German consul in Yokohama, where by this time there were as many as ten German commercial firms.

Eulenburg, *Ost-Asien, 1860–1862, in Briefen des Grafen Fritz zu Eulenburg* (1900),
   is Eulenburg's own account of the mission.
Ishinshi Gakkai, *Bakumatsu ishin gaikō shiryō shūsei* (20 vols., 1943), V, 92–131,
   contains three chapters on the Eulenburg mission and lists twenty pertinent
   documents.

Maruyama, *Shoki Nichi-Doku tsūkō shōshi* (1931), is a good Japanese account of early German-Japanese relations.

EFFORTS TO END THE UNEQUAL TREATIES, 1861-1896

The German attitude toward treaty privileges was uncompromising while the unequal treaty period lasted. From the beginning, Brandt made it clear that he would stand for no nonsense from the Japanese government. This he illustrated, rather to the amusement of his British colleague, Sir Harry Parkes, by walking one day into a bookstore in Yokohama and insisting upon obtaining a book that listed all the daimyō of Japan. The Tokugawa shogunate had forbidden access by foreigners to such information, but Brandt refused to leave the store without obtaining the desired item. After a flurry of messages from the owner of the store to government officials, permission was eventually granted and Brandt walked out, victor in the clash of wills. More serious, however, was the incident involving the steamer *Hesperia*. This was a German ship which arrived in Yokohama in 1879, at a time when a serious cholera epidemic was raging in Kobe and Osaka and when the Meiji government had put strict quarantine measures on all ships entering Japanese waters. The German minister, supported by the British, refused to abide by these Japanese regulations and, on grounds of extraterritorial privilege, insisted that the vessel be permitted to dock. When the Japanese tried to force the ship to accede to quarantine, the *Hesperia* was escorted to the dock by a German cruiser, and her passengers and cargo discharged in spite of Japanese protests.

Such unyielding attitudes displayed by the great powers toward Japan under the unequal treaty system provoked the Japanese to work untiringly for treaty revision, the main objective of Japanese foreign policy in the early Meiji years. As far as Germany was involved, the first Japanese attempt was made by Foreign Minister Inoue Kaoru in 1882. He submitted new proposals for revision of the judicial clauses in the existing treaties, so as to provide for the abolition of extraterritoriality within five years, excepting certain capital offenses and matters affecting the personal status of foreigners. In return, the Japanese government was willing to concede further rights of residence and land tenure to foreigners in treaty ports and further permission to travel within the country. Germany's reaction to this proposal was interesting, inasmuch as the German minister, K. von

Eisendecher, together with his American colleague, welcomed these ideas, whereas Sir Harry Parkes, the British envoy, was opposed to them. Parkes argued that no such cocnessions could be made until Japan had a better civil and commercial code. The attitude of the United States as well as that of Germany seems to have been to curry favor with Japan and to benefit at the expense of British trade.

The matter was reopened in 1886, when a new conference of all the treaty powers met in May in Tokyo. Foreign Minister Inoue had summoned home Aoki Shūzō, the Japanese representative in Berlin, to help him approach the German representatives in Japan. Again, as in 1882, Germany seemed prepared to support the Japanese claims to autonomy. Since the British too had been impressed with recent Japanese legal and judicial reforms, the representatives of both powers worked out a new "Anglo-German project" in June of 1886, a scheme which, analogous with Egypt, provided for a system of mixed courts. This notion produced a storm of protest within Japan, so that the negotiations once again came to nothing.

After Ōkuma Shigenobu became foreign minister in 1888, the Japanese government again renewed negotiations, approaching both Germany and the United States on the subject of treaty revision. Saionji Kimmochi, who had been appointed Japanese minister to Berlin, had a number of meetings with Count Herbert Bismarck, the German foreign secretary. In October of that year a new treaty was drawn up between Japan and Germany, providing for the abolition of consular courts within five years and the right of Japan to determine ad valorem values in customs duties. This project seemed to be headed for success, but the assassination attempt against Ōkuma suspended the work just before it was completed and caused the whole matter of treaty revision to be deferred until 1896.

The final effective treaty between Germany and Japan, which brought an end to extraterritoriality and full equality to Japan, was not signed until April 4, 1896, and did not become effective until 1899, after the Aoki-Kimberley treaty of 1894 between Japan and Britain had set the necessary precedent. The following are studies relating to treaty revision negotiations.

Documents. Germany:

American Historical Association, *A Catalogue of Files and Microfilms of the German*

Foreign Ministry Archives, 1867–1920 (1959), contains listings for *Beziehungen Deutschlands zu Japan, 1886–1920* under the file Deutschland 132, pp. 104–5. German archival material for the period of early relations has not been studied; the first few volumes of the series would seem to be pertinent, however.

Documents. Japan:

Japan, Gaimushō (Foreign Ministry), *Jōyaku kaisei kankei Nihon gaikō bunsho* (4 vols., 1941–50), Vol. I, ch. 3, sec. 5, pp. 729–82, is concerned with treaty problems with Germany during 1878–79; Vol. II has a chapter on the Inoue period dealing with attempts at treaty revision with Germany in the years 1880–87; Vol. III, ch. 5, sec. 3, has documents bearing on Ōkuma's ill-fated efforts;Vol. IV, sec. 2, covers the Mutsu Munemitsu period from 1893 to 1898.

—— *Nihon gaikō bunsho* (1936–), contains full documentary sources for the negotiations on the treaties and their revision. Beginning with Vol. I/2, which has ten documents dealing with treaty problems between Brandt and the Japanese government for the year 1868, this important series contains the following items pertaining to Japanese-German relations: Vol. II/1, 2, 3 for 1869; Vol. VII for 1874 regarding trade negotiations; Vol. XIV for 1881 (Documents 34–55) dealing with treaty revision and containing diplomatic correspondence between Aoki and Foreign Minister Inoue; and Vol. XXII for 1889 including a series of some nineteen documents relating to Ōkuma's attempt at treaty revision.

The *Hesperia* incident:

U.S., Department of State, *Foreign Relations of the United States, 1879* (1879), pp. 647–52.

Secondary accounts of the unequal treaties and treaty revision:

Inoue, *Jōyaku kaisei: Meiji no minzoku mondai* (1955).
Jones, *Extraterritoriality in Japan and the Diplomatic Relations Resulting in Its Abolition, 1853–1899* (1931).
Tōyama, *Meiji ishin* (1951).

German Influence in Japan. Although Japan's drive for treaty revision occupied most of its official relations with Germany during this period, more significant was, without doubt, the impact of German influence upon Japan.

Not only were there in Japan by 1880 at least one hundred German merchants, primarily in Yokohama, who were served by a new direct service offered since that year by the North German Lloyd, but there was also a host of German scientists, advisers, and engineers who began to play a very important role in Meiji Japan. These included German professors, such as Karl Florenz, who taught German literature at Tokyo Imperial University and who translated the *Nihongi* and *Man'yōshū*, and Raphael von Köber and Ludwig Busse, who taught philosophy at the same institution. There was also Hermann Rösler, a German adviser to Itō Hirobumi in matters concerning jurisprudence and law, who greatly contributed to the new Japanese civil and criminal codes, which were based on the German judiciary. There were many German botanists, chemists, engineers, and others, but especially important were German contributors to the fields of medicine, education, and military science.

Beginning with the arrival in 1871 of the two German military medical officers, Leopold Müller (a surgeon) and Hermann Hoffmann (an internist), German doctors occupied virtually all the chairs of medicine at Tokyo Imperial University and other Japanese medical schools until 1900. The most famous of these were Dr. Erwin Baelz, who spent twenty-three years in Japan, and Dr. Julius Scriba, who was responsible for the training of many Japanese medical doctors. Germany's preeminence in this field also caused most Japanese medical students to pursue their studies in that country.

In education the influence of Emil Hausknecht, who started teaching pedagogy at Tokyo Imperial University in 1887, was to be of considerable significance. He obtained the official support of Education Minister Mori Arinori, who himself had been educated in Europe. Mori was much taken by German ideas of education, which emphasized nationalism and the principle that an individual must be ready to sacrifice everything for the sake of the state. Hausknecht's insistence on the values of strict supervision, rigid discipline, and unquestioning obedience and his stress on man's moral character as the aim of all education were in full accord with Meiji Japan's policy of encouraging similar virtues in its subjects.

Especially important was German influence in Japan in military matters. Since German military prestige was greatly enhanced by the victories of Prussia in 1870 and 1871, the Japanese government terminated its contracts with French military advisers and switched to German officers. The most important of these were Major Klemens Wilhelm Jakob Meckel and Captain Hermann von Blankenburg, who entered the Japanese service in 1885 and imported German military methods and administration. This eventually culminated in the establishment, by Vice-Army Minister Katsura Tarō, of Japan's new army academy in 1889. Exchange of officer personnel was soon inaugurated. One of the more important language officers to be trained in Japan was Karl Haushofer, who later was to play a not inconsiderable part in Japanese-German relations with his geopolitical arguments, which he began to develop during his stay in Japan between 1908 and 1910.

Japanese interest in all things German also found expression in the establishment by Katsura of the Japanese-German Association, the Nichi-Doku Kyōkai, in 1911. German interest in Japan already had led to the formation of the Deutsche Gesellschaft für Natur- und Völkerkunde Ostasiens, which had its beginning in 1873. While Japan by then had come rather heavily under German influence in many fields, the German impression of Japan had also been a quite favorable one. In particular, Itō's visit to Germany, his indebtedness to German political theory when drawing up the Meiji constitution, and Japan's adoption of German administrative and military organizational forms for its new empire had been much praised. Yet this relationship, without much friction and some goodwill on both sides, was to be greatly transformed by the Triple Intervention in 1895.

There is very little material on the important topic of German influence in Meiji Japan. Some information may be found in:

Meissner, *Deutsche in Japan, 1639–1939* (1940).
Presseisen, *Before Aggression: Europeans Prepare the Japanese Army* (1965).

Less in:

Ostwald, *Deutschland und Japan: Eine Freundschaft zweier Völker* (1941).

Much work could be done in this field. To what degree did German political thought, German philosophy, and German military ideas contribute to the making of the new Japan? On the other hand, what was the image of Germany that was being created in the minds of the leading Japanese of this period? Another very fruitful and as yet completely unexplored area would be a study of Japanese-German trade relations for this period.

GROWING FRICTION, 1895–1914

The year 1895 ushered in a profound change in the relations between Japan and Germany. Until the accession to power of William II in 1888 and the retirement of Bismarck two years later, German diplomacy had opposed the acquisition of territories in the Far East. By 1890 this had changed. With the chancellor safely out of the way, Germany turned to global policy, *weltpolitik*, including the formulation of a definite political Far Eastern policy. It was not until the Sino-Japanese War in 1894–95, however, that Germany found the opportunity to assert its new interests, which it did by intervening actively in the territorial settlement of that conflict.

The resultant Triple Intervention of 1895, which was prompted by Germany's desire to obtain a naval base on the China coast, by the kaiser's wish to embroil Russia in Far Eastern matters in order to obtain a freer hand for himself along Germany's eastern borders and in the Balkans, and by his genuine fear of the "yellow peril," led to a reversal of the earlier and friendlier relations which had existed between Japan and Germany. After the intervention, German-Japanese relations became basically unfriendly, if not hostile, until World War I. Although Wilhelminian *machtpolitik* paid off for Germany at first, it failed in the long run. It contributed to Japan's decision to enter World War I against Germany, leading to the loss of all German possessions in the Far East; it diverted Russia only until that nation's defeat at the hands of Japan in 1905, when it renewed its activity in the Balkans; and finally, by the "yellow peril" argument, it introduced a racial question that continued to bedevil the policies of both countries until World War II.

To the Japanese, German participation in the Triple Intervention came as a great shock, made worse by the tactless behavior of the German minister to Tokyo. Having little, if any, understanding of the motives that led Germany to take this step, the Japanese were genuinely resentful and angry; they nursed a desire for revenge which finally found an outlet in World War I.

The Triple Intervention, 1895. With the outbreak of the Sino-Japanese War in 1894, the Far East became for the first time an area of the world in which great power politics were pitted against each other. The British government had attempted to bring the conflict to a close as early as October 6, 1894, when it invited Germany, France, Russia, and America to take part in a joint intervention on the basis of the independence of Korea and an indemnity for Japan. But Germany declined, for it was eager to continue maintaining friendly relations with Japan; it opposed entering into such an undertaking, and the German minister in Tokyo was advised to maintain reserve in case of any mediation attempt by either Britain or Russia. Germany, in the fall of 1894, felt that any such suggestion by the great powers would not only be futile, but worse, it would insult Japanese sensibilities and cause Japanese resentment.[1]

In November, when the hard-pressed Chinese government made a plea to the great powers, Germany refused again to be a partner in an intervention. The kaiser's marginal notes on the reports of his minister in Japan, Baron Alfred von Gutschmid, continued to reflect a tenor most favorable to Japan, evincing pleasure at its victories over China.

Yet these same Japanese victories over China served to bring into sharp focus Germany's problem of acquiring a colonial position in the Far East, especially a naval base. The absolute necessity for a German naval base in Far Eastern waters had been agreed upon by both the German Admiralty and the German Foreign Office, which had replied to such a request from the navy by agreeing that Germany was not to go away empty-handed from the situation in the Far East. The problem was which policy would be best suited to obtain for Germany what it desired. Should Germany continue a policy of nonintervention in the struggle between China and Japan and thus obtain the support of a victorious and grateful Japan? Or should Germany join other powers in an intervention against Japan, thereby profiting from Chinese gratitude? The German Foreign Office by and large was inclined toward the first course of action, as it thought that Germany could easily be compensated with bases in China through a secret understanding with a victorious Japan and that, whatever territorial changes came about in the Far East as the result of Japan's successes, they would be beneficial to German policy. This view, expressed by the new chancellor, Prince Hohenlohe-Schillingsfürst, to the kaiser on November 2, 1894, found his ready approval.

The dilemma of this situation, however, was that if Germany should not join an intervention by the powers, there was the risk that Britain and Russia might unite in any case, prevent Japan from putting forth demands

---

[1] Germany, Auswärtiges Amt, *Die grosse Politik der europäischen Kabinette, 1871–1914* (40 vols., 1922–27), IX, 239–333, is the source for this account of the German government's role in power politics in the Far East in 1894–95, unless otherwise indicated; hereafter cited as *Die grosse Politik.*

on China, and proceed to dismember China at their respective whims, leaving Germany without any territorial gains whatsoever. This possibility was sufficiently nerve-racking for the German government so that the alternative of the second policy always was kept in mind. In November both the Foreign Office and the kaiser worried about just such a possibility, William feeling that at least Germany's East Asiatic squadron ought to get Taiwan (before the French took it in a secret understanding with the Japanese), and in the same month the German ambassador in Peking proposed that Germany should obtain from China a lease in the Pescadores or Kiaochow Bay. With the coming of the new year, 1895, and continuing Japanese successes, the fear grew of China's possible dismemberment by the great powers without German participation.

From the Japanese point of view, Germany's policy of nonintervention was, of course, greatly appreciated. Late in October 1894 Aoki Shūzō, the Japanese minister to Berlin, who himself had spent many years in Germany, had married a German, and, in general, had pro-German feelings, thanked the kaiser for Germany's loyal attitude toward Japan.[2] Mutsu Munemitsu, the Japanese foreign minister, foresaw and feared the possibility of an intervention by the European powers, but he certainly did not anticipate that Germany might be a partner in such a move. Mutsu, as well as Prime Minister Itō, actually had wanted to limit Japanese demands against China, excluding territorial concessions on the mainland, precisely because they wanted to preclude such intervention. But the high military and naval officers in the government insisted on "legitimate" demands, and in a joint cabinet meeting on January 27, in the presence of the Meiji emperor, the military got its way: Japan would demand the surrender of the Liaotung Peninsula.

The German government continued to be increasingly disturbed at the thought of China's dismemberment without German participation. For a while in early March the Germans flirted with the possibility of supporting Britain in a possible intervention, but the British remained cool to such a scheme. Then, with a new direct Chinese request for German aid in its precarious situation, Germany decided to acquaint Japan more fully with developments. The German Foreign Office, fortified with a memo-

---

[2]Mutsu Hirokichi, ed., *Hakushaku Mutsu Munemitsu ikō* (1929), p. 438.

randum by the German navy stating that a Far Eastern port was an absolute necessity, issued on March 6, 1895, some "friendly advice" to Japan. In a telegram from the German foreign secretary to Gutschmid in Tokyo, he was told to inform Japan that its demand for territory on the Asian mainland would lead to intervention by the powers: "State confidentially that the kaiser recommends to the Japanese government the expediting of peace and the moderation of its terms. European great powers requested by China to intervene . . . for Japan direct and reasonable settlement most advantageous. Japanese demand for surrender of territory on mainland liable to provoke intervention."

Germany, then, for the time being continued to follow a policy of nonintervention in order to cultivate the goodwill of Japan. The advice was transmitted to the Japanese Foreign Ministry and up to Vice-Minister Hayashi Tadasu. Whether it was ever communicated to Prime Minister Itō is not clear, since he and Foreign Minister Mutsu were absent from Tokyo at the Imperial Headquarters in Hiroshima. To this communication of March 6, Hayashi replied two days later, expressing high appreciation for the friendly spirit of the German government. In an exchange of views between Hayashi and Mutsu concerning this warning and its possible consequence—intervention by the European powers—both remained rather optimistic that such an event would not come to pass, despite Aoki's constant urgings to Mutsu that the possibility of a German intervention should be taken most seriously. Aoki felt that Mutsu had developed a tendency to pay little heed to his reports.[3]

Within Japan, meanwhile, a split had developed between the military and the civilian leaders of the government regarding the peace terms to be imposed upon a prostrate China. The army and the navy stood for harsh terms: the complete humiliation of China including occupation of Peking and concessions on the mainland (not just Taiwan); and the military men forced the government to demand such concessions in the forthcoming peace negotiations with Li Hung-chang at Shimonoseki.

The Japanese refusal to heed the German warning of March 6 contributed to the final crystallization of German policy. By mid-March intervention had become inevitable. General Georg Leo von Caprivi, the former chancellor, had let lapse Germany's reassurance treaty with Russia. Hohenlohe,

---

[3] Japan, Gaimushō (Foreign Ministry), *Nihon gaikō bunsho*, XXVIII/2 (1953), 1-222 (hereafter cited as *Nihon gaikō bunsho*).

his successor, was very interested in trying to regain Russian support (he was in close touch with Bismarck) and told the kaiser in a memorandum of March 19 that Japan must be prevented from obtaining Port Arthur. Since the British government in the person of Foreign Secretary J.W. Kimberley remained distant and disinterested, Germany, the chancellor argued, must turn to Russia for an understanding. William approved, and on March 23 a telegram went off to Heinrich Leonhard von Tschirsky, the German charge d'affaires in St. Petersburg, stating that Germany was willing to cooperate with Russia in case of any joint action in the Far East.

Thus it was German overtures to London and St. Petersburg that led to the Triple Intervention and a policy of compensation through intervention. Count Sergei Witte's claim that Russia had originated the Triple Intervention against Japan seems no longer tenable.

Prince Alexis Borisovich Lobanov-Rostovsky, the Russian foreign minister, greeted this news with "great joy." Since Russia, too, had become deeply disturbed at Japan's progress, it was only too happy to obtain backing from Germany. Russia, with its interests in Manchuria, wanted Port Arthur for itself as a port and terminal for the Trans-Siberian Railway, and Witte argued that Japanese occupation of the Liaotung Peninsula would not only block Russian railway enterprise but also would be the prelude to the acquisition of all of Korea by Japan.

Russia drafted a note to the powers on April 8, suggesting that a joint address be delivered to Japan in which the powers would explain, "in a friendly way," that the annexation of Port Arthur would be a lasting obstacle to good relations between China and Japan and a constant menace to the peace in the Far East.[4] Upon receipt of this note, the German government undertook a general review of its Far Eastern policy.

By this time it had become obvious to Aoki, the Japanese minister in Berlin, that Germany's attitude toward Japan was on the verge of undergoing a drastic change.[5] The first definite indication of a shift came on March 27, when Germany supported China's request that Japan make public its peace terms before the conclusion of an armistice. But this did not deter the Japanese negotiators at Shimonoseki, who continued to put pressure on Li Hung-chang in late March and early April. Li kept the the powers well informed of these demands, and on April 2 the Japanese

---

[4] A. M. Pooley, ed., *The Secret Memoirs of Count Tadasu Hayashi* (1915), p. 85.
[5] Mutsu, *Hakushaku Mutsu Munemitsu ikō*, p. 544.

government decided that it might be wise after all to buy off Germany at the expense of Chinese territory. Aoki called upon the German Foreign Office and explained that Japan needed the Liaotung Peninsula. In return, he suggested that Germany might well claim for itself a province in southeast China.

It is certainly possible that if such an offer had been made in November 1894 or even early in March 1895, Germany might have been bought off, and the Triple Intervention might never have taken place; but by April it was too late. William II had become very nervous over the heavy Japanese demands on China, and his mind saw in the struggle in the Far East the prelude to a great conflict between the white and yellow races, between Christianity and Buddhism. By now the kaiser had convinced himself that Japanese ambitions would have to be arrested at all cost, and the German Foreign Office heartily agreed; Port Arthur in Japanese hands would be a Far Eastern Gibraltar, making China into a Japanese protectorate.

With this in mind and upon receipt of Russia's note of April 8, the Foreign Office in Berlin undertook a general review of German policy. Max von Brandt, the former German minister to Japan who had recently been appointed Far Eastern expert in the German Foreign Office, was consulted. In an important *pro memoria* Brandt threw all his influence behind a strong recommendation for cooperation with Russia. This would influence Russian attitudes toward Germany in Europe, it would result in Germany's getting a naval base from China in compensation, and it also might mean, if France could be excluded from a joint intervention, a strain on Franco-Russian relations. In thus counseling intervention, Brandt also acted on behalf of China, as it seems that he was in touch with Li Hung-chang. There is a story to the effect that Li did not sign the peace treaty at Shimonoseki until he received a coded wire from Brandt that indeed there would be intervention by the powers. This may be apocryphal, but in any case, in an interview with the kaiser on the morning of April 9, Brandt reiterated his beliefs, which were greeted with full approval by his master: it would be better to be on hand when the partition of China took place than to be left out, a German naval base in Asian waters was an absolute necessity, and "to produce as great a relief of pressures as possible upon our eastern borders . . . it is also our interest to direct Russia to the east where its true mission lies."

Rather to the disappointment of Germany, and especially of Holstein, who had hoped that the Franco-Russian alliance would get into difficulties as the result of Germany's and Russia's intervention against Japan, the French government, on April 12, also indicated its willingness to join in the intervention. The Triple Intervention had been hatched.

On the same day that China and Japan signed the peace treaty at Shimonoseki, April 17, 1895, a new note from Lobanov was addressed to all the powers asking support for Russia's position; Germany unhesitatingly gave it full backing. Precisely one week later, on April 23, the Russian, German, and French ministers in Tokyo called at the Foreign Ministry to serve on Japan their common "advice": that "the possession of the Liaotung Peninsula claimed by Japan would be a constant menace to the capital of China, and would at the same time render illusory the independence of Korea; it would henceforth be a perpetual obstacle to the peace of the Far East."[6]

Resentful Waiting, 1895–1901. The visit of the three envoys to the Japanese Foreign Ministry came as an intensely unpleasant surprise for the Japanese. They were especially taken aback and annoyed at German participation, for that country, Vice-Minister Hayashi Tadasu had supposed, had no interest whatever in the Far Eastern question. Japanese resentment was intensified by the tactless and arrogant behavior of Baron Alfred von Gutschmid in his interview with Hayashi that day. Coming after the Russian and French envoys, the German minister had caused the memorandum (identical in text with that of Russia and France) to be translated from the English and French into Japanese *rōmaji*. His secretary had trouble reading it in that form, and Hayashi found the reading difficult to understand. After having read it off, Gutschmid exceeded his instructions and supplemented the note with some explanatory remarks couched in rather threatening and peremptory language. He implied the threat of force if Japan did not comply and pointed out that there was no chance of victory for Japan should it choose to fight Russia, Germany, and France together.[7]

[6] *Die grosse Politik*, IX, 270; and *Nihon gaikō bunsho*, XXVIII/2, 15–16.
[7] *Ibid.*, p. 27; and Pooley, *Secret Memoirs*, p. 81.

This action caused intense Japanese anger. Even nine years later the distinguished Itō told Dr. Erwin Baelz in Japan that Germany's intervention had been unjustified; it had been a real insult.[8] Although Hayashi eventually persuaded Gutschmid to cancel the note in *rōmaji*, to substitute for it the original note, and to delete his additional comments, Japanese tempers were not improved when two days later the German envoy pointed out to Hayashi that, if the Japanese government had only responded to Germany's friendly advice of March 8, much annoyance and trouble would have been spared both parties. It amounted to rubbing salt into open wounds.[9]

On April 24, the day after the delivery of the "advice" by the foreign powers, a conference took place in the presence of the Meiji emperor, with Itō Hirobumi, Yamagata Aritomo, and Admiral Saigō Tsugumichi, at which the prime minister and his army and navy ministers tended toward acceptance of the proffered "advice." Itō talked to Foreign Minister Mutsu the next day. Mutsu at first hoped to be able to hold out against the intervention by securing the diplomatic support of Britain, the United States, and Italy. But since no favorable reply from Britain was forthcoming, he, too, finally acquiesced. An effort was made by Japan on May 1 to save something from the painful situation, when the Japanese government offered to retrocede all of the Liaotung Peninsula except Port Arthur.[10] Needless to say, this counter offer was rejected by the representatives of the intervening powers, and after a full-dress conference between the cabinet and leading military and naval officers in Kyoto on May 4, the next day the Japanese government yielded completely. Japan's compliance was transmitted to St. Petersburg, Berlin, and Paris, and on May 9 the three powers expressed their satisfaction with Japan's course of action. Finally, on May 10 the Triple Intervention was promulgated to the Japanese people, in an imperial rescript countersigned by all ministers, which stated that Japan's objectives had been accomplished and that the retrocession of the peninsula did not reflect upon the dignity and honor of Japan. Japan had learned how "to bear the unbearable," a memory and phrase

---

[8] Erwin Baelz, *Erwin Baelz: Das Leben eines deutschen Arztes im erwachenden Japan* (1931), p. 43.

[9] *Nihon gaikō bunsho*, XXVIII/2, 33.

[10] *Die grosse Politik*, IX, 274.

that was to be repeated under somewhat analogous circumstances on an August day in 1945, when the grandson of the Meiji emperor declared: "The decision I have reached is akin to the one forced upon my grand-father, the Emperor Meiji, at the time of the Triple Intervention. As he endured the unendurable, so shall I, and so must you."[11]

In the years after the intervention to 1901, Japanese-German relations followed a pattern of mutual hostility. German policy in the Far East remained dominated by three ideas: the acquisition of a naval base in Chinese waters, the engaging of Russia in Far Eastern affairs, and the genuine fear of the "yellow peril." In the pursuit of all of these Germany continued to cause the utmost uneasiness, if not open hostility, in Japan. Japan remained puzzled by Germany's *weltpolitik*, and what it could understand of it, Japan did not like.

As far as the creation of a German naval base in the Far East was concerned, that problem, of course, was solved with the acquisition of Kiaochow. As early as 1896, Admiral Alfred von Tirpitz had expressed his preference for that bay, and in January 1897 a German naval engineer, Georg Franzius, had been sent out to investigate the site as well as Amoy harbor. In May he came out in favor of Kiaochow, and fortunately for Germany, in November 1897 the German East Asiatic cruiser squadron was sent to Tsingtao following the murder of two German missionaries in Shantung province. On November 22, 1897, Germany demanded, and on March 8, 1898, China yielded, the desired concession at Kiaochow Bay.

German desires to keep Russia busy in the Far East, thereby keeping it out of the Balkans and European affairs and also weakening the Franco-Russian alliance, can be clearly seen in one of the famous "Willy to Nicky" letters, in which the kaiser addressed the following lines to the tsar: "To guard the rear of Russia I shall certainly do all in my power to keep Europe quiet, and also so that nobody shall hamper your action towards the Far East. For that is clearly the great task of the future for Russia to cultivate the Asian continent and to defend Europe from the inroads of the Great Yellow race. In this you will always find me on your side, ready to help you as best I can."[12]

[11]Robert J.C. Butow, *Japan's Decision to Surrender* (1954), p. 208.
[12]Isaac D. Levine, ed., *Letters from the Kaiser to the Czar* (1920), pp. 10–11.

The racial problem genuinely concerned the kaiser, but he also understood the usefulness of the argument about the "yellow peril" in his correspondence with the deeply religious Nicholas II. In 1895 the kaiser commissioned a German artist, H. Knackfuss, to draw an allegorical picture based on an imperial design, illustrating the menace from the East. When the first copy was presented to Nicholas, William explained: "It shows the powers of Europe represented by their respective genii called together by the Arch Angel Michael—sent from Heaven—to unite in resisting the inroads of Buddhism, heathenism and barbarism for the Defence of the Cross. Stress is especially laid on *united* resistance of *all* European Powers, which is just as necessary also against our common internal foes, anarchism, republicanism, and nihilism."

It does not require much imagination to arrive at an estimate of the feeling of the Japanese government in the face of Germany's grab in the Shantung peninsula, its encouragement of Russia in the Far East, and its stress on race. Unfortunately, there does not as yet seem to exist a good Japanese study of Japanese reactions to German diplomacy in this period. The following are works relating to the Triple Intervention.

Documents:

American Historical Association, *A Catalogue of Files and Microfilms of the German Foreign Ministry Archives, 1867–1920* (1959), contains a volume of the series, *Beziehungen Deutschlands zu Japan, 1886–1920* (Deutschland 132), which bears on the years 1894–95. Apparently this material has not as yet been investigated.

Germany, Auswärtiges Amt, *Die grosse Politik der europäischen Kabinette, 1871–1914*, Vol. IX (1924). Ch. 57, pp. 239–333, in this monumental undertaking deals entirely with the intervention.

Japan, Gaimushō (Foreign Ministry), *Nihon gaikō bunsho*, XXVIII/2 (1953), is the most important documentary collection; in ch. 12, pp. 1–222, some sixty documents are listed, a number of them quite important in illustrating the views of Aoki, Hayashi, Mutsu, and Itō on events leading up to the intervention and Japan's reaction to it.

—— *Nihon gaikō nempyō narabi ni shuyō bunsho* (2 vols., 1965; first published, 1955), I, 169–70, pertains to the Triple Intervention.

Biographies and memoirs:

Hohenlohe-Schillingsfürst, *Denkwürdigkeiten* (2 vols., 1907), contributes little.

Mutsu, *Kenkenroku* (1939, written in 1896), is a valuable account written by the

Japanese foreign minister and gives direct insight into the making of Japan's foreign policy at a crucial period in its history. The original version was not made public until 1929, when it became part of Mutsu, *Hakushaku Mutsu Munemitsu ikō* (1929).

Pooley, *The Secret Memoirs of Count Tadasu Hayashi* (1915), also has some interesting comments on Hayashi's negotiations with the ministers of the three powers during Mutsu's absence.

Rich and Fisher, *The Holstein Papers* (4 vols., 1955–63). Vol. III, *Correspondence, 1861–1896* (1961) is an important source of information concerning German motivation in the intervention and Japanese reaction to it.

Secondary works:

Bee, "Origins of German Far Eastern Policy" (1937), is a well-written and important article.

Brandenburg, *Von Bismarck zum Weltkriege* (1924), contains some material about the topic; it is a standard account of German diplomacy.

Franke, *Die Grossmächte in Ostasien von 1894 bis 1914* (1923), is a conventional account written from the German point of view.

Kajima, *Nihon gaikō seisaku no shiteki kōsatsu* (1951), has a chapter on the intervention largely based upon *Die grosse Politik*. Its earlier version, *Teikoku gaikō no kihon seisaku* (1938), is based on materials from the Foreign Ministry.

Langer, *The Diplomacy of Imperialism, 1890–1902* (2d ed., 1951), ch. 6, is the best and most authoritative study of the intervention in a Western language.

Ostwald, *Deutschland und Japan: Eine Freundschaft zweier Völker* (1941), also is a conventional account from the German point of view.

Rosen, "German-Japanese Relations, 1894–1902: A Study of European Imperialism in the Far East" (1956), takes up these relations, as the title suggests, as part of a study of European imperialism in the Far East. Available on microfilm, the work makes excellent use of European but not of Japanese sources.

Shinobu, *Kindai Nihon gaikōshi* (1942), a more reliable source, also has a section on the topic of the intervention.

—— *Nihon no gaikō* (1961), presents a number of recent studies by various authors.

Takeuchi, *War and Diplomacy in the Japanese Empire* (1935), has a short section on the intervention.

The Anglo-Japanese Alliance. Japanese attitudes toward Germany of distrust, suspicion, and dislike of German actions in the Far East had been shaped by the German intervention in 1895 (which Bismarck satirized as a jump into the dark). Anti-German feelings in Japan were further stimulated by the German policy of keeping Russia preoccupied in the Far East, a policy that remained consistent after the intervention. Mutual antagonism culminated in the period just prior to and during the Russo-Japanese War, when Germany's attitude was one that virtually violated its neutrality for the benefit of Russia. The unexpected victory of Japan over Russia then resulted in German inconvenience and difficulties in the Far East.

In addition, with the conclusion of the Anglo-Japanese alliance all issues between Britain and Germany became inferentially issues between Japan and Germany as well. There is some irony in this, since one German official, Hermann von Eckardstein, had proposed a joint British-German-Japanese alignment, primarily to bring Britain and Germany into a closer relationship. He failed in this objective but did facilitate the creation of the Anglo-Japanese alliance, which eventually was to be turned against Germany itself.

In the spring of 1901 it occurred to Eckardstein, then first secretary and charge d'affaires of the German embassy in London, to make use of the temporary absence due to illness of his ambassador, Hermann von Hatzfeld, to develop a scheme that would lead to an Anglo-German alliance. Eckardstein, who had married the heiress of a millionaire furniture maker, was largely motivated in this plan by his personal vanity and ambition. To open discussions with Britain, he decided to make use of Japan as an intermediary power, and in March 1901 he approached Count Hayashi Tadasu, who was serving at that time as Japanese ambassador to the Court of St. James. He suggested to Hayashi that, for maintaining peace in the Far East, a joint alliance between the three powers would be very effective indeed. Perhaps Japan might take the initiative in proposing such a plan?[13] Hayashi duly reported his conversation back to Tokyo and was then instructed by the Japanese Foreign Ministry to sound out the British government. He approached Lord Lansdowne, but only with regard to a possible Anglo-Japanese agreement.

So far the German government itself had been left in ignorance of what had gone on, but it heard, via Tokyo, of Eckardstein's talks with Hayashi and promptly demanded an explanation from the former. Eckardstein, to

---

[13]Pooley, *Secret Memoirs*, pp. 119–29, 149–50, 190–95, discusses the negotiations for the Anglo-Japanese alliance. In addition, see Hermann F. Eckardstein, *Lebenserinnerungen und politische Denkwürdigkeiten*, II (1919), 339, 342.

avoid responsibility for his unauthorized action, claimed that it was Hayashi who had made the suggestion for such an alliance, and in his denials to Berlin he even went so far as to falsify telegrams sent by him to the Wilhelmstrasse.[14]

Whether the German government really entertained the idea of a triple alliance is a moot question; certainly the service of Japan as an intermediary made direct negotiations with Britain much easier. The real goal of Eckardstein, however, was an alliance between Germany and Britain.

The British government began to take a serious interest in the Japanese aspect of the proposal, since the attraction of "splendid isolation" had considerably waned. On July 15 Sir Claude MacDonald, the British minister to Japan, in London on leave, visited Hayashi and told him that both Edward VII and Lord Salisbury were agreeable to an Anglo-Japanese alliance. He also made it known to Hayashi at that time that Eckardstein had called some days previously at the Foreign Office and expressed fears that Japan conceivably might reach an alliance with Russia instead of Britain. The kind of pressure used here by Eckardstein was to be repeated in 1915–16, and again in the relationships between Nazi Germany and militarist Japan. German diplomacy seems to have had a fondness for conjuring up the specter that an alliance might be concluded with one's possible opponent if negotiations between partners did not run along too smoothly. It suggests inconsistency and impatience, neither of which are virtues in successful diplomacy.

From the summer of 1901 on, discussions between Japan and Britain became quite serious. To the Japanese government, but not the British, there still remained the question of whether Germany would join in the proposed alliance. Itō opposed secret negotiations with Great Britain alone; he felt that Germany should be included. On November 20 Hayashi asked Lord Lansdowne about the matter.

Lansdowne replied that it might be better to wait before informing Germany about the ongoing Japanese-British discussions; if it were informed about them, Germany would only use the alliance talks as an instrument to advance its own interests (a correct enough interpretation), and furthermore, Germany, even if kept out of the alliance, would not really

---

[14]Documents 5037, 5038 in *Die grosse Politik*, XVII, 136–38.

be vexed over it, since it recognized that British and Japanese interests in China were extensive.

The question of German participation in an Anglo-Japanese alliance had been raised by Itō himself while he was in Paris. Japan was anxious to have Germany associated in that alliance, since it always worried about the possibility of a new German-French-Russian combination. The ghost of a renewed Triple Intervention continued to haunt the Japanese government, and memories of 1895 were revived during the visits of William II to France in September 1901.

In replying to Itō's query, Hayashi pointed out that Germany certainly should be informed about the Anglo-Japanese alliance, but only after the treaty had been concluded. He telegraphed Foreign Minister Komura Jutarō in Tokyo to the same effect, indicating that this was Britain's desire and thus he felt it should be followed. In his discussions with Lansdowne, Hayashi suggested that notification of Germany might best be left to Britain, since it had much closer and more important relations with Germany than did Japan; Lansdowne agreed completely. The British foreign secretary indeed was satisfied since the British government really did not want to approach Germany and since, in any case, he felt that it would be best to settle the alliance with Japan first and then consider Germany afterwards.

By December 1901 a British rapprochement with Germany had become an almost total impossibility. Chancellor Bernhard von Bülow's bitter attack in the Reichstag against British Colonial Secretary Joseph Chamberlain and the violent tenor of German press attacks against Britain over the Boer War had strained British-German relations to the utmost. Lansdowne felt that there was no longer any hope that Germany would join the Anglo-Japanese alliance. On the other hand, Germany would not disapprove of the alliance. All that was necessary was to notify the German government when the treaty had come into existence.

When the Anglo-Japanese alliance was signed in January 1902, Japan suggested that Germany should be given a week's notice in advance, but the British government turned down even that suggestion. Lord Lansdowne actually sent out instructions to postpone notification of the German ambassador in London; in this he was too late, however, since the Japanese government in Tokyo had already notified the German minister there about the existence of the new alliance. Lansdowne then followed suit by

informally notifying Count Paul von Metternich, the new German ambassador in London, without, of course, an invitation to Germany to join
the treaty.

Was Germany really interested in an alliance with Japan and Britain, or
did Eckardstein's approach represent merely an individual initiative? It is
possible, because of the tentative state of Russo-German relations at that
moment, that Germany did toy with such an idea, but basically Germany
never seriously thought along these lines. In the final analysis, ever since
1895 German policy had been to support Russia, particularly in the Far
East.

Estrangement, 1902–1914. The German policy of keeping Russia preoccupied in the Far East, even at the risk of antagonizing Japan, was
expressed in a variety of ways. In March 1901 Bülow declared that he
interpreted the Anglo-German convention on China of October 1900 as
not applying to Manchuria, thus leaving that area open to Russian penetration. Hence, Japan was left to face Russia alone in Manchuria, assisted
only by the British. Germany also refused to join the protests of the powers
against the Russian occupation of Manchuria in the wake of the Boxer
Rebellion. The German concession in Kiaochow itself served as protection
for Russia against the British, and by inference also against Japan. Germany's diplomacy remained one of pushing Russia deeper into Far Eastern
affairs, in the hope thereby of obtaining valuable concessions for itself in
Europe and the Near East, especially in connection with its cherished
Berlin-to-Baghdad railway project. This policy was calculated also to
weaken the Franco-Russian alliance. The area in which Russian ambitions
were encouraged included not only Manchuria but Korea as well. In a
letter dated January 3, 1904, the kaiser wrote to Nicholas II: "Russia to
have iceless outlet for her commerce. . . . It is evident to every unbiased
mind that Korea must and will be Russian." When and how this was to
come about was "nobody's affair and concerns only you and your country.
Russian annexation is a foregone conclusion here like the occupation of
Manchuria."[15]

Germany, in a sense, then also had a very real part in the outbreak of the
Russo-Japanese War, and once the conflict had begun, it was made clear

---

[15]Levine, *Letters from the Kaiser,* p. 100.

that Germany hoped for a Russian victory. The kaiser again professed fear of the "yellow peril" and of Japan's rapid industrialization. The professed German attitude in the conflict was that of benevolent neutrality; in fact it amounted to open support of Russia and drew sharp protests from Japan. German ships provided the Russian Baltic fleet with coal on their disastrous odyssey (ironically enough, from Cardiff), provoking a Japanese outcry, and German officers attached to the Japanese army at the front had a disconcerting habit of sending their reports directly to their government, without submitting them to Japanese scrutiny, in spite of Japanese protests.

In December 1904, when it had become clear that Japan was winning in the struggle, Germany even toyed with the idea of putting direct pressure on Japan by a joint German-French-American mediation. Conceivably Japan might be separated from Britain, which would stand isolated once again. It was a move that worried London sufficiently that the British government sounded out President Theodore Roosevelt about his ideas on the matter.

With the final collapse of Russia in 1905, German diplomacy in the Far East suffered a serious check. Germany had earned intense Japanese dislike, and as the Anglo-Japanese alliance came out of the Russo-Japanese War more strongly cemented than before, the fact that Germany loomed ever larger as the logical opponent of Britain inevitably meant that it would be so for Japan. The next step for Japan was then to enter into an understanding with the French after the Entente Cordiale had been concluded. Under the new Saionji cabinet, Hayashi signed such a Franco-Japanese agreement in 1907.

If a general war should break out, Japan would be aligned with Britain and France. Such a war would also permit Japan to revenge itself for the Triple Intervention and subsequent hostile German policies.

The following are the best existing studies on the subject of the Anglo-Japanese alliance, the Russo-Japanese War, and Germany.

Documents:

American Historical Association, *A Catalogue of Files and Microfilms of the German Foreign Ministry Archives, 1867–1920* (1959), lists *Beziehungen Deutschlands zu Japan, 1886–1920*, which, as noted above, is as yet unexplored material.

Germany, Auswärtiges Amt, *Die grosse Politik der europäischen Kabinette, 1871–1914*, XVII (1924), 133–81, is the most useful collection of German documents.

Great Britain, Foreign Office, *British Documents on the Origins of the War, 1894–1914*, Vol. II (1927), contains material about the Anglo-Japanese alliance.

Japan, Gaimushō (Foreign Ministry), *Nihon gaikō bunsho*, Vols. XXXIV–XXXV (1956–57), deals with the alliance. Supplements numbered 1, 2, and 5 to Vols. XXXVII and XXXVIII (1958–60) consider the problem of the German attitude during the Russo-Japanese War. No. 1 of this supplement, sec. 1, pp. 599–688, lists a number of reports between Foreign Minister Komura and Charge d'Affaires Inoue Katsunosuke in Berlin on Germany's support of Russia and the Japanese reaction to this development. These documents should be examined thoroughly.

Biographies and memoirs:

Eckardstein, *Lebenserinnerungen und politische Denkwürdigkeiten* (3 vols., 1919–21), is pertinent but must be used with caution, since Eckardstein was interested in presenting essentially his own personal case and did not hesitate to misrepresent when he felt it necessary.

Pooley, *The Secret Memoirs of Count Tadasu Hayashi* (1915), also is pertinent.

Secondary works:

Akagi, *Japan's Foreign Relations, 1542–1936* (1936), pp. 191–216, has a section on the Anglo-Japanese alliance.

Bloch, *German Interests and Policies in the Far East* (1940), is a very useful economic analysis of relations between Japan and Germany.

Eguchi, "Nichi-Ei dōmei no hatten to shite no Ei-Doku kōshō" (1949), is an excellent study of the alliance.

Franke, *Die Grossmächte in Ostasien von 1894 bis 1914* (1923).

Kiyosawa, *Nihon gaikōshi* (2 vols., 1942), is another analysis of the role of Germany in the origin of the alliance.

Langer, *The Diplomacy of Imperialism, 1890–1902* (2d ed., 1951), devotes ch. 23 to the alliance and Germany's role.

Zühlke, *Die Rolle des fernen Osten in den politischen Beziehungen der Mächte, 1895–1905* (1929).

A number of studies might contribute significantly to some of the topics that have only been touched upon so far. One of these might deal with the general problem of Japan's understanding of Germany's *weltpolitik*. Why was there such a lack of knowledge in Japan about German diplomacy in general, and its diplomacy in the Far East in particular? Why was the intervention such a surprise? Equally important, one might ask questions about the impact of the intervention on Japan. Did it lead to a lasting distrust of Germany? (One can catch glimpses of such distrust as late as the

1930s and 1940s when Nazi Germany and Japan concluded the Anti-Comintern Pact and the Tripartite agreement.) To what degree did the unfortunate experience of 1895 lead Japan to modify and change its diplomatic methods in the crises of 1904 and 1914?

Specifically, there does not appear to exist a study dealing with Japanese reactions to Germany's acquisition of Kiaochow Bay. Another topic which deserves some study is Japan's reaction to the problem of the "yellow peril." Did the race issue, first raised here in Germany, cause lasting Japanese trauma? To what degree did this question influence significant Japanese foreign policy decisions in future years?

In a world that stresses historical forces at the expense of the role of the individual in history, there might also be room for a good study of William II and his Far Eastern diplomacy. To what degree was Germany's diplomacy the result of his individual decisions, and to what degree was it the result of forces that propelled it in that direction in any case?

Germany's role in the Anglo-Japanese alliance has been amply covered, but this is not the case with later German-Japanese relations. Especially Germany's role in the Russo-Japanese War and Japanese reactions to it would seem to warrant further investigation. In addition, there exists practically no study of the years 1905–14 in the field of German-Japanese relations.

LIMITED WAR, 1914–1921

Japan's Decision to Enter World War I, 1914. Japan's chance to obtain revenge for Germany's role in the Triple Intervention came with the outbreak of World War I. It was an opportunity too good to let slip by. Japan's entry into the war would not only destroy German influence in the Far East but would also secure Tsingtao, greatly enhancing Japan's international position. Japanese resentment against Germany for the intervention, for encouraging Russia in Manchuria, and for supporting Russia in the Russo-Japanese War could now be paid back with interest. It was no accident that Japan's ultimatum to Germany made use of the same language, "friendly advice," that had been used by Germany against Japan in 1895. German-Japanese diplomatic hostilities resulted in Germany's eclipse in the Far East at the hands of Japan.

When it appeared, in the fateful early August days of 1914, as if the world was drifting at long last into the terrible war that many had prophesied ever since the split into two hostile camps of all the great European powers, the question also arose for Japan what stand to take in the impending conflict. On August 3 the German ambassador in Tokyo, Graf von Rex (the legation had been raised to the status of an embassy after the Russo-Japanese War), called upon Foreign Minister Katō Takaaki to ascertain Japan's attitude. Katō's answer was that Japan would maintain strict neutrality, unless Great Britain were to demand Japanese assistance—a far from reassuring answer from the point of view of Berlin. Katō gave the same reply to the British ambassador in Tokyo, who called that same day. In the evening of August 4, after Britain had declared war on Germany over the issue of Belgian neutrality, Katō met with Prime Minister Ōkuma Shigenobu and the entire Japanese cabinet and it was decided that Japan was ready to enter on Britain's side.[16]

The Japanese press itself, a good barometer of political feeling, now assumed a strong and militant anti-German tone. Germany's infamous role in the Triple Intervention was recalled to the Japanese public, and Japan's obligations to Britain under the Anglo-Japanese alliance, as well as to France and Russia under the 1907 and subsequent treaties, were stressed. The charge was made that Germany's naval power in the Pacific was a threat to all neutral shipping, and that Germany's military preparations in Kiaochow Bay were a menace to peace in the Far East. Many editorials, doubtlessly inspired by the government, advocated a Japanese attack on Germany's possessions.[17]

Whereas Japan declared its prompt readiness to join Britain in the war against the kaiser, the British government was in no hurry to request such assistance. From the beginning, Edward Grey, the British foreign secretary, had come to the conclusion that to invoke Japan's willing aid might cause infinite trouble for Britain in its position in the Far East. On August 4 Grey instructed the British ambassador in Tokyo that, while he should thank Katō for Japan's generous offer of assistance, Britain at the very most wanted only limited Japanese participation in the struggle.[18] Three

---

[16]Charles N. Spinks, "Japan's Entrance into the World War" (1936), pp. 297–311.

[17]"Why Japan Attacks Germany," *The Literary Digest*, XLIX, No. 12 (September 19, 1914), 502.

[18]Great Britain, Foreign Office, *British Documents on the Origins of the War, 1898–1914*, edited by G.P. Gooch and Harold Temperley (11 vols, 1926–38), Vol. XI.

days later, British Ambassador Conyngham Greene was told merely to request the Japanese government to aid in the destruction of German armed vessels.

Upon receipt of this request on August 7, Katō met with Ōkuma and the genrō to discuss Japan's future course of action.[19] The foreign minister advocated immediate Japanese entry into the war, thereby remaining friendly to Britain, obtaining revenge against Germany, and in general raising Japan's status in international affairs. The conference then came to the conclusion that, indeed, Japan would enter the war, but it would do more than merely destroy German armed vessels. Katō communicated this decision the next day to the Taishō emperor for approval. The emperor endorsed the decision.

Japan was particularly interested in obtaining the German leased territories in Shantung province. Consequently the negotiations which in the meantime had taken place between China and Germany, providing for the restoration of Kiaochow Bay and Tsingtao to the Chinese Republic, were disturbing to the Japanese government. Under the terms of the German-Chinese agreement of 1898, Germany possessed the right to give up its leasehold at Kiaochow at any time in return for a more suitable port elsewhere in China. Germany now indicated to Peking its willingness to evacuate for the time being, with a view to returning after the conclusion of the war. The regime in Peking, which had declared its neutrality in the European war, was of course interested in such an agreement, but neither Britain nor Japan was happy at the prospect of a Sino-German agreement concerning the leased territories. Japan now acted in such a way as to make such an agreement an impossibility. Japan having decided to go to war against Germany in a substantial way, Katō took the initiative by invoking Articles 1 and 2 of the Anglo-Japanese alliance. In addition, Japan replied to a curt German note of August 8, which requested Japan to maintain strictest neutrality, by informing Germany that such neutrality was contingent upon German conduct in the Far East and expressing Japan's concern at the mobilization of all German nationals in Tsingtao. That same day, August 8, Japanese naval units were concentrated off Tsingtao, and on

---

[19]Itō Masanori, ed., *Katō Takaaki* (1929), II, 78–81.

August 9 Katō informed Greene that Japan had decided to enter the war under the terms of the alliance. Japan would not only destroy German armed vessels, but eliminate German influence from Kiaochow as well.

The Japanese decision caused grave apprehension in London. The British government feared that the war would extend to Chinese territory and that Japan would gain great advantages in China at the expense not only of the joint enemy, Germany, but of Britain as well. Grey cabled on August 9 his advice that Japan should postpone its declaration of war and, in any case, should limit its actions to the protection of maritime trade. Two days later London followed this up by requesting that Japan suspend all military operations and withdrawing its original request of August 7 for Japanese assistance under the Anglo-Japanese alliance.[20]

Britain's afterthoughts about the effect of Japan's participation in the war in the Far East presented an embarrassing dilemma to the Japanese foreign minister and the entire Japanese government. The cabinet had made its decision, that decision had been sanctioned by the Throne; hence, a reversal of policy was not only against the interests of Japan, it was politically impossible. Katō now used as an excuse the somewhat arrogant note of Count Rex of August 8 to justify his actions to the British. Grey was told that Japan would enter on its own initiative since its interests in the Far East were sufficiently threatened by Germany.

The German government now made a belated effort to keep Japan out of the war by informing Tokyo on August 12 through Ambassador Rex that Germany would refrain from any hostile actions against Britain in the Far East if Japan were to stay neutral; but the Japanese government did not deign to reply, except to order its navy into full mobilization. The next day the British government, much to the relief of Japan, also agreed to a Japanese ultimatum to Germany that would not only demand the surrender of German armed vessels but would also require the delivery of Kiaochow. The only request London made was that Japan should state in its ultimatum that it would confine its activity to the German base in Shantung and the neighboring China seas, but on August 15 even this reservation was deleted by the British.

---

[20]Spinks, "Japan's Entrance into the World War," p. 305.

This same day, Japan issued an ultimatum to Germany. The ultimatum was a rather unique document. First, it was in the form of an "advice" (a repayment for 1895); second, it gave no overt reasons for its demands, as Germany was not accused in it of any hostile acts; and finally, it permitted a time limit of one week rather than the customary twenty-four hours for Germany's reply. The body of the document stated:

The Imperial Japanese Government sincerely believe it their duty to give advice to the Imperial German Government to carry out the following two propositions:

1. withdraw their men-of-war and armed vessels of all kinds from the Japanese and Chinese waters, and disarm at once all that cannot be withdrawn;

2. deliver up to the Japanese authorities by September 15, without condition or compensation, the entire leased territory of Kiaochow with a view to eventual restoration of the same to China.[21]

While the Japanese ultimatum was still unexpired, the British government made a further attempt to limit the sphere of Japanese action. Without any warning to Japan, a press release from London declared that Japanese action would not extend beyond the China seas and would not impinge upon the independence and integrity of China. This British statement was strongly protested by Foreign Minister Katō, and immediately afterwards Prime Minister Ōkuma issued a declaration, denying any territorial ambitions on the part of Japan and assuring the world that any warlike actions were to be limited to "self-defense."

Having received no German reply before the expiration of the ultimatum, Japan declared war on August 23. On August 26 a combined Japanese and British fleet blockaded Tsingtao, but not before the German Far Eastern fleet, commanded by Admiral Count Maximilian von Spee, had managed to leave Far Eastern waters. The German cruiser *Emden* left Tsingtao, captured a Russian auxiliary cruiser, and then turned to a most successful raiding career in the East Indies, where she accounted for a French destroyer and some twenty-three British merchantmen before being brought to bay, while the main German squadron with *Scharnhorst* and *Gneisenau* defeated the British at Coronel off the coast of Chile before being finally sunk in the battle of the Falkland Islands in early December.

Tsingtao fell to Japan on November 7, and the Japanese took over all

[21] *Ibid.*, pp. 308–9.

German interests in Shantung province, including those outside the leased area, such as the Tsinan-Tsingtao railroad, mines, and various other public and private property rights. The German Pacific islands of the Carolines, the Marshalls, and the Marianas were also taken over by Japan, which eventually obtained them as mandates from the League of Nations.

The question of whether or not Japan might have refrained from joining in the war against Germany is one that is open to some debate. A. Whitney Griswold in his *Far Eastern Policy of the United States* argues that the week's grace of the Japanese ultimatum and possible pro-German sympathies on the part of the Japanese cabinet suggest that Japan may have hoped that Germany would accept the Japanese ultimatum. While this possibility might be more fully investigated, there is no question that Japan in 1914 saw the chance to avenge itself against Germany for the Triple Intervention of 1895 and that it was determined to oust Germany from the Far East.

Given the vast quantity of unexplored documentary material available from both the German and the Japanese foreign ministries, a general review of German-Japanese relations in the period leading up to Japan's entry into World War I seems definitely indicated. Many questions need to be answered. What was Germany's attitude toward Japan's ultimatum? Did Japan really think that Germany would surrender Kiaochow Bay without a fight, and if so, would Japan otherwise not have joined Britain in the war? How strong was pro-German feeling in Japan in 1914? What was Japan's estimate of a possible German victory in the war? What was Germany's policy toward Japan during the years from 1906 to 1914?

The following works relate to Japan's entry into World War I.

Documents:

> American Historical Association, *A Catalogue of Files and Microfilms of the German Foreign Ministry Archives, 1867–1920* (1959), contains a variety of listings which seem very promising, for, as with Japan, much German source material has not as yet been explored. The file Deutschland 132, *Abbruch der Beziehugen zwischen Deutschland und Japan,* the volume of *Beziehungen Deutschlands zu Japan, 1886–1920* dealing with the year 1914 (Deutschland 132), and the files *Die Gesandtschaft in Tokyo* and *Die Gesandschaft in Peking* (Deutschland 135, No. 15) obviously are pertinent. The item cited first above, a special study concerned with Germany's break with Japan in 1914, should be valuable for determining

German actions. Secondary works that have attempted to deal with this question so far have failed.

Great Britain, Foreign Office, *British Documents on the Origins of the War, 1898–1914* (1926–38), Vol. XI, contains materials bearing on Japan's entry into World War I and German policy that led to that decision.

Japan, Gaimushō (Foreign Ministry), *Nihon gaikō nempyō narabi ni shuyō bunsho*, I (1965), 380–81, has some documents on Japan's relations with Germany in 1914.

—— *Sekai taisen kankei Nihon gaikō bunsho*, Vol. I, contains a very comprehensive and extensive Japanese documentary source for Japan's entry into World War I. These documents were compiled by the First Section of the Foreign Ministry's Research Division in March 1939. Ch. 2 lists over 160 documents relating to the opening of hostilities between Germany and Japan in 1914 and contains reports from various Japanese ambassadors abroad and instructions and memoranda of the foreign minister. This is a rich source that should yield considerable further information.

Uyehara, *Checklist of Archives in the Japanese Ministry of Foreign Affairs, Tokyo, Japan, 1868–1945, Microfilmed for the Library of Congress, 1949–1951* (1954), pp. 5, 79, lists the following: MT 1.1.4.1. series, Japanese-German relations; and UD 16 series, Berlin embassy file.

Biography:

Itō, *Katō Takaaki* (2 vols., 1929), Vol. II, is the most important biography of a statesman involved in this issue.

Secondary works:

Akagi, *Japan's Foreign Relations, 1542–1936* (1936).

Spinks, "Japan's Entrance into the World War" (1936), is an important article.

Vinacke, *A History of the Far East in Modern Times* (6th ed., 1959).

"Why Japan Attacks Germany" (1914).

Peace Negotiations during World War I, 1914–1918. The relations between Japan and Germany during World War I form a most interesting and hitherto almost unexplored chapter in the history of the foreign relations of these two countries.

As the result of German successes in 1915, Japan began to show unmistakable signs of wavering in its allegiance to the Allies, at least to the point of considering German peace overtures, which began to be made rather energetically in 1915 and continued into 1916. These promised German support for Japanese actions in the Far East at the expense of Russia.

The Japanese government made no attempt to keep these advances secret; rather, it let the proposals be known to the Allies in order to raise the price for its aid. At the same time Germany also made peace overtures to Russia, starting in the summer of 1915 and promising support for Russia against Japan. These maneuvers, however, constituted a blunder on the part of Germany, since in trying to play off Japan against Russia and Russia against Japan, it merely brought about a closer understanding between these two powers. German diplomacy, in not being able to pursue one aim consistently and in trying to negotiate a separate peace with two opponents at the same time by dangling in front of each advantages to be gained at the expense of the other, committed a serious mistake. On the other hand, Japan, by letting it be known that some of its military leaders felt that Germany might prevail in the end, was able to exact better terms for itself from the Allies, particularly concerning its claims to Kiaochow Bay and the former German islands in the Pacific Ocean.

Following the bloody stalemate in Flanders in 1914 and the apparent German successes in the battles of Ypres, Artois, and Champagne the next year, the Japanese press, probably officially inspired, began in the spring of 1915 to assume an aggressive tone against the Anglo-Japanese alliance. It was described as being one-sided and consequently unfair. At the same time, the apparent invincibility of Germany was being pointed out. Hopes for further German victories coincided with the argument that conceivably a German-Japanese alliance might be far more desirable than the maintenance of the Anglo-Japanese alliance. A number of pro-German military leaders as well as some Japanese intellectuals began to express their preference for such a turnabout.[22] The notion of a division of the whole of Manchuria and Mongolia between Japan and Russia and the possibility of further Japanese claims against China, if peace could be made with the Central Powers, exercised a powerful attraction.

Such thinking coincided with the first of a number of determined German peace-feelers to Japan. This came in January 1915, through Admiral Paul von Hintze, the German ambassador in Peking. Hintze was an astute, resolute, and cultivated naval officer, an intimate of both the kaiser and General Erich Ludendorff. His intelligence and amiability had made him

---

[22]Ishii Kikujirō, *Diplomatic Commentaries* (1936), p. 97.

a success, first at the court of Nicholas II in St. Petersburg and later as the German minister to Mexico. There his job in 1914 was to embroil that country in war with the United States, thereby cutting off much-needed supplies to the Allies in Europe. Simultaneously, Hintze began to think about persuading Japan to leave the side of the Allies, thereby frightening Russia out of the war. He reasoned that Japan would make an excellent ally for Germany, deterring both the United States and Russia.

His proposal was well received in Berlin, and late in 1914 he returned from Mexico to Germany with a new mission, that of becoming the new German ambassador to China with the objective of negotiating a separate peace with Japan. The blue-eyed, clean-shaven Hintze, who spoke English without accent, disguised himself as a steward aboard a Norwegian boat for his trip across the Atlantic. He reached Rotterdam after strolling the streets of wartime London without having been detected.

After consultations in Berlin, the new German ambassador to China, having been promoted to the rank of rear-admiral, made his way to Peking via the United States. Since the Japanese government had refused him a safe conduct for his trip across the Pacific, he sailed aboard a Norwegian freighter, the *Christian Bors*, directly from San Francisco to Shanghai without stopping in Japan and arrived in China early in January 1915. En route in Washington, Hintze had had some discussion with a number of German officials, especially the former German press attache in Tokyo, Baron Wilhelm Edward von Schoen, who had been transferred to America upon severance of Japanese-German relations. He impressed Hintze with arguments stressing that war between Japan and the United States was unavoidable and that the best chance for German diplomatic success was in fomenting trouble between both Mexico and the United States and Japan and the United States.[23]

When Hintze took up his new position in China, he felt sanguine about the possibility of detaching Japan from the ranks of the Allied powers. For the sake of further gains on the Asia mainland, Japan might be persuaded to make peace with Germany. He unofficially told an *Asahi shimbun* correspondent in Peking that Germany was definitely the victor in the war, but that Germany favored Japan and would grant it full freedom

---

[23]B.W. Tuchman, *The Zimmermann Telegram* (1958), pp. 56–58, 60–61.

of action in East Asia. In more official discussions with Hioki Eki, the Japanese minister to China, Hintze stated that he was merely voicing the personal views of the kaiser in suggesting a peace treaty with Japan. Germany would let Japan keep not only Tsingtao but also the Pacific islands and would be willing to give Japan a much freer hand in China than the Allies. Germany, he even suggested, might go so far as to finance Japan's continued expansion in China. Implied, though not expressly stated, was the idea that Japan could do as it pleased in the Far East, especially in Manchuria and Mongolia, and that Germany certainly would not restrain any such actions at the expense of Russia.[24]

Hintze's approaches were, however, only one part of a broader picture of German peace overtures to Japan. In March and early April 1915 Germany made use of the Turkish and Austrian envoys to Sweden to make contact with the Japanese minister in Stockholm, Uchida Sadatsuchi. He was told essentially the same story. Germany was ready to forgo Tsingtao in return for some compensation, and German capital would be made available for Japanese activities in China. Japan, in short, would be given carte blanche in the Far East by Germany if a separate peace could be arranged.[25]

The reception of these German peace-feelers in Japan was a most interesting one. Germany had a number of sympathetic listeners among the Japanese military, who felt that, after all, Germany might be the winner in the great struggle. The Ōkuma government made no attempt to silence these sentiments—quite the opposite. If both Germany and the Allies each suspected that Japan wavered, Japan would be in an excellent position to raise its terms. The greater the doubts concerning its loyalty, the higher the price Japan might command. Japan communicated the German proposals, those made by Hintze as well as the discussions in Stockholm, to the Allies, thereby causing considerable consternation and suspicion not only in Europe but also in America. It so happened that in April 1915 a Japanese naval vessel, the *Asama*, ran aground on the coast of Lower California, thereby contributing to American fears of a possible Japanese-Mexican understanding. These moves were sufficiently disturbing that in April 1915 the British ambassador in Washington, Cecil Spring-Rice,

[24]Otto Becker, *Der Gedanke einer Deutsch-Russisch-Japanischen Verständigung während des Weltkrieges* (1940), p. 5.

[25]Tuchman, *The Zimmermann Telegram*, p. 61.

reported that Japan was on the verge of joining Germany,[26] and the American ambassador in Berlin, James Gerard, deeply suspected a German-Japanese peace treaty in the making.

While Germany was assiduously probing for a separate peace with Japan, it also made simultaneously a number of approaches to Russia. In the summer months of 1915 the German government made use of a stranded Russian noblewoman in Austria to sound out Nicholas II about the possible conclusion of a peace treaty. Russia, the Germans argued, would benefit from such a peace by going ahead in Manchuria and Mongolia at the expense of Japan. Such devious scheming, suggesting to Japan a free hand versus Russia and to Russia a free hand versus Japan, turned out to be a serious mistake. The Russian government was fully informed about the German peace-feelers to Japan, since it had possession of the code used by Tokyo in communicating with Japanese Ambassador Motono Ichirō in St. Petersburg and since the Japanese government itself, as previously stated, leaked out all German suggestions to its allies.[27] The Russians also kept Japan closely informed about the German approaches to St. Petersburg. The possibility of a separate Russian-German peace and a possible Russian-German alliance greatly worried the Ōkuma government, always sensitive to the specter of a renewed Triple Intervention. Japan's pro-Allied ambassador in Paris, Ishii Kikujirō, especially feared such a development, and he suggested to Prime Minister Ōkuma the idea of closer ties with Russia in order to ward off a German-Russian agreement. Ōkuma, in a cabinet meeting, even went so far as to consider a Japanese invasion of Siberia in case of a German-Russian understanding.

Since Germany had been unable to conclude a separate peace with either Japan or Russia during 1915, the German government at the beginning of 1916 tried a different tack. It concentrated exclusively on Japan, using a somewhat more private and tactful approach. In March of that year Berlin sent the German industrialist Hugo Stinnes to Sweden to resume negotiations. He did this in company with the German minister to Stockholm, Hellmuth von Lucius. Talks between the German representatives and Minister Uchida were reopened on April 1 and lasted a number of

---

[26]U.S., Department of State, Archives, No. 894.20212 (hereafter cited as State Department Archives).

[27]Becker, *Deutsch-Russisch-Japanischen Verständigung*, p. 6.

weeks. At first Germany suggested a new triple alliance of Japan, Russia, and Germany. This rather breathtaking scheme was treated with considerable reserve by Uchida, but he did indicate that Japan still weighed the possibility of coming to an understanding of some sort with Germany. After some two weeks of talks, the German government, becoming increasingly desperate and eager for relief, more realistically proposed to Japan that if Japan would make a separate peace treaty, Germany was ready to surrender all of its claims in the Far East.[28]

Japan, sensing German weakness and more certain than in 1915 of eventual Allied victory, again promptly relayed these German overtures to London and St. Petersburg, with the promise that it would not sign a separate peace treaty with Germany. The diary of H.P. Hanssen, a Danish member of the German Reichstag, also reflected the declining interest of Japan. At first he was told by Gottlieb von Jagow, the German foreign secretary, that, since public opinion in Japan was increasingly more pro-German, the likelihood of a peace treaty was good, but later on, in March 1916, such optimism gave way to a more realistic appraisal of the situation: "We have put out feelers which have produced no results. I do not believe that Japan is contemplating a conflict with America. She has too many other things to do."[29]

By 1917 Japan's position had become firmly fixed. On July 3 of that year it signed a separate treaty with the Russian government in regard to their interests in China. Although Japan in 1915 had become a signatory of the London Convention, declaring that it would never make a separate peace with the Central Powers, even as late as the spring of 1917 it found the leaking of German advances a useful tool in putting pressure on the Allies. When Hintze returned home in April after China had declared war against Germany, an interview was published with him in the *Kokumin shimbun* during his call at Yokohama, in which he again expressed his hopes for an eventual Japanese-German agreement. Japanese manipulations in keeping the fear alive that Japan might conceivably come to an understanding with Germany could also be discerned in the close relations that the Japanese government maintained with Mexico. This, coupled with German efforts to bring Mexico into the war against the United States, was

---

[28]*Ibid.*, p. 7.
[29]Hans P. Hanssen, *Diary of a Dying Empire* (1955), pp. 140–41.

designed to keep America in a state of uneasiness. The Japanese envoy to Mexico, for instance, was treated with marked favor by the Mexican government, and he in turn lavishly entertained Mexican government officials. A Mexican arms-buying mission, headed by a Major Carpio, arrived in Japan in 1917 and was exceedingly well received. After visits to Kure, Sasebo, and Yokosuka, he had a number of conferences with high Japanese naval officers and was then permitted to purchase a quantity of arms for Mexico, despite a previously existing Japanese agreement with the Allies to furnish arms only to them and to no other power. Thus, Japan maintained its pressure, especially on Britain, regarding its future claims to Tsingtao and the Pacific islands.[30]

With Germany's culminating effort to bring Mexico into war against the United States, as revealed in the famous Zimmermann telegram, Japan dissociated itself completely. The Japanese ambassador in London, Chinda Sutemi, told Lord Balfour that Japan had no relations of any interest with Mexico,[31] and Viscount Ishii Kikujirō told Secretary of State Robert Lansing in Washington on November 2, 1917, that Japan had had no knowledge of that disastrous cable. Ishii not only pleaded utter ignorance but also termed the Zimmermann telegram ridiculous.

Japan had had the best from the German peace-feelers. While German diplomacy in 1915 and 1916 had tried to do too much, by playing off Japan against Russia and vice versa, Japan had been able to profit from the German advances to obtain better terms for its postwar position in the Far East from the hard-pressed Allies. German diplomacy not only blundered in its failure to deal consistently with either Japan or Russia, but it also had created in Japanese eyes a general impression of German weakness.

As had been the case in the past and would be the case in the future, the relations between Japan and Germany in this instance were conducted for purely temporary and immediate gains. There was no long-range and far-looking diplomacy on the part of either power.

As may easily be seen from the foregoing account, the whole history of German peace overtures to Japan during World War I needs studying.

[30]Tuchman, *The Zimmermann Telegram,* pp. 105–6; State Department Archives, No. 712.9417–25.

[31]Interview reported by British Ambassador Cecil Spring-Rice to Department of State, April 1915, in State Department Archives, No. 894.20212/120.

One topic that might prove most interesting would be an analysis of the reception of German peace-feelers within Japan. This is probably the most significant neglected problem in the history of Japanese-German relations. Among the questions it might be interesting to investigate are the following: Who among the Japanese military and political personalities were particularly responsive to the German approaches, and why? Did the Japanese army really entertain the idea that Germany might win, and that Japan should shift sides in midstream? To what degree did the military influence the Ōkuma government? What was the decision-making process involved that caused the Japanese cabinet to leak the German peace-feelers to the Allies? Did the German government really think that such negotiations with Japan might succeed? What caused this belief? What did Germany envisage as its postwar Far Eastern policy?

On Japanese-German relations during World War I, the following works should be consulted:

Documents:

American Historical Association, *A Catalogue of Files and Microfilms of the German Foreign Ministry Archives, 1867–1920* (1959), lists the appropriate German documents. In particular Vols. X and XI, both secret, for the years 1915 and 1916 of *Beziehungen Deutschlands zu Japan, 1886–1920* (Deutschland 132), and the secret volume WK 23, *Die Friedensaktion der Zentralmächte*, give full documentation on the as yet rather sketchy account of German peace negotiations with Japan.

Izvestia, December 30, 1917, reproduces material about German-Russian negotiations in 1915 from USSR, Krasnyi Arkhiv.

U.S., Department of State, Archives, No. 712.94, relations between Mexico and Japan; No. 862.20212, German military activities, Mexico; and No. 894.20212, Japanese military activities, Mexico, are occasionally useful.

Uyehara, *Checklist of Archives in the Japanese Ministry of Foreign Affairs, Tokyo, Japan, 1868–1945, Microfilmed for the Library of Congress, 1949–1951* (1954), lists the following materials: SP 26, "Preparatory Research Report on the Establishment of Peace between Germany and Japan"; MT 1.1.4.1, "Japanese-German Relations, 1899–1925"; and UD 16, "Pages from the Berlin Embassy File."

Young, *Checklist of Microfilm Reproductions of Selected Archives of the Japanese Army, Navy, and Other Government Agencies, 1868–1945* (1959), cites two documents: T 325, "Meetings 1–31 of Committee on Preparation for Peace in German-Japanese Hostilities" (December 1915–December 1916); and T 326,

"Written Opinions on Investigation of Peace Preparations to End German-Japanese Hostilities" (July 1915).

Memoirs:

Hanssen, *Diary of a Dying Empire* (1955), has limited usefulness.

Ishii, *Diplomatic Commentaries* (1936), offers an occasional insight, particularly in regard to Japan's reaction to the German overtures.

U.S., Department of State, *Foreign Relations of the United States: Lansing Papers, 1914–1920* (1939) has limited value.

Secondary works:

Becker, *Der Gedanke einer Deutsch-Russisch-Japanischen Verständigung während des Weltkrieges* (1940), is the only study, a rather thin one, which describes German-Japanese negotiations during World War I.

Tuchman, *The Zimmermann Telegram* (1958), touches upon some aspects of German-Japanese relations as they were reflected in Germany's activities in Mexico.

The Peace Settlement, 1918–1921. Soon after the conclusion of the armistice in early November 1918, Japanese postwar policies toward Germany were discussed in a series of conferences among officials of the Foreign, Army, and Navy ministries, although preparatory research on this topic had been done as early as 1916. An Advisory Council on Foreign Relations was set up and formulated an outline of proposals that were handed to the Japanese delegation sent to Paris. Just exactly what Japanese thinking was concerning the peace treaty to be exacted from a defeated Germany and what kind of a future Japanese-German relationship was being envisioned by the Japanese government will remain unclear until the pertinent documents in the Japanese Foreign Ministry have been studied.[32]

In any case, the Japanese delegation—headed by the genrō Marquis Saionji Kimmochi and consisting in addition of the former foreign minister, Baron Makino Nobuaki, and the three envoys to London, Paris, and Rome, Viscount Chinda Sutemi, Matsui Keishirō, and Ijūin Hikokichi respectively—was primarily instructed to refrain from purely European matters and instead to obtain from the Allies unreserved recognition

---

[32]Japan, Foreign Ministry, PVM 16 (1–5) series, as cited in Cecil H. Uyehara, *Checklist of Archives in the Japanese Ministry of Foreign Affairs, Tokyo, Japan, 1868–1945, Microfilmed for the Library of Congress, 1949–1951* (1954), p. 108.

of Japan's position in the Far East. Japan participated in the Versailles Conference as one of the five great powers, but during the stay of the delegation in Paris, from January 1919 until the signing of the treaty on June 28, the Japanese representatives remained singularly silent partners at the conference when the fate of Germany was being discussed.

What Japan pressed for were three things: 1) the transfer to Japan of the former German holdings in Shantung province; 2) the transfer to Japan of the former German islands in the Pacific north of the equator; and 3) the principle of racial equality to be written into the covenant of the League of Nations.[33] But nothing so far apparently is known about what Japan thought of its future relations with Germany or, for that matter, of the treaty settlement itself. The possibility of a future accord between Japan and Germany did not escape the attention of some politically astute observers at the conference. On September 13, 1918, New Zealand Prime Minister W.F. Massey, worried about Japan's Pacific expansion, raised precisely this point.[34]

In general, nothing at all has been done on the subject of Japan's thinking and policies vis-a-vis Germany at Versailles. This topic remains a major lacuna in a survey of the history of Japanese-German relations. Questions and problems that might come up in connection with a study of the conference and the events that followed might well deal with Japan's feelings toward the European powers in the immediate postwar period, and with Japan's ideas concerning future relations with Germany. Was there, for instance, any kind of long-range policy planning? Was there the feeling among some Japanese groups, the military possibly, that Germany might prove useful in the future (as there was among German officers, for example, Karl Haushofer)? Or, rather, was Japanese diplomacy genuinely uninterested in European affairs with the conclusion of the Versailles Conference?

The following works relate to Japan at the Paris Peace Conference:

Documents:

American Historical Association, *A Catalogue of German Foreign Ministry Files and Microfilms, 1867–1920* (1959), lists several documentary collections, notably,

[33]Japan, Foreign Ministry, SP 84, MT 2.3.1.1 (1–2), and MT 2.3.1 (4–40), as cited in *ibid.*, pp. 16, 87.
[34]David Hunter Miller, *My Diary at the Conference of Paris* (1924), XX, 314.

Friedensverhändlungen Japan, 1138; *Die Friedenskonferenz in Versailles*, 1125–1126; and *Material zu den Friedensverhändlungen*, 1095–1096.

Uyehara, *Checklist of Archives in the Japanese Ministry of Foreign Affairs, Tokyo, Japan, 1868–1945, Microfilmed for the Library of Congress, 1949–1951* (1954), includes the following important series of documents: MT 2.3.1.1.–(1–2), "Paris Peace Conference"; PVM 16–(1–5), "Documents Relating to the Paris Peace Conference, Research Papers Relating to the Development of the Paris Peace Conference, Count Makino's report on that Conference, etc."; SP 84 and SP 86, "Summary of the Paris Peace Conference."

Secondary works. Standard works on the Paris Peace Conference have little or nothing to say about Japan. The following books therefore are useful regarding this problem only as sources of background information:

Brockdorff-Rantzau, *Dokumente und Gedanken um Versailles* (1925).
Lapradelle, *La documentation internationale: La paix de Versailles* (1929).
Temperley, *A History of the Peace Conference of Paris* (6 vols., 1920–24).

THE RESUMPTION OF FRIENDLY RELATIONS, 1921–1933

Little or nothing has been done to study Japanese-German relations during the period from the Treaty of Versailles to 1930. Japan had profited from Germany's defeat by seizing all German assets in Japan during the war; moreover, Germany was forced to make reparations payments to Japan under the terms of the treaty. Diplomatic relations were resumed in 1921 when the rather well-liked William Solf arrived in Tokyo, where he served as ambassador until 1929. There does not seem to have been much in the way of bitterness between Germany and Japan, as in any case to most Germans the Pacific was far away and Germany's losses there of little value. Instead, with Germany's rapid postwar economic recovery, German-Japanese trade showed a marked increase and again became quite profitable. Many German chemists and engineers went to Japan, and in 1927 a new German-Japanese commercial treaty was concluded that reduced import duties in Germany on soybean oil, needed in industry, and established the position of the great German IG Farben complex in Japan, although the German dye industry agreed not to compete with existing Japanese dye manufacturers. During the same year a German-Japanese cultural institute was established in Tokyo.

Weimar diplomacy toward Japan and Japan's interest in Germany in the 1920s are unknown factors. Germany's Far Eastern policy during the Weimar Republic has not been examined at length. Moreover, there is need for research on Japan's interest in a revived Germany and Japan's attitudes towards Hitler's *Machtergreifung* in 1933. Especially important might be an attempt to see what connections, if any, existed between the rise of Nazi ideology in Germany and nascent militarism in Japan, and to what degree, consciously or otherwise, there was some kind of intellectual cross-fertilization. What bibliography exists at this time will be derived from the following:

Bloch, *German Interests and Policies in the Far East* (1940).

U. S., Department of State, *A Catalog of Files and Microfilms of the German Foreign Ministry Archives, 1920–1945,* I (1962), 21, 330, lists documents dealing with Japan from 1920 to 1935.

Uyehara, *Checklist of Archives in the Japanese Ministry of Foreign Affairs, Tokyo, Japan, 1868–1945, Microfilmed for the Library of Congress, 1949–1951* (1954), especially MT 1.1.4.1, a file on Japanese-German relations.

THE UNCERTAIN ALLIANCE, 1934–1941

Negotiations for the Anti-Comintern Pact, 1934–1936. The original impetus for closer cooperation between Japan and Germany stemmed from a mutual desire to find an ally against the Soviet Union in Europe and Asia. Even before 1933 there were some advocates of closer ties between these two powers, notably the German geopolitician, Karl Haushofer. It will be remembered that he had been sent to Japan in 1909 as a Bavarian artillery officer to study Japanese, and it was he who, as early as 1913, advocated in his book *Dai Nihon* an alliance between Germany and Japan. A combination of Germany, Russia, and Japan, which he considered the Eurasian bloc, meant in the jargon of geopolitics control of the heartland and hence control of the world. Haushofer's ideas certainly carried some weight with the rising Nazi ideologists. It is possible that Hitler himself in 1933 saw the value of a Japanese-German alliance directed against Russia (and possibly later against Britain) on the basis of the common hostility of both nations to the Soviet Union. Rumors heard by American diplomats of a possible Japanese-German entente go back as early as that year. The newly appointed German ambassador to Tokyo, Herbert von Dirksen, was told by Werner von Blomberg, the German war minister, in October 1933 of Hitler's conceivable interest in such a matter. Orders went out to the German press to suppress all anti-Japanese articles.[35]

The German Foreign Office had little sympathy with Hitler's pro-Japanese proclivities. Foreign Secretary Constantin von Neurath belonged to the old school, which could still vividly remember the Triple Intervention, consequent Japanese antagonism toward Germany, and the loss of Germany's Far Eastern possessions and Pacific islands. Neurath instead advocated continued close and friendly relations with China, which meant valuable trade and military aid to Chiang Kai-shek. But Joachim von Ribbentrop, who by 1934 operated his own foreign office, was greatly taken by Hitler's interest in developing friendlier relations with Japan and on his own initiative saw to it that Germany and Japan entered into closer ties. In May 1934, for instance, when a Japanese naval squadron visited German waters, President Paul von Hindenburg, Hitler, and Neurath all received its commander, Vice-Admiral Matsushita Hajime, amidst rather unprecedented ceremonies. In that year, too, a Japanischer Verein in Deutschland was founded and a new German-Japanese cultural research institute was organized in Kyoto. German newspapers launched an active pro-Japanese propaganda campaign, again giving rise to rumors of a Japanese-German alliance.

While Hitler in Berlin displayed an interest in Japan, the Japanese army in Tokyo reciprocated with an interest in Germany. Early in 1934 both powers appointed new military attaches to their respective embassies; these were individuals who were to be most important in the subsequent development of Japanese-German relations. To Berlin in March went Colonel (later General) Ōshima Hiroshi, whose father had served in an artillery regiment with Meckel, the influential early Prussian military adviser to Meiji Japan. The son had already been assistant military attache in Germany, 1921–23, and had become outspokenly pro-German. As representative of the Japanese army, Ōshima reported directly to the central military authorities in Japan; and he was given authority by the army to enter into negotiations for a military agreement with Germany. Ōshima was to be a very powerful instrument in bringing about an alliance

[35]U.S. Embassy, Berlin, to Secretary of State, February 9, 1934, in State Department Archives, No. 762.94/41.

between Nazi Germany and militarist Japan. His counterpart was Colonel Eugen Ott, who also went as military attache to the German embassy in Tokyo in March 1934.

The Japanese army became increasingly interested in the rapid rise to power of Nazi Germany. Such interest was expressed as early as November 1934 when the then Japanese ambassador in Berlin, Nagai Matsuzō, made a speech in which he pointed out that both Japan and Germany shared the same grievances and that it was only natural for both powers, isolated as they were, to unite in the pursuit of common interests. Neither Germany's announcement of its intention to rearm nor its reintroduction of military conscription met with Japanese disfavor; and in 1935 Japan also supported the legal reestablishment of a German navy equipped with submarines. This led in February 1936 to new but unfounded rumors among American diplomats stationed in Europe that a German-Japanese alliance was in the making. In fact, such an alliance was in the minds of the Japanese army on the one hand and of Ribbentrop and his special bureau on the other. In their negotiations with each other they completely bypassed the regularly established diplomatic channels of the foreign offices of both countries.

Apparently the first approach made by Ribbentrop to Ōshima in Berlin did not come until May or June 1935. At that time Ribbentrop suggested, through an intermediary, the possibility of a defensive alliance between Japan and Germany against the Soviet Union.[36] A few months later, in October, Ribbentrop had a personal interview with the Japanese military attache during which he urged him to investigate whether the Japanese army would have an interest in such a proposal. Ōshima relayed this information to Japan. The Army General Staff replied that it saw no objection to the scheme and would send to Berlin a certain Lieutenant-Colonel Wakamatsu Tadaichi, of the German division of the General Staff, with instructions from the chief of the General Staff to ascertain the views of the German army and the German government.[37] Wakamatsu arrived in Berlin in December 1935 and spent some two weeks in conversations with Ribbentrop and War Minister Blomberg. The progress of these negotia-

[36]Interrogation of Ōshima, February 1, 1946, in International Military Tribunal for the Far East (hereafter IMTFE), Exhibit 477.

[37]*Ibid.*; Harada Kumao, *Saionji kō to seikyoku* (1950–52), V, 114; for English translation, see SCAP, Civil Intelligence Section, GHQ, Far Eastern Command, *Saionji-Harada Memoirs* (hereafter cited as *Saionji-Harada Memoirs*), p. 1550.

tions was not swift but it was steady, and out of them emerged eventually the Anti-Comintern Pact.

The pact itself was a product of considerable deviousness and secrecy as far as both the Japanese and German foreign offices were concerned. In Japan the Foreign Ministry was kept completely uninformed, although Ott had been told of the talks by the Japanese General Staff. The new Japanese ambassador to Germany, Mushakōji Kintomo, knew nothing until he arrived in Berlin in April 1936, when Foreign Minister Arita Hachirō cabled him that there existed a necessity for closer relations between Japan and Germany. Until that time, neither the German ambassador in Tokyo nor the German Foreign Office knew anything of what had been going on between Ribbentrop and the Japanese army. Dirksen had heard rumors of such discussions while still in Japan, but these were not confirmed until he talked to Ribbentrop in Germany in April. The Wilhelmstrasse also was left completely in the dark until that moment, when Neurath and State Secretary Bülow expressed great skepticism and hostility. Their preference continued to be for close relations between Germany and China.

Ribbentrop forwarded the German proposals for a treaty to Japan in July 1936. Since such a treaty was desired and advocated by the Japanese army, the Hirota cabinet responded favorably. In a conference between Foreign Minister Arita and Army Minister Terauchi Hisaichi that month, the treaty was approved. The outbreak of the Spanish civil war greatly increased the pro-German sentiment in the Japanese General Staff, and Terauchi stressed the threat of Russia's military preparations: the Soviet Union's increased armaments and its alliances with France, Czechoslovakia, and the Mongolian People's Republic.

The only reservation Foreign Minister Arita expressed was that the treaty not be published until the pending Soviet-Japanese fisheries agreement had been concluded. Germany granted this request, so that the text of the treaty, which had been agreed upon in September, did not become public until November 1936. By and large, despite some opposition to the thought of an alliance against Russia from among members of the zaibatsu and from Saionji, the Hirota cabinet and the Foreign Ministry welcomed Japan's alignment with Germany. On November 20, during a meeting of the cabinet, Prime Minister Hirota Kōki expressed his opinion that the Anti-Comintern Pact would succeed in frustrating the Soviet Union's

policy of aggrandizement, would protect the common interests of both
Japan and Germany against the armed pressure of Russia, and would
contribute also to a change of policy on the part of China toward Japan.
The most important argument in defense of the agreement with Germany
was that such an arrangement would strengthen Japan vis-a-vis China
and make possible further Japanese expansion on the Asian mainland.[38]

The Anti-Comintern Pact was signed on November 25, 1936, in Berlin.
It included an appended secret agreement that provided for a limited
alliance between Germany and Japan against the USSR. This proved to be
a badly kept secret. Despite the strenuous efforts made by the Japanese
government to deny its existence and to convince the USSR that the
Anti-Comintern Pact was not directed against it, the Soviet government
was not deceived. Discussions between Arita and Russian Ambassador
Constantin Yurenev in Tokyo on that score proved fruitless, as did also an
official Foreign Ministry declaration. The Soviet Union was well informed,
partially because of the Richard Sorge contact in Japan and partially, it
appears, because Russian intelligence at The Hague had cracked the code
in use between Ōshima and Tokyo. On the very day before the pact was
concluded, the USSR informed Japan that it would not renew the fisheries
agreement, and on November 28 Foreign Minister Maxim Litvinov
denounced the pact before the Congress of Soviets. In so doing he revealed
full knowledge of the nature of the pact and the manner of its negotiation.[39]

In Germany the Anti-Comintern Pact was, of course, greeted in the
press with unanimous approval, but surprisingly enough this was not the
case in Japan. Despite the Foreign Ministry's description of the treaty as
a defensive alliance directed against an alien ideology, and despite Japan's
open invitation to China to join in it in order to curb communist activities
in the Far East, a public storm of criticism broke loose against Japan's
alliance with Germany. The intensity of adverse reaction to the Anti-
Comintern Pact surprised even America's Ambassador Joseph Grew. It was
a universally unpopular pact, especially among businessmen and members
of the Diet, who saw in it not only an instrument that would prejudice

[38]Report from the Proceedings of the Privy Council Concerning the Ratification of
Japanese-German Anti-Comintern Agreements, November 15, 1936, IMTFE, Exhibit 484.
[39]*Documents on International Affairs, 1936* (1937), p. 302.

Japan's relations with the USSR and Britain but, more importantly, one that would increase army control over Japanese political life. Fear among Japan's political parties and financial circles over the growing power of the military now found expression in bitter criticism of Hirota, who had permitted the army to conduct its own brand of diplomacy. Eventually this resulted, in February 1937, in the overthrow of the Japanese government. Army Minister Terauchi, accused in a speech by a member of the Diet of conducting dual and secret diplomacy, resigned and thereby toppled the Hirota cabinet.[40] Fear and misgivings concerning the pact as proof of the dictatorial tendencies of the Japanese army could still be expressed publicly in the press in Japan in 1936, but within a year such open criticism was to be a thing of the past.

In effect, the Anti-Comintern Pact came into being because Germany and Japan faced a common opponent. The Franco-Soviet alliance as well as Soviet aid to Spain in its civil war contributed to Germany's desire to find an ally. In the case of Japan, its actions in Manchuria and China, its withdrawal from the League of Nations, and its denunciation of the Washington and London naval limitation treaties had caused not only serious estrangement from the Western powers, but a definite deterioration in its relations with the USSR. The Soviet Union had begun to support China against Japan and to increase its military forces in the Far East. It was in these circumstances that the Japanese army, dominating the Hirota cabinet, pushed through the pact with Germany against the Soviet Union. In the short run, the Anti-Comintern Pact paid for Japan. By alleviating fears of Soviet intervention, it facilitated Japan's aggressive moves against China and particularly its exploitation of the incident that occurred near the Marco Polo Bridge on July 7, 1937.

The Sino-Japanese Conflict and Germany, July 1937-February 1938. Japan's move against China in July 1937 was based on the idea of a crushing military defeat, to be followed promptly by a generous peace formula.[41] For Germany, the Sino-Japanese war produced a serious quandary. The value of Japan as an ally against the USSR decreased immediately, and Japan's

---

[40]Tsunego Baba, "The Anti-Comintern Pact in Domestic Politics" (1937), pp. 536–39.
[41]James T.C. Liu, "German Mediation in the Sino-Japanese War, 1937–38" (1949), p. 157.

actions in China threatened German interests there. Put in a rather delicate position, the German government at first pursued a policy of strict and scrupulous neutrality. This changed when Germany, increasingly interested in an early settlement of the conflict, undertook a series of efforts at mediation. These proved to be unsuccessful, since the radical expansionist elements among the Japanese military blocked all efforts at a settlement with Nationalist China. Because they wanted the complete defeat of China, they demanded constantly harsher and harsher terms from the Nanking government, thereby rendering Germany's mediation efforts nugatory.

Moreover, as Japan sent its forces deeper into China, it paid no heed to Germany's considerable interests there. There was not even the suggestion of Japanese compensation to Germany for its support and Germany was not given any kind of a privileged economic position in Japanese-occupied China. The result was that by 1938 relations between Germany and Japan had cooled considerably.

Relations between the two powers deteriorated almost at once after the July 7 incident. On July 28 Ambassador Mushakōji Kintomo was told in Berlin by Ernst von Weizsäcker, then head of the Political Department of the German Foreign Office, that Japan's actions in China brought no benefits to Germany and, instead of leading to the elimination of communism in China, had the opposite effect.[42] Since Germany maintained a military mission with the government of Chiang Kai-shek and supplied it with sizable shipments of arms, Germany was faced with a real problem whether to support China or Japan. By August the German government had come to realize, through messages received from Dirksen and Ott in Tokyo, that Japan had become committed to the full overthrow of the Nanking regime. German opinion was divided. In general, German business circles, the Foreign Office, and the General Staff heartily disliked the conflict. They felt that German commercial interests in China were bound to suffer, that Japan had lost much of its value to Germany as an ally against the Soviet Union, and that Japan's actions stood a good chance of driving China into the hands of the Soviet Union. On the other hand, solidarity

---

[42]Document 473, in U.S., Department of State, *Documents on German Foreign Policy, 1918–1945, from the Archives of the German Foreign Ministry, Series D (1937–1945),* I (1949), 744–45 (hereafter cited as *Documents on German Foreign Policy*).

with Japan and support of its actions in China was expressed within leading Nazi circles. By October Hitler had made up his mind—he would support Japan. German arms deliveries to China were stopped at his order.[43]

At the same time, the German government agreed to try to mediate the conflict. It was probably late in August 1937 that Hirota thought first of German mediation as one solution to Japan's problem with China, since Germany was the only power friendly to both sides. In October Ōshima was requested to find out whether the German government would be ready to act in the role of a mediator. This coincided with Hitler's decision to try to end the conflict between China and Japan, and hence was most acceptable to Berlin.

Hirota gave the first set of Japanese peace terms to Ambassador Dirksen in Tokyo on November 3, 1937. These included a Japanese demand for an autonomous Inner Mongolia, a demilitarized zone and pro-Japanese administration in north China, a demilitarized zone around Shanghai, reduced customs duties, cessation of anti-Japanese policies by China, and finally, a common fight against communism. Both Dirksen and Ott thought these terms acceptable and transmitted them to German Ambassador Oskar Trautmann in Nanking, who forwarded them to Chiang Kai-shek. But Chiang flatly refused: "There would be a revolution in China if I accepted these terms."[44] Germany then extended pressure on China to accept the Japanese terms. It refused to participate in the Brussels conference, thereby indicating its diplomatic support of Japan. In addition, on November 9 Hitler made a speech in the Bürgerbräu in Munich, indicating Germany's decision to recognize Manchukuo, and the German foreign minister in Berlin urged China's ambassador to accept Japan's terms.

On December 3 Chiang Kai-shek decided to accept, but by this time it was too late. The Japanese army had become intractable, especially after the fall of Nanking on December 12. It had decided to continue the war and to end Chinese resistance to Japan once and for all. The result was that Dirksen received from Hirota on December 23 a second and much stiffer set of terms for transmittal to China. China must join Japan and

---

[43]Memorandum of German Foreign Office, October 19, 1937, Document 500, in *ibid.,* pp. 768–69.

[44]Telegram from Dirksen to German Foreign Office, November 3, 1937, Document 514, in *ibid.,* pp. 778–79; and telegram from Trautmann to German Foreign Office, November 5, 1937, Document 516, in *ibid.,* pp. 780–81.

Manchukuo in their anti-communist policies; it must join the Anti-Comintern Pact; demilitarized zones must be established "where necessary," including the Yangtze valley; a special regime was to be set up for Mongolia; China was to pay an indemnity to Japan; and there was to be closer Sino-Japanese economic cooperation.[45] These terms were transmitted to Trautmann and by him to Chiang Kai-shek on Christmas Eve. Even so, a faction of the Japanese army hoped that they would be rejected, so that Japan could proceed with the complete overthrow of the Nanking regime.

By January 1938 it had become clear that the Japanese military really did not want peace but rather the utter defeat of China. While the army was pressing for an immediate reply from Chiang Kai-shek to the terms already delivered, yet another set of demands was prepared in Tokyo. Although not delivered to China, this third set of terms was so harsh, providing for the virtual occupation of the whole country and the end of its autonomy, that it seems they were drafted purposely with the idea of rejection in mind.[46] In this way the Japanese army would be sure to be able to wreck all mediation efforts and continue the war.

On January 16, 1938, Prime Minister Konoe Fumimaro, unable to control the army in Japan, announced in a speech that Japan had ended all negotiations with China. German mediation efforts were thus abandoned, and in Germany Hitler and Ribbentrop decided to put Germany squarely on the side of Japan. A renewed German order stopped all arms shipments to China. Germany's military advisers were withdrawn from the Chiang government, much to the dislike of the German General Staff. In February 1938 Hitler, in a Reichstag speech, committed himself to the recognition of Manchukuo, and in May Germany concluded a treaty of friendship with that Japanese puppet state. Both diplomatic and commercial relations were established. Despite such German support, Japan showed no willingness to make any concessions to its partner in China. By the 1930s Germany had become the third largest trader with China while, comparatively speaking, its business relations with Japan were on a much more modest level. But despite German willingness to stop military support to China in the form of arms or advisers, an order repeated in the first week of April

[45]Telegram from Dirksen to German Foreign Office, December 23, 1937, in *ibid.*, pp. 802–4.
[46]Liu, "German Mediation," p. 165.

by Göring on specific instructions from the fuhrer, Japan let the German government know on April 8 that Germany could not be given a position of economic equality with Japan in China, not to speak of a preferential status.[47] Japan thus was fully committed to pursuing its own interests in Asia regardless of the interests of its ally.

Italy was drawn into the Anti-Comintern Pact in October 1937 because of Ribbentrop's pressure and despite opposition from the German Foreign Office and some uneasiness on the part of Italian Foreign Minister Galeazzo Ciano. But Ribbentrop did not reveal to either Ciano or Mussolini that the real nature of the pact was an alliance directed against the Soviet Union until after Italy had signed the document on November 6, when they were told of the secret annex.[48] It is possible that it was Mussolini who now began to conceive of the possibility of changing the Anti-Comintern Pact into a general tripartite alliance directed not against the Soviet Union but rather against Great Britain. At least in early December 1937 he reflected privately on such a possibility.

The Abortive Struggle for a General Alliance, February 1938–August 1939. Japan and Germany once more drew together in 1938 when Britain, France, and the United States began to loom up as the primary opponents of both countries. There ensued a long struggle for the creation of a new alliance between Japan and Germany which lasted until August 1939, when the announcement of the German-Russian nonaggression treaty produced a new crisis in Tokyo.

It so happened that Hitler decided in January 1938 to shift his foreign policy from a primarily anti-Soviet to a primarily anti-British and anti-French policy, a move that gave to Germany the remarkable victories of the Austrian *Anschluss* in March and of Munich in September. In 1938 the USSR had receded in importance to the fuhrer.

In July of the same year, the Japanese army sustained a serious defeat at the hands of the Soviet army in the Changkufeng Incident, which led to a change in Japanese policy. Japan's inability to terminate the China Incident, the marked prowess of the Soviet Union, and the powerful attraction

---

[47]Memorandum of conversation, Ribbentrop and Tōgō, April 8, 1938, Document 575, in *Documents on German Foreign Policy*, I, 851–52.

[48]Galeazzo Ciano, *Ciano's Diplomatic Papers*, edited by Malcolm Muggeridge, translated by Stuart Hood (1948), p. 141.

of Southeast Asia caused Japan to direct its expansion to the south. Its moves in south China, such as the occupation of Canton in October 1938, propelled Japan in a direction that would cause conflicts with British, French, and American interests. In this situation Germany proposed to Japan, and Japan considered, a military alliance directed not only against the USSR but against all powers.

The seeds of such negotiations were planted as early as January 1938, when Ribbentrop suggested to Ōshima the idea of a closer relationship between Germany and Japan.[49] All during the spring months of that year Germany acted to please Japan. On February 20 Germany recognized Manchukuo; Ambassador Trautmann was recalled from China soon after, as were all German military advisers serving Chiang Kai-shek; and Eugen Ott, the former military attache in the Tokyo embassy, replaced Dirksen as the new ambassador in Tokyo. The Japanese government at first hesitated to take up Ribbentrop's newest proposal, but by the spring of that year the army was in a much stronger position than before, as indicated by the general mobilization law of April 1, and by June Japan showed definite interest. By this time its relations with the West had worsened. The United States had declared a moral embargo and had suspended the export of aircraft and aviation gasoline. In June the Japanese army again bypassed the Foreign Ministry to instruct Ōshima to work for more intimate cooperation with Germany. Ōshima had a talk with Ribbentrop in early July, during which Ribbentrop proposed the draft of a treaty directed against all the powers. Ōshima agreed that he would try to find out what the Japanese army thought of the scheme for a wider alliance, and he duly transmitted Ribbentrop's draft for study in Tokyo.[50] The Japanese foreign minister and the Japanese ambassador in Berlin were kept in the usual state of ignorance during these negotiations.

The Army General Staff and many of the "young officers" had been much impressed with the strength shown by the Soviet Union at Changkufeng in July, hence Japan was now more ready to move south and to enter into an alliance directed against the Western powers. To bring this event about more easily, the General Staff demanded the appointment of Ōshima

---

[49]Interrogation of Ōshima, February 4, 6, 7, 1946, IMTFE, Exhibit 497.
[50]Affidavit of Ōshima, October 12, 1947, IMTFE, Exhibit 3508.

as the new Japanese ambassador to Berlin despite opposition from the Foreign and Navy ministries.

On August 29, 1938, a Five Ministers Conference was held to discuss the question of a general military alliance with Germany. It decided that Japan's interest continued to call for an alliance directed primarily against the USSR and only secondarily against other powers.[51] Although this was not what Ribbentrop wanted, it shows the beginning of considerations that led Japan to consider an alliance directed against powers other than the Soviet Union and thus represents the first departure from the original Anti-Comintern Pact.

Germany's great victory at Munich in September much impressed Japan with Hitler's diplomacy. Ribbentrop, although now profoundly convinced that Britain and France would never fight, continued to be eager for an alliance with Japan since such an alliance would further immobilize the Western powers. Munich convinced the Japanese army of the weakness of the West and its appeasement policy. Konoe sent a telegram of congratulation to Hitler, and the army used Munich as an excuse to occupy Canton, implying a direct threat to Hong Kong.[52]

Early in October Ōshima was made ambassador, and he and Ribbentrop continued their talks concerning a new alliance. At the suggestion of Ribbentrop, Italy was now also brought into the discussions and a new draft of a triple alliance was prepared in Berlin. This draft was sent to Tokyo, where it was studied by the Konoe cabinet, but considerable opposition to it continued to be expressed. Konoe himself, as well as Foreign Minister Arita and the leaders of the navy, were still reluctant to engage in a general alliance, arguing that Japan should first terminate the China Incident and not worsen relations with the West.[53]

As a kind of compromise, a German-Japanese cultural agreement was signed on November 25, 1938, but the Konoe cabinet's opposition to a general alliance lasted until January 1939. In that month the Hiranuma Kiichirō cabinet, more ultranationalist and more sympathetic to the wishes of the army, took power after the Konoe cabinet proved itself unable to

[51]Harada, *Saionji kō to seikyoku*, VII, 389; *Saionji-Harada Memoirs*, p. 2553.
[52]Memorandum of German Foreign Office, October 29, 1938, Document 534, in *Documents on German Foreign Policy*, IV (1951), 684–85.
[53]Telegram from Ott to German Foreign Office, October 29, 1938, Document 535, in *ibid.*, pp. 686–89.

solve the China problem. In February 1939 it sent the Itō Nobufumi mission to Rome and Berlin to discuss further the problem of an alliance with Germany and Italy. Itō talked to Shiratori Toshio, the Japanese ambassador in Rome, and to Ōshima in Berlin, pointing out that the Japanese government still thought in terms of an alliance directed primarily against the USSR, but the two ambassadors refused to transmit his message to the governments to which they were accredited and even went as far as to threaten to resign.[54] For this they were reprimanded by Foreign Minister Arita. The army backed down temporarily, but not for long. Soon the army resumed pressure on Prime Minister Hiranuma, while Japanese military units continued to advance to the south, occupying Hainan Island and the Spratley group in February and March. Impressed by the unchallenged establishment by Germany of a protectorate over Czechoslovakia, Hiranuma began to waver in his opposition to an alliance. Finally, despite Arita's objections and the expressed disinclination of the emperor, the army succeeded in getting the Five Ministers Conference to agree to try for a general military alliance with Germany. However, there were to be some reservations: its duration was to be only five years, and it was to be prefaced with an explanation to the West that it was directed against the Soviet Union and not against any of the Western nations and that aid provided to Germany would only be of a limited nature.[55] This naturally would not do for Germany, and on April 2 Ribbentrop rejected the Japanese reply. The two Japanese ambassadors in Rome and Berlin agreed fully with Ribbentrop, protesting the action of their own government as impossible. Ōshima even went so far as to tell Ribbentrop that Japan would agree to participate in a war in which Germany was involved.[56] In thus committing Japan to war, Ōshima clearly committed an act of insubordination.

A new Japanese conference met on April 8 to discuss the situation, but it could not bring itself to punish the two ambassadors or even to order them home despite the emperor's intense annoyance.[57] On the other hand, a new situation now was created by opposition to the alliance from the navy. The Japanese navy, dependent on America for fuel and supplies, opposed an alliance with Germany and Italy because it felt this could bring Japan

[54]Ciano diary entries, February 1939, IMTFE, Exhibit 501.
[55]Harada, *Saionji kō to seikyoku*, VII, 319.
[56]Telegram from Ribbentrop to Ott, April 26, 1939, IMTFE, Exhibit 502.
[57]Harada, *Saionji kō to seikyoku*, VII, 325; *Saionji-Harada Memoirs*, p. 2486.

into war against Britain and France and possibly America as well. The navy minister therefore supported Arita. The army, determined to get an agreement with Germany and demanding an unlimited military alliance, bitterly attacked the foreign minister and gradually also won over Prime Minister Hiranuma, who declared that the request of the army was "righteous." But the navy was adamant and caused a wire to be sent to Shiratori, who was still in Berlin, which made it clear that there could be no effective military aid from Japan to the Axis and that in any case Japan would reserve for itself the right to decide when to enter into war. This action infuriated the two pro-Axis ambassadors, who demanded their own recall.

Amidst this tension the army played its trump card—the threat of direct action, or army-inspired violence. The result was another Five Ministers Conference, this one on April 25, 1939, to discuss the matter of the recall of the two ambassadors and the general problem of relations with Germany. The meeting split into two factions, Prime Minister Hiranuma and Army Minister Itagaki Seishirō, who were in favor of the alliance with Germany, versus Foreign Minister Arita and Navy Minister Yonai Mitsumasa, who opposed it. Army pressure and Itagaki's threat to resign produced a new compromise, the Hiranuma declaration of May 4, which represented a new gain for the army.[58] Under its terms Japan was willing to conclude an alliance with Germany against all powers, with the understanding that military assistance on the part of Japan would not be possible immediately but would be given when circumstances were favorable.

The Hiranuma declaration proved to be again not quite enough for Germany, and Ribbentrop countered by sending to Japan a new version of the alliance, the so-called Gauss Plan, which called for an alliance without any reservations or restrictions by Japan. Arita, who actually believed the Gauss Plan to be the work of the Japanese army, submitted to Germany via Ōshima, was furious at this. He was even more outraged when he heard that Ōshima had told Ribbentrop that Japan was ready to participate in a war on the side of Germany regardless of any limitations. Arita declared that he refused to be any longer responsible for the conduct of Japan's foreign policy.[59]

---

[58]Harada, *Saionji kō to seikyoku,* VII, 344; *Saionji-Harada Memoirs,* p. 2506.
[59]Harada, *Saionji kō to seikyoku,* VII, 353; *Saionji-Harada Memoirs,* p. 2515.

At the Five Ministers Conference on May 7 Itagaki backed Ōshima. Arita wanted to resign but was kept from doing so by Navy Minister Yonai's full-hearted support, which was enough to keep Hiranuma from making a decision in favor of either side. The matter was thus kept in abeyance until two days later, when the Gauss Plan was again discussed. Yonai's firm opposition and his staunch support of Arita impressed Hiranuma, so that again nothing was accomplished beyond fruitless discussion.[60] The sharp split in the cabinet had become a measure of the two widely divergent views held by the Japanese army and the Japanese navy. The navy, fearing American entry into a war on the side of the British, which might spell ruin for Japan, continued its opposition to the alliance and its support of Arita. In this it was sustained by the emperor. The army, on the other hand, insisted on an alliance with Germany, arguing that it would help Japan to conclude the China affair and, in a war against Britain and France, enable it to seize their rich colonial possessions in Southeast Asia. Prime Minister Hiranuma stood waveringly between the two factions, unable to make up his mind.

This continued impasse between the army and navy did not please Germany at all. Ribbentrop put pressure on the Japanese government by having Ott let it be known that Germany was skeptical as to whether Japan really had the necessary strength to make such a decision. But he also added that the alliance with Germany was the best guarantee for Japan that America would stay out of a conflict in the Pacific.[61] In a speech to his service chiefs on May 23 Hitler pointed out that relations between Japan and Germany had become cool and restricted although he hoped that Japan would realize where its true interests lay.

Army Minister Itagaki decided, at the risk of the collapse of the government, to get Arita's resignation and to force through the alliance. Again the threat of violence was hinted at by the army, with the expected result— a new conference decision on June 6, which was to be Japan's last effort to come to an agreement with Nazi Germany in that year. Virtually all the German demands were conceded to by Japan, except for the sole reservation that Japan was to have the right to choose a favorable time to enter a war on the side of Germany against France and Britain.[62] After delaying it

[60]Harada, *Saionji kō to seikyoku*, VII, 354; *Saionji-Harada Memoirs*, p. 2516.
[61]Telegram from Ribbentrop to Ott, May 15, 1939, IMTFE, Exhibit 486–K.
[62]Telegram from Ott to German Foreign Office, June 5, 1939, IMTFE, Exhibit 614.

for some ten days, possibly in the hope of further army success in eliminating even this last reservation, Ōshima transmitted this decision to Ribbentrop; but Ribbentrop rejected it completely.

What Germany wanted and needed in the summer of 1939 was a full
and unconditional alliance. Only an all-out alliance without any strings
attached would satisfy Hitler, who was getting ready for the hour of his
"little war" against Poland and believed that such an alliance with Japan
would deter Britain from fighting.[63]

Germany's rejection of the June 6 terms caused a new flare-up in the Japanese cabinet, but British concessions in the Tientsin blockade issue made
an alliance directed against Britain seem less urgent, while navy opposition continued undiminished throughout the rest of June and early July.
Yonai solidly maintained his view that Japan could not fight a war with
America and that the alliance with Germany might plunge Japan into just
such a war. But the pitched battle fought at Nomonhan on the Manchukuo-
Mongolia border between the Japanese and Soviet forces on July 19, resulting in a major Russian victory, stiffened the army's insistence upon an
alliance with Germany. Itagaki was convinced that an Axis alliance was
necessary to protect Japan in the north while permitting it to expand to the
south.[64] Fear of a strong Soviet Union was also coupled with renewed
irritation against America. On July 26 the United States had abrogated the
Japanese-American commercial treaty of 1911, a step which presaged the
end to all legal obstacles to an embargo on American exports to Japan.

A new Five Ministers Conference was held on August 4, with both sides,
army and navy, more determined than ever to hold to their views. Itagaki
had been instructed by the army to force the alliance through, even at the
cost of the resignation of the government, while the Army General Staff
also prepared plans for street demonstrations in favor of the tie with Germany. No agreement on the issue having been reached that day, the ministers adjourned until August 8. At that time the conference continued
to stand by its decision of June 6. Hiranuma was being exposed to great
pressure from the throne, the navy, and the Foreign Ministry, and he
agreed not to go beyond the earlier decision. The army then asked Ott

[63]Telegram from Ribbentrop to Ott, June 17, 1939, IMTFE, International Prosecution
Section (hereafter IPS), Document 4009.
[64]Harada, *Saionji kō to seikyoku*, VII, 24; *Saionji-Harada Memoirs*, p. 2585.

for Germany's acceptance of the June 6 decision. In a frantic appeal it almost begged Germany to yield and stated that there would be no mental reservations whatever on the side of Japan in such an alliance.[65]

But by this time it was already too late. Germany had chosen the Soviet Union as its ally instead of Japan. On August 16 Vyacheslav Molotov had indicated a willingness for an agreement with Germany, and Germany was ready to accept the proffered hand in order to solve the "Polish question." It might be interesting to speculate on the fate of the proposed Japanese-German alliance had Russia not shown such a quick response, but after August 16 there was no further chance for it.

The Japanese government was kept in complete ignorance of Germany's radical turnabout. In Tokyo there was even talk of sending Prime Minister Hiranuma to Berlin for direct talks with Hitler in order to crystallize the alliance when, on August 21, Japan and the world were stunned by the news of the German-Soviet Nonaggression Pact.

The German-Soviet Nonaggression Pact and Japan, August 1939-July 1940. To invade Poland and to fight Britain and France if necessary, Hitler had wanted an alliance without any limitations. Japan had failed to provide this. Its reservations regarding the date of entry into the war (the result of navy fears of a strong United States) had doomed Japanese-German negotiations to failure.

The breakdown of Japanese-German talks did not, however, mean that Germany had given up all hope of continuing close relations with Japan. Indeed, to preserve Japan's goodwill, Ribbentrop was quite eager to comply with Molotov's expressed wish that, as the result of the German-Russian pact, Japan might be influenced by Germany to improve relations with the Soviet Union.[66] But Japan's stock had fallen low with Hitler. In a rather famous speech to his generals on August 23, he denounced Japan with great contempt. Japan's persistent refusal to accept Germany's terms had become intolerable. The Japanese emperor was weak, cowardly, and irre-

---

[65]Telegram from Ott to German Foreign Office, August 3, 1939, IMTFE, IPS, Document 4047.

[66]Telegram from Schulenburg to German Foreign Office, August 16, 1939, in U.S., Department of State, *Nazi-Soviet Relations, 1939–1941: Documents from the Archives of the German Foreign Office* (1948), p. 52.

solute; the Japanese people were lacquered half-monkeys who needed to feel the knout.[67]

The news of the German-Russian Nonaggression Pact was sprung on midnight of August 22, while Ribbentrop was actually en route to Moscow. Ōshima was called by State Secretary Ernst von Weizsäcker to his apartment, and a grey-faced but stony ambassador was told the story. It came as a shattering blow to Japan. There was a violent and unanimous reaction, particularly since Japan had been so close to an agreement with Germany. Hiranuma considered Germany's action a betrayal of Japan. He confessed that he could not cope with such an intricate and baffling development.[68]

The blow caused his resignation and the downfall of the Japanese cabinet. The Japanese army was especially resentful against Germany since, instead of strengthening Japan against the Soviet Union, the newest German diplomatic surprise permitted the Soviets to maintain large forces on the Manchurian border, threatening Japan more than ever before. The analogy between the German-Soviet Nonaggression Pact of 1939 and the kaiser's efforts to push Russia into Far Eastern affairs in 1895 and after was not lost on the Japanese. Japanese-German relations hit the lowest point since 1895.

Before the Japanese cabinet resigned on August 30, a strong protest was delivered to Ōshima for transmittal to the German Foreign Office, but Weizsäcker was able to persuade Ōshima to hold the protest back and not deliver it. If the protest were delivered, Germany would only give an ill-tempered answer, he argued, and there was no point to that. Besides, was it not Japan's fault that Germany had been kept waiting so unreasonably long? Ōshima did withhold the protest for three weeks, and it was not delivered until the end of the Polish campaign amidst Japanese congratulations on Germany's success.[69]

The Conclusion of the Tripartite Pact, July–September 1940. Japan harbored strong resentment against Germany as a result of the Nonaggression Pact. It remained distant in spite of Ribbentrop's untiring efforts to cultivate Japan's friendship. He worked hard to promote a Japanese rapprochement with the Soviet Union, but neither Japan nor the Soviet Union was much

[67]David J. Dallin, *Soviet Russia and the Far East* (1948), pp. 149–50.
[68]Harada, *Saionji kō to seikyoku*, VIII, 55; *Saionji-Harada Memoirs*, p. 2617.
[69]Memorandum by Weizsäcker, September 18, 1939, IMTFE, Exhibit 506.

interested in this. Stalin, who had his pact with Germany, now felt no need for it, and Japan continued to worry about renewed Soviet pressure. There was no fundamental change in the coolness existing between Japan and Germany until the great German victories in the west in May and June 1940. These produced a real shift of opinion in Japan by giving new and great impetus to the proponents of a Japanese-German alliance, and from July on, after Matsuoka Yōsuke had become the new foreign minister in the Konoe cabinet, the army's eagerness for a full alliance with the Axis bore fruit in negotiations leading to the Tripartite Pact of 1940, designed to keep the United States out of the war.

After the conclusion of the German-Soviet pact, Germany continued to work for closer relations with Japan. Ribbentrop told Ott to inform the Japanese government that the German-Russian pact had weakened Britain and in this way was to be interpreted as a great aid to Japan's China policy. Ott was energetically to continue to cement Japanese-German friendship. Ōshima in Berlin was told by the German foreign minister that the Soviet pact was in Japan's interest, since it would permit Japan to extend its power to the south, the direction in which Japan's vital interests were to be found.[70] But to this argument, as well as to Germany's willingness to mediate between Japan and the USSR, Japan turned a deaf ear.

In Japan, after the fall of the Hiranuma cabinet, the pro-German elements in the government lost power. The new cabinet, headed by General Abe Nobuyuki, followed a careful policy of being determined not to be drawn into the European conflict. Instead, every effort was made to bring the China conflict to an end. Ōshima was finally recalled and replaced by Kurusu Saburō, and Shiratori suffered a similar fate in being recalled from Rome. These two individuals continued actively to promote closer ties between Japan and Germany after their return to their homeland, and there was still some feeling in the Army General Staff that Japan should side with the Axis; but by and large sentiment within the Japanese government was opposed to any hasty adventure.[71] As we have noted, this sentiment did

---

[70]Telegram from German Foreign Office to Ott, August 22, 1939, IMTFE, IPS, Document 4047.

[71]Telegram from Ott to German Foreign Office, October 5, 1939, IMTFE, IPS, Document 4045.

not begin to change until the spectacular German victories in the spring months of 1940.

By this time the Abe government had been replaced by one headed by Admiral Yonai Mitsumasa. It remained rather friendly toward the British and Americans, although relations with the West had become more difficult following the establishment of the new puppet government of Wang Ching-wei in Nanking. But it was the overrunning of Holland in May and the fall of France in June that radically altered the situation. The army insisted impatiently on a full alliance with Germany, and the Yonai cabinet in July began to make attempts for renewed closer cooperation with Germany. Negotiations were begun through Ambassador Kurusu Saburō in Berlin, but Germany, in the flush of victory, was in no hurry to accommodate Japan.

Since the Yonai cabinet apparently got nowhere, the army now demanded immediate action. There was a bitter attack against Foreign Minister Arita. On July 5 there was an abortive assassination attempt by terrorists against Yonai himself. On July 14 Army Minister Hata Shunroku resigned in order to topple the government, so that Japan would not let the opportunity slip by to arrive at a full alliance with Germany without any kind of reservations.[72] Having expelled the Yonai cabinet, which had been too slow for its taste, the army supported the formation of a new government under Prince Konoe, who appointed Matsuoka as his foreign minister. It now became possible to commit Japan fully on the side of Germany.

The decision to make a definite pact with Germany was taken on July 20.[73] Matsuoka urged it on the grounds that Japan must take advantage of German victories by expanding to the south and by establishing its own new order in East Asia. Such an alliance would also facilitate Germany's victory over Britain and, above all, would prevent America from entering the war. Finally, it was agreed, such an alliance would also help to settle the interminable China Incident.

On August 1 the Konoe cabinet made approaches to Germany, both in Berlin through Kurusu and in Tokyo through Matsuoka, who called Ott to his residence. At first Germany was not very eager. The Battle of Britain was going full blast, and Hitler did not believe that he had any need for

[72] Article from the *Asahi shimbun*, July 17, 1940, IMTFE, Exhibit 3199.
[73] Telegram from Ott to German Foreign Office, July 20, 1940, IMTFE, Exhibit 536.

Japanese help. This time Germany wanted tangible and valuable advantages from Japan. Japan would have to pay a better price, especially in regard to Germany's interests in China.[74] Soon, however, the temper of Germany changed. As the Battle of Britain dragged on, with American aid to Britain taking concrete shape in the form of old American destroyers, as Hitler planned the extension of the war into the Balkans, and as Japan moved independently into French Indochina, Ribbentrop agreed to go ahead with negotiations with Japan.[75] He feared a possible separate agreement between Japan and the other powers interested in Southeast Asia, and Hitler increasingly was concerned with the need to restrain America. Once again a common denominator in the alliance between Japan and Germany had been found, this time America.

Late in August Ribbentrop sent Heinrich Stahmer as a special envoy to discuss in Tokyo the draft of a tripartite pact between Japan, Germany, and Italy. Matsuoka called a Five Ministers Conference on September 4. It was then, in the presence of Konoe and Army Minister Tōjō Hideki, that the basic outline for such a pact was agreed upon. The draft of the pact was mainly the work of the Japanese, who included in it a general outline of Japan's planned new order and continually stressed that such a pact would serve as a deterrent to the United States, thereby preventing war between Japan and America.[76] Stahmer presented Germany's viewpoint. A perfect meeting of minds was the result, each side looking upon the alliance as an excellent means of keeping America neutral. Japan finally would be free to move south, while Germany could finish off the war against Britain and secure its flanks for the attack on Russia. The pact was endorsed by the Privy Council on September 19, encountering a minimum of resistance within the ranks of government.[77] The same day Ribbentrop informed Ciano, and Italy agreed to join. The pact was signed in Berlin on September 27, 1940, and was accompanied in Japan by the publication of an imperial rescript. It was announced to the world as a defensive alliance to prevent the spread of hostilities and to keep the United States out of the world conflict.

---

[74]Telegram from Ott to German Foreign Office, August 2, 1940, IMTFE, Exhibit 622.
[75]Telegram from Ott to German Foreign Office, August 2, 1940, IMTFE, IPS, Document 4029.
[76]Affidavit of Saitō, October 3, 1947, IMTFE, Exhibit 3589.
[77]Minutes of Imperial Conference, September 16, 1940, IMTFE, Exhibit 550.

The Tripartite Pact, mainly the work of Matsuoka, was in more than one sense a blunder. It failed to achieve the purposes set for it. It was concluded at a moment when Germany already showed signs of being unable to win the Battle of Britain; hence, Germany's aid to Japan had become already much less useful. It did not intimidate America from either aiding Britain or blocking Japan's expansion southward. Moreover, the pact was an alliance in name only.

For some years the view prevailed that the Tripartite Pact was the consistent and logical culmination of a rapprochement between Japan and Germany that began in 1936, since it permitted each nation to give full play to a policy of expansion and aggression. In fact, the pact was but a very short-lived instrument. Neither Japan nor Germany was willing to make any sacrifice for the sake of the new partnership. It was, in fact, based on distrust and the desire of each to draw advantage from the other. Within a year Germany attacked the Soviet Union (June 1941) and Japan attacked America (December 1941), neither consulting the other in advance of its action. Mutual strategy was sacrificed for the sake of secrecy. Each power thought only of its own territorial interests: Hitler wanted America to become involved in the Pacific; Japan, on the other hand, wanted to move south but was not interested in furnishing aid to Germany against the Soviet Union.

Cross Purposes, September 1940-November 1941. The period immediately following the conclusion of the Tripartite Pact and lasting until November 1941 presents again an excellent example of the lack of cooperation between Nazi Germany and Japan, inasmuch as each power continued to follow its own interests without paying attention to the concerns of the other. This was not only most clearly illustrated in their relations with the Soviet Union but was also apparent in Germany's lukewarm attitude in mediating Japan's conflicts with Nationalist China and even Vichy France. On the other hand, Japan blithely managed to ignore German pleas for an attack on the British base at Singapore and conducted negotiations with America in the summer of 1941 without informing Germany.

One of the basic reasons Konoe had supported the Tripartite Pact in 1940 had been his hope that it would lead to the conclusion of a Soviet-Japanese nonaggression pact, made possible through German aid. In October 1940 Japan had approached the Russian government through its new ambassador in Moscow, Tatekawa Yoshitsugu, with the suggestion of such a treaty.[78] The Soviet government, nervous about the Tripartite Pact, had shown no inclination to pursue this feeler, but in November, during Molotov's visit to Berlin, Ribbentrop also brought up the matter. He told his Russian visitor that Japan was anxious for such an agreement and that Germany would be glad to mediate between the two powers. Yet, within a matter of weeks Hitler was to decide upon a new about-face in his relations with the Soviet Union. Russian demands in the Balkans and on Finland caused Hitler to issue his famous directive "Barbarossa" on December 18, preparing for the attack on the Soviet Union.[79] No concern for Japanese interests was visible in this monumental decision. Japan's Foreign Minister Matsuoka had also wanted to invoke German good offices in yet another attempt to reach a settlement and a compromise peace with Nationalist China. In October 1940 approaches were made to Chungking via Hong Kong, while the Japanese ambassador in Berlin, Kurusu, was instructed to seek the aid of the German Foreign Office and to discuss matters with Chiang's ambassador in Berlin. While it is true that the German government urged Chiang Kai-shek to come to terms with Japan or face the possibility of complete abandonment,[80] German efforts in this direction also remained unsuccessful. In any case, Nationalist China could count upon continuing Russian support.

German diplomatic assistance thus was not exactly spectacular even in the case of Japanese penetration into French Indochina. On June 19, 1940, at the time of the fall of France, Kurusu, pointing out to Germany that Japan had a special interest in the future of that French colony, solicited German pressure on the Vichy regime. But the German response was far from hearty. Repeatedly during the summer of 1940, Japan requested German assistance in facilitating Japan's southern advance but met with a half-hearted response. After the conclusion of the Tripartite Pact, however, Matsuoka benefited from increased German goodwill. Then, in February and March of 1941, during the conflict between French Indochina and

---

[78]Grigore Gafencu, *Prelude to the Russian Campaign, from the Moscow Pact to the Opening of Hostilities in Russia* (1945), p. 87.

[79]U.S., Department of State, *Nazi-Soviet Relations*, pp. 251, 260.

[80]Herbert Feis, *The Road to Pearl Harbor: The Coming of the War between the United States and Japan* (1950), p. 134.

Thailand, the Nazi government finally put pressure on the French, but to little effect.

Contrary then to Matsuoka's hopeful predictions, the Tripartite Pact was not a success. The Soviet Union had not been brought into line, China continued to resist, and Japanese-German diplomatic cooperation remained on rather a meager scale. Finally, the United States had also become more hostile to Japan instead of being overwhelmed at the prospect of Japanese-German solidarity.

In view of this situation, Matsuoka decided to go to Europe in person to look into the state of Soviet-German relations, to see what could be done in Moscow toward arriving at an agreement with the Soviet Union, and to overcome the deadlock in negotiations with China.[81] After accepting an invitation from Ribbentrop, Matsuoka set forth toward Berlin in March of 1941 via the Trans-Siberian Railway. En route on March 24 in Moscow, he had talks with Stalin and Molotov, opening the subject of "fundamental problems in Soviet-Japanese relations,"[82] but further discussions were deferred until after Matsuoka's return from Germany.

In the German capital Matsuoka met Hitler and Ribbentrop several times between March 26 and 29. He then left for a brief visit to Rome, returning to Berlin during the first week of April to continue his conversations with the fuhrer and his foreign minister. Ribbentrop pointed out that Germany's relations with the Soviet Union were correct but not friendly, and that there was no certainty how they might develop. In any case, if Russia made a hostile move, Germany would strike it down.[83] Ribbentrop presented this veiled warning to Matsuoka about the state of German-Soviet relations to convince him that Japan should forgo the attempt to make a pact with Russia; rather, he urged, Japan should strike at Singapore. Despite repeated urgings of this nature, Matsuoka was not convinced, and he continued above all to display concern about arriving at an agreement with the USSR. Ribbentrop, rather irritated at the obtuseness of his visitor, then warned Matsuoka that a conflict with the Soviet Union was "always within the realm of possibility."[84] The case to illustrate the

---

[81]Robert L. Craigie, *Behind the Japanese Mask* (1945), p. 115.
[82]U.S., Department of State, *Nazi-Soviet Relations*, p. 280.
[83]*Ibid.*, pp. 284–85.
[84]*Ibid.*, p. 303.

fundamental lack of cooperation between Germany and Japan could not be more clearly illustrated—Germany had already set the machinery in motion to launch its attack on Russia, while Japan was still set upon a non-aggression treaty with the same power. German lack of cooperation with its nominal partner even went so far as to prohibit any reference to the forthcoming operation "Barbarossa" in a directive issued by Hitler to the German General Staff concerning collaboration with Japan.[85]

After leaving Berlin, Matsuoka went to Moscow, where he stayed from April 7 to April 13 and from whence he returned to Japan with a signed Soviet-Japanese pact of neutrality. In fact this agreement represented a Soviet triumph and yet another in Matsuoka's series of mistakes. In view of Germany's unmistakable attitude toward the Soviet Union, there was no need for such an agreement on the part of Japan, but Matsuoka simply did not believe that a German-Soviet clash was imminent.

By and large the Japanese government was disappointed with his results, and Matsuoka's stock fell low. The real drop came with Germany's invasion of the Soviet Union on June 22, which precipitated a crisis in Japan. As soon as the news was known, Matsuoka urged an immediate Japanese attack on Russia, going even so far as to appeal directly to the emperor over the head of Konoe. But this time he went too far.

Relations between the foreign minister and Konoe became markedly strained, and Hiranuma also was bitterly hostile to Matsuoka. An Imperial Conference on July 2 went on record that Japan would continue to advance to the south, into Indochina and Thailand, and that Russia was to be informed that Japan would remain neutral.[86] Japanese resentment against Germany was most intense; Japan had been made to look ridiculous again, just as in the case of the conclusion of the Soviet-German pact a mere two years before. Matsuoka could not escape the wrath of the cabinet; the Konoe government resigned on July 18, with the avowed purpose of getting rid of him as foreign minister, and was then reconstituted two days later with Admiral Toyoda Teijirō in the post. Certainly the months since the conclusion of the Tripartite Pact had not been productive in terms of

---

[85]International Military Tribunal, Nuremberg, *Nazi Conspiracy and Aggression, Opinion and Judgment* (1946–48), I, 847–49 (hereafter cited as Nuremberg Tribunal).

[86]Joseph Grew, *Ten Years in Japan* (1944), pp. 401–2; F.C. Jones, *Japan's New Order in East Asia: Its Rise and Fall, 1937–1945* (1954), p. 279.

German cooperation. Rather, the policies of the two powers had again widely diverged.

From the point of view of Nazi Germany the same held true. Japan had not been an ideal partner.

Ever since the postponement of Germany's plan to invade Britain, Ribbentrop had urged Japan to attack Singapore. On February 23, 1941, for instance, Ribbentrop had a talk with Ōshima (again appointed Japanese ambassador to Berlin), during which he pointed out that such a move would bring Britain to its knees. Preferably, such an attack was to be undertaken with lightning speed in the midst of peace and without a declaration of war.[87] The German foreign minister continued to emphasize the need for this all during the spring of 1941, and the topic was one that undoubtedly came up during the Hitler-Matsuoka talks in Berlin. Yet, despite German urgings and insistence upon the need for a speedy attack by Japan on Singapore, Matsuoka managed to avoid definite commitments.[88] Full of reservations, his declaration on this point did not satisfy German wants at all.

Germany was not only dissatisfied with Japan's lack of energy in regard to Britain, but Berlin also became disturbed and furious at Japanese negotiations carried on with the United States, about which Japan kept Germany carefully in the dark.

Japanese negotiations with the United States had begun in April of 1941. Matsuoka, however, did not divulge their existence to the Germans until early May, and even then he communicated with Secretary of State Cordell Hull in Washington without taking cognizance of Germany's reply to the proposals that had been sent to America. A furious Ribbentrop insisted that Germany should be kept fully informed and should participate in these negotiations. But Matsuoka, after invoking again Japan's loyalty to the Tripartite Pact, would not agree to such German participation. Ōshima in Berlin was also incensed. He heard about these negotiations for the first time not from Tokyo but from Ribbentrop, a situation full of irony when one remembers what had gone on in 1939. Needless to say, he strongly remonstrated with Matsuoka against an agreement with the United States. Such a development would render the Tripartite Pact

---

[87] *Ibid.*, p. 251.
[88] U.S., Department of State, *Nazi-Soviet Relations*, pp. 289–98.

meaningless, and Japan's "two-faced" diplomacy would earn it the contempt and hatred of both sides and in the end would fully isolate it.[89] Moral indignation over two-faced diplomacy, one must confess, seems strange from the mouth of one who had practiced such diplomacy with considerable verve not so very long before. The breakdown of the American-Japanese negotiations and the coming to power of the Tōjō cabinet on October 18, 1941, ushered in the final period before Pearl Harbor, but until November 1941 Germany could hardly feel overly pleased at the actions of its ally in the Far East.

War and the Renewed Alliance, November–December 1941. In the last two months before Pearl Harbor, once Japan had made its decision to go to war against the United States, it did its best to get a German commitment to enter that war and to revive the Tripartite Pact. In this it was successful, and once again because of a mutual opponent both Japan and Germany were united in their common aims. But this was not the result of any kind of planned cooperation before the outbreak of the war; rather it came about, as in the past, because the policies of both powers happened momentarily to be the same. Indeed, in November of 1941 Japan was not at all sure of German participation in its struggle against America, but this did not deter it. Japan was ready, if necessary, to fight the United States alone.

By November 1 the Japanese supreme command had become adamant— there could no longer be any delay as to the decision for war or peace. Japan's rapidly decreasing raw material supplies, especially the crucial oil reserves, would give it no hope for a successful war unless it was launched in the very near future or unless the diplomatic negotiations with Washington were crowned with a modicum of success. On November 5 a decision was made for a last attempt at negotiations, and if these were not to be successful by November 25, Japan would fight the United States and Britain. It would then also inform Germany and Italy of its decision and ask them to join with it against the United States and agree to a "no separate peace" treaty. However, the Japanese military also decided that if Germany should demand Japanese participation in the struggle against the Soviet Union, Japan would demur.[90]

[89]Jones, *Japan's New Order*, pp. 274–75.
[90]*Ibid.*, pp. 295–98.

Upon the failure of the diplomatic negotiations in Washington, the Japanese government made its decision on December 1 for war. Until that moment and ever since the fall of Matsuoka, Japan had consistently refused to keep Germany informed about the content and progress of the negotiations in Washington and had also been careful to keep Ōshima in ignorance of what went on. In fact, Germany did know something about the conversations in Washington through secret channels, and it had become deeply suspicious about the Japanese maneuvers.

Ōshima felt his being kept in the dark quite keenly, and he reported back to Tokyo that there would be no telling what Germany might do without consulting Japan if Japan negotiated without informing Germany. Actually, Hitler did not really object to the Japanese-American conversations; what he wanted above all was to defeat the USSR first, and hence he was not eager for war with America at that stage. He continued to urge Japan to attack the Soviet Union, but on that score, as had been the case before, Germany was unable to obtain a clear-cut reply from Japan.[91]

In late November Japan began to sound out Germany about its attitude in the event of a Japanese-American war. Ribbentrop gave his assurance that Germany would join,[92] and on November 28 he repeated the German pledge to do so in a talk with Ōshima. The German foreign minister did not, however, suspect the imminent Japanese attack against the United States, and he continued to urge upon Japan either an attack against Singapore, which would finish off the British, or a Japanese invasion of the Soviet Union. There is no reason not to believe that Ribbentrop spoke the truth in his postwar trial when he declared that he did not wish for a Japanese strike against America.[93]

On November 30 Tōgō Shigenori, Japan's foreign minister, instructed Ōshima to tell Hitler and Ribbentrop that there was an extreme danger of war; it might come quicker than anyone expected. If Japan were to go to war against America, it would do so because of its quarrel with that country over the Tripartite Pact.[94] On that same day Tōgō also had an interview with Ott, the German ambassador in Tokyo. He explained to him, not

[91]*Ibid.*, pp. 323–24.
[92]Telegram from Ribbentrop to Tōjō, November 23, 1941, IMTFE, Exhibit 60.
[93]Ribbentrop statement, March 30, 1946, IMTFE, Exhibit 2692.
[94]Nuremberg Tribunal, V, 566–67.

exactly truthfully, that it was Japan's faithfulness to the Tripartite Pact that had been the main obstacle to negotiations in Washington.

Next, Ōshima was told to obtain a "no separate peace" agreement from Germany. He approached Ribbentrop on this, but the latter pointed out that it would be necessary to consult Hitler. Since the fuhrer was at the moment at the Russian front, no immediate reply was possible. Finally, on December 5 Ribbentrop gave his formal acceptance of the Japanese requests. If war broke out between Japan and the United States, Germany and Italy would join, and both powers would also agree to a "no separate peace" clause. Even so, Germany was still completely unaware of the imminence of war. Ōshima himself heard of the Pearl Harbor attack through broadcasts from London, and both to him and to an incredulous Ribbentrop it came as a complete surprise.[95]

Once war had broken out, Ribbentrop declared that of course Germany would fully subscribe to a revived Tripartite Pact. The three powers would prosecute the war until complete victory, there would be no separate armistice, and there would be cooperation for the new order after peace.[96] Such a text was drawn up and agreed upon, and on December 11 Germany and Italy declared war against the United States, in fulfillment of their treaty obligations. The alliance had been renewed, since both Japan and Germany had come up against a common opponent. But again this was a situation brought about only by the actions of the one power; one cannot speak of a consistent Japanese-German diplomacy.

In general, Japanese-German relations, 1933–41, were governed only by narrow considerations of power politics on the part of both nations. Their intense and concentrated nationalism led each to pursue goals of *machtpolitik* which frequently subordinated their real diplomatic, economic, and ideological interests to the pursuit of pure power. Only in rare instances, when the interests of both nations merged for brief periods of time, such as in 1936 in the Anti-Comintern Pact and again in 1940 in the Tripartite Pact, was there a genuine common policy that Germany and Japan both followed for their mutual interests. For the rest of the time, Japanese-

---

[95]Ribbentrop statement, March 30, 1946, IMTFE, Exhibit 2692.

[96]U.S., Congress, Joint Committee on the Investigation of the Pearl Harbor Attack, *Hearings before the Joint Committee on the Investigation of the Pearl Harbor Attack* (1946), Part 35, pp. 687–88.

German relations frequently consisted of nothing but fruitless negotiations and disappointments, each nation going its separate way.

It is true, of course, that there were many elements common to both powers. Both Germany and Japan were politically isolated after their withdrawal from the League of Nations. Both were dedicated to expansionist foreign policies, at the expense of the Soviet Union, Britain, or any other obstacle in their paths. Ideologically both had contempt for democratic procedures and dislike for communist doctrine, substituting instead respect for military achievement, aggressive ultranationalism, and totalitarianism. Both emphasized courage, soldierly virtue, and the subordination of the individual to the interests of the state, and constructed educational systems designed to accomplish these purposes. Even in the field of economics Germany and Japan had much in common. They were the two greatest "have-not" nations of Europe and Asia, overpopulated, poor in raw materials, dependent on overseas markets for their prosperity; and both were adherents of an economic philosophy which increasingly, from the 1930s on, spurned private capitalism and instead turned toward state control and regulation. Finally, both Germany and Japan felt unbounded confidence in their destinies or missions. The interesting fact is that, despite all these common factors, the diplomacies of Japan and Germany were carried on almost completely independently from each other.

One is almost tempted to propose a general hypothesis that when, as in the case of Germany or Japan, powers are brought together by the force of historical similarity in being recently unified, "have-not" nations eager to overthrow the status quo, they are inclined to develop a system of diplomacy which does not go beyond the intensely narrow aims of naked *machtpolitik*. Finally, it may be observed that in each country these policies were the product also of a somewhat revolutionary structure of power and a somewhat arbitrary process of decision-making which prevented the fullest wisdom of the nation from being brought to bear effectively on the problems of foreign relations.

Because of the defeat of Japan and Germany in World War II, a very great amount of documentary material has become available, so that the researcher actually faces an *embarras de richesse*. No attempt is made here to list all that might be available; only the most important sources are described briefly.

International Military Tribunal for the Far East:

Documents are grouped as follows: "Record of Proceedings," a narrative; "Exhibits," documents introduced in evidence; "Analysis of Documents," documents not introduced at the trial but analyzed. The latter two categories are more important than the "Record of Proceedings." Documents include files from the Foreign Ministry and the Germany embassy in Tokyo.

Asahi Shimbunsha, *Tōkyō saiban* (3 vols., 1962).
Kyokutō Kokusai Gunji Saiban, *Kyokutō kokusai gunji saiban sokkiroku* (1946–48).
Kyokutō Kokusai Gunji Saiban Kōhan Kiroku Kankōkai, *Kyokutō kokusai gunji saiban kōhan kiroku* (2 vols., 1948).

Guides to the material include the following:

Asahi Shimbun Chōsa Kenkyū Shitsu, *Kyokutō kokusai gunji saiban kiroku mokuroku oyobi sakuin* (1953).
Dull and Umemura, *The Tokyo Trials: A Functional Index to the Proceedings of the International Military Tribunal for the Far East* (1957).

International Military Tribunal, Nuremberg:

Nazi Conspiracy and Aggression (10 vols., 1946–48).

Germany:

Dokumente der deutschen Politik (9 vols., 1939–44), is useful for official statements.
U.S., Department of State, *A Catalog of Files and Microfilms of the German Foreign Ministry Archives, 1920–1945* (2 vols., 1962–64).
—— *Documents on German Foreign Policy, 1918–1945* (16 vols., 1949–57).

Japan. Microfilm reproductions of historical materials in the Foreign, Army, and Navy ministries are indicated in the following checklists:

Japan, Gaimushō (Foreign Ministry), *Nihon gaikō nempyō narabi ni shuyō bunsho* (1965), Vol. II.
Uyehara, *Checklist of Archives in the Japanese Ministry of Foreign Affairs, Tokyo, Japan, 1868–1945, Microfilmed for the Library of Congress, 1949–1951* (1954).
Young, *Checklist of Microfilm Reproductions of Selected Archives of the Japanese Army, Navy, and Other Government Agencies, 1868–1945* (1959).

United States:

U.S., Congress, Joint Committee on the Investigation of the Pearl Harbor Attack, *Hearings before the Joint Committee on the Investigation of the Pearl Harbor Attack,* 39 parts (15 vols., 1946).

U.S., Department of State, Archives, are of great value, especially for Japanese-German relations to 1939.

—— *Papers Relating to the Foreign Relations of the United States, Japan: 1931–1941* (2 vols., 1943).

Documentary series:

Royal Institute of International Affairs, *Documents on International Affairs, 1928–* (1929–), is useful for official speeches and announcements.

Biographies and memoirs:

Ciano, *The Ciano Diaries, 1939–1943* (1946), includes some very informative material on Japanese-German relations.

—— *Ciano's Diplomatic Papers* (1948), an edited translation of Ciano, *L'Europa verso la catastrofe* (1948), contains a selection of some of Ciano's notes and memoranda, occasionally of vital importance.

Craigie, *Behind the Japanese Mask* (1945), discusses events to 1941.

Dirksen, *Moscow, Tokyo, London* (1952), the record of the German ambassador to Japan, 1933–38, is very disappointing.

Grew, *Ten Years in Japan* (1944), often is useful.

Harada, *Saionji kō to seikyoku* (9 vols., 1950–52, 1956) is invaluable for behind-the-scenes insights recorded by Harada Kumao, secretary to Prince Saionji, the last of the great Japanese genrō. The work contains exceedingly fascinating glimpses into Japanese dealings with Germany. During the Occupation an English translation was prepared by SCAP, Civil Intelligence Section, GHQ, Far East Command, under the title *Saionji-Harada Memoirs*.

Kido, *Kido Kōichi nikki*, is useful. 2 vols. plus a supplementary volume of letters and documents: Kido Kōichi Nikki Kenkyūkai, *Kido Kōichi kankei bunsho* (1966). Portions of the diary were quoted in a work known as the *Kido nikki* (1947), parts of which were translated as "Kido Diary, July 11, 1931–December 9, 1945," Documents 1632 and 1768, International Prosecution Section, IMTFE.

Schwarz, *This Man Ribbentrop, His Life and Times* (1943), has quite a lot to say but little of it is reliable.

Weizsäcker, *Memoirs* (1951), on the other hand, has little to say.

German foreign policy:

Holldack, *Was wirklich geschah* (1949), is an excellent study of this topic.

Kordt, *Wahn und Wirklichkeit* (1948), contains comments by a former German diplomat that occasionally are quite penetrating.

German-Japanese relations:

Feis, *The Road to Pearl Harbor* (1950), pays some attention to this topic, particularly after the conclusion of the Tripartite Pact.

Iklé, *German-Japanese Relations, 1936–1940* (1956), approaches events from the Japanese point of view.

Jones, *Japan's New Order in East Asia: Its Rise and Fall, 1937–1945* (1954), is an excellent monograph with several first-rate sections on Japan and Germany.

Libal, *Japans Weg in den Krieg* (1971).

Nihon Kokusai Seiji Gakkai Taiheiyō Sensō Gen'in Kenkyūbu, *Taiheiyō sensō e no michi* (1962–63), Vol. IV, *Nitchū sensō II*, and Vol. V, *Sangoku dōmei: Nisso chūritsu jōyaku*, present the most thorough and authoritative treatment of German-Japanese relations during this period.

Presseisen, *Germany and Japan: A Study in Totalitarian Diplomacy, 1933–1941* (1958), uses primarily German materials.

Wiskemann, *The Rome-Berlin Axis* (1949), very ably discusses in detail relations between Berlin and Tokyo.

German-Japanese economic relations:

Bloch, *German Interests and Policies in the Far East* (1940), is a solid work.

Anti-Comintern Pact:

Baba, "The Anti-Comintern Pact in Domestic Politics" (1937).

Kajima, *Gendai no gaikō* (1937).

Sommer, *Deutschland und Japan zwischen den Mächten, 1935–1940: Vom Antikominternpakt zum Dreimächtepakt* (1962).

Japan in the 1930s:

Utley, "Japan's Inner Conflict" (1937).

Germany and the Sino-Japanese war:

Liu, "German Mediation in the Sino-Japanese War, 1937–38" (1949).

Tripartite Pact:

Hosoya, "Sangoku dōmei to Nisso chūritsu jōyaku (1939–1941)" (1963).

Kase, *Mizurī gō e no dōtei* (1951), is an interesting account of Japanese politics leading to the Tripartite Pact; the English translation is entitled *Journey to the Missouri* (1950).

Matsuo, *Sangoku dōmei to Nichi-Bei sen* (1940), is an official account of the Tripartite Pact and its effect on Japanese-American relations.

Ōhata, "Nichi-Doku-I sangoku dōmei" (1959), is based on the records of the International Military Tribunal for the Far East.

Sommer, *Deutschland und Japan zwischen den Mächten, 1935–1940: Vom Antikomin-ternpakt zum Dreimächtepakt* (1962).

Toscano, *Le origini diplomatiche del patto d'acciaio* (2d rev. ed., 1956), is a good study by an Italian writer of relations between Italy and Germany and has some reflections on the role of Japan.

Ueda, "Nichi-Doku-I sangoku dōmei" (1953), also is based on the materials of the International Military Tribunal for the Far East.

Opinions of Karl Haushofer:

Haushofer, *Dai Nihon* (1913), and *Japan baut sich sein Reich* (1941); both were important for their influence on Nazi diplomatic thought.

German-American relations and Japan, 1941:

Trefousse, *Germany and American Neutrality, 1939–1941* (1956), is a good account of German policy toward the United States in 1941 and of the role of Japan.

Germany and Japan during World War II:

Meskill, *Hitler and Japan: The Hollow Alliance* (1966).

Available material related to Japanese-German relations in the 1930s and 1940s has been well researched, so that for the time being little remains to be done. This situation arises, of course, from the intense interest aroused by the diplomatic negotiations that led to the outbreak of World War II. It would be interesting, however, to learn what the Japanese government and military thought of Germany during the period from 1939 until the end of the war. In what way did Germany's victories and failures influence Japanese attitudes? In 1940 this is apparent; in 1941 less so. In what way, for example, did the Battle of Britain influence Japan? Furthermore, it would be instructive to follow the Russian campaign through the files of the Japanese Army General Staff.

7

Japan's Policies
Toward Russia

Hosoya Chihiro

JAPAN AND TSARIST RUSSIA, 1868–1917

The history of Japanese-Russian relations from 1868 to 1917 may be divided into four periods. The first, 1868–75, was marked by recurring incidents resulting from Japan's failure to obtain an agreement with Russia for a boundary line on the island of Sakhalin for its northern frontier; it ended in 1875 with a treaty by which Japan received the Kuril Islands in exchange for recognition of Russian control of all of Sakhalin. Between 1875 and 1891, another clearly defined period, relations became more friendly as Russia gave up its active policy in the Far East and Japan turned inward. The building of the Trans-Siberian Railway, between 1891 and 1902, however, signaled the revival of Russia's interest in the Far East and set off several years of imperialist rivalry in Korea and Manchuria by both countries. Aggravated first by the Triple Intervention in 1895, relations grew increasingly hostile until they culminated in war, 1904–5. In the following years both countries attempted to demarcate their spheres of interest in Northeast Asia in order to remove this major cause of trouble and to work together to prevent a third power, especially the United States, from penetrating the region. The partnership, which took initial form in an entente in 1907 and was expanded in subsequent agreements in 1910, 1912, and 1916, grew increasingly close before the tsarist regime was overthrown in 1917.

The following are major sources of general information concerning relations between Japan and Russia from the Meiji Restoration to the Russian revolution.

Government publications:

Japan, Gaimushō (Foreign Ministry), *Nihon gaikō bunsho* (1936–). A collection of diplomatic documents beginning in 1868 which, when completed over the next several years, will contain volumes to 1945. Documents from the Meiji period have been published in forty-five volumes. There are also several special series; for example, a series dealing with the Russo-Japanese War. Several volumes for the early years of the Taishō period also have appeared.

—— "Nichi-Ro kōshō shi" (2 vols., 1944). Based chiefly on Foreign Ministry records, the work is the most important account of Japanese policy toward tsarist Russia. In addition to a detailed history of diplomatic negotiations, the study contains some information regarding the decision-making process.

—— *Nihon gaikō nempyō narabi ni shuyō bunsho* (2 vols., 1965; first published, 1955). A collection of selected documents, 1868–1945, it is the most useful reference for students of Japanese foreign policy in the modern period. Documents pertaining to Japanese-Russian relations to the end of the tsarist period are in Vol. I.

General studies:

Japan, Gaimushō (Foreign Ministry), *Nihon gaikō hyakunen shōshi* (2d rev. ed., 1958).

Kajima, *Nihon gaikō seisaku no shiteki kōsatsu* (1951), originally published as *Teikoku gaikō no kihon seisaku* (1938).

Kiyosawa, *Nihon gaikōshi* (2 vols., 1942).

Lensen, "Japan and Tsarist Russia—the Changing Relationships, 1875–1917" (1962). A succinct study that tends to discount the imperialist designs of Russian Far Eastern policy.

Numata, *Nichi-Ro gaikōshi* (1943).

Shinobu, *Kindai Nihon gaikōshi* (1942).

—— *Nihon no gaikō* (1961).

Watanabe, *Nihon kinsei gaikōshi* (1938).

DELINEATION OF THE NORTHERN FRONTIER, 1868–1875

In the latter half of the nineteenth century tsarist Russia appeared on the scene as a great power in Far Eastern politics. A policy of pushing eastward implied a grave threat to Japan's national security. In 1855, in the wake of other Western countries, Russia forced Japan to enter into commercial and diplomatic relations by a treaty of peace and friendship. Three years later the two countries signed a treaty of friendship and commerce. During the next decade Russia intensified its pressure on Japan. In the west, for example, the captain of the *Posadnik*, a Russian corvette, attempted to occupy Tsushima island for more than half of 1861 until

forced away by two British warships the shogunate had called in. And in
the north, Russian influence and power grew on the island of Sakhalin.

The question of Sakhalin was one of the most important international
issues confronting the new leaders of the Meiji government. The treaty of
1855 with the shogunate was ambiguous. It simply stipulated that Sakhalin was in the joint possession of both countries and that citizens of both
treaty nations were to be allowed to move about freely. Repeated efforts
by the Tokugawa shogunate in the 1860s to draw a border line on the
island were unsuccessful, however, and in 1868 the task was passed on to
the new Meiji government. Each year thereafter the problem became more
urgent as Russia sent more people to the island and incidents between the
two populations became more frequent.

The question for Japan was whether to maintain its position in the
southern part of Sakhalin at any cost or, with a view to securing friendly
relations with Russia, to give up its rights on the island in exchange for
compensation elsewhere. Government leaders initially were inclined to take
a strong stand against Russia, stressing the value of colonizing Sakhalin
even at the cost of taking up arms against Russia. This was the tenor of a
cabinet decision in September 1869, and as a step in this direction, the
Sakhalin Colonization Agency was set up in March 1870.

The policy of confronting Russia seems to have reflected the strong
views of Iwakura Tomomi, who wrote to Chancellor Sanjō Sanetomi
in April 1869 that the "national prosperity of Japan is contingent upon the
success of colonizing Ezo."[1] By "Ezo," of course, he meant both Hokkaido
and Sakhalin (northern [kita] or farther [oku] Ezo). This conception of
Sakhalin as a distant part of the Hokkaido area, which Japan had always
claimed, may have created in the minds of government leaders a psychological resistance to giving it up. An additional factor of importance was
Japan's lack of information concerning the contemporary international
situation, especially the strength of Russia vis-a-vis the strength of Japan,
so that no adequate judgment could be made of the relative capabilities of
the two nations. Furthermore, the decision-makers may have expected that
if Japan became involved in a serious conflict with Russia over Sakhalin,
the British would come to their aid again as they had in the case of Tsushima.

[1]Iwakura Kō Kyūseki Hozonkai, ed., Iwakura kō jikki (1927), II, 699–701.

By 1870 the Japanese government had resolved to seek a diplomatic solution to the problem. In March 1870 it approached the United States minister to Japan asking for American mediation to secure Russian acceptance of a plan to divide the island along latitude 50 degrees north. Russian unwillingness to accept the United States as mediator, however, led the Japanese government to open direct negotiations with the Russian government in November of the same year.

This new willingness of the Japanese to negotiate may have been influenced by Sir Harry Parkes, the British minister to Japan. Concerned that Russia might attempt to use incidents arising from the joint possession of Sakhalin as an excuse to occupy Hokkaido, Parkes repeatedly urged the Japanese government not to get drawn into armed conflict with the Russians over Sakhalin.

In June 1871 Soejima Taneomi was appointed special envoy to go to Siberia to talk over the matter with the Russians but failed to see the Russian delegate. The first real talks began in May 1872, when Evgenii Biutsov arrived in Japan as the Russian minister. His talks with Soejima, then foreign minister, continued to March 1873, but they failed to reach an agreement. Soejima insisted that either the island should be divided between the countries or one country should sell its rights to the other. Biutsov refused to consider giving up Sakhalin; instead he proposed that Japan exchange its rights to Sakhalin for Russian rights to the northern Kuril Islands. Soejima appeared ready to consider this proposal if, in addition, Russia would promise neutrality in the event that Japan undertook military intervention in Korea. But the talks were broken off in March 1873 when Soejima left for China to discuss the problem then arising over Taiwan.

The second round of negotiations was carried on from June 1874 to May 1875 between Enomoto Takeaki, the Japanese minister to Russia, and Petr Stremoukhov, director of the Asia Department of the Russian Foreign Office at St. Petersburg. Before sending Enomoto to the Russian capital, the Japanese government had decided to reverse its stand; it was now prepared to accept the Russian proposal to exchange its rights in Sakhalin for the northern Kuril Islands. While it is not clear when and how the Japanese government reached this decision, its changed attitude is first expressed in a draft "Order of Sending Japanese Delegates to Russia and Korea," dated February 2, 1874, which was sent by Chancellor Sanjō to Iwakura.[2] The document shows clearly that the Japanese government gave priority to the Russian question rather than the Korean question, which was also of some urgency. The exchange principle embodied in this document formed the basis of the instruction Enomoto received from the government on March 5, 1874, before leaving for Russia.

Why did Japan change its policy in the Sakhalin dispute? Several factors may be suggested. First of all, it was highly desirable for Japan to stabilize its relations with Russia before launching an active Korean policy, lest Russia oppose it or at least distract it by exerting pressure on the northern territories. Evidence of such thinking is found, for example, in a passage from a memorandum by Ōkubo Toshimichi in October 1873, urging a peace policy toward Korea. "In regard to the diplomatic situation," he wrote, "the most important countries for us are Russia and Britain. . . . Relations with them are uncertain. I fear that Russia will interfere unless we secure our independence. If we open fire on Korea, Russia will catch us both, like the fisherman who seizes both the clam and the bird while they are fighting each other. Thus we should not begin a war in Korea now."[3]

Second, there was growing feeling among the Japanese decision-makers, including Ōkubo, that Japanese resources and energies might better be expended in areas with a more favorable climate. It should be noted again that Japan undertook a military expedition to Taiwan in April 1874.

Third, rising pessimism about the value of colonizing Sakhalin, coupled with the scarcity of resources Japan could spare in developing this region, supported the argument for withdrawal. Among others, Kuroda Kiyotaka, the commissioner of colonization, repeatedly recommended that it would be much wiser for Japan to concentrate its energy on the colonization of Hokkaido than to make futile efforts to develop Sakhalin. He even went so far as to argue that pulling back from Sakhalin would strengthen the security of Hokkaido. It must be added that the Ministry of Finance, worrying about the lack of money for investing in key domestic sectors of the economy, had always been reluctant to undertake an extensive colonizing program in Sakhalin and had been inclined to abandon the island.

---

[2] *Iwakura Tomomi kankei bunsho*, VII (1934), 464–66.
[3] *Ōkubo Toshimichi bunsho*, II (1928), 53–64.

Last, there was a discernible change in the way Iwakura and other de-cision-makers perceived Japan's external setting as a result of their trip around the world in 1871–73. The observations the Iwakura Embassy brought back home seemed to help its members and others to grasp more realistically Japan's position in world politics and to establish priorities for national policy. Both Iwakura and Ōkubo, who formerly had been ex-ponents of a strong policy in the Sakhalin dispute, upon their return in 1873 argued for conciliation.

Once the Japanese government decided to give up its rights to Sakhalin, it was able to resolve its differences with Russia fairly quickly. Although a settlement was held up briefly while Enomoto tried unsuccessfully to per-suade Russia to sweeten the exchange by throwing into the bargain some Russian warships, the Sakhalin-Kuril Islands exchange treaty was finally signed in St. Petersburg on May 7, 1875. Materials for the years 1868–75 are particularly rich.

Documents and letters:

> *Iwakura Tomomi kankei bunsho*, Vols. IV–VII (1930–34). Among these documents are several letters revealing Iwakura's views on the problem of the northern territories as well as records giving an insight into the decision-making process related to the opening of talks with the Russians in 1871 and 1874.
>
> Japan, Gaimushō (Foreign Ministry), *Nihon gaikō bunsho*, Vols. I–VIII (1936–40). The basic official documents for the 1868–75 period are published here.
>
> Kido, *Kido Takayoshi nikki* (3 vols., 1967; originally published, 1932–33).
>
> *Kido Takayoshi bunsho*, Vol. III–VI (1930–31).
>
> Kuroda Kiyotaka ikken shorui, a manuscript collection at the Kensei Shiryō Shitsu of the National Diet Library, is the best source for the views of Kuroda.
>
> *Ōkubo Toshimichi bunsho*, Vols. II–VI (1927–28). This collection of materials is of significance equal to the Iwakura collection noted above. Ōkubo played the most important role in the switch in Japan's policy in 1873–74.
>
> *Ōkuma Shigenobu kankei bunsho*, Vols. I–III (1932–33).
>
> Waseda Daigaku Shakai Kagaku Kenkyūjo, *Ōkuma bunsho* (5 vols., 1958–62).

Biographies:

> Iwakura Kō Kyūseki Hozonkai, *Iwakura kō jikki* (1927), Vols. II–III, contains useful material on Iwakura's initial strong policy in the Sakhalin dispute.
>
> Kamo, *Enomoto Takeaki: Meiji Nihon no kakuretsu soseki* (1960), gives an account of Enomoto's participation in Japanese-Russian talks from June 1874 to May 1875.

Kido Kō Denki Hensansho, *Shōgiku Kido kō den* (1927), Vol. II, is of more limited value for this study.

Kiyosawa, *Gaiseika to shite no Ōkubo Toshimichi* (1942), argues that Ōkubo, who had originally taken a firm stand against Russian penetration into southern Sakhalin, changed his view to one seeking accommodation with the Russians because of his awareness of the urgency of industrializing and modernizing his country.

Maruyama, *Maruyama Sakura den* (1899), is a valuable work about a high official of the Foreign Ministry who was sent to Sakhalin in 1869 to negotiate with the Russians on the spot. He was determined to resist Russia in Sakhalin, even arguing for the use of armed force to limit Russian expansion.

Ōkuma Kō Hachijūgonenshi Hensankai, *Ōkuma kō hachijūgonenshi* (1926), Vol. I, is of less value than the Ōkubo and Iwakura studies with regard to Japanese-Russian issues in this period.

Studies:

Ayusawa, "Karafuto Chishima no shiteki kōsatsu" (1951).

Berton, "The Russo-Japanese Boundary, 1850–1875" (1951), gives a balanced account, based on Russian and Japanese sources, of the process by which the boundary problem was settled. He emphasizes two points as key factors in causing the Japanese to agree to the 1875 settlement: first, the recommendations made by Kuroda to concentrate on colonizing Hokkaido, and second, the attractiveness to other Meiji leaders of more southern areas for Japanese activities.

Hiraoka, *Ishin zengo no Nihon to Roshia* (1934), republished as *Nichi-Ro kōshō shi wa* (1944), gives an account of Okamoto Kansuke, who was active as a government official concerned with the program to develop Sakhalin and who favored an early agreement with the Russians. Okamoto himself wrote a book, *Kita Ezo shinshi* (1866), to attract public attention to the favorable prospects for developing Sakhalin and to encourage the government to move rapidly in this direction.

Hosokawa, "Karafuto Chishima kōkan mondai no temmatsu" (1941–42).

Inoue, *Nihon no gunkokushugi* (1953), Vol. II.

Japan, Gaimushō (Foreign Ministry), "Nichi-Ro kōshō shi" (1944), Vol. I, contains the most detailed account of this topic.

Karafutochō, *Karafuto enkaku shi* (1925), is a good source of information about the Japanese settlements in Sakhalin in the early Meiji period.

Lensen, *The Russian Push toward Japan: Russo-Japanese Relations, 1697–1875* (1959), also based on Russian and Japanese sources, interprets the motivation of the Japanese decision-makers in 1874–75 as follows (pp. 442–43): "The abandonment of Sakhalin reflected the feeling of the government that Japanese energies might better be expended elsewhere, not only in Hokkaido but in the warmer regions of Korea and Formosa." Moreover, Lensen expresses approval of the exchange agreement, saying (p. 446) that "Japan's legal claims to Sakhalin were not beyond question. She had been outdistanced in colonization and her military position on the island had become untenable. Russia could not be expected to pull out of northwestern Sakhalin, which dominated the Amur Estuary, while incidents arising from the joint occupation of the island made Sakhalin the Achilles' heel of Japan, endangering the security of the whole empire."

Maruyama, *Nihon hoppō hatten shi* (1942), refers to Saigō Takamori's concern with the northern territories as well as to the correlation between the Sakhalin and the Korean questions.

Nakamura, *Chishima Karafuto shinryaku shi* (2d ed., 1943).

Narochnitzkii, *Kolonial'naia politika kapitalisticheskikh derzhav na Dal'nem Vostoke, 1860–1895* (1956), is an interesting but somewhat tendentious work by a Soviet scholar. Based primarily on Russian Foreign Office archives, Narochnitzkii argues that Japan, having no rights to the southern part of Sakhalin, simply usurped the Kuril Islands and called the process an exchange of territory. Japan, he says, took advantage of the difficulties the Russians were experiencing in the Near East and in their relations with Britain. He assumes on the basis of several reports from Russian diplomatic representatives that Japan's abandonment of Sakhalin was due to the increasing interest of Japanese ruling circles in pushing toward the south. He also alleges that the United States instigated the Japanese to take a strong position against Russia on the question.

Oka, "Meiji shonen no Ezochi to Igirisu" (1943), treats the British attitude toward the Japanese-Russian conflict over the northern territories. He discusses Minister Parkes' attempt to send a British cruiser to this region in 1868 and provides a background to Parkes' moves in the following years to persuade the Japanese government to reach a settlement with the Russians.

Okamoto, *Nichi-Ro kōshō Hokkaidō shikō* (1898).

Ōta, *Nichi-Ro Karafuto gaikōsen* (1941).

Ōtomo, *Hokumon sōshō* (6 vols., 1943).

Ōyama, "Meiji shoki no hoppō ryōdo mondai" (1962), is a solid work based on Foreign Ministry records and on several of the other collections noted above. His special contribution is his account of the process by which the Japanese government shifted its position toward abandoning Sakhalin in 1873–74.

Shimomura, *Meiji ishin no gaikō* (1948), ch. 8, pp. 313–37, treats the topic under review here.

Shinobu, "Chishima Karafuto kōkan jōyaku" (1957), is an attempt to establish
the legitimacy of the Sakhalin-Kuril Islands exchange treaty in order to challenge current Soviet contentions rather than a work concerned chiefly with
analysis of a historical process.

Suematsu, *Kinsei ni okeru hoppō mondai no shinten* (1928).

Ueda, "Ryōdo kizoku kankeishi" (1953).

Watanabe, *Nihon kinsei gaikōshi* (1938), a general work already noted, is useful
in the study of the relationship between the Sakhalin and Korean questions.

There still remain some further important aspects of the subject to be
explored. Meriting attention are such topics as Japan's image of Russia or
the related question of the conception the new Meiji leaders held of the
Russian menace to Japan's national security. Whether these leaders were
worried seriously about the Russian menace or whether they deliberately
magnified the threat to attain other ends is another question that needs
more careful examination. How great, too, did they believe the Russian
threat to be in comparison with the danger some felt from Britain? An
initial attempt in this direction can be found in the following works:

Inō, "Kinsei Nihon ni okeru shinrosetsu no keifu" (1953), reviews the ideas of
leading pro-Russian Japanese from the end of the Tokugawa period to the middle of the Meiji period.

Yasuoka, "Meiji shoki no tai-Ro keikairon ni kansuru ichi kōsatsu" (1960).

There also is a need to approach the study of the decision-making process
in Japan's Russian policy, 1868–75, from a perspective that will correlate
this policy with Japanese policy in other major regions, such as Korea and
Taiwan. The fear of Russia always preyed on the minds of Japanese decision-makers when they took up Korean policy, and the settlement of the
Sakhalin dispute was assessed at least in part for its effect on Korean policy.

The influence of such Western countries as the United States and Britain
on Japan's shift in position in 1873–74 might be further investigated. It
is well known that Charles W. LeGendre, an American adviser to the
Japanese Foreign Ministry, was advising Japan on its Korean policy at the
time and on its decision to send troops to Taiwan. Is there any evidence
that he was also involved in the formulation of Japan's Russian policy,
especially the switch in position concerning the Sakhalin dispute?

CALM BEFORE THE STORM, 1875–1891

In the wake of the settlement of the Sakhalin dispute, an era of good feeling obtained in Japanese-Russian relations for about two decades. Its hands occupied with the Near Eastern question, tsarist Russia was not in a position to get deeply involved in Far Eastern politics in the 1870s and 1880s. Moreover, Russia was too handicapped by the underdeveloped condition of Siberia, above all by the poor transportation system, to undertake a policy of expansion in the Far East, where serious resistance was envisaged. On the other hand, the primary concern of the leaders of Japan, especially those who had established their power through the successful stand against invasion of Korea in 1873, was to industrialize and modernize their country rather than to expand Japan's power beyond its boundaries. They saw the most important external issue as the revision of the treaties imposed upon Japan by the Western countries. This issue was deemed one of the barriers standing in the way of achieving the supreme domestic goal. Thus, circumstances on both sides made for good relations between Japan and Russia. Even as late as 1892, instructions given to the new Russian minister to Japan show that the Russian government did not envisage any basic conflict between the two countries.

The Russian attitude toward revision of the treaties reflected these friendly attitudes. When the Japanese government approached the Russian government in July 1880 with a proposal for revising the treaties, permitting Japan to raise the tariff rate and revoke the extraterritorial privileges, Russia expressed its willingness to revise the treaties in principle but reserved commitment on the extraterritorial rights problem. This made the Russians stand out as more friendly to Japan than some other Western countries, especially Britain, which simply refused to consider a revision. In the years that followed, from 1880 to 1888, when negotiations for revision of the treaties were conducted at conferences jointly attended by representatives of the trading powers, Russia proved to be the nation most accommodating to Japanese desires. Finally, in August 1889 Russia followed Germany and the United States in signing with Japan a new treaty of friendship, commerce, and navigation, which provided for Russian abandonment of its extraterritorial rights, an increased tariff rate for Japan, and most-favored-nation treatment for Russia.

In the 1880s a new international crisis was developing in Korea out of the rivalry for influence among various Korean factions within Korea and between China and Japan from outside. Coups d'etat in 1882 and 1884 revealed the mounting intensity of the struggle and the depth of Chinese and Japanese involvement. Japan began to search for international support from Western countries, including Russia. Since Russia also feared Chinese influence in northeastern Asia and was interested in preserving the status quo, there appeared to be a mutuality of interest in opposing extension of Chinese power in Korea. In 1889 Japan and Russia took up the matter of exchanging information concerning Chinese activities there.

In 1891 an attempt by a Japanese constable to assassinate Crown Prince Nicholas shocked both governments, but it had little effect on Japanese-Russian relations. It was not this incident but the beginning of the construction of the Trans-Siberian Railway that marked the year 1891 as a turning point from which time the two powers began to move toward hostility; however, it was not until 1895 that the new current came to the surface.

While the attempt on the life of the Russian crown prince was an isolated act, completely alien to the desires of the Japanese government, it was indicative of a persistent feeling among some Japanese who remained suspicious that Russia desired to conquer their country. These were the Japanese who had been wary of Russian activities in the Far East throughout the "era of good feeling," looking upon Russian acquisition of Sakhalin and even the Russian response to the treaty revision problem as signs of evil intent.

Research related to Japan's policy toward Russia between 1875 and 1891 has been neglected. Only limited references to the question have been made in general works, and there have been very few special studies.

Japan, Foreign Ministry, "Nichi-Ro kōshō shi" (2 vols., 1944).

Lensen, "The Attempt on the Life of Nicholas in Japan" (1961), has a picturesque recital of the events surrounding the attempt to assassinate the Russian crown prince at Ōtsu, but the account reveals nothing really significant about Japanese-Russian relations.

Narochnitzkii, *Kolonial'naia politika kapitalisticheskikh derzhav na Dal'nem Vostoke, 1860–1895* (1956), contains some information about Japanese-Russian relations during the Korean crisis in the 1880s. Prime Minister Itō Hirobumi's remark to the Russian representative in the fall of 1887 to the effect that Japan, preoccupied with domestic affairs, simply desired to see peace and tranquillity in Korea is cited. Foreign Minister Ōkuma Shigenobu's design for a "close partnership" among Japan, Russia, and China to preserve the status quo in the Far East also is noted. Narochnitzkii is inclined to assume that Japanese policy concerning the Korean question was essentially anti-Russian, while its Far Eastern policy until 1895 was aimed chiefly at preserving the status quo and preventing a Sino-Japanese rapprochement.

The most significant results of research in depth for this period would seem to come from a study of the relationship between Japan's policy toward Russia and the struggle between Japan and China in Korea.

THE ROAD TO WAR, 1891–1905

Search for a Modus Vivendi, 1891–1900. The beginning of the construction of the Trans-Siberian Railway in 1891 signaled a turning point in Russo-Japanese relations. It indicated Russian intention to carry on an extensive drive toward the Far East, and it increased a feeling of misgiving toward Russia among Japanese civil and military leaders, who viewed the railroad as a potential threat to Japan's national security and expansion. This feeling is clearly expressed in two memoranda drawn up in 1890. In one, dated March 1890, Prime Minister Yamagata Aritomo called attention to the new Russian move as it related to the Korean situation and suggested that the Japanese government accelerate the building of Japan's military strength, make diplomatic overtures seeking cooperation from Great Britain and Germany, in a joint effort to check Russian expansion, and cooperate with the Chinese government to oppose Russian imperialism.

Another is a memorandum written by Foreign Minister Aoki Shūzō on May 15, 1890. Aoki argued that the construction of the Siberian railroad amounted to a real buildup of Russian military strength in Siberia that would endanger Japan's safety. He recommended that Japan and China cooperate to forestall Russian expansion and to expel Russian power from eastern Siberia. He also urged Japan to approach the British and the Germans to ask for their cooperation against Russian expansion.

The rising wariness of the Japanese leaders toward the Russian advance in the east did not, however, lead to the implementation of an anti-Russian policy as suggested in the above memoranda. In fact, the intensification of Japan's conflict with China over the stakes in Korea obliged Japan to give up the idea of cooperating with China against Russia and instead to seek Russian understanding in the increasingly likely event of an armed clash with China.

The intervention of the three powers, Russia, France, and Germany, in April 1895 at the end of the Sino-Japanese War, requiring Japan to renounce its recently acquired territorial rights in the Liaotung Peninsula, aroused an intense feeling of national indignation among the Japanese people. Popular resentment was especially directed toward Russia, which was perceived as the initiator of the affair.

Within the circle of Japanese decision-makers, three alternative responses to this challenge were considered: 1) to ignore the demand and proceed to the conclusion of the peace treaty as agreed to between Japan and China; 2) to submit the matter to an international conference to be deliberated; or 3) to meet the demand to give up Japan's foothold in the Liaotung Peninsula. Foreign Minister Mutsu Munemitsu, looking forward to securing the diplomatic support of Britain, the United States, and Italy, and seeing the possibility of playing off the French and Germans against the Russians, stood for rejection of the demand. Prime Minister Itō was inclined toward holding an international conference, despite the strong opposition of the foreign minister. Failure to receive a favorable answer from the British government made Mutsu's stand untenable, and the final decision to renounce the right to perpetual occupation of the Liaotung Peninsula, except for its southern part, was reached at an Imperial Conference on April 29, 1895. When Russia stood firm in its original demand, the Japanese government, not aware that the Russian military demonstration was a bluff, retreated further and gave up its right to hold any part of the Liaotung Peninsula.

The Triple Intervention brought to the surface the basic conflict in the objectives Japan and Russia were trying to achieve on the continent. In addition, it intensified the widespread anti-Russian feeling among the Japanese public. Nevertheless, Japan's decision-makers did not press for war. Realizing that Japan was militarily too weak and diplomatically too isolated for that, they decided to follow a conciliatory policy and look for a modus vivendi with the Russians.

The attempt to reach an agreement with the Russians was first sought on the Korean question. Military victory over China did not bring the settlement of the Korean problem Japan desired. The Russians took the place of the Chinese in Korea. The struggle between the pro-Japanese party and the pro-Russian party became intense in 1895 and erupted in the murder of Queen Min by Japanese intrigue in October of that year; her death was followed by the assassination of Premier Kim Hong-jip (also known as Kim Koeng-jip), leader of the pro-Japanese party, and the flight of King Kojong into the Russian legation in February 1896.

In a letter that spring, Mutsu Munemitsu, who was to head the Foreign Ministry once again in April 1896, referred to two alternative courses open to Japan: if Russia were to attempt to extend the Trans-Siberian Railway into the Liaotung Peninsula or to turn Korea into a protectorate, Japan should strongly counter these steps, even if it meant resorting to war; or alternatively, if Russia were to take such steps, Japan should refrain from going beyong lodging diplomatic protest and instead should concentrate its energy on building up the nation's strength at home. Mutsu favored the latter course. Komura Jutarō, the Japanese minister to Korea, also outlined alternatives. He thought they were: 1) to press Japan's own solution on the Korean government without regard for the intentions of other countries; 2) to find a settlement by consultations with other countries concerned with Korean affairs; 3) to seek a modus vivendi with the Russian government as to the Korean problem. Of these, like Mutsu, he seemed to prefer the third course.

The feasibility of Komura's second alternative, a multilateral agreement, was probed, but when the British government made clear its intention not to get involved in Korean affairs, the Japanese government decided to search for a modus vivendi with the Russians. The first effort in this direction took the form of talks between Komura and Weber, the Russian minister to Korea, in Seoul, which resulted in the signing on May 14, 1896, of a joint memorandum. This agreement stipulated that both countries were to advise the Korean king to return to his own palace, that Japan was entitled to maintain a limited number of military police to safeguard its telegraph line between Pusan and Seoul, and that each country was entitled to maintain an equal number of its own troops at several places to protect its nationals and its legation against attack by the Koreans.

The second effort took the form of higher-level talks at St. Petersburg between Yamagata and Russian Foreign Minister Lobanov, which resulted in the agreement of June 9, 1896. There was a controversy within the Japanese government concerning the sending of Yamagata to the Russian capital, and Prime Minister Itō was at first inclined to assume the responsibility himself. Nishi Tokujirō, Japanese minister to Russia, was against the appointment of the special envoy and tendered his resignation in protest. On the other hand, Mutsu favored the plan and set forth his own idea for an agreement.

At the start of the talks, Yamagata proposed his own plan to Lobanov to the effect that both countries should divide Korea into two spheres of influence, the line of division to be the thirty-eighth parallel of latitude; this was rejected by Lobanov. Lobanov's insistence that Russia was entitled to train Korean troops threatened to disrupt the conference, but an agreement was finally reached by which both parties pledged to undertake joint efforts to reform Korean internal politics and to extend military and financial assistance on the basis of mutual consultation. The agreement contained a secret convention which stipulated that each party had the right to maintain a limited number of soldiers in Korea necessary to safeguard its nationals and legation from attack by the Koreans, and to send additional forces in the event of political disturbances, provided that there be left an unoccupied zone between the forces of the two countries.

The Yamagata-Lobanov agreement did not, however, bring the competition between the two countries in Korea to a halt. In disregard of the objection Yamagata had voiced at the talks, the Russian government proceeded to send army officers to Seoul in the summer of 1896 to reorganize the Korean army. Russian economic activities in north Korea also were gaining ground during the period 1896–97, as was first demonstrated by a concession the Russians acquired to exploit the timber and mineral resources on the Korean bank of the Yalu River. The Japanese decision-makers viewed the Russian penetration into Korea with considerable misgiving. In the meantime, the Russians were also stepping up their activities in Manchuria, capitalizing on the secret agreement they had made with the Chinese in 1896. To achieve their long-cherished desire to gain an ice-free port on the Pacific, the Russians sent warships to Port Arthur at the end of 1897 and then demanded long-term leases at Dairen and Port Arthur in the beginning of 1898.

The intensification of the Russian drive toward Manchuria, along with their increased activities in Korea, led the Japanese decision-makers to envision the possibility of dealing with the Russians upon a new basis. In place of the old idea that Japan and Russia should either establish joint control in Korea or divide it into spheres of influence, a new concept began to gain acceptance among Japan's leaders, that of seeking a modus vivendi with Russia on the basis of an "exchange policy," meaning that Russia would recognize Japan's freedom of action in Korea and in return Japan would regard Manchuria as lying outside Japanese interests. This new policy toward Russia, strongly supported by Prime Minister Itō and Foreign Minister Nishi Tokujirō and endorsed by such leading statesmen as Yamagata and Inoue Kaoru, received formal approval at a cabinet meeting in March 1898.

Foreign Minister Nishi immediately explored this new proposal with Rosen, the Russian minister in Tokyo. The Russian government, however, was not prepared to commit itself to abandoning its hold in Korea. It rejected Japan's exchange proposal. On the other hand, the talks between Nishi and Rosen resulted in the Nishi-Rosen agreement of April 25, 1898, which stipulated that the Russian government would not obstruct the development of commercial and industrial relations between Japan and Korea. The Japanese decision-makers thus had to satisfy themselves with securing Russian recognition of the preponderance of Japan's economic interests in Korea instead of a more exclusive sphere of influence.

Yamagata memorandum, March 1890:

Ōyama, "Yamagata Aritomo ikensho" (1957).

Aoki memorandum, May 15, 1890:

Japan, Gaimushō (Foreign Ministry), *Nihon gaikō bunsho*, XXIII (1952), 538–43.

Japanese decision-making and the Trans-Siberian Railway:

Itō and Hiratsuka, *Hisho ruisan: gaikō hen*, Vol. III (1935).

Triple Intervention, 1895:

Mutsu, *Hakushaku Mutsu Munemitsu ikō* (1929), contains an extremely valuable memoir, the *Kenkenroku*, for studying the decision-making process immediately following the Triple Intervention. Written in 1896 but not published until 1929 as part of this study, the *Kenkenroku* represents a rare case in the history of Japanese foreign policy when a foreign minister left a detailed account of the course of talks among policy-makers. It also gives an insight into Mutsu's definition or value perception of the situation. Accounts based on the *Kenkenroku* include:

Fukaya, *Nisshin sensō to Mutsu gaikō: Mutsu Munemitsu no "Kenkenroku"* (1940), is based entirely on Mutsu's memoir.

Shinobu, *Mutsu gaikō: Nisshin sensō no gaikō shiteki kenkyū* (1935), first published as *Nisshin sensō* (1934), is an outstanding work that utilizes the *Kenkenroku* and other sources. Shinobu contends that Mutsu took a firm position concerning the conditions for peace on the basis of his estimate of the domestic situation.

Diplomacy following the demands of the three powers:

Abe, "Nisshin kōwa to sangoku kanshō" (1961).

Japan, Gaimushō (Foreign Ministry), *Nihon gaikō bunsho*, XXVIII/2 (1953), brings to light some aspects of Mutsu's diplomacy, especially his efforts to enlist assistance from Britain, the United States, and Italy and to play off the Germans and French against the Russians.

Pooley, *The Secret Memoirs of Count Tadasu Hayashi* (1915), is of value for its account of the negotiations between the Japanese Foreign Ministry and the ministers of the three powers in Tokyo. While Mutsu was ill, Hayashi directed the negotiations.

Search for a modus vivendi with Russia in 1896:

Itō and Hiratsuka, *Hisho ruisan: gaikō hen*,Vol. III(1935), is important for Mutsu's views on sending a special envoy to Russia, Nishi's report on the talks at Petrograd, and other information related to the Yamagata-Lobanov agreement.

Japan, Gaimushō (Foreign Ministry), *Komura gaikōshi* (2 vols., 1953), and *Nihon gaikō bunsho*, Vol. XXIX (1954), both furnish information relevant to how the Japanese government, following Komura's advice, took the course of agreement with the Russian government after making a fruitless effort to secure British intervention. These works also represent the best sources on the Komura-Weber and the Yamagata-Lobanov talks.

——— "Nichi-Ro kōshō shi" (1944), Vol. I, is the best account of Japan's efforts to realize a modus vivendi.

Keikōkai, *Tsuzuki Keiroku den* (1926), represents an important private source concerning the Yamagata mission. Little known as it is, it is significant for its accounts of the plan presented by Yamagata for a Russo-Japanese rapprochement and of the negotiations between Yamagata and Lobanov. Tsuzuki, son-in-law of the genrō Inoue, accompanied Yamagata on his trip to Russia.

Malozemoff, *Russian Far Eastern Policy, 1881–1904* (1958), is a valuable work on Russian Far Eastern policy and Russo-Japanese relations in the period leading up to the Russo-Japanese War. His account of the two agreements Japan made with Russia in 1896 is based largely on the Romanov work below.

Nagaoka, "Yamagata Aritomo no Rokoku haken to Nichi-Ro kyōtei" (1953), is the only special study to appear in Japanese about the efforts to realize a modus vivendi. It is especially interesting for information concerning

Yamagata's idea of dividing Korea into two areas where each of the parties could send their forces and the proposal's subsequent rejection by the Russian government.

Romanov, *Rossiia v Man'chzhurii, 1892–1906* (1928), was one of the first scholars to point out that Yamagata's original idea was to divide Korea along the thirty-eighth parallel and that this was turned down by Lobanov. He argues that the real significance of the agreements for Japan lay in the fact that Russia agreed thereafter not to give Korea separate advice and aid of a financial and military nature. This work has been translated into English by Susan Wilbur Jones as *Russia in Manchuria, 1892–1906* (1952). The postwar edition of the book in Russian is known as *Ocherki diplomaticheskoi istorii Russko-Iaponskoi voiny, 1895–1907* (1947).

Tokutomi, *Kōshaku Yamagata Aritomo den* (1933), Vol. III, relates how Yamagata was chosen as special envoy to Russia in spite of Itō's desire to assume responsibility for the negotiations.

Nishi-Rosen agreement, April 25, 1898:

Itō, *Katō Takaaki* (1929), Vol. II, is useful for its account of the objections of Minister Katō in London to the rapprochement policy.

Japan, Gaimushō (Foreign Ministry), *Nihon gaikō bunsho*, XXXI/1 (1954), 109–85, is the most relevant source. It reveals that the Russian government took the initiative for negotiations in January 1898.

Maejima, "Nisshin Nichi-Ro sensō ni okeru tai-Kan seisaku" (1961), reveals the influence of two pro-Russian elder statesmen, Itō and Inoue, on the plan to exchange Manchuria for Korea.

Malozemoff, *Russian Far Eastern Policy, 1881–1904* (1958), gives a good account of the topic. He assumes, however, that the initiative for the negotiations was taken by the Japanese government. Malozemoff explains the factors making for the rapprochement as follows: "The obscurity of political alignments, the numerical superiority of the Japanese army over the Russian forces in the Far East, and the delicate balance in naval forces, influenced Russia and Japan to act cautiously and pushed them toward a compromise on Korea."

Oka, "Nisshin sensō to tōji ni okeru taigai ishiki" (1954–55), deals with the perceptions Japan's national leaders in the 1890s had of their country's external setting and with the goal structure of national policy. Oka points out that the pro-Russian policy expounded by the leaders was connected with their idea of turning Japan's future course in a southward direction.

Yamaguchi, "Kenseitō naikaku no seiritsu to kyokutō jōsei" (1961), deals with the foreign policy of the Ōkuma cabinet, which succeeded the Itō cabinet in June 1898. He argues that the foreign policy of the Ōkuma cabinet was designed principally to secure a foothold on the continent, that it had the backing of Britain and America, and that it was essentially pro-Anglo-Saxon and anti-Russian in nature.

There still remain to be explored many aspects of Japanese-Russian relations and of Japan's Russian policy in the 1890s. Of these, Japan's search for a modus vivendi in the period 1896–98 represents perhaps the most interesting. In spite of its importance, there have been no extensive studies on the subject based on Japanese primary sources. Kajima, *Nihon gaikō seisaku no shiteki kōsatsu* (1951), originally published under the title *Teikoku gaikō no kihon seisaku* (1938), for example, is a general work that refers only to the substance of the Yamagata-Lobanov agreement. The other two writers of general works based on pre-World War II scholarship, Kiyosawa Kiyoshi and Shinobu Seizaburō, devoted but little attention to these events.

Kiyosawa, *Nihon gaikōshi* (2 vols., 1942).
Shinobu, *Kindai Nihon gaikōshi* (1942).

More light is needed on the process by which the Manchuria-Korea exchange policy was formulated and on the objectives the leaders were pursuing in this policy.

Since Yamagata's strong influence seems to have been important in the formulation of Japan's Russian policy in the period under review, his attitude toward Russia must be more carefully studied, particularly the shift in his position from advocating an anti-Russian alignment before 1895 to supporting a rapprochement with Russia after 1895.

More study is needed also of the perceptions of Japan's leaders as to Japanese military capability vis-a-vis Russia and its external setting. In addition, an analysis of changes in public attitudes toward Russia after 1895 might prove significant.

Shift to a Firm Stand, 1900–1903. The search for a modus vivendi was continued in 1900. Minister Komura Jutarō in St. Petersburg was instructed by the Yamagata cabinet to undertake negotiations with the Russian government in the summer of 1900. Moved by a plan to take advantage of the Boxer Rebellion to extend Japanese power in Fukien, Yamagata wanted to maintain tranquillity in Korea.

The rise of a new tendency in Japan's Russian policy can be observed after the plan to occupy Amoy failed to be implemented when Foreign Minister Aoki Shūzō addressed a memorandum to the emperor urging the necessity to send armed forces to Korea with full resolve to face an armed struggle with the Russians. This step was in line with the mounting demands of army officials and nationalist groups to occupy Korea with armed forces as a countermeasure to the armed occupation of southern Manchuria by the Russians. Aoki's action, however, aroused strong opposition among political leaders and caused the resignation of the Yamagata cabinet.

The firm stand against the Russians taken by Aoki was renewed by the next foreign minister, Katō Takaaki of the Itō cabinet. Katō had opposed a rapprochement based on an exchange of Manchuria for Korea and had advocated working with the British against the Russians. When the Russian minister in Tokyo approached Katō in January 1901, the latter stood firm in his opposition and insisted upon the withdrawal of Russian power from Korea. Katō further declined to acquiesce in Russia's advance into Manchuria following the Boxer Rebellion. In his view, Manchuria and Korea could not be separated from each other and preservation of the former was equally as important to Japanese interests as preservation of the latter.

When it was reported that the Russian government had pressed an agreement on the Chinese government demanding Russian control over Manchuria, Japanese leaders were greatly shocked. At a cabinet meeting on March 12 Katō advocated a strong response, recommending the adoption of one of the following alternatives: 1) send a protest openly and resort to arms if Russia did not make a favorable response; 2) begin the military occupation of Korea after declaring the purpose to be one of self-defense, in disregard of the existing Japanese-Russian understanding; or 3) send a protest and consider the next step after receiving the Russian response. The Japanese government finally decided to follow the most moderate course and on March 25 registered a protest with the Russian government asking that an international conference be held at Peking to discuss the whole matter. At the same time Katō pressed for rejection of Russian demands upon the Chinese government.

The Russians turned down the Japanese demand, and Japanese decision-makers were forced to consider the next step. A series of top-level meetings among government and military leaders was held from the end of March to the beginning of April. Although Katō, who favored a strong policy, was prepared to take up arms, Prime Minister Itō's argument for sending another strong protest prevailed during the meetings. It is not certain how the Russian government weighed the Japanese protest, but the retraction by Russia of its demands on China, on April 5, averted a showdown.

In support of the new hard line, various elements in the Japanese government became increasingly attracted to the idea of strengthening Japan's hand by seeking an alliance with Britain. Thus, an alliance with Britain or an entente with Russia were the alternatives pressed on Japanese decision-makers in the period from mid-1901 to the beginning of 1902. While Foreign Minister Komura of the Katsura Tarō cabinet continued Katō's firm stand against Russia and favored the idea of working with Britain for the common purpose of checking the Russian advance into the Far East, there were still some influential political figures who urged that a way be sought to live with Russia before committing Japan to the Western countries. A serious split of opinion among political leaders developed around this issue. Prime Minister Katsura and Foreign Minister Komura, supported by elder statesman Yamagata and most officials of the Foreign Ministry, wanted to take the path of British alignment. On the other hand, elder statesmen Itō and Inoue and Minister Kurino Shin'ichirō in St. Petersburg stood for a new entente with Russia instead of running the risk of a deterioration in Japan's relations with Russia.

Itō, with a view to realizing an entente with Russia, proceeded to St. Petersburg to submit a draft entente of his own devising to the Russian government on December 4, 1901. The Japanese government, however, did not see the likelihood of reaching an agreement with Russia on the conditions they desired and finally chose to conclude an alliance with Britain. The Anglo-Japanese alliance was signed on January 30, 1902.

Japan's leaders did not intend by the new alignment to close the door to further negotiations with the Russians. Instead, they hoped it would strengthen their bargaining position, enabling them to extract the concessions that Russia had hitherto withheld. In November 1902 Foreign Minister Komura instructed Minister Kurino to start the new negotiations and informed him of the essential points he hoped would form the basis of an agreement. In the meantime, Kurino was so eager to achieve an entente that he had already begun talks with the Russian foreign minister in September, presenting his own draft of an agreement, without a governmental instruction. But the talks at St. Petersburg did not bear fruit, and relations between the two countries became more strained.

Primary source:

Japan, Gaimushō (Foreign Ministry), *Nihon gaikō bunsho*, Vols. XXXIV–XXXV (1957), constitute the most important primary sources. The volumes contain several telegrams to Katō from Minister Komura and Minister Chinda Sutemi concerning the Russian proposal for the neutralization of Korea, as well as several telegrams reporting German and British attitudes in support of a free hand for Japan in Korea in 1901. They also provide a detailed account of the opinions exchanged among decision-makers over the choice between the two alternatives, alliance with Britain or entente with Russia.

General:

Kuzuu, *Tōa senkaku shishi kiden*, Vol. I (1933), is useful for an understanding of the strong policy toward Russia advocated in 1900.

Policy related to internal developments:

Fujimura, "Gumbi kakuchō to kaikyū mujun no tenkai" (1959).
—— "Tai-Sen seisaku no tenkan" (1959). In these two articles Fujimura contends that fundamental to the change in Japan's Russian policy was mounting internal unrest and increasing financial difficulties arising from social contradictions inherent in the Japanese political structure.

Role of Katō Takaaki:

Itō, *Katō Takaaki* (2 vols., 1929), is a valuable source concerning Katō's firm stand.
Maejima, "Ro-Shin mitsuyaku to Katō gaikō" (1960), places Katō's firm stand toward Russia in the context of a popular movement in Japan manipulated by the National Alliance (Kokumin Dōmeikai) and of pressure from the Kenseihontō. Beyond this, he suggests a connection between Katō's policy and the interests of the monopolistic bourgeoisie.
Nakayama, "Hokushin jihen go ni okeru Chōsen mondai to Manshū mondai no setsugō" (1959), tries to make it clear that it was not until 1901, when Katō was in charge of the Foreign Ministry, that Japanese decision-makers saw the Manchurian problem as being closely connected to the Korean problem. He also asserts that Katō tried, but failed, to take advantage of the conclusion of the Anglo-German agreement in October 1900 to align Britain and Germany with Japan in order to forestall Russian control over Manchuria.

Japanese naval supremacy:

Gal'perin, *Anglo-Iaponskii soiuz, 1902–1921 gg* (1947).

Alliance with Britain or entente with Russia. Memoranda:

Hayashi, "Nichi-Ei dōmei kyōyaku teiketsu shimatsusho ichibu sōfu no ken," a report to the Foreign Ministry, constitutes the most significant source concerning the negotiations between Hayashi and the British Foreign Office. Pooley, *The Secret Memoirs of Count Tadasu Hayashi* (1915), is based on this report.

Ishii, "Nichi-Ei dōmei kyōyaku teiketsu shimatsusho ichibu sōfu no ken: fuki Nichi-Ei kyōtei kōshō shimatsu," also is important.

Itō Hirobumi, "Nichi-Ei dōmei to Nichi-Ro kyōshō," in Hiratsuka, *Zoku Itō Hirobumi hiroku* (1930), pp. 1–59, is valuable for the account of Itō's talks with government leaders and his negotiations with the Russian government.

Itō and Hiratsuka, *Hisho ruisan: zassan* (1936), II, 299–302, has an interesting memorandum, "Ei-Doku kyōshō to Nichi-Ro dōmei," which was submitted to the Itō cabinet in 1900 with a view to urging the cabinet to conclude an alliance with Russia in order to achieve the ultimate goal of extending Japan's control over Fukien and Korea.

Yamagata Aritomo, "Tōyō dōmei ron," in Tokutomi, *Kōshaku Yamagata Aritomo den* (1933), III, 494–96, was drawn up in April 1901. Yamagata expounds on the necessity for Japan to join with Britain and Germany to check the Russian advance.

Biographies:

Inoue Kaoru Kō Denki Hensankai, *Segai Inoue kō den*, Vol. V (1934).

Japan, Gaimushō (Foreign Ministry), *Komura gaikōshi* (1953), Vol. I.

Tokutomi, *Kōshaku Katsura Tarō den* (1917), Vol. I.

—— *Kōshaku Yamagata Aritomo den* (1933), Vol. III.

Studies:

Chang, *The Anglo-Japanese Alliance* (1931), is a solid work.

Dennis, *The Anglo-Japanese Alliance* (1923), along with Shinobu's book listed below, is a pioneering work on the subject.

Gal'perin, *Anglo-Iaponskii soiuz, 1902–1921 gg* (1947), is the most comprehensive work written on the subject after World War II.

Imai, "Nichi-Ei dōmei kōshō ni okeru Nihon no shuchō" (1957).

—— "Nichi-Ei dōmei to Kurino Shin'ichirō" (1962). In these two articles, Imai tries to make the point that there was no basic divergence of views between the pro-British group and the pro-Russian group among Japanese leaders. Both sides agreed on the basic objective to be pursued—to secure a free hand for Japan in Korea. The controversy was related only to the strategic problem of how best to achieve this objective. Another point made by Imai is that the government leaders who advocated the bond with Britain did not reject the idea of seeking a rapprochement with Russia after Japan formed an alliance with Britain.

Malozemoff, *Russian Far Eastern Policy, 1881–1904* (1958), makes the point that the Russian minister in Tokyo, Izvolskii, took the initiative to achieve a Russo-Japanese entente; this work is useful for the talks between Itō and Lamsdorff and the Russian response to Itō's proposal.

Murashima, "Nichi-Ei dōmei to Man-Sen mondai" (1959), reaches the same conclusion as Imai. Basing his work on British and Japanese documents, Murashima asserts that through the alliance with Britain, Japanese decision-makers intended to strengthen Japan's position vis-a-vis Russia in the coming negotiations over Korea in order to obtain a free hand in Korea. He thus takes into account the relationship between the Anglo-Japanese and the Russo-Japanese negotiations in the fall of 1901.

Nish, *The Anglo-Japanese Alliance* (1966).

Shinobu, *Nidai gaikō no shinsō* (1928), written on the basis of partial use of the archives of the Foreign Ministry and, as such, a pioneering work, still is useful.

There are several research topics in connection with Japan's Russian policy from 1900 to 1903 to be more thoroughly explored. The issue confronting the Yamagata cabinet in the summer of 1900 as a result of the outbreak of the Boxer Rebellion, that is, the choice of two alternatives—active policy in Fukien or active policy in Korea, in other words, southern advance or northern advance—constitutes the most interesting topic. On this subject, see:

Nish, "Japan's Indecision during the Boxer Disturbances" (1961). Nish argues that the most crucial factor affecting Japan's decision to drop the southern project and take a more cautious attitude toward the northern project in Korea was the intimation that Russia was going to withdraw its troops into Manchuria. He further points out that "disagreements over Korea and south China contributed to the disunity of the ministry and to its downfall."

What made Japan's Russian policy shift to a hard line in 1901? What powerful figures supported Katō's stand from behind the scenes? Although as noted there have been some works treating this question, the subject requires more careful study. In this connection, too, there is the important question of why Prime Minister Itō selected Katō as foreign minister when Katō envisioned a foreign policy rather different from Itō's.

There are conflicting views concerning the initiative in January 1901 for the proposal on neutralization of Korea. Gal'perin ascribes the initiative to Korea, and Malozemoff to Japan. The Foreign Ministry's *Nichi-Ro kōshō shi* states that Korean Minister Chō Byong-sik in Tokyo approached the

Japanese government in the summer of 1900 with the idea of neutralizing Korea and that Russian Minister Izvolskii then took up the matter in his talk with Katō in December 1900.

As to the Itō mission to Russia in November 1901, there are still many points left unclarified. How well informed were the government leaders before Itō left concerning his intention to seek an agreement with Russia? Did they consciously use the Itō mission as a maneuver in negotiating with the British?

War and Peace, 1903–1905. The conclusion of the Anglo-Japanese alliance seemed to check the Russian advance toward the east. In an agreement with the Chinese government in April 1902, the Russians pledged to evacuate their forces from Manchuria within two years in three successive withdrawals to occur at six-month intervals. However, this turned out to be a passing phase. In April 1903, when the time limit for the second evacuation came, the Russians not only failed to carry out the terms of the Russo-Chinese agreement but also entered upon a new venture in north Korea by obtaining lumber concessions and putting forces along the Russian-Korean border.

Japanese policy-makers convened at least three important top-level meetings to consider the steps Japan should take. The first was held on March 15 and was attended by the five genrō, namely, Yamagata, Itō, Ōyama, Inoue, and Matsukata Masayoshi. The second was held on April 21, with Prime Minister Katsura, Foreign Minister Komura, Itō, and Yamagata attending. Four ministers—Katsura, Komura, Army Minister Terauchi Masatake, and Navy Minister Yamamoto Gonnohyōe—and the five genrō attended the last session on June 23, which met in the emperor's presence. The basic policy decided on, which the Japanese government would follow to meet the new Russian advance, was as follows: 1) while Japan recognized the superior position of Russian rights in Manchuria, it could not permit Russian forces to stay there; 2) Japan claimed preeminent rights for itself in Korea and could not allow the Russians to extend their influence there; and 3) Japan would enter into negotiations with the Russian government to reach a final settlement regarding the question of Manchuria and Korea.

While the elder statesmen were deliberating the appropriate course of action, pressures for war were building up within Japan. In May 1903 a group called the Kogetsukai, organized by middle-grade officers of both the army and the navy and officials of the Foreign Ministry, met to exert pressure on the decision-makers to take up arms. On June 22 General Ōyama Iwao, chief of the General Staff, presented a memorandum to the emperor which explained the army's stand in the following way: Japan should realize an early solution of the Korean question; it now had the advantage from a strategic point of view and a few years' delay would place Russia in a superior position. In addition to increasing pressure from officials within the government, there was a movement among the Japanese public in support of a strong Russian policy. The government leaders, in order to watch the progress of the diplomatic negotiations, however, took time before reaching a final decision.

Japanese-Russian talks at the last stage prior to the war were broached by a statement submitted to the Russian government by Minister Kurino on July 31, 1903. The progress of the negotiations, first in St. Petersburg and then in Tokyo, failed to narrow the gap existing between the basic stands of the two countries. By the end of December 1903, Japanese decision-makers, convinced of the hopelessness of the talks, had almost decided to resort to arms to escape the stalemate. The final decision to go to war was made on January 12, 1904.

In spite of initial military success in the field, Japanese military and civil leaders were not optimistic about total victory over tsarist Russia. They were all aware that the Japanese economy was incapable of carrying the heavy burden of prolonged war and that diplomatic weapons should be employed along with military efforts to bring an early termination of the war. When the war began, General Kodama Gentarō, chief of staff of the expeditionary forces in Manchuria, expressed his outlook for the war in the following way: "There is a good chance for Japan to win six victories out of ten on the battlefield, and if that is the case, some country can be expected to step forward to offer good offices."[4] Conscious of the intrinsic vulnerability of their military and economic strength, civil and military leaders were concerned with the problem of when and how to terminate the war.

In July 1904, before the first large battle was fought in Liaoyang, Foreign Minister Komura presented a memorandum to the prime minister that

[4]Kaneko Kentarō, *Nichi-Ro sensō hiroku* (1929), pp. 27–28.

pointed out the necessity of studying peace problems and expressed his own view on the terms for peace. Prime Minister Katsura was also interested in a peace treaty at this time and set forth his ideas regarding it. At a cabinet meeting in August there was talk about war aims and the conditions for peace, and it was decided to pursue the following four objectives: 1) to preserve the integrity of Manchuria and Korea; 2) to obtain new concessions in the area of Korea, Manchuria, and Siberia; 3) to establish Japan's preponderance in China; and 4) to extend Japan's protectorate over Korea and include Manchuria in its sphere of interest.

To terminate the war by diplomacy, Japan's leaders faced a variety of alternatives, including: 1) holding an international conference of the powers concerned in order to discuss the conditions for peace; 2) counting on mediation by one of the countries allied with the belligerents— Britain and France; 3) asking for the good offices of a neutral power, especially the United States; or 4) negotiating directly with Russia. The first alternative failed to rally much support from Japanese decision-makers, who still held strong memories of the Triple Intervention. The means the Japanese government first favored was direct negotiations, and an approach was made in July 1904 by the Japanese minister in Britain, Hayashi Tadasu, to Count Witte, who was visiting Berlin. There is no account available of further developments following Hayashi's peace-feeler. For a time, some leaders were inclined to seek mediation, particularly in April 1905, when the French government expressed its willingness to serve, but the choice finally fell upon the third alternative, seeking the good offices of the United States.

The Japanese government began to consider the possibility of United States mediation in the early stages of the war, and after the capture of Port Arthur early in January 1905 it began to feel out President Theodore Roosevelt's views through Japan's minister in Washington as well as through a special envoy, Kaneko Kentarō. Following Japan's victory in the battle of Mukden, which began on March 10 and lasted for several days, the government engaged in serious discussions concerning peace and the resort to diplomatic means to achieve it. This was due to an increasing awareness among political leaders, especially such elder statesmen as Itō, Yamagata, and Inoue, of the nation's critical economic situation. Japan had almost exhausted its war resources and was in no position to continue the war for another year. When General Kodama came to Tokyo to inform

Japanese decision-makers of the difficulty of gaining additional victories on the field, they were brought to realize even more strongly the necessity for making peace overtures in the near future. Kodama's appearance was followed by a letter from Ōyama, commander-in-chief of the expeditionary forces, addressed to Yamagata, indicating the necessity for taking some diplomatic action.

A series of heated discussions developed among decision-makers about the steps to be taken toward early termination of the war, producing a split of opinion between the high government authorities and the elder statesmen. Finally an agreement was reached, and the cabinet on April 21, 1905, decided upon the necessary conditions for peace. At the same time it was agreed that Japan would ask President Roosevelt for his good offices, and on May 31, 1905, an official step for the request was taken.

President Roosevelt brought the belligerent countries together on August 9, 1905, at Portsmouth, New Hampshire. A deadlock ensued over Japan's demand for two concessions, the cession of Sakhalin and the payment of an indemnity. The Japanese government could either insist upon its original demands and be prepared for a breakdown of the peace conference, or withdraw its demands to save it. At an Imperial Conference on August 28, the Japanese government chose the latter course based on the strong advice of President Roosevelt to concede plus the request of the high military authorities to conclude a peace at any cost. Just after the Imperial Conference was over, the Japanese government received new information to the effect that the Russian government was prepared to cede the southern half of Sakhalin, and the Japanese government sent last-minute revised instructions to its delegate. The treaty was finally signed on September 5, 1905.

Decision for war:

Japan, Gaimushō (Foreign Ministry), *Komura gaikōshi* (1953), Vol. I, is the most important source for the activities of Foreign Minister Komura.
—— *Nihon gaikō bunsho*, Vols. XXXVI and XXXVII (1960), are the most relevant sources for the study of Japan's decision to go to war.
Katsura Tarō Papers, a manuscript collection at the Kensei Shiryō Shitsu, National Diet Library, Tokyo, cites letters exchanged between Katsura and Yamagata revealing that, as late as December 1903, Yamagata had been hesitant to take up arms against Russia. The papers in this collection and materials in Tokutomi, *Kōshaku Katsura Tarō den* (1917), Vol. II, show that Prime Minister

Katsura took a more positive attitude than the genrō concerning war policy. *Katsura Tarō kankei bunsho mokuroku* is a catalog of the collection.

Ko Hakushaku Yamamoto Kaigun Taishō Denki Hensankai, *Hakushaku Yamamoto Gonnohyōe den*, Vol. II (1938), is useful for an account of the Imperial Conferences of June 23, 1903, and January 12, 1904. Yamamoto was navy minister and acted for the prime minister at the latter conference.

Biographies of elder statesmen:

Inoue Kaoru Kō Denki Hensankai, *Segai Inoue kō den*, Vol. V (1934).

Ono Sanenobu, *Gensui kōshaku Ōyama Iwao* (1935), is the source for the memorandum Ōyama presented to the emperor on June 22, 1903.

—— *Gensui kōshaku Ōyama Iwao nempu* (1935).

Shumpō Kō Tsuishōkai, *Itō Hirobumi den* (1940), Vol. III.

Tokutomi, *Kōshaku Yamagata Aritomo den* (1933), Vol. III.

Attitude of the army:

Fukushima Shōgun Jiseki Kankōkai, *Fukushima Yasumasa shōgun jiseki* (1941), is useful for an account of a memorandum written by General Fukushima, director of the Second Section of the Army General Staff. He estimated that Japan's military strength at the time was such as to be able to challenge the Russian army with some chance of victory but that it would be inadequate to do so later. He also asserted that unless Japan could settle the Korean problem at once, it would be unable to curb the Russian advance in the near future.

Activities of the Kogetsukai:

Kuroita, *Fukuda taishō den* (1937), contains materials concerning the Kogetsukai. Kuzuu, *Tōa senkaku shishi kiden*, Vol. I (1933), refers extensively to the activities of the Kogetsukai. The book thus is a useful source for learning about the strong policy toward Russia expounded by middle-grade officers in the army and navy and supported by the radical nationalist movement outside the government.

Comprehensive studies of developments leading to the war:

Malozemoff, *Russian Far Eastern Policy, 1881–1904* (1958), makes the point that the Russian government adopted the "new course" in the period from February to August 1903 with "the unmistakable objectives of abandoning the Yalu enterprise, lest it incur the antagonism of Japan and thus prejudice future negotiations regarding Korea as a whole, of retreating from Manchuria gracefully, but as slowly as possible, to the position held before the Boxer Rebellion, and of trying to obtain certain guarantees." He further states that "the history of the negotiations is still of importance in substantiating the fact that the 'new course' of Russian policy was still in force and that the conduct of the negotiations was never dominated by Alexeev and the Bezobrazob 'group.' "

Studies in agreement with Malozemoff's thesis include:

Krupinski, *Russland und Japan* (1940).

Lensen, "Japan and Tsarist Russia—the Changing Relationships, 1875–1917" (1962), states that "the Russians, who wished to keep the Japanese out of north Korea, away from their own frontier, were willing to go on negotiating, the Japanese not. Fearing that time was against them, the Japanese struck while striking was good."

Romanov, *Rossiia v Man'chzhurii, 1892–1906* (1928), is the most extensive study of the historical background of the Russo-Japanese War. The work was based on the archives of the Russian Foreign Office and Finance Ministry. This is an exhaustive treatment of Russian policy relating to the causes of the war, with special reference to the active role Witte played in the process, but it pays scant attention to Japanese policy. The post-World War II edition of the book, *Ocherki diplomaticheskoi istorii Russko-Iaponskoi voiny, 1895–1907* (1947), puts more emphasis on what the author terms the aggressive, plundering nature of Japanese imperialistic policy. The rewriting, however, was chiefly designed to offer a new version of Russian Far Eastern policy during the period under review, identifying the true instigators of Russian aggressive policy as the bourgeoisie, who sought a new market, and the most reactionary landlords.

Negotiations with Russia prior to the war:

Hiratsuka, *Shishaku Kurino Shin'ichirō den* (1942), is valuable for its account of Kurino's handling of the negotiations; it also indicates his pro-Russian view.

—— *Zoku Itō Hirobumi hiroku* (1930), pp. 153–68, contains Itō's memoir, "Nichi-Ro kōshō haretsu no temmatsu," concerning negotiations with the Russian government.

Japan, Gaimushō (Foreign Ministry), "Nichi-Ro kōshō shi" (1944), Vol. I, is the most extensive account of Russo-Japanese negotiations prior to the war.

Ōhata, "Nichi-Ro kaisen gaikō (1961).

—— "Nichi-Ro sensō to Man-Kan mondai" (2 parts, 1958). In these two articles, based on the Foreign Ministry archives and the Katsura Tarō papers, Ōhata states that Foreign Minister Komura was ready to take up arms if the negotiations should fail (see the instructions he had H. W. Denison, a foreign adviser to the Foreign Ministry, draw up after the Imperial Conference of June 23, 1904, to be sent to Minister Kurino) and that on December 16 Prime Minister Katsura told the other decision-makers that the negotiations were hopeless.

The character of the Russo-Japanese War:

Shimomura, "Nichi-Ro sensō to Manshū shijō" (1956).

—— "Nichi-Ro sensō no seikaku" (1957).

—— "Kaisen gaikō" (1959).

In these articles, based on the archives of the Foreign Ministry, Shimomura is preoccupied with defining the character of the Russo-Japanese War. He argues that Japan was chiefly concerned with keeping an "open door" in Manchuria, deterring the Russians from establishing monopolistic control there, and preventing them from utilizing it as a strategic base for advancing into Korea.

Shinobu, "Nichi-Ro sensō no kenkyū shi, I: Nihon" (1959), examines certain other questions that have concerned Japanese historians. Was the war imperialistic or nationalistic? And was Korea or Manchuria the market at stake for Japanese capitalism?

Studies of the movement for war among the Japanese public:

Fujimura, "Kaisen yoron no kōzō" (1959).

Somura, "Nihon no shiryō kara mita Nichi-Ro sen zen no Manshū-Shiberia mondai" (1958). Both studies treat the movement among the Japanese public as a force agitating for a more decisive policy toward Russia.

Events leading to peace overtures:

Japan, Foreign Ministry, *Komura gaikōshi* (1953), Vol. II.

—— *Nichi-Ro sensō*, Vol. V (1960), supplement to *Nihon gaikō bunsho*, Vol. XXXVII–XXXVIII, is most important for accounts of the Japanese approach to the American government, the resolutions at cabinet meetings, and the letters exchanged among civil and military leaders.

—— *Nihon gaikō nempyō narabi ni shuyō bunsho* (1965), Vol. I.

Kaneko, *Nichi-Ro sensō hiroku* (1929), is the memoir of the man sent to the United States to seek President Roosevelt's good offices.

Tokutomi, *Kōshaku Katsura Tarō den* (1917), Vol. II.

—— *Kōshaku Yamagata Aritomo den* (1933), Vol. III.

Japanese-American relations during the war:

Dennett, *Roosevelt and the Russo-Japanese War* (1925).

Ueda, "Nichi-Ro sensō to Rūzuveruto" (1956). Both works focus on Japan and the United States during the war and on President Roosevelt's move for good offices.

Portsmouth Conference. Proceedings:

Japan, Gaimushō (Foreign Ministry), "Nichi-Ro kōshō shi" (1944), Vol. II, is the most extensive Japanese account of the conference.

Korostovetz, *Pre-War Diplomacy: The Russo-Japanese Problem* (1920), a detailed account of the proceedings of the conference, is based upon the diary of a member of the Russian delegation.

Last-minute revised Japanese instructions:

Ishii, *Gaikō yoroku* (1930).

Shidehara, *Gaikō gojūnen* (1951). Each of these diplomats, both of whom served in the Foreign Ministry at the time the Japanese government sent revised last-minute instructions to the delegation at Portsmouth, relates the episode in his memoir.

Some recent studies:

Ishida, "Pōtsumasu jōyaku to hoppō ryōdo mondai" (1962), is based on some of the materials published in the relevant volumes of *Nichi-Ro sensō*, Vol. V (1960), supplement to *Nihon gaikō bunsho*, Vols. XXXVII–XXXVIII.

Ogiso, "Pōtsumasu kōwa kaigi" (1959), is most valuable for an account of the attitudes of the powers toward the peace problem, of Roosevelt's moves, and of developments at the peace conference itself.

White, *The Diplomacy of the Russo-Japanese War* (1964).

Yoshimura, "Nichi-Ro kōwa mondai no ichi sokumen: Nihon no tai-Shin taido o chūshin ni" (1961), also is based on materials from *Nichi-Ro sensō*, Vol. V (1960), supplement to *Nihon gaikō bunsho*, Vols. XXXVII–XXXVIII.

Malozemoff and others have revealed that the Russian government, hoping to avert a showdown with Japan, was willing to take whatever steps were necessary to avoid war and during 1903 adopted the "new course" of abandoning economic interests in north Korea. This was not what Japanese decision-makers understood Russian intentions and moves to be; rather, Japanese leaders felt increasingly that, owing to the intensification of Russia's aggressive policy, Japan's national security was on the verge of being destroyed. How did this happen? Were there any deliberate efforts to distort the reality of Russian Far Eastern policy, or were there weaknesses of communication? This is an important issue to be explored in future research.

From the decision-making approach, many questions still remain to be more intensively studied. Among others, the question of the role played by the military in Japan's decision to go to war remains to be clarified. Would it not be possible to explore whether the strong views of middle-grade officers were reflected in the official stand taken by military leaders, which, in turn, shaped government policy? How did the leaders calculate the relative military strengths of Japan and Russia?

Gal'perin, *Anglo-Iaponskii soiuz, 1902–1921 gg* (1947), argues that the Japanese government entered into negotiations with Russia only to acquire a semblance of legality and justification for its subsequent attack on Russia. Although the records relevant to the Imperial Conference of June 23, 1903, where the decision to begin negotiations was made, do not support this thesis, what was the real intent of the Japanese government when it started the negotiations?

There is need to explore further why Japan turned from war to peace. There is good reason to believe that the reports presented by the high authorities in the field influenced Yamagata's judgment of the military situation considerably, and in turn acted as a decisive factor in Japan's moving toward a peace conference.

DRIFT TOWARD PARTNERSHIP, 1905–1917

Settlement of the Old Feud, 1905–1907: The First Russo-Japanese Entente. The military victory of Japan over Russia changed the structure of power politics in the Far East and marked the start of new relations between the two countries. Instead of long-standing conflict and struggle, there appeared a prospect of mutual respect for each other's interests in Manchuria. Japan's Russia policy after the war aimed first to remove the causes of future trouble between the two countries by defining the sphere of interest each country could claim and then to strengthen Japan's ties with Russia. This was done with a view to building a future bond between the two countries so that they might work together to safeguard their spheres of interest from economic encroachment by a third power, particularly the United States.

In the years following the victory, Japanese military leaders were concerned over the possibility of a war of revenge and felt the need to reach an understanding with Russia. Under their sponsorship, a top-level secret conference was held on May 22, 1906, with four government ministers, all the elder statesmen, and military leaders attending. They included Itō, Yamagata, Ōyama, Matsukata, Inoue, Saionji, Terauchi, Sakatani Yoshirō, Hayashi Tadasu, Saitō Makoto, Katsura, Yamamoto, and Kodama. The conference adopted a resolution providing that measures be taken immediately in Manchuria to prepare against Russian revenge and that, at the same time, efforts be made to win over Russia and cause it to forget the past.

In accord with this decision, the Army General Staff set to work to create a basic plan for Japan's national defense. The resulting "Imperial National Defense Policy," drawn up by Lieutenant-Colonel Tanaka Giichi and redrafted by Yamagata, was completed in 1907. Although this plan specified Russia as the main target of Japanese military preparedness, the Japanese army was eager to settle the old feud with the Russians and was prepared to reach an understanding with them. The elder statesmen were no less anxious than the army to bring about a reconciliation with the Russians, and it is said that "Prince Yamagata and Prince Itō, as soon as the treaty had been concluded, commenced working for the conclusion of a Russo-Japanese convention which would supplement the treaty of Portsmouth."[5]

But before the Japanese government had clearly formulated the terms it would seek in the new relationship, the Russians themselves proposed an agreement. The initiative was taken by Russian Foreign Minister A.P. Izvolskii in a talk with Japanese Ambassador to Russia Motono Ichirō in December 1906. This move seemingly reflected the new postwar orientation of Russian foreign policy toward the West, which required that relations with Japan be eased. In preparing their response, Japanese leaders found themselves divided. Itō, then resident-general in Korea, in particular had views at odds with those of others within the government. As a long-time protagonist of an entente, Itō was eager to accept the Russian proposal, which placed Outer Mongolia within Russia's sphere of interest. On the other hand, influential opinion within the government, especially within the Foreign Ministry, was reluctant to reach an agreement if it entailed recognizing the special status of Russia in Outer Mongolia. In addition to this another controversy arose between Itō and various government leaders over the clause regarding Korea. As a consequence, a number of messages were exchanged between Seoul and Tokyo before an understanding was reached, thanks to Yamagata's mediation.

The treaty was signed on July 30, 1907. It stipulated mutual recognition of each other's spheres of interest in Manchuria, Russian recognition of

[5] A.M. Pooley, ed., *The Secret Memoirs of Count Tadasu Hayashi* (1915), p. 231.

Japan's control over Korea, and Japanese recognition of Russia's special status in Outer Mongolia.

It is surprising how little attention this subject was given by Japanese scholars in the older general histories of diplomacy; for example:

Kajima, *Nihon gaikō seisaku no shiteki kōsatsu* (1951), first published as *Teikoku gaikō no kihon seisaku* (1938), notes the initiative on the Russian side and the pressure exerted by the British and French governments on the Japanese government but does not discuss what Japanese decision-makers understood the problem to be and how they acted on it.

Kiyosawa, *Nihon gaikōshi* (2 vols., 1942), ignores the entente entirely.

Shinobu, *Kindai Nihon gaikōshi* (1942), treats the problem in the same cursory manner as Kajima.

Standard biographies also are of little help. The following, for example, do not refer to the rapprochement at all:

Shumpō Kō Tsuishōkai, *Itō Hirobumi den* (3 vols., 1940).

Tokutomi, *Kōshaku Katsura Tarō den* (2 vols., 1917).

—— *Kōshaku Yamagata Aritomo den* (3 vols., 1933).

The few documentary collections and studies of value include:

Edwards, "The Far Eastern Agreement of 1907" (1954), is based on British and French documents.

Iswolski, *Au service de la Russie: Alexandre Iswolski, correspondance diplomatique, 1906–1911* (1937), focuses on Izvolskii's activities and makes some contribution in analyzing the role of French diplomacy in bringing about the Russo-Japanese entente, but it lacks information concerning the moves of Japanese decision-makers.

Japan, Gaimushō (Foreign Ministry), "Nichi-Ro kōshō shi" (1944), a valuable source, has a detailed account of the Russian proposal and the Japanese counterproposal and of the negotiations that followed leading to the conclusion of the treaty.

—— *Nihon gaikō bunsho*, XL/1 (1960), contains several documents not referred to in sources cited here; as yet no study has made use of this publication.

Matsumoto, *Kinsei Nihon gaikōshi kenkyū* (1942), was the first significant study of the rapprochement and revealed divisions of opinion among civil and military leaders concerning the appropriate response to the Russian proposal for an entente.

Nakayama, *Nichi-Ro sensō igo* (1957), emphasizes the role of French diplomacy in the process of reaching an entente.

Pooley, *The Secret Memoirs of Count Tadasu Hayashi* (1915), the memoirs of the then Japanese foreign minister, was the first important book containing information on the rapprochement. The Hayashi materials make it clear that Russian Foreign Minister Izvolskii was eager to come to an understanding with Japan and took up the matter with the Japanese ambassador, making allusions to articles by Dillon, the correspondent in St. Petersburg for the *Daily Telegraph*, which pointed out the usefulness of a Russo-Japanese entente. Pooley also notes the eagerness of Japanese statesmen immediately after the war to effect a rapprochement with Russia.

Price, *The Russo-Japanese Treaties of 1907–1916 concerning Manchuria and Mongolia* (1933), is the most useful of the books published following the disclosure by the Bolshevik government, shortly after the 1917 revolution, of the secret convention of the treaty. But Price did not have access to Japanese primary sources, and therefore his conclusions about the policy-making process within the Japanese government are faulty. He also wrongly assumes that the delay in the negotiations was caused by the difficulty of reaching an agreement concerning the demarcation of spheres of interest in Manchuria.

Siebert, *Entente Diplomacy and the World* (1921).

Tanaka, "Nichi-Ro kyōshō ron" (1956), points out that there was a strong desire on the Japanese as well as the Russian side for a rapprochement. He also presents a new account of the discussions at the conference of the genrō in 1907.

Yakhontoff, *Russia and the Soviet Union in the Far East* (1931).

What is the real meaning of the first Russo-Japanese entente? Was it a supplement to the Portsmouth Treaty for the purpose of enabling the two countries to coexist in Northeast Asia? Or did it signalize the first major step for the two countries to work together in an effort to counter a common rival that threatened their economic interests in this area? In this connection, the question of how Japanese decision-makers perceived the American threat to Japan's interests in Manchuria should be more carefully studied. It would be interesting to examine the process by which the American threat emerged and grew in the Japanese mind, overshadowing the Russian threat. It must be recalled here that there occurred a controversy between the army and the navy over the imaginary enemy against whom the Japanese national defense plan was to be made in 1907. The army looked upon Russia as the most likely enemy; the navy, upon the United States. The national defense plan gave emphasis to measures to cope with possible renewed conflict with Russia.

What made the Japanese Foreign Ministry take a rather cool attitude toward a rapprochement with Russia in 1907? There is scope for further research in the archives of the Foreign Ministry on the process by which the decision to conclude this treaty was reached.

Cooperation to Resist American Penetration, 1907–1912. The conclusion of the Russo-Japanese agreement, enabling the Russians to shift the emphasis of expansion from east to west and allowing the Japanese to dispel their apprehension over a war of revenge, had a favorable effect on Russo-Japanese relations. It was not the Russian drive eastward but rather the American economic advance in Manchuria in the late 1900s that gradually attracted the attention of Japanese policy-makers as a new barrier to their continental policy.

Discernment of the change in the roles being played by Russia and the United States led Japanese political leaders to consider the feasibility of working more closely with the Russians. In 1909 an attempt to explore the idea of collaboration with Russia was made by Itō, then president of the Privy Council, and a visit to Harbin was designed for the purpose of conferring with Russian Minister of Finance V.N. Kokovtsov. Itō's assassination prevented the meeting's taking place.

In July 1910 Russo-Japanese talks (provided direct impetus by the proposal made by U.S. Secretary of State Knox to neutralize the Manchurian railroads and form an international syndicate to extend a loan to China) gave rise to the second entente. This time Foreign Minister Komura took the initiative, seeking to consolidate the Japanese position in southern Manchuria. After getting approval at a cabinet meeting in March 1910, Komura entered into the negotiations with Russia and was successful in signing the second Russo-Japanese entente on July 4, 1910.

The essential points of the entente can be found in its secret convention: "Each of the two High Contracting Parties undertake not to hinder in any way the consolidation and further development of the special interests of the other Party. . . . In the event that these special interests should come to be threatened, the two High Contracting Parties will agree upon the measures to be taken with a view to common action or to the support to be accorded for the safeguarding and the defense of those interests."[6]

[6]Japan, Gaimushō (Foreign Ministry), *Nihon gaikō nempyō narabi ni shuyō bunsho* (1965), I, 336–37 (hereafter cited as *Nihon gaikō nempyō*).

Developments in Mongolia, occasioned by the overthrow of the Ch'ing dynasty in October 1911, prompted Foreign Minister Uchida Yasuya to seek to extend the line dividing the Japanese and Russian spheres of interest into Mongolia. He took the initiative with the Russians and on July 8, 1912, finally concluded the third Russo-Japanese entente.

The second entente, July 1910. Motono-Izvolskii talks, April-May 1910:

> Kajima, *Nihon gaikō seisaku no shiteki kōsatsu* (1951), first published as *Teikoku gaikō no kihon seisaku* (1938).
>
> Tokutomi, *Kōshaku Katsura Tarō den* (1917), Vol. II.

Negotiations:

> Japan, Gaimushō (Foreign Ministry), "Nichi-Ro kōshō shi" (1944), provides a fairly detailed account of the negotiations.
>
> ——*Komura gaikōshi* (1953), Vol. II, is the most important work on this subject because it has a more detailed description of the course of the negotiations than the previously-cited work and also contains clear evidence that Foreign Minister Komura took the initiative in the negotiations. Moreover, according to this account it was Komura's hope that the agreement would be followed by similar agreements with Britain and France.
>
> —— *Nihon gaikō bunsho*, Vol. XLIII (1962), covers this period, but it has not yet been used for a scholarly work.
>
> Matsumoto, *Kinsei Nihon gaikōshi kenkyū* (1942), was the first to note the cabinet meeting in March at which the decision was made to enter into negotiations with Russia and the fundamental principles upon which a treaty was to be concluded were agreed upon.
>
> Tanaka, "Nichi-Ro kyōshō ron" (1956), also points out that Komura took the initiative in the negotiations.

The origins of the third entente between Japan and Russia have been less well defined than those of the second entente. Other than Matsumoto, who pointed out the significance of new developments in Mongolia, most scholars until the 1950s tended to characterize the agreement solely as a countermeasure to an American-sponsored four-power loan to China, which was signed in April 1911.

The third entente, July 1912:

Documents:

> Japan, Gaimushō (Foreign Ministry), *Nihon gaikō bunsho*, Vol. XLV (1963); with the publication of this volume the entire subject of the third entente should be restudied.

As a countermeasure to the four-power loan:

> Kajima, *Nihon gaikō seisaku no shiteki kōsatsu* (1951), first published as *Teikoku gaikō no kihon seisaku* (1938), discusses the loan in detail as a cause of the agreement but offers no description of the process leading to the conclusion of the entente.
>
> Shinobu, *Kindai Nihon gaikōshi* (1942), asserts, "Japan and Russia signed the agreement . . . with a view to taking a countermeasure against the offensive of the Four Power Consortium, which had come into existence as a result of their participation."

Developments in Manchuria and Mongolia:

> Matsumoto, *Kinsei Nihon gaikōshi kenkyū* (1942).
>
> Tanaka, "Nichi-Ro kyōshō ron" (1956), makes it clear that Foreign Minister Uchida took the initiative in the talks and indicates that three developments prompted the Japanese government to take this course: 1) the American attempt to have Manchuria included in the area where the Four Power Consortium was to operate; 2) the Russian moves to annex northern Manchuria; and 3) the support given by Russia to the movement for independence in Mongolia.

The process of strengthening Japan's ties with Russia was paralleled by a slackening of its tie with Britain. When the Anglo-Japanese treaty was changed into a weaker alignment in 1911, the Russo-Japanese entente developed into a stronger partnership. It appears that Japan was shifting its partnership from Britain to Russia. Significant research might well be done on the relationships between the pro-Russian group and pro-Anglo-Saxon group within the power elite at this time.

Is it not possible that Japan's shift in policy had something to do with the increasing interest among decision-makers for advancing into southern China, where political life was in turmoil? Such motivation seems particularly likely to have influenced Foreign Minister Uchida in concluding the third entente.

Toward a Russo-Japanese Alliance, 1912–1916. The outbreak of World War I in 1914 had immediate repercussions on power relations in the Far East. The major powers involved in this area—Great Britain, France, and Russia—were now tied down in a life-and-death struggle in Europe. The retreat of Western political influence from China, along with the state of political turmoil that followed the overthrow of the Ch'ing dynasty, was welcomed by Japanese political leaders as creating favorable conditions for

Japan to advance its imperialistic policy on the continent without serious interruptions. The Japanese move in this direction was to present the Twenty-One Demands to the Chinese government in January 1915, intending not only to strengthen Japan in its sphere of interest in China but also to extend its influence outward and to exact new concessions from China.

Although the Russian government was deeply disturbed by Japan's increasing activities in China, it was in no position to take strong measures to curb them. Rather, it deemed it necessary to make Russia's relationship with Japan more friendly in order to lessen the danger of a German-Japanese rapprochement. As the war developed, the desire of the Russian government for closer collaboration with the Japanese government increased, with the hope of obtaining military aid, especially munitions, from the Japanese government. The Russian policy in this direction first took the form, shortly after the war broke out, of applying for admission to the Anglo-Japanese alliance.

This proposition aroused serious discussion among Japanese decision-makers. Communications among the elder statesmen and government leaders in the period from the summer of 1914 to the beginning of 1915 revealed that there was a divergence of opinion between the elder statesmen and Foreign Minister Katō Takaaki, who represented the view of the Foreign Ministry. Inoue emerged as the elder statesman most strongly in favor of keeping close ties with the Russians and of forming a four-power alliance to include France. In spite of the efforts of the elder statesmen, Foreign Minister Katō did not change his stand. He argued for shelving the question until after the war because of his concern about its possible weakening effect upon the Anglo-Japanese alliance.

In February 1915 Yamagata drafted a long memorandum in which he advocated an alliance with Russia; a copy was sent to each of the elder statesmen for his approval. Encouraged by the complete agreement shown by the genrō, Yamagata presented the memorandum to Prime Minister Ōkuma Shigenobu who, in turn, called upon the government to take the course indicated in it. This memorandum constitutes an interesting document for abstracting several variables underlying the Russian policy of Yamagata, the single most powerful figure among Japanese leaders: his image of the situation surrounding Japan, his predictions of the development of the war, the influence upon him of the historical experience of the Triple Intervention, and his view of the objectives to be achieved through the alliance.

It might not be too great a mistake to predict that the war will end in a 50–50 or 60–40 settlement. . . . It is undeniable that though the immediate cause of the present European war is the struggle for power, the real cause is the struggle between the Slavic and Germanic races. Seeing this, it can easily be imagined how much fiercer the struggle between the yellow and white races would be . . . it is extremely important, therefore, to make plans to prevent the establishment of a white alliance against the yellow people. . . . Probably reliance upon the Anglo-Japanese alliance alone would not be a foolproof policy for maintaining perpetual peace in Eastern Asia. . . . Russia is throwing all its forces to the west and has no leisure to think of the east. Furthermore, the fact that Japan has been helping Russia causes the Russians to feel grateful to Japan, and the past feelings of resentment have now been forgotten. . . . In other words this is the best time to conclude a Russo-Japanese alliance.[7]

The memorandum, however, did not cause Katō to change his stand, so Yamagata tried in vain to convince him in person. This issue contributed to the animosity between the genrō and the foreign minister, which in turn forced the prime minister either to oust Katō from the cabinet or to alienate himself from the elder statesmen. Ōkuma selected the former alternative.

Shortly after Ishii Kikujirō took Katō's place, the Russian government took another step to bring about an alliance with Japan. Grand Duke Georgii came to Tokyo with a new proposal: he offered Japan a sector of the Russian-controlled Chinese Eastern Railway in Manchuria. When the proposal for an alliance was made to Foreign Minister Ishii by the Russian mission, a conflict again developed between the Japanese government and Yamagata because of Ishii's cool attitude toward this proposal. In spite of Ishii's reluctance, the government finally decided, as a result of Yamagata's insistence, to enter into negotiations.

After a series of talks, the Japanese and Russian governments reached an agreement. An alliance treaty was concluded and signed by Russian Foreign Minister S.D. Sazonov and Japanese Ambassador Motono on July 3, 1916. It stipulated that:

Article 1. The two High Contracting Parties, recognizing that their vital

---

[7]Tokutomi Iichirō, ed., *Kōshaku Yamagata Aritomo den* (1933), III, 942–46; Ono Sanenobu, ed., *Gensui kōshaku Ōyama Iwao* (1935), pp. 830–33.

interests demand that China should not fall under the political domination of any third Power hostile to Russia or Japan, will frankly and loyally enter into communication whenever circumstances may demand and will agree upon the measures to be taken to prevent such a situation being brought about.

Article 2. In the event that, in consequence of the measures taken by mutual agreement as provided in the preceding article, war should be declared between one of the Contracting Parties and one of the third Powers contemplated by the preceding article, the other Contracting Party will, upon the demand of its ally, come to its aid.[8]

The elder statesmen and the secret alliance:

Inoue Kaoru Kō Denki Hensankai, *Segai Inoue kō den*, Vol. V (1934).

Ono Sanenobu, *Gensui kōshaku Ōyama Iwao* (1935).

Takahashi, *Sankō iretsu* (1925), contains a good account of Yamagata's efforts to effectuate the alliance and the differences of opinion between him and the Foreign Ministry.

Tokutomi, *Kōshaku Yamagata Aritomo den* (1933), III, 942–53.

Events leading to the alliance:

Japan, Gaimushō (Foreign Ministry), "Nichi-Ro kōshō shi" (1944), supplements Matsumotó by providing a more detailed story of the developments after the arrival of Grand Duke Georgii in Tokyo.

Kajima, *Nihon gaikō seisaku no shiteki kōsatsu* (1951), originally published as *Teikoku gaikō no kihon seisaku* (1938), relates some of the developments from the summer of 1914 to the summer of 1915 in Japan's response to the Russian proposal for an alliance.

Matsumoto, *Kinsei Nihon gaikōshi kenkyū* (1942), utilizing the archives of the Foreign Ministry, presents a comprehensive picture of the steps leading to the alliance.

Shinobu, *Kindai Nihon gaikōshi* (1942), also has some of the information Kajima includes.

Tanaka, "Nichi-Ro kyōshō ron" (1956).

The most difficult interpretive problem is to determine against whom the alliance was directed. The most extensive and valuable work on this question, based on the archives of the Foreign Ministry and on Russian diplomatic correspondence, is:

Berton, "The Secret Russo-Japanese Alliance of 1916" (1956). Berton argues forcefully that the alliance was not simply an extension of the preceding

---

[8] *Nihon gaikō nempyō*, I, 420–21.

anti-American alignment but represented a new departure, fundamentally an anti-German measure taken by the elder statesmen, who dreaded a postwar "all-white" alliance. Berton's dissertation is further useful for its detailed account of the four months of negotiations in Petrograd which, in July 1916, finally produced a compromise. Berton's view differs from the generally accepted thesis that the alliance was directed principally against the United States.

Price, *The Russo-Japanese Treaties of 1907–1916 concerning Manchuria and Mongolia* (1933), states: "Yet it seems reasonably clear that whatever the 'third power' was, it must answer to the following characteristics: it must be a power seeking or which might seek 'political domination' over China, and be 'hostile to Russia or Japan'. . . . If Germany were the nation indicated, one queries why was Germany not specifically named."

Shinobu, *Nihon no gaikō* (1961), takes the same position, stating that the purpose of the alliance was to unite Russia and Japan more intimately in opposition to Britain and the United States, especially the latter.

Although Berton's argument is the most convincing, it has not yet found general acceptance. Alternatively, it might be assumed that the alliance was designed to detach Russia from a suspected "all-white" alliance rather than to take measures directed toward a specific country, the United States or Germany.

JAPANESE POLICY TOWARD SOVIET RUSSIA, 1917–1941

The Bolshevik revolution and subsequent collapse of Russian power in Northeast Asia was looked upon favorably by Japanese decision-makers. They saw in the upheaval conditions that might enable Japan to achieve its aim of seeing Russia so weakened it could no longer furnish a serious obstacle to the execution of Japan's continental policy, including the extension of its economic interests in this area. After several months of deliberations, Japanese decision-makers, having received an American proposal for sending joint forces, finally decided in July 1918 to join in the Siberian expedition. Thus, the first period of Japanese-Soviet relations, 1918–22, may be characterized as Japan's attempt to pursue its goals—the elimination of the Russian menace, the extension of its own economic interests, and the forestalling of the spread of bolshevism—by means of armed force.

The second period, 1922–25, was characterized by efforts to establish normal intercourse between both countries and by a gradual shift of attitude on the part of Japanese decision-makers to accept recognition of the revolutionary regime. The change was completed in January 1925 with the conclusion of the Japanese-Soviet treaty.

Opening of normal intercourse, however, did not affect the basic antagonistic attitude of Japanese decision-makers. During the third period, 1925–39, they still looked upon the USSR with feelings of distrust and hatred and were reluctant to enter into closer political relations with the Soviet government. Their main concern was to retain securely and to exploit the economic concessions the USSR had pledged to grant in the treaty of 1925. As the Soviet Union built up its military strength in the Far East in the early 1930s, demands for taking countermeasures increased noticeably, resulting in a strengthened Kwantung army and the conclusion of the Anti-Comintern Pact with Germany. Antagonism toward the USSR among Japanese decision-makers heightened as border disputes recurred in the late 1930s, but Japan was in no position, after plunging into the China War, to resort to all-out war.

In the fourth period, 1939–41, Japan sought a rapprochement with the Russians. The Nazi-Soviet Nonaggression Pact marked a turning point. Japanese decision-makers thereafter modified their attitude toward the USSR and, under pressures from Germany as well as from the Japanese army, became receptive to the opening of new relations with Russia. The first positive move in this direction was a proposal by the Yonai cabinet to the Soviet government in July 1940 for a neutrality pact. The Konoe cabinet which followed, however, favored a more encompassing scheme of rapprochement with the USSR, such as the formation of a four-power entente, consisting of Japan, Germany, Italy, and the USSR, designed to demarcate each nation's respective spheres of interest and to prevent American interference in their efforts to bring a "new order" to the world. Deterioration of German-Soviet relations, however, made it impossible to effectuate this grand plan, whereupon Foreign Minister Matsuoka Yōsuke, during visits to Berlin and Moscow, came back to the original idea of a neutrality pact as a means of rapprochement with the USSR. The Japanese-Soviet Neutrality Pact was signed in Moscow on April 13, 1941.

The Nazi attack on the USSR in June 1941 brought a radical change to the external setting in which Japan was placed. Japanese decision-makers had to decide whether to join the German action or not. Heated debates developed during the several days immediately following the receipt of the report of the German attack. Finally, at an Imperial Conference, Japan's leaders decided not to go to war with the USSR at that time but to make extensive preparations to enable Japan to take up arms against the Russians at an opportune moment.

Little work has been done as yet to study Japan's Soviet policy. The only book that reviews Japanese-Soviet relations for this period places emphasis on the process of negotiation:

Japan, Gaimushō (Foreign Ministry), "Nisso kōshō shi" (1942).

Except for the following studies, most of the general works dealing with the history of Japanese foreign policy do not discuss this problem.

Japan, Gaimushō (Foreign Ministry), *Nihon gaikō hyakunen shōshi* (1958).
Shinobu, *Nihon no gaikō* (1961).

ARMED INTERVENTION IN SIBERIA, 1917–1922

The Decision to Intervene, 1917–1918. How was the Bolshevik revolution perceived by Japanese decision-makers and to what extent were its profound implications recognized by them? What goals were they trying to achieve in response to the chaotic situation they understood to exist in Russia? What means were seen as effective for attaining their objectives? What alternatives were considered by the decision-makers and how did the debates develop? Was there any strong pressure, internal or external, brought on the policy-making process? What finally led to the commitment to intervention in Siberia in the summer of 1918?

It has been argued in Soviet and other historical literature that Japanese political leaders responded immediately to the revolution with a project for armed intervention in Siberia, that their desire was to strangle the young Bolshevik regime in its embryonic stage, and that they were motivated by their hatred toward this regime and their fear of spreading revolutionary influence in their own country. It is true that the Japanese army drew up a plan for sending Japanese troops into northern Manchuria and Far Eastern Russia shortly after the revolution and then undertook the building up of a pro-Japanese self-governing Russian body in Far Eastern Russia. But did this mean that they purposefully sought to overthrow the Bolshevik regime? And was the execution of the army's plan sanctioned by government leaders?

Most Japanese sources tell us that decision-makers were informed about the situation in Russia and for several months following the revolution did not demonstrate serious concern over the potential consequences of the revolution for Japan or other parts of the Far East. Instead, they portrayed the Bolsheviks as agents of the German government. Consequently, the problem as they saw it during this period was not whether to intervene in the development of the revolution, but rather how to make best use of the opportunity to extend Japan's influence into northern Manchuria and Far Eastern Russia. Of concern also was the possibility that the Bolsheviks might help the Germans extend their influence to the Far East. In short, the following were the problems with which Japanese decision-makers were most concerned: to take advantage of the political collapse of the tsarist state to eliminate the Russian threat to Japan's national security, to extend Japanese control over additional natural resources considered necessary for the growth of the economy, and to forestall the spread of German influence in the Far East.

To achieve these ends, the army argued in favor of sending armed forces to the Russian Far East and for establishing a pro-Japanese Russian regime. This proposal divided the decision-makers, and in the spring of 1918, when the army asserted that Japan should engage in a Siberian expedition regardless of the willingness of the Allied powers to participate and even without their cooperation, an especially heated debate arose among Japan's leaders. Foreign Minister Motono supported the army's stand, but the majority preferred a cautious course. Hara Takashi, the leader of the most influential political party, the Seiyūkai, voiced the strongest opposition and at meetings of the Advisory Council on Foreign Relations insisted on the necessity of reaching an understanding with the United States.

On March 19, 1918, when the Japanese government sent a note to the United States government to inform it of Japan's intention not to take any military action without prior American agreement, it became evident that the anti-interventionists had scored a victory in the controversy. In this decision-making process, Yamagata, discerning that Japan was not equipped to conduct a large-scale war without economic aid from the United States and Britain, appears to have played a major role.

Thus, Japanese decision-makers, dependent upon the willingness of the

American government to act, did not find themselves in a position to send armed forces to Siberia until they had received, on July 8, a note from the American government inviting Japan to undertake joint armed intervention, limited in the number of military personnel and area of operations. A long debate at meetings of the Advisory Council on Foreign Relations followed. Whether Japan should limit the expedition as asked by the American government or whether an independent course, in disregard of the American proposal, should be pursued was the point of controversy. The resolution finally agreed upon seemingly favored the former course, but in time the army preempted the situation and justified its actions in terms of strategic need.

General studies.

Before World War II most Japanese scholars tended to avoid this topic, exceptions being brief accounts in the following narrative histories:

Ōtsu, *Dai Nihon kenseishi* (10 vols., 1927–28).
Shinobu, *Taishō gaikō jūgonenshi* (1927).

Since World War II several serious general studies have appeared:

Hosoya, *Shiberia shuppei no shiteki kenkyū* (1955), is based on extensive use of the archives of the Foreign Ministry, on the diary of Itō Miyoji for this period, "Sui'usō nikki," and on other pertinent sources. Hosoya makes it clear that divergent viewpoints existed among the decision-makers, that the American attitude greatly influenced the Japanese decision-making process, and that dualism of policy was manifested in the execution of Japan's Siberian policy.
—— "Origin of the Siberian Intervention" (1958) is an abridgement of the foregoing book.
Inoue, *Nihon no gunkokushugi* (1953), Vol. II, in line with some Soviet historical literature, emphasizes the feeling of hostility held by the Japanese ruling class toward the Bolshevik regime and interprets as the mainspring of their intervention their opposition to the Bolshevik revolution.
Morley, *The Japanese Thrust into Siberia, 1918* (1957), focusing on the policy-making process and making wide use of archival as well as published materials, argues that the Japanese interventionists, such as Motono and the Army General Staff, wanted an expedition in support of a pro-Japanese regime, so as to establish Japan's political and economic hegemony in the Amur region, while the anti-interventionists, like Hara Takashi and Makino Nobuaki, believing that Japan's security lay first of all in understanding with the West,

refused to support an expedition until the invitation was extended by the United States.

Ōura, "Kyokutō-Roshia ni taisuru Bei-Nichi kanshō to sono hatan ni tsuite no ichi kōsatsu" (1954–55), is merely a reflection of Soviet historical literature during the Cold War.

Shinobu, *Taishō seijishi*, Vol. II (1951), follows the same line as Inoue and stresses the Japanese initiative in undertaking the intervention, but it is more useful and reliable.

White, *The Siberian Intervention* (1950), describes developments leading to the Siberian intervention. He explains the motives of the Japanese decision-makers in this venture as an attempt to transform the Japan Sea into a Japanese "inland sea." His conclusions, however, are not based on Japanese primary sources.

Specialized studies and materials relating to the roles of certain elements in the decision-making process:

Individuals:

Hara, *Hara Takashi nikki*, Vol. VII (1951).

Suda, "Shihaisō ni okeru seiji rinri no keisha: Nisso kōshō shi o chūshin to shite" (1957), is a study of four men, politicians and diplomats, who were deeply involved in formulating and executing Japan's policy toward Soviet Russia during the period 1917–56, namely Motono Ichirō, Gotō Shimpei, Shigemitsu Mamoru, and Kōno Ichirō. Suda asserts that Motono argued strongly for armed intervention because of the affection he felt for a "good old neighbor" and his desire to extend help to his respectable friends in Russia. Suda's view makes Motono stand out as a unique figure among the interventionists.

Tokutomi, *Kōshaku Yamagata Aritomo den* (1933), Vol. III.

Tsurumi, *Gotō Shimpei*, Vol. III (1938).

The Advisory Council on Foreign Relations:

Hara, *Hara Takashi nikki*, Vols. VII–VIII (1951).

Itō, "Sui'usō nikki: Nichi-Bei shuppei teigi mondai" and "Gaikō Chōsakai kaigi hikki Hara naikaku seiritsu go" (1918–19). Both documents are also in his *Sui'usō nikki*, edited by Kobayashi Tatsuo (1966).

The army:

Araki, *Gensui Uehara Yūsaku den* (1937), Vol. II.

Hosoya, "Japanese Documents on the Siberian Intervention, 1917–1922: Part 1, November 1917-January 1919" (1960).

Ishimitsu, *Dare no tame ni* (1960), relates some of the activities by which the army tried to inspire anti-Bolshevik elements.

Japan, Sambō Hombu (Army General Staff), "Taishō shichinen naishi jūichinen Shiberia shuppei shi" (1924), Vols. I-III, is a good source for information about the significant role the army played in the process of decision-making, how it worked out a plan to dispatch troops, and how it engineered anti-Bolshevik movements in northern Manchuria and Far Eastern Russia.

Takakura, *Tanaka Giichi denki*, Vol. II (1960).

Dispatch of warships to Vladivostok in January 1918:

Hosoya, "Nihon kaigun rikusentai no Uradivostokku jōriku: tai-So kanshō sensō no purorōgu" (1959).

Japan, Gunreibu (Navy General Staff), "Taishō yonen naishi kyūnen kaigun senshi" (1924), Vol. I.

Katō Kanji Denki Hensankai, *Katō Kanji taishō den* (1941).

Negotiations with allied powers:

Japan, Gaimushō (Foreign Ministry), "Shiberia shuppei ni itaru kōshō keika," Vol. I of "Shiberia shuppei mondai" (1922).

Tsurumi, *Gotō Shimpei*, Vol. III (1938).

Invitation from the United States for a joint expedition:

Kennan, *Russia Leaves the War* (1956).

——*The Decision to Intervene* (1958).

Unterberger, *America's Siberian Expedition, 1918-1920* (1956).

The revolution in Harbin:

Seki, "1917 nen Harubin kakumei: Harubin sobietto juritsu o meguru kokusai seijigaku teki ichi kōsatsu" (1958), deals with the struggle for power between Horvat and local Bolshevik leaders at Harbin. While the emphasis is placed on the formulation of the strategy employed by Horvat, the work is also useful for insights into Japanese policy as it was directed toward the revolution at Harbin.

Although various aspects of the process by which Japan decided to intervene in Siberia are extensively explored by both Morley and Hosoya, some important questions still remain for further study. Among them the most important is how the Japanese decision-makers regarded the Bolshevik revolution. There also is need for more intensive study of the significant bearing domestic politics seem to have had on the political process leading to the intervention. The study of Tanaka Giichi's role in the intervention might shed more light on the topic.

Execution and Termination of the Siberian Expedition, 1918–1922. Once having embarked upon the Siberian Expedition, Japanese government leaders soon came to realize that there were great difficulties blocking achievement of their purposes in Northeast Asia. The Bolsheviks, successful in rallying popular support among the people in Siberia by taking advantage of national sentiment aroused by the allied intervention, exhibited powerful and unexpected resistance. The anti-Bolshevik groups, on the other hand, constantly struggled among themselves and lost popular support. Under the circumstances Japan, in order to pave the way for establishment of its influence in eastern Siberia, would have to dispatch a much larger armed force; however, it could not afford to do so. Besides, it was increasingly evident that the American government was dissatisfied with the way the Japanese army was behaving in Siberia. Rather than expanding the expeditionary forces, the Japanese government decreased them in December 1918 after the American government protested strongly that their number exceeded the original agreement for the intervention.

When it became apparent that the situation, external and internal, which Japanese decision-makers faced was not conducive to pursuing their defined goals in Northeast Asia, how did they adapt themselves? Here the question arises of why the Japanese expeditionary forces remained until as late as October 1922, far beyond the termination of the allied intervention. Even today no satisfactory answer has been given for this development. Two factors can be isolated as acting to prevent Japanese decision-makers from putting an end to the intervention. First, they were seriously concerned over the spread of bolshevism, which they also related to the rice riots in Japan and the national independence movement in Korea. They felt constrained to take countermeasures against the Bolsheviks. Thus, it can be suggested that from the fall of 1918 Japanese decision-makers saw a new purpose for the expedition, that of forestalling the spread of bolshevism, to which they gradually gave priority. A significant step was taken in this direction on May 16, 1919, when the Japanese government granted de facto recognition to the Kolchak regime in western Siberia. The Kolchak regime collapsed by the end of 1919, but Japanese decision-makers still did not want to give up the idea of establishing a buffer state or *cordon sanitaire* against the advance of Bolshevik power in the east.

The second factor that may have delayed withdrawal of Japanese troops was related to the originally defined objectives of the intervention. With their armed forces remaining in Siberia, it seemed to Japanese decision-makers, their bargaining position for acquiring economic concessions was strengthened. Moreover, the army felt it important for reasons of its prestige to secure some compensation for withdrawing from Siberia.

Domestic and international pressures against Japan's Siberian policy increased, however. Japanese delegates at the Washington Conference were sharply criticized by the powers. On the domestic scene, there was strong feeling that the heavy burden the expedition placed on national finances should be relieved before catastrophe resulted. The leader of the opposition political party, Katō Takaaki, scored the government on this point.

Furthermore, when efforts were unsuccessful at both the Dairen conference and the Changchung conference to come to an understanding with the Far Eastern Republic on the question of setting up a neutrality zone or obtaining some economic concessions, Japan's decision-makers had to admit that the policy they had pursued in Siberia was a failure. In October 1922 they withdrew the entire Japanese expeditionary force from Siberian soil.

General studies of the intervention:

Japan, Gaimushō (Foreign Ministry,), "Nisso kōshō shi" (1942).
——— "Shiberia shuppei mondai" (1922), Vol. II.
Japan, Sambō Hombu (Army General Staff), "Taishō shichinen naishi jūichinen Shiberia shuppei shi" (1924), Vols. I–IV.
Shinobu, *Nihon no gaikō* (1961).
——— *Taishō seijishi*, Vols. II–III (1951–52).
Ueda, "Shiberia shuppei to kita Karafuto mondai" (1962).

Opposition to the spread of bolshevism:

Hosoya, "Nihon to Koruchaku seiken shōnin mondai" (1961), asserts that under the Hara cabinet the emphasis of Japan's Siberian policy shifted to attempts to forestall the spread of bolshevism, and that following this course the cabinet first supported the Kolchak regime and then decided to grant de facto recognition to it. Hosoya emphasizes the following as major factors influencing the Siberian policies of the Hara cabinet: 1) growing concern over social unrest as an aftermath of the August 1918 rice riots in Japan and the 1919 national independence movement in Korea; 2) interest in gaining economic concessions in Siberia; and 3) the intention to cooperate with the intervention policy of the United States.
——— "Shiberia shuppei o meguru Nichi-Bei kankei" (1961), states that the anti-

Bolshevik policies of the United States and Japan were in tandem but that the two nations were in conflict over Japan's disposition to extend its power into Northeast Asia, and he traces the development of these two facets in Japanese-United States relations during the course of the joint intervention.

Kobayashi, "Shiberia kanshō to Nikoraefusuku jiken" (1956–58), suggests that two events made Japan disinclined to evacuate troops as early as it had intended: the appearance of a Bolshevik-controlled government in Vladivostok at the end of January 1920, and the subsequent Nikolaevsk massacre of May 25, 1920.

—— "Tai-So seisaku no suii to Mammō mondai" (1963), writes about the Dairen conference and matters related to the evacuation of Japanese troops.

Kobayashi has studied Japanese Siberian policy as it was carried out after the termination of the allied intervention. But the process by which Japan's decision-makers responded to the sudden announcement of the American government that it was withdrawing its forces, and by which they finally decided to recall the Japanese army, should be analyzed further. Japan's relations with the Far Eastern Republic also require much more study.

THE ROAD LEADING TO RECOGNITION OF THE SOVIET GOVERNMENT, 1922–1925

The Gotō-Joffe Talks. Although the Japanese government finally put an end to the expedition to Siberia, it neither immediately recognized the Soviet government nor attempted to open official intercourse with it. Before Japanese decision-makers took steps in this direction, they had to come to realize that it would be necessary for them to undo the damage of the intervention, especially in view of the change in power politics in the Far East and the international political climate in general.

The first significant move in this direction was made at the beginning of 1923 by Gotō Shimpei, then mayor of the city of Tokyo. Gotō invited A.A. Joffe, a leading figure of the Soviet Foreign Office, to Tokyo for talks with him. They met for a series of conferences from February to June 1923 and exchanged opinions on the conditions each deemed prerequisite to reaching an understanding between the two countries. The discussions were sufficiently fruitful for the Japanese government to enter the talks, although still professing that they were unofficial.

Gotō was the first leading political figure who strongly advocated a policy of rapprochement with the USSR and worked for realization of talks between representatives of both countries. He seems to merit being called Itō Hirobumi's successor in advocating friendly relations with the Russians and even the necessity of collaborating with them. Gotō wrote two memoranda in February and March 1923 which suggest something of his perception of conditions in the Far East and of the objectives he sought. The first one reads as follows:

> If a Japanese-Soviet rapprochement can be realized, it will be instrumental, in the first place, in forestalling the plot the Chinese are now engineering and, second, in bringing about a favorable situation for us for getting easy access to economic concessions. To advance national interests, Japan took steps to establish friendship with Russia in the days of tsarist Russia without questioning its aggressive policy. Since communist Russia has stood for the cause of opposition to aggression and of coexistence and coprosperity with other nations, there is no reason to fear bad effects from a rapprochement and to hesitate to open trade with Soviets.

The second memorandum reads as follows:

> The settlement of the question will not only help advance Japan's economic interests but will also contribute to the solution of key problems in Japan's policy toward China and the United States. . . . If we need to be concerned over the spread of communism, it means we have weaknesses inside our own country to be taken care of. . . . The urgent tasks for Japanese foreign policy are the following: 1) to solidify the foundations for undertaking economic development in Asiatic Russia; 2) to eliminate the source of future troubles by forestalling possible American moves toward Russia; and 3) to prevent any machinations on the part of the Chinese before they can achieve a rapprochement with Russia.[9]

The dominant factor which drove Gotō toward ties with the Russians apparently was his fear of a Russo-Chinese rapprochement and the consequent isolation of Japan in the Far East. The nightmare of isolation linked with the historical experience of the Triple Intervention seemed to influence his behavior as it had Itō, Yamagata, and the other genrō.

Gotō Shimpei:

> Shinobu, *Gotō Shimpei* (1941), presents Gotō's view of history by which he interpreted recent developments as a struggle for hegemony between the old and

---

[9]Tsurumi Yūsuke, ed., *Gotō Shimpei*, IV (1938), 420-34.

the new continents; Shinobu strongly suggests that Gotō's Russian policy was deeply rooted in this view.

Tsurumi, *Gotō Shimpei*, Vol. IV (1938), is the most important source for Gotō's perceptions, values, and attitudes.

Gotō-Joffe talks:

Kobayashi, "Nisso kokkō chōsei no ichi dammen: Gotō-Yoffe kōshō kaishi no keika" (1958).

—— "Sobietto Roshia no kyokutō tōitsu to gyogyō mondai" (1959). In both of these articles Kobayashi suggests that concern over a possible Sino-Russian rapprochement motivated Gotō to invite Joffe to Japan. Kobayashi also pays special attention to fishery interests, which he assumes acted as a pressure group to influence Gotō's deliberations with Joffe.

Naitō, *Tsutsumi Seiroku no shōgai* (1937), provides a penetrating account of the activities of the fishery interests to bring about an early normalization of Japanese-Soviet relations. Naitō makes it clear that the provisional convention on fisheries signed by Gotō and Joffe was a result of the active work of those concerned with Japanese fisheries in Asiatic Russia.

Suda, "Shihaisō ni okeru seiji rinri no keisha: Nisso kōshō shi o chūshin to shite" (1957), also stresses that concern over a possible Sino-Russian rapprochement directly motivated Gotō to initiate his talks with Joffe.

The Japanese navy was agreeable to an early establishment of normal relations between the two governments. The navy traditionally had been concerned with the preservation of tranquillity in Northeast Asia and now was concerned with the stabilization of Japan's relations with the USSR. At the same time, it was very much interested in obtaining access to oil concessions in northern Sakhalin. In this connection it must be noted that Prime Minister Katō Tomosaburō, an admiral, gave his consent in advance to Gotō's move to invite Joffe.

Despite Gotō's efforts and the navy's willingness to change the status of Japan's relations with the Soviet Union, resistance to a rapprochement persisted among government leaders, particularly in the Foreign Ministry, represented by Foreign Minister Uchida Yasuya and Matsudaira Tsuneo, the director of the Europe-America Bureau, and attempts were even made to interrupt the Gotō-Joffe talks. Tōgō Shigenori, then chief of a section under Matsudaira, explained the basis for divergent opinions among the decision-makers as follows: "While Prime Minister Katō and Mr. Gotō did not seriously concern themselves with communist activities, preferring to consider policy toward the Soviet Union in terms of accommodating conflicting interests in the Far East, the Foreign Ministry approached the Russian question more broadly, insisting that ideological issues also be taken into account."[10] The split between Gotō and the Foreign Ministry is dealt with in detail by Kobayashi in "Tai-So seisaku no suii to Mammō mondai" (1963). Kobayashi's is the most suggestive work available on Japan's efforts to normalize its relations with the Soviet Union in the period 1922–25.

Gotō Shimpei is one of the most intriguing figures in the history of Japanese foreign policy. He should be studied from the viewpoint of his unique outlook on world affairs and his deep concern for friendship with the Soviet Union.

The attitudes of Japanese business leaders toward rapprochement with the Soviet Union constitutes another interesting topic. Some displayed ideological prejudices, while others were so eager to establish normal relations that they exerted pressure on the administration. The question of what the strongest factors operating against the realization of Gotō's design were also might be more intensively explored.

Conclusion of the Japanese-Soviet Treaty. As a result of the groundwork laid by the Gotō-Joffe talks, Kawakami Toshihiko and Joffe held discussions in Tokyo from June to July 1923. They were not successful, however, in bringing about an agreement between the two countries. In May 1924 Yoshizawa Kenkichi, minister to China, met with Soviet Minister Karakhan in Peking. Their discussions ended finally in an agreement in January 1925 to establish official intercourse between the two countries.

What factors made for a more positive attitude on the part of Japanese decision-makers for settling the Russian problem? And what considerations made them agree to the Japanese-Soviet treaty in spite of the fact that it did not satisfy some of their demands? Japan's new course seems to be related largely to a change of opinion within the Foreign Ministry. The view favoring British and Italian moves toward recognition of the USSR, anticipating also that the Chinese would act similarly, prevailed over a policy based on ideological antagonism.

---

[10]Tōgō Shigenori, *Jidai no ichimen* (1952), pp. 35–36.

Studies of the modification of Japan's Soviet policy:

Kobayashi, "Nihon tai-So gaikō seisaku kateiron josetsu" (1960), focuses on the Yoshizawa-Karakhan talks as they were related to the foreign policy-making process in Japan. Kobayashi shows that concern over the rapid development of Sino-Soviet talks acted to bring about the change in Japan's Soviet policy.

—— "Nisso kokkō juritsu no ichi dammen" (1961), indicates that in the fall of 1923 the Yamamoto cabinet initiated the shift in Japanese policy and that succeeding cabinets continued this policy. Kobayashi assumes the new policy reflected the views of the navy and the influence of Gotō, who served as home minister in the Yamamoto cabinet.

—— "Pekin kaigi to Pōtsumasu jōyaku: Nihon gaikō seisaku kettei katei ni kansuru shiron teki oboegaki" (1959), points out the significance of the Pekin Kaigi Jumbi Uchiawasekai, created within the Foreign Ministry to direct an overall examination of the Russian problem. He also describes a related controversy between the Treaties Bureau and the Europe-America Bureau.

Kawakami-Joffe talks:

Japan, Gaimushō (Foreign Ministry), "Nisso kōshō shi" (1942), contains a brief description of the talks.

Kobayashi, "Tai-So seisaku no suii to Mammō mondai" (1963).

The question of how the Japanese government moved toward the decision to establish normal relations with the Soviet Union is a topic to be studied further. The development of Japanese policy provides an excellent example of how international and domestic political pressures can overrule policy-makers' instinctive hostility toward a communist country. More attention, therefore, should be paid to the activities of business groups in Japan who were interested in Soviet trade and in the demands of fishery interests. Another interesting topic to be examined is the degree to which Japanese domestic politics became involved in the process of opening formal relations with the Soviet Union.

REJECTION OF RAPPROCHEMENT, 1925–1939

Settlement of Pending Questions, 1925–1931. The conclusion of the Japanese-Soviet treaty did not in fact bring about a radical change in the way Japanese decision-makers viewed Soviet leaders or dealt with them. They were distrustful of Soviet moves, a suspicion somewhat increased by Comintern activities in Japan. This would seem to explain Japan's rejection in August 1926 of Soviet proposals for a neutrality pact and in May 1927 for a nonaggression pact.

In truth, Japanese decision-makers concerned with Asia paid relatively little attention to Russia itself but concentrated chiefly on developments in China. The USSR, suffering from economic difficulties, was not successful in building up military strength sufficient to pose a threat to Japan's national security. In addition, no grave incidents occurred between Japan and the Soviet Union calling for Japanese leaders to make major decisions. They were most concerned with the signing of pacts that would affirm the right of Japan to exploit those economic concessions pledged by the Soviet government in the treaty of 1925.

When the negotiations concerning an agreement on fisheries bogged down, Prime Minister Tanaka Giichi asked Gotō Shimpei to proceed to Moscow to settle the problem. In Moscow in January 1928 Gotō expanded the discussions and urged Stalin to consider an entente among Japan, the USSR, and China.

Actually, Gotō represented a minority view among Japanese political leaders. The majority, suspicious of Soviet direction of growing communist activities in Japan, opposed any form of political rapprochement with the Soviet Union. Indeed, some military leaders, out of concern over communist penetration of northern Manchuria, argued that Japan should take advantage of internal disputes in the Soviet Union to eliminate totally the Russian threat from Northeast Asia and to cut off assumed close contacts between the Chinese communists and the Soviet Union.

Japan's Soviet policy:

Kobayashi, "Tai-So seisaku no suii to Mammō mondai" (1963).

Gotō's mission to Moscow:

Tsurumi, *Gotō Shimpei*, Vol. IV (1938).

The role of anti-bolshevism in Japan's policy toward the Soviet Union constitutes the most important problem to be explored. How deeply were Japanese decision-makers concerned with the threat of communism to their domestic and continental policies? Did they make use of this threat for other purposes?

The response of the Japanese government to the Sino-Soviet armed conflict in 1929 represents another interesting topic on which no work has been done.

Japanese attitudes toward the Sino-Soviet conflict, 1929:

Shidehara, *Gaikō gojūnen* (1951).

The Manchurian Incident and the Anti-Comintern Pact, 1931–1936. The Manchurian Incident created a new element in Japanese-Soviet relations. The Kwantung army extended its military control over northern Manchuria, and the buffer zone between the armed forces of the two countries disappeared. Soviet leaders reacted to the incident in a conciliatory manner on the one hand, proposing a nonaggression pact with Japan and offering to sell the Soviet share of the Chinese Eastern Railway, but on the other hand they hastened the buildup of military strength in Asiatic Russia.

How did Japanese decision-makers perceive the new situation in Northeast Asia in terms of their Soviet policy? The response to the Soviet proposal for a nonaggression pact is suggestive. Serious controversy arose over this question among officials in the Foreign Ministry. The argument favoring acceptance arose from concern over Japan's isolated position and the possibility of joint intervention by Western countries. The opposition stated that once the pact was signed, the Soviet government, taking advantage of the Japanese government's inability to take strong measures, would increase pressure detrimental to Japanese economic activities in Asiatic Russia. Some also argued that Japan was destined sooner or later to become involved in armed clashes with the Russians.

Within military circles, the twofold problem of coping simultaneously with the buildup of Soviet military strength and the Soviet conciliatory policy engendered heated discussion. One group, known as the Imperial Way faction and led by Army Minister Araki Sadao, opposed any reconciliation with the Russians because of the incompatibility of interests and ideologies. This group even went so far as to express readiness for preventive war. Another group, the Control faction, represented by Colonel Nagata Tetsuzan, strongly opposed running the risk of war with the Soviets and wanted to accommodate Soviet policy by purchasing the Chinese Eastern Railway. The Control faction argued that Japan should concentrate its efforts on solidifying its military foothold in Northeast Asia and on developing natural resources and heavy industry and should avoid trouble with the Russians.

In the first round a relatively firm stand prevailed, and the Japanese government in December 1932 sent a note to the Soviet government declining the proposal for a nonaggression pact. It is not certain whether or not the idea of resorting to preventive war was seriously discussed at top-level meetings, but it is evident that a strong policy such as that advocated by the Imperial Way faction and General Araki did not have the support of a majority of the leaders of the Japanese government. When the government decided to enter negotiations respecting the Chinese Eastern Railway, the strong policy suffered another setback. Agreement on this problem was finally reached between the two countries in March 1935.

In the meantime, Japanese military leaders in response to the Soviet buildup of military strength took measures to strengthen the army in Manchuria. The Japanese army also began to prod the government to seek another country that would cooperate with Japan regarding policies toward the Soviet Union. The idea of an anti-Comintern pact with Germany thus originated with the desire of the Army General Staff to strengthen Japan's military stand relative to the USSR. The initiative for the talks was taken by Ōshima Hiroshi, the Japanese military attache in Berlin. In its essential meaning, this alignment was directed against Russia, and as such the pact could be called a new version of the Anglo-Japanese alliance.

On the study of Japanese Soviet policy during this period, there are few primary sources available. Most of the relevant documents of the Foreign Ministry were destroyed during World War II. Manuscript materials kept by Araki and others, however, throw some light on the problem. Part of the Araki materials are on deposit at the Military History Office of the National Defense Agency.

Japan, Gaimushō (Foreign Ministry), "Nisso kōshō shi" (1942), provides a rather detailed account of the negotiations related to the purchase of the Chinese Eastern Railway.

Ōhashi, *Taiheiyō sensō yuraiki* (1952), is also useful on this topic.

The study of the Anti-Comintern Pact has been viewed in both Japan and Western countries as part of the study of Japanese-German relations.

Iklé, *German-Japanese Relations, 1936–1940* (1956), properly states that "the original impetus for cooperation stemmed from the mutual desire to find an ally against Russia in Europe and in Asia," but he is wrong in asserting that "the basic idea originated with the Germans" and that the negotiations were directed completely by them.

Presseisen, *Germany and Japan: A Study in Totalitarian Diplomacy, 1933–1941* (1958).

The following works are based on the records of the International Military Tribunal for the Far East but do not give much insight into the origins of the pact.

Ōhata, "Nichi-Doku-I sangoku dōmei" (1959).
Ueda, "Nichi-Doku-I sangoku dōmei" (1953).

In another study Ōhata reveals some new facts relating to the process by which the Anti-Comintern Pact was concluded.

Ōhata, "Nichi-Doku bōkyō kyōtei dō kyōka mondai (1935–1939)" (1963).

But even with the testimony of some of the participants, the destruction of relevant documents deprives the historian of important information.

The topic of preventive war appears interesting if it is considered in conjunction with the attitude of the Imperial Way faction toward the Soviet Union. Japanese military planning directed toward the Soviet Union also should be studied in order to gain insight into Japan's Soviet policy. This is true since the army played a significant role in Japan's foreign policy-making process, especially with regard to Japan's policy toward the Soviet Union.

Although the question of negotiations about the Chinese Eastern Railway also should be intensively explored, given the scarcity of relevant materials it is not certain whether the results would be worth the effort.

Recurring Border Disputes, 1936–1939. Conclusion of the Anti-Comintern Pact resulted directly in action by the Soviet government to cancel the signing of a Japanese-Soviet fisheries convention. Soviet leaders saw the pact in effect as a military alliance destined to result in a combined German-Japanese attack on Soviet Russia. Moreover, two important factors— relative military strength and the balance of international politics—now favored the Soviet Union. Subsequent events further embittered Japanese-Soviet relations. The Soviet government, for example, detained Japanese fishing vessels, hindered the work of the Japanese oil concession in northern Sakhalin, and closed the Japanese consulates at Novosibirsk and Odessa. Recurring border disputes, which had begun in 1933 along the Soviet-Manchukuo frontier, increased in intensity after 1936 and verged on all-out war in the Changkufeng Incident (1938) and the Nomonhan Incident (1939).

Among Japanese military leaders and nationalist groups there still was strong support for an active policy toward the USSR. Proponents of this view stood for the cause of anti-communism and stressed the need to meet the Soviet military challenge. General Araki declared in October 1937 that it would probably be necessary for Japan to strike directly against Russia in order to eliminate communism in the Far East. He further stated that America and Britain should cooperate with Japan in solving world problems.

Japanese decision-makers, however, tied down by military engagements in China since the summer of 1937, were in no position to engage in an all-out war with Soviet Russia, no matter how heavily the threat of communism hung over their heads. Even though Japanese military leaders, such as Army Minister Itagaki Seishirō and Vice-Army Minister Tōjō Hideki, boasted in the fall of 1938 of Japan's military capability to engage in a two-front war, there was a general feeling among decision-makers that as long as the China War lasted, Japan must avoid war with the Soviets at any cost. The increased tendency within Japan in the late 1930s toward pushing the drive for southward expansion also acted as a restraining influence on the move toward a military attack or any other active steps against the USSR.

It has not yet been established which country started the two grave border incidents at Changkufeng and Nomonhan. But there is no doubt that Japanese middle-grade army officers in both the Kwantung and Korea armies were prepared to magnify the scale of fighting and were eager to strike a heavy blow at the Soviet army. In contrast with the officers on the spot, military leaders in Tokyo made every effort to localize the armed clash and to solve the problem through diplomatic channels.

Few primary sources are available for the study of Japan's Soviet policy during this period. Only a small number of documents are to be found in the archives of the Foreign Ministry. The appropriate sections of the following work are useful for a general view of Japanese-Soviet relations in the late 1930s:

Japan, Gaimushō (Foreign Ministry), "Nisso kōshō shi" (1942).

Regarding Japanese-Soviet border disputes, there are some relevant materials in the form of diaries and memoirs of military leaders, such as Hata Shunroku and Nakajima Tetsuzō, who were involved in the Changkufeng and Nomonhan incidents. These papers are deposited in the Military History Office of the National Defense Agency in Tokyo. They are valuable in shedding light on the conflict between the Army General Staff and army officers on the spot over the conduct of military operations and in revealing the emperor's opposition to their enlargement.

Harada, *Saionji kō to seikyoku*, Vol. VII (1952), should be consulted for information about the reaction of political leaders to the incidents.

Hata, "Nitchū sensō no gunjiteki tenkai (1937–1941)" (1963), based on military materials, supplies a description of the border disputes and clarifies the nature of the conflicting views between military leaders in Tokyo and military commanders in the field.

Hata, "Nikki Shōwa yonen jūgatsu shichinichi kara Shōwa nijūnen sangatsu nijūhachinichi."

Inada, "Soren kyokutō gun to no taiketsu" (1956), traces the development of the Changkufeng Incident.

Nakajima, "Kaisō roku" (1940).

Sevost'yanov, *Politika velikikh derdzav na Dal'nem Vostoke* (1961), is concerned with Japanese military aggression in the Far East, 1937–39.

Shigemitsu, *Gaikō kaisōroku* (1953), who served as Japanese ambassador to the Soviet Union, offers some comment on the incidents.

Shishkin, *Khalkhin-gol* (1954), provides the most detailed account of military developments during the Nomonhan Incident, stresses that the Kwantung army took the initiative in the fighting, and relates the extent of the defeat sustained by the Kwantung troops.

For the period 1937–39 in Japan's policy toward the Soviet Union, two important questions should be examined: 1) how Japanese military and political leaders assessed the developing purge in the Soviet Union, and 2) how and why they arrived at the decision to avoid an all-out war with the Soviet Union.

THE ROAD TO THE JAPANESE-SOVIET NEUTRALITY PACT, 1939–1941

The announcement that Germany and Soviet Russia had concluded a nonaggression pact shocked Japan's decision-makers. They feared that the USSR would take advantage of its new international position to exert added pressure on Japan in Northeast Asia. As events developed, however, pressure came from Germany to induce Japan to reach a rapprochement with the Russians and enter a new alignment with Germany, Italy, and the USSR.

The Hiranuma cabinet resigned following the German switch from alliance with Japan to cooperation with the USSR. The new Abe cabinet, seeing that the Japanese-Soviet balance of power had shifted against Japan and desirous of taking advantage of the outbreak of the European war to end the stalemate between China and Japan, made friendly gestures to Russia. Hoping to create an atmosphere conducive to reconciliation, Japanese decision-makers moved toward a settlement of the Nomonhan Incident and agreed to the establishment of a joint committee to deal with demarcation of the border between Outer Mongolia and Manchukuo. Despite strong pressure from Germany, however, Japan was not prepared to enter into negotiations for a nonaggression pact with the USSR.

In the meantime, from the fall of 1939 to the spring of 1940 three sets of internal pressures were operating that eventually forced Japanese decision-makers to effectuate a rapprochement with the USSR. The first came from pro-Axis elements, led by Ambassador Shiratori Toshio, who clamored for a military alliance with Germany and Italy after obtaining a Soviet-Japanese nonaggression pact. The second came from Ambassador Tōgō in Moscow, who foresaw in Japanese-Soviet reconciliation a favorable impact on the conduct of the China War and an effective diplomatic weapon in Japan's relations with the United States. The third originated with the Army General Staff, which hoped that a nonaggression pact would stop the shipment of Soviet arms to the Chinese government. In addition, young officials within the Foreign Ministry favored such a pact.

Germany's sweep through Denmark, Norway, Holland, and Belgium in April and May 1940 further changed the international power balance.

The Yonai cabinet began to reexamine Japan's policy toward the Soviet Union. Yet, despite this development and increasing pressure from young officials within the Foreign Ministry urging a nonaggression pact with the USSR, Foreign Minister Arita Hachirō was reluctant to take such a course. He feared deterioration of Japan's relations with the United States and Britain, and he had deeply ingrained anti-communist feelings. Meanwhile, events in Europe had been developing in such a manner as to make a rapprochement policy seem advantageous. Finally, Arita reached a compromise with the Army General Staff, which in turn had unofficial ties with the young officials of the Foreign Ministry, in support of a neutrality pact with the USSR. In May 1940 a meeting of high-level officials decided upon this course. On July 2 Ambassador Tōgō proposed the neutrality pact to the Soviet government. In the light of Japan's rejection of past Soviet proposals for a nonaggression pact, this represented a new course for Japan's Soviet policy.

Shortly after Ambassador Tōgō talked with Soviet Foreign Minister Molotov, a political reshuffling took place in Japan and the Konoe cabinet was formed. The new cabinet decided to continue the policy of rapprochement with the USSR but in a more positive way. The new foreign minister, Matsuoka Yōsuke, tended to formulate Japan's Soviet policy in a wider perspective than had the former government, in harmony with his grand design for establishing a "new world order." Matsuoka believed steadfastly in Germany's ability to influence Russia, and he also expected German help to be extended since Japan was meeting the German demand for an alliance.

First, however, Japan had to decide to join the Axis powers in Europe. Once the negotiations for the Tripartite Pact were completed in September 1940, Foreign Minister Matsuoka was free to work for a four-power entente that would include the Axis nations and the USSR. He looked upon his task as a design for reaching an agreement on demarcation of spheres of interest in East Asia and on mutual cooperation in building a "new world order." He first instructed Ambassador Tatekawa Yoshitsugu in Moscow to make a new proposal for a nonaggression pact to the Soviet government. When Matsuoka discovered that the Soviet Union insisted upon Japanese renunciation of northern Sakhalin as its price, he decided to attempt to negotiate the pact himself. Still believing that Germany maintained friendly relations with the USSR, he drew up a draft plan of an "Outline for Negotiations with Germany, Italy, and the USSR."[11] In February 1941 the Liaison Conference accepted his plan.

In Berlin, where he went first for talks, German leaders stated there was no hope for the four-power entente, and furthermore they discouraged any plan for a Japanese-Soviet rapprochement. Disregarding the advice of the German authorities, Matsuoka went on to Moscow and proposed a nonaggression pact. On April 13 he actually reached an agreement with Soviet leaders for a neutrality pact.

After Matsuoka realized there was no chance for achieving his grand design, what objectives did he have in the Japanese-Soviet Neutrality

[11] *Nihon gaikō nempyō*, II, 480–82.

Pact? Two have been advanced: 1) Matsuoka intended to strengthen Japan's bargaining position vis-a-vis the United States by way of rapprochement with the Soviet Union; and 2) he found it necessary to secure Japan's northern outposts before driving toward the south.

The outbreak of the Soviet-German war in June 1941 forced Japanese decision-makers to completely reconsider Japan's relations with the USSR. A series of Liaison Conferences were held to decide upon the final choice between alternatives: whether Japan should join the attack on the Soviet Union in Asiatic Russia or stay out of the war. Matsuoka and Major-General Tanaka Shin'ichi, director of the Operations Division of the Army General Staff, favored the former course. The majority of Japan's civil and military leaders, however, were cautious and inclined to watch developments for a while. Finally, at an Imperial Conference on July 2, Japan's leaders chose the latter course. At the same time, they decided to try to build up the Kwantung army rapidly to facilitate an attack on the Soviet army when a favorable situation, such as the transfer westward of half of the Soviet Far East army, should present itself.

The buildup of the Kwantung army continued, but the Army General Staff finally decided in August not to start operations against the Soviet army that year. This decision stemmed directly from an analysis of reports on the movements of the Soviet army. After the Pacific War started, the Japanese army clearly could no longer consider opening another front in Siberia.

Japan's Soviet policy, 1939–1941:

Gol'dberg, *Vneshniaia politika Iaponii, Sentiabr' 1939–Dekabr' 1941 gg* (1959), for the most part is based on secondary Japanese sources and on materials of the International Military Tribunal for the Far East. The work is designed chiefly to reveal the aggressive character of Japan's policy toward the Soviet Union.

Hosoya, "Sangoku dōmei to Nisso chūritsu jōyaku (1939–1941)" (1963), is based on documents of the Foreign Ministry and materials deposited in the Military History Office of the National Defense Agency in Tokyo. Hosoya describes the positive attitude of the Army General Staff in the first half of 1940 toward an accommodation with the Soviet Union, Matsuoka's grand design for a four-power entente, and Japan's response to the outbreak of the Soviet-German war in June 1941.

Lupke, *Japans Russlandpolitik von 1939 bis 1941* (1962), is a solid work based on extensive use of Japanese Foreign Ministry documents.

Biographies and memoirs of decision-makers:

Arita, *Hito no me no chiri o miru: gaikō mondai kaikoroku* (1948).

—— *Bakabachi to hito wa iu: gaikōkan no kaisō* (1959). Both works are memoirs of Arita Hachirō; unfortunately, neither contains specific information about Japanese policy toward the USSR.

Harada, *Saionji kō to seikyoku*, Vol. VIII (1952), is very helpful for studying the reaction in court circles and among other pro-Anglo-Saxon elements to the policy of rapprochement with the Soviet Union.

Yabe, *Konoe Fumimaro* (1952), Vol. II, is useful for an account of the so-called Ogikubo Conference on July 19, 1940, and of other meetings in which discussions of basic policy took place.

Matsuoka Yōsuke has no authentic biography or memoir, but two memoirs written by his associates are instructive in that they give hints of Matsuoka's view of the world situation and of his conduct of foreign policy. They are:

Ōhashi, *Taiheiyō sensō yuraiki* (1952).
Saitō, *Azamukareta rekishi: Matsuoka to sangoku dōmei no rimen* (1955).

Proposal for the neutrality pact with the Soviet Union, July 1940:

Japan, Gaimushō (Foreign Ministry), "Gaikō shiryō" (1946), contains an important account of this proposal based mostly on diplomatic archives saved from destruction during and immediately after World War II.

Kōtani, "Nisso chūritsu jōyaku ni tsuite no kokuhaku" (1956).

Tanemura, *Daihon'ei kimitsu nisshi* (1952), an abridged and somewhat edited version of Tanemura's original diary, is helpful for understanding discussions within the Army General Staff which followed the proposal for a neutrality pact.

Tōgō, *Jidai no ichimen* (1952).

Tsuchihashi, "Sambō Hombu dainibuchō jidai no omoide" (1957), is in the Military History Office, National Defense Agency.

The Japanese-Soviet Neutrality Pact, April 1941:

Gordon, "The Russo-Japanese Neutrality Pact of April, 1941" (1956), is a study of Japan's policy leading to the pact with a view to "throwing light on the tactics and calculations of both Russia and Japan in their relations with each other and with other states, particularly Germany and China; and to giving some insight into the division within the Japanese leadership over relations with the USSR."

Liaison Conferences, June 1941:

Hattori, *Dai Tōa sensō zenshi*, Vol. I (1953), is especially valuable on the question of reactions to the Nazi attack on Soviet Russia.

8

Japan's Policies
Toward the United States

Akira Iriye

❖

In studying Japanese policy toward the United States between the Meiji
Restoration and Pearl Harbor, one becomes aware of the absence of long-
range and clearly definable policy formulations. To be sure there were
general attitudes or orientations. After 1917, at any rate, the Japanese navy
came to regard the United States as the foremost imaginary enemy, and
in the 1920s the army also accepted such a view, while Meiji and Taishō
bureaucrats tended to view the United States as one of the most important
sources of capital for Japanese industrialization.

Apart from these broad conceptions, however, there was not worked out
a systematic formulation of policy specifically aimed at the United States.
It would seem that there were always Japanese-American relations but not
Japanese policies toward America. There were specific decisions made
vis-a-vis Washington, but these were more often responses to specific
situations than reflections of an overall policy. Thus we find Japanese
officials taking a very pragmatic attitude toward the United States; they
would deal with each issue as it arose but they would not work out a clear
formulation of policy alternatives to the extent that they did with respect
to China, Russia, or even Britain. This may have been a reflection of Japan's
overall interest in continental affairs, and in fact Japan's policy toward the
United States seems primarily to have been a function of Japanese relations
with these countries. This is remarkable, considering the definite dependence of the Japanese economy on the United States. Perhaps here lay the
essential problem—Japan failed to bridge the gap between its general
orientation toward the United States and specific, year-to-year decisions.

The absence of clear policy toward the United States has had marked
impact on historical scholarship. Historians have generally accepted one
form or another of determinism concerning the inevitability of conflict

between the two countries. But they have found it difficult to apply this determinism to each specific circumstance. Even in the late 1930s there were events for which it would be extremely difficult to do so. So much depended on happenings in Europe and on developments within the United States.

In this essay, Japanese "policy" is discussed as though there were consciously formulated policies specifically toward the United States. Such was not the case. However, something more than a mere cataloging of facts is needed, and I have tried to "find" policies even when these were not enunciated as such. The review of existing literature reveals that much further research is needed before we can discuss the subject with greater clarity.

TREATY REVISION, 1868–1894

It is now well recognized that Japanese policy before the first Sino-Japanese War (1894–95) was motivated by a desire to emerge as a unified and independent nation. Japan's America policy can also be best examined in this context.

The United States played a unique role in the story of Japanese treaty revision. Americans such as Townsend Harris, Henry Wheaton, and Francis Wayland did much, through residence in Japan or through their books, to acquaint the Japanese with concepts and procedures of international law. It is also interesting to note that the American system of protective tariffs greatly impressed Itō Hirobumi while he was in the United States in 1870, and that Japan's interest in tariff revision for protective purposes may have dated from this time.[1] There were, of course, other, more pressing reasons for treaty revision: the government's need for additional revenues from customs receipts, and its need for greater control over foreign merchants who at first monopolized trade transactions. Here again we may say that Japan's contact with American merchants and the American market provided an important background for treaty revision negotiations.

The American visit of the Iwakura Embassy of 1871–73 is extremely significant, since it was in Washington that the Japanese first had a taste

---

[1] *Iwakura Tomomi kankei bunsho*, VII (1934), 333–35.

of the difficulties awaiting them in the task of treaty revision. They had thought that the United States would be one of the powers most disposed to revision, and they used the United States as a test case. The result was disappointing, but the rich experience in Washington gave them valuable lessons in diplomatic negotiation. After 1873 the Japanese government continued to believe that America would be one of the easier powers to deal with in connection with treaty revision. This was primarily because the groundwork had been laid by Iwakura's mission. Moreover, it was because the United States had proved more willing to release tariff control than extraterritoriality that the Meiji government, under the foreign policy leadership of Terajima Munenori, decided to tackle the tariff problem first. The result was the conclusion of a new convention in 1878, in which the United States restored tariff autonomy to Japan. This may have reinforced the feeling of Japanese officials that they could always count on a sympathetic attitude from the United States on the issue of treaty revision.

There is no evidence, however, that Japan sought to establish particularly close ties with the United States or that it applied a different set of policies to the United States from those applied to other countries. During the above-mentioned negotiation for a new convention, for example, the Japanese government at first hesitated to proceed with the negotiation for fear of antagonizing the European powers.[2] The feeling seems to have been that American sympathy was appreciated but that it was not overly useful unless other powers, too, could be persuaded to follow suit. Such realization led to Inoue Kaoru's strategy of multinational negotiation, dealing simultaneously with all countries. During his tenure of office no systematic effort was made to cultivate American friendship. After Inoue's resignation in 1887, his successor, Ōkuma Shigenobu, reverted to the method of individual negotiations. Here again the United States was the first major power to sign a new treaty with Japan, conditionally surrendering extraterritoriality. By this time, however, Japan seems to have realized the basic need to define its attitude toward Great Britain, as the latter continued to be the greatest obstacle in the path of treaty revision. Ōkuma and his successors (Aoki Shūzō, Enomoto Takeaki, and Mutsu Munemitsu) bent their efforts in this direction, consciously taking advantage of Anglo-Russian rivalry in Asia. They seem to have taken for granted that the

---

[2]Japan, Gaimushō (Foreign Ministry), *Jōyaku kaisei kankei Nihon gaikō bunsho*, I (1941), 447ff.

United States would be willing to negotiate a new treaty at any moment. They did have a foretaste of the immigration question, however, as the United States government had begun to take measures to restrict Chinese immigration. Consequently, Japan formally recognized, in a new treaty signed in 1894, America's right to regulate the immigration of Japanese laborers.

The indispensable documentary collection for Japanese-American negotiations on treaty revision is:

Japan, Gaimushō (Foreign Ministry), *Jōyaku kaisei kankei Nihon gaikō bunsho* (4 vols., 1941–50).

The following is a supplementary volume to this collection that contains a convenient summary of the negotiations between the two countries over treaty revision:

Japan, Gaimushō (Foreign Ministry), *Jōyaku kaisei keika gaiyō* (1950).

Other useful documents include the following:

Iwakura Kō Kyūseki Hozonkai, *Iwakura kō jikki* (3 vols., 1927; first published, 1906).
Iwakura Tomomi kankei bunsho (8 vols., 1927–35).
Kido, *Kido Takayoshi nikki* (3 vols., 1967).
Ōkubo Toshimichi bunsho (10 vols., 1927–29).
Waseda Daigaku Shakai Kagaku Kenkyūjo, *Ōkuma bunsho* (5 vols., 1958–62).
  Vol. I contains a diary kept by Katō Takaaki, Ōkuma's secretary during the period of negotiations for treaty revision.

The following collections of Itō Hirobumi's papers suffer from censorship but contain memoranda and other important materials on treaty revision:

Hiratsuka, *Itō Hirobumi hiroku* (1929).
——*Zoku Itō Hirobumi hiroku* (1930).
Itō and Hiratsuka, *Hisho ruisan: gaikō hen* (3 vols., 1934–35).

Official, semi-official, and nonofficial Japanese biographies are as a rule useful sources of information. On Japanese-American relations during this period, however, there are surprisingly few such works of value. Only the following contain more than perfunctory reference to treaty revision, and even then there is little fresh information concerning Japanese attitudes toward the United States:

Inoue Kaoru Kō Denki Hensankai, *Segai Inoue kō den* (5 vols., 1933–34).
Itō, *Katō Takaaki* (2 vols., 1929).

Katsuta, *Ōkubo Toshimichi den* (3 vols., 1910–11).
Ōkuma Kō Hachijūgonenshi Hensankai, *Ōkuma kō hachijūgonenshi* (3 vols., 1926).
Shinobu, *Mutsu Munemitsu* (1938).
Shumpō Kō Tsuishōkai, *Itō Hirobumi den* (3 vols., 1940).
Watanabe, *Monjo yori mitaru Ōkuma Shigenobu kō* (1932).
—— *Mutsu Munemitsu den* (1934).
—— *Ōkuma Shigenobu* (1952).

There are many studies of treaty revision, but only the following are specifically concerned with Japanese-American negotiations:

Kajima, *Nichi-Bei gaikōshi* (1958).
Kamikawa, *Nichi-Bei bunka kōshō shi, I: sōsetsu gaikō hen* (1956).
Shimomura, *Meiji shonen jōyaku kaisei shi no kenkyū* (1962).

Of these three works, Shimomura's is undoubtedly the best, as the author effectively compares Japanese and American sources and carefully analyzes the Iwakura mission's negotiations in 1872. Kajima's study has some documents, but little analysis. Part II of the work edited by Kamikawa, which was written by Hanabusa Nagamichi, concerns the early Meiji period. It is primarily a digest of main events and similarly lacks analysis. For a systematic study of Japanese-American relations encompassing the entire period before the Sino-Japanese War one would still have to consult Treat, although the approach is primarily from the American side. To obtain the Japanese side of the picture for the early 1870s, a doctoral dissertation by Marlene J. Mayo at Columbia University is useful:

Mayo, "The Iwakura Embassy and the Unequal Treaties" (1961).
Treat, *Diplomatic Relations between the United States and Japan, 1853–1895* (2 vols., 1932).

For treaty revision in general, the following works should be consulted:

Hattori, *Kindai Nihon gaikōshi* (1954).
Inoue, *Jōyaku kaisei: Meiji no minzoku mondai* (1955).
Jones, *Extraterritoriality in Japan and the Diplomatic Relations Resulting in Its Abolition, 1853–1899* (1931).
Kiyosawa, *Nihon gaikōshi* (2 vols., 1942).
Moriya, *Jōyaku kaisei* (1934).
Nakamura, *Kindai Nihon no hōteki keisei: jōyaku kaisei to hōten hensan* (1956).
Ōyama, "Iwakura kaisei sōan to Terajima kaisei sōan" (1957).
Tabohashi, *Meiji gaikōshi* (1934).
Watanabe, *Nihon kinsei gaikōshi* (1938).

—— *Gaikō to gaikōka* (1939).
Yamamoto, *Jōyaku kaisei shi* (1943).

There has been a trend among some scholars, as exemplified by Hattori and Inoue, to explain treaty revision as an aspect either of Japan's "bourgeois revolution" or its development as an "absolutistic state." No doubt there was a close relationship between the Japanese government's effort to win equal treaty status and its policy of military and industrial modernization. Such an approach, however, does not seem to help much when we consider specifically Japan's policy toward the United States. Now that basic Japanese documents have been published and American records are readily available, the time seems opportune to go beyond the works cited here to develop a new interpretation of Japanese-American relations before the Sino-Japanese War.

IMPERIAL KINSHIP, 1894–1905

The successful consummation of treaty revision negotiations coincided with the coming of the era of the "diplomacy of imperialism" in the Far East. Japanese-American relations, consequently, entered a new phase, as both countries came to take part in power politics in Asia. The "diplomacy of imperialism" must be distinguished from "imperialism" as such, which has been traced back to antiquity. What characterized the 1890s and the subsequent decade was the advanced nations' overriding concern with power, measured in terms of colonial possessions and spheres of influence. The Far East, as elsewhere on the globe, was divided between those countries which expanded and those which were expanded into. Exclusive rights and particularistic arrangements, obtained by the former at the expense of the latter, distinguished this age, rather than the most-favored-nation treatment clauses that had been a unique feature of the foregoing "treaty system."

The diplomacy of imperialism, however, was more than an expression of the advanced nations' naked thirst for power. It also provided a framework for international action. While it may not be accurate to describe the new situation as a "system," it is possible to say that the powers on the whole tried to maintain an equilibrium by means of a series of alliances, ententes, and agreements designed to affirm their mutual spheres of influence and check any potential threat to the balance of power. Such a balance, though precarious, was maintained because of the very multiplicity of imperial powers with global interests. Their Far Eastern policies were never isolated but were intimately linked to their overall power considerations—another factor that tended to discourage too radical a break in the balance of power. War, and the threat of war, always existed, but it should be noted that military action was taken by an imperialist power primarily to prevent an upset in the status quo in colonial areas which was considered detrimental to its interests.

Japanese leaders in this period consciously resolved to join the ranks of the imperialists and play their game. In the words of Fukuzawa Yukichi, Japan was to "leave Asia" and act like a respectable Western nation. Many factors were responsible for such a decision: the feeling of superiority over Chinese and Koreans, reinforced by the vogue of Social Darwinism; the Triple Intervention episode, which more than anything else taught Japanese the lesson that might was right; and the need for Western capital and machines, which necessitated a greater degree of integration of the Japanese economy into the Western economic system, as well as political accord with some, if not all, of the powers.

Japanese-American relations were developed in such a context. When discussing Japanese policy, one must keep in mind that Japanese officials thought and acted in that milieu. For them the United States was just another imperialist power that was expected to play a role in maintaining an equilibrium in the Far East. Japan and the United States were imperial neighbors. There was no thought that the latter was significantly different from the former or from any other power in the Far East.

During and immediately following the Sino-Japanese War, Japanese policy toward the United States was dictated by the need to have the latter maintain benevolent neutrality and, if possible, even a friendly attitude toward the Japanese undertaking in Asia. Foreign Minister Mutsu's interest in maintaining Japan's good reputation in the United States was such that, when the New York *World* printed a story of an atrocity at Port Arthur, he immediately offered an explanation.[3] It was to the United States that Japan turned for protection of its officials and other nationals in China during the war. Basic to these decisions was the belief that the

[3]Komatsu Midori, *Meiji gaikō hiwa* (1936), pp. 103–6.

United States could be counted upon to offer Japan its helping hands, just as it had during the treaty revision negotiations. In the *Kenkenroku*, written in 1895, Mutsu called the United States the country most favorably disposed to Japan. He decided, accordingly, that Japan should turn to America if it should become necessary to open peace talks with China. When, however, the State Department actually offered mediation in November 1894, the Tokyo government politely declined the offer, thinking that the proper moment for peace had not yet arrived. It was five months later, at the time of the episode of the Triple Intervention, that Japan turned in earnest to the United States. The Japanese minister at Berlin, Aoki, telegraphed Mutsu, "Lose no time to employ [the] U.S. to create division in our favor." This strategy proved ineffective, however. As Mutsu realized, the United States could not be expected to intervene on behalf of Japan because of its policy of noninvolvement. Nevertheless, the episode, if anything, confirmed the image of America held by Japanese officials as a fair-minded and friendly nation.[4]

With America's emergence as a Pacific power following the Spanish-American War, Japanese policy toward the United States became more sharply defined. Since both Japan and the United States were now imperialists, it was naturally considered to the advantage of both to define mutual spheres of influence. Regarding the Hawaiian Islands, Japan showed some modest resistance to the American annexation, reflecting the Japanese government's self-confidence that as a great power expanding in all directions it should protest against the westward expansion of another power. Regarding the Philippines, Japan's main concern was with the islands' political stability and the maintenance of the balance of power in Asia. For these reasons it expressed its desire that either the United States annex the Philippines or, barring that development, the United States, Japan, and another power (presumably Britain) cooperate in administering the territory. Though Philippine insurgents turned to Japan for leadership, it was felt most essential to discourage such moves and to act within the framework of imperialist diplomacy.

In 1899 Japan responded favorably to John Hay's first Open Door note. From the Japanese point of view it connoted an agreement among the

---

[4]Japan, Gaimushō (Foreign Ministry), *Nihon gaikō bunsho*, XXVIII/2 (1953), 35, 89–92 (hereafter cited as *Nihon gaikō bunsho*); Mutsu Munemitsu, *Kenkenroku* (1939), chap. 15.

imperialists to respect the status quo and safeguard each other against economic discrimination in China. Such policies naturally suited Japan, and the Tokyo government could be reassured that it could continue to count on the United States in carrying out its policies in the Far East. A year later, with the outbreak of the Boxer Rebellion, Japan took pains to coordinate action with the powers, although it appears that it was most concerned with obtaining Britain's consent before dispatching its troops to China. Japan was particularly interested in allaying the suspicions of Russia and Germany, and there is no evidence that it was overly concerned with American reaction. The second Hay note, affirming America's interest in maintaining the territorial integrity of China, may have impressed Japanese officials as a veiled warning, as it was issued just as Japan was contemplating the dispatch of a division to China. But it does not seem that Japan took the note very seriously, certainly not as one calculated to undermine the basic framework of Japanese-American understanding.

At the beginning of the twentieth century, therefore, it could be said that the Japanese government regarded the United States as one of the imperialist powers in the Far East, and one with which it was to its advantage to remain in friendly relations and to cooperate where practicable. Such cooperation was most noted in Manchuria, which American merchants had entered with avidity. In their negotiations for new treaties with China following the Boxer Rebellion, Japanese and American officials coordinated their actions and both pressed China to open new ports in Manchuria, overriding Russian objections.[5] From the Japanese point of view, a joint stand with the United States was particularly useful as it could strengthen the Anglo-Japanese alliance and probably serve to counter Russian preponderance in Manchuria.

It now seems well established that Japan's Far Eastern policy at this time was directed at claiming Korea as its sphere of influence and, to a lesser and less certain degree, extending Japanese influence in southeast China, namely the provinces of Fukien and Chekiang.[6] In such an undertaking

---

[5]Shimomura Fujio, "Nichi-Ro sensō no seikaku" (1957), pp. 139–41.

[6]Imai Shōji, "Nichi-Ro sensō to tai-Shin seisaku no tenkai" (1960); Shimomura, "Nichi-Ro sensō no seisaku" and "Nichi-Ro sensō to Manshū shijō" (1956). Among recent studies of Japanese imperialism and expansionism at the turn of the century are Akira Iriye, "Imperialism in East Asia" (1970) and *Pacific Estrangement* (1972); and I.H. Nish, *The Anglo-Japanese Alliance* (1966).

Japan expected no difficulty from any quarter except Russia, and certainly it was not felt that the United States would object. The Tokyo government was rather surprised, therefore, when the State Department in 1900 intimated that it might ask for the use of Samsah Bay, in Fukien province, as an American naval base. It is characteristic of Japanese policy at this time that, while Minister Takahira Kogorō in Washington welcomed such a step as further evidence of Japanese-American friendship, Foreign Minister Katō Takaaki vehemently objected to it, saying Japan should not be guided by friendly sentiments alone.[7] But this was a minor incident, and before 1904 the two imperialists across the Pacific managed to maintain cordial relations, each confining its political action to its own spheres of influence. Elsewhere in the Far East, such as Manchuria, the United States and Japan were primarily interested in seeking equal commercial opportunities, although the former did not go as far as the latter in trying to counter the particularistic policies of the tsarist government.

The Russo-Japanese War (1904–5) was typical of the age in that it was a limited war designed, from the Japanese point of view, to check the Russian threat to Japanese interests in Korea. Once the war was started, however, the top policy-makers in Tokyo were emboldened to utilize the war to effect a partial redefinition of the status quo in Asia. While only the army and a handful of civilian bureaucrats had hitherto advocated the extension of Japan's sphere of interest to Manchuria, now the government itself, headed by Prime Minister Katsura Tarō and Foreign Minister Komura Jutarō, decided to add south Manchuria to the Japanese zone of influence. In so doing they were certainly breaking their previous commitment to an open door in Manchuria, now that they called for Japan's succession to Russia's political as well as economic rights in south Manchuria. Strikingly enough, there was apparently little thought given to this problem at the time. Possible conflict with American policy does not seem to have entered the consideration of the Japanese government as it drafted its peace terms with Russia, including the transfer of the Liaotung leasehold to Japan. This was probably because it was not felt that the mere

[7] *Nihon gaikō bunsho*, XXXIII (1956), 276. The Open Door policy has been treated more recently by these works: Thomas J. McCormick, *China Market: America's Quest for Informal Empire, 1893–1901* (1967); William Appleman Williams, *Roots of the Modern American Empire* (1969); Marilyn B. Young, *The Rhetoric of Empire: American China Policy, 1895–1901* (1968).

transfer of Russian title would be upsetting the basic principle of under-standing between Japan and the United States. It can be documented that initially at least the Japanese government believed it was fighting Russia not only for its own security in Korea but also in the interest of the powers. Throughout the war Japan continued to assure President Roose-velt that its basic policy was cooperation with the West in China. There was, of course, an element of propaganda in such assurances. Desperately in need of money to finance the war, Japanese officials had to convince American and British bankers that they had no evil designs after the war. What is most striking, however, was the basic assumption in Tokyo that Japan's succession to the Russian rights in south Manchuria entailed merely a minor redefinition of the power balance and would not upset the status quo to the detriment of third powers.[8]

The fact that it was to the United States that Japan finally looked for mediation indicated Japan's continued confidence in American sympathy. The Japanese expectation that President Theodore Roosevelt would be instrumental in procuring a peace treaty favoring Japan was not totally justified, but there is no evidence that Japanese officials were disillusioned with American policy during the Portsmouth Peace Conference. Actually they were grateful for Roosevelt's efforts, which they fondly believed to have been made to present Japan's case to the tsar. Their confidence in the strategy of imperial understanding with the United States must have been confirmed when the President told Kaneko Kentarō, both during and after the peace conference, that Japan should carry out a Monroe Doctrine in Asia.[9]

Japanese-American relations in this period are fully documented in the following collection:

Japan, Gaimushō (Foreign Ministry), *Nihon gaikō bunsho* (1936–   ).

Such episodes as American mediation efforts during the Sino-Japanese and Russo-Japanese wars, the Philippine annexation, the Open Door, the

---

[8]Kamikawa Hikomatsu, ed., *Nichi-Bei bunka kōshō shi, I: sōsetsu gaikō hen* (1956), pp. 438ff. For Japanese diplomacy during and immediately after the Russo-Japanese War there are two excellent recent studies: Shumpei Okamoto, *The Japanese Oligarchy and the Russo-Japanese War* (1970); and Tsunoda Jun, *Manshū mondai to kokubō hōshin* (1967).

[9]Roosevelt's diplomacy during the war is well described by John A. White, *The Diplomacy of the Russo-Japanese War* (1964); and Raymond A. Esthus, *Theodore Roosevelt and Japan* (1966).

Samsah Bay incident, and the Portsmouth Peace Conference can now be studied in the light of this collection.

The publication of these volumes has made other sources, notably biographies, much less useful than formerly. Nevertheless, the following biographies and memoirs contain direct reference to Japanese policy toward the United States during this period:

Hara, *Hara Takashi nikki* (9 vols., 1950–51).
Honda, *Tamashii no gaikō: Nichi-Ro sensō ni okeru Komura kō* (1941).
Japan, Foreign Ministry, *Komura gaikōshi* (2 vols., 1953).
Mutsu, *Kenkenroku* (1939).
Takahashi, *Takahashi Korekiyo jiden* (1936).

Most general histories of Japanese diplomacy contain chapters dealing with American mediation efforts during the Sino-Japanese and the Russo-Japanese wars. But they do little more than reprint basic documents exchanged between the two governments. In this category we may list the following works:

Hanabusa, *Meiji gaikōshi* (1960).
Kajima, *Nihon gaikō seisaku no shiteki kōsatsu* (1951), first published as *Teikoku gaikō no kihon seisaku* (1938).
—— *Nichi-Bei gaikōshi* (1958).
Kamikawa, *Nichi-Bei bunka kōshō shi, I: sōsetsu gaikō hen* (1956), presents a detailed account of American policy toward Japan during the Russo-Japanese War.
Komatsu, *Meiji gaikō hiwa* (1936).
Shinobu, *Nidai gaikō no shinsō* (1928).
Shinobu, *Mutsu gaikō: Nisshin sensō no gaikō shiteki kenkyū* (1935), first published as *Nisshin sensō* (1934).

The works noted above, however, are essentially digests of main events plus collections of documents. At best they supplement, but more often they repeat, noted works by Western historians, such as the following:

Beale, *Theodore Roosevelt and the Rise of America to World Power* (1956).
Conroy, *The Japanese Seizure of Korea, 1868–1910* (1960).
Dennett, *Americans in Eastern Asia: A Critical Study of the Policy of the United States with Reference to China, Japan and Korea in the 19th Century* (1922).
—— *Roosevelt and the Russo-Japanese War* (1925).
Griswold, *Far Eastern Policy of the United States* (1962; first published, 1938).
Langer, *The Diplomacy of Imperialism, 1890–1902* (2d ed., 1951).

Vagts, *Deutschland und die Vereinigten Staaten in der Weltpolitik* (2 vols., 1935).
Zabriskie, *American-Russian Rivalry in the Far East: A Study in Diplomacy and Power Politics, 1895–1914* (1946).

None of these works is specifically concerned with Japanese policy toward the United States. The result has been an abundance of books on United States policy toward Japan, not vice versa. Some of the works, notably Langer's and Vagts' monographs, carefully analyze the diplomacy of imperialism in the Far East, however, and they provide constructive frameworks in which Japanese policy can be discussed intelligently.

When historians generalize about Japanese policy at this time, going beyond the presentation of data, they have done so almost invariably in terms of the "character" of Japanese imperialism or of Japan's wars with China and Russia. In this connection they have been inclined to explain Japan's actions as a function either of its internal politics (determined by the unfolding "absolutism of the emperor system"), of its economy (characterized as "capitalism"), or of the overall international system of "power politics." Here the influence of Marxist thought and Russian historiography has been notable. The following is a list of several influential Soviet books and some representative works on these questions by Japanese writers:

Avarin, *Imperializm v Man'chzhurii* (1934).
Dobrov, *Dal'nevostochnaia politika SShA v period Russko-Iaponskoi voiny* (1952).
Eguchi, "Nihon teikokushugi no kokusaiteki keiki" (1954).
Kantorovich, *Amerika v bor'be za Kitai* (1935).
Kuroba, *Sekaishijō yori mitaru Nichi-Ro sensō* (1960).
Romanov, *Ocherki diplomaticheskoi istorii Russko-Iaponskoi voiny, 1895–1907* (rev. ed., 1955).
Shinobu and Nakayama, *Nichi-Ro sensō shi no kenkyū* (1959).

While some Japanese writers have tended to indulge in academic discussion of the domestic factors presumably determining the character of the Russo-Japanese War, some others, notably Shimomura Fujio, have contributed to restoring clear thinking on the matter because of their relative freedom from Marxist biases.

Imai, "Nichi-Ro sensō to tai-Shin seisaku no tenkai" (1960).
Shimomura, "Nichi-Ro sensō to Manshū shijō" (1956).
—— "Nichi-Ro sensō no seikaku" (1957).

Japanese historiography on the question of expansion into Manchuria is well summarized in:

Ogiso, Sakurai, Fujimura, and Yoshii, "Nisshin Nichi-Ro sensō kenkyūshi" (1961).

While the works thus far mentioned deal only incidentally with Japanese policy toward the United States, the following monographs treat specific aspects of Japanese-American relations. They are valuable as they show what objective scholarship can do in this field.

Inō, "Giwadan jihen to Nihon no shuppei gaikō: daigo shidan shutsudō ni itaru made no keii" (1952).
Yamaguchi, "Kenseitō naikaku no seiritsu to kyokutō jōsei" (1961).
Yoshimura, "Nichi-Ro kōwa mondai no ichi sokumen: Nihon no tai-Shin taido o chūshin ni" (1961).

Yamaguchi discusses Japan's response to the Spanish-American War, and Yoshimura's is one of the few monographs that raises the question of Japan's view of possible American reaction to its peace terms during the war with Russia.

It seems obvious that the writing on this period has been confined largely to Japan's two wars, with little attention paid to the interwar years. These years have too often been treated simply as a period in transition, of preparation for an eventual conflict between Russia and Japan. But these years are particularly relevant to the study of American-Japanese relations in view of the rift between the two countries after the war. It would seem that a series of monographs could be written on Japanese policy from a fresh point of view. Such monographs might examine Japanese views of the Far East in this period of imperialist diplomacy and relate them to Japan's attitude toward the United States. The question would have to be asked as to how Japan visualized its postwar relations with the United States when, in 1904, it was decided to succeed to Russian rights in south Manchuria. Since American capital was beginning to play an increasingly important role in Japan as well as in China, it would be extremely interesting, for example, to see how Japanese businessmen reacted to the complexities of power politics in the Far East.

PARTING OF THE WAY, 1905–1914

The years between the Portsmouth Peace Conference and World War I may be taken as a distinctive period in Japanese-American relations. It was during these years that the two countries became for the first time aware of their different interests and goals in the Far East. At the same time conflict between the two was still definable in terms of the diplomacy of imperialism.

Personal factors seem to have been as important as other factors in the developing rift between the two countries. Foreign Minister Komura had been instrumental in Japan's decision to claim south Manchuria as its sphere of influence. To this end he would promote active trade and investment activities by Japanese in that region. Gotō Shimpei, the first president of the South Manchuria Railway Company, also promoted such a scheme. Komura's opposition to having American financiers participate in the South Manchuria Railway project is a good example of his policy. Under such encouragement Japanese merchants became actively interested in exporting cotton piece-goods to Manchuria. All this meant competition with and eventual predominance over American merchants, the most influential non-Russian foreign group in south Manchuria before the Russo-Japanese War.

In the United States too there arose a group of businessmen and officials who were determined to expand American influence in Manchuria. Among them, men like E.H. Harriman, Willard Straight, and F.M. Huntington Wilson were actively interested in countering the trend toward Japanese predominance in south Manchuria. They would do so by introducing capital and building railways in Manchuria. Their ideas were incorporated in Philander Knox's China policy.

Apart from these personal and related factors there were others that served to intensify the sense of rivalry between the two countries. After the Russo-Japanese War and as a result of the second Anglo-Japanese alliance, the Japanese navy became predominant in the western Pacific and able therefore to challenge American colonial possessions. The navies in both countries began to study plans for a future naval conflict between them.[10]

[10]Kobayashi Tatsuo, "Kaigun gunshuku jōyaku, 1921–1926" (1963), pp. 7–14. See also Hata Ikuhiko, "Meiji ikō ni okeru Nichi-Bei Taiheiyō senryaku no hensen" (1968).

Another important factor, the immigration dispute, does not seem to have been necessarily related to Japanese-American rivalry in the Far East after 1905. Race prejudice and the nature of California politics, which have essentially nothing to do with a given international situation, were more important factors. Nevertheless, California exclusionists could and did argue that after Manchuria their state was the next target of Japanese expansionism.[11] Thus the immigration issue could easily lead to a war scare in both countries.

Given this potential animosity, Japanese policy toward the United States could choose from several alternatives. It could either ignore American opposition and extend its influence in the Far East, seek rapprochement with the United States, or strike a compromise between these positions. Japan's choice, of course, depended in part on the policies of other imperialist powers. The willingness of Russia, France, and Britain at this time to recognize Japanese rights in south Manchuria reduced the value of American goodwill. On the other hand, the United States was believed to be most important for Japanese trade. It was therefore undesirable to antagonize or unnecessarily irritate the United States. For these reasons Japanese policy toward the United States took the alternative of seeking a workable relationship between the two countries, one which would uphold Japanese rights in the Far East but would not alienate the United States to the detriment of Japanese-American trade.

There are two important documents in this period which exemplify such a policy. One is the minutes of the famous "conference on Manchurian problems," held in Tokyo in May 1906. There Itō Hirobumi expressed the view that Japan should endeavor to allay the suspicion of the powers that it was closing the door in Manchuria. He was well aware of Japan's financial dependence on Britain and the United States, and he believed it was to Japan's advantage to remain on good terms with them. The conferees then decided to abolish the military government of the Kwantung Leased Territory and to reopen the door of economic opportunity in Manchuria, for example by making Dairen a free port and permitting

[11]See Roger Daniels, *The Politics of Prejudice: The Anti-Japanese Movement in California and the Struggle for Japanese Exclusion* (1962), p. 70. The subject of the immigration crisis is covered by two recent monographs: Charles E. Neu, *An Uncertain Friendship: Theodore Roosevelt and Japan, 1906–1909* (1967); and Iriye, *Pacific Estrangement* (1972).

foreigners residence and business activities in certain areas along the South Manchuria Railway.[12] The second document is a cabinet decision on foreign policy, adopted in September 1908, after Komura came back as foreign minister in the second Katsura cabinet. "It is necessary," the decision stated, "for Japan not only to maintain good relations with the United States politically but also to promote friendly relations in view of America's predominant position in our trade." Under the heading "Activities Abroad," the cabinet concluded that it was most essential to maintain and cultivate closer trade relations with the United States and China. Furthermore, "while trade competition with the powers is unavoidable, as Japanese foreign trade develops, Japan should take heed not to let this commercial competition affect its political relations with other countries. . . . Trade competition should be carried out through fair and moderate means, and Japan should avoid employing unfair tactics and obtaining improper advantages." On the immigration issue, the government thought it best not to jeopardize Japan's trade relations with the United States by irritating Americans with a policy of encouraging emigration to their country.[13]

This policy of seeking to maintain good relations with the United States was behind Japan's decision to minimize the impact of the immigration dispute, in 1907 by concluding a gentleman's agreement and in 1911 by expressing a willingness as part of the new commercial treaty to control the emigration of laborers to the United States. It was also behind the Root-Takahira agreement of November 1908, which upheld the principle of the Open Door in China as well as the status quo in mutual territorial possessions in the Pacific.

It is evident, however, that the policy of seeking understanding with the United States was never an end in itself but a tactic to safeguard the Japanese empire. The defense and economic development of the empire required increased foreign borrowing, which amounted to over ¥760 million between 1905 and 1913. The importance of the United States as a market and a supplier of capital was obvious. The same considerations of empire, however, precluded the possibility of arriving at an arrangement with the United States at the cost of sacrificing Japan's imperial interests. Thus

[12]Japan, Gaimushō (Foreign Ministry), *Nihon gaikō nempyō narabi ni shuyō bunsho* (1965; first published, 1955), I, 260–69 (hereafter cited as *Nihon gaikō nempyō*).
[13]*Ibid.*, pp. 305–9.

Japan acted strongly to prevent Americans from undermining its influence in Manchuria through their several projects. It tried to prevent the United States from coming to the assistance of the Ch'ing government, which at that time was trying to nationalize all railways in China, including those granted as concessions to foreigners. The Japanese government put pressure on China not to seek American support in such an undertaking. There is little evidence that Japanese officials were overly alarmed by the rumored moves toward an entente among Germany, the United States, and China, but Japan acted swiftly and resolutely whenever there was such a possibility. It agreed to the American-inspired construction of the Chinchow-Aigun railway only on condition that Japanese capital participate in it equally. Knox's scheme for "railway neutralization" in Manchuria, which may be regarded as the most spectacular attempt by the United States to challenge the Japanese empire, was strenuously opposed by Japan, confident that its allies would support its rights, as indeed they did.

The emphasis on the defense of the empire led the Japanese military to devise plans for a possible conflict with the United States. While there was no overall governmental planning, the Japanese navy resolved in 1907 to consider the United States a hypothetical enemy in future warfare. This was because American policy in Asia at the time impressed Japan's naval strategists as intent upon redefining the status quo to the detriment of the Japanese empire. The naval preparedness against the United States, coupled with financial dependence on the latter for the maintenance of the empire, typifies Japanese foreign policy in this heyday of imperialist politics.

Japanese-American relations in the early 1910s remained basically the same as in the previous five years, but they were necessarily affected by the Chinese upheaval. Japanese policy concerning the republican revolution in 1911–12 and the recognition of the Yuan Shih-k'ai regime indicates that Japan was still interested in maintaining basic solidarity with the imperialist powers in the Far East. Since, however, the United States under President Woodrow Wilson was prone to act independently, as evidenced by its eagerness to extend speedy recognition to the Yuan government and its decision to withdraw from the international banking consortium, there was created an impression of further divergence between Japanese and American policies. The rift was widened as a result of measures taken in 1913 by the California state legislature to prohibit ownership of land by Japanese immigrants, and by the Magdalena Bay episode of 1911–12, during which the United States objected to negotiations between a Japanese company and an American syndicate for a huge tract of land near this bay in Lower California.[14]

It can be said, then, that the basic Japanese policy toward the United States between 1905 and 1914 was motivated by the need to preserve the newly acquired empire. Japan viewed itself and the United States as imperialists, as members of the Far Eastern world order that had come into existence after the Sino-Japanese War. This is another way of saying that Japanese leaders fully identified their country as one of the advanced powers engaged in imperialistic ventures in Asia. While some of those not in policy-making positions were inclined toward various forms of Pan-Asianism and some others began to call for a union of Asian peoples under Japanese leadership in opposition to the dominating white race, the government's policy was to discourage such talk which, it was feared, would arouse Western suspicions. When leaders, notably Ōkuma Shigenobu, talked of the "harmony of East and West" to which Japan should contribute, this merely implied Japan's mission as a representative of the West to civilize Asians. There was no thought of abandoning the basic orientation of foreign policy, to act like a Western power by building, consolidating, and, if possible, expanding an empire.[15]

The official documentary collection in the Foreign Ministry contains the basic source materials. In addition, the following series takes up treaty revision negotiations after 1907:

Japan, Gaimushō (Foreign Ministry), *Tsūshō jōyaku kankei Nihon gaikō bunsho* (3 vols., 1954).

The following is a supplement and contains a useful summary of the negotiations:

Japan, Gaimushō (Foreign Ministry), *Tsūshō jōyaku to tsūshō seisaku no hensen* (1951).

The following among biographical works are relevant:

Kikuchi, *Hakushaku Chinda Sutemi den* (1938).

[14]Thomas A. Bailey, *A Diplomatic History of the American People* (7th ed., 1964), pp. 588-89; Kamikawa, *Nichi-Bei bunka kōshō shi*, I, pp. 537-42. The most recent treatment of the Magdalena Bay episode is William R. Braisted, *The United States Navy in the Pacific, 1909-1922* (1971).

[15]Nomura Kōichi, "Kokuminteki shimeikan no shoruikei to sono tokushitsu" (1961), pp. 140-46. For an overall discussion of Japanese-American estrangement, see Iriye, *Pacific Estrangement*.

Ko Hakushaku Yamamoto Kaigun Taishō Denki Hensankai, *Hakushaku Yama-moto Gonnohyōe den* (2 vols., 1938).

Considering the importance of this period for Japanese-American relations, there is surprisingly little that is of value among secondary works. Much has been written on such episodes as Harriman's railway scheme in Manchuria, Knox's "dollar diplomacy," the Chinchow-Aigun railway project, and the recognition of Yuan Shih-k'ai. These, however, have been treated primarily from the American angle and only as isolated incidents in Japanese-American relations. While the general worsening of relations between the two countries after the Russo-Japanese War is universally recognized, few have bothered to consider this phenomenon in terms of Japanese policy toward the United States. The following are several of the more intelligent and useful monographs analyzing this problem:

Baba, "Nichi-Ro sensō go no tairiku seisaku" (1961).
Bailey, *Theodore Roosevelt and the Japanese-American Crises* (1964; first published, 1934).
Braisted, *The United States Navy in the Pacific, 1897–1909* (1958).
Clinard, *Japan's Influence on American Naval Power, 1897–1917* (1947).
Croly, *Willard Straight* (1924).
Daniels, *Politics of Prejudice: The Anti-Japanese Movement in California and the Struggle for Japanese Exclusion* (1962).
Dulles, *Forty Years of American-Japanese Relations* (1937).
Harrington, *God, Mammon and the Japanese* (1944).
Hatano, "Nichi-Ro sensō go ni okeru kokusai kankei no dōin: Nichi-Bei kankei o chūshin to suru" (1957).
Irie, "Shingai kakumei to shinseifu no shōnin" (1956).
Kachi, "Nichi-Bei tsūshō kōkai jōyaku to Kariforunia-shū tochi hō" (1961).
Nakayama, *Nichi-Ro sensō igo* (1957).
Tupper and McReynolds, *Japan in American Public Opinion* (1937).

Croly and Harrington emphasize the role of personality in the unfolding drama of Japanese-American hostility, while Braisted describes American naval thinking on Japanese expansionism up to 1909. Daniels' monograph has been superseded by Neu's *An Uncertain Friendship* (1967) but is still useful. It correlates California's racism with Japanese-American antagonism in Manchuria. One must not forget, in this connection, the relevant chapters in Griswold's classic study of American Far Eastern policy.

None of the works thus far cited adequately analyzes the issue of Japan's economic dependence on the United States. Studies of the economic history of Japan, such as those listed below, point to the need for fresh thinking about this problem in order to arrive at a more rounded interpretation of Japanese policy toward the United States. Many questions remain, such as the Japanese leaders' apprehension of a possible future conflict with the United States, their image of Sino-American relations, and their effort to square Japanese-British understanding with Anglo-American amity.

Lockwood, *The Economic Development of Japan: Growth and Structural Change, 1868–1938* (1954).

Takahashi, *Taishō Shōwa zaikai hendō shi* (3 vols., 1954–55).

CRISIS AND RECONCILIATION, 1914–1922

In the years between World War I and the Washington Conference, radical changes occurred in the diplomacy of imperialism in the Far East and, concomitantly, in Japanese-American relations. The existing framework of power politics was destroyed, first, by Japan's active expansionism, which destroyed the precarious balance among the imperialists, and, second, by the anti-imperialist or nonimperialist policies of China, the Soviet Union, the United States, and Germany. Given these two forces undermining the prewar balance, it was natural that the foremost representatives of these two trends—Japan and the United States—should come to oppose each other openly.

Economic historians have pointed out that the Japanese empire was facing a grave financial crisis in 1914, since foreign financiers, on whose loans the maintenance of the empire had depended, had become less and less willing to lend money to Japan unless it clearly followed a policy of economic retrenchment. The Japanese government was caught in a vicious circle of having to borrow money to pay interest on the money borrowed earlier. Even within Japan, voices began to be heard that the nation's imperial responsibilities should be reduced to restore financial stability. But the outbreak of World War I providentially saved the empire; from the end of 1914 on, Japan's trade deficits disappeared and there was a net inflow of capital as orders came pouring in for Japanese arms, merchandise, and ships, not only from the European belligerents but also from the United States, alike profiting from the war, and from Asian countries, hitherto consumers of European goods. Japan's leaders were now emboldened to consolidate and expand the empire.

The Tokyo government decided to take advantage of Europe's distress and seek to perpetuate Japanese rights in the Liaotung Peninsula and the South Manchuria Railway. This could be done by expelling German influence from Shantung and restoring the peninsula to China, in return for the latter's agreement to perpetuate Japan's rights in Manchuria beyond the terms set in the original leases to Russia. To this extent, it may be said that Japanese policy was primarily designed to preserve the existing empire. Actually, of course, Japan went much further. In 1915 it sought to have China recognize Japan's special rights in Inner Mongolia, which had already been sanctioned by the third Russo-Japanese entente (1912), and to succeed to German rights in Shantung. Also in 1915 and early 1916 the Ōkuma cabinet did its best to frustrate Yuan Shih-k'ai's efforts to centralize authority in China. The cabinet of General Terauchi Masatake (1916–18), on the other hand, financially and politically assisted the Peking government, but with the intention of establishing Japanese tutelage over China. Finally, Japan sought to displace Russian influence in north Manchuria as well as in eastern Siberia and took advantage of the American suggestion for a joint expedition in order to fulfill these ends. By the time of the armistice in Europe, the Japanese empire had been so expanded that the prewar balance was unrecognizable.

The old framework of imperialist power rivalry was also undermined by the defection of Germany and Austria from the imperialist ranks, President Wilson's active policy of the "new diplomacy," Bolshevik Russia's anti-imperialist propaganda, and China's awakened nationalism. These were all connected with the war, although it is possible to date Wilson's new diplomacy from before the war. His tendency to act alone had been evident in his attitude toward Yuan Shih-k'ai. It was the war in Europe, however, which enabled him to formulate the new concepts of international relations such as "national sovereignty" and the "self-determination of peoples." These principles were primarily applicable to eastern Europe and were not to be taken literally elsewhere on the globe. Nevertheless, Wilsonian policy had a tremendous impact in the Far East where the prewar balance had been upset by Japanese action. First of all, the United States under Wilson made it explicit that it was opposed to Japan's wartime expansionism. Such opposition itself was nothing new; imperialist powers had opposed each other whenever one seemed to encroach upon the prerogative of another. This time, however, American policy was couched in a new language, that of the new diplomacy. The United States would oppose Japanese expansion, not because it was interested in restoring a prewar balance of power in the Far East, but fundamentally because it was intent on demolishing the very system of imperialist diplomacy. The United States would attack such practices of the old diplomacy as secret and open alliances and agreements among the powers at the expense of China, mutual recognition of spheres of influence, and exclusive bilateral arrangements with China to the detriment of free and open competition. It was not that the United States had turned against the existing treaty structure—it was not yet ready to endorse China's national sovereignty immediately and unconditionally. But it was definitely opposed to particularistic policies and power rivalries at the expense of weaker countries. The American proposal for a new banking consortium and insistence on the abrogation of the Anglo-Japanese alliance provide the best examples of this attitude.

Such a trend in American policy was at first only dimly recognized in Tokyo. This explains why there was no fundamental change in the basic tenet of Japanese policy toward the United States during these years. Japan still wished to be on good terms with the United States. As examples of this attitude, we may cite Japan's sensitivity to American reaction to the Twenty-One Demands, Ishii Kikujirō's attempt to define a workable agreement with Secretary of State Robert Lansing, and the Tokyo government's interest, at least initially, in coordinating action with the United States for a Siberian expedition. On the Twenty-One Demands episode, it is possible to argue that care was taken to put the most radical demands in group five primarily so as not to alarm the powers, including the United States. Japan was worried lest China should turn to the United States for help, and it did its best to assure the latter of its mild intentions.[16] Since the United States nevertheless responded with the caveat of May 11, 1915, it became a primary task of the Japanese government to patch over differences between the two countries as best it could. While General Terauchi was prime minister, it is true, some began strongly advocating an independent course of action in the Far East. Nishihara Kamezō's activities in China and Gotō Shimpei's proposal for bilateral arrangements

---

[16]Kwan Ha Yim, "Japanese Policy toward China during World War I" (1963), a provocative reinterpretation of the Twenty-One Demands. See also I.H. Nish, *Alliance in Decline* (1972).

between China and Japan are examples. Foreign Minister Motono Ichirō and his staff, however, continued to consider it imperative for Japan to operate within the framework of understanding with the West. Their views of Japan and of other powers had not changed; they were all imperialists playing their game according to its ground rules. Whereas the American government was taking steps to extricate itself from the framework of imperialist diplomacy, the Japanese government continued to regard the United States as a member of the system. In such a context, understanding with the United States was considered essential, in view of the latter's relatively enhanced power status during the war.

Between the episode of the Twenty-One Demands and the signing of the Lansing-Ishii agreement in November 1917, Japan consistently sought to negotiate a modus vivendi with the United States. In such an agreement Japan would recognize America's free hand in the immigration matter and agree to respect the Open Door in China, but in return the United States would be asked to recognize Japan's special interests in Manchuria and eastern Inner Mongolia. Foreign Minister Motono's private instructions to Ishii, as he set out for the United States in the summer of 1917, stated, "Japan possesses no intention of hindering the economic activities of the United States in China, so long as they do not infringe upon Japan's special interests." This was the basic philosophy behind the negotiations for an agreement with Washington.[17] The Lansing-Ishii compromise, ambiguous as it was, especially as it included a secret protocol upholding the status quo in China, was accepted by Japan since it could be utilized to impress China with the utter hopelessness of courting American assistance against Japan.[18]

Finally, some, if not all, of the most influential policy-makers in Tokyo were strongly convinced of the need to cooperate with the United States vis-a-vis Bolshevik Russia. Men such as Uehara Yūsaku and Tanaka Giichi insisted on unilateral action in Siberia to take advantage of the power vacuum there, and some others, like Foreign Minister Motono, were interested in granting Britain's and France's proposal for a Japanese expedition to create an eastern front. But it was the views of men like Yamagata Aritomo, Hara Takashi, and Makino Nobuaki that modified Japanese policy

---

[17] *Nihon gaikō nempyō*, I, 434–37.
[18] Sadao Asada, "Japan and the United States, 1915–1925" (1963).

toward Siberia. They reasoned that in view of America's importance in Far Eastern matters as well as in Japanese trade, cooperation with the United States was absolutely necessary before Japan could undertake such an expedition. Wilson's proposal for a joint expedition in July 1918 solved the impasse within governmental circles in Tokyo. Once the expedition was underway, the army acted on its own initiative, augmenting its forces and widening its sphere of operation beyond the Vladivostok area. Here again it is essential to remember that as soon as Hara came to power in September 1918 he set about conciliating the United States by reducing the size of Japanese troops.[19]

Why was Japan at all interested in maintaining a degree of understanding with the United States? There are certain obvious reasons. First, the importance of the United States for the Japanese economy was still widely recognized. Realistically noting the superiority of American financial power, Japanese leaders believed it to Japan's advantage to invite U.S. capital in China to work in cooperation with Japanese capital.[20] Second, and connected with this reason, there was the Japanese officials' vision of the postwar world. In his famous diagnosis Yamagata visualized the Far East once again dominated by a combination of Western powers. Because of the very successes of Japanese imperialism, he feared that the advanced Western nations would come back to the Far East and confront Japan in unity.[21] His vision of a racial conflict in the future may not have been shared by other leaders, and some of them in fact argued that because of such a possibility Japan should take unilateral steps in China and Siberia to forestall the return of Western influence. Most civilian officials, however, seem to have been agreed that this was an untenable alternative and that the best thing was to come to terms with one or more Western powers, including the United States. Finally, after November 1917 Japan could no longer count on Russia's solid support of its spheres of influence and had to compensate for this loss by turning to the United States.

These are important factors, but we should note that underlying them all was the assumption that the United States was just another imperialist power. As noted above, Japanese officials continued to visualize

---

[19]Hosoya Chihiro, "Shiberia shuppei o meguru Nichi-Bei kankei" (1961), pp. 78–79.
[20]Asada, "Japan and the United States," p. 27.
[21]Tokutomi Iichirō, ed., *Kōshaku Yamagata Aritomo den* (1933), III, 919–28.

Japanese-American relations in terms of rivalry or entente between two imperialists. That is why they were so intent on mutual deals, on having the United States recognize Japanese prerogatives in return for certain Japanese concessions. It was this assumption that was put to a severe test during the Paris Peace Conference and thereafter, since the United States had now clearly attacked the practices of the old diplomacy and sought to bring about a new set of rules to govern the conduct of nations. Japanese policy toward the United States during the peace conference becomes intelligible in such a context. Japan had expected that its wartime negotiations with China would be upheld by America. Regarding the League of Nations as an instrument of big-power diplomacy, Japanese officials thought they were offering a reasonable deal when they agreed to participate in it if the Japanese position in Shantung were upheld.

It soon became apparent to Japanese leaders, however, that the United States was not only seeking to roll back the tide of Japan's wartime expansionism but even to undermine the basic framework of power diplomacy in the Far East. The clearest expressions of this attitude, as noted above, were the American policies on the new consortium and the renewal of the Anglo-Japanese alliance. Here again Japan at first acted under the same assumptions as earlier. It agreed to join the consortium on condition that its preserves in Manchuria and Inner Mongolia should be excluded from the consortium's sphere of operation. On the alliance with Britain, the Japanese government sought to placate American sensibilities by inviting the United States to join the alliance or to participate in a substitute triple agreement. It was only when these attempts failed that Japan began seriously reconsidering its overall strategy.

In the course of the Washington Conference (1921–22), Japanese officials apparently made up their minds that their adherence to the diplomacy of imperialism was no longer adequate in their conduct of foreign policy and that Japan might as well proclaim its willingness to abide by the new rules of the game being developed under the American initiative. There were various factors behind this decision: the need to put an end to the dangerous naval race; the reassertion of power by civilian bureaucrats in Tokyo who were more oriented toward agreement with the United States than were the military; and the overall consideration that Japan's postwar economic adjustment needed solid affiliation with the Western economies. To be sure, the Japanese government accepted the sweeping renunciation of the spheres of influence and other particularistic practices in China in the Nine Power Treaty only after it persuaded itself that the "security clause" in the treaty—expressing the signatories' agreement not to infringe upon each other's rights in China—was tantamount to the powers' tacit recognition of Japanese influence in Manchuria.

Nevertheless, private and public expressions by Japanese officials make it amply evident that by 1922 Japan had become definitely aware of the passing of the old order of things in international relations. This does not mean, of course, that imperialism as such was gone. The Japanese empire, now including some of the former German islands in the Pacific, was solidly preserved, and it was not challenged even by the United States. Empires remained, but the old concepts and practices defining their mutual relationships had been discarded. It is in this sense that the Washington Conference may be said to have put an end to the diplomacy of imperialism in the Far East. Japan was a witness, though at first reluctant, to the passing of an epoch.[22]

The study of Japanese foreign policy during and after World War I suffers from the fact that the official published documentary collection only recently reached the war period. One could turn to the following shorter collection, which has the most vital documents between 1840 and 1945:

Japan, Gaimushō (Foreign Ministry), *Nihon gaikō nempyō narabi ni shuyō bunsho* (2 vols., 1965; first published, 1955).

The number of documents printed in this collection, however, is extremely limited. Ideally, the researcher should have access to unpublished records in the Foreign Ministry as well as extant military archives. Microfilm reproductions of some of these documents are indicated in the following checklists:

Uyehara, *Checklist of Archives in the Japanese Ministry of Foreign Affairs, Tokyo, Japan, 1868–1945, Microfilmed for the Library of Congress, 1949–1951* (1954).
Young, *Checklist of Microfilm Reproductions of Selected Archives of the Japanese Army, Navy, and Other Government Agencies, 1868–1945* (1959).

The official documents may be supplemented by certain autobiographical

---

[22]Sadao Asada, "Japan's 'Special Interests' and the Washington Conference, *1921–1913*" (1961). See also Akira Iriye, *After Imperialism: The Search for a New Order in the Far East, 1921–1931* (1965).

and biographical sketches, among which the following are relevant to the
study of Japanese policy toward the United States:

Arai, *Katō Tomosaburō* (1958).
Araki, *Gensui Uehara Yūsaku den* (2 vols., 1937).
Gensui Katō Tomosaburō Denki Hensan Iinkai, *Gensui Katō Tomosaburō den* (1928).
Hara, *Hara Takashi nikki* (9 vols., 1950–51).
Ishii, *Gaikōkan no isshō* (1950).
Ishii, *Gaikō yoroku* (1930).
Itō, "Sui'usō nikki: Nichi-Bei shuppei teigi mondai" (1962).
—— *Sui'usō nikki: Rinji Gaikō Chōsa Iinkai kaigi hikki nado* (1966).
Katō Kanji Denki Hensankai, *Katō Kanji taishō den* (1941).
Kurihara, *Hakushaku Itō Miyoji* (2 vols., 1938).
Kuroda, *Gensui Terauchi hakushaku den* (1920).
Obata Yūkichi Denki Kankōkai, *Obata Yūkichi* (1957).
Oka, *Yamagata Aritomo: Meiji Nihon no shōchō* (1958).
Shibusawa Seien Kinen Zaidan Ryūmonsha, *Shibusawa Eiichi denki shiryō* (58 vols., 1955–65).
Shidehara Heiwa Zaidan, *Shidehara Kijūrō* (1955).
Shidehara, *Gaikō gojūnen* (1951).
Takakura, *Tanaka Giichi denki* (2 vols., 1958–60).
Tanaka, *Yoshino Sakuzō* (1958).
Tokutomi, *Kōshaku Yamagata Aritomo den* (3 vols., 1933).
Tsurumi, *Gotō Shimpei* (4 vols., 1937–38).

These biographies and autobiographies are of varying merit, but they all contain some discussion of Japan's attitude toward the United States in this period. Most of them, however, single out the Siberian expedition and the Washington Conference for treatment and pay little attention to minor but equally significant events. Uehara's biography contains an interesting observation by the general on the South Pacific islands as part of the Japanese defense system. Volume 33 of the Shibusawa biographical materials contains information about Shibusawa's tour of the United States in 1916 to popularize his idea of Japanese-American financial cooperation. The diary of Hara Takashi is perhaps the most valuable source on the thinking of Japanese leaders on Japanese-American relations.

There are certain competent monographs dealing with aspects of Japanese policy toward the United States, such as the Twenty-One Demands, the Lansing-Ishii agreement, the Siberian Expedition, the Paris Peace

Conference, and the Washington Conference. Here the list is limited to those directly concerned with Japan's America policy:

Ōhata, "Washinton kaigi Nihon seifu kunrei ni tsuite no kōsatsu" (1952).
—— "Washinton kaigi kaisai to Nichi-Bei kankei" (1961).
Rōyama, "Manshū mondai o meguru Nichi-Bei gaikō no sōten" (1956).
Shinobu, *Taishō seijishi* (4 vols., 1951–52).
—— *Taishō demokurashii shi* (3 vols., 1954–59).
Somura, "Washinton kaigi no ichi kōsatsu: Ozaki Yukio no gumbi seigen ron o chūshin ni shite" (1958).
Yim, "Japanese Policy toward China during World War I" (1963).

The Washington Conference has been studied in the following monographs:

Asada, "Japan and the United States, 1915–1925" (1963).
Buckley, *The United States and the Washington Conference* (1970).
Louis, *British Strategy in the Far East, 1919–1939* (1971).
Nish, *Alliance in Decline, 1908–1923* (1972).

The monographs indicate that a fair degree of research has been done on various aspects of Japanese policy toward the United States during this critical period. It would seem, however, that since so many of the works presuppose an underlying conflict between Japanese and American policies, they undoubtedly were influenced by subsequent events. While such a conflict was perhaps unavoidable, given Japan's wartime expansionism and particularistic diplomacy, one should not necessarily suppose that there was a logical connection between Japanese-American hostilities in the late 1930s and those in the 1910s. Future research will have to go much beyond a simple description of the clash between Japanese expansionism and the American policy of the Open Door. One would have to examine how Japanese leaders visualized their country's economic stake and its implications in Japanese-American relations. In addition, one would need to study specifically how changes in American policy under Wilson affected Japanese thinking on Far Eastern matters.

THE SEARCH FOR A NEW ORDER, 1922–1931

For some time after the Washington Conference, Japanese leaders consistently spoke of the "new epoch" in international relations. Prime Minister Takahashi Korekiyo, for instance, stated that the Washington

Conference had ushered in a "new stage" in international politics and opened up a "new vista" in the foreign policies of the powers. It was not very clear what specifically was "new," but these expressions revealed the feeling that the old order of things had passed. As discussed earlier, the old framework of power politics had in fact been undermined beyond recognition, and Japanese leaders had realized the futility of resisting this trend. The problem they faced in the 1920s was, therefore, how to define a new framework in which Japanese interests would be promoted. Should it take the form of close cooperation with the United States and/or Britain? What if these countries had their own ideas other than that of joint action with Japan? Should Japan, instead, seek to safeguard its interests by reverting to the practice of the 1910s, by entering into bilateral arrangements with China? But were Japan's interests in China so important that Japanese relations with other countries were of a secondary nature? What should Japan's attitude be toward the powers, such as the Soviet Union and Germany, which were not members of the new multilateral treaty structure set up by the Washington Conference? What form should Japan's relationship with the League of Nations take?

These were the problems that vexed Japan's policy-makers throughout the 1920s. It is too often assumed that some of them, notably Shidehara Kijūrō, advocated and practiced "internationalism," while others, like Tanaka Giichi, chose the alternative of independent action in China. It is essential to note, however, that both Shidehara and Tanaka grappled with the same fundamental question of finding a new basis for foreign policy and that their solutions to the problem were as much influenced by happenings outside of Japan over which they had little control as by their own ideas and other domestic factors.

Since Japan's leaders during the 1920s were groping for a viable foreign policy, it is extremely difficult to characterize Japanese-American relations in a coherent manner. It is possible, however, to postulate that there were at least three phases through which Japan's foreign policy passed during the years between the Washington Conference and the Manchurian Incident. In each phase the Japanese government tried to define new principles and to found a new basis of foreign policy so as to protect and extend what it took to be national interests. Japanese policy toward the United States was an essential aspect of such a search.

The first phase, immediately following the Washington Conference, probably lasted until the middle of 1925. It was during these three years that the successive foreign ministers—Uchida Yasuya, Ijūin Hikokichi, Matsui Keishirō, and Shidehara—spoke of the "new era," the "spirit of the Washington Conference," "international cooperation," "coexistence and coprosperity," and "constructive, pacific policy." Translated into practice, these phrases meant a general policy of understanding with the "Washington powers," in particular the United States and Britain. The framework for such understanding was no longer that of bilateral alliances and ententes but was believed to have been provided by the Washington Conference. In accordance with the treaties and resolutions of the conference, therefore, Japan proceeded to withdraw its troops from Shantung, north Manchuria, and Siberia, and it agreed to the abrogation of the Lansing-Ishii agreement. It consistently refused to interfere in the civil strife in China. It no longer sought to uphold its rights in the Far East by means of secret protocols.

Even outside of the Far East, Japanese policy was more eager to maintain a spirit of friendship with the United States than during the 1910s. During the immigration crisis following the passage of America's Oriental exclusion act in 1924, the Foreign Ministry took a cautious and patient attitude, believing that the feeling of racial insult should not be allowed to interfere with the basic policy of understanding with the United States. Most Japanese officials were also unenthusiastic about reopening talks with Russia to normalize their relations, in view of America's and Britain's initial policies of nonrecognition.

Such a policy of basic understanding with the United States reflected the realization that the Japanese economy still depended on America's capital and market. The need was increased after the earthquake of 1923. This was an era of "economic diplomacy." Since the old aggressive practices had been renounced, Japan was to expand economically. It was believed that the United States had much to offer to Japan as it strove to be more fully affiliated with the Western economies.

The principle of Japanese-American understanding did much to improve the atmosphere between the two countries. State Department officials, who had earlier strongly denounced Japanese policy, were by 1925 talking of the good faith and honorable intentions of Japan. But the new approach did not totally satisfy the Japanese leaders groping for a constructive alternative to the diplomacy of particularism. By 1925 it was obvious that the Washington

powers had totally failed to placate the increasingly radical Chinese nationalism. They had virtually looked the other way while Soviet officials,
agents, and advisers entered the field and assiduously cultivated Chinese
friendship. The feeling of desperation grew not only in Tokyo but also in
London and Washington. It was no accident, then, that from about the time
of the May 30 incident in China in 1925 all three governments began to
reformulate their China policies.

In Japan this reformulation took the form of reversion to bilateralism.
This was to be expected. Since it appeared that the renunciation of particularistic diplomacy had served no useful purpose in reconciling Chinese
nationalism and Japanese interests, it was natural that the government in
Tokyo once again decided to act independently in China and enter into
bilateral arrangements with it. Unlike the period 1905–22, however, no
conflict with the United States was visualized as a consequence of such
a policy. This point will be discussed shortly.

The new course of Japanese policy can be illustrated briefly. During the
Peking Tariff Conference (1925–26) Japan absolutely refused to grant an
unconditional and immediate customs increase to China, despite the fact
that the United States and other powers were agreed on this minimum
concession to China. In 1926, with the beginning of the Northern Expedition by the Nationalists, Japan refused to cooperate with the United States
and Britain in protecting the foreign nationals in the path of the revolutionary army. Japan began instead unilaterally to approach the right-wing
Nationalists in order to undercut radical nationalism in China. Meanwhile,
in Peking, Japan had sought to negotiate a bilateral tariff treaty with China,
even while the Tariff Conference was still in session, so as to establish close
economic ties between the two countries.

Such a policy of unilateral action in China was carried out under both
Shidehara and Tanaka. It was in fact the former who initiated this approach.
The best expression of this is a small episode during the Peking Tariff
Conference. There the Japanese delegates objected to Tokyo's stiff stand
on the customs surtax question and suggested that Japan consent to a small
tariff increase in China in order not to sabotage the principle of working
with the United States. To this plea the Foreign Ministry replied sharply,
"It is sentimentalism and not national policy to argue that we give up our
long-held and cardinal principles and agree to the irrational and haphazard
device of effecting a 2.5 percent surtax simply in order to repay American

kindness and save the face of the country that initiated the Washington Conference."[23]

While Tanaka's handling of the China question was undoubtedly more severe than Shidehara's, as evidenced by such measures as the sending of forces to Shantung and the issuing of a warning to Chinese troops against disturbing the peace in Manchuria, it does not follow that Tanaka's policy was less concerned to reach an understanding with the United States than Shidehara's. It was, if anything, Tanaka who realized anew the need for coordinating action with the powers in China. The sending of the futile Uchida Yasuya mission to London and Washington in the late summer of 1928 is a case in point.

As mentioned above, in taking recourse to independent tactics in China, neither Shidehara nor Tanaka anticipated friction with the United States. This distinguishes Japanese policy in the mid-1920s from that in the heyday of imperialistic diplomacy. Between 1905 and 1922 the Japanese government had visualized international relations in terms of the imperialists' struggle for power. As discussed earlier, such a struggle was conducive to the creation of a temporary status quo, a subtle though precarious balance which was maintained by means of bilateral arrangements. But conflict among the imperialists was always a possibility, whenever one appeared to encroach upon the preserved sphere of influence of another. When Japan extended its influence in Manchuria and China, therefore, its leaders were aware that they needed to obtain the prior consent of other imperialists and that even then some of the latter might resent such an upset in the balance of power. In the 1920s, on the other hand, the Japanese did not think that their unilateral action in China would necessarily imply a clash with the United States or other powers. This was because Japanese-Chinese relations were no longer viewed as affecting Japan's relations with other countries. Japan started to act unilaterally in China, but it continued to seek understanding with the United States, without realizing that these actions might contradict each other. Japan's participation in the Geneva disarmament conference (1927) and in the Kellogg-Briand Pact (1928) are good examples of this type of thinking. It may be said that the Far East

[23]Japan, Gaimushō (Foreign Ministry), PVM 12–57 series, as cited in Cecil H. Uyehara, *Checklist of Archives in the Japanese Ministry of Foreign Affairs, Tokyo, Japan, 1868–1945, Microfilmed for the Library of Congress, 1949–1951* (1954), p. 107.

had become isolated in world politics. Or it may be postulated that there had developed a polarization of Japanese policy: one set of policies was applied in China, while another was carried out elsewhere. All the same, such a trend in Japanese foreign policy in the mid-1920s testifies to the passing of the old order and Japan's ad hoc response to the situation.

By the time Shidehara came back to the Foreign Ministry in July 1929, the failure of the unilateral approach in China had become apparent. The result of seeking bilateral arrangements with China and refusing to coordinate action with the United States and Britain on matters relating to China was disastrous. Not only had Japan failed to stop the spread of revolutionary nationalism to north China and Manchuria, but Japanese exports to China had suffered a decline and Japanese business interests in China were hurt tremendously. Moreover, the United States and Britain were far in advance of Japan in closer relations with the Nationalist regime. Japan had gotten nowhere with the policy of pursuing a set of policies in China irrespective of its policies elsewhere.

After the middle of 1929, consequently, another period of groping for policy began. It seems fair to say that in this period Shidehara decided to try reverting to the principle of understanding with the United States and Britain in China. He and his staff reasoned that the radical nationalism of the Nanking government made it imperative for the treaty powers to take a common stand so as to meet the challenge in unity. Japan's particular interests in China were to be subordinated to this larger goal. The Japanese government decided, for instance, to cooperate with the United States, Britain, and others to protect their nationals in the interior of China during the civil war of 1930. It also decided to coordinate policy with London and Washington on the question of abrogating extraterritoriality. The London Naval Conference of 1930, of course, gave a unique opportunity to Shidehara to display Japan's earnest desire to achieve solid understanding with Britain and the United States.

There was a compelling economic reason for the renewed interest in understanding with the United States. The Minseitō government had decided to lift the gold embargo, which had been imposed in 1917 as a war measure and, unlike in other countries, had never been repealed, and to reintegrate the Japanese economy more fully into the world economy as a solution to long-standing economic problems at home. Such measures called for credit from the West to enable smooth transition to a gold stand-

ard and competitive trade. The same economic forces compelling Japan
in this direction and prompting it to adopt a foreign policy of understanding with the West, however, doomed the new policy to failure. There was
little opportunity for coordinating action with the United States and
Britain at a time when the world economic crisis gripped the attention of
their officials. If anything, they tended to look at the Far East in terms of
their own domestic economic needs. They were in no mood to work out
a program of joint action in China that would benefit all countries.

By the early 1930s, moreover, Shidehara's foreign policy had come under
fire from the most powerful critics within Japan, the military. It is interesting to note that throughout the 1920s the Japanese military had advocated
a global foreign policy, even while the civilian government experimented
with one set of policies in China and another elsewhere. Military strategists
such as Ishiwara Kanji, Itagaki Seishirō, and Nagata Tetsuzan believed that
the next war would be truly global and "total," claiming all the resources
of the nation. Such a war, in their opinion, was likely to be fought between
Japan, the most powerful nation in Asia, and the United States, the might-
iest Western power. For this reason, Japan's foreign policy should also be
global; it should aim at strong action in China as an integral part of the
fundamental national goal of preparing for war against the United States.
"We must take resolute steps to gain control over the Manchurian government in preparation for war with the United States," said Ishiwara in July
1929.[24] From such a point of view, Shidehara's policy after 1929 was untenable because he seemed to base it on the unwarranted assumption that
Japan could count on the goodness of the West and that Japan and the
United States could continue to live in peace. Shidehara might have
silenced these critics if his policy had brought about tangible results in
China. Such was not the case, and in time he realized that the search for
a new order through peaceful means, serving the enlightened self-interests
of Japan as well as satisfying the needs of other countries, had ended in
failure.

These conceptions are presented more fully in the following work:

Iriye, *After Imperialism: The Search for a New Order in the Far East, 1921–1931* (1965).

[24]Seki Hiroharu, "Manshū jihen zenshi" (1963), p. 367.

Among biographies and collections of biographical materials, the following volumes are relevant to Japan's relations with the United States during this period:

Aoki, *Wakatsuki Reijirō Hamaguchi Osachi* (1958).
Hara, *Yamamoto Jōtarō denki* (1942).
Harada, *Saionji kō to seikyoku* (9 vols., 1950–52, 1956).
Ishigami, *Seitō shiron: Hara Takashi botsugo* (1960).
Kodama, *Ware yaburetari* (1949).
Morishima, *Imbō ansatsu guntō: gaikōkan no kaisō* (1950).
Okada Taishō Kiroku Hensankai, *Okada Keisuke* (1956).
Sekine, *Hamaguchi Osachi den* (1931).
Ugaki, *Ugaki nikki* (1954).
Wakatsuki, *Kofūan kaikoroku* (1950).
Yamaura, *Mori Kaku* (1940).

Because of the authors' efforts to correlate existing Japanese materials, *Manshū jihen zen'ya* (1962), Vol. I of the following series, is the most useful source among secondary works taking up problems in the late 1920s. While the series emphasizes the period after the Manchurian crisis, the authors have uncovered many interesting documents for the 1920s. Particularly fascinating are the writings of Ishiwara Kanji on Japan's future conflict with the United States and the records of the Japanese navy on the London Naval Treaty.

Nihon Kokusai Seiji Gakkai Taiheiyō Sensō Gen'in Kenkyūbu, *Taiheiyō sensō e no michi* (8 vols., 1962–63).

For a rather lengthy review of the series, see the following article:

Iriye, "Japanese Imperialism and Aggression: Reconsiderations, II" (1963).

There are only a handful of monographs dealing with Japanese-American relations during the 1920s. The following are all excellent:

Asada, "Amerika no tai-Nichi kan to 'Washinton taisei' " (1967).
Etō, "Nankin jiken to Nichi-Bei" (1959).
Imai, "Shidehara gaikō ni okeru seisaku kettei" (1959).
Satō "Kyōchō to jiritsu no aida—Nihon" (1967).
Unno, "Rondon kaigun gunshuku kaigi" (1959).
Usui, *Nitchū gaikōshi: Hokubatsu no jidai* (1971).

The trend in historiography has been to interpret the 1920s primarily as a period of transition in which Japanese expansionism temporarily "retreated" from the aggressive excesses of the 1910s in preparation for a fresh assault. Such a unilinear approach has too often failed to consider adequately changes outside of Japan as well as those affecting the decision-making processes within Japan. It is essential to grasp the significance of the forces that had put an end to the old form of imperialist power rivalry in the Far East. At the same time, the nature of conflict between the various elite groups comprising the second-generation leadership of modern Japan must be sufficiently explored. It may be, for example, that the military attacked Shidehara's policy of understanding with the West not only for what it was but also for what it represented; the military may have opposed Japan's America policy at least partially because it was being pursued by civilian bureaucrats who failed to assign constructive roles to army and navy officers in the decision-making process. Japanese policy toward the United States will be comprehended fully only when we have analyzed the search for a new order both in the Far East and in Japan itself.

UNEASY COEXISTENCE, 1931–1938

The Manchurian crisis marked the first stage in Japan's road toward the creation of a self-sufficient empire, toward the formation of a "national defense state." An outline of these ideas had already been developed in the late 1920s by such military strategists as Ishiwara and Nagata, as noted earlier. It will be recalled that their basic assumption was the inevitability of another war, which would be global and "total." For them, action in Manchuria was simply a first step in preparing for that conflict, not an end in itself. Few civilian bureaucrats agreed with their prognosis at first, though it seems fair to say that, probably for other reasons, the civilians did support their policy toward Manchuria and China. As the decade wore on, however, the military succeeded in imposing their idea of a national defense state on the government, so that after 1936 we find Japanese leaders —civilian, military, and business—in basic agreement on the value of an economically self-sufficient and militarily well-prepared empire.

The enlarged empire of the 1930s included Korea, Taiwan, Manchuria, Jehol, and, after 1935, north China. It supplied most of the foodstuffs for home consumption, and its relative importance in Japan's export trade increased steadily. Foreign policy statements and decisions by the Japanese government indicated that it sought to impose a new definition of the international order upon the Far East. Compared with the groping and the uncertainties of the 1920s, Japanese leaders were now much bolder and more self-confident. The withdrawal from the League of Nations which became effective in 1935, the abrogation of the Washington Naval Treaty in 1934, the failure of the London Naval Conference of 1935, Hirota Kōki's "three principles of peace," the cabinet decision of August 1936 on the essentials of Japanese foreign policy, Konoe Fumimaro's proclamation of a New Order in East Asia in November 1938, all marked Japan's step-by-step withdrawal from the framework of acting with the understanding of the West. Japan, which had "left" Asia after the Sino-Japanese War, was going back to it and was less and less concerned with Western opinion. Japan's decision to move in this direction was not, of course, totally voluntary. It was encouraged by the world economic crisis, which stimulated economic nationalism and the vogue of bilateral trade agreements. On the other hand, Japan's role in accelerating such trends cannot be doubted. After the outbursts of hysterical putschism by young officers and terrorists came to an end in 1936, Japan began a national task of mobilizing its total resources for imperial consolidation and military preparedness.

There was something anomalous about Japanese-American relations during this period. The architects of the Manchurian crisis had believed that they were adding Manchuria to Japan's imperial domain in order to prepare for war against the United States. After 1931, however, their attention turned more and more to the Soviet Union. It may be said that the latter now replaced the United States as the foremost imaginary enemy in the minds of army officers. For one thing, this was an inevitable response to the buildup of Soviet armed forces in Siberia. Equally significant was the realization that the United States now occupied an economically crucial position vis-a-vis the Japanese empire. Despite its growing self-sufficiency, the empire was still dependent on raw materials from the United States and the British empire, and after the drop in American purchases of Japanese silks, Japan's trade deficit vis-a-vis the United States grew year after year. It may be said, therefore, that its economic dependence on the United States was the weakest and most vulnerable part of the Japanese empire. Unless an alternative source of raw materials, especially oil and iron, could be found, Japan was compelled to take cognizance of American policy, despite its basic decision for an economic autarchy and predominance in the Far East. This did not mean, of course, that Japan would seek positive understanding with the United States. Rather, Japan would see to it that the latter would acquiesce in the new situation in the Far East without inviting an open rift between the two countries. It would try to reduce American influence in Asia without risking a fatally strong American retaliation.

Within this broad framework, Japanese policy toward the United States in this period can briefly be summarized. When the Manchurian Incident broke out, the Tokyo government immediately decided on nonextension of hostilities. For Shidehara, laboring to bring about a framework of understanding with the United States, the Kwantung army's action was a serious blow. He struggled hard to repair the damages done, but his preoccupation with reaction in the United States was not shared by his colleagues in the cabinet. They had begun to lose confidence in the soundness of the Western economies and in the wisdom of depending on the West for settlement of Far Eastern matters. After Shidehara left the Foreign Ministry in December 1931, the idea of working together with the United States and Britain as a basic tenet of Japanese action was never again revived. From then on the United States became something less than a wealthy partner. It was a power to be reckoned with, especially since Henry L. Stimson had made his stand unmistakably clear. But Japan would deal with the United States as much from a position of strength as possible.

Among Shidehara's successors there was little interest in achieving genuine understanding with America. Their primary preoccupation was with Manchuria and China. In the cabinet meeting of August 27, 1932, the basic idea of military preparedness and national mobilization was put down as fundamental policy. With respect to the United States, it was decided to lessen the tension between the two countries "by an appropriate allocation of the principle of the Open Door." But this innocuous statement was coupled with another, stating the need "to proceed swiftly with preparations vis-a-vis the United States in view of the fact that the greatest obstacle to our policy in Manchuria and Mongolia comes from that country."[25] Here was a clear departure from the terminology of the 1920s. The Japanese government was intent upon imposing a fait accompli on the United States and believed it could do so with impunity. Here was clearly a diplomacy of new imperialism. In the boldness of Japanese action

[25] *Nihon gaikō nempyō*, II, 206–10.

it went much beyond the earlier imperialist power struggle and was undoubtedly encouraged by the caution and timidity of Japan's potential antagonists.

The foreign policy of Hirota Kōki, who both as foreign minister and as prime minister played the most important civilian role between 1933 and 1938, was in line with such a trend. In his telegraphic instruction to the Japanese minister in China, dated April 13, 1934, he stated that Japan's position in China was different from that of other countries and that "Japan must do everything it can to accomplish its mission in East Asia, regardless of whether other powers will recognize it or not." He went on to say that it was Japan's responsibility to maintain peace and order in Asia. Accordingly, he concluded, Japan should be prepared to "destroy" other countries' programs of military, political, and economic assistance to China. These ideas were incorporated into the famous Amō declaration.[26] In May 1934 Hirota tried to obtain America's recognition of Japanese predominance in the Far East by proposing a new agreement between the two countries that would more or less divide the Pacific into American and Japanese spheres of influence. This was entirely in accord with the developing concept of imperial self-sufficiency, but it had nothing to recommend itself to the United States. Throughout the year 1935 Japan sought to obstruct the Nationalist government's attempt at financial reform through foreign assistance, and in October the foreign, army, and navy ministers agreed anew that, to maintain peace in the Far East, it would be essential to press China to give up the policy of dependence on Europe and America.[27]

Japanese officials, in particular the military, were compelled to sharpen their views of Japanese-American relations in the mid-1930s as the two countries entered an "era of no treaties" in 1936, the Washington and London naval treaties having finally expired that year. The year 1935 had seen the resumption of Japanese military action in north China, followed in 1936 by Sino-Japanese clashes in Inner Mongolia. For some men, in particular Ishiwara Kanji, chief of the Operations Section of the Army General Staff, the time was opportune to effect a rapprochement with the United States so as to devote full national energy to preparedness against the Soviet Union. Such a recommendation, however, was strongly op-

---

[26]Shimada Toshihiko, "Kahoku kōsaku to kokkō chōsei, 1933–1937" (1962), pp. 73–78.
[27]*Nihon gaikō nempyō*, II, 303–4.

posed by the navy, which was intent upon an extended armament program now that the naval treaties had expired. Partly such opposition reflected a built-in rivalry and jealousy between the two services, and partly it was a logical expression of the urge for imperial self-sufficiency. From the navy's point of view, the control of key strategic areas in south China, offshore islands, French Indochina, and ultimately the Dutch East Indies was essential if the new Japanese empire was to become truly self-sufficient economically and impregnable militarily.[28]

The celebrated "Fundamentals of National Policy," adopted by the Five Ministers Conference on August 7, 1936, betrayed the basic conflict of views between army and navy. It was here stated that Japan's basic policy was to maintain its predominant position in the Far East and further to expand into the South Seas. Japan would cooperate closely with Manchukuo and China, prepare against the United States and Britain, and defend Manchuria against the Russian menace. Toward Southeast Asia, Japan would still maintain peaceful and gradualist policies. The ministers also decided that Japan's naval strength should be augmented to the extent necessary for control of the western Pacific. In "The Foreign Policy of Imperial Japan" which accompanied this decision, it was stated that Japan's immediate objective should be the removal of the Soviet threat to the empire. Consequently, Japan was to adopt an attitude of caution toward the United States, in view of the latter's ability to obstruct Japanese policies toward Russia and China. "Japan should respect America's trade interests in China so that the United States may understand our fair policy, promote good relations between the two countries on the basis of Japanese-American economic compatibility, and try to prevent American interference with Japanese policy in East Asia," the document concluded. The contradictory statements on Japanese policy toward the United States were never reconciled, and there was no thorough analysis of the possible causal relationship between Japan's southward advance and the worsening of Japanese-American relations.[29]

The general direction of Japanese policy and the contradictions it contained were not altered by the outbreak of war with China in July 1937.

---

[28]Shimada, "Kahoku kōsaku to kokkō chōsei," pp. 206–12; and Tsunoda Jun, "Kaidai" (1963), pp. 430–37.

[29]*Nihon gaikō nempyō*, II, 344–45; also Hata Ikuhiko, "Futsu-In shinchū to gun no nanshin seisaku (1940–1941)" (1963), pp. 148, 150, 168.

It is possible to argue that the navy's fixation with southward advance was a crucial factor behind the extension of hostilities to south China. In 1937 and the greater part of 1938, however, neither the navy nor the army wanted trouble with the United States. The Japanese military were aware that American policy at this time hardly went beyond moral condemnation of their actions and therefore that they could take certain measures in China without anticipating American retaliation. They closed the Yangtze River to foreign navigation, bombarded Chinese cities with foreign populations, and blockaded the China coast south of Shanghai. Only once, during the Panay Incident of December 1937, the Japanese thought the matter was grave enough to require their prompt apology to the United States as well as a payment of compensation. On the whole it can be said, therefore, that before the end of 1938 Japan continued its policy of proceeding with imperial designs without endangering the supply of needed raw materials from the United States.

Useful sources for this period are found in the transcripts of the International Military Tribunal for the Far East and in unpublished documents in the Foreign Ministry. Care must be taken, however, in using the trial materials, since so many of the documents are personal testimonies of doubtful accuracy. The following are published records of the trial:

Asahi Shimbunsha, *Tōkyō saiban* (3 vols., 1962).
Kyokutō Kokusai Gunji Saiban, *Kyokutō kokusai gunji saiban sokkiroku* (1946–48).
Kyokutō Kokusai Gunji Saiban Kōhan Kiroku Kankōkai, *Kyokutō kokusai gunji saiban kōhan kiroku* (2 vols., 1948).

The diary of Kido Kōichi is useful:

Kido, *Kido Kōichi nikki* (2 vols., 1966), plus a supplementary volume of letters and documents: Kido Kōichi Nikki Kenkyūkai, *Kido Kōichi kankei bunsho*. Portions of the diary were quoted in a work known as the *Kido nikki* (1947), parts of which were translated as "Kido Diary, July 11, 1931–December 9, 1945," Documents 1632 and 1768, IMTFE, International Prosecution Section.

A few biographical works are relevant to this period:

Aritake, *Saitō Makoto* (1958).
Imamura, *Kōzoku to kashikan* (1960).
Mitarai, *Minami Jirō* (1957).
Saitō Shishaku Kinenkai, *Shishaku Saitō Makoto den* (4 vols., 1941–42).
Shigemitsu, *Gaikō kaisōroku* (1953).
Yoshizawa, *Gaikō rokujūnen* (1958).

Despite the relative richness of source materials for this period, there has been little systematic study of Japanese policy toward the United States after 1931. It would, of course, be impossible completely to isolate Japanese-American relations, but it seems possible to discuss the matter as something other than the story of an inevitable conflict between the two countries, whether in terms of two imperialisms or of the clash between Japanese expansionism and the American doctrine of collective security. No doubt the Japanese empire did expand and was opposed by the American policy of nonrecognition and numerous protests against the violation of the Open Door in China. But such a macroscopic view would have to be supplemented, if not modified, by a careful analysis of the way the two governments, including the military, tried to determine priorities in their respective foreign policies, and the way such priorities affected their views of each other. The increasing importance of Japanese-American trade in each nation's economy, as well as the beginnings of renewed naval construction programs in both countries, would have to be fitted into an over-all discussion of Japanese-American relations.

The following monographs, with the exception of Tansill's work, are not specifically concerned with Japanese-American relations between 1931 and 1938, but they all supply basic data from which interpretations could be drawn. Tansill presents one interpretation, and while the author commits a grave sin in quoting documents out of context and is a captive of his own brand of determinism, the book at least raises a few serious questions that merit careful analysis.

Butow, *Tojo and the Coming of the War* (1961).
Crowley, *Japan's Quest for Autonomy* (1966).
Feis, *The Road to Pearl Harbor* (1950).
Iriye, "The Failure of Military Expansionism" (1971).
Jones, *Japan's New Order in East Asia: Its Rise and Fall, 1937–1945* (1954).
Kurihara, *Tennō: Shōwashi oboegaki* (1955).
Langer and Gleason, *The Challenge to Isolation* (1953).
Thorne, *The Limits of Foreign Policy* (1972).
Tansill, *Back Door to War: The Roosevelt Foreign Policy, 1933–1941* (1952).

The series concerned with Japan's road to the Pacific War:

Nihon Kokusai Seiji Gakkai Taiheiyō Sensō Gen'in Kenkyūbu, *Taiheiyō sensō e no michi* (8 vols., 1962–63), singularly contains no systematic examination of Japanese policy toward the United States before 1938. Nevertheless, Vol. II, on the Manchurian crisis, *Manshū jihen* (1962), and Vols. III–IV, concerned with the Sino-Japanese War, *Nitchū sensō*, Parts I–II (1962–63), have an impressive number of hitherto little known documents, in particular from the army and navy archives. These documents might be studied with a view to tracing the evolution of Japan's policy toward the United States.

It would make a fascinating study to take a few individuals, such as Ishiwara Kanji in the army, Yonai Mitsumasa in the navy, and Shigemitsu Mamoru or Arita Hachirō among professional diplomats, and trace their ideas on Japanese-American relations. Such a study would go a long way to clarify the still engrossing subject of war guilt and help us better to understand the complex problem of individual responsibility versus economic and military necessities.

WAR OR ACCOMMODATION, 1938–1941

The year 1938 saw the beginning of involvement of the Far Eastern crisis in the deteriorating situation in Europe. Japan had tried to avoid such an involvement, seeking instead to settle Far Eastern matters without interference by extra-Far Eastern considerations. The Munich crisis and Germany's and Italy's decisions to upset the status quo, however, inevitably forced the merging of the Far Eastern and European crises. This was because Germany began actively to press Japan for an alliance against the Western democracies as well as against the Soviet Union, and because the United States came to identify itself as a determined foe of aggressors, including both Japan and Germany.

Such a development presented a difficulty and an opportunity for Japan's foreign relations in general and Japanese policy toward the United States in particular. Japan had to formulate a clear stand on such issues as the protection of American rights in China now that the United States began to show signs of a determination to oppose aggression, taking recourse to economic, if not military, sanctions. The fact that the United States linked Japan with Germany meant that Japan had to tread carefully before it should decide to identify its cause with that of Germany. At the same time, from the point of view of achieving the goal of a self-sufficient empire, there was much to be gained from the merging of the Far Eastern with the European conflict. Japan could take advantage of German victories in Europe to expand into the European powers' colonial possessions in Asia, which could possibly replace the United States as a source of much-needed raw materials.

Japanese policy toward the United States after the end of 1938 reflected this duality of difficulty and opportunity presented by the European conflict. In the end it was decided to round out the empire by capturing the rich resources of Southeast Asia, thus inviting war with the United States. This eventuality was unavoidable, given America's determination to defend the Dutch and British colonial possessions in Asia. The inevitability of conflict with the United States, once Japan expanded into Southeast Asia, was also recognized by the Japanese, although there persisted a division of opinion concerning the point at which Japanese expansion would cause the United States to intervene forcefully. But there was a singular lack of determination on the part of Japanese officials either to avoid such a conflict with the United States or to meet the American challenge squarely. This indecision was due to a great extent to difference of views and professional rivalries among the army, the navy, and the Foreign Ministry. More fundamentally, however, it was but another manifestation of the fatal weakness in Japanese policy toward the United States, mentioned at the outset, namely its pragmatism and lack of carefully thought-out calculations. Because of these factors it is misleading to talk of Japan's road to the Pacific War as though it were a straight road, expressing a logically arrived at decision of its leaders. Here some examples will suffice to illustrate the complex problems of decision-making and the impact of external affairs upon relations between the two countries.

The first indication of a clear rift between Japan and the United States was the exchange of notes in late 1938. To the American protest against the constant infringements on American rights in China, Foreign Minister Arita bluntly replied, on November 18, 1938, that, since Japan was at war, there might be some difficulty in carrying out its intention to respect American rights. The note clearly stated that Japan was building a new order in East Asia and that the old ideas and principles of diplomacy would no longer serve to establish permanent peace in the Far East. The Arita note, coming on the heels of Konoe's declaration of a New Order in East Asia, issued on November 3, definitely stiffened American policy. The State Department now decided to go beyond the negative policy of refusing to recognize Japan's New Order or to accept British and French suggestions for an understanding with Japan. Beginning at the end of the year, the United States slowly but firmly put into effect various retaliatory measures, such as extending small-scale loans to China and imposing an embargo, at first moral but later legal, on export of strategic materials to Japan. One climax came in July 1939, when the United States announced its intention to abrogate the existing treaty of commerce with Japan. The abrogation went into effect in January 1940.

This definite American counteroffensive forced a clear decision by the Japanese government. The abrogation of the commercial treaty left the American export of strategic materials to Japan at the mercy of the Washington government, and that government's embargo policy revealed its readiness to use its power to deprive Japan of the materials essential for the empire. Japan's response to this new challenge was at first vacillating. As early as August 1936, as noted above, the Tokyo government had visualized Japanese penetration of Southeast Asia with a view to utilizing the natural resources of the region for the developing empire. But no systematic effort had been made in this direction, since Japan could still obtain raw materials peacefully from the United States and the British empire. Even the Konoe government's proclamation of a New Order had primarily referred to the new situation in the Far East, embracing particularly Japan, Manchukuo, and China. The American abrogation of the commercial treaty necessitated a change in this basic approach, but until the spring of 1940 the Japanese government groped for a suitable policy without finding it. On the one hand, the cabinets of Hiranuma Kiichirō, Abe Nobuyuki, and Yonai Mitsumasa tried to maintain at least a degree of understanding with the United States. Foreign Minister Nomura Kichisaburō, in particular, desperately tried to improve Japanese-American relations. He sought in vain to use the partial reopening of the Yangtze River to foreign ships late in 1939 as evidence of Japan's good intentions and thereby to persuade the United States to reconsider its policy of economic retaliation. The Yonai cabinet, coming to office in January 1940, continued to seek rapprochement with the United States by inviting the latter's good offices to solve the Sino-Japanese impasse.[30]

The outbreak of war in Europe in September 1939 initially did not affect the general trend in Japanese policy. The Abe cabinet discouraged

---

[30]Usui Katsumi, "Nitchū sensō no seijiteki tenkai, 1937–1941" (1963), pp. 184–98. See also Usui, *Nitchū sensō* (1967).

talk of rapprochement with the Soviet Union, which began to be heard among the "new bureaucrats," as it would run counter to the policy of avoiding further worsening of Japanese-American relations.[31] The Yonai cabinet also held out stubbornly against an alliance with Germany as long as it was aimed at the United States. Nevertheless, it was inevitable that the war in Europe should be viewed in Japan in connection with its relations with the United States and its ambition of southern expansion. In fact, it was under Prime Minister Yonai that definite steps were initiated to take advantage of the European conflict and reformulate Japanese foreign policy in the light of the conflict. One of the basic documents in this regard is the "Outline of Overall National Policies," drafted soon after the formation of the Yonai cabinet. This outline was written by senior- and middle-grade staff members of the army, navy, and civilian agencies and called for a national effort to construct a New Order in Greater East Asia based on the spirit of the "eight corners of the world under our roof." It visualized the creation of a huge economic bloc embracing the Far East, Southeast Asia, and India. Recognizing Japan's continued dependence on American economic resources, the outline stressed the need to prevent the unnecessary worsening of relations with the United States; but also it stated that Japan needed to reduce such dependence as it built its new economic empire.[32]

The resumption of hostilities in Europe in the spring of 1940 and the almost instantaneous fall of France and the Netherlands finally brought Japan to decide to help itself to the resources of the French and Dutch colonies in Asia and to work toward the formation of a truly self-sufficient and impregnable empire. Prime Minister Yonai and Foreign Minister Arita, while still opposed to a military alliance with Germany, took steps to secure a continued supply of oil, tin, rubber, and other materials from the Dutch East Indies. They also pressed France to agree to the installation of Japanese inspectors in northern French Indochina to seal it off from Chungking. Likewise, Britain was warned to stop sending supplies to Chungking through Hong Kong and Burma. It is important to note that Yonai's and Arita's opposition to the Axis alliance idea did not

---

[31]Hosoya Chihiro, "Sangoku dōmei to Nisso chūritsu jōyaku (1939–1941)" (1963), pp. 238–42.

[32]Tanaka Sōgorō, *Nihon fashizumu shi* (1960), pp. 202ff.

prevent them from taking these crucial steps—another indication of pragmatism in Japanese policy.

Despite these concrete measures, the Yonai cabinet was brought down by the army, primarily because the latter felt the government was not moving fast enough. By mid-1940 key army officials had become convinced of the desirability of an advance into Southeast Asia, which would be facilitated by an alliance with Germany and a neutrality pact with the Soviet Union. Such ideas had, of course, for some time been advocated by men like Shiratori Toshio and Matsuoka Yōsuke, and were incorporated into the decision of the so-called Ogikubo Conference, held on July 19, 1940, and attended by the prospective prime, foreign, army, and navy ministers of the second Konoe cabinet. The adopted program envisaged the attainment of imperial self-sufficiency by an advance southward, alliance with Germany and Italy, and neutralization of the Soviet Union and the United States.[33] The basic assumption in such a policy was the idea that the world was divided into several blocs, each bloc under one or two supreme powers. Japan would form its own bloc and have others recognize this fact, just as it would pledge to respect their blocs.

For Matsuoka these various steps were calculated to enable Japan to negotiate with the United States from a position of strength. The Japanese military were more realistic and aware that these measures would exacerbate the deteriorating Japanese-American relations. But there were subtle differences of opinion between various military groups as to the inevitability as well as the desirability of war with the United States. Army officials were most eager to strike southward and capture the British and Dutch colonies, and they reasoned that this could be done without necessarily inviting war with the United States. Should the latter stand up against Japanese expansionism, however, the army believed that Japan should fight. Navy officials, on the other hand, doubted that Britain and the United States could be so separated; the two countries were considered to be equally committed to the defense of the status quo in Southeast Asia. Consequently, while agreeing in principle to the policy of southward expansion, top naval officials at first were unwilling to carry it out because of fear of war with the United States as well as with Britain.

---

[33]Hosoya, "Sangoku dōmei," pp. 182–84. The best study of Matsuoka's personality and thinking is Miwa Kimitada, *Matsuoka Yōsuke* (1971).

They also persisted in their refusal to approve a military alliance with Germany against these countries.

The picture began to change in the fall of 1940. Staff officers of the Navy Ministry and the Navy General Staff began pushing for a strong policy toward the United States. The "first committee," organized by section chiefs at this time, was probably the most influential single group prodding Japanese leaders to take a more belligerent attitude toward America. Its members believed that, sooner or later, war with the United States was unavoidable and that Japan therefore should advance into southern Indochina and the Dutch East Indies to secure naval bases and strategic raw materials. Their reasoning was obviously circular; they thought war with the United States was inevitable because of America's retaliatory economic measures, which had been and would further be directed against Japanese policy in China and Southeast Asia. For these naval strategists, however, the fundamental causes of the Japanese-American antagonism were irrelevant. They were technicians concerned with the problem of how a war against the United States could be won and when it should be started.[34]

All these crosscurrents of military thinking and diplomatic maneuver continued to flow in the year 1941, but in time two major streams, running in opposite directions, became clearly discernible. One stream emphasized that the point of no return had been reached in Japanese-American relations and that Japan therefore should worry only about how to wage war against the United States. Strongly advocated by section chiefs in the Navy Ministry and General Staff, who imposed their views on their superiors, such determinism won the adherence of the army in the spring of 1941. From this time on, both services were in virtual agreement on the inevitable logic of events: Japan would expand into southern French Indochina and elsewhere in Southeast Asia, the United States would retaliate by imposing a total embargo on exports to Japan, and Japan would finally make up its mind to fight the United States. The German attack on the Soviet Union in late June briefly revived the army's interest in war against Japan's northern neighbor, but it did not affect the logic of events, once

[34]Tsunoda Jun, "Nihon no tai-Bei kaisen, 1940–1941" (1963), pp. 201–13. Akira Iriye, *Across the Pacific: An Inner History of American-East Asian Relations* (1967), gives a broad survey of Japanese-American relations during the period preceding the outbreak of the Pacific War.

the government decided to undertake an expedition into southern Indochina.

The second stream expressed the last-minute efforts by the Japanese government to avoid war with the United States. Such efforts, too, were supported by logic. Since Japan's southward advance had been called for in order to enable Japan to do without American oil and iron, it could be reasoned that the empire might be voluntarily limited if its *raison d'être* no longer existed, that is, if the United States would restore trade in strategic raw materials. These ideas presented the justification, from the Japanese point of view, for starting conversations in Washington in the spring of 1941. General Tōjō Hideki, too, after becoming prime minister in October, was willing to continue talks with the United States, as he was doubtful that the Japanese navy could successfully wage war against the American navy. The last-minute negotiations between the two governments, details of which need not be repeated here, can be characterized as an attempt to determine the degree to which the Japanese self-sufficient empire might be reduced. Japan was willing to give up its southward advance if the United States would consent to the resumption of trade.

The United States, as is well known, almost accepted such a compromise settlement in November 1941, primarily in order to buy time. But at the last moment the Washington government decided to challenge the basic idea of the Japanese empire and presented the "Hull note" of November 26. Since this visualized a return to the status quo, not of 1940, 1939, or even of 1937, but virtually of 1931, the Tōjō cabinet regarded it as an ultimatum. The same note, however, pleased the Japanese exponents of war, now that any hope of accommodation with the United States had evaporated. Throughout the month of November the military had made detailed plans for military action if no satisfactory compromise was achieved in Washington by the end of the month. It was ironic that the surprise attack on Pearl Harbor, not on Manila or Guam, had been advocated by Admiral Yamamoto Isoroku, who had also been the strongest exponent of rapprochement with the United States.

War was perhaps the only way through which Japan's military and civilian bureaucrats could test, and eventually recognize, the futility of the idea of a self-sufficient empire. The idea itself, however, was rooted in the historical experience of a nation not blessed with rich natural resources and a late-comer to the arena of international power politics. The

Japanese-American conflict of the late 1930s and early 1940s illustrates, perhaps better than anything else, the strains of modern Japanese society standing uneasily between East and West.

The period of the final road to war is rich in sources, especially biographical materials. The following volumes contain valuable documents connected with the Privy Council and the Imperial Headquarters, respectively:

Fukai, *Sūmitsuin jūyō giji oboegaki* (1953).
Tanaka, *Nihon fashizumu shi* (1960).
Tanemura, *Daihon'ei kimitsu nisshi* (1952).

The general works on the road to war written before the early 1960s have been superseded by the last three volumes of *Taiheiyō sensō e no michi*:

Vol. V, *Sangoku dōmei: Nisso chūritsu jōyaku* (1963).
Vol. VI, *Nampō shinshutsu* (1963).
Vol. VII, *Nichi-Bei kaisen* (1963).

The following studies in this series are especially excellent and pertinent to Japanese-American relations:

Hosoya, "Sangoku dōmei to Nisso chūritsu jōyaku (1939–1941)," in V, 157–331, on the Axis alliance.
Hata, "Futsu-In shinchū to gun no nanshin seisaku (1940–1941)," in VI, 143–274, on the southern advance.
Tsunoda, "Nihon no tai-Bei kaisen, 1940–1941," in VII, 1–387, on naval thinking and strategy toward the United States.

The authors have combed through thousands of pages of archival documents and interviewed an impressive number of men active during the 1930s and 1940s. These volumes can be used profitably as documentary histories from which the researcher can draw his own interpretations.

Among biographical publications, the following may be noted. Each contains discussions of Japanese-American relations, valuable for descriptions of personalities rather than of official relations between the two governments:

Arita, *Hito no me no chiri o miru: gaikō mondai kaikoroku* (1948).
—— *Bakahachi to hito wa iu: gaikōkan no kaisō* (1959).
Fukudome, *Kaigun no hansei* (1951).
Kazama, *Aru hangyaku: Ozaki Hotsumi no shōgai* (1959).
Kodama, *Akusei jūsei ransei: fūun yonjūnen no kiroku* (1961).

Konoe, *Heiwa e no doryoku* (1946).

—— *Ushinawareshi seiji* (1946).

Kurusu, *Hōmatsu no sanjūgonen* (1948).

Miwa, *Matsuoka Yōsuke* (1971).

Morishima, *Shinjuwan Risubon Tōkyō: zoku ichi gaikōkan no kaisō* (1950).

Nomura, *Beikoku ni shishite: Nichi-Bei kōshō no kaiko* (1946).

Ogata, *Ichi gunjin no shōgai: kaisō no Yonai Mitsumasa* (1955).

Ōhashi, *Taiheiyō sensō yuraiki* (1952).

Okada, *Okada Keisuke kaikoroku* (1950).

Saitō, *Azamukareta rekishi: Matsuoka to sangoku dōmei no rimen* (1955).

Sakuta, *Tennō to Kido* (1948).

Satō, *Tōjō Hideki to Taiheiyō sensō* (1960).

Suma, *Gaikō hiroku* (1956).

Takagi, *Yamamoto Isoroku to Yonai Mitsumasa* (1950).

Tanaka, *Taisen totsu'nyū no shinsō* (1955).

Tōgō, *Jidai no ichimen* (1952).

Tomita, *Haisen Nihon no uchigawa: Konoe kō no omoide* (1962).

Watanabe, *Ugaki Kazushige no ayunda michi* (1948).

Yabe, *Konoe Fumimaro* (2 vols., 1952).

These works have been the basis of several general works on the road to war, among which the following are examples:

Aoki, *Taiheiyō sensō zenshi* (3 vols., 1953).

Ashida, *Dainiji sekai taisen gaikōshi* (1960).

Fukudome, *Shikan Shinjuwan kōgeki* (1955).

Kūmagiri, "Nichi-Bei kōshō" (1953).

Okada, *Konoe Fumimaro: tennō to gumbu to kokumin* (1959).

Ōtaka, *Kishū ka bōryaku ka: Shinjuwan no sekinin* (1954).

—— *Dainiji taisen sekinin ron* (1959).

Rekishigaku Kenkyūkai, *Taiheiyō sensō shi* (5 vols., 1954).

Saitō, "Sen-kyūhyaku-yonjūichinen no Nichi-Bei kankei ni tsuite no oboegaki" (1954).

Takamiya, *Tennō heika* (1951).

Tsunoda, "Nichi-Bei kōshō" (1959).

Most of the above writers have utilized works by non-Japanese historians, especially by "revisionist" American writers. The following is a limited list of the most important works on the subject, orthodox and revisionist:

Beard, *President Roosevelt and the Coming of the War, 1941: A Study in Appearances and Realities* (1948).

Burns, *Roosevelt: The Soldier of Freedom* (1970).

Heinrichs, *American Ambassador* (1966).

Langer and Gleason, *The Undeclared War, 1940–1941* (1953).

Morton, *Strategy and Command: The First Two Years* (1962).

Schroeder, *The Axis Alliance and Japanese-American Relations, 1941* (1958).

Toland, *The Rising Sun* (1969).

Tuchman, *Stilwell and the American Experience in China* (1971).

Wilson, *The First Summit* (1969).

Wohlstetter, *Pearl Harbor: Warning and Decision* (1962).

Some of these authors, notably Schroeder, have raised an important question on the inflexibility of the American stand on China in 1941 in the last-minute negotiations in Washington. It is argued that the Pacific War would have been postponed, if not totally avoided, if the United States had compromised on the issue of Japanese troops in China, since it had never meant to fight for the Open Door or the integrity of China before 1941, and since Chiang Kai-shek was incapable of defending his country at any rate.

Such an argument misses the essential point of difference between the United States and Japan. It is true that America's insistence on the withdrawal of Japanese troops from China, coupled with the demand that Japan totally repudiate the alliance with Germany, proved to be the major stumbling block in the efforts toward peace, since the Japanese army was adamant on the issue of China. But the China question was never isolated. From the American point of view, Japanese evacuation of troops not only from Indochina but also from China would serve as definite evidence of a change of heart, as insurance against the recurrence of aggression, which was a prerequisite before trade could be resumed between the two countries. The Japanese insisted, of course, that the United States simply talked about principles and went on cutting off supplies essential for the survival of Japan. To which the makers of American policy replied that Japan could always have these supplies if only it repented. Thus the Hull note of November 26 was a direct challenge aimed at the Japanese conception of empire. In this sense the Japanese-American conflict was a struggle between two different definitions of peace and order in the Far East.

PART TWO

Bibliography of
Japan's Foreign Policy
1868–1941

9

Bibliography of Foreign Policy Standard Works

◆

A selected list of books and articles as cited in the Critical Essays and published generally before 1963.*

Abe Kōzō 阿部光藏. "Nisshin kōwa to sangoku kanshō" 日清講和と三国干渉 (The Sino-Japanese peace and the Triple Intervention), *Kokusai seiji: Nihon gaikōshi kenkyū—Nisshin Nichi-Ro sensō*, 1961, pp. 52–70.

Aichi Daigaku Kokusai Mondai Kenkyūjo 愛知大学国際問題研究所. *Ko Naitō Konan sensei chojutsu mokuroku* 故内藤湖南先生著述目録 (List of the writings of the late Professor Naitō Konan). Tokyo, Keisō Shobō, 1954.

Aida Tsutomu 会田勉. *Kawashima Naniwa ō* 川島浪速翁. Tokyo, Bunsuikaku, 1936.

Aishingyōro Kō 愛親覚羅浩. *Ruten no ōbi: Manshū kyūtei no higeki* 流転の王妃満州宮廷 の悲劇 (Wandering princess: A Manchurian imperial court tragedy). Tokyo, Bungei Shunjū Shinsha, 1959.

Ajia rekishi jiten アジア歴史事典 (Dictionary of Asian history). Tokyo, Heibonsha, 1959–62.

Akagi, Roy. *Japan's Foreign Relations, 1542–1936*. Tokyo, Hokuseido, 1936.

Akimoto Ikuo 秋本育夫. "Bōeki shōsha" 貿易商社 (Foreign trade companies), in Matsui Kiyoshi 松井清, ed., *Kindai Nihon bōekishi* 近代日本貿易史 (A history of modern Japan's foreign trade), II, 129–240. Tokyo, Yūhikaku, 1961.

Allen, Bernard M. *The Rt. Hon. Sir Ernest Satow: A Memoir*. London, Kegan Paul, Trench, and Trübner, 1933.

Allen, G. C. "Factors in Japan's Economic Growth," in C. D. Cowan, ed., *The Economic Development of China and Japan*, pp. 192–204. New York, Praeger, 1964.

Allen, G. C. and Audrey G. Donnithorne. *Western Enterprise in Far Eastern Development: China and Japan*. London, Allen and Unwin, 1954.

Altman, Albert. "Guido Verbeck and the Iwakura Embassy," *Japan Quarterly*, XIII, No. 1 (January-March 1966), 54–62.

* Note: Japanese characters for titles of periodicals will be found in the listing at the end of the Bibliography of Standard Works. Where an article appears without a full citation complete publication information and Japanese characters are listed under the relevant author or editor elsewhere in the Bibliography of Standard Works.

American Historical Association. *A Catalogue of Files and Microfilms of the German Foreign Ministry Archives, 1867-1920.* Washington, The American Historical Association Committee for the Study of War Documents, 1959.

Andō Hikotarō 安藤彦太郎, ed. *Mantetsu: Nihon teikokushugi to Chūgoku* 満鉄日本帝国主義と中国 (The South Manchuria Railway Company: Japanese imperialism and China). Tokyo, Ochanomizu Shobō, 1965.

—— "Nichi-Ro sensō shi kenkyū no kadai: shu to shite Nitchū kankeishi no shiten kara" 日露戦争史研究の課題：主として日中関係史の視点から (Research topics on the history of the Russo-Japanese War, from the viewpoint of the history of Sino-Japanese relations), *Rekishigaku kenkyū*, No. 238 (1960), pp. 29-33.

Andō Hikotarō and Yamada Gōichi 山田豪一. "Kindai Chūgoku kenkyū to Mantetsu Chōsabu" 近代中国研究と満鉄調査部 (Studies of modern China and the Research Department of the South Manchuria Railway Company), *Rekishigaku kenkyū*, No. 270 (November 1962), pp. 36-43.

Andō Minoru 安藤実. "Mantetsu Kaisha no sōritsu ni tsuite" 満鉄会社の創立について (The establishment of the South Manchuria Railway Company), *Rekishi hyōron*, No. 117 (May 1960) pp. 13-32; No. 118 (June 1960), pp. 13-36.

Andō Tokki 安藤徳器, ed. and trans. *Ō Chōmei jijoden* 汪兆銘自叙伝 (Autobiography of Wang Chao-ming). Tokyo, Gannandō, 1940.

Andō Yoshio. "Development of Heavy Industry," in Shibusawa Keizo, ed., *Japanese Society in the Meiji Era*, pp. 305-46. Tokyo, Ōbunsha, 1958.

—— "Development of Mining Industry," in Shibusawa Keizo, ed., *Japanese Society in the Meiji Era*, pp. 347-67. Tokyo, Ōbunsha, 1958.

The Annual Register: A Review of Public Events at Home and Abroad for the Year 1937. London, Longmans, Green, 1938.

Aoki Shūzō 青木周蔵. *Aoki Shūzō jiden* 青木周蔵自伝 (The autobiography of Aoki Shūzō). Edited by Sakane Yoshihisa 坂根義久. Tokyo, Heibonsha, 1970.

—— *Jōyaku kaisei kiji* 條約改正記事 (Records on treaty revision). Tokyo, Foreign Ministry, 1891.

Aoki Tokuzō 青木得三. *Taiheiyō sensō zenshi* 太平洋戦争前史 (The historical background of the Pacific War). 3 vols. Tokyo, Gakujutsu Bunken Fukyūkai, 1953.

—— *Wakatsuki Reijirō Hamaguchi Osachi* 若槻礼次郎　浜口雄幸. Tokyo, Jiji Tsūshinsha, 1958.

Aoyama Hidehiko 青山秀彦. "Ōkuma zaisei to fukoku kōsō" 大隈財政と富国構想 (Ōkuma's fiscal policy and the "rich country" concept), in Shōshikai Sanjisshūnen Kinen Rombunshū 昭史会三十周年記念論文集, *Nihon rekishi ronkyū* 日本歴史論究 (Discussions on Japanese history), I, 491-509. 2 vols. Tokyo, Ninomiya Shoten, 1963-64.

Aoyama Kazuo 青山和夫 [Kuroda Zenji 黒田善治]. *Bōryaku jukurenkō* 謀略熟練工 (A skilled schemer). Tokyo, Myōgi Shuppan, 1957.

Arai Tatsuo 新井達夫. *Katō Tomosaburō* 加藤友三郎. Tokyo, Jiji Tsūshinsha, 1958.

Araki Sadao 荒木貞夫, ed. *Gensui Uehara Yūsaku den* 元帥上原勇作伝 (Biography of Marshal Uehara Yūsaku). 2 vols. Tokyo, Gensui Uehara Yūsaku Denki Kankō-kai, 1937.

Arita Hachirō 有田八郎. *Bakahachi to hito wa iu: gaikōkan no kaisō* 馬鹿八と人はいう外交官の回想 (People call me "Hachi" the fool: Memoirs of a diplomat). Tokyo, Kōwasha, 1959.

—— *Hito no me no chiri o miru: gaikō mondai kaikoroku* 人の目の塵を見る外交問題回顧録 (Beholding the mote in other men's eyes: Memoirs of diplomatic problems). Tokyo, Kōdansha, 1948.

Aritake Shūji 有竹修二. *Ishiwata Sōtarō* 石渡荘太郎. Tokyo, Ishiwata Sōtarō Denki Hensankai, 1954.

—— *Okada Keisuke* 岡田啓介. Tokyo, Okada Taishō Kiroku Hensankai, 1956.

—— *Saitō Makoto* 斉藤実. Tokyo, Jiji Tsūshinsha, 1958.

Asada Sadao 麻田貞雄. "Amerika no tai-Nichi kan to 'Washinton taisei' " アメリカの対日観と「ワシントン体制」(America's attitude toward Japan and the "Washington Conference system"), *Kokusai seiji: Nihon gaikōshi no shomondai*, III, 1968, pp. 96–115.

—— "Japan and the United States, 1915–1925." Unpublished doctoral dissertation, Yale University, 1963.

—— "Japan's 'Special Interests' and the Washington Conference, 1921–1922," *American Historical Review*, LXVI, No. 1 (October 1961), 62–70.

Asahi Shimbun Chōsa Kenkyū Shitsu 朝日新聞調査研究室, ed. *Kyokutō kokusai gunji saiban kiroku mokuroku oyobi sakuin* 極東国際軍事裁判記録目録及び索引 (Catalog and index to the records of the International Military Tribunal for the Far East). Tokyo, Asahi Shimbunsha, privately printed, 1953.

Asahi Shimbunsha 朝日新聞社, ed. *Tōkyō saiban* 東京裁判 (The Tokyo trials). 3 vols. Tokyo, Asahi Shimbunsha, 1962.

Asai Seiichi 浅居誠一. *Nisshin Kisen Kabushiki Kaisha sanjūnenshi oyobi tsuiho* 日清汽船株式会社三十年史及追補 (Thirty-year history of the Sino-Japanese Steamship Company, and supplement). Tokyo, Nisshin Kisen Kabushiki Kaisha, 1941.

Asakura Kōkichi 朝倉孝吉. *Meiji zenki Nihon kin'yū kōzōshi* 明治前期日本金融構造史 (The structure of Japanese finance in early Meiji). Tokyo, Iwanami Shoten, 1962.

Asano Torajirō 浅野虎次郎. *Daigensui Chō Sakurin* 大元帥張作霖 (Field Marshal Chang Tso-lin). Dairen, Nikka Jitsugyōsha, 1928.

Ashida Hitoshi 芦田均. *Dainiji sekai taisen gaikōshi* 第二次世界大戦外交史 (Diplomatic history of World War II). Tokyo, Jiji Tsūshinsha, 1960.

Avarin, B. *Imperializm v Man'chzhurii* (Imperialism in Manchuria). 2 vols. Moscow and Leningrad, Gosudarstvennoe Sotsial'noekonomicheskoe Izdatel'stvo, 1934.

Aya Tetsuichi 綾哲一 and Furuichi Kenzaburō 古市賢三郎. "Nichi-Man jidō no rekkoku kan" 日満児童の列国観 (Images of foreign countries held by children in Japan and Manchuria), *Ōyōshinri kenkyū*, III, No. 1 (November 1934), 93–116.

Ayusawa Shintarō 鮎沢信太郎. "Karafuto Chishima no shiteki kōsatsu" 樺太千島 の史的考察 (A historical study of Sakhalin and the Kuril Islands), *Nihon rekishi*, No. 42 (November 1951), pp. 2–5.

Baba Akira 馬場明. "Nichi-Ro sensō go no tairiku seisaku" 日露戦争後の大陸政策 (Japan's policy toward the continent after the Russo-Japanese War), *Kokusai seiji: Nihon gaikōshi kenkyū—Nisshin Nichi-Ro sensō*, 1961, pp. 134–50.

Baba, Tsunego. "The Anti-Comintern Pact in Domestic Politics," *Contemporary Japan*, V, No. 4 (March 1937), 536–44.

Baelz, Erwin. *Erwin Baelz: Das Leben eines deutschen Arztes im erwachenden Japan*. Stuttgart, J. Engelhorns nachf., 1931.

Baelz, Toku, ed. *Awakening Japan: The Diary of a German Doctor: Erwin Baelz*. New York, Viking Press, 1932.

Bailey, Thomas A. *A Diplomatic History of the American People*. 7th ed. New York, Appleton-Century-Crofts, 1964.

—— *Theodore Roosevelt and the Japanese-American Crises*. Gloucester, Mass., Peter Smith, 1964 (first published Stanford, Stanford University Press, 1934).

Banno Masataka 坂野正高. "Nihonjin no Chūgoku kan: Oda Yorozu hakushi no 'Shinkoku gyōseihō' o megutte" 日本人の中国観—織田萬博士の「清国行政法」をめ ぐって (Japanese images of China: Dr. Oda Yorozu's "Administrative Laws of the Ch'ing Dynasty"), *Shisō*, No. 452 (February 1962), pp. 69–78; No. 456 (June 1962), pp. 64–85.

Beale, Howard K. *Theodore Roosevelt and the Rise of America to World Power*. Baltimore, Johns Hopkins Press, 1956.

Beard, Charles A. *President Roosevelt and the Coming of the War, 1941: A Study in Appearances and Realities*. New Haven, Yale University Press, 1948.

Becker, Otto. *Der Gedanke einer Deutsch-Russisch-Japanischen Verständigung während des Weltkrieges*. Neumünster, Wachholtz, 1940.

Beckmann, George M. *The Making of the Meiji Constitution: The Oligarchs and the Constitutional Development of Japan, 1868–1891*. Lawrence, University of Kansas, 1957.

Bee, Minge C. "Origins of German Far Eastern Policy," *Chinese Social and Political Science Review*, XXI (April 1937), 65–97.

Berton, Peter A. "The Russo-Japanese Boundary, 1850–1875." Unpublished master's essay, Columbia University, 1951.

—— "The Secret Russo-Japanese Alliance of 1916." Unpublished doctoral dissertation, Columbia University, 1956.

Bland, J. O. P. *Recent Events and Present Policies in China.* Philadelphia, Lippincott, 1912.

Bloch, Kurt. *German Interests and Policies in the Far East.* New York, Institute of Pacific Relations, 1940.

Braisted, William R. *The United States Navy in the Pacific, 1897–1909.* Austin, University of Texas Press, 1958.

—— *The United States Navy in the Pacific, 1909–1922.* Austin, University of Texas Press, 1971.

Brandenburg, Erich. *Von Bismark zum Weltkriege.* Berlin, Deutsche Verlagsgesellschaft für Politik und Geschichte, 1924.

Brockdorff-Rantzau, U. K. C. *Dokumente und Gedanken um Versailles.* Berlin, Verlag für Kulturpolitik, 1925.

Brown, Sidney Devere. "Ōkubo Toshimichi: His Political and Economic Policies in Early Meiji Japan," *Journal of Asian Studies,* XXI, No. 2 (February 1962), 183–97.

Buckley, Thomas H. *The United States and the Washington Conference, 1921–1922.* Knoxville, University of Tennessee Press, 1970.

Buell, Raymond Leslie. "The Development of the Anti-Japanese Agitation in the United States," *Political Science Quarterly,* XXXVII (December 1922), 605-38.

—— *Japanese Immigration.* Boston, World Peace Foundation, 1924.

Burns, James MacGregor. *Roosevelt: The Soldier of Freedom, 1940–1945.* New York, Harcourt Brace Jovanovich, 1970.

Butow, Robert J. C. *Japan's Decision to Surrender.* Stanford, Stanford University Press, 1954.

—— *Tojo and the Coming of the War.* Princeton, Princeton University Press, 1961.

Chang, Chung-fu. *The Anglo-Japanese Alliance.* Baltimore, Johns Hopkins Press, 1931.

Chō Yukio 長幸男. "Ōkuma Shigenobu no shihei taisaku—sono mujun to shokusan kōgyō to no kanren ni tsuite" 大隈重信の紙幣対策その矛盾と殖産興業との関聯について (Ōkuma Shigenobu's currency policy—its contradictions and connection with the encouragement of production), in Chō Yukio, *Nihon keizai shisōshi kenkyū* 日本経済思想史研究 (Studies in the history of Japanese economic thought), pp. 65–118. Tokyo, Miraisha, 1963.

Chōsen Ginkō 朝鮮銀行. *Chōsen Ginkō nijūgonenshi* 朝鮮銀行二十五年史 (Twenty-five year history of the Bank of Korea). Seoul, Chōsen Ginkō, 1934.

Chōsen Ginkō Shi Hensan Iinkai 朝鮮銀行史編纂委員会. *Chōsen Ginkō ryakushi* 朝鮮銀行略史 (A brief history of the Bank of Korea). Tokyo, Chōsen Ginkō, 1960.

Churchill, W. S. *The Second World War.* 6 vols. Boston, Houghton Mifflin, 1948–53.

Chyne, W. Y. [Chuang Wen-ya], ed. *Handbook of Cultural Institutions in China.* Shanghai, Chinese National Committee on Intellectual Co-operation, 1936.

Ciano, Galeazzo. *The Ciano Diaries, 1939–1943*. Edited by Hugh Gibson. Garden City, Doubleday, 1946.

—— *Ciano's Diplomatic Papers*. Edited by Malcolm Muggeridge, translated by Stuart Hood. London, Odhams Press, 1948. An edited translation of Galeazzo Ciano, *L'Europa verso la catastrofe*. Verona, A. Mondadori, 1948.

Clifford, Nicholas R. *Retreat from China: British Policy in the Far East, 1937–1941*. Seattle, University of Washington Press, 1967.

Clinard, O. J. *Japan's Influence on American Naval Power, 1897–1917*. Berkeley, University of California Press, 1947.

Conroy, F. Hilary. *The Japanese Seizure of Korea, 1868–1910: A Study of Realism and Idealism in International Relations*. Philadelphia, University of Pennsylvania Press, 1960.

Cowan, C. D., ed. *The Economic Development of China and Japan*. New York, Praeger, 1964.

Craigie, Robert L. *Behind the Japanese Mask*. London, Hutchinson, 1945.

Croly, Herbert. *Willard Straight*. New York, Macmillan, 1924.

Crowley, James B. "Japanese Army Factionalism in the Early 1930's," *Journal of Asian Studies*, XXI, No. 3 (May 1962), 309–26.

—— *Japan's Quest for Autonomy: National Security and Foreign Policy, 1930–1938*. Princeton, Princeton University Press, 1966.

—— "A Reconsideration of the Marco Polo Bridge Incident," *Journal of Asian Studies*, XXII, No. 3 (May 1963), 277–91.

Dallin, David J. *Soviet Russia and the Far East*. New Haven, Yale University Press, 1948.

Daniels, Roger. *The Politics of Prejudice: The Anti-Japanese Movement in California and the Struggle for Japanese Exclusion*. Berkeley, University of California Press, 1962.

Deconde, Alexander, ed. *Isolation and Security: Ideas and Interests in Twentieth Century American Foreign Policy*. Durham, Duke University Press, 1957.

Dennett, Tyler. *Americans in Eastern Asia: A Critical Study of the Policy of the United States with Reference to China, Japan and Korea in the 19th Century*. New York, Macmillan, 1922.

—— *Roosevelt and the Russo-Japanese War: A Critical Study of American Policy in Eastern Asia in 1902–05, Based Primarily upon the Private Papers of Theodore Roosevelt*. New York, Doubleday, Page, 1925.

Dennis, Alfred L.P. *The Anglo-Japanese Alliance*. Berkeley, University of California Press, 1923.

Dickins, F.V. and S. Lane Poole. *The Life of Sir Harry Parkes, Sometime Her Majesty's Minister to China and Japan*. 2 vols. London, Macmillan, 1894.

Dirksen, Herbert von. *Moscow, Tokyo, London: Twenty Years of German Foreign Policy*. Norman, University of Oklahoma Press, 1952.

"D. Mare" D. マレー (D. Murray), in Shōwa Joshi Daigaku Kindai Bungaku Kenkyū Shitsu 昭和女子大学近代文学研究室, ed., *Kindai bungaku kenkyū sōsho* 近代文学研究叢書 (Studies in modern literature), VIII, 71–118. Tokyo, Shōwa Joshi Daigaku Kōyōkai, 1958.

Documents on International Affairs, 1928—. London, Oxford University Press, 1929—.

Dobrov, A.S. *Dal'nevostochnaia politika SShA v period Russko-Iapanskoi voiny* (The Far Eastern policy of the United States in the period of the Russo-Japanese War). Moscow, Gosudarstvennoe Izdatel'stvo Politicheskoi Literatury, 1952.

Dokumente der deutschen Politik. 9 vols. Berlin, Deutsches Auslandswissenschaftliches Institut, 1939–44.

Dugdale, Blanche E.C. *Arthur James Balfour, First Earl of Balfour*. 2 vols. London, Hutchinson, 1936.

Dull, Paul A. "The Assassination of Chang Tso-lin," *Far Eastern Quarterly*, XI, No. 4 (August 1952), 453–63.

Dull, Paul A. and Michael T. Umemura. *The Tokyo Trials: A Functional Index to the Proceedings of the International Military Tribunal for the Far East*. Ann Arbor, University of Michigan Press, 1957.

Dulles, F.R. *Forty Years of American-Japanese Relations*. New York, Appleton-Century, 1937.

Eckardstein, Hermann F. *Lebenserinnerungen und politische Denkwürdigkeiten*. 3 vols. Leipzig, Paul List, 1919–21.

Eden, Anthony. *The Memoirs of Anthony Eden, Earl of Avon: Facing the Dictators*. Boston, Houghton Mifflin, 1962.

Edwards, E.W. "The Far Eastern Agreement of 1907," *Journal of Modern History*, XXVI, No. 4 (December 1954), 340–55.

Egashira Tsuneharu 江頭恒治. "Takashima Tankō ni okeru Nichi-Ei kyōdō jigyō" 高島炭坑に於ける日英共同事業 (The Takashima Coal Mine, a joint Anglo-Japanese venture), in Nihon Keizaishi Kenkyūjo 日本経済史研究所, ed., *Bakumatsu keizaishi kenkyū* 幕末経済史研究 (Studies in the economic history of the late Tokugawa period), pp. 23–58. Tokyo, Yūhikaku, 1935.

Eguchi Bokurō 江口朴郎. "Giwadan jiken no igi ni tsuite" 義和団事件の意義について (The significance of the Boxer Rebellion), *Rekishigaku kenkyū*, No. 150 (March 1951), pp. 74–83.

—— "Nichi-Ei dōmei no hatten to shite no Ei-Doku kōshō" 日英同盟の発展としての英独交渉 (British-German negotiations and the development of the Anglo-Japanese alliance), in Eguchi Bokurō, Hayashi Kentarō 林健太郎, and Takahashi Kōhachirō 高橋幸八郎, *Kokusai kankei no shiteki bunseki* 国際関係の史的分析 (Historical analysis of international relations). Tokyo, Ochanomizu Shobō, 1949.

—— "Nihon teikokushugi no kokusaiteki keiki" 日本帝国主義の国際的契機 (The international setting of Japanese imperialism), in Eguchi, *Teikokushugi to minzoku*, pp. 70–140.

—— *Teikokushugi to minzoku* 帝国主義と民族 (Imperialism and the nation). Tokyo, Tōkyō Daigaku Shuppankai, 1954.

Eguchi Keichi 江口圭一. "Kaku Shōrei jiken to Nihon teikokushugi" 郭松齢事件と日本帝国主義 (The Kuo Sung-ling incident and Japanese imperialism), *Jimbun gakuhō*, No. 17 (November 1962), pp. 71–88.

Emi, Kōichi, *Government Fiscal Activity and Economic Growth in Japan, 1868–1960.* Tokyo, Kinokuniya, 1963.

—— "The Growth of the Japanese Economy in the First Half of the Meiji Period," *Hitotsubashi Journal of Economics*, III, No. 2 (June 1963), 6–15.

Endō Shōkichi 遠藤湘吉, Katō Toshihiko 加藤俊彦, and Takahashi Makoto 高橋誠. *Nihon no ōkura daijin* 日本の大藏大臣 (Japan's finance ministers). Tokyo, Nihon Hyōronsha, 1964.

Esthus, Raymond A. *Theodore Roosevelt and Japan.* Seattle, University of Washington Press, 1966.

Etō Shinkichi 衛藤瀋吉. "Chūgoku ni taisuru sensō shūketsu kōsaku" 中国に対する戦争終結工作 (Japanese peace maneuvers toward China), in Nihon Gaikō Gakkai 日本外交学会, ed., *Taiheiyō sensō shūketsu ron* 太平洋戦争終結論 (Collected essays on the termination of the Pacific War), pp. 383–423. Tokyo, Tōkyō Daigaku Shuppankai, 1958.

—— "Keihōsen shadan mondai no gaikō katei" 京奉線遮断問題の外交過程 (The diplomatic negotiations concerning the suspension of traffic on the Peking-Mukden Railway), in Shinohara and Mitani, *Kindai Nihon no seiji shidō*, pp. 375–429.

—— "Nankin jiken to Nichi-Bei" 南京事件と日米 (Japan and the United States during the Nanking Incident), in Saitō Makoto 斉藤眞, ed., *Takagi Yasaka sensei koki kinen: gendai Amerika no naisei to gaikō* 高木八尺先生古稀記念現代アメリカの内政と外交 (Commemorating the seventieth birthday of Professor Takagi Yasaka: American domestic politics and diplomacy), pp. 299–324. Tokyo, Tōkyō Daigaku Shuppankai, 1959.

—— "Nihonjin no Chūgoku kan: Suzue Gen'ichi o megutte" 日本人の中国観鈴江言一をめぐって (Japanese images of China: Suzue Gen'ichi), *Shisō*, No. 445 (July 1961), pp. 11–15.

—— "Shidehara gaikō kara Tanaka gaikō e: gaikō mondai o midari ni tōsō no gu ni suru to dō naru ka" 幣原外交から田中外交へ外交問題をみだりに党争の具にするとどうなるか (From Shidehara diplomacy to Tanaka diplomacy: A lesson taken from party quarrels over diplomatic problems), *Sekai keizai*, No. 82 (June 1963), pp. 2–12.

Eulenburg, Fritz. *Ost-Asien, 1860–1862, in Briefen des Grafen Fritz zu Eulenburg.* Berlin, E.S. Mittler, 1900.

Feis, Herbert. *The Road to Pearl Harbor: The Coming of the War between the United*

States and Japan. Princeton, Princeton University Press, 1950.

Ferrell, Robert H. *American Diplomacy in the Great Depression: Hoover-Stimson Foreign Policy, 1929–1933.* New Haven, Yale University Press, 1957.

Fifield, Russell. *Woodrow Wilson and the Far East: The Diplomacy of the Shantung Question.* New York, Crowell, 1952.

Flowers, Montaville. *The Japanese Conquest of American Opinion.* New York, Doran, 1917.

France, Ministère des affaires étrangères. *Documents diplomatiques français, 1871– 1914.* 41 vols. Paris, Imprimerie Nationale, 1929–59.

Franke, Otto. *Die Grossmächte in Ostasien von 1894 bis 1914.* Braunschweig, Westermann, 1923.

Friedman, Irving S. *British Relations with China, 1931–1939.* New York, Institute of Pacific Relations, 1940.

Fujii Mitsuo 藤井光男 and Fujii Harue 藤井治枝. "1880 nendai no sanshi kin'yū ni tsuite" 1880 年代の蚕糸金融について (Silk yarn financing in the 1880s), *Tochi seido shigaku,* No. 13 (1961), pp. 29–46.

Fujii Shigeru 藤井茂. "Nihon keizai no hatten to bōeki seisaku" 日本経済の発展と 貿易政策 (Foreign trade policy and Japan's economic growth), *Kokumin keizai zasshi,* CX, No. 2 (August 1964), 1–17.

—— "The Development of the Japanese Cotton Industry and the Import of American Cotton," in Ohara, *Japanese Trade and Industry in the Meiji-Taishō Era,* pp. 299–394.

Fujii Shōichi 藤井松一. "Teikokushugi no seiritsu to Nichi-Ro sensō" 帝国主義の 成立と日露戦争 (The rise of imperialism and the Russo-Japanese War), in Rekishigaku Kenkyūkai Taikai Hōkoku 歴史学研究会大会報告, ed., *Jidai kubun jō no rironteki shomondai* 時代區分上の理論的諸問題 (Theoretical problems concerning periodization), pp. 44–59. Tokyo, Iwanami Shoten, 1956.

Fujii Shōzō 藤井昇三. "Sen-kyūhyaku-nijūnen An-Choku sensō o meguru Nitchū kankei no ichi kōsatsu: Hembōgun mondai o chūshin to shite" 1920年安直戦争 をめぐる日中関係の一考察辺防軍問題を中心として (A note on Sino-Japanese relations during the 1920 Anhwei-Chihli war and the problem of the Pien-fang army), in *Kokusai seiji: Nihon gaikōshi kenkyū—Nitchū kankei no tenkai,* 1960, pp. 56–70.

Fujimoto Haruki 藤本治毅. *Ningen Ishiwara Kanji* 人間石原莞爾 (Ishiwara Kanji, the man). Tokyo, Taichi Sangyōsha, 1959.

Fujimoto Jitsuya 藤本実也. *Kaikō to kiito bōeki* 開港と生糸貿易 (The opening of the ports and the foreign trade in raw silk). 3 vols. Tokyo, Kaikō to Kiito Bōeki Kankōkai, 1939.

Fujimura Michio 藤村道生. "Gumbi kakuchō to kaikyū mujun no tenkai" 軍備拡張と 階級矛盾の展開 (Arms expansion and class contradictions), in Shinobu and

Nakayama, *Nichi-Ro sensōshi no kenkyū*, pp. 67–89.

—— "Kaisen yoron no kōzō" 開戦世論の構造 (Public opinion at the outbreak of the war), in Shinobu and Nakayama, *Nichi-Ro sensōshi no kenkyū*, pp. 179–216.

—— "Nichi-Ro sensō no seikaku ni yosete" 日露戦争の性格に寄せて (On the nature of the Russo-Japanese War), *Rekishigaku kenkyū*, No. 195 (1956), pp. 1–13.

—— "Tai-Sen seisaku no tenkan" 対鮮政策の転換 (The turning point in policy toward Korea), in Shinobu and Nakayama, *Nichi-Ro sensōshi no kenkyū*, pp. 143–60.

Fujimura Satoru 藤村通. "Ōkurakyō Ōkuma Shigenobu no zaisei keizai seisaku kihon kōryō" 大蔵卿大隈重信の財政経済政策基本綱領 (The basic principles of Finance Minister Ōkuma Shigenobu's fiscal and economic policy), *Ibaragi daigaku bunri gakubu kiyō (shakai kagaku)*, No. 11 (December 1960), pp. 113–42.

—— "Seinan sensō go no Ōkuma no zaisei seisaku" 西南戦争後の大隈の財政政策 (Ōkuma's fiscal policy after the Satsuma Rebellion), *Ibaragi daigaku seikei gakkai zasshi*, No. 11 (June 1962), pp. 39–70.

Fujisaki Yoshirō 藤崎嘉郎. *Manshū to Aioi Yoshitarō* 満州と相生由太郎 (Manchuria and Aioi Yoshitarō). Dairen, Ōsakayagō Shoten, 1932.

Fujita Akerō 藤田明郎. "Meiji zenki ni okeru shokusan kōgyō seisaku to shōgyōteki nōgyō no hatten" 明治前期における殖産興業政策と商業的農業の発展 (The policy of encouraging production and the development of commercial agriculture in early Meiji), *Rekishi hyōron*, No. 135 (November 1961), pp. 62–75.

Fujita Masahiro. "The Banking System in the Middle Meiji Era (1870–1910)," *Kobe Economic and Business Review*, No. 3 (1956), pp. 55–85.

—— "The Development of Overseas Banking System in Japan in the Meiji Era," *Kobe Eeonomic and Business Review*, No. 4 (1957), pp. 69–90.

Fujiwara Akira 藤原彰. *Gunjishi* 軍事史 (History of the Japanese military). Tokyo, Tōkyō Keizai Shimpōsha, 1961.

Fukai Eigo 深井英五. *Sūmitsuin jūyō giji oboegaki* 枢密院重要議事覚書 (Notes on important sessions of the Privy Council). Tokyo, Iwanami Shoten, 1953.

Fukaya Hiroshi 深谷博治. *Nisshin sensō to Mutsu gaikō: Mutsu Munemitsu no "Kenkenroku"* 日清戦争と陸奥外交陸奥宗光の蹇蹇録 (The Sino-Japanese War and Mutsu diplomacy: Mutsu Munemitsu's "Kenkenroku"). Tokyo, Nihon Hōsō Shuppan Kyōkai, 1940.

Fukudome Shigeru 福留繁. *Kaigun no hansei* 海軍の反省 (A self-examination by the navy). Tokyo, Nihon Shuppan Kyōdō Kabushiki Kaisha, 1951.

—— *Shikan Shinjuwan kōgeki* 史観真珠湾攻撃 (A historical view of the attack on Pearl Harbor). Tokyo, Ajiasha, 1955.

Fukushima Masao 福島正夫. "Meiji shonen no keizai seisaku to shihon chikuseki no mondai—Ōkubo Ōkuma kōsō to Matsukata kōsō" 明治初年の経済政策と資本蓄積の問題 大久保大隈構想と松方構想 (Economic policy and the problem of capital accumulation in early Meiji—the Ōkubo-Ōkuma conception and the Matsukata conception), *Tōyō bunka*, No. 9 (June 1952), pp. 1-20.

Fukushima Shōgun Jiseki Kankōkai 福島将軍事蹟刊行会. *Fukushima Yasumasa shōgun jiseki* 福島安正将軍事蹟 (Biography of General Fukushima Yasumasa). Tokyo, Tōa Kyōkai, 1941.

Furushima Toshio 古島敏雄. *Sangyōshi* 産業史 (History of industry), III. Vol. XII of *Taikei Nihonshi sōsho* 体系日本史叢書 (A systematic anthology of Japanese history). 3 vols. Tokyo, Yamakawa Shuppansha, 1966.

Furuta Ryōichi 古田良一. *Nihon kaiunshi gaisetsu* 日本海運史概説 (An outline history of Japanese maritime transportation). Tokyo, Dōbun Shoin, 1955.

Furuya Tetsuo 古屋哲夫. "Nihon teikokushugi no seiritsu o megutte" 日本帝国主義の成立を繞って (On the rise of Japanese imperialism), *Rekishigaku kenkyū*, No. 202 (1956), pp. 40-56.

Fuse Katsuji 布施勝治. *Shina kokumin kakumei to Hyō Gyokushō* 支那国民革命と馮玉祥 (The Chinese national revolution and Feng Yü-hsiang). Tokyo, Ōsakayagō Shoten, 1929.

Fuse Shimpei 布勢信平. *Mammō ken'eki yōroku* 満蒙權益要録 (A summary of Japanese rights and interests in Manchuria and Mongolia). Tokyo, Seibunkan, 1932.

Gafencu, Grigore. *Prelude to the Russian Campaign, from the Moscow Pact to the Opening of Hostilities in Russia.* London, E. Mueller, 1945.

Gaimushō Hyakunenshi Hensan Iinkai 外務省百年史編纂委員会, ed. *Gaimushō no hyakunen* 外務省の百年 (A century of the Japanese Foreign Ministry). 2 vols. Tokyo, Hara Shobō, 1969.

Gal'perin, A.L. *Anglo-Iaponskii soiuz, 1902–1921 gg* (The Anglo-Japanese alliance, 1902–1921). Moscow, Gosudarstvennoe Izdatel'stvo Politicheskoi Literatury, 1947.

Gensui Katō Tomosaburō Denki Hensan Iinkai 元帥加藤友三郎伝記編纂委員会, ed. *Gensui Katō Tomosaburō den* 元帥加藤友三郎伝 (Biography of Katō Tomosaburō). Tokyo, Gensui Katō Tomosaburō Den Hensan Iinkai, 1928.

Germany, Auswärtiges Amt. *Die grosse Politik der europäischen Kabinette, 1871–1914.* 40 vols. Berlin, Deutsche Verlagsgesellschaft für Politik, 1922–27.

Gol'dberg, D.I. *Vneshniaia politika Iaponii, Sentiabr' 1939–Dekabr' 1941 gg* (Foreign policy of Japan, September 1939–December 1941). Moscow, Izdatel'stvo Vostochnoi Literatury, 1959.

Gordon, Joseph. "The Russo-Japanese Neutrality Pact of April, 1941." Unpublished master's essay, Columbia University, 1956.

Great Britain, Foreign Office. *British Documents on the Origins of the War, 1898–1914.* Edited by G. P. Gooch and Harold Temperley. 11 vols. London, H. M. Stationery Office, 1926–38.

Vol. II: *The Anglo-Japanese Alliance and the Franco-British Entente* (1927).

Vol. IV: *The Anglo-Russian Rapprochement, 1903–1907* (1929).

Vol. VIII: *Arbitration, Neutrality, and Security* (1932).

Vol. XI: *The Outbreak of War* (1938).

—— *Documents on British Foreign Policy, 1919–1939.* Edited by E. L. Woodward, Rohan Butler, and J. P. T. Bury. London, H. M. Stationery Office, 1947–

Grew, Joseph. *Ten Years in Japan.* New York, Simon and Schuster, 1944.

—— *Turbulent Era: A Diplomatic Record of Forty Years, 1904–1945.* 2 vols. Boston, Houghton Mifflin, 1952.

Grey, Edward. *Twenty-five Years, 1892–1916.* 2 vols. New York, Frederick A. Stokes, 1925.

Griffis, William Elliot. *Verbeck of Japan, a Citizen of No Country: A Life Story of Foundation Work Inaugurated by Guido Fridolin Verbeck.* New York, Fleming H. Revell, 1900.

Griswold, A. Whitney. *Far Eastern Policy of the United States.* New Haven, Yale University Press, 1962 (first published New York, Harcourt, Brace, 1938).

Haji Seiji 土師清二 [Akamatsu Seita 赤松静太]. *Ginkō sobyō* 吟香素描 (A sketch of Ginkō). Tokyo, Tōhō Shoin, 1959.

Hakurankai Kyōkai (Exposition Society). *Japan and Her Exhibits at the Panama-Pacific International Exhibition, 1915.* Tokyo, Japan Magazine, 1915.

Hall, Ivan. "Mori Arinori: The Formative Years," *Papers on Japan,* III, 52–124. Cambridge, East Asian Research Center, Harvard University, November 1965.

Hamano Suetarō 浜野末太郎 (pen name, Tonan 斗南). *Shinajin katagi* 支那人気質 (Chinese spirit). Tokyo, Sekai Shuppansha, 1926.

Hanabusa Nagamichi 英修道. "Manshū jihen kara Nihon no Kokusai Remmei dattai made" 満州事変から日本の国際連盟脱退まて (From the Manchurian Incident to Japan's withdrawal from the League of Nations), in Nihon Gaikō Gakkai 日本外交学会, ed., *Taiheiyō sensō gen'in ron* 太平洋戦争原因論 (Origins of the Pacific War), pp. 231–70. Tokyo, Shimbun Gekkansha, 1953.

—— *Meiji gaikōshi* 明治外交史 (Meiji diplomatic history). Tokyo, Shibundō, 1960.

—— "Okinawa kizoku no enkaku" 沖縄帰属の沿革 (A history of sovereignty over Okinawa), *Kokusaihō gaikō zasshi,* LIV, Nos. 1–3 (April 1955), 3–40.

—— "Santō mondai no kaiketsu ni kansuru Nikka kōshō" 山東問題の解決に関する日華交渉 (Sino-Japanese negotiations to settle the Shantung problem), *Hōgaku kenkyū,* XXXIII, No. 2 (1960), 47–91.

Hanawa Kunzō 塙薫蔵, ed. *Ura Keiichi* 浦敬一. Tokyo, Jumpū Shoin, 1924.

Hanaya Tadashi 花谷正. "Manshū jihen wa kōshite keikaku sareta" 満州事変はこうして計画された (Thus was plotted the Manchurian Incident), *Bessatsu chisei, V: himerareta Shōwashi,* December 1956, pp. 40–50.

Hanssen, Hans P. *Diary of a Dying Empire.* Bloomington, Indiana University Press, 1955.

Hanzawa Hiroshi 判沢弘. " 'Manshūkoku' no isan wa nani ka" 「満州国」の遺産

は何か (What is the legacy of 'Manchukuo'?), *Chūō kōron*, LXXIX, No. 7 (July 1964), 114–25.

Hara Heizō 原平三. "Tokugawa bakufu no Eikoku ryūgakusei: Bakumatsu ryūgakusei no kenkyū" 徳川幕府の英国留学生幕末留学生の研究 (Students sent to England by the Tokugawa shogunate: A study of Japanese students abroad in the last years of the shogunate), *Rekishi chiri*, LXXIX, No. 5 (May 1942), 345–74.

Hara Keiichirō 原奎一郎, ed. *Hara Takashi nikki* 原敬日記 (Diary of Hara Takashi). 9 vols. Tokyo, Kengensha, 1950–51.

Hara Shirō 原司郎. "Daini Daishichijūshi Kokuritsu Ginkō no chokin ginkōka" 第二第七十四国立銀行の貯金銀行化 (The transformation into savings banks of the Second and the Seventy-Fourth National Banks), in Yokohama Shi Shi Henshūshitsu, *Yokohama shi shi*, III, Part 2, 438–93. Yokohama, Yūrindō, 1963.

—— "Daini Kokuritsu Ginkō oboegaki" 第二国立銀行覚書 (Memorandum on the Second National Bank), *Kin'yū keizai*, No. 50 (1958), pp. 58–82.

—— "Infurēshonki no ginkō" インフレーション期の銀行 (Banks during the inflation), in Yokohama Shi Shi Henshūshitsu, *Yokohama shi shi*, III, Part 2, 411–37. Yokohama, Yūrindō, 1963.

—— "Meiji chūki ni okeru Yokohama Daini Kokuritsu Ginkō no seikaku" 明治中期における横浜第二国立銀行の性格 (The character of the Yokohama Second National Bank in middle Meiji), in *Shōkeihō ronsō*, XI, No. 3 (November 1960), 45–70. Also in *Kin'yū keizai*, No. 65 (December 1960), pp. 57–80.

—— "Meiji shoki kin'yūshi e no ichi kōsatsu—kawase kaisha no setsuritsu o chūshin to shite" 明治初期金融史への一考察 為替会社設立を中心として (A note on the financial history of early Meiji—the establishment of exchange companies), *Ginkō kenkyū*, No. 300 (February 1957), pp. 31–46.

—— "Meiji shoki Yokohama kin'yūshi oboegaki" 明治初期横浜金融史覚書 (Memorandum on the financial history of Yokohama in early Meiji), *Shōkeihō ronsō*, XII, No. 4 (February 1962), 55–116.

—— *Meiji zenki kin'yūshi* 明治前期金融史 (The financial history of the early Meiji period). Tokyo, Tōyō Keizai Shimpōsha, 1965.

—— "Shin kin'yū kikō no sōsetsu" 新金融機構の創設 (Establishment of new financial institutions), in Yokohama Shi Shi Henshūshitsu, *Yokohama shi shi*, III, Part 1, 166–226. Yokohama, Yūrindō, 1961.

—— "Yokohama Shōkin Ginkō no setsuritsu to sono seikaku" 横浜正金銀行の設立とその性格 (The establishment and character of the Yokohama Specie Bank), in Yokohama Shi Shi Henshūshitsu, *Yokohama shi shi*, III, Part 2, 494–571. Yokohama, Yūrindō, 1963.

—— "Yokohama Shōkin Ginkō shoki no tokushitsu" 横浜正金銀行初期の特質 (The character of the Yokohama Specie Bank in its early years), *Shōkeihō ronsō*, XIV,

No. 3 (January 1964), 97–147.

Hara Yasusaburō 原安三郎. *Yamamoto Jōtarō denki* 山本条太郎伝記 (Biography of Yamamoto Jōtarō), Tokyo, Yamamoto Jōtarō Ō Denki Hensankai, 1942.

—— *Yamamoto Jōtarō ronsaku* 山本条太郎論策 (Policies of Yamamoto Jōtarō), I–II. Tokyo, Yamamoto Jōtarō Ō Denki Hensankai, 1939.

Hara Yoshio. "On Japanese Students Abroad, 1854 to 1873." New York, Columbia University Seminar on Modern East Asia: Japan, May 15, 1965 (mimeographed for distribution to members and guests of the seminar).

Harada Katsumasa 原田勝正. "Chōsen heigō to shoki no shokuminchi keiei" 朝鮮併合と初期の植民地経営 (The annexation of Korea and the early period of colonization by Japan), in *Iwanami kōza Nihon rekishi gendai* 岩波講座日本歴史現代 (Iwanami lectures on contemporary Japanese history), I, 197–244. Tokyo, Iwanami Shoten, 1963.

Harada Kumao 原田熊雄. *Saionji kō to seikyoku* 西園寺公と政局 (Prince Saionji and politics). 8 vols., 1 supplementary vol. Tokyo, Iwanami Shoten, 1950–52, 1956.

Harada Mikio 原田三喜雄. "Shokusan kōgyō seisaku kenkyū no tōmen suru kadai" 殖産興業政策研究の当面する課題 (Immediate problems in studying the encouragement of production policy), *Shakai keizai shigaku*, XXIX, No. 1 (1963), 88–98.

Harrington, F. H. *God, Mammon and the Japanese: Dr. Horace N. Allen and Korean-American Relations, 1884–1905.* Madison, University of Wisconsin Press, 1944.

Hata Ikuhiko 秦郁彦. "Futsu-In shinchū to gun no nanshin seisaku (1940–1941)" 仏印進駐と軍の南進政策 (一九四〇年〜一九四一年) (The occupation of French Indochina and the military advance southward [1940–1941]), in *Nampō shinshutsu* 南方進出 (The southward advance), pp. 143–274. Vol. VI of Nihon Kokusai Seiji Gakkai Taiheiyō Sensō Gen'in Kenkyūbu, ed., *Taiheiyō sensō e no michi.* Tokyo, Asahi Shimbunsha, 1963.

—— "Kōdōha to Tōseiha" 皇道派と統制派 (The Imperial Way faction and the Control faction), *Jiyū*, III, No. 5 (1961), 78–90.

—— "Meijiki ikō ni okeru Nichi-Bei Taiheiyō senryaku no hensen" 明治期以降における日米太平洋戦略の変遷 (Changes in Japanese and American strategies in the Pacific after the Meiji period), *Kokusai seiji: Nichi-Bei kankei no imēji*, 1966, pp. 36–57.

—— "Nikka jihen" 日華事変 (The Sino-Japanese War), *Kokusai seiji: Nihon gaikōshi kenkyū—Shōwa jidai*, 1959, pp. 71–84.

—— "Ni-ni-roku jiken" 二二六事件 (The February 26 Incident), *Jiyū*, III, No. 6 (1961), 96–108.

—— "Nitchū sensō no gunjiteki tenkai (1937–1941)" 日中戦争の軍事的展開一九三七年〜一九四一年 (Military developments during the Sino-Japanese War [1937–1941]), in *Nitchū sensō II* 日中戦争 (The Sino-Japanese War, Part 2), pp. 1–110. Vol. IV of Nihon Kokusai Seiji Gakkai Taiheiyō Sensō Gen'in Kenkyūbu, *Taiheiyō sensō e no michi.* Tokyo, Asahi Shimbunsha, 1963.

—— *Nitchū sensōshi—Nihon tairiku seisaku no tenkai* 日中戦争史日本大陸政策の展開 (A history of the Sino-Japanese War—the development of Japanese continental policy). Tokyo, Kawade Shobō Shinsha, 1961.

—— "Rikugun no habatsu 'Sakurakai' " 陸軍の派閥「櫻会」(The 'Cherry Blossom Society' clique in the army), *Jiyū*, III, No. 3 (1961), 88–101.

—— "Sakurakai shuisho" 櫻会趣意書 (Declaration of the Cherry Blossom Society), *Rekishi kyōiku*, IV, No. 2 (1958), 65, 81–88.

—— "Umezu Ka Ōkin kyōtei keii" 梅津何応欽協定経緯 (The conclusion of the Ho-Umezu agreement), *Ajia kenkyū*, IV, No. 2 (1957), 65–114.

Hata Ikuhiko and Shimizu Setsurō 清水節郎. "Rokōkyō jiken" 蘆溝橋事件 (The Marco Polo Bridge Incident), *Ajia kenkyū*, III, No. 2 (1956), 80–97.

Hata Shunroku 畑俊六. "Nikki Shōwa yonen jūgatsu shichinichi kara Shōwa nijūnen sangatsu nijūhachinichi" 日記昭和四年十月七日〜昭和二十年三月二十八日 (Diary, October 7, 1929—March 28, 1945). National Defense Agency, Military History Office, Archives, unpublished, n.d.

Hatada Takashi 旗田巍. *Chōsen shi* 朝鮮史 (History of Korea). Tokyo, Iwanami Shoten, 1951.

—— "Meijiki no Nihon to Chōsen" 明治期の日本と朝鮮 (Japan and Korea in the Meiji era), in *Kokusai seiji: Nikkan kankei no tenkai*, 1962, pp. 1–12.

Hatano Yoshihiro 波多野善大. "Nichi-Ro sensō go ni okeru kokusai kankei no dōin: Nichi-Bei kankei o chūshin to suru" 日露戦争後に於ける国際関係の動因—日米関係を中心とする (Motives in international relations after the Russo-Japanese War: Japanese-American relations), in *Kokusai seiji: Nihon gaikōshi kenkyū—Meiji jidai*, 1957, pp. 153–82.

—— "Nishihara shakkan no kihonteki kōsō" 西原借款の基本的構想 (The fundamental idea behind the Nishihara loan), *Nagoya daigaku bungakubu jisshūnen kinen ronshū*, March, 1959, pp. 393–416.

—— "Ri Kōshō sen-happyaku-hachijūnendai ni okeru tai-Nichi seisaku ni tsuite" 李鴻章 1880年代における対日政策について (Li Hung-chang and China's policy toward Japan in the 1880s), *Rekishigaku kenkyū*, No. 253 (May 1961), pp. 38–42.

—— "Shimonoseki jōyaku dairokujō daiyonkō no seiritsu shita haikei ni tsuite" 下関条約第六条第四項の成立した背景について (Determining factors in the writing of Article 6, Clause 4 of the Treaty of Shimonoseki, 1895), *Kindai Chūgoku kenkyū*, No. 1 (January 1958), pp. 137–211.

—— "Shingai kakumei to Nihon" 辛亥革命と日本 (The Chinese revolution of 1911 and Japan), *Rekishi kyōiku*, II, No. 2 (February 1954), 96–103.

Hattori Kazuma 服部一馬. "Bakumatsu Meiji shoki no gaikoku shihon no katsudō to taiō keitai" 幕末明治初期の外国資本の活動と対応形態 (The reaction to the activity of foreign capital in late Tokugawa and early Meiji), *Keizai to bōeki*, No. 87 (November 1965), pp. 32–42; No. 91 (November 1966), pp. 1–9.

—— "Bōeki no hatten" 貿易の発展 (The development of foreign trade), in Yoko-hama Shi Shi Henshūshitsu, *Yokohama shi shi*, III, Part 2, 195–279. Yokohama, Yūrindō, 1963.

—— "Kaikō to Nihon shihonshugi" 開港と日本資本主義 (The opening of the ports and Japanese capitalism), in *Nihon keizaishi taikei* 日本経済史大系 (Japanese econo-mic history series), V, 3–32. 6 vols. Tokyo, Tōkyō Daigaku Shuppankai, 1965.

Hattori Shisō 服部之總. *Kindai Nihon gaikōshi* 近代日本外交史 (Modern Japanese diplomatic history). Tokyo, Kawade Shobō, 1954.

Hattori Takushirō 服部卓四郎. *Dai Tōa sensō zenshi* 大東亞戰爭全史 (A history of the Greater East Asia war). 8 vols. Tokyo, Masu Shobō, 1953–56.

Hattori, Yukimasa. *The Foreign Commerce of Japan since the Restoration.* Baltimore, Johns Hopkins Press, 1904.

Haushofer, Karl. *Dai Nihon, Betrachtungen über Gross-Japans Wehrkraft, Weltstellung und Zukunft.* Berlin, E.S. Mittler, 1913.

—— *Japan baut sich sein Reich.* Berlin, Zeitgeschichteverlag, 1941.

Hayashi Gonsuke 林権助. *Waga shichijūnen o kataru* わが七十年を語る (Story of my seventy years). Tokyo, Daiichi Shobō, 1935.

Hayashi Masakazu 林正和. "Kantō mondai ni kansuru Nisshin kōshō no keii" 間島問題に関する日清交渉の経緯 (History of the Sino-Japanese negotiations con-cerning the Chien-tao problem), *Sundai shigaku*, No. 10 (March 1960).

Hayashi Saburō 林三郎. *Taiheiyō sensō rikusen gaishi* 大平洋戦争陸戦概史 (History of the Pacific War). Tokyo, Iwanami, 1957.

Hayashi Tadasu 林董. "Nichi-Ei dōmei kyōyaku teiketsu shimatsusho ichibu sōfu no ken: Fuzokusho Hayashi kōshi Nichi-Ei dōmei kyōyaku teiketsu shimatsu" 日英同盟協約締結始末書一部送付の件—附属書林公使日英同盟協約締結始末 (Report from Minister Hayashi on conclusion of the Anglo-Japanese alliance), in Japan, Foreign Ministry, *Nihon gaikō bunsho*, XXXV, 32–61.

Hayashi Takeji 林竹二. "Bakumatsu no kaigai ryūgakusei" 幕末の海外留学生 (Students who went overseas at the end of the Tokugawa), *Nichi-Bei forum* (Japanese-American forum), Parts 1–3. Tokyo, U.S. Embassy Publications, January, February, April 1963.

—— "Mori Arinori to Tōmasu Rēku Harisu" 森有礼とトマス・レーク・ハリス (Mori Arinori and Thomas Lake Harris), *Nichi-Bei forum* (Japanese-American forum). Tokyo, U.S. Embassy Publications, March 1963.

Heinrichs, Waldo H. Jr. *American Ambassador: Joseph C. Grew and the Development of the United States Diplomatic Tradition.* Boston, Little, Brown, 1966.

Higo Kazuo 肥後和夫. "Jumbikin o meguru Meiji zenki no zaisei kin'yū seisaku" 「準備金」をめぐる明治前期の財政金融政策 (The reserve fund in early Meiji fiscal and financial policy), in *Itō Hanya hakushi taikan kinen rombunshū: zaiseigaku no kihon mondai* 井藤半彌博士退官記念論文集—財政学の基本問題 (Collected essays commemorating the retirement of Dr. Itō Hanya: Fundamental problems in the study of fiscal policy), pp. 223–51. Tokyo, Chikura Shobō, 1960.

—— "Matsukata defure ni kansuru oboegaki" 松方デフレに関する覚書 (Memorandum on the Matsukata deflation), *Seiji keizai ronsō* 政治経済論叢, VIII, No. 1 (1958) 46–55.

—— "Meiji shoki ni okeru enka antei seisaku ni tsuite" 明治初期における円貨安定政策について (The policy of stabilizing the value of the yen in early Meiji), *Seiji keizai ronsō*, IX, No. 1 (1959), 111–34.

—— "Shōwa shoki made no waga kuni seika seisaku to zaisei" 昭和初期までの我が国正貨政策と財政 (Japan's fiscal and specie policy until early Shōwa), *Seiji keizai ronsō*, X, No. 1 (1960), 23–67.

Higuchi Hiroshi 樋口弘. *Nihon tōgyōshi* 日本糖業史 (History of Japan's sugar industry). Tokyo, Naigai Keizaisha, 1956.

Hikiage Engo Chō 引揚援護庁. *Hikiage engo no kiroku* 引揚援護の記録 (A record of relief for repatriated citizens). Tokyo, Hikiage Engo Chō, 1950.

Hirano Reiji 平野零児. *Manshū no imbōsha: Kōmoto Daisaku no unmeiteki na ashiato* 満州の陰謀者河本大作の運命的な足あと (A conspirator in Manchuria: The life of Kōmoto Daisaku). Tokyo, Jiyū Kokuminsha, 1959.

Hiraoka Masahide 平岡雅英. *Ishin zengo no Nihon to Roshia* 維新前後の日本とロシア (Japan and Russia at the time of the Restoration). 1934. Republished as *Nichi-Ro kōshō shi wa* 日露交渉史話 (A historical account of Russo-Japanese negotiations). Tokyo, Chikuma Shobō, 1944.

Hiratsuka Atsushi 平塚篤, ed. *Itō Hirobumi hiroku* 伊藤博文秘録 (Private papers of Itō Hirobumi). Tokyo, Shunjūsha, 1929.

—— *Shishaku Kurino Shin'ichirō den* 子爵栗野慎一郎伝 (Biography of Viscount Kurino Shin'ichirō). Tokyo, Kōbunsha, 1942.

—— ed. *Zoku Itō Hirobumi hiroku* 續伊藤博文秘録 (Private papers of Itō Hirobumi, supplement). Tokyo, Shunjūsha, 1930.

Hirschmeier, Johannes. *The Origins of Entrepreneurship in Meiji Japan.* Cambridge, Harvard University Press, 1964.

Hō Takushū 彭沢周 [P'eng Tse-chou]. "Chōsen mondai o meguru Jiyūtō to Furansu —shu to shite Yamabe shi setsu ni taisuru hihan" 朝鮮問題をめぐる自由党とフランス—主として山辺氏説に対する批判 (The Liberal Party and France over Korean questions: Critical comments on Mr. Yamabe's view), *Rekishigaku kenkyū*, No. 265 (June 1962), pp. 19–27.

—— "Kōshin jihen o meguru Inoue gaimukyō to Furansu kōshi to no kōshō" 甲申事変をめぐる井上外務卿とフランス公使との交渉 (Negotiations between Foreign Minister Inoue and the French minister over the incident of 1884 in Korea), *Rekishigaku kenkyū*, No. 282 (November 1963), pp. 34–44.

—— "Shimonoseki jōyaku ni tsuite" 下関条約について (On the Treaty of Shimonoseki), *Nihonshi kenkyū*, No. 56 (September 1961), pp. 27–48.

—— "Shin-Futsu sensōki ni okeru Nihon no tai-Kan seisaku" 清仏戦争期における日本の対韓政策 (Japanese policy toward Korea at the time of the Sino-French war) *Shirin*, XLIII, No. 3 (May 1960), 124–43.

Hohenlohe-Schillingsfürst, Alexander. *Denkwürdigkeiten*. 2 vols. Stuttgart and Leipzig, Deutsche Verlags-anstalt, 1907.

Holldack, Heinz. *Was wirklich geschah*. Munich, Nymphenburger Verlagshandlung, 1949.

Honda Kumatarō 本多熊太郎. *Tamashii no gaikō: Nichi-Ro sensō ni okeru Komura kō* 魂の外交―日露戦争に於ける小村侯 (Spirited diplomacy: Marquis Komura and the Russo-Japanese War). Tokyo, Chikura Shobō, 1941.

Honjō Eijirō 本庄栄治郎. "O-yatoi gaikokujin to waga kuni no keizai oyobi keizai-gaku" 御雇外国人とわが国の経済及び経済学 (Foreign employees and Japan's economy and economics), *Dōshisha daigaku keizaigaku ronsō*, VI, No. 1 (February 1955), 1–19.

Hora Tomio 洞富雄. "Meiji jūnendai no yōgin sōba" 明治十年代の洋銀相場 (The value of the Mexican dollar in the second decade of the Meiji era), in Yokohama Shi Shi Henshūshitsu, *Yokohama shi shi*, III, Part 2, 346–409. Yokohama, Yūrindō, 1963.

—— "Meiji shonen no yōgin sōba" 明治初年の洋銀相場 (The value of the Mexican dollar in early Meiji), in Yokohama Shi Shi Henshūshitsu, *Yokohama shi shi*, III, Part 2, 280–345. Yokohama, Yūrindō, 1963.

—— "Yōgin sōba to naikoku tsūka" 洋銀相場と内国通貨 (The domestic currency and the value of the Mexican dollar), *Ōkuma kenkyū*, No. 4 (March 1954), pp. 81–117; No. 5 (October 1954), pp. 167–239.

Hori Tsuneo 堀経夫. *Meiji keizaigakushi: jiyūshugi hogoshugi o chūshin to shite* 明治経済学史―自由主義保護主義を中心として (A history of economics in the Meiji period: free trade versus protectionism). Tokyo, Kōbundō, 1935.

Horiba Kazuo 堀場一雄. *Shina jihen sensō shidō shi* 支那事変戦争指導史 (A history of military strategy in the Sino-Japanese War). 2 vols. Tokyo, Jiji Tsūshinsha, 1962.

Horie Eiichi 堀江英一, ed. *Kindai sangyō no seisei* 近代産業の生成 (The rise of modern industry). Tokyo, Ochanomizu Shobō, 1958.

Horie Yasuzō 堀江保蔵. "Foreign Trade Policy in the Early Meiji Era," *Kyoto University Economic Review*, XXII, No. 2 (October 1952), 1–21.

—— *Gaishi yu'nyū no kaiko to tembō* 外資輸入の回顧と展望 (The history and future prospects of foreign capital imports). Tokyo, Yūhikaku, 1950.

—— "Ishin go no taigai keizai hatten" 維新後の対外経済発展 (The development of overseas economic relations after the Restoration), *Keizaishi kenkyū*, XXVII, No. 4 (April 1942), 321–46.

—— "Japanese-American Financial Relations," in Ohara, *Japanese Trade and Industry in the Meiji-Taishō Era*, pp. 395–480.

—— "Japan's Balance of International Payments in the Early Meiji Period," *Kyoto University Economic Review*, XXIV, No. 1 (April 1954), 16–33.

—— *Meiji ishin to keizai kindaika* 明治維新と経済近代化 (The Meiji Restoration and economic modernization). Tokyo, Shibundō, 1963.

—— "Meiji shonen no kan'ei sangyō ni tsuite" 明治初年の官営産業に就いて (Government industries in early Meiji), *Keizai ronsō*, XLIV, No. 5 (May 1937), 164–81.

—— "Meiji shonen no kangyō kikan" 明治初年の勧業機関 (Agencies to encourage industry in early Meiji), *Keizai ronsō*, LVIII, Nos. 1–2 (1944), 157–71.

—— "Meiji yonen no heisei kaikaku" 明治四年の幣制改革 (The reform of the currency system in 1871), in Honjō Eijirō 本庄栄治郎, ed., *Meiji ishin keizaishi kenkyū* 明治維新経済史研究 (Studies in the economic history of the Meiji Restoration), pp. 485–527. Tokyo, Kaizōsha, 1930.

—— "Meiji zenki no bōeki seisaku" 明治前期の貿易政策 (Foreign trade policy in early Meiji), *Keizai ronsō*, LXXI, No. 1 (1953), 1–20.

—— "Meiji zenki no gaishi haijo ni tsuite" 明治前期の外資排除に就いて (The elimination of foreign capital in early Meiji), *Keizai ronsō*, LVI, No. 1 (January 1943), 107–14.

—— "Meiji zenki no kokusai shūshi" 明治前期の国際収支 (The balance of payments in early Meiji), *Shakai keizai shigaku*, XX, No. 1 (1954), 1–16.

Horikawa Takeo 堀川武夫. *Kyokutō kokusai seijishi josetsu: nijūikkajō yōkyū no kenkyū* 極東国際政治史序説—二十一箇条要求の研究 (Introduction to the history of international politics in the Far East: A study of the Twenty-One Demands). Tokyo, Yūhikaku, 1958.

Horiuchi Tateki 堀内干城. *Chūgoku no arashi no naka de: Nikka gaikō sanjūnen yawa* 中国の嵐の中で—日華外交三十年夜話 (Through storms in China: A diplomatic memoir of thirty years of Japanese-Chinese relations). Tokyo, Kengensha, 1950.

Hosaka Yūichirō 穂坂唯一郎. *Dōjinkai yonjūnenshi* 同仁会四十年史 (A forty-year history of the Universal Benevolence Association). Tokyo, Dōjinkai, 1943.

Hosokawa Kameichi 細川亀市. "Karafuto Chishima kōkan mondai no temmatsu" 樺太千島交換問題の顛末 (A detailed account of the Sakhalin-Kuril islands exchange problem), *Hōgaku shirin*, XLIII, No. 12 (December 1941), 23–38; XLIV, No. 1 (January 1942), 70–93; XLIV, No. 2 (February 1942), 47–67.

Hosoya Chihiro 細谷千博. "Japanese Documents on the Siberian Intervention, 1917–1922: Part 1, November 1917–January 1919," *Hitotsubashi Journal of Law and Politics*, I, No. 1 (April 1960), 30–53.

—— "Nihon kaigun rikusentai no Uradivostokku jōriku: tai-So kanshō sensō no purorōgu" 日本海軍陸戦隊のウラディヴォストック上陸—対ソ干渉戦争のプロローグ

(The question of landing Japanese marines at Vladivostok: Prologue to the Siberian intervention), *Rekishi kyōiku*, VII, No. 1 (January 1959), 38-45.

—— "Nihon to Koruchaku seiken shōnin mondai" 日本とコルチャク政権承認問題 (Japan and the issue of recognizing the Kolchak regime), *Hitotsubashi daigaku hōgaku kenkyū*, No. 3 (March 1961), pp. 13-135.

—— "Origin of the Siberian Intervention," *Annals of the Hitotsubashi Academy*, IX, No. 1 (October 1958), pp. 91-108.

—— "Sangoku dōmei to Nisso chūritsu jōyaku (1939-1941)" 三国同盟と日ソ中立条約 (The Tripartite Pact and the Japanese-Soviet neutrality treaty, 1939-1941), in *Sangoku dōmei: Nisso chūritsu jōyaku* 三国同盟—日ソ中立条約 (The Tripartite Pact: The Japanese-Soviet neutrality treaty), pp. 157-331. Vol. V of Nihon Kokusai Seiji Gakkai Taiheiyō Sensō Gen'in Kenkyūbu, *Taiheiyō sensō e no michi*. Tokyo, Asahi Shimbunsha, 1963.

—— *Shiberia shuppei no shiteki kenkyū* シベリア出兵の史的研究 (A historical study of the Siberian expedition). Tokyo, Yūhikaku, 1955.

—— "Shiberia shuppei o meguru Nichi-Bei kankei" シベリア出兵をめぐる日米関係 (The Siberian expedition and Japanese-American relations), in *Kokusai seiji: Nihon gaikōshi kenkyū—Nichi-Bei kankei no tenkai*, 1961, pp. 73-90.

Hōten Shōkō Kaigisho 奉天商工会議所 (Mukden Chamber of Commerce and Industry). *Hōten keizai sanjūnenshi* 奉天経済三十年史 (A thirty-year history of economic activities in Mukden). Mukden, Hōten Shōkō Kaigisho, 1940.

Hummel, Arthur W., ed. *Eminent Chinese of the Ch'ing Period (1644-1912)*. 2 vols. Washington D.C., U.S. Government Printing Office, 1943-44.

Ichihashi, Yamato. *Japanese in the United States: A Critical Study of the Problems of the Japanese Immigrants and Their Children*. Stanford, Stanford University Press, 1932.

Ichiko Chūzō 市古宙三. "Giwaken no seikaku" 義和拳の性格 (The character of the Boxer Rebellion), *Kindai Chūgoku kenkyū*, October 1948, pp. 245-67.

Ichimata Masao 一又正雄. "Nichi-Bei imin mondai to 'kokunai mondai' " 日米移民問題と「国内問題」 (Japanese Emigration and the Jurisdictional Question in the United States), in Ueda Toshio 植田捷雄, ed., *Kamikawa sensei kanreki kinen: kindai Nihon gaikōshi no kenkyū* 神川先生還暦記念—近代日本外交史の研究 (Commemorating the sixtieth birthday of Professor Kamikawa: Studies in modern Japanese diplomatic history), pp. 423-39. Tokyo, Yūhikaku, 1956.

Igarashi Tamae 五十嵐珠恵. "Shingai kakumei to Nihon oyobi Nihonjin: namboku dakyō e no katei ni okeru Nihon no taiō" 辛亥革命と日本および日本人—南北妥協への過程における日本の対応 (The 1911 Revolution, Japan, and the Japanese: Japanese response to the compromise between north and south), *Shisō*, No. 1 (February 1961), pp. 6-31.

Ike Kyōkichi 池享吉. *Shina kakumei jikkenki* 支那革命実見記 (Memoirs of the Republican revolution in China). Tokyo, Kaneo Bun'endō, 1911.

Ikeda Kōtarō 池田浩太郎. "Chitsuroku shobun no keika to kōsai kōfu—Meiji shoki kōsai seisaku no issetsu" 秩禄処分の経過と公債交付—明治初期公債政策の一節 (Pension capitalization and the delivery of the bonds—an aspect of national debt policy in early Meiji), *Seijō daigaku keizai kenkyū*, No. 12 (May 1960), pp. 265–93.

—— "Kankin suitō no tenkai katei—Meiji shoki ni okeru kankin suitō no kin'yūteki igi" 官金出納の展開過程—明治初期に於ける官金出納の金融的意義 (The receipt and disbursement of government funds—their financial significance in early Meiji), *Seijō daigaku keizai kenkyū*, No. 16 (October 1962), pp. 55–80; No. 17 (March 1963), pp. 41–58. Also reprinted in Okada Shumpei 岡田俊平, ed., *Meiji shoki no zaisei kin'yū seisaku* 明治初期の財政金融政策 (Financial and fiscal policy in early Meiji), pp. 175–219. Tokyo, Seimeikai, 1964.

—— "Kyūhansai shobun to shinkyū kōsai no kōfu—Meiji shoki kōsai seisaku no issetsu" 旧藩債処分と新旧公債の交付—明治初期公債政策の一節 (The disposition of the old domain debts and the exchange of bonds—an aspect of national debt policy in early Meiji), in *Itō Hanya hakushi taikan kinen rombunshū: zaiseigaku no kihon mondai* 井藤半彌博士退官記念論文集—財政学の基本問題 (Collected essays commemorating the retirement of Dr. Itō Hanya: Fundamental problems in the study of fiscal policy), pp. 253–69. Tokyo, Chikura Shobō, 1960.

—— "Meiji shoki ni okeru kankin toriatsukai no zaiseiteki igi" 明治初期における官金取扱いの財政的意義 (The fiscal significance of the handling of government funds in early Meiji), *Seijō daigaku keizai kenkyū*, No. 14 (November 1961), pp. 23–46. Also reprinted in Okada Shumpei 岡田俊平, ed., *Meiji shoki no zaisei kin'yū seisaku* 明治初期の財政金融政策 (Financial and fiscal policy in early Meiji), pp. 147–74. Tokyo, Seimeikai, 1964.

—— "Waga kuni kōsai no seiritsu—Meiji shoki kōsai seisaku" 我が国公債の成立—明治初期公債政策 (The establishment of Japan's national debt—national debt policy in early Meiji), *Seijō daigaku keizai kenkyū*, Nos. 8–9 (September 1958), pp. 237–66.

Ikeda Makoto 池田誠. "Naitō Konan no En Seigai ron" 内藤湖南の袁世凱論 (Naitō Konan's comments on Yuan Shih-k'ai), *Ritsumeikan hōgaku*, No. 44 (February 1963), pp. 71–103.

Ikeda Toshio 池田敏雄. "Ningen kiroku shomoku" 人間記録書目 (Bibliography of biographies). 2 vols. Mimeographed and privately circulated, n.d.

Ikei Masaru 池井優. "Daiichiji Hō-Choku sensō to Nihon" 第一次奉直戰爭と日本 (The first Mukden-Chihli war and Japan), in Hanabusa Nagamichi Hakushi Kanreki Kinen Rombunshū Henshū Iinkai 英修道博士還暦記念論文集編集委員会, ed., *Hanabusa Nagamichi hakushi kanreki kinen rombunshū: gaikōshi oyobi kokusai seiji no shomondai* 英修道博士還暦記念論文集—外交史及び国際政治の諸問題 (Essays commemorating the sixtieth birthday of Dr. Hanabusa Nagamichi: Studies in diplomatic history and international politics). Tokyo, Keiō Tsūshin, 1962.

—— "Dainiji Hō-Choku sensō to Nihon" 第二次奉直戰爭と日本 (The second Mukden-Chihli war and Japan), *Hōgaku kenkyū*, XXXVII, No. 3 (March 1964), 48–75.

—— "Funatsu Shin'ichirō zen Hōten sōryōji yori Debuchi gaimujikan ate Manshū Chūgoku shutchō genchi hōkoku shokan Taishō 14.12.5 yori dō 15.2 made" 船津辰一郎前奉天総領事より出淵外務次官宛満州中国出張現地報告書簡大正 14. 12. 5 より同 15.2 まで (Letters sent from Manchuria and China by Funatsu Shin'ichirō, former consul in Mukden, to Vice Foreign Minister Debuchi, December 5, 1925 to February 1926), *Hōgaku kenkyū*, XXXVI, No. 7 (July 1963), 81–98.

—— "Nihon no tai-En gaikō: shingai kakumeiki" 日本の対袁外交—辛亥革命期 (Japan's diplomacy toward Yuan Shih-k'ai at the time of the 1911 revolution), *Hōgaku kenkyū*, XXXV, No. 4 (April 1962), 64–93; No. 5 (May 1962), 49–83.

Iklé, Frank William. *German-Japanese Relations, 1936–1940.* New York, Bookman Associates, 1956.

Imai Seiichi 今井清一. "Shidehara gaikō ni okeru seisaku kettei" 幣原外交における 政策決定 (Decision-making in Shidehara diplomacy), in *Nempō seijigaku*, pp. 92–112. Tokyo, Iwanami Shoten, 1959.

—— "Taishōki ni okeru gumbu no seijiteki chii" 大正期に於ける軍部の政治的地位 (The political position of the military during the Taishō period), *Shisō*, No. 399 (September 1957), pp. 3–21; No. 402 (December 1957), pp. 106–22.

Imai Shōji 今井庄次. "Nichi-Ei dōmei kōshō ni okeru Nihon no shuchō" 日英同盟 交渉における日本の主張 (Japan's demands during the negotiations for the Anglo-Japanese alliance), *Kokusai seiji: Nihon gaikōshi kenkyū—Meiji jidai*, 1957, pp. 119–36.

—— "Nichi-Ei dōmei to Kurino Shin'ichirō" 日英同盟と栗野慎一郎 (The Anglo-Japanese alliance and Kurino Shin'ichirō), *Rekishi kyōiku*, X, No. 2 (February 1962), 39–44.

—— "Nichi-Ro sensō to tai-Shin seisaku no tenkai" 日露戰爭と対清政策の展開 (The Russo-Japanese War and the development of Japanese policy toward China), *Kokusai seiji: Nihon gaikōshi kenkyū—Nitchū kankei no tenkai*, 1960, pp. 17–28.

—— "Nichi-Ro sensō zengo Manshū zairyū Nihonjin no bumpu jōtai" 日露戰爭 前後満州在留日本人の分布状態 (The distribution of Japanese in Manchuria during the Russo-Japanese War), *Rekishi chiri*, LXXXIX, No. 3 (January 1960), 41–53.

Imamura Hitoshi 今村均. *Kōzoku to kashikan* 皇族と下士官 (The imperial family and noncommissioned officers). Tokyo, Jiyū Ajiasha, 1960.

—— "Manshū hi o fuku koro" 満州火を噴く頃 (The outbreak of the Manchurian Incident), *Bessatsu chisei, V: himerareta Shōwashi*, December 1956, pp. 60–71.

In Memoriam: David Murray, Ph.D., LL.D., Superintendent of Educational Affairs in the Empire of Japan and Adviser to the Japanese Imperial Minister of Education, 1873–1879. New York, privately printed, 1915.

Inada Masazumi 稲田正純. "Senryakumen kara mita Shina jihen no sensō shidō" 戦略面から見た支那事変の戦爭指導 (Military strategy of the Sino-Japanese

War), in *Kokusai seiji: Nihon gaikōshi kenkyū—Nitchū kankei no tenkai,* 1960, pp. 150–69.

—— "Soren kyokutō gun to no taiketsu" ソ連極東軍との対決 (Confrontation with the Soviet Far Eastern army), *Bessatsu chisei, V: himerareta Shōwashi,* December 1956, pp. 276–98.

Inagaki Tomomi 稲垣友美. "Gakkan Dabiddo Marē no kenkyū" 学監ダビッド・マレーの研究 (A study of Superintendent of Educational Affairs David Murray), *Firosofia,* No. 29 (December 1955), pp. 100–23.

The Independent and The Weekly Review. 121 vols. New York, National Weekly Corporation, December 7, 1848–October 13, 1928.

Inō Kanori 伊能嘉矩. *Taiwan bunkashi* 台湾文化志 (Cultural history of Taiwan). 3 vols. Tokyo, Tōkō Shoin, 1928.

Inō Tentarō 稲生典太郎. "Giwadan jihen to Nihon no shuppei gaikō: daigo shidan shutsudō ni itaru made no keii" 義和団事変と日本の出兵外交—第五師団出動に至るまでの経緯 (The Boxer Rebellion and the negotiations for the sending of Japanese troops: To the dispatch of the Fifth Division), in Kaikoku Hyakunen Kinen Bunka Jigyōkai 開国百年記念文化事業会, ed., *Kaikoku hyakunen kinen Meiji bunkashi ronshū* 開国百年記念明治文化史論集 (Collected papers on Meiji cultural history commemorating the centennial of the opening of the country), pp. 497–562. Tokyo, Kengensha, 1952.

—— "Kinsei Nihon ni okeru shinrosetsu no keifu" 近世日本に於ける親露説の系譜 (Genealogy of Russophilism in Japan), *Kokushigaku,* No. 60 (March 1953), pp. 44–59.

—— " 'Tanaka jōsōbun' o meguru ni san no mondai" 「田中上奏文」をめぐる二, 三の問題 (Some problems raised by the 'Tanaka Memorial'), *Kokusai seiji: Nihon gaikōshi kenkyū—Nihon gaikōshi no shomondai,* No. 1, 1963, pp. 72–87.

Inouchi Hirobumi 井内弘文. "Meijiki keizai seisaku shisō no kichō" 明治期経済政策思想の基調 (The main current of thought on economic policy in the Meiji period), *Mie daigaku gakugei gakubu kenkyū kiyō,* No. 25 (March 1962), pp. 47–61.

Inoue Kaoru Kō Denki Hensankai 井上馨侯伝記編纂会. *Segai Inoue kō den* 世外井上公伝 (Biography of Marquis Inoue Kaoru). 5 vols. Tokyo, Naigai Shoseki Kabushiki Kaisha, 1933–34.

Inoue Kiyoshi 井上清. *Jōyaku kaisei: Meiji no minzoku mondai* 条約改正—明治の民族問題 (Treaty revision: the national task during the Meiji period). Tokyo, Iwanami Shoten, 1955.

—— "Nichi-Ro sensō ni tsuite: Shimomura Fujimura shi ni taisuru han hihan" 日露戦争について—下村・藤村氏に対する反批判 (On the Russo-Japanese War: A rebuttal of Messrs. Shimomura and Fujimura), *Nihonshi kenkyū,* No. 38 (September 1958), pp. 1–16.

—— *Nihon no gunkokushugi* 日本の軍国主義 (Militarism in Japan). 2 vols. Tokyo,

Tōkyō Daigaku Shuppankai, 1953.

—— "Taiheiyō sensō shikan" 太平洋戰爭史観 (A historical view of the Pacific War), *Gendaishi kenkyū*, December 1961.

Inoue Masaji 井上雅二. *Kyojin Arao Sei* 巨人荒尾精 (Arao Sei, a great man). Tokyo, Sakura Shobō, 1910.

Inoue Yōichirō 井上洋一郎. "Meijiki zōsen seisaku no igi to sono kōka" 明治期造船政策の意義とその効果 (The significance and effectiveness of shipbuilding policy in the Meiji period), *Shakai keizai shigaku*, XXXII, No. 1 (May 1966), 31–50.

"International Expositions," in *Encyclopedia of the Social Sciences*, VI (1931), 24–26.

International Military Tribunal, Nuremberg. *Nazi Conspiracy and Aggression, Opinion and Judgment*. 8 vols., 2 supplementary vols. 1946–48.

International Military Tribunal for the Far East. *Record of the Proceedings, Documents, Exhibits, Judgment, Dissenting Judgments, Preliminary Interrogations, Miscellaneous Documents*. Tokyo, mimeographed, 1946–49.

Inukai Ken 犬養健. *Yōsukō wa ima mo nagarete iru* 揚子江は今も流れている (The Yangtze still flows). Tokyo, Bungeishunjū Shinsha, 1960.

Irie Keishirō 入江啓四郎. "Shingai kakumei to shinseifu no shōnin" 辛亥革命と新政府の承認 (On the 1911 revolution in China and recognition of the new government), in Ueda Toshio 植田捷雄, ed., *Kamikawa sensei kanreki kinen: kindai Nihon gaikōshi no kenkyū* 神川先生還暦記念—近代日本外交史の研究 (Commemorating the sixtieth birthday of Professor Kamikawa: Studies in modern Japanese diplomatic history), pp. 231–94. Tokyo, Yūhikaku, 1956.

Irimajiri Yoshinaga 入交好脩. "Meiji seifu no shokusan kōgyō seisaku" 明治政府の殖産興業政策 (The encouragement of production policy of the Meiji government), *Nihon rekishi*, No. 147 (September 1960), pp. 131–34.

Iriye, Akira. *Across the Pacific: An Inner History of American-East Asian Relations*. New York, Harcourt, Brace and World, 1967.

—— *After Imperialism: The Search for a New Order in the Far East, 1921–1931*. Cambridge, Harvard University Press, 1965.

—— "Chang Hsüeh-liang and the Japanese," *Journal of Asian Studies*, XX, No. 1 (November 1960), 33–43.

—— "Imperialism in East Asia," in James B. Crowley, ed., *Modern East Asia: Essays in Interpretation*, pp. 122–50. New York, Harcourt, Brace and World, 1970.

—— "Japanese Imperialism and Aggression: Reconsiderations, II," *Journal of Asian Studies*, XXIII, No. 1 (November 1963), 103–13.

—— "Japan's China Policy in the Twenties." Mimeographed paper presented to the University Seminar on Modern East Asia: Japan, Columbia University, March 9, 1962.

—— *Pacific Estrangement: Japanese and American Expansion, 1897–1911*. Cambridge, Mass., Harvard University Press, 1972.

—— "The Failure of Military Expansionism," in James William Morley, ed., *The Dilemmas of Growth in Prewar Japan*, pp. 107–38. Princeton, Princeton University Press, 1971.

Ishida Hideo 石田栄雄. "Nijūikkajō mondai o terasu kokusai kaigi: Parī kaigi, Washinton kaigi o tsūjite" 二十一箇条問題を照す国際会議―巴里会議華府会議を通じて (International conferences shed light on the problem of the so-called Twenty-One Demands: The Paris Conference and the Washington Conference), *Gakujutsu kenkyū (jimbun shakai shizen)*, No. 7 (November 1958), pp. 79–87.

—— "Ōkuma rōkō to tai-Shi gaikō: iwayuru nijūikkajō mondai o megurite toku ni daigokō kibō jōkō ni tsuite" 大隈老侯と対支外交―所謂二十一箇条問題を繞りて特に第五項希望条項に就いて (Marquis Ōkuma and Japan's policy toward China: The problem of the so-called Twenty-One Demands, in particular group five), *Ōkuma kenkyū*, No. 5 (October 1954), pp. 126–66; No. 6 (May 1955), pp. 86–142; No. 7 (March 1956).

—— "Pōtsumasu jōyaku to hoppō ryōdo mondai" ポーツマス条約と北方領土問題 (The Portsmouth Treaty and the question of the northern territories), *Kokusaihō gaikō zasshi*, LX, Nos. 4–6 (March 1962), 68–98.

—— "Tai-Ka nijūikkajō mondai to rekkoku no teikō" 対華二十一箇条問題と列国の低抗 (The problem of the Twenty-One Demands and the opposition of the powers), *Kokusai seiji: Nihon gaikōshi kenkyū—Taishō jidai*, 1958, pp. 39–51.

Ishida Kōhei 石田興平. "Meiji zenki ni okeru bōsekigyō no hattatsu to shokumin-chiteki kōshinkoku e no yushutsu" 明治前期における紡績業の発達と植民地的後進国への輸出 (The development of the cotton-spinning industry in early Meiji and exports to semi-colonial underdeveloped countries), *Hikone ronsō*, No. 112 (June 1965), pp. 1–21.

—— "Meiji zenki ni okeru kindaiteki kōtsū to bōeki oyobi kinu kōgyō—Nihon shihonshugi no keisei ni taisuru igi" 明治前期における近代的交通と貿易および絹工業―日本資本主義の形成に対する意義 (The silk industry, foreign trade, and modern communications in early Meiji—their significance for the establishment of Japanese capitalism), *Hikone ronsō*, No. 110 (March 1965), pp. 1–23.

Ishigami Ryōhei 石上良平. *Seitō shiron: Hara Takashi botsugo* 政党史論―原敬歿後 (A historical essay on political parties: After the death of Hara Takashi). Tokyo, Chūō Kōronsha, 1960.

Ishii Itarō 石射猪太郎. *Gaikōkan no isshō* 外交官の一生 (The life of a diplomat). Tokyo, Yomiuri Shimbunsha, 1950.

Ishii Kenji 石井謙治, Matsuki Tetsu 松木哲, and Osada Tetsuo 小佐田哲男. "Meiji shoki ni okeru kaiun kindaika ni kansuru shiryō" 明治初期における海運近代化に関する史料 (Materials related to the modernization of maritime transportation in early Meiji), *Kaijishi kenkyū*, No. 5 (October 1965), pp. 75–86; No. 6 (April 1966), pp. 86–101.

Ishii Kikujirō 石井菊次郎. *Diplomatic Commentaries*. Baltimore, Johns Hopkins Press, 1936.

—— *Gaikō kaisō dampen* 外交回想断片 (Miscellaneous reminiscences about diplomacy). Tokyo, Kinseidō, 1939.

—— *Gaikō yoroku* 外交餘録 (Diplomatic commentaries). Tokyo, Iwanami Shoten, 1930.

—— "Nichi-Ei dōmei kyōyaku teiketsu shimatsusho ichibu sōfu no ken: fuki Nichi-Ei kyōtei kōshō shimatsu" 日英同盟協約締結始末書一部送付ノ件—附記 日英協定交渉始末 (Report on negotiations for the Anglo-Japanese alliance), in Japan, Foreign Ministry, *Nihon gaikō bunsho*, XXXV, 62–92.

Ishii Ryōsuke, ed. *Japanese Legislation in the Meiji Era*. Translated and adapted by William J. Chambliss. Tokyo, Pan-Pacific Press for the Centenary Culture Council, 1958.

Ishii Takashi 石井孝. *Bakumatsu bōekishi no kenkyū* 幕末貿易史の研究 (Studies in the history of foreign trade during the late Tokugawa period). Tokyo, Nihon Hyōronsha, 1944.

—— "Bakumatsu kaikō go ni okeru bōeki dokusen kikō no hōkai 幕末開港後における貿易独占機構の崩壊 (The collapse of the foreign trade monopoly mechanism after the opening of the ports in the late Tokugawa period), *Shakai keizai shigaku*, XI, No. 10 (January 1942), 47–90.

—— "Chihō jichi no hatten to bōekishō" 地方自治の発展と貿易商 (The foreign trade merchants and the development of regional autonomy), in Yokohama Shi Shi Henshūshitsu, *Yokohama shi shi*, III, Part 2, 1–194. Yokohama, Yūrindō, 1963.

—— *Meiji ishin no kokusaiteki kankyō* 明治維新の国際的環境 (The international situation at the time of the Meiji Restoration). Tokyo, Yoshikawa Kōbunkan, 1957; 2d rev. ed., 1966.

—— "Meiji seifu no sanshi bōeki kisoku" 明治政府の蚕糸貿易規則 (The Meiji government's regulations for foreign trade in silk yarn), in Yokohama Shi Shi Henshūshitsu, *Yokohama shi shi*, III, Part 1, 62–165. Yokohama, Yūrindō, 1961.

—— "Rengō Kiito Niazukarijo jiken o meguru shomondai" 聯合生糸荷預所事件を めぐる諸問題 (Various problems related to the Federated Raw Silk Warehouse incident), *Rekishigaku kenkyū*, No. 313 (June 1966), pp. 30–36.

—— "Rengō Kiito Niazukarijo jiken sairon" 聯合生糸荷預所事件再論 (A reexamination of the Federated Raw Silk Warehouse incident), *Nihon rekishi*, No. 234 (November 1967), pp. 19–29.

—— "Shoki ni okeru bōeki no shinchō" 初期における貿易の伸張 (The expansion of foreign trade in the early period), in Yokohama Shi Shi Henshūshitsu, *Yokohama shi shi*, II, 279–576. Yokohama, Yūrindō, 1959.

—— "The Opening of the Ports and Early Trade Relations between Japan and the

United States," in Ohara, *Japanese Trade and Industry in the Meiji-Taishō Era*, pp. 55-148.

Ishikawa Shingo 石川信吾. *Shinjuwan made no keii: kaisen no shinsō* 眞珠湾までの経緯—開戦の眞相 (To Pearl Harbor: The truth about the outbreak of the war). Tokyo, Jiji Tsūshinsha, 1960.

Ishimitsu Makiyo 石光眞清. *Dare no tame ni* 誰のために (For whom?). Tokyo, Ryūsei-kaku, 1960.

Ishinshi Gakkai 維新史学会, ed. *Bakumatsu ishin gaikō shiryō shūsei* 幕末維新外交史料集成 (Diplomatic materials on the Bakumatsu and Restoration periods). 20 vols. Tokyo, Zaisei Keizai Gakkai, 1943.

Ishizaka Tomiji 石坂富司. "Kita Ikki kenkyūshi josetsu" 北一輝研究史序説 (An introduction to the history of studies on Kita Ikki), *Nihon rekishi*, No. 178 (March 1963), pp. 73-85.

Ishizaki Teruhiko 石崎昭彦. "Nihon no shihonshugika to gaishi, 1868-1914" 日本の資本主義化と外資 1868-1914 (Foreign capital and the development of Japanese capitalism, 1868-1914), *Shōkei ronsō*, II, No. 1 (June 1966), 209-49.

Ishizuka Hiromichi 石塚裕道. "Ōkubo seiken no seiritsu to kōzō: shokusan seisaku tenkai no seijiteki zentei ni tsuite" 大久保政権の成立と構造—殖産政策展開の政治的前提について (The establishment and structure of the Ōkubo regime: The political prerequisites for the development of the encouragement of production policy), in *Tōkyō toritsu daigaku jisshūnen kinen rombunshū* 東京都立大学十周年記念論文集 (Essays commemorating the tenth anniversary of Tokyo Metropolitan University), pp. 117-240. Tokyo, 1960.

——"Shokusan kōgyō seisaku no tenkai" 殖産興業政策の展開 (The development of the encouragement of production policy), in *Nihon keizaishi taikei* 日本経済史大系 (Japanese economic history series), V, 35-103. 6 vols. Tokyo, Tōkyō Daigaku Shuppankai, 1965.

Islam, Nural. *Foreign Capital and Economic Development: Japan, India, and Canada*. Rutland, Vt., Charles M. Tuttle, 1960.

Iswolski, Hélène, ed. *Au service de la Russie: Alexandre Iswolski, correspondance diplomatique, 1906-1911*. Paris, Les Editions internationales, 1937.

Itani Zen'ichi 猪谷善一. "Meiji shonen ni okeru sanshu yushutsu" 明治初年における蚕種輸出 (Silk-worm egg card exports in early Meiji), *Shakai keizai shigaku*, VI, No. 10 (February 1937), 185-222.

Itō Hirobumi 伊藤博文, ed., and Hiratsuka Atsushi 平塚篤, rev. *Hisho ruisan* 秘書類纂 (A collection of secret documents). 27 vols. Tokyo, Hisho Ruisan Kankōkai, 1933-36.

Itō Masanori 伊藤正徳. *Gumbatsu kōbōshi* 軍閥興亡史 (Rise and fall of the military). 3 vols. Tokyo, Bungei Shunjūsha, 1957-58.

—— ed. *Katō Takaaki* 加藤高明. 2 vols. Tokyo, Katō Haku Denki Hensan Iinkai, 1929.

Itō Miyoji 伊藤巳代治. "Gaikō Chōsakai kaigi hikki Hara naikaku seiritsu go" 外交調査会会議筆記原内閣成立後 (Notes from meetings of the Advisory Council on Foreign Relations after the establishment of the Hara cabinet), item No. 663 in Kokuritsu Kokkai Toshokan 国立国会図書館, comp., *Kenseishi hensankai shūshū bunsho mokuroku: Kensei Shiryō Shitsu shozō mokuroku daiichi* 憲政史編纂会収集文書目録―憲政資料室所蔵目録第一 (Catalog of documents collected by the Committee for the Compilation of the History of Constitutional Government in Japan: The first catalog of materials deposited in the Kensei Shiryō Shitsu, National Diet Library). Tokyo, by the compiler, 1960.

—— "Sui'usō nikki: Nichi-Bei shuppei teigi mondai" 翠雨荘日記―日米出兵提議問題 (From the Sui'usō diary: The proposal for a Japanese-American expeditionary force), *Kokusai seiji: Nihon gaikōshi kenkyū—daiichiji sekai taisen*, 1962, pp. 1–89.

—— *Sui'usō nikki: Rinji Gaikō Chōsa Iinkai kaigi hikki nado* 翠雨荘日記―臨時外交調査委員会会議筆記等 (From the Sui'usō diary: Notes from meetings of the Advisory Council on Foreign Relations and other matters). Edited by Kobayashi Tatsuo 小林龍夫. Vol. VII of *Meiji hyakunenshi sōsho* 明治百年史叢書 (Historical materials of the century since the Meiji Restoration). Tokyo, Hara Shobō, 1966.

Itō Takeo 伊藤武雄. *Kōryū to tōfū* 黄竜と東風 (Yellow dragon and east wind). Tokyo, Kokusai Nihon Kyōkai, 1964.

Itō Yanosuke 伊東彌之助. "Tsūshōshi seisaku ni okeru kawase kaisha" 通商司政策に於ける為替会社 (The role of the exchange companies in Trade Control Office policy), in Keiō Gijuku Keizaishi Gakkai 慶応義塾経済史学会, ed., *Meiji shoki keizaishi kenkyū* 明治初期経済史研究 (Studies in the economic history of early Meiji), II, 305–35. 2 vols. Tokyo, Ganshōdō, 1937.

Iwabuchi Tatsuo 岩淵辰雄. *Gumbatsu no keifu* 軍閥の系譜 (Militarism in the Shōwa period). Tokyo, Chūō Kōronsha, 1948.

Iwakura Kō Kyūseki Hozonkai 岩倉公旧蹟保存会, ed. *Iwakura kō jikki* 岩倉公実記 (True record of Prince Iwakura). 3 vols. Tokyo, Iwakura Kō Kyūseki Hozonkai, 1927 (first published, 1906).

Iwakura Tomomi kankei bunsho 岩倉具視関係文書 (Papers of Iwakura Tomomi). Edited by Ōtsuka Takematsu 大塚武松. 8 vols. Tokyo, Nihon Shiseki Kyōkai, 1927–35.

Izu Kimio 伊豆公夫 and Matsushita Yoshio 松下芳男. *Nihon gunji hattatsushi* 日本軍事発達史 (History of the Japanese army). Tokyo, Mikasa Shobō, 1938.

Jane's Fighting Ships, 1914. London, S. Low, Marston, 1914.

Jansen, Marius B. *The Japanese and Sun Yat-sen*. Cambridge, Harvard University Press, 1954.

—— *Sakamoto Ryōma and the Meiji Restoration*. Princeton, Princeton University Press, 1961.

Japan, Commission impériale à l'Exposition universelle de Paris, 1878. *Le Japon à l'Exposition universelle de 1878, publié sous la direction de la Commission impériale Japonaise*. Paris, Commission impériale de Japon, 1878.

Japan, Commission impériale à l'Exposition universelle de Paris, 1900. *Catalogue spécial officiel du Japon*. Paris, Lemercier, 1900.

—— *Histoire de l'industrie de la pêche maritime et fluviale au Japon, par la Bureau des produits maritimes et fluviaux du Ministère d'agriculture et commerce (rédigé pour l'Exposition universelle de Paris en 1900)*. Tokyo, Nōshōmushō, 1900.

—— Empire du Japon, Ministère de l'agriculture et du commerce, Station centrale agronomique. *Notice des objets exposés*. Tokyo, Insatsu Kabushiki Kaisha, 1900.

Japan, Gaimushō 外務省 (Foreign Ministry). "Beikoku ni okeru hai-Nichi mondai ikken" 米国ニ於ケル排日問題一件 (Documents relating to anti-Japanese problems in the United States), 1911–14, cited in Uyehara, *Checklist*, p. 25, Reel MT 3.8.2.274 (1–7).

—— "Gaikō shiryō" 外交資料 (Materials on foreign relations). Tokyo, unpublished, 1946.

—— "Hokubei Gasshūkoku ni oite hompōjin tokō seigen oyobi haiseki ikken" 北米合衆国ニ於イテ本邦人渡航制限及ビ排斥一件 (Documents relating to the limitation and exclusion of Japanese immigrants by the United States), 1891–1909, cited in Uyehara, *Checklist*, p. 24, Reel MT 3.8.2.21.

—— *Jōyaku kaisei kankei Nihon gaikō bunsho* 條約改正関係日本外交文書 (Japanese diplomatic documents on treaty revision). 4 vols. Tokyo, Nihon Gakujutsu Shinkōkai, 1941–50.

—— *Jōyaku kaisei kankei Nihon gaikō bunsho, tsuiho* 條約改正関係日本外交文書追補 (Japanese diplomatic documents related to treaty revision, supplement). Tokyo, Nihon Kokusai Rengō Kyōkai, 1953.

—— *Jōyaku kaisei keika gaiyō* 條約改正経過概要 (A summary of the development of treaty revision). Supplement to *Jōyaku kaisei kankei Nihon gaikō bunsho* 條約改正関係日本外交文書 (Japanese diplomatic documents on treaty revision). Tokyo, Nihon Kokusai Rengō Kyōkai, 1950.

—— *Komura gaikōshi* 小村外交史 (History of Komura diplomacy). 2 vols. Tokyo, Shimbun Gekkansha, 1953. Reprinted as Vol. VII of *Meiji hyakunenshi sōsho* 明治百年史叢書 (Historical materials of the century since the Meiji Restoration). Tokyo, Hara Shobō, 1966.

—— "Matsumoto kiroku: Shina jihen" 松本記録—支那事変 (Matsumoto Record: The China Incident), cited in Uyehara, *Checklist*, p. 109, Reel PVM 42.

—— "Nichi-Ei gaikōshi" 日英外交史 (History of diplomatic relations between Japan and Great Britain), 2 vols. Tokyo, printed for private circulation, 1937. Cited in Uyehara, *Checklist*, p. 83, Reel Sp. 2.

—— "Nichi-Ro kōshō shi" 日露交渉史 (History of Russo-Japanese relations). 2 vols. Tokyo, unpublished, 1944. Cited in Uyehara, *Checklist*, p. 83, Reel Sp. 3. (See Chap. 10, "Recent Works.")

—— *Nihon gaikō bunsho* 日本外交文書 (Documents on Japanese foreign relations). Tokyo, Nihon Kokusai Rengō Kyōkai, 1936- .

—— *Nihon gaikō hyakunen shōshi* 日本外交百年小史 (A short history of the past one hundred years of Japanese diplomacy). 2d rev. ed. Tokyo, Yamada Shoin, 1958.

—— *Nihon gaikō nempyō narabi ni shuyō bunsho* 日本外交年表並主要文書 (Chronology and major documents of Japanese foreign relations). 2 vols. Tokyo, Hara Shobō, 1965 (first published by Nihon Kokusai Rengō Kyōkai, 1955).

—— *Nihon gaikō nenkan* 日本外交年鑑 (Yearbook of Japanese diplomacy). Tokyo, Nihon Gaikō Nenkansha, 1943.

—— "Nisso kōshō shi" 日ソ交渉史 (History of Soviet-Japanese relations). Tokyo, unpublished, 1942. Cited in Uyehara, *Checklist*, p. 83, Reel Sp. 4. (See Chap. 10, "Recent Works.")

—— "Rokoku kakumei ikken" 露国革命一件 (The Russian revolution), cited in Uyehara, *Checklist*, Reel MR 1.6.3.24 (1–31).

—— *Sekai taisen kankei Nihon gaikō bunsho* 世界大戦関係日本外交文書 (Documents related to Japanese diplomacy and World War I, subtitled "Documents diplomatiques japonais relatifs à la guerre mondiale de 1914–1918"). Tokyo, 1939.

—— "Shiberia shuppei mondai" シベリア出兵問題 (The Siberian expedition question). 2 vols. Tokyo, 1922.

—— *Shūsen shiroku* 終戦史録 (Historical record of the end of the war). Tokyo, Shimbun Gekkansha, 1952.

—— "Tai-Bei keihatsu undō ikken" 対米啓発運動一件 (Documents relating to efforts to enlighten U.S. public opinion), 1913–20, cited in Uyehara, *Checklist*, p. 25, Reel MT 3.8.2.287 (0–2).

—— "Tai-Bei keihatsu undō jigyō hōkoku" 対米啓発運動事業報告 (Official reports on efforts to enlighten U.S. public opinion), 1914–19, cited in Uyehara, *Checklist*, pp. 25–26, Reel MT 3.8.2.290 (1–2).

—— "Tai-Bei keihatsu undō jigyō hōkoku: zai-Nyūyōku sōryōjikan" 対米啓発運動事業報告—在ニューヨーク總領事館 (Official reports on efforts to enlighten U.S. public opinion: New York Consulate-General), 1914–19, cited in Uyehara, *Checklist*, pp. 1712–15, Reel MT 3.8.2.290–2.

—— "Teikoku no taigai seisaku kankei ikken" 帝国の対外政策関係一件 (Documents on Japanese foreign policy). 7 vols. Unpublished, n.d.

—— "Teikoku no tai-Shi seisaku kankei ikken" 帝国の対支政策関係一件 (Documents on Japanese policy toward China). 8 vols. Unpublished, n.d.

—— "Tōhō Bunka Jigyōbu kankei kaikei zakken" 東方文化事業部関係会計雑件 (Miscellaneous documents relating to the finances of the Cultural Affairs

Division in the Orient), 1922–41, cited in Uyehara, *Checklist*, p. 69, Reel S 8.2. 1.0–1.

—— "Tōhō bunka jigyō kankei zakken" 東方文化事業関係雑件 (Miscellaneous documents relating to cultural work in the Orient), 1922–41, cited in Uyehara, *Checklist*, p. 69, Reel S 8.0.0.0–1.

—— *Tsūshō jōyaku kankei Nihon gaikō bunsho* 通商條約関係日本外交文書 (Japanese diplomatic documents related to commercial treaties). 3 vols. Tokyo, Nihon Kokusai Rengō Kyōkai, 1954.

—— *Tsūshō jōyaku to tsūshō seisaku no hensen* 通商條約と通商政策の変遷 (Changes in trade treaties and trade policy). Edited by Kawashima Nobutarō 川島信太郎. Supplement to *Jōyaku kaisei kankei Nihon gaikō bunsho* 條約改正関係日本外交文書 (Japanese diplomatic documents on treaty revision). Tokyo, Sekai Keizai Chōsakai, 1951.

Japan, Gaimushō, Amerika Kyoku 外務省亜米利加局 (Foreign Ministry, America Bureau). *Hokubei Nikkei shimin gaikyō* 北米日系市民概況 (Condition of American citizens of Japanese descent in North America). Tokyo, Gaimushō, 1936.

Japan, Gaimushō, Bunka Jigyōbu 外務省文化事業部 (Foreign Ministry, Cultural Affairs Division). *Chūka Minkoku kyōiku sono ta no shisetsu gaiyō* 中華民国教育その他の施設概要 (Outline of educational and other facilities in the Republic of China). Tokyo, Gaimushō, 1931.

Japan, Gaimushō, Tsūshō Kyoku 外務省通商局 (Foreign Ministry, International Trade Bureau). "Tai-Bei imin mondai ni kansuru Nichi-Bei kōshō keika" 対米移民問題ニ関スル日米交渉経過 (Japanese-American negotiations on the problem of Japanese immigration into the United States), 1933, cited in Uyehara, *Checklist*, p. 85, Reel Sp. 50.

Japan, Gunreibu 軍令部 (Navy General Staff). "Kahoku mondai 'Shinsei jiken' keii" 華北問題新生事件経緯 (Particulars of the "New Life" incident). Unpublished, 1935.

—— *Meiji sanjūshichi-hachinen kaisenshi* 明治三十七八年海戦史 (Naval history of the Russo-Japanese War). 3 vols. Tokyo, Gunreibu, 1909–10.

—— Records of the Navy General Staff, collected at the Zaidan Hōjin Shiryō Chōsakai 財団法人資料調査会 (Historical Materials Research Association).

—— "Taishō yonen naishi kyūnen kaigun senshi" 大正四年乃至九年海軍戦史 (History of naval warfare, 1915–20). 6 vols. Tokyo, unpublished, 1924.

Japan, Imperial Japanese Commission to the International Exhibition at Philadelphia. *Official Catalogue of the Japanese Section, and Descriptive Notes on the Industry and Agriculture of Japan*. Philadelphia, Japanese Commission, 1876.

Japan, Imperial Japanese Government Commission to the Japan-British Exhibition. *An Illustrated Catalogue of Japanese Old Fine Arts Displayed at the Japan-British Exhibition, London, 1910*. Tokyo, Shimbi Shoin, 1910.

Japan, Imperial Japanese Commission to the Louisiana Purchase Exposition. *The Exhibit of the Empire of Japan: Official Catalogue, International Exposition, St. Louis, 1904.* St. Louis, Woodward and Tiernan, 1904.

—— *Japan in the Beginning of the Twentieth Century.* Edited by Yamawaki Haruki for the Ministry of Agriculture and Commerce. Tokyo, Tōkyō Shoin, 1904.

Japan, Imperial Japanese Commission to the New York World's Fair, 1939. *Directory and Catalogue of Exhibits at the Japanese Pavilion and Japanese Section of the Hall of Nations.* (No publication information given.)

Japan, Imperial Japanese Commission to the Panama-Pacific International Exhibition, San Francisco, 1915. *Japan as It Is.* Tokyo, Kokusai Tsūshinsha, 1915.

Japan, Imperial Japanese Commission to the World's Columbian Exposition, Chicago, U.S.A., 1893. *History of the Empire of Japan.* Translated by Capt. F. Brinkley. Tokyo, Dai Nippon Tosho Kabushiki Kaisha at the direction of the Ministry of Education, 1893.

Japan, Mombushō 文部省 (Ministry of Education). *Meiji ikō kyōiku seido hattatsushi* 明治以降教育制度発達史 (History of the development of the educational system since the beginning of the Meiji era). 12 vols. Tokyo, Mombushō Nai Kyōikushi Hensankai, 1938–39.

—— *Mombushō daisan nempō* 文部省第三年報 (Third annual report of the Ministry of Education). Tokyo, Mombushō, 1875; reprinted in 2 vols., Tokyo, Senbundō Shoten, 1964.

—— *An Outline History of Japanese Education, Literature and Arts; Prepared by the Mombushō for the Philadelphia International Exhibition, 1876, Reprinted for the Paris Exposition, 1878.* Tokyo, Ministry of Education, 1877.

—— *Riji kōtei* 理事功程 (Introduction to Western education). 15 vols. Tokyo, Mombushō, 1873.

Japan, Mombushō, Kambō, Hōkokuka 文部省官房報告課 (Ministry of Education, Secretariat, Information Section). *Catalogue of Objects Exhibited at the World's Columbian Exposition, Chicago, U.S.A., 1893.*

Japan, Mombushō, Shakai Kyōikukyoku 文部省社会教育局 (Ministry of Education, Bureau of Social Education), ed. *Sōtei shisō chōsa gaiyō* 壮丁思想調査概要 (Summary of a survey of the ideas of young men of military age). Tokyo, by the editor, 1931.

Japan, Nōshōmushō 農商務省 (Ministry of Agriculture and Commerce). *A Descriptive Catalogue of the Agricultural Products Exhibited in the World's Columbian Exposition.* Tokyo, Seishibunsha, 1893.

Japan, Nōshōmushō, Shōmukyoku 農商務省商務局 (Ministry of Agriculture and Commerce, Bureau of Commerce), ed. *Dai Nihon gaikoku bōeki* 大日本外国貿易 (The foreign trade of Japan). Tokyo, 1911.

Japan, Rikugunshō 陸軍省 (Army Ministry), *Meiji sanjūshichi-hachinen sen'eki rikugun seishi* 明治三十七八年戦役陸軍政史 (Official army history of the Russo-Japanese

War). 10 vols. Tokyo, Rikugunshō, 1911.

—— *Rikugun enkaku yōran* 陸軍沿革要覧 (A handbook of the army). Tokyo, Rikugun-shō, 1890.

Japan, Sambō Hombu 参謀本部 (Army General Staff). *Meiji nijūshichi-hachinen Nisshin senshi* 明治二十七八年日清戦史 (History of the Sino-Japanese War). 8 vols. Tokyo, Ikueisha, 1904, 1907.

—— *Sambō enkakushi* 参謀沿革誌 (History of the Army General Staff). Tokyo, Sambō Hombu, 1882.

—— *Shōwa sannen Shina jihen shuppei shi* 昭和三年支那事変出兵史 (History of the military expedition during the incident of 1928 in China). Tokyo, Sambō Hombu, 1930.

—— "*Taishō shichinen naishi jūichinen Shiberia shuppei shi*" 大正七年乃至十一年シベリア出兵史 (History of the Siberian Expedition, 1918–22). 7 vols. Tokyo, Sambō Hombu, 1924.

Japan, Tetsudōshō 鉄道省 (Ministry of Railways). *Nihon tetsudōshi* 日本鉄道史 (History of Japanese railroads). 3 vols. Tokyo, Tetsudōshō, 1921.

Japan Times Weekly and Trans-Pacific, 1938–41.

Japan Trade Center. *How to See the Japan Pavilion (The New York World's Fair, 1964–1965).* New York, Japan Trade Center, prepared under the supervision of the Japan External Trade Organization, 1964.

Japan, Tsūshō Sangyōshō 通商産業省 (Ministry of International Trade and Industry), ed. *Shōkō seisakushi V: bōeki (jō)* 商工政策史貿易(上) (A history of commercial and industrial policy, V: Foreign trade, part 1). Tokyo, 1965.

Japan Weekly Chronicle, August 28, 1924–October 16, 1941.

Japanese Association of America, San Francisco. *Facts in the Case; They Will Be Carefully Weighed in Considering the Proposed Alien Land Initiative Law.* San Francisco, Japanese Association of America, 1920.

—— *The Proposed Land Bills: The Other Side.* San Francisco, Japanese Association of America, 1913.

—— *Statistics Relative to Japanese Immigration and the Japanese in California.* San Francisco, Japanese Association of America, 1921.

Jones, F.C. *Extraterritoriality in Japan and the Diplomatic Relations Resulting in Its Abolition, 1853–1899.* New Haven, Yale University Press, 1931.

—— *Japan's New Order in East Asia: Its Rise and Fall, 1937–1945.* London, Oxford University Press, 1954.

Kabayama Aisuke ō 樺山愛輔翁 (The venerable Kabayama Aisuke). Tokyo, Kokusai Bunka Kaikan, 1955.

Kachi Teruko 佳知晃子. "Nichi-Bei tsūshō kōkai jōyaku to Kariforunia-shū tochi hō" 日米通商航海条約とカリフォルニア州土地法 (The treaty of 1911 and the

California land law), *Kokusai seiji: Nihon gaikōshi kenkyū—Nichi-Bei kankei no tenkai*,· 1961, pp. 21–45.

—— "The Treaty of 1911 and the Immigration and Alien Land Law Issue between the United States and Japan, 1911–1913." Unpublished doctoral dissertation, University of Chicago, 1957.

Kaikoku Hyakunen Kinen Bunka Jigyōkai 開国百年記念文化事業会, ed. *Nichi-Bei bunka kōshō shi* 日米文化交渉史 (History of Japanese-American cultural relations). 6 vols. Tokyo, Yōyōsha, 1954–56.

Kaizuma Haruhiko 海妻玄彦. "Shōwa gaikōshi sōsetsu" 昭和外交史総説 (A general survey of the diplomatic history of the Shōwa period), *Kokusai seiji: Nihon gaikō-shi kenkyū—Shōwa jidai*, 1959, pp. 1–13.

Kaji Wataru 鹿地亘. *Dasshutsu* 脱出 (Escape). Tokyo, Kaiōsha, 1948.

—— *Hansen shiryō* 反戦資料 (Research materials opposing war). Tokyo. Dōseisha, 1964.

—— ed., *Nihon jimmin hansen dōmei* 日本人民反戦同盟 (Japanese people's alliance against war). 9 vols., microfilm. Tokyo, Kyokutō Shoten, 1961.

Kajima Morinosuke 鹿島守之助. *Gendai no gaikō* 現代の外交 (Contemporary diplomatic relations). Tokyo, Gaikō Jihōsha, 1937.

—— *Nichi-Bei gaikōshi* 日米外交史 (A history of Japanese-American diplomatic relations). Tokyo, Kajima Kenkyūjo, 1958.

—— *Nichi-Ei gaikōshi* 日英外交史 (A history of Anglo-Japanese diplomatic relations). Tokyo, Kajima Kenkyūjo, 1957.

—— *Nihon gaikō seisaku no shiteki kōsatsu* 日本外交政策の史的考察 (A historical view of Japan's foreign policy). Tokyo, Kajima Kenkyūjo, 1951. Originally published as *Teikoku gaikō no kihon seisaku* 帝国外交の基本政策 (Basic foreign policies of the empire). Tokyo, Ganshōdō Shoten, 1938.

Kajinishi Mitsuhaya 楫西光速. "Development of Light Industry," in Shibusawa, *Japanese Society in the Meiji Era*, pp. 237–303.

—— "Development of Transportation and Communication Systems," in Shibusawa, *Japanese Society in the Meiji Era*, pp. 369–400.

—— "Meiji shonen no sangyō shihon" 明治初年の産業資本 (Industrial capital in early Meiji), *Shakai keizai shigaku*, XXV, No. 1 (1959), 1–25.

—— "Nihon jūkōgyō no seisei" 日本重工業の生成 (The genesis of Japan's heavy industry), *Keizaigaku ronshū*, XXVI, Nos. 1–2 (1959), 1–24.

—— *Nihon kindai mengyō no seiritsu* 日本近代綿業の成立 (The establishment of Japan's modern cotton industry). Tokyo, Kadokawa Shoten, 1950.

—— "Shihonshugi no ikusei" 資本主義の育成 (The nurturing of capitalism), in *Iwanami kōza Nihon rekishi kindai* 岩波講座日本歴史近代 (Iwanami lectures on modern Japanese history), III, 1–51. Tokyo, Iwanami Shoten, 1962.

—— "Shokusan kōgyō seisaku to sangyō shihon no seisei" 殖産興業政策と産業資本

の生成 (The encouragement of production policy and the formation of industrial capital), *Keizai kenkyū*, IX, No. 3 (July 1958), 191–97.

Kajinishi Mitsuhaya, Katō Toshihiko 加藤俊彦, Ōshima Kiyoshi 大島清, and Ōuchi Tsutomu 大内力. *Nihon shihonshugi no hatten* 日本資本主義の発展 (Development of capitalism in Japan). 3 vols. Tokyo, Tōkyō Daigaku Shuppankai, 1957–59.

——— *Nihon shihonshugi no seiritsu* 日本資本主義の成立 (The establishment of Japanese capitalism). 2 vols. *Sōsho Nihon ni okeru shihonshugi no hattatsu* 叢書日本における 資本主義の発達 (Series on the development of capitalism in Japan). Tokyo, Tōkyō Daigaku Shuppankai, 1956.

Kajinishi Mitsuhaya and Kobayashi Masaaki 小林正彬. "Shokusan kōgyō seisaku to sangyō shihon no seiritsu" 殖産興業政策と産業資本の成立 (The encouragement of production policy and the establishment of industrial capital), in Rekishigaku Kenkyūkai 歴史学研究会, ed., *Meiji ishin shi kenkyū kōza* 明治維新史研究講座 (Studies in the history of the Meiji Restoration), V, 3–30. 6 vols. Tokyo, Heibonsha, 1958–59.

Kamei Kan'ichirō 亀井貫一郎. *Dai Tōa minzoku no michi* 大東亜民族の途 (The way of the peoples of Greater East Asia). Tokyo, Seiki Shobō, 1941.

Kamikawa Hikomatsu 神川彦松. *Japan-American Diplomatic Relations in the Meiji-Taisho Era*. Translated by Kimura Michiko. Tokyo, Pan-Pacific Press, 1958.

——— *Nichi-Bei bunka kōshō shi, I: sōsetsu gaikō hen* 日米文化交渉史I—総説外交編 (History of Japanese-American cultural relations, I: Introduction and diplomatic relations). Tokyo, Yōyōsha, 1956.

Kamimura Shin'ichi 上村伸一. *Gaikō gojūnen* 外交五十年 (Fifty years of diplomacy). Tokyo, Jiji Tsūshinsha, 1960.

Kamisaka Torizō 上坂酉三. "Kaikoku jidai ni okeru bōeki to yōgin to no kōryū kankei" 開国時代における貿易と洋銀との交流関係 (The relationship between trade and Mexican silver at the time of the opening of Japan), *Ōkuma kenkyū*, XXIX, No. 4 (1954).

Kamiyama Shigeo 神山茂夫. *Gendai Nihon kokka no shiteki kyūmei* 現代日本国家の史的究明 (Historical analysis of the modern Japanese state). Tokyo, Ashikai, 1953.

Kamo Giichi 加茂儀一. *Enomoto Takeaki: Meiji Nihon no kakuretaru soseki* 榎本武揚 明治日本の隠れたる礎石 (Enomoto Takeaki: Meiji Japan's hidden cornerstone). Tokyo, Chūō Kōronsha, 1960.

Kanaya Mahito 金谷眞人. "Waga kuni taigai tsūshō seisaku to sono konnichi ni itaru made no enkaku" 我国対外通商政策とその今日に至るまでの沿革 (The development of Japan's international trade policy up to the present), *Gaikō jihō*, LXX, No. 1 (1934), 156–84.

Kaneko Kentarō 金子堅太郎. *Nichi-Ro sensō hiroku* 日露戦争秘録 (Secret records of the Russo-Japanese War). Tokyo, Hakubunkan, 1929.

Kanno Watarō 管野和太郎. *Bakumatsu ishin keizaishi kenkyū* 幕末維新経済史研究

(Studies in the economic history of the late Tokugawa and the Meiji Restoration). Vol. I of *Nihon keizaishi kenkyūjo sōsho* (Japanese Economic History Institute series). Tokyo, Mineruba Shobō, 1961.

—— "Bakumatsu no shōsha" 幕末の商社 (Trading firms at the end of the Tokugawa period), in Honjō Eijirō 本庄栄治郎, ed., *Meiji ishin keizaishi kenkyū* 明治維新経済史研究 (Studies in the economic history of the Meiji Restoration), pp. 63–103. Tokyo, Kaizōsha, 1930.

—— "Tsūshō kaisha kawase kaisha" 通商会社為替会社 (Foreign trade companies and exchange companies), in Honjō Eijirō 本庄栄治郎, ed., *Meiji ishin keizaishi kenkyū* 明治維新経済史研究 (Studies in the economic history of the Meiji Restoration), pp. 105–300. Tokyo, Kaizōsha, 1930.

Kantōchō 関東庁 (Kwantung Government-General), ed. *Kantōchō shisei nijūnenshi* 関東庁施政二十年史 (A twenty-year history of the administration of the Kwantung leased territory). Dairen, Kantōchō, 1926.

—— ed. *Kantōchō shisei sanjūnenshi* 関東庁施政三十年史 (A thirty-year history of the administration of the Kwantung leased territory). Dairen, Kantōchō, 1936.

Kantōchō, Chōkan Kambō, Bunshoka 関東庁長官官房文書課 (Kwantung Government-General, Secretariat, Records Section), ed. *Kantōchō yōran* 関東庁要覧 (Handbook of the Kwantung Government-General). Dairen, Kantōchō, 1925, 1927, 1928, 1934.

Kantorovich, A. *Amerika v bor'be za Kitai* (America in the battle for China). Moscow, Gosudarstvennoe Sotsial'noekonomicheskoe Izdatel'stvo, 1935.

Karafutochō 樺太庁 (Government of Sakhalin), ed. *Karafuto enkaku shi* 樺太沿革史 (History of Sakhalin). Karafuto, Karafutochō, 1925.

Karasawa Tomitarō 唐沢富太郎. *Kyōkasho no rekishi: kyōkasho to Nihonjin no keisei* 教科書の歴史—教科書と日本人の形成 (History of textbooks: Textbooks and the development of the Japanese character). Tokyo, Sōbunsha, 1956.

Kasai Takashi 笠井孝. *Ura kara mita Shina minzokusei* 裏から見た支那民族性 (An international view of the Chinese national character). Tokyo, Nihon Gaiji Kyōkai, 1935.

Kase Toshikazu 加瀬俊一. *Mizurī gō e no dōtei* ミズリー号への道程 (Journey to the U.S.S. Missouri). Tokyo, Bungei Shunjū Shinsha, 1951. Translated as *Journey to the Missouri*. New Haven, Yale University Press, 1950.

Katakura Chū 片倉衷. "Ugaki naikaku ryūzansu" 宇垣内閣流産す (An Ugaki cabinet fell through), *Bessatsu chisei, V: himerareta Shōwashi*, December 1956, pp. 160–68.

Katō Kanji Denki Hensankai 加藤寛治伝記編纂会, ed., *Katō Kanji taishō den* 加藤寛治大將伝 (Biography of Admiral Katō Kanji). Tokyo, Katō Kanji Denki Hensankai, 1941.

Katō Toshihiko 加藤俊彦. "Development of Foreign Trade," in Shibusawa, *Japanese Society in the Meiji Era*, pp. 473–509.

—— "Development of the Monetary System," in Shibusawa, *Japanese Society in the Meiji Era*, pp. 181–235.

—— *Hompō ginkō shiron* 本邦銀行史論 (Treatise on the history of Japanese banking). Tokyo, Tōkyō Daigaku Shuppankai, 1957.

Katsura Tarō kankei bunsho mokuroku: Kensei shiryō mokuroku daisan 桂太郎関係文書目録—憲政資料目録第三 (Catalog of documents related to Katsura Tarō: The third catalog of constitutional materials deposited in the Kensei Shiryō Shitsu, National Diet Library, Tokyo). Tokyo, Kokuritsu Kokkai Toshokan, 1965.

Katsura Tarō Papers 桂太郎関係文書. Tokyo, Kensei Shiryō Shitsu, National Diet Library.

Katsuta Magoya 勝田孫彌. *Ōkubo Toshimichi den* 大久保利通伝 (Biography of Ōkubo Toshimichi). 3 vols. Tokyo, Dōbunkan, 1910–11.

Kawakami, Kiyoshi K. *Jokichi Takamine: A Record of His American Achievements.* New York, William Edwin Rudge, 1928.

Kawamura Kazuo 河村一夫. "Hokushin jihen to Nihon" 北清事変と日本 (The north China incident and Japan), *Kokusai seiji: Nihon gaikōshi kenkyū—Meiji jidai*, 1957, pp. 93–118.

Kawamura Zenjirō 川村善二郎. "Hara Takashi naikaku" 原敬内閣 (The Hara cabinet), *Rekishi kyōiku*, VIII, No. 2 (1902), 35–40.

Kawashima Isami 川島伊佐美. *Nichi-Bei gaikōshi* 日米外交史 (A History of Japanese-American diplomatic relations). San Francisco, Hatae Minoru, 1934.

Kawashima Naniwa 川島浪速. "Hokushi no jōsei ni nagaruru kihon seishin" 北支の情勢に流るる基本精神 (The basic spirit underlying the present situation in north China). Unpublished materials in the Araki Sadao papers, Tōkyō Daigaku Hōgakubu (Tokyo University, Faculty of Law), 1937.

—— "Tai-Shi narabi ni tai-Mammō no komponteki keirin" 対支並に対満蒙の根本的経綸 (Fundamental policy toward China, Manchuria, and Mongolia). Unpublished materials in the Araki Sadao papers, Tōkyō Daigaku Hōgakubu (Tokyo University, Faculty of Law), 1926.

Kawashima Nobutarō 川島信太郎. *Hompō tsūshō seisaku jōyaku shi gairon* 本邦通商政策條約史概論 (An introduction to the history of Japanese trade policy and trade treaties). Tokyo, Ganshōdō, 1941.

Kayano Nagatomo 萱野長知. *Chūka Minkoku kakumei hikyū* 中華民国革命秘笈 (Secret memoirs of the Chinese revolution). Tokyo, Kōkoku Seinen Kyōiku Kyōkai, 1941.

Kazama Michitarō 風間道太郎. *Aru hangyaku: Ozaki Hotsumi no shōgai* ある反逆—尾崎秀実の生涯 (Treason: The life of Ozaki Hotsumi). Tokyo, Shinseidō, 1959.

Kazami Akira 風見章. *Konoe naikaku* 近衞内閣 (The Konoe cabinets). Tokyo, Nihon Shuppan Kyōdō, 1951.

Kazankai 霞山会, ed. *Konoe Kazan kō* 近衞霞山公 (Prince Konoe Atsumaro). Tokyo, Kazankai, 1924.

Keikōkai 馨光会, ed. *Tsuzuki Keiroku den* 都筑馨六伝 (Biography of Baron Tsuzuki Keiroku). Tokyo, Keikōkai, 1926.

Kennan, George. *American Diplomacy, 1900-1950.* Chicago, University of Chicago Press, 1951.

—— *The Decision to Intervene.* Vol. II of *Soviet-American Relations, 1917-1920.* Princeton, Princeton University Press, 1958.

—— *Russia Leaves the War.* Vol. I of *Soviet-American Relations, 1917-1920.* Princeton, Princeton University Press, 1956.

Kiba Kōsuke 木場浩介, ed. *Nomura Kichisaburō* 野村吉三郎. Tokyo, Nomura Kichisaburō Denki Kankōkai, 1961.

Kido Kō Denki Hensansho 木戸公伝記編纂所, ed. *Shōgiku Kido kō den* 松菊木戸公伝 (Biography of Kido Takayoshi). 2 vols. Tokyo, Meiji Shoin, 1927.

Kido Kōichi 木戸幸一. "Kido [Kōichi] Diary, July 11, 1931-December 9, 1945," Documents 1632 and 1768, International Prosecution Section, International Military Tribunal for the Far East, includes extracts from the *Kido nikki* (1947). IPS Document 1632, an English translation, and IPS Document 1768, Japanese text and English translation, are cited as IMT 2 and IMT 398, respectively, in Uyehara, *Checklist*, pp. 112 and 132. See following item.

—— *Kido Kōichi nikki* 木戸幸一日記 (Kido Kōichi diary). 2 vols. plus supplementary volume of documents: Kido Kōichi Nikki Kenkyūkai 木戸幸一日記研究会, comp. *Kido Kōichi kankei bunsho* 木戸幸一関係文書 (Kido Kōichi papers). Tokyo, Tōkyō Daigaku Shuppankai, 1966.

—— *Kido nikki* 木戸日記 (Kido diary). Edited by Kyokutō Kokusai Gunji Saiban Kenkyūkai 極東国際軍事裁判研究会. Tokyo, Heiwa Shobō, 1947.

Kido Takayoshi 木戸孝允. *Kido Takayoshi nikki* 木戸孝允日記 (Kido Takayoshi diary). 3 vols. Tokyo, Tōkyō Daigaku Shuppankai, 1967. Originally published Tokyo, Nihon Shiseki Kyōkai, 1932-33.

Kido Takayoshi bunsho 木戸孝允文書 (Kido Takayoshi papers). Edited by Tsumaki Chūta 妻木忠太. 8 vols. Tokyo, Nihon Shiseki Kyōkai, 1929-31.

Kikkawa Gaku 橘川学. *Arashi to tatakau tesshō Araki: Rikugun rimenshi* 嵐と闘ふ哲将荒木一陸軍裏面史 (Biography of General Araki: Inside story of the army). Tokyo, Denki Hemponkai, 1955.

Kikkawa Hidezō 吉川秀造. "Maeda Masana" 前田正名, *Keizaishi kenkyū*, XXV, No. 4 (April 1941), 251-72.

—— "Maeda Masana no shokusan kōgyō undō" 前田正名の殖産興業運動 (Maeda Masana's efforts to encourage production), *Dōshisha shōgaku*, XIV (1962), 54-81.

—— *Meiji ishin shakai keizaishi kenkyū* 明治維新社会経済史研究 (Studies in the social and economic history of the Meiji Restoration). Tokyo, Nihon Hyōronsha, 1943.

—— "Meiji jidai no seika seisaku" 明治時代の正貨政策 (Specie policy in the Meiji period), *Dōshisha shōgaku*, V, No. 3 (1953), 43–64; No. 6 (1954), 21–47.

—— "Meiji seifu no kashitsuke kin" 明治政府の貸付金 (Loans made by the Meiji government), in Honjō Eijirō 本庄栄治郎, ed., *Meiji ishin keizaishi kenkyū* 明治維新経済史研究 (Studies in the economic history of the Meiji Restoration), pp. 407–84. Tokyo, Kaizōsha, 1930.

Kikuchi Akishirō 菊地秋四郎 and Nakajima Ichirō 中島一郎. *Hōten nijūnenshi* 奉天二十年史 (History of Mukden, 1895–1915). Mukden, Hōten Nijūnenshi Kankōkai, 1926.

Kikuchi Takaharu 菊地貴晴. "Ampō tetsudō kōchiku mondai to tai-Nichi boikotto ni tsuite" 安奉鉄道工築問題と対日ボイコットについて (The building of the Mukden-Antung railroad and the anti-Japanese boycott), *Fukushima daigaku gakugei gakubu ronshū*, No. 11, Part 1 (March 1960), pp. 53–69.

—— "Daini Tatsu Maru jiken no tai-Nichi boikotto" 第二辰丸事件の対日ボイコット (The Chinese anti-Japanese boycott at the time of the Daini Tatsu Maru incident, 1908), *Rekishigaku kenkyū*, No. 209 (July 1957), pp. 1–13.

Kikuchi Takenori 菊地武徳, ed. *Hakushaku Chinda Sutemi den* 伯爵珍田捨巳伝 (Biography of Count Chinda Sutemi). Tokyo, Kyōmei Kaku, 1938.

Kikuchi Teiji 菊地貞二. *Chōkyōrō mampitsu* 丁杏盧漫筆 (Essays from my Chōkyōrō villa). Hsinking, Shinkyō Nichinichi Shimbunsha, 1936.

Kimiya Yasuhiko 木宮泰彦. *Nikka bunka kōryūshi* 日華文化交流史 (History of Sino-Japanese cultural relations). Tokyo, Fuzambō, 1955.

Kimura, Motokazu. "Fiscal Policy and Industrialization in Japan, 1868–1895," *Annals of the Hitotsubashi Academy*, No. 6 (1955), pp. 12–28.

Kimura Yoshito 木村義人. "Manshū jihen to Ishiwara Kanji" 満州事変と石原莞爾 (The Manchurian Incident and Ishiwara Kanji). Unpublished doctoral dissertation, Tokyo University, 1962. (Deposited in Etō Shinkichi's office.)

Kin'yū Keizai Kenkyūjo 金融経済研究所. *Meiji zenki no ginkō seido* 明治前期の銀行制度 (The banking system in early Meiji). Tokyo, Tōyō Keizai Shimpō, 1965.

—— *Nihon no ginkō seido kakuritsu shi* 日本の銀行制度確立史 (History of the consolidation of the Japanese banking system). Tokyo, Tōyō Keizai Shimpō, 1966.

"Kishida Ginkō" 岸田吟香, in Shōwa Joshi Daigaku Kindai Bungaku Kenkyūshitsu 昭和女子大学近代文学研究室, ed., *Kindai bungaku kenkyū sōsho* 近代文学研究叢書 (Studies in modern literature), VIII, 217–63. Tokyo, Shōwa Joshi Daigaku Kōyōkai, 1958.

Kita Ikki 北一輝. *Shina kakumei gaishi* 支那革命外史 (An unofficial history of the Chinese revolution). Tokyo, Daitōkaku, 1921.

—— *Zōho Shina kakumei gaishi* 増補支那革命外史 (An unofficial history of the Chinese revolution, revised and enlarged). Tokyo, Utsumi Bunkōdō, 1937.

Kita Shina Kaihatsu Kabushiki Kaisha 北支那開発株式会社. *Kita Shina Kaihatsu Kabushiki Kaisha oyobi kankei kaisha gaiyō* 北支那開発株式会社及関係会社概要 (An outline of the North China Development Company and related companies). Peking, Kita Shina Kaihatsu Kabushiki Kaisha, 1940–44.

Kita Teikichi 喜多貞吉, ed. *Wada Toyoji den* 和田豊治伝 (Biography of Wada Toyoji). Tokyo, Wada Toyoji Den Hensansho, 1926.

Kitamura Hironao 北村敬直. "Kōtsū Ginkō shakkan no seiritsu jijō" 交通銀行借款の成立事情 (Circumstances leading to the supply of credit to the Communication Bank), *Shakai keizai shigaku*, XXVII, No. 3 (December 1961), 39–58.

Kitazaki Toyoji 北崎豊二. "Meijiki ni okeru matchi seizōgyō no hatten" 明治期におけるマッチ製造業の発展 (The development of match manufacturing in the Meiji period), *Hisutoria*, No. 26 (February 1960), pp. 18–33.

Kiyosawa Kiyoshi 清沢洌. *Gaiseika to shite no Ōkubo Toshimichi* 外政家としての大久保利通 (Ōkubo Toshimichi as a diplomat). Tokyo, Chūō Kōronsha, 1942.

—— *Nihon gaikōshi* 日本外交史 (Diplomatic history of Japan). 2 vols. Tokyo, Tōkyō Keizai Shimpōsha, 1942.

Knatchbull-Hugessen, Sir Hughe. *Diplomat in Peace and War*. London, John Murray, 1949.

Ko Hakushaku Yamamoto Kaigun Taishō Denki Hensankai 故伯爵山本海軍大将伝記編纂会, ed. *Hakushaku Yamamoto Gonnohyōe den* 伯爵山本権兵衛伝 (Biography of Count Yamamoto Gonnohyōe). 2 vols. Tokyo, Yamamoto Hakushaku Denki Hampukai, 1938.

Kobayashi Masaaki 小林正彬. "Kindai sangyō no keisei to kangyō haraisage" 近代産業の形成と官業拂下げ (The development of modern industry and the sale of government enterprises), in *Nihon keizaishi taikei* 日本経済史大系 (Japanese economic history series), V, 291–355. 6 vols. Tokyo, Tōkyō Daigaku Shuppankai, 1965.

Kobayashi Tatsuo 小林龍夫. "Kaigun gunshuku jōyaku, 1921–1926" 海軍軍縮条約 (一九二一年〜一九二六年) (Naval disarmament treaties, 1921–1926), in *Manshū jihen zen'ya* 満州事変前夜 (On the eve of the Manchurian Incident), pp. 7–15. Vol. I of Nihon Kokusai Seiji Gakkai Taiheiyō Sensō Gen'in Kenkyūbu, *Taiheiyō sensō e no michi*. Tokyo, Asahi Shimbunsha, 1963.

—— "Parī heiwa kaigi to Nihon no gaikō" パリー平和会議と日本の外交 (The Paris Peace Conference and Japanese diplomacy), in Ueda Toshio 植田捷雄, ed., *Kamikawa sensei kanreki kinen: kindai Nihon gaikōshi no kenkyū* 神川先生還暦記念—近代日本外交史の研究 (Commemorating the sixtieth birthday of Professor Kamikawa: Studies in modern Japanese diplomatic history), pp. 365–422. Tokyo, Yūhikaku, 1956.

Kobayashi Ushisaburō 小林丑三郎 and Kitasaki Susumu 北崎進. *Meiji Taishō zaiseishi*

明治大正財政史 (A fiscal history of the Meiji and Taishō periods). Tokyo, Ganshōdō, 1927.

Kobayashi Yoshimasa 小林良正. *Meiji ishin ni okeru shōkōgyō no shohenkaku* 明治維新における商工業の諸変革 (Changes in commerce and industry during the Meiji Restoration). Tokyo, Iwanami Shoten, 1932.

Kobayashi Yukio 小林幸男. "Nihon tai-So gaikō seisaku kateiron josetsu" 日本対ソ外交政策過程論序説 (Introduction to a discussion of the policy-making process in Japan's relations with the Soviet Union), *Kinki daigaku*, VIII, Nos. 3–4 (March 1960), 1–30.

—— "Nisso kokkō chōsei no ichi dammen: Gotō-Yoffe kōshō kaishi no keika" 日ソ国交調整の一断面—後藤ヨッフェ交渉開始の経過 (One aspect of the adjustment of Japanese-Soviet relations: Developments at the beginning of the Gotō-Joffe negotiations), *Kokusai seiji: gaikōshi kenkyū—Taishō jidai*, 1958, pp. 130–42.

—— "Nisso kokkō juritsu no ichi dammen" 日ソ国交樹立の一断面 (One aspect of the establishment of relations between Japan and the Soviet Union), *Rekishi kyōiku*, IX, No. 2 (February 1961), 25–31.

—— "Pekin kaigi to Pōtsumasu jōyaku: Nihon gaikō seisaku kettei katei ni kansuru shironteki oboegaki" 北京会議とポーツマス条約. 日本外交政策決定過程に関する試論的覚書 (The Peking conference and the Portsmouth Treaty: A memorandum on the process of Japanese foreign policy-making), *Kokusai seiji: Nihon gaikōshi kenkyū—Shōwa jidai*, 1959, pp. 14–25.

—— "Shiberia kanshō to Nikoraefusuku jiken" シベリア干渉とニコラエフスク事件 (The Siberian intervention and the Nikolaevsk incident), *Kinki daigaku hōgaku*, V, No. 3 (December 1956), 181–223; V, No. 4 (March 1957), 91–133; VI, No. 1 (July 1957), 93–134; VI, Nos. 2–3 (November 1957), 121–66; VI, No. 4 (March 1958), 105–34; VII, No. 1 (June 1958), 79–111.

—— "Sobietto Roshia no kyokutō tōitsu to gyogyō mondai" ソビエットロシアの極東統一と漁業問題 (The Soviet Union's consolidation of territory in the Far East and the dispute over fisheries), *Kinki daigaku hōgaku*, VII, Nos. 2–4 (February 1959), 85–153.

—— "Tai-So seisaku no suii to Mammō mondai" 対ソ政策の推移と満蒙問題 (The development of policy toward the Soviet Union and the Manchuria-Mongolia problem), in *Manshū jihen zen'ya* 満州事変前夜 (On the eve of the Manchurian Incident), pp. 161–284. Vol. I of Nihon Kokusai Seiji Gakkai Taiheiyō Sensō Gen'in Kenkyūbu, *Taiheiyō sensō e no michi*. Tokyo, Asahi Shimbunsha, 1963.

Kodama Yoshio 児玉誉士夫. *Akusei jūsei ransei: fūun yonjūnen no kiroku* 悪政銃声乱世—風雲四十年の記録 (Misrule, gunshots, perilous days: A record of forty years of troubled times). Tokyo, Kōbundō, 1961.

—— *Ware yaburetari* われ敗れたり (I am defeated). Tokyo, Kyōbunsha, 1949.

Kodan Bun'ichi 小段文一 and Yoshinobu Susumu 吉信肅. "Bōeki to shōhin keizai no hattatsu" 貿易と商品経済の発達 (Foreign trade and the development of a commodity economy), in Matsui Kiyoshi 松井清, ed., *Kindai Nihon bōekishi* 近代日本貿易史 (A history of modern Japan's foreign trade), I, 31–225. 3 vols. Tokyo, Yūhikaku, 1959–63.

Koiso Kuniaki Jijoden Kankōkai 小磯国昭自叙伝刊行会. *Katsuzan Kōsō* 葛山鴻爪 (pen name of Koiso Kuniaki). Tokyo, Chūō Kōron Jigyō, 1963.

Kojima, Kiyoshi. "Japanese Foreign Trade and Economic Growth," *Annals of the Hitotsubashi Academy*, No. 8 (1958), pp. 143–68.

Kojima Tsunehisa 小島恒久. "Meiji shoki no Miike Tankō—tankō kan'ei ni kansuru ichi kōsatsu" 明治初期の三池炭鉱―炭鉱官営に関する一考察 (The Miike Coal Mine in early Meiji—an inquiry into the government operation of coal mines), *Shakai kagaku ronshū*, No. 5 (March 1965), pp. 1–43.

Kokusai Bunka Shinkōkai 国際文化振興会 (Society for International Cultural Relations), ed. *Catalogue of Japanese Art in the Palace of Fine and Decorative Arts at the Golden Gate International Exposition, Treasure Island, San Francisco, California, 1939.* Tokyo, Kokusai Bunka Shinkōkai, 1939.

—— ed. *Nichi-Doku bunka kyōtei* 日独文化協定 (The Japanese-German cultural agreement). Tokyo, Kokusai Bunka Shinkōkai, 1939.

—— ed. *Nichi-I bunka kyōtei* 日伊文化協定 (The Japanese-Italian cultural agreement). Tokyo, Kokusai Bunka Shinkōkai, 1939.

—— *K.B.S. Quarterly.*

Kokusai Keizai Gakkai 国際経済学会. *Nihon bōeki no kōzō to tenkai* 日本貿易の構造と展開 (The structure and development of Japan's foreign trade). No. 10 of *Kokusai keizai* 国際経済 (International economics). Tokyo, Nihon Hyōronsha, 1958.

Komai Tokuzō 駒井徳三. *Dai Manshūkoku kensetsu roku* 大満州国建設録 (The establishment of Manchukuo). Tokyo, Chūō Kōronsha, 1933.

—— *Tairiku e no higan* 大陸への悲願 (My hopes for the mainland). Tokyo, Kōdansha, 1952.

Komatsu Midori 小松緑. *Meiji gaikō hiwa* 明治外交秘話 (Secret history of Meiji diplomacy). Tokyo, Chikuma Shobō, 1936.

Konoe Fumimaro 近衛文麿. *Heiwa e no doryoku* 平和への努力 (My struggle for peace). Tokyo, Nihon Dempō Tsūshinsha, 1946.

—— *Ushinawareshi seiji* 失はれし政治 (Politics that failed). Tokyo, Asahi Shimbunsha, 1946.

Kordt, Erich. *Wahn und Wirklichkeit.* Stuttgart, Union deutsche Verlagsgesellschaft, 1948.

Korostovetz, J.J. *Pre-War Diplomacy: The Russo-Japanese Problem, Treaty Signed at*

Portsmouth, U.S.A., 1905; Diary of J.J. Korostovetz. London, British Periodicals, 1920.

Kōtani Etsuo 甲谷悦雄. "Nisso chūritsu jōyaku ni tsuite no kokuhaku" 日ソ中立條約についての告白 (The truth concerning the Russo-Japanese neutrality pact). Unpublished pamphlet, 1956.

Koyama Ichirō 小山一郎. *Tōa senkaku Arao Sei* 東亜先覚荒尾精 (Arao Sei, pioneer activist of East Asia). Tokyo, Tōa Dōbunkai, 1938.

Koyūkai 滬友会, ed. *Tōa Dōbun Shoin Daigaku shi* 東亜同文書院大学史 (History of the East Asia Common Culture University). Tokyo, Koyūkai, 1955.

Krupinski, Kurt. *Russland und Japan, ihre Beziehungen bis zum Frieden von Portsmouth.* Berlin, Ost-Europa verlag, 1940.

Kudō Eiichi 工藤英一. "Taguchi Ukichi to kaiungyō hogo mondai" 田口卯吉と海運業保護問題 (Taguchi Ukichi and the problem of protection for the maritime transport industry), *Meiji gakuin ronsō*, No. 85 (October 1963), pp. 37–62.

Kudō Takeshige 工藤武重. *Konoe Atsumaro kō* 近衛篤麿公 (Prince Konoe Atsumaro). Tokyo, Dainichisha, 1938.

Kumagiri Nobuo 熊切信男. "Nichi-Bei kōshō" 日米交渉 (Japanese-American negotiations), in Nihon Gaikō Gakkai 日本外交学会, ed., *Taiheiyō sensō gen'in ron* 太平洋戦争原因論 (On the origins of the Pacific War), pp. 347–82. Tokyo, Shimbun Gekkansha, 1953.

Kume Kunitake 久米邦武, ed. *Tokumei zenken taishi Bei-Ō kairan jikki* 特命全権大使米欧回覧実記 (Authentic record of the embassy to the United States and Europe). 5 vols. Tokyo, Hakubunsha, 1878.

Kuo Ting-yee, comp., and James W. Morley, ed. *Sino-Japanese Relations, 1862–1927: A Checklist of the Chinese Foreign Ministry Archives.* New York, The East Asian Institute, Columbia University, 1965.

Kurihara Hirota 栗原広太, ed. *Hakushaku Itō Miyoji* 伯爵伊東巳代治 (Biography of Count Itō Miyoji). 2 vols. Tokyo, Shinteikai, 1938.

Kurihara Ken 栗原健. "Abe Gaimushō seimukyokuchō ansatsu jiken to tai-Chūgoku (Mammō) mondai" 阿部外務省政務局長暗殺事件と対中国「満蒙」問題 (The assassination of Abe, director of the Political Affairs Bureau of the Foreign Ministry, and the problem of China [Manchuria and Mongolia] policy), *Kokusaihō gaikō zasshi*, LV, No. 5 (November 1956), 50–76.

—— "Daiichiji dainiji Mammō dokuritsu undō" 第一次　第二次満蒙独立運動 (The first and second independence movements in Manchuria and Mongolia), *Kokusai seiji: Nihon gaikōshi kenkyū—Taishō jidai*, 1958, pp. 52–65.

—— "Hayashi Tadasu gaimudaijin no 'Tai-Shin seiryaku kanken' " 林董外務大臣の「対清政略管見」 (Foreign Minister Hayashi Tadasu's proposal concerning Japan's China policy), *Kokusai seiji: Nihon gaikōshi kenkyū—Meiji jidai*, 1957, pp. 195–203.

—— "Nichi-Ro sensō go ni okeru Manshū zengo sochi mondai no ippan" 日露戦爭後における満州善後措置問題の一斑 (An aspect of the issue of policy toward Manchuria after the Russo-Japanese War), *Kokusaihō gaikō zasshi*, LIX, No. 6 (March 1961), 1–25.

—— "Nikka jihen keika gaiyō" 日華事変経過概要 (A brief history of the China Incident), *Rekishi kyōiku*, VI, No. 4 (1958), 43–51; No. 5, 70–76; No. 6, 82–89.

—— *Tennō: Shōwashi oboegaki* 天皇—昭和史覚書 (The emperor: A note on the history of the Shōwa period). Tokyo, Yūshindō, 1955.

Kuroba Shigeru 黒羽茂. "Iwayuru Nunobiki Maru jiken ni tsuite" いわゆる布引丸事件について (Concerning the so-called Nunobiki Maru incident), *Shigaku zasshi*, LXXI, No. 9 (September 1962), 51–65.

—— *Sekaishijō yori mitaru Nichi-Ro sensō* 世界史上より見たる日露戦爭 (The Russo-Japanese War as seen from the standpoint of world history). Tokyo, Shibundō, 1960.

Kuroda Kiyotaka ikken shorui 黒田清隆一件書類 (Kuroda Kiyotaka papers). Manuscript collection at the Kensei Shiryō Shitsu, National Diet Library, Tokyo.

Kuroda Kōshirō 黒田甲子郎, ed. *Gensui Terauchi hakushaku den* 元帥寺内伯爵伝 (Biography of Count Marshal Terauchi Masatake). Tokyo, Gensui Terauchi Hakushaku Denki Hensanjo, 1920.

Kuroita Katsumi 黒板勝美, ed. *Fukuda taishō den* 福田大将伝 (Biography of General Fukuda Masatarō). Tokyo, Fukuda Taishō Den Kankōkai, 1937.

Kurusu Saburō 來栖三郎. *Hōmatsu no sanjūgonen* 泡沫の三十五年 (Vain endeavor). Tokyo, Bunka Shoin, 1948.

Kuzuu Yoshihisa 葛生能久, ed. *Tōa senkaku shishi kiden* 東亜先覚志士記伝 (Biographical sketches of pioneer patriots in East Asia). 3 vols. Tokyo, Kokuryūkai Shuppanbu, 1933–36. Reprinted in *Meiji hyakunenshi sōsho* 明治百年史叢書 (Historical materials of the century since the Meiji Restoration), Vols. XXII–XXIV. Tokyo, Hara Shobō, 1966.

Kyokutō Kokusai Gunji Saiban 極東国際軍事裁判 (International Military Tribunal for the Far East). *Kyokutō kokusai gunji saiban sokkiroku* 極東国際軍事裁判速記録 (Stenographic record of the International Military Tribunal for the Far East). Tokyo, Asahi Shimbunsha, 1946–48.

Kyokutō Kokusai Gunji Saiban Kōhan Kiroku Kankōkai 極東国際軍事裁判公判記録刊行会, ed. *Kyokutō kokusai gunji saiban kōhan kiroku* 極東国際軍事裁判公判記録 (Records of the International Military Tribunal for the Far East). 2 vols. Tokyo, Fuzambō, 1948.

La Fargue, Thomas E. *China and the World War*. Stanford, Stanford University Press, 1937.

Langer, William L. *The Diplomacy of Imperialism, 1890–1902*. 2d ed. New York, Knopf, 1951.

Langer, William L. and S. Everett Gleason. *The Challenge to Isolation*. New York, Harper, 1953.

—— *The Undeclared War, 1940–1941*. New York, Harper, 1953.

Lapradelle, Albert. *La documentation internationale: la paix de Versailles* (International documents: The Peace of Versailles). Paris, 1929.

Lensen, George A. "The Attempt on the Life of Nicholas in Japan," *The Russian Review*, XX, No. 3 (July 1961), 232–53.

—— "Japan and Tsarist Russia—the Changing Relationships, 1875–1917," *Jahrbücher für Geschichte osteuropas*, X (1962), 337–48.

—— *The Russian Push toward Japan: Russo-Japanese Relations, 1697–1875*. Princeton, Princeton University Press, 1959.

Levine, Isaac D., ed. *Letters from the Kaiser to the Czar*. New York, Frederick A. Stokes, 1920.

Libal, Michael. *Japans Weg in den Krieg: die Aussenpolitik der Kabinette Konoye, 1940–1941*. Dusseldorf, Droste Verlag, 1971.

Link, Arthur S. *Wilson: The Struggle for Neutrality, 1914–1915*. Princeton, Princeton University Press, 1960.

Lippmann, Walter. "The London Naval Conference: An American View," *Foreign Affairs*, VIII, No. 4 (July 1930), 499–518.

Liu, James T.C. "German Mediation in the Sino-Japanese War, 1937–38," *Far Eastern Quarterly*, VIII, No. 2 (February 1949), 157–71.

Lockwood, William W. *The Economic Development of Japan: Growth and Structural Change, 1868–1938*. Princeton, Princeton University Press, 1954.

—— ed. *The State and Economic Enterprise in Modern Japan*. Princeton, Princeton University Press, 1965.

Louis, Wm. Roger. *British Strategy in the Far East, 1919–1939*. London, Oxford University Press, 1971.

Lowe, Peter. *Great Britain and Japan, 1911–1915*. New York, St. Martin's Press, 1969.

Lu, David J. *From the Marco Polo Bridge to Pearl Harbor: Japan's Entry into World War II*. Washington D.C., Public Affairs Press, 1961.

Lupke, Hubertus. *Japans Russlandpolitik von 1939 bis 1941*. Frankfurt, A. Metzner Verlag, 1962.

McCormick, Thomas J. *China Market: America's Quest for Informal Empire, 1893–1901*. Chicago, Quadrangle Books, 1967.

McMaster, John. "Japanese Gold Rush of 1859," *Journal of Asian Studies*, XIX, No. 3 (1960), 273–87.

—— "The Takashima Mine: British Capital and Japanese Industrialization," *Business History Review*, XXXVII, No. 3 (Autumn 1963), 217–39.

McWilliams, Carey. *Prejudice—Japanese-Americans: Symbol of Racial Intolerance*. Boston, Little Brown, 1944.

Maeda Unosuke 前田卯之助. "Iwayuru shōken kaifukusen no ato o kaerimite" 所謂商権恢復戦の跡を顧みて (Reflections on the effects of the battle to restore commercial rights), *Kigyō to shakai*, No. 10 (1927), pp. 20–72.

Maejima Shōzō 前島省三. "Kanjō seihen: Hokushin jihen ni itaru Nihon 'teikoku' gaikō no ichi sokumen" 漢城政変—北清事変にいたる日本「帝国」外交の一側面 (The Han-ch'eng [Kyong-song] incident: A phase of imperial Japanese diplomatic policy at the time of the Boxer Rebellion), *Ritsumeikan hōgaku*, Nos. 29–30 (September 1959), pp. 226–29.

—— *Nihon fashizumu to gikai* 日本ファシズムと議会 (Japanese fascism and the Diet). Kyoto, Hōritsubunkasha, 1956.

—— "Nisshin Nichi-Ro sensō ni okeru tai-Kan seisaku" 日清日露戦争における対韓政策 (Policy toward Korea during the Sino-Japanese and Russo-Japanese wars), in *Kokusai seiji: Nihon gaikōshi kenkyū—Nisshin Nichi-Ro sensō*, 1961, pp. 71–86.

—— "Ro-Shin mitsuyaku to Katō gaikō" 露清密約と加藤外交 (The Russo-Chinese secret pact and Katō diplomacy), *Ritsumeikan hōgaku*, No. 34 (1960), pp. 239–81.

Majima Ken 馬島健. *Gumbatsu antō hishi* 軍閥暗闘秘史 (Secret history of factional feuds within the army). Tokyo, Kyōdō Shuppansha, 1946.

Malozemoff, Andrew. *Russian Far Eastern Policy, 1881–1904, with Special Emphasis on the Causes of the Russo-Japanese War*. Berkeley and Los Angeles, University of California Press, 1958.

Mamiya Kunio 間宮国夫. "Meiji shoki ni okeru chokuyushutsu kaisha no setsuritsu to tenkai" 明治初期における直輸出会社の設立と展開 (The establishment and development of direct export companies in early Meiji), *Shakai kagaku tōkyū*, IX, No. 2 (March 1964), 71–99.

—— "Meiji shonen ni okeru shōhōshi seisaku no tenkai" 明治初年における商法司政策の展開 (The development of commercial company policy in the early Meiji period), *Shakai kagaku tōkyū*, XI, No. 3 (January 1966), 83–117.

—— "Meiji zenki no kin'yūshi ni tsuite" 明治前期の金融史について (On monetary policy during early Meiji), in Shakai Keizai Shigakkai 社会経済史学会, ed., *Saikin jūnenkan ni okeru shakai keizai shigaku no hattatsu* 最近10年間における社会経済史学の発達 (Developments in the study of socio-economic history during the last ten years). Special issue of *Shakai keizai shigaku*, XXXI, Nos. 1–5 (February 1966), 137–48.

—— "Shōhōshi no soshiki to kinō" 商法司の組織と機能 (The structure and functioning of the Commerce Control Office), *Shakai keizai shigaku*, XXIX, No. 2 (December 1963), 30–50.

Manshikai 満史会, ed. *Manshū kaihatsu yonjūnenshi* 満州開発四十年史 (A forty-year history of the development of Manchuria). 2 vols. plus supplement. Tokyo, Manshū Kaihatsu Yonjūnenshi Kankōkai, 1964.

Mantetsu Sōsaishitsu Chihōbu Zammu Seiri Iinkai 満鉄総裁室地方部残務整理委員会,

ed. *Mantetsu fuzokuchi keiei enkaku zenshi* 満鉄附属地経営沿革全史 (A complete history of the management of the Japanese settlement attached to the South Manchuria Railway Company). 3 vols. Dairen, Minami Manshū Tetsudō Kabushiki Kaisha, 1939.

Maruyama Kunio 丸山国雄. *Nihon hoppō hatten shi* 日本北方発展史 (A history of Japanese expansion to the north). Tokyo, Suisansha, 1942.

—— *Shoki Nichi-Doku tsūkō shōshi* 初期日独通交小史 (A short history of early Japanese-German relations). Tokyo, Nichi-Doku Bunka Kyōkai, 1931.

Maruyama Masahiko 丸山正彦, ed. *Maruyama Sakura den* 丸山作楽伝 (Biography of Maruyama Sakura). Tokyo, Chūaisha, 1899.

Maruyama Masao 丸山眞男. "Nihon fashizumu no shisō to undō" 日本ファシズムの思想と運動 (The ideology and dynamics of Japanese fascism), in Maruyama, *Gendai seiji no shisō to kōdō* 現代政治の思想と行動 (Thought and behavior in contemporary politics), pp. 28–87. Tokyo, Miraisha, 1965. English translation in Masao Maruyama, *Thought and Behaviour in Modern Japanese Politics*, pp. 25–83. Edited by Ivan Morris. New York, Oxford University Press, 1963.

Masubuchi Tatsuo 増淵龍夫. "Nihon no kindai shigakushi ni okeru Chūgoku to Nihon, II" 日本の近代史学史における中国と日本 II (China and Japan in modern Japanese historiography, Part 2), *Shisō*, No. 468 (June 1963), pp. 97–110.

Matsuda Tomoo 松田智雄. *Igirisu shihon to tōyō* イギリス資本と東洋 (English capital and the Far East). Tokyo, Nihon Hyōronsha, 1950.

Matsui Kiyoshi 松井清. "Hōhōron to dankai kubun" 方法論と段階區分 (Methodology and periodization), in Matsui, *Kindai Nihon bōekishi* 近代日本貿易史 (A history of modern Japan's foreign trade), I, 3–30. 3 vols. Tokyo, Yūhikaku, 1959–63.

—— *Nihon bōekiron* 日本貿易論 (A treatise on Japan's foreign trade). Tokyo, Yūhikaku, 1950.

—— "Sangyō shihonshugi to gaikoku bōeki" 産業資本主義と外国貿易 (Industrial capitalism and foreign trade), *Keizai ronsō*, LXV, No. 6 (June 1950), pp. 1–47.

Matsumoto Tadao 松本忠雄. *Kinsei Nihon gaikōshi kenkyū* 近世日本外交史研究 (A diplomatic history of modern Japan). Tokyo, Hakukōdō, 1942.

—— *Nisshi shin kōshō ni yoru teikoku no riken* 日支新交渉に依る帝国の利権 (The rights and interests of Japan, with reference to the recent Sino-Japanese negotiations). Tokyo, Shimizu Shoten, 1915.

—— *Taishō yonen Nisshi kōshōroku* 大正四年日支交渉録 (A record of Sino-Japanese relations in 1915). Tokyo, Shimizu Shoten, 1921.

Matsumura Kenzō 松村謙三, ed. *Nagai Ryūtarō* 永井柳太郎. Tokyo, Keisō Shobō, 1959.

Matsunaga Yasuzaemon 松永安左衛門. *Shina gakan* 支那我観 (My view of China). Tokyo, Jitsugyō no Sekaisha, 1919.

Matsunari Yoshie 松成義衛, Miwa Teizō 三輪悌三, and Chō Yukio 長幸男. *Nihon ni okeru ginkō no hattatsu* 日本における銀行の発達 (The development of banking in Japan). Tokyo, Aoki Shoten, 1959.

Matsuo Jumei 松尾樹明. *Sangoku dōmei to Nichi-Bei sen* 三国同盟と日米戦 (The Tripartite Pact and the Japanese-American war). Tokyo, Kasumigaseki Shobō, 1940.

Matsuoka Yōsuke 松岡洋右. *Mantetsu o kataru* 満鉄を語る (An account of the South Manchuria Railway Company). Tokyo, Daiichi Shuppansha, 1937.

—— *Tōa zenkyoku no dōyō* 東亜全局の動揺 (Disturbances throughout East Asia). Tokyo, Senshinsha, 1931.

—— *Ugoku Mammō* 動く満蒙 (Changing Manchuria and Mongolia). Tokyo, Senshinsha, 1931.

Matsushita Yoshio 松下芳男. *Meiji gunsei shiron* 明治軍制史論 (History of the Meiji military system). 2 vols. Tokyo, Yūhikaku, 1956.

Matsuyoshi Sadao 松好貞夫. "Hompō seika seisaku no henkō to jisseki" 本邦正貨政策の変更と実績 (The results achieved by changes in Japan's specie policy), *Keizaishi kenkyū*, XIX, No. 4 (April 1938), 440–56.

—— *Meiji ishin go ni okeru ryōgaeshō kin'yū* 明治維新後に於ける両替商金融 (Money exchangers and finance after the Meiji Restoration). Tokyo, Kinyū Kenkyūkai, 1937.

Matsuzaka Heisaburō 松坂兵三郎. "Nihon keizai no seichō to bōeki kōzō no suii" 日本経済の成長と貿易構造の推移 (Economic growth and changes in the foreign trade structure of Japan), *Seijō daigaku keizai kenkyū*, VIII, No. 9 (September 1958), 295–326. Reprinted in Okada Shumpei 岡田俊平, ed., *Meiji shoki no zaisei kin'yū seisaku* 明治初期の財政金融政策 (Financial and fiscal policy in early Meiji), pp. 302–34. Tokyo, Seimeikai, 1964.

Maxon, Yale C. *Control of Japanese Foreign Policy: A Study of Civil-Military Rivalry, 1930–1945*. Berkeley, University of California Press, 1957.

Mayo, Marlene J. "The Iwakura Embassy and the Unequal Treaties." Unpublished doctoral dissertation, Columbia University, 1961.

—— "The Iwakura Mission to the United States and Europe, 1871–1873," *Researches in the Social Sciences on Japan*, II, 28–47. New York, East Asian Institute, Columbia University, 1959.

—— "Rationality in the Restoration," in Bernard Silberman and Harry D. Harootunian, eds., *Modern Japanese Leadership*, pp. 323–69. Tucson, University of Arizona Press, 1966.

Medlicott, W. Norton. *The Economic Blockade*. 2 vols. London, H. M. Stationery Office, 1952 and 1959.

Meiji Shiryō Kenkyū Renrakkai 明治史料研究連絡会, ed. *Kindai sangyō no seisei* 近代産業の生成 (The development of modern industry). Vol. II of *Meijishi kenkyū sōsho* 明治史研究叢書 (Studies in Meiji history), Second Series. Tokyo, Ochanomizu Shobō, 1960.

Meiji Zaiseishi Hensankai 明治財政史編纂会, ed. *Meiji zaiseishi* 明治財政史 (A fiscal history of the Meiji period). 15 vols. Tokyo, Maruzen, 1904-5.

Meissner, Kurt. *Deutsche in Japan, 1639-1939, dreihundert Jahre Arbeit für Wirtsland und Vaterland.* Stuttgart and Berlin, Deutsche Verlags-anstalt, 1940.

Meskill, Johanna Menzel. *Hitler and Japan: The Hollow Alliance.* New York, Atherton Press, 1966.

Mibe Seiichirō 三辺清一郎. "Meiji shoki ni okeru waga kuni menka seisan no chōraku" 明治初期に於ける我国綿花生産の凋落 (The decline of Japanese cotton production in early Meiji), in Keiō Gijuku Keizaishi Gakkai 慶応義塾経済史学会, ed., *Meiji shoki keizaishi kenkyū* 明治初期経済史研究 (Studies in the economic history of early Meiji), II, 79-125. 2 vols. Tokyo, Ganshōdō, 1937.

Michida Toshishichi 満田俊七. "Waga kuni bōeki kin'yū no kigen" 我国貿易金融の起源 (The beginning of the financing of Japan's foreign trade), *Tōyō keizai shimpō*, No. 1954 (1941), pp. 36-38.

Mikami Akiyoshi 三上昭美. "Gaimushō setchi no keii" 外務省設置の経緯 (The establishment of the Foreign Ministry), *Kokusai seiji: Nihon gaikōshi kenkyū— Nihon gaikōshi no shomondai*, 1963, pp. 1-21.

Miller, David Hunter. *My Diary at the Conference of Paris.* 21 vols. New York, printed for the author by the Appeal Printing Company, 1924.

Minami Kashū Nikkeijin Shōgyō Kaigisho 南加州日系人商業会議所, ed. *Minami Kashū Nihonjin shichijūnenshi* 南加州日本人七十年史 (A seventy-year history of the Japanese in southern California). Los Angeles, Minami Kashū Nikkeijin Shōgyō Kaigisho, 1960.

Minami Manshū Tetsudō 南満州鉄道 and Mantetsu Sangyōbu 満鉄産業部, eds. *Mantetsu chōsa kikan yōran* 満鉄調査機関要覧 (Handbook of the research organs of the South Manchuria Railway Company). Dairen, Mantetsu Sangyōbu, 1936.

Minami Manshū Tetsudō Kabushiki Kaisha 南満州鉄道株式会社, ed. *Minami Manshū Tetsudō Kabushiki Kaisha dainiji jūnenshi* 南満州鉄道株式会社第二次十年史 (A history of the second decade of the South Manchuria Railway Company). Dairen, Minami Manshū Tetsudō Kabushiki Kaisha, 1928.

—— ed. *Minami Manshū Tetsudō Kabushiki Kaisha jūnenshi* 南満州鉄道株式会社十年史 (A ten-year history of the South Manchuria Railway Company). Dairen, Minami Manshū Tetsudō Kabushiki Kaisha, 1919.

—— ed. *Minami Manshū Tetsudō Kabushiki Kaisha nijūnen ryakushi* 南満州鉄道株式会社二十年略史 (A short twenty-year history of the South Manchuria Railway Company). Dairen, Minami Manshū Tetsudō Kabushiki Kaisha, 1927.

—— ed. *Minami Manshū Tetsudō Kabushiki Kaisha sanjūnen ryakushi* 南満州鉄道株式会社三十年略史 (A short thirty-year history of the South Manchuria Railway Company). Dairen, Minami Manshū Tetsudō Kabushiki Kaisha, 1937.

Minami Tokuko 南とく子. "Nisshin sensō to Chōsen bōeki" 日清戰爭と朝鮮貿易 (The Sino-Japanese War and Korean trade), *Rekishigaku kenkyū*, No. 149 (January 1951), pp. 43–45.

Minobe Tatsukichi 美濃部達吉. "Rikugunshō happyō no kokubōron o yomu" 陸軍省発表の国防論を読む (On reading the essay on national defense issued by the Army Ministry), *Chūō kōron*, November 1934, pp. 125–32. Reprinted in *Chūō kōron*, November 1959, pp. 328–35.

Mitani Katsumi 三谷克巳. *Kokusai shūshi to Nihon no seichō* 国際収支と日本の成長 (The balance of payments and Japan's economic growth). Tokyo, Heibonsha, 1957.

Mitani Taichirō 三谷太一郎. " 'Tenkanki' (1918–1921) no gaikō shidō" 「転換期」 (1918–1921) の外交指導 (1918–1921: A 'turning point' in diplomatic leadership), in Shinohara and Mitani, *Kindai Nihon no seijishidō*, pp. 293–374.

Mitarai Tatsuo 御手洗辰雄, ed. *Minami Jirō* 南次郎. Tokyo, Minami Jirō Denki Kankōkai, 1957.

Mitsui Bussan gojūnenshi 三井物産五十年史 (A fifty-year history of Mitsui Bussan). Tokyo, by the editor, 1935.

Mitsui Ginkō gojūnenshi 三井銀行五十年史 (A fifty-year history of the Mitsui Bank). Tokyo, by the editor, 1926.

Mitsui Ginkō Hachijūnenshi Hensan Iinkai 三井銀行八十年史編纂委員会. *Mitsui Ginkō hachijūnenshi* 三井銀行八十年史 (An eighty-year history of the Mitsui Bank). Tokyo, by the editor, 1957.

Mitsuoka Takeo 三岡丈夫. *Yuri Kimimasa den* 由利公正伝 (Biography of Yuri Kimimasa). Tokyo, Yūkōkan, 1916.

Miura Hiroyuki 三浦周行. *Meiji ishin to gendai Shina* 明治維新と現代支那 (The Meiji Restoration and contemporary China). Tokyo, Tōkō Shoin, 1931.

—— "Meiji jidai ni okeru Ryūkyū shozoku mondai" 明治時代における琉球所属問題 (Problems of sovereignty over the Ryukyu islands in the Meiji era), *Shigaku zasshi*, XVII, No. 7 (July 1931), 1–14; No. 12 (December 1931), 1–35.

Miwa Kimitada 三輪公忠. *Matsuoka Yōsuke* 松岡洋右. Tokyo, Chūō Kōronsha, 1971.

Miwa Ryōichi 三和良一. "1880 nendai no shihonka dantai—Tōkyō Shōkōkai no setsuritsu to sono katsudō" 1880年代の資本家団体—東京商工会の設立とその活動, (A capitalist organization in the 1880s—the establishment and activities of the Tokyo Chamber of Commerce and Industry), *Aoyama keizai ronshū*, XVI, No. 1 (July 1964), 51–89.

Miyamoto Gennosuke 宮本源之助, ed. *Meiji un'yushi* 明治運輸史 (History of transportation in the Meiji era). Tokyo, Un'yu Nippōsha, 1913.

Miyamoto Mataji 宮本又次. "Meijiki ni okeru bōeki shōsha no seiritsu katei to bōeki shihon no sangyō ikusei (keiei shiteki kōsatsu)" 明治期における貿易商社の成立過程と貿易資本の産業育成（経営史的考察）(The process of establishing foreign trade companies in the Meiji period and the nurturing of industry by foreign trade capital—an inquiry into management history), *Ōsaka daigaku keizaigaku*, XII, Nos. 3–4 (March 1963), 166–207.

—— "Meiji shoki no kawase to Ono Gumi" 明治初期の為替と小野組 (The Ono Combine and foreign exchange in early Meiji), *Bankingu*, No. 218 (May 1966), pp. 49–64; No. 219 (June 1966), pp. 65–83; No. 220 (July 1966), pp. 49–57; No. 221 (August 1966), pp. 68–85.

Miyazaki Tōten (Torazō) 宮崎滔天 (寅藏). *Sanjūsannen no yume* 三十三年の夢 (The thirty-three-year dream). Tokyo, Kokkō Shobō, 1902.

Mizunuma Tomoichi 水沼知一. "Meiji zenki ni okeru Yokohama Shōkin Ginkō no gaikoku kawase kin'yū" 明治前期における横浜正金銀行の外国為替金融 (Foreign exchange financing by the Yokohama Specie Bank in early Meiji), *Tochi seido shigaku*, No. 15 (1963), pp. 17–36.

—— "Meiji zenki Takashima Tankō ni okeru gaishi to sono haijo katei no tokushitsu" 明治前期高島炭鉱における外資とその排除過程の特質 (The elimination of foreign capital from the Takashima Coal Mine in early Meiji), *Rekishigaku kenkyū*, No. 273 (February 1963), pp. 28–37.

Mori Kahē 森嘉兵衛 and Itabashi Gen 板橋源. *Kindai tetsusangyō no seiritsu—Kamaishi Seitetsujo zenshi* 近代鉄産業の成立―釜石製鉄所前史 (The establishment of the modern iron industry—the early history of the Kamaishi Ironworks). Tokyo, Fujiseitetsu, 1957.

Mori Taikichirō. "Raw Silk Trade with the United States and Our Country's Silk-Reeling Industry," in Ohara, *Japanese Trade and Industry in the Meiji-Taisho Era*, pp. 203–98.

Mori Yoshizō 森芳三. "Meiji nijūkyūnen Nisshin tsūshō jōyaku to shihon yushutsu" 明治二十九年日清通商条約と資本輸出 (The Sino-Japanese commercial treaty of 1894 and the export of Japanese capital to China), *Yamagata daigaku kiyō (shakai kagaku)*, I, No. 3 (December 1961), 1–36.

Morishima Morito 森島守人. *Imbō ansatsu guntō: gaikōkan no kaisō* 陰謀暗殺軍刀―外交官の回想 (Intrigue, assassination, and swords: Reminiscences of a diplomat). Tokyo, Iwanami Shoten, 1950.

—— *Shinjuwan Risubon Tōkyō: zoku ichi gaikōkan no kaisō*. 眞珠湾リスボン東京―続一外交官の回想 (Pearl Harbor, Lisbon, Tokyo: Reminiscences of a diplomat, continued). Tokyo, Iwanami Shoten, 1950.

Morison, Elting E. *Turmoil and Tradition: A Study of the Life and Times of Henry L. Stimson*. Boston, Houghton Mifflin, 1960.

Moriya Hidesuke 森谷秀亮. *Jōyaku kaisei* 條約改正 (Treaty revision). Vol. IX of *Iwanami kōza Nihon rekishi* 岩波講座日本歴史 (Iwanami lectures on Japanese history). Tokyo, Iwanami Shoten, 1934.

Morley, James W. *The Japanese Thrust into Siberia, 1918.* New York, Columbia University Press, 1957; reprinted Freeport, N.Y., Books for Libraries, 1972.

—— "Review of R. J. C. Butow, *Tojo and the Coming of the War,*" *Political Science Quarterly,* LXXXVII, No. 1 (March 1962), 95–97.

Morris, Ivan I. *Nationalism and the Right Wing in Japan: A Study of Post-War Trends.* New York, Oxford University Press, 1960.

Morton, Louis. "Historia Mentem Armet: Lessons of the Past," *World Politics,* XII, No. 2 (January 1960), 155–64.

—— *Strategy and Command: The First Two Years.* Vol. X of *United States Army in World War II: The War in the Pacific.* Washington D.C., Office of the Chief of Military History, Department of the Army, 1962.

Morton, William F. "Sainan jihen, 1928–1929" 済南事変 1928-29 (The Tsinan Incident, 1928–1929), in *Kokusai seiji: Nihon gaikōshi kenkyū—Nitchū kankei no tenkai,* 1960, pp. 103–18.

Motoki Mitsuyuki 元木光之. *Naigaimen Kabushiki Kaisha gojūnenshi* 内外綿株式会社五十年史 (A fifty-year history of the Naigaimen Company). Osaka, Naigaimen Kabushiki Kaisha, 1937.

Mukōyama Hiroo 向山寛夫. "Nihon tōchika ni okeru Taiwan minzoku undō shi" 日本統治下における台湾民族運動史 (A history of the Taiwan people's movement under Japanese rule). Unpublished manuscript, March 1961.

Munakata Kingo 宗像金吾, ed. *Tōa no senkakusha Sanshū Nezu sensei narabi ni fujin* 東亜の先覚者山洲根津先生並夫人 (Pioneer activists of East Asia, Mr. Nezu [pen name, Sanshū] and his wife). Published privately by Munakata, 1943.

Murashima Shigeru 村島滋. "Nichi-Ei dōmei to Man-Sen mondai" 日英同盟と満鮮問題 (The Anglo-Japanese alliance and the Manchuria-Korea problem), in Shinobu and Nakayama, *Nichi-Ro sensō shi no kenkyū,* pp. 114–41.

Mushakōji Kinhide 武者小路公秀. "From Fear of Dependence to Fear of Independence," *Japan Annual of International Affairs,* No. 3 (1964), pp. 68–86.

——"Nihonjin no taigai ishiki: apurōchi settei no tame no nōto" 日本人の対外意識—アプローチ設定のためのノート (Japanese attitudes toward foreign countries: A note to determine approaches to the problem), *Shisō,* No. 444 (June 1961), pp. 86–102.

Mutsu Hirokichi 陸奥広吉, ed. *Hakushaku Mutsu Munemitsu ikō* 伯爵陸奥宗光遺稿 (Posthumous works of Count Mutsu Munemitsu). Tokyo, Iwanami Shoten, 1929.

Mutsu Munemitsu 陸奥宗光. *Kenkenroku* 蹇蹇録 (Memoirs of a devoted subject). Tokyo, Iwanami Shoten, 1939.

Mutsu Munemitsu Papers 陸奥宗光文書. Kensei Shiryō Shitsu, National Diet Library, Tokyo. (See Chap. 10, "Recent Works.")

Nagai Hideo 永井秀夫. "Shokusan kōgyō seisakuron" 殖産興業政策論 (Views on the encouragement of production policy), *Hokkaidō daigaku bungakubu kiyō*, No. 10 (November 1961), pp. 131–58.

Nagai Michio 永井道雄. "Nihon o tazuneru shōgai no tabi: Tsunoda Ryūsaku" 日本をたずねる生涯の旅角田柳作 (Tsunoda Ryūsaku's search for Japan), in Nagai, *Ishoku no ningenzō* 異色の人間像 (Outstanding personalities). Tokyo, Kōdansha, 1965.

Nagaoka Shinjirō 長岡新次郎. "Ōshū taisen sanka mondai" 欧州大戦参加問題 (The issue of entering World War I), *Kokusai seiji: Nihon gaikōshi kenkyū—Taishō jidai*, 1958, pp. 26–38.

—— "Yamagata Aritomo no Rokoku haken to Nichi-Ro kyōtei" 山県有明の露国派遣と日露協定 (Yamagata Aritomo as envoy to Russia and the Russo-Japanese agreement), *Nihon rekishi*, No. 59 (April 1953), pp. 16–19.

Nagata Masaomi 永田正臣. *Keizai dantai hattenshi* 経済団体発展史 (History of the development of economic organizations). Tokyo, Kotōshoten, 1956.

—— "Meiji seifu no kanshō seisaku to shōhō kaigisho" 明治政府の勧商政策と商法会議所 (The Meiji government's policy of encouraging commerce and the chambers of commerce), *Komazawa daigaku kenkyū ronshū*, No. 4 (October 1963), pp. 111–29.

—— "Shokusan kōgyō seisaku to shōkō kaigisho" 殖産興業政策と商法会議所 (The encouragement of production policy and the chambers of commerce and industry), *Shakai keizaishi kenkyūjo kenkyū kiyō*, No. 1 (October 1963), pp. 37–77.

Naitō Chishū 内藤智秀. "Meiji jidai ni okeru Nihon no keizaiteki haikei" 明治時代における日本の経済的背景 (The economic background of Japan in the Meiji period), *Seishin joshi daigaku ronsō*, No. 18 (March 1962), pp. 17–24.

Naitō Juntarō 内藤順太郎. *Seiden En Seigai* 正伝袁世凱 (Biography of Yuan Shih-k'ai). Tokyo, Hakubunkan, 1913.

Naitō Tamiji 内藤民治. *Tsutsumi Seiroku no shōgai* 堤清六の生涯 (Biography of Tsutsumi Seiroku). Hakodate, Nichi-Ro Gyogyō nai Shokōkai, 1937.

Nakai Seizō 中井省三. *Nihon ni okeru bōeki shisō no hensen to sono rekishiteki haikei* 日本における貿易思想の変遷とその歴史的背景 (The historical background of changes in Japanese thought on foreign trade). Tokyo, Seki Shoin, 1957.

Nakajima Kōzaburō 中島幸三郎. *Fūunji Sogō Shinji den* 風雲児十河信二伝 (Biography of Sogō Shinji). Tokyo, Kōtsū Kyōdō Shuppansha, 1955.

Nakajima Tetsuzō 中島鉄藏. "Kaisō roku" 回想録 (Reminiscences). Unpublished, 1940. On deposit at National Defense Agency, Military History Office, Archives.

Nakamura Kikuo 中村菊男. *Kindai Nihon no hōteki keisei: jōyaku kaisei to hōten hensan* 近代日本の法的形成—条約改正と法典編纂 (Development of law in modern Japan: Treaty revision and codification of laws). Tokyo, Yūshindō, 1956.

—— "Nikka jihen no gen'in to hatten no yurai" 日華事変の原因と発展の由来 (The cause of the China Incident), *Hōgaku kenkyū*, XXX, No. 1 (January 1960), 1–12.

—— "Rokōkyō jiken no boppatsu to hatten" 蘆溝橋事件の勃発と発展 (The outbreak and development of the Marco Polo Bridge Incident), *Hōgaku kenkyū*, XXX, No. 2 (February 1960), 201–21.

—— *Shōwa seijishi* 昭和政治史 (Political history of the Shōwa period). Tokyo, Keiō Tsūshin, 1958.

Nakamura Kyūshirō 中村久四郎. *Gendai Nihon ni okeru Shinagaku kenkyū no jitsujō* 現代日本に於ける支那学研究の実状 (The present state of Chinese studies in modern Japan). Tokyo, Gaimushō Bunka Jigyōbu, 1928.

Nakamura Naomi 中村尚美. "Meiji jūyonen no seihen" 明治十四年の政変 (The political change of 1881), *Rekishi kyōiku*, XIII, No. 2 (February 1965), 17–24.

—— "Meiji shoki no keizai seisaku—tsūshō kawase ryōkaisha no yakuwari" 明治初期の経済政策--通商為替両会社の役割 (Economic policy in early Meiji —the role of the foreign trade companies and the exchange companies), *Shigaku zasshi*, LXVIII, No. 1 (January 1959), 38–58.

—— "Meiji zenki ni okeru zeiken kaifuku undō" 明治初期における税権回復運動 (The movement for tariff autonomy in early Meiji), *Shakai kagaku tōkyū*, XII, No. 1 (August 1966), 31–70.

—— "Ōkuma's Financial Policy and the Political Change of the 14th Year of Meiji," *Waseda Bulletin of Social Sciences*, 1962, pp. 49–58.

—— "Ōkuma zaisei tenkaiki no shokusan kōgyō seisaku" 大隈財政展開期の殖産興業政策 (The encouragement of production policy during the shift in Ōkuma's fiscal policy), *Shakai kagaku tōkyū*, IX, No. 1 (March 1964), 95–141.

—— "Ōkuma zaisei to jūyonen seihen" 大隈財政と十四年政変 (Ōkuma's fiscal policy and the political change of 1881), *Shakai kagaku tōkyū*, VII, No. 3—VIII, No. 1 (1962), 201–75.

—— "Ōkuma zaisei to kaiun—Mitsubishi no seiritsu" 大隈財政と海運－三菱の成立 (Ōkuma's fiscal policy and maritime transportation—the establishment of Mitsubishi), *Waseda daigakushi kiyō*, I, No. 1 (June 1965), 83–118.

—— "Seinansen go no infurēshon to sono taisaku" 西南戦後のインフレーションとその対策 (The post-Satsuma Rebellion inflation and the measures adopted to deal with it), *Shakai kagaku tōkyū*, VI, No. 1 (June 1961), 145–72.

—— "Yuri zaisei no taijō" 由利財政の退場 (The end of Yuri's fiscal policy), *Nihon rekishi*, No. 204 (May 1965), pp. 2–11.

Nakamura Takafusa 中村隆英. "Go-sanjū jiken to zaikabō" 五・三十事件と在華紡 (The May 30 Incident and the Japanese cotton industry in China), in Kindai Chūgoku Kenkyū Iinkai 近代中国研究委員会, ed., *Kindai Chūgoku kenkyū* 近代中国研究 (Studies on contemporary China), No. 6, pp. 99–169. Tokyo, Tōkyō Daigaku Shuppankai, 1964.

Nakamura Zentarō 中村善太郎. *Chishima Karafuto shinryaku shi* 千島樺太侵略史 (History of aggression in the Kuril Islands and Sakhalin). 2d ed. Osaka, Sōgensha, 1943.

Nakatsuka Akira 中塚明. "Nisshin sensō" 日清戦爭 (The Sino-Japanese War), in *Iwanami kōza Nihon rekishi kindai* 岩波講座日本歴史近代 (Iwanami lectures on modern Japanese history), IV, 119–65. Tokyo, Iwanami Shoten, 1962.

—— "Nisshin sensō to Chōsen mondai" 日清戦爭と朝鮮問題 (The Sino-Japanese War and the Korean question), *Nihonshi kenkyū*, No. 66 (May 1963), pp. 34–51.

Nakatsumi Tomokata 中津海知方. *Yokimbu hishi* 預金部秘史 (A secret history of the Deposit Division of the Finance Ministry). Tokyo, Tōyō Keizai Shimpōsha Shuppanbu, 1928.

Nakayama Jiichi 中山治一. "Hokushin jihen go ni okeru Chōsen mondai to Manshū mondai no setsugō" 北清事変後における朝鮮問題と満州問題の接合 (The connection between the Manchurian and Korean problems following the Boxer Rebellion), in Shinobu and Nakayama, *Nichi-Ro sensōshi no kenkyū*, pp. 90–113.

—— *Nichi-Ro sensō igo: Higashi Ajia o meguru teikokushugi no kokusai kankei* 日露戦爭以後東アジアをめぐる帝国主義の国際関係 (After the Russo-Japanese War: The East Asian view of the international relations of imperialism). Tokyo, Sōgensha, 1957.

—— "Saionji shushō no Manshū ryokō ni tsuite: Nichi-Ro sen go no Manshū mondai, sono ni" 西園寺首相の満州旅行について—日露戦後の満州問題そのニ (A trip to Manchuria by Prime Minister Saionji: The Manchurian problem after the Russo-Japanese War, Part 2), *Jimbun kenkyū*, XIII, No. 7 (August 1962), 12–25.

Nakayama Masao 中山正男. *Ichi gunkokushugisha no chokugen* 一軍国主義者の直言 (Candid opinions of a militarist). Tokyo, Masu Shobō, 1956.

Narochnitzkii, A.L. *Kolonial'naia politika kapitalisticheskikh derzhav na Dal'nem Vostoke, 1860–1895* (Colonial politics of the capitalist powers in the Far East, 1860–1895). Moscow, Izdatel'stvo Akademii Nauk SSSR, 1956.

Nashimoto Yūhei 梨本祐平. *Chūgoku no naka no Nihonjin* 中国の中の日本人 (Japanese in China). 2 vols. Tokyo, Heibonsha, 1958.

Natsume Sōseki 夏目漱石. *Botchan* 坊ちゃん. Tokyo, Iwanami Shoten, 1942. First published, 1907.

—— *Man-Kan tokoro-dokoro* 満韓ところどころ (Impressions of Manchuria and Korea). Tokyo, Shun'yōdō, 1910.

Nawa Tōichi 名和統一. *Nihon bōsekigyō no shiteki bunseki* 日本紡績業の史的分析 (Historical analysis of the spinning industry in Japan). Tokyo, Chōryūsha, 1948. Originally published as Nawa, *Nihon bōsekigyō to gemmen mondai kenkyū* 日本紡績業と原綿問題研究 (Studies of the Japanese spinning industry and its raw cotton problem). Osaka, Daidōshoin, 1937.

Nawata Eijirō 縄田栄次郎. "Fukoku kyōhei" 富国強兵 (Rich country, strong army), *Ronsō*, No. 11 (1955), pp. 1–21.

Neu, Charles. *An Uncertain Friendship: Theodore Roosevelt and Japan, 1906–1909.* Cambridge, Mass., Harvard University Press, 1967.

Nichi-Bei Shūkō Tsūshō Hyakunen Kinen Gyōji Un'eikai 日米修好通商百年記念行事運営会, ed. *Man'en gannen kem-Bei shisetsu shiryō shūsei* 万延元年遣米使節史料集成 (Historical materials on the 1860 mission to the United States). 7 vols. Tokyo, Kazama Shobō, 1960–61.

Nihon Gakujutsu Kaigi Daiichibu 日本学術会議第一部, ed. *Bunkakei bunken mokuroku 14: Nihon kindaishi—denki hen* 文化系文献目録14—日本近代史伝記編 (Bibliography of works in the social sciences and humanities, No. 14: Modern Japanese history —biographies and autobiographies). Tokyo, Nihon Gakujutsu Kaigi, 1963.

Nihon Ginkō Chōsa Kyoku 日本銀行調査局. *Nihon kin'yūshi shiryō: Meiji Taishō* 日本金融史資料明治大正 (Materials for a financial history of Japan: The Meiji and Taishō periods). 25 vols. Tokyo, Ōkurashō Insatsu Kyoku, 1954–61.

Nihon Jimbun Gakkai 日本人文学会, ed. *Shakaiteki kinchō no kenkyū* 社会的緊張の研究 (Studies of social tensions). Tokyo, Yūhikaku, 1953.

Nihon Kanzei Kyōkai 日本関税協会, ed. *Nihon no kanzei* 日本の関税 (Japan's tariff). Tokyo, by the editor, 1959.

Nihon Kokusai Seiji Gakkai 日本国際政治学会, ed. *Kokusai seiji: Nihon gaikōshi kenkyū —Meiji jidai* 国際政治日本外交史研究明治時代 (International relations: Studies in the diplomatic history of Japan—the Meiji era). Tokyo, Yūhikaku, 1957.

—— ed. *Kokusai seiji: Nihon gaikōshi kenkyū—Nisshin Nichi-Ro sensō* 国際政治日本外交史研究日清日露戦争 (International relations: Studies in the diplomatic history of Japan—the Sino-Japanese and Russo-Japanese wars). Tokyo, Yūhikaku, 1962.

—— ed. *Kokusai seiji: Nihon gaikōshi kenkyū—Shōwa jidai* 国際政治日本外交史研究昭和時代 (International relations: Studies in the diplomatic history of Japan—the Shōwa era). Tokyo, Yūhikaku, 1960.

Nihon Kokusai Seiji Gakkai Taiheiyō Sensō Gen'in Kenkyūbu 日本国際政治学会太平洋戦争原因研究部, ed. *Taiheiyō sensō e no michi* 太平洋戦争への道 (The road to the Pacific War). 7 vols., 1 supplementary vol. of documents. Tokyo, Asahi Shimbunsha, 1962–63. A major portion of this work is being translated under the general editorship of James William Morley and will be published in 5 vols. by Columbia University Press as *Japan's Road to the Pacific War*.

Nihon rekishi daijiten 日本歴史大辞典 (Encyclopedia of Japanese history). 20 vols., 2 supplementary vols. Tokyo, Kawade Shobō Shinsha, 1956–60.

Nihon Zaisei Keizai Kenkyūjo 日本財政経済研究所, ed. *Nihon kin'yū zaiseishi* 日本金融財政史 (A fiscal and financial history of Japan). Tokyo, by the editor, 1957.

Ningen Kankei Sōgō Kenkyūdan 人間関係総合研究団, ed. *Nihonjin: bunka to pāso-nariti no jisshōteki kenkyū* 日本人文化とパーソナリティの実証的研究 (The Japanese:

Studies of personality and culture). Nagoya, Reimei Shobō, 1962.

Nish, I.H. *Alliance in Decline, 1908–1923*. London, Athlone Press, 1972.

—— "Japan and the Ending of the Anglo-Japanese Alliance," in K. Bourne and D.C. Watt, eds., *Studies in International History*, pp. 369–84. London, Longmans 1967.

—— "Japan's Indecision during the Boxer Disturbances," *Journal of Asian Studies*, XX, No. 4 (August 1961), 449–61.

—— *The Anglo-Japanese Alliance: The Diplomacy of Two Island Empires, 1894–1907*. London, Athlone Press, 1966.

Nishihara Kamezō 西原亀三. *Yume no shichijūyonen: Nishihara Kamezō jiden* 夢の七十余年—西原亀三自伝 (A dream of over seventy years: The autobiography of Nishihara Kamezō). Edited by Murashima Nagisa 村島渚. Kyoto, Kumohara-mura Amata-gun, 1949.

Niwa Kunio 丹羽邦男. *Meiji ishin no tochi henkaku* 明治維新の土地変革 (Land reform during the Meiji restoration). Tokyo, Ochanomizu Shobō, 1962.

Noguchi Yonejirō 野口米次郎. *Chū-Nichi Jitsugyō Kabushiki Kaisha sanjūnenshi* 中日実業株式会社三十年史 (A thirty-year history of the Sino-Japanese Business Company). Tokyo, Chū-Nichi Jitsugyō Kabushiki Kaisha, 1943.

Nomura Kichisaburō 野村吉三郎. *Beikoku ni shishite: Nichi-Bei kōshō no kaiko* 米国に使して—日米交渉の回顧 (Ambassador to the United States: Reminiscences of the Japanese-American negotiations). Tokyo, Iwanami Shoten, 1946.

Nomura Kōichi 野村浩一. "Kokuminteki shimeikan no shoruikei to sono tokushitsu" 国民的使命観の諸類型とその特質 (Various patterns in Japanese concepts of the national mission), in *Kindai Nihon shisōshi kōza I: rekishiteki gaikan* 近代日本思想史講座 I—歴史的概観 (Lectures on the history of modern Japanese thought, I: Historical outline), pp. 137–73. Tokyo, Chikuma Shobō, 1961.

—— "Manshū jihen chokuzen no Tōsanshō mondai" 満州事変直前の東三省問題 (The problem of the Three Eastern Provinces just before the Manchurian Incident,) *Kokusai seiji: Nihon gaikōshi kenkyū—Nitchū kankei no tenkai*, 1960, pp. 71–86.

—— "Son Bun no minzokushugi to tairiku rōnin: sekaishugi minzokushugi dai-Ajiashugi no kanren ni tsuite" 孫文の民族主義と大陸浪人—世界主義民族主義大アジア主義の関連について (Sun Yat-sen's nationalism and the China activists: The relationships among nationalism, pan-Asianism, and cosmopolitanism), *Shisō*, No. 396 (June 1957), pp. 11–26.

Norman, E.H. "The Genyōsha: A Study in the Origins of Japanese Imperialism," *Pacific Affairs*, XVII (September 1944), 261–84.

Nozawa Yutaka 野沢豊, ed. "Nihon ni okeru Son Bun kankei bunken mokuroku" 日本における孫文関係文献目録 (A bibliography of works published in Japan about Sun Yat-sen), *Shisō*, No. 396 (June 1957), pp. 79–93.

—— "Shingai kakumei to Taishō seihen" 辛亥革命と大正政変 (The 1911 revolution and the political struggle in Japan in 1913), in Tōkyō Kyōiku Daigaku Ajiashi Kenkyūkai Chūgoku Kindaishi Bukai 東京教育大学アジア史研究会中国近代史部会, ed., *Chūgoku kindaika no shakai kōzō: shingai kakumei no shiteki chii* 中国代近化の社会構造—辛亥革命の史的地位 (The social structure and modernization in China: The historical position of the 1911 revolution), *Kyōiku shoseki Tōyō shigaku ronshū*, August 1960, pp. 173–223.

Numata Ichirō 沼田市郎. *Nichi-Ro gaikōshi* 日露外交史 (A history of Russo-Japanese diplomatic relations). Tokyo, Ōsakayagō Shoten, 1943.

Obata Yūkichi Denki Kankōkai 小幡酉吉伝記刊行会, ed. *Obata Yūkichi* 小幡酉吉. Tokyo, Obata Yūkichi Denki Kankōkai, 1957.

Ōdachi Shigeo denki 大達茂雄伝記 (Biography of Ōdachi Shigeo). 2 vols. Tokyo, Ōdachi Shigeo Denki Kankōkai, 1956.

Ōe Shinobu 大江志乃夫. "Chūō shūken kokka no seiritsu" 中央集権国家の成立 (The establishment of the centralized state), in *Iwanami kōza Nihon rekishi kindai* 岩波講座日本歴史近代 (Iwanami lectures on modern Japanese history), II, 53–96. Tokyo, Iwanami Shoten, 1962.

—— "Jōyaku kaisei hōshin no keizaiteki haikei" 條約改正方針の経済的背景 (The economic background of treaty revision policy), in Shōshikai Sanjisshūnen Kinen Rombunshū 昭史会三十周年記念論文集, *Nihon rekishi ronkyū* 日本歴史論究 (Discussions on Japanese history), I, 511–25. 2 vols. Tokyo, Ninomiya Shoten, 1963.

—— *Meiji kokka no seiritsu* 明治国家の成立 (The establishment of the Meiji state). Tokyo, Minerubā, 1959.

—— "Nihon shihonshugi no seiritsu katei—toku ni 1880 nendai o megutte" 日本資本主義の成立過程—特に1880年代をめぐって (The establishment of Japanese capitalism—especially during the 1880s), *Rekishigaku kenkyū*, Supplement, November 1961, pp. 28–38.

—— "Nihon shihonshugi no seiritsushi o meguru watashi no hansei" 日本資本主義の成立史をめぐるわたしの反省 (Second thoughts on the history of the establishment of Japanese capitalism), *Rekishigaku kenkyū*, No. 250 (February 1961), pp. 39–46.

—— "Ōkubo seikenka no shokusan kōgyō seisaku seiritsu no seiji katei" 大久保政権下の殖産興業政策成立の政治過程 (The political background of Ōkubo's encouragement of production policy), in Inada Masaji 稲田正次, ed., *Meiji kokka keisei katei no kenkyū* 明治国家形成過程の研究 (Studies in the formation of the Meiji state), pp. 375–427. Tokyo, Ochanomizu Shobō, 1966.

—— "Ōkubo seiken to Nihon shihonshugi" 大久保政権と日本資本主義 (The Ōkubo government and Japanese capitalism), *Nihonshi kenkyū*, No. 87 (November 1966), pp. 41–64.

Office of the Chief of Military History, Japanese Research Division, United States

Army Forces, Far East, and the Eighth United States Army. *Far East History Source File: "Important National Policy Decisions."*

Official Report of the Japan British Exhibition, 1910, at the Great White City, Shepherd's Bush, London. London, Unwin, 1911.

Ogata Hiroyasu 尾形裕康. *Seiyō kyōiku i'nyū no hōto* 西洋教育移入の方途 (Ways of introducing Western education). Tokyo, Kōdansha, 1961.

Ogata, Sadako N. *Defiance in Manchuria: The Making of Japanese Foreign Policy, 1931–1932.* Berkeley, University of California Press, 1964.

Ogata Taketora 緒方竹虎. *Ichi gunjin no shōgai: kaisō no Yonai Mitsumasa* 一軍人の生涯―回想の米内光政 (The life of a soldier: Reminiscences of Yonai Mitsumasa). Tokyo, Bungei Shunjū Shinsha, 1955.

Ogiso Teruyuki 小木曾照行. "Pōtsumasu kōwa kaigi" ポーツマス講和会議 (The Portsmouth Peace Conference), in Shinobu and Nakayama, *Nichi-Ro sensōshi no kenkyū*, pp. 377–417.

Ogiso Teruyuki, Sakurai Toshiteru 櫻井敏照, Fujimura Michio 藤村道生, and Yoshii Hiroshi 義井博. "Nisshin Nichi-Ro sensō kenkyūshi" 日清日露戦争研究史 (A history of studies on the Sino-Japanese and Russo-Japanese wars), *Kokusai seiji: Nihon gaikōshi kenkyū—Nisshin Nichi-Ro sensō*, 1961, pp. 151–69.

Ohara Keishi. "General Outline: A Historical Survey of Economic Relations between Japan and the United States," in Ohara, *Japanese Trade and Industry in the Meiji-Taisho Era.* pp. 1–52.

—— ed. *Japanese Trade and Industry in the Meiji-Taisho Era.* Translated and adapted by Ōkata Tamotsu. Centenary Cultural Council Series: A History of Japanese-American Cultural Relations, 1853–1926. Tokyo, Ōbunsha, 1957.

Ōhashi Chūichi 大橋忠一. *Taiheiyō sensō yuraiki* 太平洋戦争由来記 (Origins of the Pacific War). Tokyo, Kaname Shobō, 1952.

Ōhata Tokushirō 大畑篤四郎. "Nichi-Doku bōkyō kyōtei dō kyōka mondai (1935–1939)" 日独防共協定同強化問題 (一九三五年～一九三九年) (The Japanese-German Anti-Comintern Pact and the problem of strengthening it), in *Sangoku dōmei: Nisso chūritsu jōyaku* 三国同盟日ソ中立条約 (The Tripartite Pact: The Japanese-Soviet neutrality treaty), pp. 1–156. Vol. V of Nihon Kokusai Seiji Gakkai Taiheiyō Sensō Gen'in Kenkyūbu, *Taiheiyō sensō e no michi.* Tokyo, Asahi Shimbunsha, 1963.

—— "Nichi-Doku-I sangoku dōmei" 日独伊三国同盟 (The Tripartite Pact among Japan, Germany, and Italy), *Kokusai seiji: Nihon gaikōshi kenkyū—Shōwa jidai*, 1959, pp. 85–98.

—— "Nichi-Ro kaisen gaikō" 日露開戦外交 (Diplomatic negotiations prior to the Russo-Japanese War), *Kokusai seiji: Nihon gaikōshi kenkyū—Nisshin Nichi-Ro sensō*, 1961, pp. 102–18.

—— "Nichi-Ro sensō to Man-Kan mondai" 日露戦争と満韓問題 (The Russo-

Japanese War and the problem of Korea and Manchuria), *Kindai Nihonshi kenkyū*, No. 5 (April 1958), pp. 1–9; No. 6 (September 1958), pp. 9–16.

—— "Nihon no Washinton kaigi sanka" 日本のワシントン会議参加 (Japan's participation in the Washington Conference), *Waseda hōgakkaishi: hōritsu hen*, X (July 1960), 21–48.

—— "Washinton kaigi kaisai to Nichi-Bei kankei" ワシントン会議開催と日米関係 (Japanese-American relations at the opening of the Washington Conference), *Kokusai seiji: Nihon gaikōshi kenkyū–Nichi-Bei kankei no tenkai*, 1961, pp. 91–106.

—— "Washinton kaigi Nihon seifu kunrei ni tsuite no kōsatsu: gumbi seigen mondai ippan narabi ni rikugun gumbi seigen mondai" ワシントン会議日本政府訓令についての考察―軍備制限問題一般ならびに陸軍軍備制限問題 (A study of the Japanese government's instructions for the Washington Conference: The problem of general arms limitations and of limits on military armaments), in Hanabusa Nagamichi Hakushi Kanreki Kinen Rombunshū Henshū Iinkai 英修道博士還暦記念論文集編集委員会, ed., *Hanabusa Nagamichi hakushi kanreki kinen rombunshū: gaikōshi oyobi kokusai seiji no shomondai* 英修道博士還暦記念論文集―外交史及び国際政治の諸問題 (Essays commemorating the sixtieth birthday of Dr. Hanabusa Nagamichi: Studies in diplomatic history and international politics), pp. 257–74. Tokyo, Keiō Tsūshin, 1952.

Ohsawa, J.G. *Two Great Indians in Japan: Rashbehari Bose and Subhas Chandra Bose*. Calcutta, K.C. Das, 1954.

Ōishi Kaichirō 大石嘉一郎. "Ishin seiken to Ōkuma zaisei―Ōe Shinobu shi no shinsetsu o chūshin to shite" 維新政権と大隈財政―大江志乃夫氏の新説を中心として (The Restoration regime and Ōkuma's fiscal policy―the new theory of Ōe Shinobu), *Rekishigaku kenkyū*, No. 240 (April 1960), pp. 25–31.

—— "Matsukata zaisei to jiyū minkenka no zaiseiron" 松方財政と自由民権家の財政論 (Matsukata's fiscal policy and the fiscal theory of the popular rights advocates), *Shōgaku ronshū*, XXX, No. 2 (January 1962), 380–442.

—— "Ōkuma zaisei to Matsukata zaisei" 大隈財政と松方財政 (Ōkuma's fiscal policy and Matsukata's fiscal policy), *Rekishigaku kenkyū*, Supplement, November 1961, pp. 62–67.

Oka Yoshitake 岡義武. "Meiji shonen no Ezochi to Igirisu" 明治初年の蝦夷地と英吉利 (Ezo and Great Britain in the early Meiji era), *Kokka gakkai zasshi* 国家学会雑誌, LVII, No. 6 (1943), 1–37.

—— "Nisshin sensō to tōji ni okeru taigai ishiki" 日清戦争と当時における対外意識 (The Sino-Japanese War and Japanese attitudes toward foreign countries), *Kokka gakkai zasshi*, LXVIII, Nos. 3–4 (October–December 1954), 1–29; Nos. 5–6 (January–March 1955), 1–32.

—— *Yamagata Aritomo: Meiji Nihon no shōchō* 山県有朋―明治日本の象徴 (Yamagata Aritomo: Symbol of Meiji Japan). Tokyo, Iwanami Shoten, 1958.

Okada Keisuke 岡田啓介. *Okada Keisuke kaikoroku* 岡田啓介回顧錄 (Reminiscences of Okada Keisuke). Tokyo, Mainichi Shimbunsha, 1950.

Okada Shumpei 岡田俊平. *Bakumatsu ishin no kahei seisaku* 幕末維新の貨幣政策 (Currency policy in the late Tokugawa and Restoration periods). Tokyo, Moriyama Shoten, 1955.

—— "Dajōkansatsu kachi antei hōan ni tsuite" 太政官札価値安定法案について (The plan to stabilize the value of government bills), *Seijō daigaku keizai kenkyū*, No. 17 (March 1963), pp. 17–40. Reprinted in Okada, ed., *Meiji shoki no zaisei kin'yū seisaku* 明治初期の財政金融政策 (Financial and fiscal policy in early Meiji), pp. 66–91. Tokyo, Seimeikai, 1964.

—— "Dajōkansatsu no ryūtsū jōkyō" 大政官札の流通状況, in Okada, ed., *Meiji shoki no zaisei kin'yū seisaku* 明治初期の財政金融政策 (Financial and fiscal policy in early Meiji). Tokyo, Seimeikai, 1964.

—— "Kinsatsu kachi ronsō ni tsuite" 金札価値論爭について (The debate over the value of the gold bill), *Seijō daigaku keizai kenkyū*, No. 13 (December 1960), pp. 85–110.

—— "Meijiki ni okeru bōeki kin'yū" 明治期における貿易金融 (Foreign trade finance in the Meiji period), *Kin'yū keizai*, No. 57 (August 1959), pp. 19–37.

—— "Meiji shoki heisei kaikaku ni okeru Ōkuma kō no kōken" 明治初期幣制改革における大隈侯の貢献 (The contribution of Marquis Ōkuma to monetary reform in early Meiji), *Ōkuma kenkyū*, No. 4 (March 1954), pp. 1–26.

—— "Meiji shoki ni okeru fukuhon'isei no seiritsu" 明治初期における複本位制の成立 (The establishment of a bimetallic standard in early Meiji), *Seijō daigaku keizai kenkyū*, No. 20 (October 1964), pp. 29–54.

—— "Meiji shoki ni okeru nigawase kin'yū" 明治初期における荷爲替金融 (Documentary bill finance in early Meiji), *Seijō daigaku keizai kenkyū*, Nos. 8–9 (September 1958), pp. 207–35.

—— "Meiji shoki no tsūka kyōkyū seisaku" 明治初期の通貨供給政策 (Currency supply policy in early Meiji), in Okada, ed., *Meiji shoki no zaisei kin'yū seisaku* 明治初期の財政金融政策 (Financial and fiscal policy in early Meiji), pp. 3–143. Tokyo, Seimeikai, 1964.

—— "Meiji shoki no yōgin taian" 明治初期の洋銀対案 (Mexican dollar counterproposals in early Meiji), *Keizai to bōeki*, LIV, No. 5 (1952), 1–21.

—— *Meiji zenki no seika seisaku* 明治前期の正貨政策 (Specie policy in early Meiji). Tokyo, Tōyō Keizai Shimpōsha, 1958.

—— "Nihon bōekigin" 日本貿易銀 (Japan's foreign trade silver yen), *Seijō daigaku keizai kenkyū*, No. 5 (February 1956), pp. 100–28.

—— "Nihon engin no kaigai ryūtsūsaku—Honkon o chūshin to shite" 日本円銀の海外流通策—香港を中心として (The policy of circulating the Japanese silver yen abroad—with focus on Hong Kong), *Seijō daigaku keizai kenkyū*, No. 6 (September 1956), pp. 101–28.

—— *Nihon shihonshugi sōseiki ni okeru kin'yū seisaku* 日本資本主義創生期における金融政策 (Financial policy in the formative period of Japanese capitalism). Tokyo, Seijō Daigaku Keizai Gakkai, 1960.

—— "Ōkuma Shigenobu no kokusai shūshi kinkōron" 大隈重信の国際収支均衡論 (Ōkuma's theory of balancing the international accounts), *Seijō daigaku keizai kenkyū*, No. 21 (March 1965), pp. 29–41; No. 22 (October 1965), pp. 23–39; No. 23 (March 1966), pp. 19–36.

—— "Ōkuma Shigenobu no zaisei keizai seisaku no kichō" 大隈重信の財政経済政策の基調 (The basis of Ōkuma Shigenobu's fiscal and economic policies), *Waseda daigakushi kiyō*, I, No. 1 (June 1965), 65–81.

—— "Shōhōshi ni yoru dajōkansatsu kashitsuke hōshiki" 商法司による太政官札貸付方式 (The method of advancing government bill loans through the Commerce Control Office), *Seijō daigaku keizai kenkyū*, No. 16 (October 1962), pp. 1–30.

—— "Shōhōshi Tsūshōshi ni yoru tsūka kyōkyū seisaku" 商法司・通商司による通貨供給政策 (The policy of supplying currency through the Commerce Control Office and the Trade Control Office), *Seijō daigaku keizai kenkyū*, No. 18 (November 1963), pp. 73–94. Reprinted in Okada, ed., *Meiji shoki no zaisei kin'yū seisaku* 明治初期の財政金融政策 (Financial and fiscal policy in early Meiji), pp. 3–20. Tokyo, Seimeikai, 1964.

—— "'Shōken kaifuku' to Rengō Kiito Niazukarijo" 「商権恢復」と聯合生糸荷預所 (The "restoration of commercial rights" and the Federated Raw Silk Warehouse), *Seijō daigaku keizai kenkyū*, No. 12 (May 1960), pp. 133–52.

—— "Waga kuni ni okeru daiikki kinhon'isei jidai no tsūka mondai" 我国における第一期金本位制時代の通貨問題 (The currency problem during Japan's first period on the gold standard), *Seijō daigaku keizai kenkyū*, No. 19 (March 1964), pp. 23–44.

Okada Taishō Kiroku Hensankai 岡田大將記録編纂会, ed. *Okada Keisuke* 岡田啓介. Tokyo, Okada Taishō Kiroku Hensankai, 1956.

Okada Takeo 岡田丈夫. *Konoe Fumimaro: tennō to gumbu to kokumin* 近衛文麿―天皇と軍部と国民 (Konoe Fumimaro: The emperor, the military, and the people). Tokyo, Shunjūsha, 1959.

—— "Nitchū sensō ni tsuite" 日中戦争について (On the Sino-Japanese War), *Rekishi hyōron*, No. 134 (October 1961), pp. 8–17; No. 135 (November 1961), pp. 21–27.

Okahashi Tamotsu 岡橋保. "Matsukata zaisei kin'yū seisaku no rekishiteki igi" 松方財政金融政策の歴史的意義 (The historical significance of Matsukata's fiscal and financial policy), *Keizaigaku kenkyū*, XXXI, No. 1 (April 1965), 1–35.

Okakura, Kakuzō. *The Hō-ōden [Phoenix Hall]: An Illustrated Description of the Buildings Erected by the Japanese Government at the World's Columbian Exposition, Jackson Park, Chicago.* Tokyo, K. Ogawa, 1893.

Okamoto Kansuke 岡本監輔. *Kita Ezo shinshi* 北蝦夷新誌 (A new account of Japan's northern territory). Tokyo, Hokumonsha, 1866.

Okamoto Ryūnosuke 岡本柳之助, ed. *Nichi-Ro kōshō Hokkaidō shikō* 日露交渉北海道史稿 (History of Russo-Japanese negotiations about Hokkaido). Tokyo, Mujin Fūgetsu Shooku, 1898.

Okamoto, Shumpei. *The Japanese Oligarchy and the Russo-Japanese War.* New York, Columbia University Press, 1970.

Okano Masujirō 岡野増次郎, ed. *Go Haifu* 呉佩孚 (Wu P'ei-fu). Yamanashi-ken Minamitsuru-gun Mizuho-mura, Banseikaku, 1939.

Oki Shūji 沖修二. *Ningen Yamashita Tomoyuki* 人間山下奉文 (Biography of Yamashita Tomoyuki). Tokyo, Nihonshūhōsha, 1959.

Ōkubo Toshimichi bunsho 大久保利通文書 (Papers of Ōkubo Toshimichi). Edited by Hayakawa Junzaburō 早川純三郎. 3 vols. Tokyo, Nihon Shiseki Kyōkai, 1927-29.

Okudaira Takehiko 奥平武彦. *Chōsen kaikoku kōshō shimatsu* 朝鮮開国交渉始末 (Diplomatic negotiations concerning the opening of Korea). Tokyo, Tōkō Shoin, 1935.

Ōkuma Kō Hachijūgonenshi Hensankai 大隈侯八十五年史編纂会, ed. *Ōkuma kō hachijūgonenshi* 大隈侯八十五年史 (The life of Ōkuma Shigenobu). 3 vols. Tokyo, Ōkuma Kō Hachijūgonenshi Hensankai, 1926.

Ōkuma Shigenobu kankei bunsho 大隈重信関係文書 (Documents concerning Ōkuma Shigenobu). 6 vols. Tokyo, Nihon Shiseki Kyōkai, 1932-35.

Ōkuma Shigenobu Papers 大隈重信文書. Shakai Kagaku Kenkyūjo, Waseda University.

Ong Yok-tek 王育徳. *Taiwan: Kumon suru sono rekishi* 台湾—苦悶するその歴史 (Taiwan: A history of agony). Tokyo, Kubundō, 1964; rev. ed. 1970.

Ōnishi Rihei 大西理平, ed. *Asabuki Eiji kun den* 朝吹英二君伝 (Biography of Asabuki Eiji). Tokyo, 1928.

Ono Giichi. *War and Armament Expenditures of Japan.* New York, Oxford University Press, 1922.

Ono Kazuichirō 小野一一郎. "Kindaiteki kahei seido no seiritsu to sono seikaku" 近代的貨幣制度の成立とその性格 (The establishment and character of the modern currency system), in Matsui Kiyoshi 松井清, ed., *Kindai Nihon bōekishi* 近代日本貿易史 (A history of modern Japan's foreign trade), I, 297-346. 3 vols. Tokyo, Yūhikaku, 1959-63.

—— "Nihon ni okeru Mekishiko doru no ryūnyū to sono kōzai" 日本におけるメキシコドルの流入とその功罪 (The good and bad aspects of the influx of Mexican dollars into Japan), *Keizai ronsō*, LXXXI, No. 3 (March 1958), 1-17; No. 4 (April 1958), 38-52; No. 5 (May 1958), 24-37; No. 6 (June 1958), 37-55.

Ono Kazuichirō and Namba Heitarō 難波平太郎. "Nihon tekkōgyō no seiritsu to genryō mondai" 日本鉄鋼業の成立と原料問題 (The establishment of the Japanese iron and steel industry and the raw materials problem), *Keizai ronsō*, LXXIII, No. 4 (April 1954), 38–51.

Ono Sanenobu 尾野実信, ed. *Gensui kōshaku Ōyama Iwao* 元帥公爵大山巌 (Biography of Prince Marshal Ōyama Iwao). Tokyo, Ōyama Gensui Den Kankōkai, 1935.

—— ed. *Gensui kōshaku Ōyama Iwao nempu* 元帥公爵大山巌年譜 (Chronology of the life of Prince Marshal Ōyama Iwao). Tokyo, Ōyama Gensui Den Kankōkai, 1935.

Ono Tokujirō 小野得二郎. *Dōjinkai sanjūnenshi* 同仁会三十年史 (A thirty-year history of the Universal Benevolence Association). Tokyo, Dōjinkai, 1932.

Ono Zentarō 小野善太郎. *Ishin no gōshō—Ono Gumi shimatsu* 維新の豪商―小野組始末 (A merchant prince of the Restoration period—the Ono Combine), with explanatory introduction by Miyamoto Mataji. Tokyo, Seiabō, 1966.

Onoe Kazuo 尾上一雄. "Kaikō to Nichi-Bei bōeki kankei no hottan" 開港と日米貿易関係の発端 (The opening of the ports and the beginning of Japanese-American trade relations), *Seijō daigaku keizai kenkyū*, No. 11 (December 1959), pp. 46–73.

Ōoka Hazama 大岡破挫魔, ed. *Kita Matazō kun den* 喜多又藏君伝 (Biography of Kita Matazō). Osaka, Nihon Menka Kabushiki Kaisha, 1933.

Oriental Economist. *The Foreign Trade of Japan*. Tokyo, Oriental Economist, 1935.

Osatake Takeshi 尾佐竹猛. "Yuri zaisei ni tsuite" 由利財政について (Yuri's fiscal policy), *Shakai keizai shigaku*, XIII, Nos. 11–12 (March 1943), 18–38.

Ōshima Hideji 大島英二. "Meiji shoki no zaisei" 明治初期の財政 (Fiscal policy in early Meiji), in Keiō Gijuku Keizaishi Gakkai 慶応義塾経済史学会, ed., *Meiji shoki keizaishi kenkyū* 明治初期経済史研究 (Studies in the economic history of early Meiji), I, 263–304. 2 vols. Tokyo, Ganshōdō, 1937.

Ostwald, Paul. *Deutschland und Japan: Eine Freundschaft zweier Völker*. Berlin, Junker und Dünnhaupt, 1941.

Ōta Saburō 太田三郎. *Nichi-Ro Karafuto gaikōsen* 日露樺太外交戦 (The Japanese-Russian diplomatic dispute over Sakhalin). Tokyo, Kōbunsha, 1941.

Ōtaka Shōjirō 大鷹正次郎. *Dainiji taisen sekinin ron* 第二次大戦責任論 (The debate over responsibility for World War II). Tokyo, Jiji Tsūshinsha, 1959.

—— *Kishū ka bōryaku ka: Shinjuwan no sekinin* 奇襲か謀略か―真珠湾の責任 (Surprise attack or plot: Responsibility for Pearl Harbor). Tokyo, Jiji Tsūshinsha, 1954.

Ōtomo Kisaku 大友喜作, ed. *Hokumon sōsho* 北門叢書 (Collected works on the northern territories). 6 vols. Tokyo, Hokkō Shobō, 1943.

Ōtsu Jun'ichirō 大津淳一郎. *Dai Nihon kenseishi* 大日本憲政史 (Constitutional history of Japan). 10 vols. Tokyo, Hōbunkan, 1927–28.

Ott, David J. "The Financial Development of Japan, 1878–1958," *Journal of Political Economy*, No. 69 (1961), pp. 122–41.

Ōuchi Hyōe 大内兵衛. *Nihon zaiseiron: kōsaihen* 日本財政論―公債篇 (Treatise on Japanese fiscal policy: The national debt). Vol. XXII of *Keizaigaku zenshū* 経済学全集 (Complete collection on economics). Tokyo, Kaizōsha, 1932.

—— "Yuri Kimimasa" 由利公正, *Sekai*, No. 109 (January 1955), pp. 103–16.

Ōuchi Hyōe and Tsuchiya Takao 土屋喬雄, eds. *Meiji zenki zaisei keizai shiryō shūsei* 明治前期財政経済史料集成 (Historical materials on the finance and economy of early Meiji Japan). 21 vols. Tokyo, Kaizōsha, 1931–36.

Ōuchi Tsutomu 大内力. *Nihon keizairon* 日本経済論 (Treatise on the Japanese economy). Vols. VII-VIII of *Keizaigaku taikei* 経済学大系 (Outline of economics). Tokyo, Tōkyō Daigaku Shuppankai, 1962–63.

Ōura Toshihiro 大浦敏弘. "Kyokutō-Roshia ni taisuru Bei-Nichi kanshō to sono hatan ni tsuite no ichi kōsatsu" 極東ロシアに対する米日干渉とその破綻についての一考察 (A study of the American-Japanese intervention in Far Eastern Russia and the failure of the expedition), *Handai hōgaku*, No. 12 (November 1954), pp. 1–25; No. 15 (August 1955), pp. 23–59.

The Outlook. January 1870–April 1932. Merged with *The Independent* as *The Outlook and The Independent*, October 1928–February 1932.

Ōyama Azusa 大山梓. "Iwakura kaisei sōan to Terajima kaisei sōan" 岩倉改正草案と寺島改正草案 (Drafts on treaty revision by Iwakura Tomomi and Terajima Munemori), in *Kokusai seiji: Nihon gaikōshi kenkyū—Meiji jidai*, Fall Special Issue, October 1957, pp. 51–66.

—— "Meiji shoki no hoppō ryōdo mondai" 明治初期の北方領土問題 (The problem of the northern frontier at the beginning of the Meiji era), *Kokusaihō gaikō zasshi*, LX, Nos. 4–6 (1962), 39–67.

—— "Yamagata Aritomo ikensho" 山県有朋意見書 (Collected memoranda by Yamagata Aritomo), *Kokusai Seiji: Nihon gaikōshi kenkyū—Meiji jidai*, 1957, pp. 183–95.

—— "Yamagata Aritomo teikoku kokubō hōshin an" 山県有朋帝国国防方針案 (Yamagata Aritomo's plan for national defense), *Kokusai seiji: Nihon gaikōshi kenkyū—Nisshin Nichi-Ro sensō*, 1961, pp. 170–77.

O-yatoi gaikokujin ichiran 御雇外国人一覧 (Summary of foreigners employed by the government). Tokyo, Chūgaidō, 1872. Reprinted in Yoshino Sakuzō, *Gaikoku bunkahen*, pp. 347–62.

Ozaki Hotsumi 尾崎秀実. "Tōa kyōdōtai no rinen to sono seiritsu no kyakkanteki kiso" 東亜協同体の理念とその成立の客観的基礎 (Idea of an East Asia cooperative community and the objective basis for its establishment). Written in 1939. Reprinted in *Chūō kōron*, Supplement, November 1954, pp. 400–10.

Panama Taiheiyō Bankoku Daihakurankai パナマ太平洋万国大博覧会, *The Panama Pacific International Exposition* (in English and Japanese). San Francisco, The New World, 1912.

Parlett, Harold. "In Piam Memoriam," in Charles Eliot, *Japanese Buddhism*, pp. 7–34. London, Routledge and Kegan Paul, 1959.

Patrick, Hugh. "External Equilibrium and Internal Convertibility: Financial Policy in Meiji Japan," *Journal of Economic History*, XXV, No. 2 (June 1965), 187–213.

—— "Japan, 1868–1914," in Rondo Cameron, ed., *Banking in the Early Stages of Industrialization: A Study in Comparative Economic History*, pp. 239–89. New York, Oxford University Press, 1967.

Pooley, A.M. *Japan's Foreign Policies*. London, Allen and Unwin, 1920.

—— ed. *The Secret Memoirs of Count Tadasu Hayashi*. New York and London, Putnam, 1915.

Pratt, John T. *War and Politics in China*. London, Jonathan Cape, 1943.

Pratt, Julius W. *A History of United States Foreign Policy*. Englewood Cliffs, N.J., Prentice-Hall, 1955.

Presseisen, Ernst L. *Before Aggression: Europeans Prepare the Japanese Army*. Tucson, University of Arizona Press, 1965.

—— *Germany and Japan: A Study in Totalitarian Diplomacy, 1933–1941*. The Hague, Martinus Nijhoff, 1958.

Price, Ernst B. *The Russo-Japanese Treaties of 1907–1916 concerning Manchuria and Mongolia*. Baltimore, Johns Hopkins Press, 1933.

Reiss, Ludwig. "Deutschland und Japan," *Preussische Jahrbücher*, CLXVIII (April-June 1917), 203–29.

Rekishigaku Kenkyūkai 歴史学研究会, ed. *Taiheiyō sensō shi* 太平洋戦争史 (History of the Pacific War). 5 vols. Tokyo, Tōyō Keizai Shimpōsha, 1954.

Reubens, Edwin P. "Foreign Capital and Domestic Development in Japan," in Simon Kuznets, *Economic Growth: Brazil, India and Japan*, pp. 179–228. Durham, Duke University Press, 1955.

Rich, Norman and H.M. Fisher, eds. *The Holstein Papers*. 4 vols. Cambridge, Cambridge University Press, 1955–63.

Ritter, Gerhard. "Staatskunst und Kriegshandwerk, das Problem des 'Militarismus' in Deutschland," reviewed in *American Historical Review*, LXVII, No. 2 (January 1962), 405–7.

Romanov, B.A. *Ocherki diplomaticheskoi istorii Russko-Iaponskoi voiny, 1895–1907* (An outline diplomatic history of the Russo-Japanese War, 1895–1907). Moscow and Leningrad, Izdatel'stvo Akademii Nauk SSSR, 1947; rev. ed., 1955.

—— *Rossiia v Man'chzhurii, 1892–1906* (Russia in Manchuria, 1892–1906). Leningrad, A.S. Enukidze Oriental Institute, 1928.

—— *Russia in Manchuria, 1892–1906*. Translated by Susan Wilbur Jones. Ann Arbor, by J.W. Edwards for the American Council of Learned Societies, 1952.

Rosen, Oscar. "German-Japanese Relations, 1894–1902: A Study of European Imperialism in the Far East." Unpublished doctoral dissertation, University of Wisconsin, 1956.

Rosovsky, Henry, ed. *Industrialization in Two Systems*. New York, Wiley, 1966.

—— "Japan's Transition to Economic Growth," in Rosovsky, *Industrialization in Two Systems*, pp. 91-139.

Rōyama Masamichi 蠟山政道. "Manshū mondai o meguru Nichi-Bei gaikō no sōten" 満州問題をめぐる日米外交の争点 (The Manchurian problem as the point of issue in Japanese-American diplomacy), in Ueda Toshio 植田捷雄, ed., *Kamikawa sensei kanreki kinen: kindai Nihon gaikōshi no kenkyū* 神川先生還暦記念—近代日本外交史の研究 (Commemorating the sixtieth birthday of Professor Kamikawa: Studies in modern Japanese diplomatic history), pp. 541-62. Tokyo, Yūhikaku, 1956.

Saigō Kōsaku 西郷鋼作 (pen name of Tamura Shinsaku 田村真作). *Itagaki Seishirō* 板垣征四郎. Tokyo, Seiji Chishikisha, 1938.

Saigusa Hiroto 三枝博音, Nozaki Shigeru 野崎茂, and Sasaki Shun 佐々木峻. *Kindai Nihon sangyō gijutsu no seiōka* 近代日本産業技術の西欧化 (Westernization of industrial technology in modern Japan). Tokyo, Tōyō Keizai Shimpōsha, 1960.

Saitō Shishaku Kinenkai 斉藤子爵記念会, ed. *Shishaku Saitō Makoto den* 子爵斉藤実伝 (Biography of Viscount Saitō Makoto). 4 vols. Tokyo, Saitō Shishaku Kinenkai, 1941-42.

Saitō Tadashi 斉藤正. "Meiji shoki no kangyō to mingyō" 明治初期の官業と民業 (Government enterprise and private enterprise in early Meiji), *Seijō daigaku keizai kenkyū*, No. 14 (November 1961), pp. 47-74; No. 16 (October 1962), pp. 31-54; No. 18 (November 1963), pp. 95-118. Reprinted in Okada Shumpei 岡田俊平, ed. *Meiji shoki no zaisei kin'yū seisaku* 明治初期の財政金融政策 (Financial and fiscal policy in early Meiji), pp. 223-99. Tokyo, Seimeikai, 1964.

Saitō Takashi 斉藤孝. "Sen-kyūhyaku-yonjūichinen no Nichi-Bei kankei ni tsuite no oboegaki" 1941年の日米関係についての覚書 (A memorandum concerning Japanese-American relations in 1941), *Rekishigaku kenkyū*, No. 175 (1954), pp. 31-42.

Saitō Yoshie 斉藤良衛. *Azamukareta rekishi: Matsuoka to sangoku dōmei no rimen* 欺かれた歴史—松岡と三国同盟の裏面 (History deceived: The inside story of Matsuoka and the Tripartite Pact). Tokyo, Yomiuri Shimbunsha, 1955.

—— "Chō Sakurin bakushi no zengo, sono 1" 張作霖爆死の前後，其の一 (Before and after the assassination of Chang Tso-lin, Part 1), *Aizu tanki daigaku gakuhō*, No. 4 (January 1955).

—— "Chō Sakurin no shi" 張作霖の死 (The death of Chang Tso-lin), *Aizu tanki daigaku gakuhō*, No. 5 (December 1955).

—— *Saikin Shina kokusai kankei* 最近支那国際関係 (Recent international relations concerning China). Tokyo, Kokusai Remmei Kyōkai, 1931.

—— *Shina kokusai kankei gaikan* 支那国際関係概観 (A survey of China's international relations). Tokyo, Kokusai Remmei Kyōkai, 1924.

Sakairi Chōtarō 坂入長太郎. "Meiji shoki ni okeru zaisei" 明治初期における財政

(Fiscal policy in early Meiji), *Keizaikei*, No. 28 (April 1956), pp. 1-23.

Sakatani Yoshirō 阪谷芳郎. *Segai Inoue kō den* 世外井上公伝 (A biography of Marquis Inoue Kaoru). 5 vols. Tokyo, Naigai Shoseki, 1933-34.

Sakudō Yōtarō 作道洋太郎. "Bōeki shōsha no hatten to Kansaikei kigyō no keisei" 貿易商社の発展と関西系企業の形成 (The development of foreign trade companies and the formation of Kansai enterprises), *Ōsaka daigaku keizaigaku*, XII, Nos. 3-4 (March 1963), 208-55.

Sakurai Yoshiyuki 櫻井義之. "Chōsen no kindaika to Nisshin sensō" 朝鮮の近代化と日清戦争 (The modernization of Korea and the Sino-Japanese War), *Rekishi kyōiku*, X, No. 2 (February 1962), 33-38.

—— "Kindai Nikkan kankei shiryō kaidai" 近代日韓関係資料解題 (An annotated bibliography of sources for the study of modern Japanese-Korean relations), *Kokusai seiji: Nikkan kankei no tenkai*, 1962, pp. 128-40.

Sakuta Takatarō 作田高太郎. *Tennō to Kido* 天皇と木戸 (The emperor and Kido). Tokyo, Heibonsha, 1948.

Sanetō Keishū 実藤恵秀. *Chūgokujin Nihon ryūgakushi* 中国人日本留学史 (History of Chinese students in Japan). Tokyo, Kuroshio Shuppan, 1960.

—— *Chūgokujin Nihon ryūgaku shikō* 中国人日本留学史稿 (Draft history of Chinese students in Japan). Tokyo, Nikka Gakkai, 1939.

—— *Meiji Nisshi bunka kōshō* 明治日支文化交渉 (Cultural relations between Japan and China in the Meiji period). Tokyo, Kōfūkan, 1943.

Sansom, Katharine. *Sir George Sansom and Japan: A Memoir*. Tallahassee, Diplomatic Press, 1972.

Sasaki Seiji 佐々木誠治. *Nihon kaiun kyōsōshi josetsu* 日本海運競争史序説 (Prolegomena to a history of competition in Japan's maritime transportation). Kobe, Kaiji Kenkyūkai, 1954.

—— *Nihon kaiungyō no kindaika* 日本海運業の近代化 (The modernization of Japan's maritime transportation industry). Tokyo, Kaibundō, 1961.

—— "Nihon kaiunshi kenkyū no saikin dōkō" 日本海運史研究の最近動向 (Recent trends in the study of Japan's maritime transportation industry), *Kokumin keizai zasshi*, CXII, No. 1 (July 1965), 94-113.

—— "The Maritime Competition in the Early Meiji Era," *Kobe Economic and Business Review*, No. 1 (1954), pp. 38-51.

Sasaki Tōichi 佐々木到一. *Aru gunjin no jiden* ある軍人の自伝 (Autobiography of a military officer). Tokyo, Keisō Shobō, 1963.

Satō Kenryō 佐藤賢了. *Tōjō Hideki to Taiheiyō sensō* 東条英機と太平洋戦争 (Tōjō Hideki and the Pacific War). Tokyo, Bungei Shunjū Shinsha, 1960.

Satō Kōseki 佐藤垢石. *Bōryaku shōgun Aoki Norizumi* 謀略將軍青木宣純 (The scheming general, Aoki Norizumi). Tokyo, Bokusui Shobō, 1943.

Satō Saburō 佐藤三郎. "Kōakai ni kansuru ichi kōsatsu" 興亜会に関する一考察 (A study of the Kōakai), *Yamagata daigaku kiyō (jimbun kagaku)*, No. 4 (August 1951), pp. 1–14.

―― "Meiji sanjūsannen no Amoi jiken ni kansuru kōsatsu: kindai Nitchū kōshō shijō no hitokoma to shite" 明治三十三年の厦門事件に関する考察―近代日中交渉史上の一駒として (A study of the Amoy incident of 1900: a page in the history of modern Sino-Japanese relations), *Yamagata daigaku kiyō (jimbun kagaku)*, No. 2 (March 1963).

Satō Seizaburō 佐藤誠三郎. "Kyōchō to jiritsu no aida―Nihon" 協調と自立の間―日本 (Between cooperation and autonomy―the case of Japan), in Nihon Seiji Gakkai 日本政治学会, ed., *Nempō seijigaku 1969: kokusai kinchō kanwa no seiji katei* 年報政治学1969―国際緊張緩和の政治過程 (The annals of the Japan Political Science Association, 1969: The political process in the reduction of international tensions), pp. 99–144. Tokyo, Iwanami Shoten, 1970.

Satō Shōichirō 佐藤昌一郎. "Kigyō bokkōki ni okeru gunkaku zaisei no tenkai" 企業勃興期における軍拡財政の展開 (The formulation of a fiscal policy for military expansion during the period of rapid industrial development in the 1880s), *Rekishigaku kenkyū*, No. 295 (December 1964), pp. 11–30.

―― "Matsukata zaisei to gunkaku zaisei no tenkai" 松方財政と軍拡財政の展開 (Matsukata's fiscal policy and the formulation of a fiscal policy for military expansion), *Shōgaku ronshū*, XXXII, No. 3 (December 1963), 43–89.

Satō Yasunosuke 佐藤安之助. *Mammō mondai o chūshin to suru Nisshi kankei* 満蒙問題を中心とする日支関係 (Sino-Japanese relations centering on Manchurian and Mongolian problems). Tokyo, Nihon Hyōronsha, 1931.

Satow, E.M. *A Diplomat in Japan*. London, Seeley Service, 1921.

Sawada Akira 澤田章. "Dajōkansatsu hakkō no shushi to shokusan kōgyō" 太政官札発行の趣旨と殖産興業 (The encouragement of production and the significance of the government note issue), *Shakai keizai shigaku*, III, No. 7 (October 1932), 679–702.

―― *Meiji zaisei no kisoteki kenkyū* 明治財政の基礎的研究 (Basic studies in Meiji fiscal policy). Tokyo, Hōbunkan, 1934.

Sawada Ken 沢田謙. *Joden Ō Chōmei* 叙伝汪兆銘 (Biography of Wang Chao-ming [Ching-wei]). Tokyo, Shunjūsha, 1939.

Scalapino, Robert. *Democracy and the Party Movement in Prewar Japan: The Failure of the First Attempt*. Berkeley and Los Angeles, University of California Press, 1962; first published in 1953.

Schroeder, Paul W. *The Axis Alliance and Japanese-American Relations, 1941*. Ithaca, Cornell University Press, 1958.

Schwantes, Robert S. *Japanese and Americans: A Century of Cultural Relations*. New York, Harper, for the Council on Foreign Relations, 1955.

Schwarz, Paul. *This Man Ribbentrop, His Life and Times.* New York, Messner, 1943.

Sekai no naka no Nihon 世界のなかの日本 (Japan in the world). Vol. VIII of *Kindai Nihon shisōshi kōza* 近代日本思想史講座 (Lectures on the history of modern Japanese thought). Tokyo, Chikuma Shobō, 1961.

Seki Hiroharu 関寛治. "Manshū jihen zenshi" 満州事變前史 (A history of the developments leading to the Manchurian Incident), in *Manshū jihen zen'ya* 満州事變前夜 (On the eve of the Manchurian Incident), pp. 287–440. Vol. I of Nihon Kokusai Seiji Gakkai Taiheiyō Sensō Gen'in Kenkyūbu, *Taiheiyō sensō e no michi.* Tokyo, Asahi Shimbunsha, 1963.

—— "1917 nen Harubin kakumei: Harubin sobietto juritsu o meguru kokusai seijigakuteki ichi kōsatsu" 一九一七年ハルビン革命—ハルビン・ソビエット樹立をめぐる国際政治学的一考察 (The revolution in Harbin in 1917: A study in international politics centering on the establishment of the Harbin soviet), *Kokusaihō gaikō zasshi*, LVII, No. 3 (August 1958), 36–83.

—— "Tairiku gaikō no kiki to sangatsu jiken" 大陸外交の危機と三月事件 (The March Incident and the crisis in Japan's China policy), in Shinohara and Mitani, *Kindai Nihon no seijishidō*, pp. 433–90.

Sekine Minoru 関根実, ed. *Hamaguchi Osachi den* 浜口雄幸伝 (Biography of Hamaguchi Osachi). Tokyo, Hamaguchi Osachi Den Kankōkai, 1931.

Sekiya Jūrō 関矢充郎. *Kaiketsu En Seigai* 快傑袁世凱 (The heroic Yuan Shih-k'ai). Tokyo, Jitsugyō no Nihonsha, 1913.

Sekiyama Naotarō 関山直太郎. "Eikoku Tōyō Ginkō to waga kuni to no kankei tansho" 英国東洋銀行と我国との関係端緒 (The beginning of the relation between Japan and Britain's Oriental Bank), *Keizaishi kenkyū*, XVIII, No. 3 (September 1937), 207–19.

—— "Kyūshohan no gaikoku fusai shobun" 旧諸藩の外国負債処分 (The disposition of the foreign debts of the former domains), *Shakai keizai shigaku*, I, No. 2 (1931), 349–74.

—— *Nihon kahei kin'yūshi kenkyū* 日本貨幣金融史研究 (Studies in the history of Japanese currency and finance). Tokyo, Shin Keizaisha, 1943.

Sevost'yanov, E.N. *Politika velikikh derdzav na Dal'nem Vostoke* (Policies of the great powers in the Far East). Moscow, 1961.

Shanhai Kyoryū Mindan 上海居留民団. *Mindan sōritsu sanjūgoshūnen kinenshi* 民団創立三十五周年記念史 (A history commemorating the thirty-fifth anniversary of the founding of the Japanese Shanghai Residents Association). Shanghai, Shanhai Kyoryū Mindan, 1942.

Shanhai Zasshisha 上海雑誌社, ed. *Hakusen Nishimoto kun den* 白川西本君伝 (Biography of Nishimoto Hakusen). Shanghai, privately printed by Ashizawa Tamiji, 1934.

Shi Mei 史明. *Taiwanjin yonhyakunenshi* 台湾人四百年史 (A four-hundred-year history of the people of Taiwan). Tokyo, Otowa Shobō, 1962.

Shibata Motohiro 柴田固弘. "Shihon chikuseki ni okeru gaishi no yakuwari" 資本蓄積における外資の役割 (The role of foreign capital in capital accumulation), in Matsui Kiyoshi 松井清, ed., *Kindai Nihon bōekishi* 近代日本貿易史 (A history of modern Japan's foreign trade), I, 275–96. 3 vols. Tokyo, Yūhikaku, 1959–63.

Shibusawa Hideo 澁沢秀雄. *Jōi ronsha no to-Ō* 攘夷論者の渡欧 (A trip to Europe by an advocate of expelling the barbarians). Tokyo, Sōgabō, 1941.

Shibusawa Keizō, ed. *Japanese Society in the Meiji Era.* Translated by S.H. Culbertson and Kimura Michiko. Vol. IV of Centenary Cultural Council series, *Japanese Culture in the Meiji Era.* Tokyo, Ōbunsha, 1958.

Shibusawa Seien Kinen Zaidan Ryūmonsha 澁沢青淵記念財団龍門社, ed. *Shibusawa Eiichi denki shiryō* 澁沢栄一伝記資料 (Materials for a biography of Shibusawa Eiichi). 58 vols. Tokyo, Shibusawa Seien Kinen Zaidan Ryūmonsha, 1955–65.

Shidehara Heiwa Zaidan 幣原平和財団, ed. *Shidehara Kijūrō* 幣原喜重郎. Tokyo, Shidehara Heiwa Zaidan, 1955.

Shidehara Kijūrō 幣原喜重郎. *Gaikō gojūnen* 外交五十年 (Fifty years as a diplomat). Tokyo, Yomiuri Shimbunsha, 1951.

Shigefuji Takeo 重藤威夫. *Nagasaki kyoryūchi bōeki jidai no kenkyū* 長崎居留地貿易時代の研究 (Studies on foreign trade during the period of the Nagasaki concession). Tokyo, Sakai Shoten, 1961.

Shigemitsu Mamoru 重光葵. *Gaikō kaisōroku* 外交回想録 (Diplomatic reminiscences). Tokyo, Mainichi Shimbunsha, 1953.

—— *Japan and Her Destiny: My Struggle for Peace.* Edited by F. S. G. Piggott. New York, E. P. Dutton, 1958.

—— *Shōwa no dōran* 昭和の動乱 (Turbulence during the Shōwa period). 2 vols. Tokyo, Chūō Kōronsha, 1952.

Shima Yasuhiko 島恭彦. "Meiji zaisei no gensoku to shite no kōki hōken zaisei" 明治財政の原則としての後期封建財政 (Late feudal fiscal policy as the basis for Meiji fiscal policy), *Naigai kenkyū*, XIV, No. 2 (1941), 151–73.

—— *Ōkura daijin* 大蔵大臣 (Finance ministers). Tokyo, Iwanami Shoten, 1949.

Shimada Toshihiko 島田俊彦. "Kahoku kōsaku to kokkō chōsei, 1933–1937" 華北工作と国交調整 (一九三三年〜一九三七年) (Operations in north China and readjustment of diplomatic relations, 1933–1937), in *Nitchū sensō I* 日中戦争 I (The Sino-Japanese War, Part I), pp. 73–78. Vol. III of Nihon Kokusai Seiji Gakkai Taiheiyō Sensō Gen'in Kenkyūbu, *Taiheiyō sensō e no michi*. Tokyo, Asahi Shimbunsha, 1962.

—— "Kawagoe-Chō Gun kaidan no butai ura" 川越・張郡会談の舞台裏 (Background information on the Kawagoe-Chang Chün talks in September 1936), *Ajia kenkyū*, X, No. 1 (April 1963), 49–68; No. 3 (October 1963), 23–49.

—— "Manshū jihen no tenkai" 満州事變の展開 (The development of the Manchurian crisis), in *Manshū jihen* 満州事變 (The Manchurian Incident), pp. 1–188. Vol.

II of Nihon Kokusai Seiji Gakkai Taiheiyō Sensō Gen'in Kenkyūbu, *Taiheiyō sensō e no michi*. Tokyo, Asahi Shimbunsha, 1962.

—— "Shanhai teisen kyōtei shimpan mondai" 上海停戦協定侵犯問題 (Violation of the Shanghai cease-fire agreement), *Musashi daigaku ronshū*, III, No. 1 (December 1955), 60–110.

—— "Shiryō: Shōwa shichinen Shanhai teisen kyōtei seiritsu no keii" 資料—昭和七年上海停戦協定成立の経緯 (Materials concerning the 1932 Shanghai cease-fire agreement), *Ajia kenkyū*, I, No. 3 (March 1955), 76–99; No. 4 (March 1955), 77–96.

—— "Umezu-Ka Ōkin kyōtei no seiritsu" 梅津何応欽協定の成立 (Conclusion of the Ho-Umezu agreement), *Kokusai seiji: Nihon gaikōshi kenkyū—Shōwa jidai*, 1959, pp. 50–70.

Shimbō Hiroshi 新保博. "Ishinki no shin'yō seido—Ōsaka Kawase Kaisha o chūshin to shite" 維新期の信用制度—大阪為替会社を中心として (The credit system during the Restoration period—the Osaka Exchange Company), *Keizaigaku kenkyū* (Kobe Daigaku nempō), No. 9 (July 1962), pp. 125–84.

—— "Ishinki no shōgyō kin'yū seisaku—tsūshō kaisha kawase kaisha o megutte" 維新期の商業金融政策—通商会社為替会社をめぐって (Commercial and economic policy in the Restoration period—the foreign trade companies and the exchange companies), *Shakai keizai shigaku*, XXVII, No. 5 (1962), 1–28.

—— "Tōkyō Kawase Kaisha" 東京為替会社 (The Tokyo Exchange Company), *Kokumin keizai zasshi*, CVII, No. 1 (January 1963), 17–34; No. 2 (February 1963), 59–76.

Shimoda Hiroshi 下田博. "Ishin zengo gaikoku bōekiron" 維新後前外国貿易論 (Foreign trade at the time of the Restoration), in Keiō Gijuku Keizaishi Gakkai 慶応義塾経済史学会, ed., *Meiji shoki keizaishi kenkyū* 明治初期経済史研究 (Studies in the economic history of early Meiji), II, 382–432. 2 vols. Tokyo, Ganshōdō, 1937.

Shimomura Fujio 下村富士男. "Kaisen gaikō" 開戦外交 (Diplomacy at the outset of the war), in Shinobu and Nakayama, *Nichi-Ro sensō shi no kenkyū*, pp. 161–78.

—— *Meiji ishin no gaikō* 明治維新の外交 (Diplomacy of the Meiji Restoration). Tokyo, Ōyashima Shuppan Kabushiki Kaisha, 1948.

—— *Meiji shonen jōyaku kaisei shi no kenkyū* 明治初年條約改正史の研究 (A study of the history of treaty revision at the beginning of the Meiji period). Tokyo, Yoshikawa Kōbunkan, 1962.

—— "Nichi-Ro sensō ni tsuite: Manshū shijō" 日露戦争について—満州市場 (The Russo-Japanese War: Markets in Manchuria), *Rekishi kyōiku*, IV, No. 1 (January 1956), 50–54.

—— "Nichi-Ro sensō no seikaku" 日露戦争の性格 (The character of the Russo-Japanese War), *Kokusai seiji: Nihon gaikōshi kenkyū—Meiji jidai*, 1957, pp. 137–52.

—— "Nichi-Ro sensō to Manshū shijō" 日露戦争と満州市場 (The Russo-Japanese

War and the Manchuria market), *Nagoya daigaku bungakubu kenkyū ronshū*, No. 14 (March 1956), pp. 1-16.

Shin Kuk-ju 申国柱. "Kankoku no kaikoku: Unyō gō jiken o megutte" 韓国の開国―雲揚号事件をめぐって (The opening of Korea as seen through the Unyō incident), in *Kokusai seiji: Nihon gaikōshi kenkyū—Bakumatsu ishin jidai*, 1960, pp. 124-42.

—— "Kōka jōki chokugo no Kan-Nichi gaikō" 江華条規直後の韓日外交 (Korean-Japanese diplomatic relations just after the conclusion of the Treaty of Kanghwa) *Kokusai seiji: Nikkan kankei no tenkai*, 1962, pp. 13-34.

Shindō Motoichi 真藤素一. "Meiji shoki no infurēshon" 明治初期のインフレーション (Inflation in early Meiji), *Keizai ronsō*, LXXIV, No. 6 (December 1954), 18-37.

Shindō Toyoo 進藤豊夫. "Shokusan kōgyō seisaku to kōzangyō—Miike kōzan no kanshū o megutte" 殖産興業政策と鉱山業―三池鉱山の官収をめぐって (The mining industry and the encouragement of production policy—government income from the Miike mine), *Rekishi to gendai*, No. 7 (May 1965), pp. 14-32.

Shinjo Hiroshi. *History of the Yen*. Kobe, Kobe University, 1962.

Shinobu Jumpei 信夫淳平. *Mammō tokushu ken'eki ron* 満蒙特殊権益論 (Japan's special rights and interests in Manchuria and Mongolia). Tokyo, Nihon Hyōronsha, 1932.

—— *Nidai gaikō no shinsō* 二大外交の真相 (A true history of two great diplomatic events). Tokyo, Banrikaku Shobō, 1928.

—— *Taishō gaikō jūgonenshi* 大正外交十五年史 (Foreign relations during the fifteen years of the Taishō era). Tokyo, Kokusai Remmei Kyōkai, 1927.

Shinobu Seizaburō 信夫清三郎. "Chishima Karafuto kōkan jōyaku" 千島樺太交換条約 (Sakhalin-Kuril Islands exchange treaty), *Kokusai Seiji: Nihon gaikōshi kenkyū—Meiji jidai*, 1957, pp. 40-50.

—— *Gotō Shimpei* 後藤新平. Tokyo, Hakubunkan, 1941.

—— *Kindai Nihon gaikōshi* 近代日本外交史 (Diplomatic history of modern Japan). Tokyo, Chūō Kōronsha, 1942.

—— *Mutsu gaikō: Nisshin sensō no gaikō shiteki kenkyū* 陸奥外交―日清戦争の外交史的研究 (Mutsu diplomacy: A historical study of the diplomacy of the Sino-Japanese War). Tokyo, Sobunkaku, 1935. First published as *Nisshin sensō* 日清戦争 (The Sino-Japanese War). Tokyo, Fukuda Shobō, 1934.

—— *Mutsu Munemitsu* 陸奥宗光. Tokyo, Hakuyōsha, 1938.

—— "Nichi-Ro sensō no kenkyū shi, I: Nihon" 日露戦争の研究史 I―日本 (History of research on the Russo-Japanese War, I: Japan), in Shinobu and Nakayama, *Nichi-Ro sensō shi no kenkyū*, pp. 2-34.

—— ed. *Nihon no gaikō* 日本の外交 (Japanese diplomacy). Tokyo, Mainichi Shimbunsha, 1961.

—— "Nisso chūritsu jōyaku" 日ソ中立条約 (The Japanese-Soviet Neutrality Pact), in *Kokusai seiji: Nihon gaikōshi kenkyū—Shōwa jidai*, 1959, pp. 99-110.

—— *Taishō demokurashii shi* 大正デモクラシー史 (History of Taishō democracy). 3 vols. Tokyo, Nihon Hyōron Shinsha, 1954-59.

—— "Taishō gaikōshi no kihon mondai" 大正外交史の基本問題 (Fundamental problems in the diplomatic history of the Taishō period), *Kokusai seiji: Nihon gaikōshi kenkyū—Taishō jidai*, 1958, pp. 1-12.

—— *Taishō seijishi* 大正政治史 (A political history of the Taishō era). 4 vols. Tokyo, Kawade Shobō, 1951-52.

Shinobu Seizaburō and Nakayama Jiichi 中山治一, eds. *Nichi-Ro sensō shi no kenkyū* 日露戦争史の研究 (Studies on the history of the Russo-Japanese War). Tokyo, Kawade Shobō Shinsha, 1959.

Shinohara Hajime 篠原一 and Mitani Taichirō 三谷太一郎, eds. *Kindai Nihon no seiji-shidō* 近代日本の政治指導 (Modern Japanese political leadership). Tokyo, Tōkyō Daigaku Shuppankai, 1965.

Shinohara, Miyohei. "Economic Development and Foreign Trade in Pre-War Japan," in Cowan, *The Economic Development of China and Japan*, pp. 220-48. Also in Miyohei Shinohara, *Growth and Cycles in the Japanese Economy*, pp. 43-75. Tokyo, Kinokuniya, 1962.

Shionoya Yūichi 塩野谷祐一. "Nihon no kōgyōka to gaikoku bōeki" 日本の工業化と外国貿易 (The industrialization of Japan and its foreign trade), *Hitotsubashi ronsō*, LVI, No. 5 (November 1966), 72-93.

Shirayanagi Shūko 白柳秀湖. *Konoe ke oyobi Konoe kō* 近衛家及び近衛公 (The Konoe family and Prince Konoe). Nagoya, Kokumin Shimbunsha, 1941.

Shiroiwa Ryūhei 白岩龍平. *Konoe Kazan kō no dai-Ajia keirin* 近衛霞山公の大亜細亜経綸 (The pan-Asian policies of Prince Konoe Kazan [Atsumaro]). Tokyo, Dai Ajia Kyōkai, 1933.

Shishkin, S. N. *Khalkhin-gol* (The Nomonhan Incident). Moscow, 1954.

Shizuta Ujiharu 志津田氏治. *Kaiji rippō no hatten* 海事立法の発展 (The development of maritime legislation). Kobe, Kaibundō, 1959.

Shōda Kazue 勝田主計. *Kiku no newake: Nisshi keizaijō no shisetsu ni tsuite* 菊の根分け—日支経済上の施設に就て (Dividing the chrysanthemum's roots: On the establishment of a Sino-Japanese economy). Tokyo, Jijokai, 1918.

Shōda Ken'ichirō 正田健一郎. "Bakumatsu Meiji shoki no keizai hatten" 幕末明治初期の経済発展 (Economic development in the late Tokugawa and early Meiji periods), *Waseda seiji keizaigaku zasshi*, CLXII (June 1960), 71-94.

Shumpō Kō Tsuishōkai 春畝公追頌会, ed. *Itō Hirobumi den* 伊藤博文伝 (Biography of Itō Hirobumi). 3 vols. Tokyo, Shumpō Kō Tsuishōkai, 1940.

Siebert, B. de, trans. *Entente Diplomacy and the World: Matrix of the History of Europe, 1909-41*. Arranged and annotated by G. A. Schreiner. New York and London, G. P. Putnam's, 1921.

Siebold, Baron Alexander von. *Japan's Accession to the Comity of Nations.* Translated with an introduction by Charles Lowe. London, Kegan Paul, Trench, Trübner, 1901.

The Sino-Japanese Negotiations of 1915: Japanese and Chinese Documents and Chinese Official Statement. Washington D. C., Carnegie Endowment for Peace, 1921.

Smith, Thomas C. *Political Change and Industrial Development in Japan: Government Enterprise, 1868–1880.* Stanford, Stanford University Press, 1955.

Snyder, Richard C., H. W. Bruck, and Burton Sapin, eds. "Decision-Making as an Approach to the Study of International Politics," in *Foreign Policy Decision-Making: An Approach to International Politics.* New York, Free Press, 1962.

Someya Yoshitarō 染谷孝太郎. "Shokusan kōgyō seisakka no gairai sangyō to zairai sangyō" 殖産興業政策下の外来産業と在来産業 (Foreign-style and native industry under the encouragement of production policy), *Meidai shōgaku ronsō,* XLVII, No. 2 (November 1963), 29–58.

Sommer, Theo. *Deutschland und Japan zwischen den Mächten, 1935–1940: Vom Antikominternpakt zum Dreimächtepakt.* Tübingen, J. C. B. Mohr (Paul Siebeck), 1962.

Somura Yasunobu 曾村保信. "Nihon no shiryō kara mita Nichi-Ro senzen no Manshū-Shiberia mondai" 日本の資料から見た日露戦前の満州シベリア問題 (The Manchuria-Siberia problem before the Russo-Japanese War as seen from Japanese materials), in Somura, *Kindaishi kenkyū, I: Nihon to Chūgoku* 近代史研究 I— 日本と中国 (Studies in modern history, I: Japan and China). Tokyo, Komine Shoten, 1958.

—— "Shingai kakumei to Nihon" 辛亥革命と日本 (The 1911 revolution and Japan), *Kokusai seiji: Nihon gaikōshi kenkyū—Nitchū kankei no tenkai,* 1960, pp. 43–55.

—— "Tairiku seisaku ni okeru imēji no tenkan" 大陸政策におけるイメージの転換 (Changing images in Japan's policy toward the mainland), in Shinohara and Mitani, *Kindai Nihon no seijishidō,* pp. 253–92.

—— "Uchida Ryōhei no Chūgoku kan—shingai kakumei yori Taishō shoki made" 内田良平の中国観—辛亥革命より大正初期まで (Uchida Ryōhei's views on China, from the 1911 revolution to the beginning of the Taishō era), *Hōgaku shimpō,* LXIV, No. 6 (June 1957), 61–76.

—— "Washinton kaigi no ichi kōsatsu: Ozaki Yukio no gumbi seigen ron o chūshin ni shite" ワシントン会議の一考察—尾崎行雄の軍備制限論を中心として (A study of the Washington Conference centered on Ozaki Yukio's essay on limitation of armaments), *Kokusai seiji: Nihon gaikōshi kenkyū—Taishō jidai,* 1958, pp. 118–29.

Sonoda Kazuki 園田一亀. *Chō Sakurin* 張作霖 (Chang Tso-lin). Tokyo, Chūkadō, 1923.

—— *Tōsanshō no seiji to gaikō* 東三省の政治と外交 (The politics and foreign relations of the Three Eastern Provinces). Mukden, Hōten Shimbunsha, 1925.

Spinks, Charles N. "Behind Japan's Anglophobia," *Contemporary Japan*, VII, No. 2 (September 1938), 237–42.

—— "Japan's Entrance into the World War," *Pacific Historical Review*, V, No. 4 (1936), 297–311.

Starr, Frederick. *The Ainu Group at the St. Louis Exposition.* Chicago, Open Court, 1904.

Stimson, Henry L. *The Far Eastern Crisis: Recollections and Observations.* New York, Harper, 1936.

Storry, Richard. *The Double Patriots: A Study of Japanese Nationalism.* Cambridge, Riverside Press, and Boston, Houghton, Mifflin, 1957.

—— "The Mukden Incident of September 18–19, 1931," in St. Anthony's Papers, No. 2: *Far Eastern Affairs*, No. 1 (1957), pp. 1–12.

Suda Teiichi 須田禎一. "Shihaisō ni okeru seiji rinri no keisha: Nisso kōshō shi o chūshin to shite" 支配層における政治倫理の傾斜—日ソ交渉史を中心として (Decline in the political ethics of the ruling class: Centering on the Japanese-Soviet negotiations), *Shisō*, No. 391 (January 1957), pp. 75–87.

Suematsu, Kencho. *The Risen Sun.* London, Constable, 1905.

Suematsu Yasukazu 末松保和. *Kinsei ni okeru hoppō mondai no shinten* 近世に於ける北方問題の進展 (Development of issues on Japan's northern frontier in modern times). Tokyo, Shibundō, 1928.

Sugii Rokurō 杉井六郎. "Chitsuroku shobun to shichibu ritsuki gaishi boshū" 秩禄処分と七分利付外資募集 (Pension capitalization and the raising of the 7 percent foreign loan), in Kyōto Daigaku Bungakubu Dokushikai 京都大学文学部読史会, ed., *Dokushikai sōritsu gojisshūnen kinen kokushi ronshū* 読史会創立五十周年記念国史論集 (Essays on Japanese history commemorating the fiftieth anniversary of the founding of the Dokushikai), pp. 1493–1510. 2 vols. Kyoto, by the editor, 1959.

—— "Jōyaku kaiseishi jō no engan bōeki" 条約改正史上の沿岸貿易 (Coastal trade from the standpoint of the history of treaty revision), *Bunka shigaku*, No. 13 (1957), pp. 44–63; No. 14 (1958), pp. 34–46.

—— "Meiji jidai no kaiun seisaku—seifu no Mitsubishi kan" 明治時代の海運政策—政府の三菱観 (Maritime transportation policy in the Meiji period—the government's view of Mitsubishi), *Rekishi kyōiku*, XII, No. 1 (January 1964), 28–34.

—— "Meiji seifu no kaiun seisaku" 明治政府の海運政策 (The maritime transportation policy of the Meiji government), *Geirin*, VII, No. 5 (1956), 258–94.

Sugiyama Kazuo 杉山和雄. "Kahei kin'yū seido no kakuritsu" 貨幣金融制度の確立 (The establishment of the currency and financial system), in Rekishigaku Kenkyūkai 歴史学研究会, ed., *Meiji ishin shi kenkyū kōza* 明治維新史研究講座 (Studies in the history of the Meiji Restoration), IV, 190–214. 6 vols. Tokyo, Heibonsha, 1958.

—— "Kin'yū seido no sōsetsu" 金融制度の創設 (The founding of the financial system), in *Nihon keizaishi taikei* 日本経済史大系 (Japanese economic history series), V, 177–231. 6 vols. Tokyo, Tōkyō Daigaku Shuppankai, 1965.

Sugiyama Sakae 杉山栄. *Senkusha Kishida Ginkō* 先駆者岸田吟香 (Kishida Ginkō, the pioneer). Tsuyama, Tomatsu Gakuen, 1952.

Suma Yakichirō 須磨彌吉郎. *Gaikō hiroku* 外交秘録 (A confidential record of diplomacy). Tokyo, Shōkō Zaimu Kenkyūkai, 1956.

Supreme Commander for the Allied Powers, Civil Intelligence Section, General Headquarters, Far East Command. *Saionji-Harada Memoirs.* Mimeographed. Tokyo, n.d.

Supreme Commander for the Allied Powers, Education Research Branch, Civil Information and Education Section, General Headquarters, Far East Command. *Foreign Students in Japan, 1896–1947.* Mimeographed. Tokyo, 1948.

Survey of International Affairs, 1920– . London, Oxford University Press, 1925–

Suzue Gen'ichi 鈴江言一. *Chūgoku kaihō tōsōshi* 中国解放闘争史 (A history of China's struggle for liberation). Tokyo, Ishizaki Shoten, 1953.

—— *Son Bun den* 孫文伝 (Biography of Sun Yat-sen). Tokyo, Iwanami Shoten, 1950.

Suzuki Kantarō den 鈴木貫太郎伝 (Biography of Suzuki Kantarō). Tokyo, Suzuki Kantarō Denki Hensan Iinkai, 1960.

Suzuki Ken'ichi 鈴木健一. "Shanhai jihen no suii ni tsuite: toku ni seifu to gumbu no dōkō" 上海事變の推移について—とくに政府と軍部の動向 (Development of the Shanghai Incident: The activities of the Japanese government and the military), *Rekishi hyōron*, No. 134 (October 1961), pp. 65–77.

Suzuki Ryō 鈴木良. "Meiji jūnendai ni okeru gaikoku bōeki to burujoajii—Kiito Niazukarijo jiken o megutte" 明治10年代における外国貿易とブルジョアジー—生糸荷預所事件をめぐって (Foreign trade and the bourgeoisie in the second decade of Meiji—the Raw Silk Warehouse incident), *Nihonshi kenkyū*, No. 35 (January 1958), pp. 19–39.

Suzuki Takeo 鈴木武雄. "Meiji shoki no kōsai seisaku" 明治初期の公債政策 (National debt policy in early Meiji), *Keizai kenkyū*, III, No. 1 (1926), 129–90.

Tabe Toshirō 田辺敏郎. "Meiji seifu no kōsai seisaku" 明治政府の公債政策 (The national debt policy of the Meiji government), *Rekishi kagaku*, II, No. 5 (1933), 30–34.

Tabohashi Kiyoshi 田保橋潔. "Kindai Chōsen ni okeru kaikō no kenkyū" 近代朝鮮に於ける開港の研究 (A study of the opening of the ports of modern Korea), in *Oda sensei shōju kinen Chōsen ronshū* 小田先生頌寿記念朝鮮論集 (Commemorating Professor Oda: Essays on Korea). Seoul, Ōsakayagō Shoten, 1934.

—— *Kindai Nissen kankei no kenkyū* 近代日鮮関係の研究 (A study of modern Japanese-

Korean relations). 2 vols. Tokyo, Sokō Shobō, 1929.

—— "Kindai Nis-Shi-Sen kankei no kenkyū: Tenshin jōyaku yori Nisshi kaisen ni itaru" 近代日支鮮関係の研究―天津条約より日支開戦に至る (A critical study of Japan's diplomatic relations with China and Korea: From the Treaty of Tientsin to the beginning of the Sino-Japanese War), *Keijō teikoku daigaku hōbungakubu kenkyū chōsa sasshi*, No. 3 (1930).

—— *Meiji gaikōshi* 明治外交史 (A diplomatic history of the Meiji era). Vol. IX of *Iwanami kōza Nihon rekishi* 岩波講座日本歴史 (Iwanami lectures on Japanese history). Tokyo, Iwanami, 1934.

—— *Nisshin sen'eki gaikōshi no kenkyū* 日清戦役外交史の研究 (A study of the diplomatic history of the Sino-Japanese War). Tokyo, Tōkō Shoin, 1951.

—— "Ryūkyū hammin bangai jiken ni kansuru kōsatsu 琉球藩民番害事件に関する 考察 (Remarks on the murder of Ryukyuan natives by aborigines in Formosa), in *Ichimura hakushi koki kinen Tōyōshi ronsō* 市村博士古稀記念東洋史論叢 (Commemorating Professor Ichimura: Essays on Far Eastern history). Tokyo, Fuzambō, 1933.

Tai-Shi Kōrōsha Denki Hensankai 対支功労者伝記編纂会, ed. *Tai-Shi kaikoroku* 対支 回顧録 (Recollections of China). 2 vols. Tokyo, Tai-Shi Kōrōsha Denki Hensankai, 1936.

—— *Zoku tai-Shi kaikoroku* 続対支回顧録 (Recollections of China, supplement). 2 vols. Tokyo, Dai Nihon Kyōka Tosho Kabushiki Kaisha, 1941–42.

Taiwan Ginkō 台湾銀行. *Taiwan Ginkō jūnen kōshi* 台湾銀行十年後史 (A history of the Bank of Taiwan during the past decade). Tokyo, Taiwan Ginkō, 1916.

—— *Taiwan Ginkō jūnenshi* 台湾銀行十年史 (A ten-year history of the Bank of Taiwan). Tokyo, Taiwan Ginkō, 1910.

—— *Taiwan Ginkō nijūnenshi* 台湾銀行二十年史 (A twenty-year history of the Bank of Taiwan). Taihoku, Taiwan Ginkō, 1919.

—— *Taiwan Ginkō yonjūnenshi* 台湾銀行四十年史 (A forty-year history of the Bank of Taiwan). Tokyo, Taiwan Ginkō, 1939.

Taiwan seinen (also known as *Taiwan chinglian*) 台湾青年 (The young Formosan). Tokyo, Taiwan Toklip Lianbeng (United Formosans for Independence), a monthly publication.

Takagaki Torajirō 高垣寅次郎. *Kindai Nihon kin'yūshi* 近代日本金融史 (A financial history of modern Japan). Tokyo, Zenkoku Chihōginkō Kyōkai, 1955.

—— "Kōhon 'shihei shōkyakusetsu' no shuchō—Nihon kindai kin'yūshi kenkyū no issetsu" 稿本「紙幣消却説」の主張―日本近代金融史研究の一節 (On the draft "Theory of Currency Redemption": An aspect of the history of modern Japanese finance), in *Itō Hanya hakushi taikan kinen rombunshū: zaiseigaku no kihon mondai* 井藤半彌博士退官記念論文集―財政学の基本問題 (Collected essays commemorating the retirement of Dr. Itō Hanya: Fundamental problems in the study of fiscal policy), pp. 185–208. Tokyo, Chikura Shobō, 1960.

—— ed. *Meiji shoki ni okeru zaisei kin'yū seisaku to gaikoku shihon no kankei* 明治初期における財政金融政策と外国資本の関係 (The relation of foreign capital to fiscal and financial policy in early Meiji). Tokyo, 1958.

Takagi Sōkichi 高木惣吉. *Taiheiyō sensō kaisenshi* 太平洋戦争海戦史 (Naval history of the Pacific War). Tokyo, Iwanami, 1949.

—— *Yamamoto Isoroku to Yonai Mitsumasa* 山本五十六と米内光政 (Yamamoto Isoroku and Yonai Mitsumasa). Tokyo, Bungei Shunjū Shinsha, 1950.

Takahashi Kamekichi 高橋亀吉. *Taishō Shōwa zaikai hendō shi* 大正昭和財界変動史 (History of changes in the financial world in the Taishō and Shōwa eras). 3 vols. Tokyo, Tōyō Keizai Shimpōsha, 1954–55.

Takahashi Korekiyo 高橋是清. *Takahashi Korekiyo jiden* 高橋是清自伝 (Autobiography of Takahashi Korekiyo). Tokyo, Chikura Shobō, 1936.

Takahashi Kyūichi 高橋久一. "Meiji shoki ni okeru shōsha to shōgyō shihon" 明治初期における商社と商業資本 (Commercial companies and commercial capital in early Meiji), *Hikone ronsō*, No. 97 (May 1963), pp. 43–55.

Takahashi Makoto 高橋誠. "Jumbikin no zaiseiteki igi ni tsuite" 準備金の財政的意義について (The fiscal significance of the reserve fund), *Keizai shirin*, XXVIII, No. 3 (1960), 31–96.

—— *Meiji zaiseishi kenkyū* 明治財政史研究 (Studies in the fiscal history of the Meiji period). Tokyo, Aoki Shoten, 1964.

—— "Meiji zenki bōeki kin'yū kikō ni kansuru shiron" 明治前期貿易金融機構に関する試論 (An essay on the foreign trade finance structure in early Meiji), *Keizai shirin*, XXVII, No. 2 (1959), 31–50.

—— "Meiji zenki ni okeru zaisei seisaku no tenkai" 明治前期における財政政策の展開 (The development of fiscal policy in early Meiji), *Keizai shirin*, XXII, No. 2 (1954), 60–99.

Takahashi Yoshio 高橋義雄. *Sankō iretsu* 山公遺烈 (Recollections of Prince Yamagata Aritomo). Tokyo, Keibundō Shoten, 1925.

Takakura Tetsuichi 高倉徹一, ed. *Tanaka Giichi denki* 田中義一伝記 (Biography of Tanaka Giichi). 2 vols. Tokyo, Tanaka Giichi Denki Kankōkai, 1958–60.

Takamiya Tahei 高宮太平. *Gunkoku taiheiki* 軍国太平記 (Chronicle of a military nation). Tokyo, Kantōsha, 1951.

—— *Tennō heika* 天皇陛下 (The emperor). Tokyo, Kantōsha, 1951.

Takamura Naosuke 高村直助. "Kigyō bokkōki ni okeru bōsekigyō no kōzō—Ōsaka Bōseki Kaisha no seiritsu" 企業勃興期における紡績業の構造—大阪紡績会社の成立 (The structure of the cotton spinning industry during the period of rapid industrial development in the 1880s—the establishment of the Osaka Spinning Company), *Shigaku zasshi*, LXXII, No. 8 (August 1963), 1–30; No. 9 (September 1963), 23–40.

Takasaki Tatsunosuke 高崎達之助. *Manshū no shūen* 満州の終焉 (The death of Manchuria). Tokyo, Jitsugyō no Nihonsha, 1953.

Takase Tamotsu 高瀬保. "Meijiki ni okeru kaiun no kindaika" 明治期における海運の近代化 (The modernization of maritime transportation in the Meiji period), *Etchū shidan,* No. 30 (January 1965), pp. 69–75.

Takeda Taijun 武田泰淳 and Takeuchi Minoru 竹内実. *Mō Takutō: sono shi to jinsei* 毛澤東―その詩と人生 (Mao Tse-tung: His poetry and life). Tokyo, Asahi Shimbunsha, 1965.

Takeda Tetsurō 武田鉄郎. "Meiji shonen no shokusan kōgyō seisaku to kaigai tenrankai sandō" 明治初年の殖産興業政策と海外展覧会参同 (The encouragement of production policy and participation in overseas expositions in early Meiji), *Keizaishi kenkyū,* XXVIII, No. 5 (1942), 524–37.

Takeuchi, Kenji. "The 'Classical' Theories of International Trade and the Expansion of Foreign Trade in Japan from 1859 to 1892." Unpublished doctoral dissertation, Duke University, 1962.

Takeuchi Minoru 竹内実. "Kangakusha no Chūgoku kikō: Nihonjin no Chūgoku zō, nōto 1" 漢学者の中国紀行―日本人の中国像ノート① (Memoirs of a Japanese scholar of the Chinese classics: A note on Japanese images of China, 1), *Hokuto,* IV, No. 1 (January 1959), 1–13.

—— "Sōseki no 'Man-Kan tokoro-dokoro': Nihonjin no Chūgoku zō, nōto 2" 漱石の「満韓ところどころ」―日本人の中国像ノート② (Sōseki's "Impressions of Manchuria and Korea": A note on Japanese images of China, 2), *Hokuto,* IV, No. 2 (April 1959), 1–10.

Takeuchi, Tatsuji. *War and Diplomacy in the Japanese Empire.* Garden City, N.Y., Doubleday, Doran, 1935.

Takeuchi Yoshimi 竹内好, ed. *Ajiashugi* アジア主義 (Pan-Asianism). Tokyo, Chikuma Shobō, 1963.

Takezoe Seisei (Shin'ichirō) 竹添井井 (進一郎). *Dokuhōrō shibun kō: fu Sen'unkyō'u nikki* 独抱樓詩文稿―附棧雲峡雨日記 (Dokuhōrō poems and the Sen'unkyō diary). Tokyo, Yoshikawa Kōbunkan, 1912.

—— *Gen Isan monzen* 元遺山文選 (Selected poems of Yüan I-shan). Tokyo, Kaibun Shooku, 1883.

Takigawa Masajirō 滝川政次郎. *Hōritsu kara mita Shina kokuminsei* 法律から見た支那国民性 (Chinese national character from a legal point of view). Tokyo, Daidō Inshokan, 1941.

Tamashima Nobuyoshi 玉嶋信義, ed. and trans. *Chūgoku no me* 中国の眼 (In the eyes of the Chinese). Tokyo, Kōbundō, 1959.

Tanaka Giichi kankei bunsho mokuroku 田中義一関係文書目録 (Catalog of documents relating to Tanaka Giichi). Yamaguchi, Yamaguchiken Kenritsu Monjokan, 1961.

Tanaka Giichi Papers. Yamaguchiken Kenritsu Monjokan, Yamaguchi. The papers have been microfilmed and are available in the Kensei Shiryō Shitsu, National Diet Library.

Tanaka Naokichi 田中直吉. "Nichi-Ro kyōshō ron" 日露協商論 (An essay on the Russo-Japanese agreement), in Ueda Toshio 植田捷雄, ed., *Kamikawa sensei kanreki kinen: kindai Nihon gaikōshi no kenkyū* 神川先生還暦記念―近代日本外交史の研究 (Commemorating the sixtieth birthday of Professor Kamikawa: Studies in modern Japanese diplomatic history), pp. 295-364. Tokyo, Yūhikaku, 1956.

—— "Nissen kankei no ichi dammen: Keijō jingo no hen" 日鮮関係の一断面―京城壬午の變 (A facet of Korean-Japanese relations: The incident of 1882 at Kyŏngsŏng, Imo pyon), *Kokusai seiji: Nihon gaikōshi kenkyū—Meiji jidai*, 1957, pp. 67-92.

Tanaka Ryūkichi 田中隆吉. *Haiin o tsuku* 敗因を衝く (Why defeated?). Tokyo, Sansuisha, 1946.

Tanaka Shin'ichi 田中新一. *Taisen totsu'nyū no shinsō* 大戦突入の眞相 (The truth about the plunge into the Pacific War). Tokyo, Gengensha, 1955.

Tanaka Sōgorō 田中惣五郎. *Kita Ikki* 北一輝. Tokyo, Miraisha, 1959.

—— *Nihon fashizumu no genryū: Kita Ikki no shisō to shōgai* 日本ファシズムの源流―北一輝の思想と生涯 (Foundations of Japanese fascism: Kita Ikki's thought and life). Tokyo, Hakuyōsha, 1949.

—— *Nihon fashizumu shi* 日本ファシズム史 (History of Japanese fascism). Tokyo, Kawade Shobō Shinsha, 1960.

—— "Yokohama Kiito Niazukarijo jiken" 横浜生糸荷預所事件 (The Yokohama Raw Silk Warehouse incident), *Meiji daigaku tanki daigaku kiyō*, No. 1 (February 1957), pp. 101-29.

—— *Yoshino Sakuzō* 吉野作造. Tokyo, Miraisha, 1958.

Tanaka Tokihiko 田中時彦. *Meiji ishin no seikyoku to tetsudō kensetsu* 明治維新の政局と鉄道建設 (Railroad construction and the political situation during the Meiji Restoration). Tokyo, Yoshikawa Kōbunkan, 1963.

—— "Nihon ni okeru tetsudō dō'nyū seisaku no keisei katei" 日本における鉄道導入政策の形成過程 (The process of policy formation in the introduction of the railroad into Japan), *Toritsudai hōgakkai zasshi*, II, No. 2 (March 1962), 36-72.

—— "Nihon ni okeru tetsudō dō'nyū seisaku no seijiteki haikei" 日本における鉄道導入政策の政治的背景 (The political background of the policy of introducing the railroad into Japan), *Toritsudai hōgakkai zasshi*, III, Nos. 1-2 (March 1963), 465-501.

—— "Seisaku kettei no shiten kara mita Nihon no tetsudō sōsetsu" 政策決定の視点から見た日本の鉄道創設 (The inauguration of the railroad in Japan from the viewpoint of decision-making), *Kōtsū bunka*, No. 4 (October 1964), pp. 23-34.

Tanaka Toyoki 田中豊喜. "Meiji zettaishugi to shokusan kōgyō seisaku josetsu" 明治絶対主義と殖産興業政策序説 (Introduction to Meiji absolutism and the encouragement of production policy), *Meidai shōgaku ronsō*, XLVII, No. 3 (December 1963), 35–71.

Tanemura Sakō 種村佐孝. *Daihon'ei kimitsu nisshi* 大本営機密日誌 (Confidential record of the Imperial Headquarters). Tokyo, Daiyamondosha, 1952.

Taniguchi Ō Denki Hensan Iinkai 谷口翁伝記編纂委員会, ed. *Taniguchi Fusazō den* 谷口房蔵伝 (Biography of Taniguchi Fusazō). Osaka, Taniguchi Ō Denki Hensan Iinkai, 1934.

Tansill, Charles C. *Back Door to War: The Roosevelt Foreign Policy, 1933–1941*. Chicago, H. Regnery, 1952.

Tatemoto Masahiro 建元正弘. "Meiji 1–34 nen no kokusai shūshi suikei sagyō hōkoku" 明治 1–34 年の国際収支推計作業報告 (A working report on balance of payments estimates, 1868–1901), plus supplement, *Kyōto daigaku keizai kenkyūjo disukasshon pēpā* 6610 京都大学経済研究所ディスカッションペーパー 6610 (Kyoto University Economic Research Institute discussion paper 6610). Kyoto, 1966.

—— "Meiji shoki ni okeru keizai seichō to shigen haibun" 明治初期における経済成長と資源配分 (Economic growth and resource allocation in early Meiji), *Kyōto daigaku keizai kenkyūjo disukasshon pēpā* 6505 京都大学経済研究所ディスカッションペーパー 6505 (Kyoto University Economic Research Institute discussion paper 6505). Kyoto, 1965.

Tatemoto Masahiro and Baba Masao 馬場正雄. "Meiji gaikoku bōeki tōkei (Meiji 1–20 nen)" 明治外国貿易統計（明治 1〜20年）(Meiji foreign trade statistics, 1868–87), *Kyōto daigaku keizai kenkyūjo disukasshon pēpā* 6603 京都大学経済研究所ディスカッションペーパー 6603 (Kyoto University Economic Research Institute discussion paper 6603). Kyoto, 1966.

Taylor, George E. *The Struggle for North China*. New York, Institute of Pacific Relations, 1940.

Teichman, Eric. *Affairs of China: A Survey of the Recent History and Present Circumstances of the Republic of China*. London, Methuen, 1938.

Teikoku Zaigō Gunjinkai 帝国在郷軍人会. *Teikoku Zaigō Gunjinkai sanjūnenshi* 帝国在郷軍人会三十年史 (A thirty-year history of the Imperial Reservists Association). Tokyo, Teikoku Zaigō Gunjinkai Hombu, 1944.

Tejima Seiichi sensei den 手島精一先生伝 (Biography of Professor Tejima Seiichi). Tokyo, Tejima Kōgyō Kyōiku Shikindan, 1929.

Temperley, Harold W. V., ed. *A History of the Peace Conference of Paris*. 6 vols. London, H. Frowde, and Hodder and Stoughton, 1920–24.

Tenshin Kyoryū Mindan 天津居留民団. *Tenshin Kyoryū Mindan nijisshūnen kinenshi* 天津居留民団二十周年記念誌 (A twenty-year commemorative record of the Tientsin Residents Association). Tientsin, Tenshin Kyoryū Mindan, 1930.

Terahiro Akio 寺広映雄. "Chūgoku kakumei ni okeru Chū-Nichi kōshō no ichi kōsatsu: Miyazaki Tōten o chūshin ni shite" 中国革命に於ける中日交渉の一考察—

宮崎滔天を中心にして (Comments on Sino-Japanese relations during the Chinese revolution: Centering on Miyazaki Tōten), *Hisutoria*, No. 9 (October 1954), pp. 9–17.

—— "Chūgoku kakumei to Miyazaki Tōten" 中国革命と宮崎滔天 (The Chinese revolution and Miyazaki Tōten), *Hisutoria*, No. 7 (August 1953).

Thompson, Richard Austin. "The Yellow Peril, 1890–1924." Unpublished doctoral dissertation, University of Wisconsin, 1957.

Thorne, Christopher. *The Limits of Foreign Policy: The West, the League and the Far Eastern Crisis of 1931–1933.* London, Hamish Hamilton, 1972.

Tilley, John. *London to Tokyo.* London, Hutchinson, 1944.

Tōa Dōbunkai 東亜同文会, ed. *Konoe Kazan kō kinenshi* 近衛霞山公記念誌 (Commemorating Prince Konoe Kazan [Atsumaro]), *Shina*, Nos. 2–3 (February 1934).

—— *Tōa Dōbunkai kiyō* 東亜同文会紀要 (Bulletin of the East Asia Common Culture Association). Tokyo, Tōa Dōbunkai, 1937.

Tōa Dōbun Shoin 東亜同文書院 (Shanghai). *Sōritsu sanjisshūnen kinen Tōa Dōbun Shoin shi* 創立三十周年記念東亜同文書院志 (A record commemorating the thirtieth anniversary of the founding of the East Asia Common Culture Academy). Shanghai, Tōa Dōbun Shoin, 1930.

Tōa Dōbun Shoin Koyū Dōsōkai 東亜同文書院滬友同窓会, ed. *Sanshū Nezu sensei den* 山洲根津先生伝 (Biography of Sanshū [Nezu Hajime]). Tokyo, Nezu Sensei Denki Hensanbu, 1930.

Tōa Kenkyūsho (Itō Yū) 東亜研究所 (伊藤斌). *Tōken seika tekiyō* 東研成果摘要 (Outline of the results of research by the East Asia Research Institute). Tokyo, Tōa Kenkyūsho, 1943.

Togai Yoshio 栂井義雄. "Meiji ishin zengo no Mitsui" 明治維新前後の三井 (Mitsui at the time of the Meiji Restoration), *Senshūdai ronshū*, No. 35 (December 1964), pp. 76–84.

Tōgō Shigenori 東郷茂徳. *Jidai no ichimen* 時代の一面 (An aspect of the Shōwa era). Tokyo, Kaizōsha, 1952.

—— *The Cause of Japan.* Translated and edited by Togo Fumihiko and B.B. Blakeney. New York, Simon and Schuster, 1956. A partial translation of *Jidai no ichimen.*

Tōkei Sūri Kenkyūsho Kokuminsei Chōsa Iinkai 統計数理研究所国民性調査委員会, ed. *Nihonjin no kokuminsei* 日本人の国民性 (The Japanese national character). Tokyo, Chiseidō, 1961.

Tokinoya Katsu 時野谷勝. "Kyōikurei seitei no rekishiteki haikei" 教育令制定の歴史的背景 (Historical background of the establishment of the educational regulations [of 1897]), in Kaikoku Hyakunen Kinen Bunka Jigyōkai 開国百年記念文化事業会, ed., *Kaikoku hyakunen kinen Meiji bunkashi ronshū* 開国百年記念明治文化史論集 (Collected papers on Meiji cultural history commemorating the centennial of the opening of the country), pp. 123-51. Tokyo, Kangensha, 1952.

Tokutomi Iichirō 德富猪一郎, ed. *Kōshaku Katsura Tarō den* 公爵桂太郎伝 (Biography of Prince Katsura Tarō). 2 vols. Tokyo, Kō Katsura Kōshaku Kinen Jigyōkai, 1917.

—— *Kōshaku Matsukata Masayoshi den* 公爵松方正義伝 (Biography of Prince Matsukata Masayoshi). 2 vols. Tokyo, Kōshaku Matsukata Masayoshi Denki Hakkōkai, 1935.

—— ed. *Kōshaku Yamagata Aritomo den* 公爵山県有朋伝 (Biography of Prince Yamagata Aritomo). 3 vols. Tokyo, Yamagata Aritomo Kō Kinen Jigyōkai, 1933.

Tōkyō Shisei Chōsakai 東京市政調査会. *Tōkyō Shisei Chōsakai yonjūnenshi* 東京市政調査会四十年史 (A forty-year history of the Tokyo Institute of Municipal Research). Tokyo, Tōkyō Shisei Chōsakai, 1962.

Toland, John. *The Rising Sun: The Decline and Fall of the Japanese Empire*. New York, Random House, 1970.

Tomimura Shin'en 富村真演. "Ryūkyū ōchō no chōkō bōeki saku" 琉球王朝の朝貢貿易策 (The tribute trade policy of the Liu-chiu dynasty), *Ryūkyū daigaku bunri gakubu kiyō jimbun shakai*, No. 5 (December 1960), pp. 1-26.

Tominaga Yūji 富永祐治. *Kōtsū ni okeru shihonshugi no hatten* 交通における資本主義の発展 (The development of capitalism in communications). Tokyo, Iwanami Shoten, 1953.

Tomita Kenji 富田健治. *Haisen Nihon no uchigawa: Konoe kō no omoide* 敗戦日本の内側—近衛公の想い出 (Inside defeated Japan: Recollections of Prince Konoe). Tokyo, Kokon Shoin, 1962.

Tōmiya Taisa Kinen Jigyō Iinkai 東宮大佐記念事業委員会, ed. *Tōmiya Kaneo den* 東宮鉄男伝 (Biography of Tōmiya Kaneo). Tokyo, Tōmiya Taisa Kinen Jigyō Iinkai, 1940.

Toscano, Mario. *Le origini diplomatiche del patto d'acciaio* (Diplomatic origins of the pact of steel). 2d rev. ed. Florence, Sansoni, 1956. Translated as *The Origins of the Pact of Steel*. Baltimore, Johns Hopkins Press, 1968.

Tōyama Shigeki 遠山茂樹. *Meiji ishin* 明治維新 (The Meiji Restoration). Tokyo, Iwanami Shoten, 1951.

Tōyama Shigeki, Imai Seiichi 今井清一, and Fujiwara Akira 藤原彰. *Shōwashi* 昭和史 (A history of the Shōwa period). 2d rev. ed. Tokyo, Iwanami Shoten, 1959.

Tōyama Shigeki and Satō Shin'ichi 佐藤進一. *Nihonshi kenkyū nyūmon* 日本史研究入門 (Introduction to the study of Japanese history). 2 vols. Tokyo, Tōkyō Daigaku Shuppankai, 1963.

Tōyō Bunko 東洋文庫. *Tōyō Bunko shozō kindai Nihon kankei bunken bunrui mokuroku: Washo maikurofuirumu no bu* 東洋文庫所蔵近代日本関係文献分類目録—和書マイクロフィルムの部 (Classified catalogue of books in the Tōyō Bunko on modern Japan:

Japanese books and microfilms). Tokyo, Tōyō Bunko Kindai Nihon Kenkyū Shitsu, 1961–63.

Tōyō Takushoku Kabushiki Kaisha 東洋拓殖株式会社. *Tōyō Takushoku Kabushiki Kaisha sanjūnenshi* 東洋拓殖株式会社三十年誌 (A thirty-year history of the Oriental Development Company). Tokyo, Tōyō Takushoku Kabushiki Kaisha, 1939.

Treat, Payson J. *Diplomatic Relations Between the United States and Japan, 1853–1895.* 2 vols. Stanford, Stanford University Press, 1932.

Trefousse, H.L. *Germany and American Neutrality, 1939–1941.* New York, Bookman Associates, 1956.

Tsuchihashi Yūitsu 土橋勇逸. "Sambō Hombu dainibuchō jidai no omoide" 参謀本部第二部長時代の思い出 (Recollection of events while Director of the Second Division of the Army General Staff). Unpublished handwritten document, 1957.

Tsuchiya Tadao 土屋忠雄. *Meiji jūnendai no kyōiku seisaku* 明治十年代の教育政策 (Educational policies in the second decade of the Meiji era). Tokyo, Kōdansha, 1956.

Tsuchiya Takao 土屋喬雄. *Ishin keizaishi* 維新経済史 (An economic history of the Restoration period). Tokyo, Seikatsusha, 1942.

—— "Keizai seisakka to shite no Ōkubo Toshimichi" 経済政策家としての大久保利通 (Ōkubo Toshimichi as an economic policy-maker), *Chūō kōron*, LX, No. 4 (April 1935), 95–110.

—— "Meiji shoki no bōeki seisaku" 明治初期の貿易政策 (Foreign trade policy in early Meiji), *Shakai keizai shigaku*, VI, No. 10 (February 1937), 168–84.

—— *Meiji zenki keizaishi kenkyū* 明治前期経済史研究 (Studies in the economic history of early Meiji). Tokyo, Nihon Hyōronsha, 1944.

—— "Meiji zenki no infurēshon to sono kokufuku" 明治前期のインフレーションとその克服 (The successful cure for the early Meiji inflation), *Keizaigaku ronshū*, XXIV, No. 2 (1958), 1–27; No. 3 (1958), 80–90.

—— "Transition and Development of Economic Policy," in Shibusawa, *Japanese Society in the Meiji Era*, pp. 103–79.

Tsuji, Masanobu. *Singapore: The Japanese Version.* Sydney, O. Smith, 1960.

Tsukatani Akihiro 塚谷晃弘. "Daiikkai Naikoku Kangyō Hakurankai to Meiji shoki tōjiki kōgyō" 第一回内国勧業博覧会と明治初期陶磁器工業 (The first Domestic Enterprise Encouragement Exposition and the early Meiji ceramics industry), *Kokugakuin daigaku seikei ronsō*, XIV, No. 1 (July 1965), 1–30.

Tsunoda Jun 角田順. "Kaidai" 解題 (Explanatory note), in *Nampō shinshutsu* 南方進出 (The southward advance), pp. 430–37. Vol. VI of Nihon Kokusai Seiji Gakkai Taiheiyō Sensō Gen'in Kenkyūbu, ed., *Taiheiyō sensō e no michi.* Tokyo, Asahi Shimbunsha, 1963.

—— *Manshū mondai to kokubō hōshin* 満洲問題と国防方針 (The Manchurian question and Japanese defense policy). Tokyo, Hara Shobō, 1967.

—— "Nichi-Bei kōshō: Nihon gawa no mondai ten" 日米交渉―日本側の問題点 (Japanese-American negotiations before Pearl Harbor: The problems on the Japanese side), *Kokusai seiji: Nihon gaikōshi kenkyū—Shōwa jidai,* 1959, pp. 111–37.

—— "Nihon no tai-Bei kaisen, 1940–1941" 日本の対米開戦 (一九四〇年〜一九 四一年) (Japanese-American relations, 1940–1941), in *Nichi-Bei kaisen* 日米開戦 (Outbreak of war between Japan and the United States), pp. 1–387. Vol. VII of Nihon Kokusai Seiji Gakkai Taiheiyō Sensō Gen'in Kenkyūbu, ed., *Taiheiyō sensō e no michi.* Tokyo, Asahi Shimbunsha, 1963.

Tsurumi Sakio 鶴見佐吉雄. *Nihon bōeki shikō* 日本貿易史綱 (An outline history of Japan's foreign trade). Tokyo, Ganshōdō, 1939.

Tsurumi Yūsuke 鶴見祐輔, ed. *Gotō Shimpei* 後藤新平. 4 vols. Tokyo, Gotō Shimpei Haku Denki Hensankai, 1937–38.

Tuchman, Barbara W. *Stilwell and the American Experience in China, 1911–45.* New York, Macmillan, 1971.

—— *The Zimmermann Telegram.* New York, Viking Press, 1958.

Tupper, Eleanor, and G.E. McReynolds. *Japan in American Public Opinion.* New York, Macmillan, 1937.

Uchida Naosaku 内田直作. "Ansei kaikoku to Igirisu shihon—sono kyōdō hōshiki ni kansuru oboegaki" 安政開国とイギリス資本―その協同方式に関する覚書 (English capital and the opening of the ports in the Ansei period—a memorandum on its cooperative form), *Seijō daigaku keizai kenkyū,* Nos. 8–9 (September 1958), pp. 327–46. Reprinted in Okada Shumpei 岡田俊平, ed., *Meiji shoki no zaisei kin'yū seisaku* 明治初期の財政金融政策 (Financial and fiscal policy in early Meiji), pp. 365–84. Tokyo, Seimeikai, 1964.

Uchida Ryōhei 内田良平. *Nihon no san dai kyūmu* 日本の三大急務 (Three urgent tasks before Japan). Tokyo, Kokuryūkai, 1912.

—— *Shina kaizō ron* 支那改造論 (Reconstructing China). Tokyo, Kokuryūkai, 1911.

—— *Zen Mammō tetsudō tōitsu ikensho* 全満蒙鉄道統一意見書 (Views on the unification of railroads in Manchuria and Mongolia). Tokyo, Kokuryūkai Shuppanbu, 1930.

Uchiyama Kanzō 内山完造. *Heikin yūsen: Chūgoku no konjaku* 平均有銭―中国の今昔 (Neither wealth nor poverty: China's present and past). Tokyo, Dōbunkan, 1955.

—— *Kakō roku* 花甲録 (My life). Tokyo, Iwanami Shoten, 1960.

Uchiyama Masakuma 内山正熊. "Nichi-Doku sensō to Santō mondai" 日独戦争と 山東問題 (The German-Japanese war and the Shantung problem), *Hōgaku kenkyū,* XXXIII, No. 2 (February 1960), 243–91.

Ueda Toshio 植田捷雄. "Daiichiji taisen ni okeru Nihon no sansen gaikō" 第一次大戦 に於ける日本の参戦外交 (The negotiations concerning Japan's entrance into World War I), in Gakujutsu Kenkyū Kaigi Gendai Chūgoku Kenkyū Tokubetsu Iinkai 学術研究会議現代中国研究特別委員会, ed., *Kindai Chūgoku kenkyū* 近代中国 研究 (Research on modern China), pp. 327–61. Tokyo, Kōgakusha, 1948.

—— "Nichi-Doku-I sangoku dōmei" 日独伊三国同盟 (The Tripartite Pact among Japan, Germany, and Italy), in Nihon Gaikō Gakkai 日本外交学会, ed., *Taiheiyō sensō gen'in ron* 太平洋戦争原因論 (Origins of the Pacific War). Tokyo, Shimbun Gekkansha, 1953.

—— "Nichi-Ro sensō to Rūzuvieruto" 日露戦争とルーズヴェルト (The Russo-Japanese War and Roosevelt), in Ueda Toshio 植田捷雄, ed., *Kamikawa sensei kanreki kinen: kindai Nihon gaikōshi no kenkyū* 神川先生還暦記念—近代日本外交史の研究 (Commemorating the sixtieth birthday of Professor Kamikawa: Studies in modern Japanese diplomatic history). Tokyo, Yūhikaku, 1956.

—— *Nikka kōshō shi: Nihon no tairiku hatten to sono hōkai katei* 日華交渉史—日本の大陸発展とその崩壊過程 (A history of Sino-Japanese negotiations: Japan's expansion on the mainland and the process of its collapse). Tokyo, Nomura Shoten, 1948.

—— "Nisshin sen'eki to kokusaihō" 日清戦役と国際法 (The Sino-Japanese War and international law), in Hanabusa Nagamichi Hakushi Kanreki Kinen Rombunshū Henshū Iinkai 英修道博士還暦記念論文集編集委員会, ed., *Hanabusa Nagamichi hakushi kanreki kinen rombunshū: gaikōshi oyobi kokusai seiji no shomondai* 英修道博士還暦記念論文集—外交史及び国際政治の諸問題 (Essays commemorating the sixtieth birthday of Dr. Hanabusa Nagamichi: Studies in diplomatic history and international politics). Tokyo, Keiō Tsūshin, 1962.

—— "Ryōdo kizoku kankeishi" 領土帰属関係史 (A history of Japan's territorial settlements), in Kokusaihō Gakkai 国際法学会, ed., *Heiwa jōyaku no sōgō kenkyū* 平和条約の綜合研究 (A comprehensive study of the peace treaty), Vol. I. Tokyo, Yūhikaku, 1953.

—— "Ryūkyū no kizoku o meguru Nisshin kōshō" 琉球の帰属を繞る日清交渉 (Sino-Japanese negotiations concerning the disputed sovereignty over the Ryukyu islands), *Tōyō bunka kenkyūjo kiyō*, No. 2 (September 1951), pp. 151–201.

—— "Shiberia shuppei to kita Karafuto mondai" シベリア出兵と北樺太問題 (The Siberian Expedition and the question of northern Sakhalin), *Kokusaihō gaikō zasshi*, LX, Nos. 4–6 (March 1962), 99–126.

Ueyama Shumpei 上山春平. "Taiheiyō sensō no shisō shiteki igi" 太平洋戦争の思想史的意義 (Ideological significance of the Pacific War), *Chūō kōron*, September 1961, pp. 98–107.

Ugaki Kazushige 宇垣一成. *Ugaki nikki* 宇垣日記 (Ugaki diary). Tokyo, Asahi Shimbunsha, 1954.

Ullman, Richard H. *Intervention and the War*. Vol. I of *Anglo-Soviet Relations, 1917–1921*. Princeton, Princeton University Press, 1961.

Umetani Noboru 梅溪昇. "Kindai Nihon guntai no seikaku keisei to Nishi Amane" 近代日本軍隊の性格形成と西周 (The formation of the character of the modern Japanese army and Nishi Amane), *Jimbun gakuhō*, No. 4 (1954), pp. 19–44.

—— *Meiji zenki seijishi no kenkyū* 明治前期政治史の研究 (A study of early Meiji political history). Tokyo, Miraisha, 1963.

—— *O-yatoi gaikokujin* 御雇い外国人 (Foreigners employed by the government). Tokyo, Nihon Keizai Shimbunsha, 1965.

Umezu Kazurō 梅津和郎. "Keizai hattenki ni okeru bōeki seisaku shisō" 経済発展期 における貿易政策思想 (Thought on foreign trade policy during the period of economic development), in Matsui Kiyoshi 松井清, ed., *Kindai Nihon bōekishi* 近代日本貿易史 (A history of modern Japan's foreign trade), II, 241–316. 3 vols. Tokyo, Yūhikaku, 1959–63. Also in Umezu, *Nihon no bōeki shisō*, pp. 77–181.

—— "Meiji shoki no bōeki seisaku to bōeki shisō" 明治初期の貿易政策と貿易思想 (Foreign trade thought and policy in early Meiji), in Matsui Kiyoshi 松井清, ed., *Kindai Nihon bōekishi* 近代日本貿易史 (History of modern Japan's foreign trade), I, 347–404. 3 vols. Tokyo, Yūhikaku, 1959–63. Also in Umezu, *Nihon no bōeki shisō*, pp. 12–76.

—— *Nihon no bōeki shisō: Nihon bōeki seisaku shisōshi kenkyū* 日本の貿易思想―日本貿易政策思想史研究 (Foreign trade thought in Japan: Studies in the history of Japanese foreign trade policy thought). Kyoto, Minerubā Shobō, 1963.

Union of Soviet Socialist Republics. *Krasnyi arkiv* (Red Archive). 106 vols. Moscow, Gosudarstvennoe Izdatel'stvo, 1922–41.

United States, Congress, Joint Committee on the Investigation of the Pearl Harbor Attack. *Hearings before the Joint Committee on the Investigation of the Pearl Harbor Attack.* 39 parts in 15 vols. Washington D.C., U.S. Government Printing Office, 1946.

United States, Congress, Senate. *Treaty on the Limitation of Naval Armaments: Hearings before the Committee on Foreign Relations.* Washington D.C., U.S. Government Printing Office, 1930.

—— *London Naval Treaty of 1930: Hearings before the Committee on Naval Affairs.* Washington D.C., U.S. Government Printing Office, 1930.

United States, Department of the Army, Office of Military History. 14 reels of microfilm. Washington D.C., Library of Congress, 1964.

Japanese Monograph, No. 45, History of Imperial General Headquarters Army Section. Rev. ed.

Japanese Monograph, No. 77, Japanese Preparations for Operations in Manchuria (prior to 1943).

Japanese Monograph, No. 145, Outline of Naval Armament and Preparations for War, Part I.

Japanese Monograph, No. 146, Political Strategy Prior to the Outbreak of War, Part II.

Japanese Monograph, No. 147 (Japanese), Political Strategy Prior to the Outbreak of War, Part III. Rev. ed.

Japanese Monograph, No. 150, Political Strategy Prior to the Outbreak of War, Part IV.

Japanese Monograph, No. 160, Outline of Naval Armament and Preparations for War, Part III.

United States, Department of State. *A Catalog of Files and Microfilms of the German Foreign Ministry Archives, 1920–1945.* 2 vols. Stanford, Hoover Institution, 1962–64.

—— *Documents on German Foreign Policy, 1918–1945, from the Archives of the German Foreign Ministry.* 16 vols. Washington D.C., U.S. Government Printing Office, 1949–57.

—— *Foreign Relations of the United States, 1879.* Washington D.C., U.S. Government Printing Office, 1879.

—— *Foreign Relations of the United States, 1934,* Vol. III, *The Far East.* Washington D.C., U.S. Government Printing Office, 1950.

—— *Foreign Relations of the United States: Lansing Papers, 1914–1920.* Washington D.C., U.S. Government Printing Office, 1939.

—— *Nazi-Soviet Relations, 1939–1941: Documents from the Archives of the German Foreign Office.* Washington D.C., U.S. Government Printing Office, 1948.

—— *Papers Relating to the Foreign Relations of the United States, Japan: 1931–1941.* 2 vols. Washington D.C., U.S. Government Printing Office, 1943.

Unno Fukuju 海野福寿. "Bōekishijō ni okeru 1880 nendai" 貿易市場における1880年代 (The 1880s in the history of foreign trade), *Rekishigaku kenkyū,* No. 253 (May 1963), pp. 21–30.

—— "Chihō chokuyushutsu kaisha no setsuritsu to tenkai" 地方直輸出会社の設立と展開 (The establishment and development of regional direct export companies), in Yokohama Shi Shi Henshūshitsu, *Yokohama shi shi,* III, Part 1, 689–752. Yokohama, Yūrindō, 1961.

—— "Chokuyushutsu no tenkai" 直輸出の展開 (The development of direct exports) in Yokohama Shi Shi Henshūshitsu, *Yokohama shi shi,* III, Part 1, 615–88. Yokohama, Yūrindō, 1961.

—— "Meiji bōekishi kenkyū to dōkō" 明治貿易史研究と動向 (Trends in the study of the history of foreign trade during the Meiji period), in Shakai Keizai Shigakkai 社会経済史学会, ed., *Saikin jūnenkan ni okeru shakai keizai shigaku no hattatsu* 最近十年間における社会経済史学の発達 (Developments in the study of socio-economic history during the last ten years). Special issue of *Shakai keizai shigaku,* XXXI, Nos. 1–5 (February 1966), 149–60.

—— "Meiji nijūnendai ni okeru 'shōken kaifuku' undō ni tsuite" 明治二十年代における「商権回復」運動について (The "restoration of commercial rights" movement, 1887–97), *Hōkei ronshū* (Shizuoka Daigaku Hōkei Tankidaibu), No. 20 (November 1965), pp. 77–138.

—— *Meiji no bōeki: kyoryūchi bōeki to shōken kaifuku* 明治の貿易—居留地貿易と商権回復

(Meiji foreign trade: Foreign concession trade and the restoration of commercial rights). Tokyo, Hanawa Shobō, 1967.

—— "Seishi seichagyō no hatten" 製糸製茶業の発展 (The development of the silk-reeling and tea industries), in Yokohama Shi Shi Henshūshitsu, *Yokohama shi shi*, III, Part 1, 465–558. Yokohama, Yūrindō, 1961.

—— "Seishigyō chagyō kumiai no setsuritsu" 製糸業茶業組合の設立 (The establishment of silk-reeling and tea associations), in Yokohama Shi Shi Henshūshitsu, *Yokohama shi shi*, III, Part 1, 799–852. Yokohama, Yūrindō, 1961.

—— "Yokohama bōeki ichiba no kikō" 横浜貿易市場の機構 (The structure of the Yokohama foreign trade market), in Yokohama Shi Shi Henshūshitsu, *Yokohama shi shi*, III, Part 1, 559–614. Yokohama, Yūrindō, 1961.

—— "Yokohama Rengō Kiito Niazukarijo jiken" 横浜聯合生糸荷預所事件 (Yokohama Federated Raw Silk Warehouse incident), in Yokohama Shi Shi Henshūshitsu, *Yokohama shi shi*, III, Part 1, 753–98. Yokohama, Yūrindō, 1961.

—— "Yokohama Rengō Kiito Niazukarijo jiken" 横浜聯合生糸荷預所事件 (Yokohama Federated Raw Silk Warehouse incident), *Rekishigaku kenkyū*, No. 310 (March 1966), pp. 35–44.

Unno Fukuju and Morita Shirō 守田志郎. "Kaikō igo no shōhin seisan to jinushisei" 開港以後の商品生産と地主制 (The landlord system and the production of commercial goods after the opening of the ports), in *Iwanami kōza Nihon rekishi kindai* 岩波講座日本歴史近代 (Iwanami lectures on modern Japanese history), II, 97–140. Tokyo, Iwanami Shoten, 1962.

Unno Yoshirō 海野芳郎. "Rondon kaigun gunshuku kaigi: Nihon no tachiba to shuchō" ロンドン海軍軍縮会議—日本の立場と主張 (The London Naval Disarmament Conference: Japan's point of view), *Kokusai seiji: Nihon gaikōshi kenkyū—Shōwa jidai*, 1959, pp. 36–49.

Unterberger, Betty. *America's Siberian Expedition, 1918–1920: A Study of National Policy.* Durham, Duke University Press, 1956.

Usui Chūzō 臼井忠三, ed. *Tenshin Kyoryū Mindan sanjisshūnen kinenshi* 天津居留民團三十周年記念誌 (Thirty-year commemorative record of the Tientsin Residents Association). Tientsin, Tientsin Residents Association, 1941.

Usui Katsumi 臼井勝美. "Chōsa jiken" 長沙事件 (The Changsha incident), *Rekishi kyōiku*, IX, No. 2 (February 1961), 53–58.

—— "Chō Sakurin bakushi no shinso" 張作霖爆死の眞相 (The facts concerning the assassination of Chang Tso-lin), *Bessatsu chisei, V: himerareta Shōwashi*, December 1956, pp. 26–38.

—— "Chūgoku no taisen sanka to Nihon no tachiba" 中国の大戦参加と日本の立場 (China's entrance into World War I and the position of Japan), *Rekishi kyōiku*, VIII, No. 2 (February 1960), 22–28.

—— "Go-sanjū jiken to Nihon" 五・三〇事件と日本 (The May 30 Incident and

Japan), *Ajia kenkyū*, IV, No. 2 (October 1957), 43–64.

—— "Jōyaku kaisei to Chōsen mondai" 条約改正と朝鮮問題 (Treaty revision and the Korean question), in *Iwanami kōza Nihon rekishi kindai* 岩波講座日本歴史近代 (Iwanami lectures on modern Japanese history), Vol. IV. Tokyo, Iwanami Shoten, 1962.

—— "Nihon to shingai kakumei: sono ichi sokumen" 日本と辛亥革命―その一側面 (One facet of the relationship between Japan and the Chinese revolution of 1911), *Rekishigaku kenkyū*, No. 207 (May 1957), pp. 49–52.

—— *Nitchū gaikōshi: Hokubatsu no jidai* 日中外交史―北伐の時代 (A history of Sino-Japanese diplomatic relations: The Northern Expedition period). Tokyo, Hanawa Shobō, 1971.

—— "Nitchū sensō no seijiteki tenkai, 1937–1941" 日中戦争の政治的展開（一九三七年～一九四一年） (The historical development of the Sino-Japanese War, 1937–1941), in *Nitchū sensō II* 日中戦争 II (The Sino-Japanese War, Part 2). Vol. IV of Nihon Kokusai Seiji Gakkai Taiheiyō Sensō Gen'in Kenkyūbu, ed., *Taiheiyō sensō e no michi*. Tokyo, Asahi Shimbunsha, 1963.

—— *Nitchū sensō* 日中戦争 (The Second Sino-Japanese War). Tokyo, Chūō Kōronsha, 1967.

—— "Ōshū taisen to Nihon no tai-Man seisaku: Namman Tōmō jōyaku no seiritsu zengo" 欧州大戦と日本の対満政策―南満東蒙条約の成立前後 (World War I and Japanese policy toward Manchuria: The conclusion of the southern Manchuria-eastern Mongolia treaty), *Kokusai seiji: Nihon gaikōshi kenkyū—daiichiji sekai taisen*, 1962, pp. 15–27.

—— " 'Shidehara gaikō' oboegaki" 「幣原外交」覚書 (A note on "Shidehara diplomacy"), *Nihon rekishi*, No. 126 (December 1958), pp. 62–68 and 11.

—— " 'Shina jihen' zen no Chū-Nichi kōshō" 「支那事変」前の中日交渉 (Sino-Japanese negotiations prior to the China Incident), *Kokusai seiji: Nihon gaikōshi kenkyū—Nitchū kankei no tenkai*, 1960, pp. 119–33.

—— "Tanaka gaikō ni tsuite no oboegaki" 田中外交についての覚書 (A memorandum on Tanaka diplomacy), *Kokusai seiji: Nihon gaikōshi kenkyū—Shōwa jidai*, 1959, pp. 26–35.

Utley, Freda. "Japan's Inner Conflict," *Asia*, XXXVII, No. 5 (May 1937), 325–28.

Uyehara, Cecil H. *Checklist of Archives in the Japanese Ministry of Foreign Affairs, Tokyo, Japan, 1868–1945, Microfilmed for the Library of Congress, 1949–1951*. Washington D.C., Library of Congress, 1954.

Vagts, Alfred. *Deutschland und die Vereinigten Staaten in der Weltpolitik*. 2 vols. New York, Macmillan, 1935.

Vevier, Charles. *The United States and China, 1906–1913: A Study of Finance and Diplomacy*. New Brunswick, Rutgers University Press, 1955.

Vinacke, Harold. *A History of the Far East in Modern Times.* 6th ed. New York, Appleton-Century-Crofts, 1959.

Vinson, J. Chal. "The Imperial Conference of 1921 and the Anglo-Japanese Alliance," *Pacific Historical Review,* XXXI, No. 3 (August 1962), 257–66.

Waguneru sensei tsuikaishū ワグネル先生追懐集 (Reminiscences of Professor Gottfried Wagner). Tokyo, Ko Waguneru Hakushi Kinen Jigyōkai, 1938.

Wakatsuki Reijirō 若槻礼次郎. *Kofūan kaikoroku* 古風庵回顧録 (Memoirs of Wakatsuki Reijirō). Tokyo, Yomiuri Shimbunsha, 1950.

Wagatsuma Hiroshi 我妻洋 and Yoneyama Toshinao 米山俊直. *Henken no kōzō: Nihonjin no jinshukan* 偏見の構造—日本人の人種観 (The structure of prejudice: Japanese views of race). Tokyo, Nihon Hōsō Shuppan Kyōkai, 1967.

Wang Yun-sheng 王芸生, ed. *Liu-shih-nien lai Chung-kuo yü Jih-pen* 六十年来中国與日本 (China and Japan in the past sixty years). 7 vols. Tientsin, Tientsin Ta Kung Pao She, 1932–34.

Waseda Daigaku Shakai Kagaku Kenkyūjo 早稲田大学社会科学研究所, ed. *Ōkuma bunsho* 大隈文書 (Papers of Ōkuma Shigenobu). 5 vols. Tokyo, by the editor, 1958–62.

Watanabe Gizan (Shūhō) 渡辺岐山 (秀方). *Shina kokuminsei ron* 支那国民性論 (An essay on Chinese national character). Tokyo, Ōsakayagō Shoten, 1922.

Watanabe Ikujirō 渡辺幾治郎. *Gaikō to gaikōka* 外交と外交家 (Diplomacy and diplomats). Tokyo, Chikura Shobō, 1939.

—— *Monjo yori mitaru Ōkuma Shigenobu kō* 文書より観たる大隈重信侯 (Marquis Ōkuma Shigenobu as seen through documents). Tokyo, Ko Ōkuma Kō Kokumin Reibokai, 1932.

—— *Mutsu Munemitsu den* 陸奥宗光伝 (Biography of Mutsu Munemitsu). Tokyo, Kaizōsha, 1934.

—— *Nihon kinsei gaikōshi* 日本近世外交史 (A history of modern Japanese diplomacy). Tokyo, Chikura Shobō, 1938.

—— *Ōkuma Shigenobu* 大隈重信. Tokyo, Ōkuma Shigenobu Kankōkai, 1952.

—— ed. *Ōkuma Shigenobu kankei monjo* 大隈重信関係文書 (Documents related to Ōkuma Shigenobu). 6 vols. Tokyo, Nihon Shiseki Kyōkai, 1932–35.

Watanabe Shigeo 渡辺茂雄. *Ugaki Kazushige no ayunda michi* 宇垣一成の歩んだ道 (The path of Ugaki Kazushige). Tokyo, Shintaiyōsha, 1948.

Wazaki Kōzō 和崎皓三. "Fukoku kyōhei—shokusan kōgyō" 富国強兵—殖産興業 (Rich country, strong army—the encouragement of production), in Rekishigaku Kenkyūkai Nihonshi Kenkyūkai 歴史学研究会日本史研究会, ed., *Nihon rekishi kōza* 日本歴史講座 (Lectures on Japanese history), V, 75–97. 8 vols. Tokyo, Tōkyō Daigaku Shuppankai, 1956.

Weizsäcker, Ernst von. *Memoirs.* Chicago, Regnery, 1951.

White, John Albert. *The Diplomacy of the Russo-Japanese War.* Princeton, Princeton

University Press, 1964.

—— *The Siberian Intervention*. Princeton, Princeton University Press, 1950.

"Why Japan Attacks Germany," *The Literary Digest*, XLIX, No. 12 (September 19, 1914), 502.

Williams, William Appleman. *Roots of the Modern American Empire: A Study of the Growth and Shaping of a Social Consciousness in a Marketplace Society*. New York, Random House, 1969.

Wilson, Theodore A. *The First Summit: Roosevelt and Churchill at Placentia Bay, 1941*. Boston, Houghton Mifflin, 1969.

Wiskemann, Elizabeth. *The Rome-Berlin Axis: A History of the Relations between Hitler and Mussolini*. New York, Oxford University Press, 1949.

Wohlstetter, Roberta. *Pearl Harbor: Warning and Decision*. Stanford, Stanford University Press, 1962.

Wood, G. Z. *China, the United States and the Anglo-Japanese Alliance*. New York, Fleming H. Revell, 1921.

Woodward, Ernest L. *British Foreign Policy in the Second World War*. London, H. M. Stationery Office, 1962.

Wright, Stanley F. *China's Customs Revenue since the Revolution of 1911*. 3d ed. Shanghai, Statistical Department of the Inspectorate of Customs, 1935.

Yabe Teiji 矢部貞治, ed. *Konoe Fumimaro* 近衛文麿. 2 vols. Tokyo, Kōbundō, 1952.

Yagisawa Zenji 八木沢善次. "Meiji shoki no defurēshon to nōgyō kyōkō" 明治初期のデフレーションと農業恐慌 (The early Meiji deflation and agricultural depression), *Shakai keizai shigaku*, II, No. 3 (1932), 257-98.

—— "Seinan sen'eki go no infurēshon" 西南戦役後のインフレーション (The post-Satsuma Rebellion inflation), *Keizaishi kenkyū*, No. 7 (1932), pp. 101-17, 255-70.

Yakhontoff, V. A. *Russia and the Soviet Union in the Far East*. New York, Coward-McCann, 1931.

Yamabe Kentarō 山辺健太郎. "Chōsen kaikaku undō to Kin Gyokukin: Kōshin jihen ni kanren shite" 朝鮮改革運動と金玉均—甲申事変に関連して (Korean reform movements and Kim Ok-kyun: The Korean incident of 1884), *Rekishigaku kenkyū*, No. 247 (November 1960), pp. 31-46.

—— "Itsubi no hen ni tsuite" 乙未の変について (The Korean incident of 1895), *Kokusai seiji: Nikkan kankei no tenkai*, 1962, pp. 69-81.

—— "Jingo gunran ni tsuite" 壬午軍乱について (On the Korean incident of 1882), *Rekishigaku kenkyū*, No. 257 (September 1961), pp. 13-25.

—— "Kōshin jihen ni tsuite: toku ni 'Jiyūtō shi' no ayamari ni kanren shite" 甲申事変について—とくに「自由党史」のあやまりに関連して (The Korean incident of 1884, with special emphasis on the errors in the "History of the Liberal Party"), *Rekishigaku kenkyū*, No. 244 (August 1960), pp. 23-34.

—— "Kōshin jihen to Tōgaku no ran" 甲申事変と東学の乱 (The Korean incident of 1884 and the Tonghak uprising), in Chikuma Shobō Henshūbu 筑摩書房編集部, ed., *Yuragu Chūka teikoku* ゆらぐ中華帝国 (The shaken Chinese empire), pp. 261–81. Vol. XI of *Sekai no rekishi* 世界の歴史 (A history of the world). Tokyo, Chūō Kōronsha, 1961.

—— "Kōshin nichiroku no kenkyū" 甲申日録の研究 (A study of a diary of the Korean incident of 1884), *Chōsen gakuhō*, No. 17 (October 1960), pp. 117–42.

——"Nihon teikokushugi to shokuminchi" 日本帝国主義と植民地 (Japanese imperialism and Japanese colonies), in *Iwanami kōza Nihon rekishi gendai* 岩波講座日本歴史現代 (Iwanami lectures on contemporary Japanese history), II. Tokyo, Iwanami Shoten, 1963.

—— "Nisshin Tenshin jōyaku ni tsuite" 日清天津條約について (On the Sino-Japanese Treaty of Tientsin), *Ajia kenkyū*, VII, No. 2 (November 1960), 1–46.

Yamada Shōji 山田昭次. "Yokohama Rengō Kiito Niazukarijo jiken to jiyū minken shoshimbun no ronchō" 横浜聯合生糸荷預所事件と自由民権諸新聞の論調 (Comments of the popular rights newspapers on the Yokohama Federated Raw Silk Warehouse incident), *Shien*, XXVI, No. 1 (July 1965), 60–81; XXVII, No. 1 (June 1966), 44–59; XXVII, No. 3 (March 1967), 53–60.

Yamaguchi Kazuo 山口和雄. *Bakumatsu bōekishi* 幕末貿易史 (History of foreign trade in the late Tokugawa period). Tokyo, Seikatsusha, 1943.

—— "Manufacture and Export of Tea," in Ohara, *Japanese Trade and Industry in the Meiji-Taisho Era*, pp. 151–200.

—— "Meiji jidai no seishi kin'yū" 明治時代の製糸金融 (Silk reeling finance in the Meiji period), *Keizaigaku ronshū*, XXVIII, No. 2 (1962), 1–45.

—— "Meiji shoki no gaikoku kaiun to Mitsubishi Kaisha" 明治初期の外国海運と三菱会社 (Foreign maritime transport in early Meiji and the Mitsubishi Company), in *Wakimura Yoshitarō kanreki kinen rombunshū sekai keizai bunseki* 脇村義太郎還暦記念論文集世界経済分析 (Analysis of the world economy: Essays commemorating the sixtieth birthday of Wakimura Yoshitarō), pp. 120–57. Tokyo, Iwanami Shoten, 1962.

—— "Meiji shonen Beikoku Taiheiyō Yūsen Kaisha no tai-Nichi shūkōsen" 明治初年米国太平洋郵船会社の対日就航船 (The beginning of navigation to Japan by the American Pacific Mail Steamship Company in early Meiji), *Nihon rekishi*, No. 179 (April 1963), pp. 86–87.

—— *Meiji zenki keizai no bunseki* 明治前期経済の分析 (Analysis of the early Meiji economy). Tokyo, Tōkyō Daigaku Shuppankai, 1956.

—— *Nihon keizaishi kōgi* 日本経済史講義 (Lectures on Japanese economic history). Tokyo, Tōkyō Daigaku Shuppankai, 1960.

—— ed. *Nihon sangyō kin'yūshi kenkyū—seishi kin'yū hen* 日本産業金融史研究―製糸金融篇 (Studies in the history of Japanese industrial finance—silk reeling finance).

Tokyo, Tōkyō Daigaku Shuppankai, 1966.

—— "The Opening of Japan at the End of the Shogunate and Its Effects," in Shibusawa, *Japanese Society in the Meiji Era*, pp. 1–46.

Yamaguchi Kazuyuki 山口一之. "Kenseitō naikaku no seiritsu to kyokutō jōsei" 憲政党内閣の成立と極東情勢 (Formation of a Kenseitō cabinet and the Far Eastern situation), *Kokusai seiji: Nihon gaikōshi kenkyū—Nisshin Nichi-Ro sensō*, 1961, pp. 87–101.

Yamaguchi Shigeji 山口重次. *Higeki no shōgun Ishiwara Kanji* 悲劇の将軍石原莞爾 (The tragic General Ishiwara Kanji). Tokyo, Sekaisha, 1952.

Yamamoto Hirobumi 山本弘文. "Shokusan kōgyō: sono kenkyū dōkō to mondaiten" 殖産興業—その研究動向と問題点 (Trends and issues in the study of industrialization in Japan), in Shakai Keizai Shigakkai 社会経済史学会, ed., *Saikin jūnenkan ni okeru shakai keizai shigaku no hattatsu* 最近十年間における社会経済史学の発達 (Developments in the study of socio-economic history during last ten years). Special issue of *Shakai keizai shigaku*, XXXI, Nos. 1–5 (February 1966), 115–25.

Yamamoto, Hiromasa. "Development of the Marine Insurance Industry in Japan," *Kobe Economic and Business Review*, No. 5 (1958), pp. 77–88.

Yamamoto Shigeru 山本茂. *Jōyaku kaisei shi* 條約改正史 (A history of treaty revision). Tokyo, Takayama Shoin, 1943.

Yamamoto Shingo 山本慎吾. "Washinton kaigi ni okeru Chūgoku mondai: kaigi ni taisuru Nihon no taido o chūshin to shite" ワシントン会議における中国問題—会議に対する日本の態度を中心として (The Chinese question at the Washington Conference and the Japanese attitude toward the conference), *Rekishi kyōiku*, IX, No. 2 (February 1961), 19–24.

Yamamura, Kozo. "The Founding of Mitsubishi: A Case Study in Japanese Business History," *Business History Review*, XLI, No. 2 (Summer 1967), 141–60.

—— "The Role of the Samurai in the Development of Modern Banking in Japan," *Journal of Economic History*, XXVII, No. 2 (June 1967), 198–220.

Yamanaka Minetarō 山中峯太郎. *Jitsuroku: Ajia no akebono daisan kakumei no shinsō* 実録アジアの曙第三革命の真相 (Dawn in Asia: The truth concerning the third revolution. A memoir). 2 vols. Tokyo, Bungei Shunjūsha, 1961–62.

Yamashita Yukio 山下幸男. "Manshū jihen no hassei" 満州事変の発生 (The outbreak of the Manchurian Incident), *Chūkyō shōgaku ronsō*, VIII, Nos. 3–4 (March 1962), 91–152.

Yamaura Kan'ichi 山浦貫一. *Mori Kaku* 森恪. Tokyo, Mori Kaku Denki Hensankai, 1940.

Yamawaki Shigeo 山脇重雄. "Mazampo jiken" 馬山浦事件 (The Mazampo incident), *Tōhoku daigaku bungakubu kenkyū nempō*, IX (January 1959), 1–45; X (February 1960), 138–87; XIII (February 1963), 47–125.

Yanaga, Chitoshi. *Japan since Perry*. New York, McGraw-Hill, 1949.

Yanaihara Tadao 矢内原忠雄. *Manshū mondai* 満州問題 (The Manchurian problem). Tokyo, Iwanami Shoten, 1934.

—— *Teikoku shugika no Taiwan* 帝国主義下の台湾 (Taiwan under imperialism). Tokyo, Iwanami Shoten, 1929.

Yano Jin'ichi 矢野仁一. *Nisshin eki go Shina gaikōshi* 日清役後支那外交史 (A diplomatic history of China since the Sino-Japanese War). Vol. IX of *Tōhō Bunka Gakuin Kyōto Kenkyūsho Kenkyūshitsu hōkoku* 東方文化学院京都研究所研究室報告 (Bulletin of the Academy of Oriental Culture, Kyoto Institute). Kyoto, Tōhō Bunka Gakuin Kyōto Kenkyūsho, 1937.

Yasuoka Akio 安岡昭男. "Meiji shoki no tai-Ro keikairon ni kansuru ichi kōsatsu" 明治初期の対露警戒論に関する一考察 (A study of the advocates of vigilance toward Russia at the beginning of the Meiji period), *Hōsei shigaku*, No. 13 (October 1960), pp. 49–58.

—— "Ryūkyū shozoku o meguru Nisshin kōshō no shomondai" 琉球所属を繞る日清交渉の諸問題 (Problems related to the Sino-Japanese negotiations concerning the disputed sovereignty over the Ryukyu islands), *Hōsei shigaku*, No. 9 (January 1957), pp. 107–16.

Yazawa Kōyū 矢澤康祐. "Sen-kyūhyaku-sanjūgo-rokunen ni okeru Kokumintō no tai-Nichi seisaku to shimbun no kō-Nichi ronchō" 1935–6 年における国民党の対日政策と新聞の抗日論調 (Kuomintang policy toward Japan and press comments attacking Japan, 1935–36), *Jimbun gakuhō*, No. 25 (March 1961), pp. 209–44.

Yim, Kwan Ha. "Japanese Policy toward China during World War I." Unpublished doctoral dissertation, Fletcher School of Law and Diplomacy, 1963.

—— "Yüan Shih-k'ai and the Japanese," *Journal of Asian Studies*, XXIV, No. 1 (November 1964), 63–73.

Yokohama Shi Shi Henshūshitsu 横浜市史編集室, ed. *Yokohama shi shi* 横浜市史 (History of the city of Yokohama). 5 vols. Yokohama, Yūrindō, 1958–63.

Yokohama Shōkin Ginkō 横浜正金銀行, ed. *Yokohama Shōkin Ginkō shi* 横浜正金銀行史 (History of the Yokohama Specie Bank). 5 vols. Yokohama, by the editor, 1920.

Yokoyama Kendō 横山健堂. *Matsui taishō den* 松井大將伝 (Biography of General Matsui Iwane). Tokyo, Hakkōsha, 1938.

Yonezawa Hideo 米沢秀夫. "Shanhai hōjin hattenshi" 上海邦人発展史 (A history of Japanese development in Shanghai), *Tōa keizai kenkyū*, XXII, No. 3 (July 1938), 50–64; XXIII, No. 1 (January-February 1939), 112–26.

Yoshida, Ken'ichi, trans. *The Yoshida Memoirs: The Story of Japan in Crisis.* Boston, Houghton Mifflin, 1962. Partial translation of Yoshida Shigeru, *Kaisō jūnen* (1957).

Yoshida Shigeru 吉田茂. *Kaisō jūnen* 回想十年 (Reminiscences of ten years). 4 vols. Tokyo, Shinchōsha, 1957.

Yoshihashi, Takehiko. *Conspiracy at Mukden: The Rise of the Japanese Military*. New Haven, Yale University Press, 1963.

Yoshikawa Mitsuharu 吉川光治. "Meiji kin'yūshi kanken" 明治金融史管見 (My views on Meiji financial history), *Bankingu*, No. 165 (December 1961), pp. 26–43.

—— "Meiji ni okeru kyūheika kaikin to heika kirisage" 明治における旧平価開禁と平価切下げ (The Meiji government's lowering of the par value and resumption of gold payments at the old par), *Kin'yū jānaru*, II, No. 10 (October 1961), 91–97.

Yoshimura Michio 吉村道男. "Nichi-Ro kōwa mondai no ichi sokumen: Nihon no tai-Shin taido o chūshin ni" 日露講和問題の一側面―日本の対清態度を中心に (One aspect of the problem of peace talks between Japan and Russia: Japan's view of China), *Kokusai seiji: Nihon gaikōshi kenkyū—Nisshin Nichi-Ro sensō*, 1961, pp. 119–33.

Yoshino Sakuzō 吉野作造, ed. *Gaikoku bunkahen* 外国文化篇 (Foreign culture). Vol. XVI of *Meiji bunka zenshū* 明治文化全集 (Complete collection on Meiji culture). Tokyo, Nihon Hyōronsha, 1928.

—— *Keizaihen* 経済篇 (Economics). Vol. IX of *Meiji bunka zenshū* 明治文化全集 (Complete collection on Meiji culture). Tokyo, Nihon Hyōronsha, 1929.

—— *Nikka kokkō ron* 日華国交論 (Essays on Sino-Japanese relations). Tokyo, Shinkigensha, 1948.

—— *Nisshi kōshō ron* 日支交渉論 (Essays on Sino-Japanese negotiations). Tokyo, Keiseisha Shoten, 1915.

Yoshizawa Kenkichi 芳沢謙吉. *Gaikō rokujūnen* 外交六十年 (Sixty years as a diplomat).Tokyo, Jiyū Ajiasha, 1958.

Young, A. Morgan. *Imperial Japan, 1926–1938*. New York, William Morrow, 1938.

—— *Japan under Taisho Tenno, 1912–1926*. London, Allen and Unwin, 1928.

Young, George. *Ten Years at the Court of St. James, 1895–1905*. New York, Dutton, 1922. A translation and adaptation of H. F. Eckardstein, *Lebenserinnerungen und politische Denkwürdigkeiten*. Leipzig, Paul List, 1919.

Young, John. *Checklist of Microfilm Reproductions of Selected Archives of the Japanese Army, Navy, and Other Government Agencies, 1868–1945*. Washington D. C., Georgetown University Press, 1959.

—— *The Research Activities of the South Manchurian Railway Company, 1907–1945: A History and Bibliography*. New York, East Asian Institute, Columbia University, 1966.

Young, Marilyn Blatt. *The Rhetoric of Empire: American China Policy, 1895–1901*. Cambridge, Mass., Harvard University Press, 1968.

Yuasa Akira 湯浅晃. "Kindai Nitchō kankei no ichi kōsatsu: burujoajii no tai-Chōsen seisaku o chūshin to shite" 近代日朝関係の一考察―ブルジョアジーの対朝

鮮政策を中心として (An examination of recent Korean-Japanese relations, with emphasis on bourgeois policy toward Korea), *Chōsen gakuhō*, No. 24 (July 1962), pp. 160–82.

Yukizawa Kenzō 行沢健三. "Ishin seifu to shihon chikuseki" 維新政府と資本蓄積 (The Restoration government and capital accumulation), in Matsui Kiyoshi 松井清, ed., *Kindai Nihon bōekishi* 近代日本貿易史 (A history of modern Japan's foreign trade), I, 227–74. 3 vols. Tokyo, Yūhikaku, 1959–63.

Yuri Masamichi 由利正通. *Shishaku Yuri Kimimasa den* 子爵由利公正伝 (Biography of Viscount Yuri Kimimasa). Tokyo, by the author, 1940.

Zabriskie, E. H. *American-Russian Rivalry in the Far East: A Study in Diplomacy and Power Politics, 1895–1914*. Philadelphia, University of Pennsylvania Press, 1946.

Zai-Bei Nihonjinkai 在米日本人会, ed. *Zai-Bei Nihonjin shi* 在米日本人史 (A history of the Japanese in the United States). San Francisco, Zai-Bei Nihonjinkai, 1940.

Zai-Ka Nihon Bōseki Dōgyōkai 在華日本紡績同業会, ed. *Funatsu Shin'ichirō* 船津辰一郎. Tokyo, Tōhō Kenkyūsha, 1958.

Zaisei Keizai Gakkai 財政経済学会, ed. *Meiji Taishō zaiseishi* 明治大正財政史 (The fiscal history of the Meiji and Taishō periods). 20 vols. Tokyo, by the editor, 1936–40.

Zōsen Kyōkai 造船協会, ed. *Nihon kinsei zōsenshi* 日本近世造船史 (History of Japanese shipbuilding in modern times). Tokyo, by the editor, 1911.

Zühlke, Herbert. *Die Rolle des fernen Osten in den politischen Beziehungen der Mächte, 1895–1905*. Berlin, Ehering, 1929.

JAPANESE-LANGUAGE PERIODICALS

Aizu tanki daigaku gakuhō 会津短期大学学報
Ajia kenkyū アジア研究
Aoyama keizai ronshū 青山経済論集
Bankingu バンキング
Bessatsu chisei, V: himerareta Shōwashi 別冊知性 5 秘められた昭和史
Bunka shigaku 文化史学
Chōsen gakuhō 朝鮮学報
Chūkyō shōgaku ronsō 中京商学論叢
Chūō kōron 中央公論
Dōshisha daigaku keizaigaku ronsō 同志社大学経済学論叢
Dōshisha shōgaku 同志社商学
Etchū shidan 越中史壇
Firosofia (Philosophia) フィロソフィア
Fukushima daigaku gakugei gakubu ronshū 福島大学学芸学部論集

Gaikō jihō 外交時報

Gakujutsu kenkyū (jimbun shakai shizen) 学術研究（人文社会自然）

Geirin 芸林

Gendaishi kenkyū 現代史研究

Ginkō kenkyū 銀行研究

Handai hōgaku 阪大法学

Hikone ronsō 彦根論叢

Hitotsubashi daigaku hōgaku kenkyū 一橋大学法学研究

Hitotsubashi ronsō 一橋論叢

Hisutoria ヒストリア

Hōgaku kenkyū 法学研究

Hōgaku shimpō 法学新報

Hōgaku shirin 法学志林

Hōkei ronshū (Shizuoka Daigaku hōkei tankidaibu) 法経論集（静岡大学法経短期大部）

Hokkaidō daigaku bungakubu kiyo 北海道大学文学部紀要

Hokuto 北斗

Hōsei shigaku 法政史学

Ibaragi daigaku bunri gakubu kiyo (shakai kagaku) 茨城大学文理学部紀要（社会科学）

Ibaragi daigaku seikei gakkai zasshi 茨城大学政経学会雑誌

Jimbun gakuhō 人文学報

Jimbun kenkyū 人文研究

Jiyū 自由

Kaijishi kenkyū 海事史研究

Keijō teikoku daigaku hōbungakubu kenkyū chōsa sasshi 京城帝国大学法文学部研究調査冊子

Keizai kenkyū 経済研究

Keizai ronsō 経済論叢

Keizai shirin 経済志林

Keizai to bōeki 経済と貿易

Keizaigaku kenkyū (Kyūshū Daigaku) 経済学研究（九州大学）

Keizaigaku kenkyū (Kōbe Daigaku nempō) 経済学研究（神戸大学年報）

Keizaigaku ronshū 経済学論集

Keizaikei 経済系

Keizaishi kenkyū 経済史研究

Kigyō to shakai 企業と社会

Kindai Chūgoku kenkyū 近代中国研究

Kindai Nihonshi kenkyū 近代日本史研究

Kinki daigaku hōgaku 近畿大学法学

Kin'yū jānaru 金融ジャーナル

Kin'yū keizai 金融経済

Kokka gakkai zasshi 国家学会雑誌

Kokugakuin daigaku seikei ronsō 国学院大学政経論叢

Kokumin keizai zasshi 国民経済雑誌

Kokusai seiji: Nichi-Bei kankei no imēji 国際政治—日米関係のイメージ

Kokusai seiji: Nihon gaikōshi kenkyū—Bakumatsu ishin jidai 国際政治—日本外交史研究—幕末維新時代

Kokusai seiji: Nihon gaikōshi kenkyū—daiichiji sekai taisen 国際政治—日本外交史研究—第一次世界大戦

Kokusai seiji: Nihon gaikōshi kenkyū—Meiji jidai 国際政治—日本外交史研究—明治時代

Kokusai seiji: Nihon gaikōshi kenkyū—Nichi-Bei kankei no tenkai 国際政治—日本外交史研究—日米関係の展開

Kokusai seiji: Nihon gaikōshi kenkyū—Nihon gaikōshi no shomondai 国際政治—日本外交史研究—日本外交史の諸問題

Kokusai seiji: Nihon gaikōshi kenkyū—Nisshin Nichi-Ro sensō 国際政治—日本外交史研究—日清日露戦争

Kokusai seiji: Nihon gaikōshi kenkyū—Nitchū kankei no tenkai 国際政治—日本外交史研究—日中関係の展開

Kokusai seiji: Nihon gaikōshi kenkyū—Shōwa jidai 国際政治—日本外交史研究—昭和時代

Kokusai seiji: Nihon gaikōshi kenkyū—Taishō jidai 国際政治—日本外交史研究—大正時代

Kokusai seiji: Nihon gaikōshi no shomondai, I 国際政治—日本外交史の諸問題 I

Kokusai seiji: Nikkan kankei no tenkai 国際政治—日韓関係の展開

Kokusaihō gaikō zasshi 国際法外交雑誌

Kokushigaku 国史学

Komazawa daigaku kenkyū ronshū 駒澤大学研究論集

Kōtsū bunka 交通文化

Kyōiku shoseki Tōyō shigaku ronshū 教育書籍東洋史学論集

Meidai shōgaku ronsō 明大商学論叢

Meiji daigaku tanki daigaku kiyō 明治大学短期大学紀要

Meiji gakuin ronsō 明治学院論叢

Mie daigaku gakugei gakubu kenkyū kiyō 三重大学学芸学部研究紀要

Musashi daigaku ronshū 武蔵大学論集

Nagoya daigaku bungakubu jisshūnen kinen ronshū 名古屋大学文学部十周年記念論集

Nagoya daigaku bungakubu kenkyū ronshū 名古屋大学文学部研究論集

Naigai kenkyū 内外研究

Nempō seijigaku 年報政治学

Nichi-Bei forum 日米フォルム

Nihon rekishi 日本歴史

Nihonshi kenkyū 日本史研究

Ōkuma kenkyū 大隈研究

Ōsaka daigaku keizaigaku 大阪大学経済学

Ōyōshinri kenkyū 応用心理研究

Rekishi chiri 歴史地理

Rekishi hyōron 歴史評論

Rekishi kagaku 歴史科学

Rekishi kyōiku 歴史教育

Rekishi to gendai 歴史と現代

Rekishigaku kenkyū 歴史学研究

Ritsumeikan hōgaku 立命館法学

Ronsō 論叢

Ryūkyū daigaku bunri gakubu kiyō jimbun shakai 琉球大学文理学部紀要人文社会

Seiji keizai ronsō 政治経済論叢

Seijō daigaku keizai kenkyū 成城大学経済研究

Seishin joshi daigaku ronsō 聖心女子大学論叢

Sekai 世界

Sekai keizai 世界経済

Senshūdai ronshū 専修大論集

Shakai kagaku ronshū 社会科学論集

Shakai kagaku tōkyū 社会科学討究

Shakai keizai shigaku 社会経済史学

Shakai keizaishi kenkyūjo kenkyū kiyō 社会経済史研究所研究紀要

Shien 史苑

Shigaku zasshi 史学雑誌

Shina 支那

Shirin 史林

Shisō 思想

Shōgaku ronshū 商学論集

Shōkei ronsō 商経論叢

Shōkeihō ronsō 商経法論叢

Sundai shigaku 駿台史学

Tōa keizai kenkyū 東亜経済研究

Tochi seido shigaku 土地制度史学

Tōhoku daigaku bungakubu kenkyū nempō 東北大学文学部研究年報

Toritsudai hōgakkai zasshi 都立大法学会雑誌

Tōyō bunka 東洋文化

Tōyō bunka kenkyūjo kiyō 東洋文化研究所紀要

Tōyō keizai shimpō 東洋経済新報

Waseda daigakushi kiyō 早稲田大学史紀要

Waseda hōgakkaishi: hōritsu hen 早稲田法学会誌—法律編
Waseda seiji keizaigaku zasshi 早稲田政治経済学雑誌
Yamagata daigaku kiyō (shakai kagaku) 山形大学紀要（社会科学）
Yamagata daigaku kiyō (jimbun kagaku) 山形大学紀要（人文科学）

10

Bibliography of Recent Works

Shumpei Okamoto

❖

A selected list of books published generally between 1963 and 1971.

BIBLIOGRAPHICAL GUIDES

Hanabusa Nagamichi 英修道, comp. *Nihon gaikōshi kankei bunken mokuroku* 日本外交史関係文献目録 (A list of materials relating to Japanese diplomatic history). Tokyo, Keiō Gijuku Daigaku Hōgaku Kenkyūkai, 1961.

—— comp. *Nihon gaikōshi kankei bunken mokuroku: tsuiho hen* 日本外交史関係文献目録—追補篇 (A list of materials relating to Japanese diplomatic history: Supplement). Tokyo, Keiō Gijuku Daigaku Hōgaku Kenkyūkai, 1968.

Kokuritsu Kokkai Toshokan 国立国会図書館 (National Diet Library), comp. *Itō Miyoji kankei bunsho mokuroku: Kensei Shiryō Shitsu shozō shiryō mokuroku daini* 伊東巳代治関係文書目録—憲政資料室所蔵資料目録第二 (Catalog of documents relating to Itō Miyoji: The second catalog of materials deposited in the Kensei Shiryō Shitsu, National Diet Library, Tokyo). Tokyo, by the compiler, 1962.

—— comp. *Kenseishi Hensankai shūshū bunsho mokuroku: Kensei Shiryō Shitsu shozō shiryō mokuroku daiichi* 憲政史編纂会収集文書目録—憲政資料室所蔵資料目録第一 (Catalog of documents collected by the Committee for the Compilation of the History of Constitutional Government in Japan: The first catalog of materials deposited in the Kensei Shiryō Shitsu, National Diet Library, Tokyo). Tokyo, by the compiler, 1960.

—— comp. *Mutsu Munemitsu kankei bunsho mokuroku: Kensei shiryō mokuroku daiyon* 陸奥宗光関係文書目録—憲政資料目録第四 (Catalog of documents relating to Mutsu Munemitsu: The fourth catalog of materials deposited in the Kensei Shiryō Shitsu, National Diet Library, Tokyo). Tokyo, by the compiler, 1966. (See also *Katsura Tarō kankei bunsho mokuroku* in chap. 9).

Ōhata Tokushirō 大畑篤四郎. *Kokusai kankyō to Nihon gaikō* 国際環境と日本外交 (The international situation and Japanese diplomacy). Tokyo, Azuma Shuppan, 1966.

Shulman, Frank J., comp. and ed. *Japan and Korea: An Annotated Bibliography of Doctoral Dissertations in Western Languages, 1877–1969*. Chicago, American Library Association, 1970.

Webb, Herschel, with the assistance of Marleigh Ryan. *Research in Japanese Sources: A Guide*. New York, Columbia University Press, 1965.

SOURCE MATERIALS (INCLUDING DOCUMENTS, AUTOBIOGRAPHIES, DIARIES, AND MEMOIRS)

Abrikossow, Dmitrii I. *Revelations of a Russian Diplomat: The Memoirs of Dmitrii I. Abrikossow*. Edited by George Alexander Lensen. Seattle, University of Washington Press, 1964.

Aoki Shūzō 青木周蔵. *Aoki Shūzō jiden* 青木周蔵自伝 (The autobiography of Aoki Shūzō). Edited by Sakane Yoshihisa 坂根義久. Tokyo, Heibonsha, 1970.

D'Anethan, Baron Albert. *The D'Anethan Dispatches from Japan, 1894–1910*. Selected, translated, and edited with a historical introduction by George Alexander Lensen. Tokyo, Sophia University, 1967.

Gendaishi shiryō 現代史資料 (Source materials on contemporary history). Tokyo, Misuzu Shobō, 1962– . Volumes relating to Japan's foreign policy, 1868–1941:

Vols. I–III and XLII: *Zoruge jiken* ゾルゲ事件 (The Sorge case). Compiled and edited with explanatory notes by Obi Toshito 小尾俊人.

Vols. IV–V and XXIII: *Kokkashugi undō* 国家主義運動 (Nationalist movements). Compiled and edited with explanatory notes by Imai Seiichi 今井清一 and Takahashi Masae 高橋正衛.

Vols. VII and XI: *Manshū jihen* 満州事変 (The Manchurian Incident) and *Zoku Manshū jihen* 続満州事変 (The Manchurian Incident, continued). Compiled and edited with explanatory notes by Tsunoda Jun 角田順, Kobayashi Tatsuo 小林竜夫, Shimada Toshihiko 島田俊彦, and Inaba Masao 稲葉正夫.

Vols. VIII–X and XII–XIII: *Nitchū sensō* 日中戦争 (The Second Sino-Japanese War). Compiled and edited with explanatory notes by Tsunoda Jun 角田順, Shimada Toshihiko 島田俊彦, Inaba Masao 稲葉正夫, Usui Katsumi 臼井勝美, and Kobayashi Tatsuo 小林竜夫.

(For a review of the Manchurian Incident and Sino-Japanese War volumes, see Akira Iriye, "Japan's Foreign Policies between World Wars—Sources and Interpretations," *Journal of Asian Studies*, XXVI, No. 4 (August 1967), 677–82.

Vols. XXXI–XXXIII: *Mantetsu* 満鉄 (The South Manchuria Railway Company). Compiled and edited with explanatory notes by Itō Takeo 伊藤武雄, Ogiwara Kiwamu 荻原極, and Fujii Masuo 藤井満洲男.

Vols. XXXIV–XXXVI and XXXVIII–XXXIX: *Taiheiyō sensō* 太平洋戦争 (The Pacific War). Compiled and edited by Sanematsu Yuzuru 実松譲, Fujii Hiroshi 藤井博, and Inaba Masao 稲葉正夫.

Vol. XXXVII: *Daihon'ei* 大本営 (The Imperial Headquarters). Compiled and edited with an explanatory note by Inaba Masao 稲葉正夫.

Vols. XLIII and XLIV: *Kokka sōdōin* 国家總動員 (National mobilization). Compiled and edited with explanatory notes by Nakamura Takafusa 中村隆英 and Hara Akira 原朗.

Hayashi Tadasu 林董. *Nochi wa mukashi no ki* 後は昔の記 (Recollections). Edited by Yui Masaomi 由井正臣. Tokyo, Heibonsha, 1971.

Heusken, Henry. *Japan Journal, 1855–1861.* Translated and edited by Jeannette C. van der Corput and Robert A. Wilson. New Brunswick, Rutgers University Press, 1964.

Higashikuni Naruhiko 東久邇稔彦. *Higashikuni nikki: Nihon gekidōki no hiroku* 東久邇日記—日本激動期の秘録 (Higashikuni Naruhiko diary: A record of turbulent Japan). Tokyo, Tokuma Shoten, 1968.

Ike, Nobutaka, trans. and ed., with an introduction. *Japan's Decision for War: Records of the 1941 Policy Conferences.* Stanford, Stanford University Press, 1967.

Imai Takeo 今井武夫. *Shina jihen no kaisō* 支那事変の回想 (Recollections of the China Incident). Tokyo, Misuzu Shobō, 1964.

Ishii Kikujirō 石井菊次郎. *Ishii Kikujirō ikō: gaikō zuisō* 石井菊次郎遺稿—外交随想 (A posthumous manuscript by Ishii Kikujirō: A diplomatic memoir). Compiled by Kajima Heiwa Kenkyūjo 鹿島平和研究所. Tokyo, Kajima Kenkyūjo Shuppankai, 1967.

Japan, Gaimushō 外務省 (Foreign Ministry), ed. *Nisso kōshō shi* 日ソ交渉史 (A history of Japanese-Soviet relations). Tokyo, Gannandō, 1969. Originally issued in 1942.

Kamikawa Hikomatsu 神川彦松, ed., and Kim Chong-myong 金正明, comp. *Nikkan gaikō shiryō shūsei* 日韓外交資料集成 (Collection of materials relating to Japanese-Korean diplomatic relations). 8 vols. in 10 books, Tokyo, Gannandō, 1963–67.

Kiyosawa Kiyoshi 清沢洌. *Ankoku nikki* 暗黒日記 (Diary of a dark era). Edited with explanatory notes by Hashikawa Bunsō 橋川文三. 3 vols. Tokyo, Hyōronsha, 1970–71.

Kojima Iken 児島惟謙. *Ōtsu jiken nisshi* 大津事件日誌 (Diary of the Ōtsu incident). Tokyo, Heibonsha, 1971.

Konoe Atsumaro 近衛篤麿. *Konoe Atsumaro nikki* 近衛篤麿日記 (Konoe Atsumaro diary). Edited by Konoe Atsumaro Nikki Kankōkai 近衛篤麿日記刊行会. 5 vols. plus supplementary vol. of source materials. Tokyo, Kajima Kenkyūjo Shuppankai, 1968–69.

Lensen, George Alexander. *Japanese Diplomatic and Consular Officials in Russia: A Handbook of Japanese Representatives in Russia from 1874 to 1968.* Compiled on the basis of Japanese and Russian sources with a historical introduction. Tallahassee, Diplomatic Press, 1968.

Meiji hyakunenshi sōsho 明治百年史叢書 (Historical materials of the century since the

Meiji Restoration). Tokyo, Hara Shobō, 1965– . Volumes relating to Japan's foreign policy, 1868–1941:

Honjō Shigeru 本庄繁. *Honjō nikki* 本庄日記 (Honjō Shigeru diary).

Itō Hirobumi 伊藤博文, comp. *Kimitsu Nisshin sensō* 機密日清戦争 (Confidential records of the First Sino-Japanese War).

Japan, Gaimushō 外務省 (Foreign Ministry), ed. *Nichi-Ro kōshō shi* 日露交渉史 (A history of Russo-Japanese relations). Originally issued in 1944.

Japan, Kaigunshō 海軍省 (Navy Ministry), ed. *Yamamoto Gonnohyōe to kaigun* 山本権兵衛と海軍 (Yamamoto Gonnohyōe and the navy).

Japan, Rikugunshō 陸軍省 (Army Ministry), comp. *Meiji tennō godenki shiryō: Meiji gunjishi* 明治天皇御伝記史料―明治軍事史 (Biographical materials relating to the Meiji emperor: A military history of the Meiji era). 2 vols.

Japan, Sambō Hombu 参謀本部 (Army General Staff), comp. *Haisen no kiroku* 敗戦の記録 (Records of the lost war).

—— comp. *Sugiyama memo* 杉山メモ (Sugiyama Gen memorandum). 2 vols.

Ōyama Azusa 大山梓, comp. *Yamagata Aritomo ikensho* 山県有朋意見書 (Collected memoranda by Yamagata Aritomo).

Tsunoda Jun 角田順, comp. *Ishiwara Kanji shiryō* 石原莞爾資料 (Materials on Ishiwara Kanji). 2 vols.

Ugaki Matome 宇垣纏. *Sensōroku* 戦藻録 (War diary). Edited by Ogawa Kanji 小川貫璽 and Yokoi Toshiyuki 横井俊之.

Nakano Masao 中野雅夫, ed. *Hashimoto taisa no shuki* 橋本大佐の手記 (Memoirs of Colonel Hashimoto Kingorō). Tokyo, Misuzu Shobō, 1963.

Nihon Kindai Shiryō Kenkyūkai 日本近代史料研究会, comp. *Nihon riku-kaigun no seido soshiki jinji* 日本陸海軍の制度組織人事 (System, organization, and personnel administration of the Japanese army and navy). Tokyo, Tōkyō Daigaku Shuppankai, 1971.

Nishi Haruhiko 西春彦. *Kaisō no Nihon gaikō* 回想の日本外交 (Diplomatic memoirs). Tokyo, Iwanami Shoten, 1965.

Nishihara Kamezō 西原亀三. *Yume no shichijūyonen: Nishihara Kamezō jiden* 夢の七十余年西原亀三自伝 (A dream of over seventy years: The autobiography of Nishihara Kamezō). Edited by Kitamura Hironao 北村敬直. Tokyo, Heibonsha, 1965.

Pineau, Roger, ed. *The Japan Expedition, 1852–1854: The Personal Journal of Commodore Matthew C. Perry*. Washington D.C., Smithsonian Institution, distributed by Random House, New York, 1969.

Satō Naotake 佐藤尚武. *Kaiko hachijūnen* 回顧八十年 (Recollections of eighty years). Tokyo, Jiji Tsūshinsha, 1963.

Satow, Sir Ernest. *Korea and Manchuria between Russia and Japan, 1895–1904*. Selected and edited with a historical introduction by George Alexander Lensen. Tallahassee, Diplomatic Press, 1966.

Shiōden Nobutaka 四王天延孝. *Shiōden Nobutaka kaikoroku* 四王天延孝回顧錄 (Memoirs of Shiōden Nobutaka). Tokyo, Misuzu Shobō, 1964.

Suematsu Tahei 末松太平. *Watakushi no Shōwashi* 私の昭和史 (A personal history of the Shōwa era). Tokyo, Misuzu Shobō, 1963.

Suzuki Kantarō 鈴木貫太郎. *Suzuki Kantarō jiden* 鈴木貫太郎自伝 (The autobiography of Suzuki Kantarō). Edited by Suzuki Hajime 鈴木一. Tokyo, Jiji Tsūshinsha, 1968.

Ugaki Kazushige 宇垣一成. *Ugaki Kazushige nikki* 宇垣一成日記 (Ugaki Kazushige diary). Edited by Tsunoda Jun 角田順. 3 vols. Tokyo, Misuzu Shobō, 1968–71.

Yoshizawa Kenkichi 芳沢謙吉. *Yoshizawa Kenkichi jiden* 芳沢謙吉自伝 (The autobiography of Yoshizawa Kenkichi). Edited by Nakano Keishi 中野敬止. Tokyo, Jiji Tsūshinsha, 1964.

(See also the supplementary volume of source materials in Nihon Kokusai Seiji Gakkai Taiheiyō Sensō Gen'in Kenkyūbu, ed. *Taiheiyō sensō e no michi,* cited in Chap. 9).

BIOGRAPHIES

Hackett, Roger F. *Yamagata Aritomo in the Rise of Modern Japan, 1838–1922.* Cambridge, Mass., Harvard University Press, 1971.

Heinrichs, Waldo H. Jr. *American Ambassador: Joseph C. Grew and the Development of the United States Diplomatic Tradition.* Boston, Little, Brown, 1966.

Hirota Kōki Denki Kankōkai 広田弘毅伝記刊行会, ed. *Hirota Kōki* 広田弘毅. Tokyo, by the editor, 1966.

Iwata, Masakazu. *Ōkubo Toshimichi: The Bismarck of Japan.* Berkeley, University of California Press, 1964.

Johnson, Chalmers. *An Instance of Treason: Ozaki Hotsumi and the Sorge Spy Ring.* Stanford, Stanford University Press, 1964.

Kuroki Yūkichi 黒木勇吉. *Komura Jutarō* 小村寿太郎. Revised and enlarged. Tokyo, Kōdansha, 1968. Originally published in 1941.

Meiji hyakunenshi sōsho 明治百年史叢書 (Historical materials of the century since the Meiji Restoration). Tokyo, Hara Shobō, 1965. Biographies relating to Japan's foreign policy, 1868–1941:

Kokuryū Kurabu 黒龍倶楽部, ed. *Kokushi Uchida Ryōhei den* 国士内田良平伝 (A biography of the patriot Uchida Ryōhei).

Komori Tokuji 小森徳治. *Akashi Motojirō* 明石元二郎. 2 vols.

Ozawa Jisaburō Teitoku Den Kankōkai 小沢治三郎提督伝刊行会, ed. *Teitoku Ozawa Jisaburō* 提督小沢治三郎 (Admiral Ozawa Jisaburō).

Sugiyama Gensui Denki Kankōkai 杉山元帥伝記刊行会, ed. *Sugiyama gensui den* 杉山元帥伝 (A biography of Sugiyama Gen).

Miwa Kimitada 三輪公忠. *Matsuoka Yōsuke* 松岡洋右. Tokyo, Chūō Kōronsha, 1971.
Oka Yoshitake 岡義武. *Konoe Fumimaro* 近衛文麿. Tokyo, Iwanami Shoten, 1972.
Oki Shūji 沖修二. *Anami Korechika* 阿南惟幾. Tokyo, Kōdansha, 1970.
Shimada Kinji 島田謹二. *Amerika ni okeru Akiyama Saneyuki* アメリカにおける秋山真之 (Akiyama Saneyuki in America). Tokyo, Asahi Shimbunsha, 1969.
—— *Roshiya ni okeru Hirose Takeo* ロシヤにおける広瀬武夫 (Hirose Takeo in Russia). Tokyo, Kōbundō, 1962.
Uchida Yasuya Denki Hensan Iinkai 内田康哉伝記編纂委員会 and Kajima Heiwa Kenkyūjo 鹿島平和研究所, eds. *Uchida Yasuya* 内田康哉. Tokyo, Kajima Kenkyūjo Shuppankai, 1969.
Wilson, George M. *Radical Nationalist in Japan: Kita Ikki, 1883–1937*. Cambridge, Mass., Harvard University Press, 1969.

MONOGRAPHIC STUDIES

Banno Masataka 坂野正高 and Etō Shinkichi 衛藤瀋吉, eds. *Ueda Toshio sensei kanreki kinen: Chūgoku o meguru kokusai seiji* 植田捷雄先生還暦記念—中国をめぐる国際政治 (Commemorating the sixtieth birthday of Professor Ueda Toshio: China in international politics). Tokyo, Tōkyō Daigaku Shuppankai, 1968.
Blacker, Carmen. *The Japanese Enlightenment: A Study of the Writings of Fukuzawa Yukichi*. London, Cambridge University Press, 1964.
Borg, Dorothy. *The United States and the Far Eastern Crisis of 1933–1938: From the Manchurian Incident through the Initial Stage of the Undeclared Sino-Japanese War*. Cambridge, Mass., Harvard University Press, 1964.
Borg, Dorothy and Shumpei Okamoto, eds., with the assistance of Dale K.A. Finlayson. *Pearl Harbor as History: Japanese-American Relations, 1931–1941*. New York, Columbia University Press, 1973.
Borton, Hugh. *Japan's Modern Century from Perry to 1970*. 2d. ed. New York, Ronald Press, 1970.
Boyle, John Hunter. *China and Japan at War, 1937–1945: The Politics of Collaboration*. Stanford, Stanford University Press, 1972.
Coox, Alvin D. *Year of the Tiger*. Tokyo, Orient/West, 1964.
Craig, Albert M. and Donald H. Shively, eds. *Personality in Japanese History*. Berkeley, University of California Press, 1970.
Crowley, James B. *Japan's Quest for Autonomy: National Security and Foreign Policy, 1930–38*. Princeton, Princeton University Press, 1966.
—— ed. *Modern East Asia: Essays in Interpretation*. New York, Harcourt, Brace and World, 1970.
Deakin, F.W. and G.R. Storry. *The Case of Richard Sorge*. New York, Harper and Row, 1966.
Dulles, Foster Rhea. *Yankees and Samurai: America's Role in the Emergence of Modern

Japan, 1791–1900. New York, Harper and Row, 1965.

Esthus, Raymond A. *Theodore Roosevelt and Japan.* Seattle, University of Washington Press, 1966.

Etō Shinkichi 衛藤瀋吉. *Higashi Ajia seijishi kenkyū* 東アジア政治史研究 (Studies in the political history of East Asia). Tokyo, Tōkyō Daigaku Shuppankai, 1968.

Feuerwerker, Albert, Rhoads Murphey, and Mary C. Wright, eds. *Approaches to Modern Chinese History.* Berkeley, University of California Press, 1967. (See particularly the articles by Marius B. Jansen, "Japanese Views of China during the Meiji Period," and Robert A. Scalapino, "Prelude to Marxism: The Chinese Student Movement in Japan, 1900–1910.")

Fox, Grace. *Britain and Japan, 1858–1883.* London, Oxford University Press, 1969.

Fukuda Shigeo 福田茂夫. *Amerika no tai-Nichi sansen* アメリカの対日参戦 (America's road to war with Japan). Kyoto, Mineruba Shobō, 1967.

Goodman, Grant K., comp. *Imperial Japan and Asia: A Reassessment.* New York, East Asian Institute, Columbia University, 1967.

Hata, Ikuhiko. *Reality and Illusion: The Hidden Crisis between Japan and the U.S.S.R., 1932–1934.* New York, East Asian Institute, Columbia University, 1967.

Hō Takushū 彭沢周 [P'eng Tse-chou]. *Meiji shoki Nik-Kan-Shin kankei no kenkyū* 明治初期日韓清関係の研究 (Studies of relations among Japan, Korea, and China during the early Meiji period). Tokyo, Hanawa Shobō, 1969.

Hosoya Chihiro 細谷千博, Saitō Makoto 斉藤眞, Imai Seiichi 今井清一, and Rōyama Michio 蠟山道雄, eds. *Nichi-Bei kankeishi: kaisen ni itaru jūnen (1931–41)* 日米関係史——開戦に至る十年一九三一年～一九四一年 (A history of Japanese-American relations: The decade preceding the war, 1931–41). 4 vols. Tokyo, Tōkyō Daigaku Shuppankai, 1971.

Ikeda Kiyoshi 池田清. *Nihon no kaigun* 日本の海軍 (The Japanese navy). 2 vols. Tokyo, Shiseidō, 1966–67.

Imai Takeo 今井武夫. *Shōwa no bōryaku* 昭和の謀略 (Intrigues in the Shōwa era). Tokyo, Hara Shobō, 1967.

Inō Tentarō 稲生典太郎. *Nihon gaikō shisō shi ronkō* 日本外交思想史論考 (Studies of the history of diplomatic thought in Japan). 2 vols. Tokyo, Komine Shoten, 1966–67.

Iriye, Akira. *Across the Pacific: An Inner History of American-East Asian Relations.* New York, Harcourt, Brace and World, 1967.

—— 入江昭. *Nihon no gaikō* 日本の外交 (Japanese diplomacy). Tokyo, Chūō Kōronsha, 1966.

—— *Pacific Estrangement: Japanese and American Expansion, 1897–1911.* Cambridge, Mass., Harvard University Press, 1972.

Itō Takashi 伊藤隆. *Shōwa shoki seijishi kenkyū* 昭和初期政治史研究 (A study of the political history of the early Shōwa era: The London Naval Conference controversy). Tokyo, Tōkyō Daigaku Shuppankai, 1969.

Jansen, Marius B., ed. *Changing Japanese Attitudes toward Modernization*. Princeton, Princeton University Press, 1965.

Jimbutsu Nihon no rekishi 人物日本の歴史 (Leading figures in Japanese history). 14 vols. Tokyo, Yomiuri Shimbunsha, 1966. Volumes relating to Japan's foreign policy, 1868–1941: Vol. XI, edited by Tōyama Shigeki 遠山茂樹; Vols. XII–XIII, edited by Konishi Shirō 小西四郎; Vol. XIV, edited by Hayashi Shigeru 林茂.

Kajima Heiwa Kenkyūjo 鹿島平和研究所, ed. *Nihon gaikōshi* 日本外交史 (A diplomatic history of Japan). 33 vols. plus 5 supplementary vols. Tokyo, Kajima Kenkyūjo Shuppankai, 1970–   . Volumes relating to Japan's foreign policy, 1868–1941:

Vol. I: Kajima Morinosuke 鹿島守之助. *Bakumatsu gaikō: kaikoku to ishin* 幕末外交 ―開国と維新 (Diplomacy at the end of the Tokugawa era: The opening of the country and the Meiji Restoration).

Vol. II: ―― *Jōyaku kaisei mondai* 條約改正問題 (Treaty revision).

Vol. III: ―― *Kinrin shokoku oyobi ryōdo mondai* 近隣諸国及び領土問題 (Neighboring countries and territorial issues).

Vol. VI: ―― *Nisshin sensō to sangoku kanshō* 日清戦争と三国干渉 (The First Sino-Japanese War and the Triple Intervention).

Vol. V: ―― *Shina ni okeru rekkyō no kakuchiku* 支那における列強の角逐 (International rivalry for rights and interests in China).

Vol. VI: ―― *Daiikkai Nichi-Ei dōmei to sono zengo* 第一回日英同盟とその前後 (The first Anglo-Japanese alliance).

Vol. VII: ―― *Nichi-Ro sensō* 日露戦争 (The Russo-Japanese War).

Vol. VIII: ―― *Dainikai Nichi-Ei dōmei to sono jidai* 第二回日英同盟とその時代 (The second Anglo-Japanese alliance).

Vol. IX: ―― *Daisankai Nichi-Ei dōmei to sono jidai* 第三回日英同盟とその時代 (The third Anglo-Japanese alliance).

Vol. X: ―― *Daiichiji sekai taisen sanka oyobi kyōryoku mondai* 第一次世界大戦参加及び協力問題 (Japan in World War I).

Vol. XI: ―― *Shina mondai* 支那問題 (The China question).

Vol. XII: ―― *Parī kōwa kaigi to shomondai* パリー講和会議と諸問題 (The Paris Peace Conference and Japan).

Vol. XIII: ―― *Washinton kaigi to shomondai* ワシントン会議と諸問題 (The Washington Conference and Japan).

Vol. XIV: Satō Naotake 佐藤尚武. *Kokusai remmei ni okeru Nihon no katsudō* 国際連盟における日本の活動 (Japanese activities in the League of Nations).

Vol. XV: Nishi Haruhiko 西春彦, ed. *Nisso kokkō mondai 1917–1945* 日ソ国交問題 一九一七～一九四五 (Japanese-Soviet relations, 1917–1945).

Vol. XVI: Horinouchi Kensuke 堀内謙介. *Kaigun gunshuku kōshō* 海軍軍縮交渉 (Naval reduction negotiations).

Vol. XVII: Kamimura Shin'ichi 上村伸一. *Chūgoku nashonarizumu to Nikka kankei no tenkai* 中国ナショナリズムと日華関係の展開 (The Development of Chinese nationalism and Sino-Japanese relations).

Vol. XVIII: Morishima Gorō 守島伍郎 and Yanai Tsuneo 柳井恒夫. *Manshū jihen* 満洲事変 (The Manchurian Incident).

Vols. XIX and XX: Kamimura Shin'ichi. *Nikka jihen* 日華事変 (The China Incident).

Vol. XXI: Horinouchi Kensuke, ed. *Nichi-Doku-I dōmei oyobi Nisso chūritsu jōyaku* 日独伊同盟及び日ソ中立條約 (The Tripartite Pact and the Japanese-Soviet Neutrality Pact).

Vol. XXII: Matsumoto Shun'ichi 松本俊一. *Nampō mondai* 南方問題 (The question of the southern advance).

Vol. XXIII: Kase Toshikazu 加瀬俊一. *Nichi-Bei kōshō* 日米交渉 (The Japanese-American negotiations).

Vol. XXIV: Ōta Ichirō 太田一郎. *Dai Tōa sensō kaishi, dai Tōa seisaku* 大東亜戦争開始 大東亜政策 (The outbreak of the Greater East Asia War and the Greater East Asia policy).

Kajima Morinosuke. *A Brief Diplomatic History of Modern Japan.* Rutland, Vt., Tuttle, 1965.

—— *The Emergence of Japan as a World Power, 1895–1925.* Rutland, Vt., Tuttle, 1968.

Kennedy, Malcolm D. *The Estrangement of Great Britain and Japan, 1917–1935.* Berkeley, University of California Press, 1969.

Kim, C.I. Eugene and Han-kyo Kim. *Korea and the Politics of Imperialism, 1876–1910.* Berkeley, University of California Press, 1967.

Kindai Nihon gaikōshi sōsho 近代日本外交史叢書 (Series on Modern Japanese diplomacy). 10 vols. Tokyo, Hara Shobō, 1968– .

Vol. I: Yoshimura Michio 吉村道男. *Nihon to Roshia* 日本とロシア (Japan and Russia).

Vol. IV: Hosoya Chihiro 細谷千博. *Roshia kakumei to Nihon* ロシア革命と日本 (The Russian revolution and Japan).

Vol. VI: Unno Yoshirō 海野芳郎. *Kokusai remmei to Nihon* 国際連盟と日本 (The League of Nations and Japan).

Vol. VII: Usui Katsumi 臼井勝美. *Nihon to Chūgoku—Taishō jidai* 日本と中国―大正時代 (Japan and China during the Taishō period).

Vol. VIII: Iriye Akira 入江昭. *Kyokutō shin chitsujo no mosaku* 極東新秩序の模索 (The search for a new order in the Far East).

Vol. X: Heinrichs, Waldo H. Jr. *Nichi-Bei gaikō to Gurū* 日米外交とグルー (Japanese-American diplomacy and Ambassador Joseph C. Grew). Translated by Asada Sadao 麻田貞雄.

Kindai Nihon shisōshi taikei 近代日本思想史大系 (Series on the history of modern Japanese thought). 8 vols. Tokyo, Yūhikaku, 1968– . Volumes relating to Japan's foreign policy, 1868–1941:

Vols. I–II: Furuta Hikaru 古田光, Sakuta Keiichi 作田啓一, and Ikematsu Keizō 生松敬三, eds. *Kindai Nihon shakai shisōshi* 近代日本社会思想史 (A history of social thought in modern Japan).

Vols. III–IV: Hashikawa Bunsō 橋川文三 and Matsumoto Sannosuke 松本三之介, eds. *Kindai Nihon seiji shisōshi* 近代日本政治思想史 (A history of political thought in modern Japan).

Vols. V–VI: Chō Yukio 長幸男 and Sumiya Kazuhiko 住谷一彦, eds. *Kindai Nihon keizai shisōshi* 近代日本経済思想史 (A history of economic thought in modern Japan).

Kinoshita Hanji 木下半治. *Nihon kokkashugi undō shi* 日本国家主義運動史 (A history of nationalist movements in Japan). 2 vols. Tokyo, Fukumura Shuppan, 1971.

Kuga Katsunan 陸羯南. *Kuga Katsunan zenshū* 陸羯南全集 (The complete works of Kuga Katsunan). Compiled by Nishida Taketoshi 西田長寿 and Uete Michiari 植手通有. 8 vols., 1 supplementary vol. Tokyo, Misuzu Shobō, 1968– .

Kuroba Shigeru 黒羽茂. *Nichi-Ei dōmei no kenkyū* 日英同盟の研究 (A study of the Anglo-Japanese alliance). Sendai, Tōhoku Kyōiku Tosho, 1968.

——— *Taiheiyō o meguru Nichi-Bei kōsō shi* 太平洋をめぐる日米抗争史 (A history of Japanese-American rivalry in the Pacific). Tokyo, Nansōsha, 1968.

Lensen, George Alexander. *Japanese Recognition of the U.S.S.R.: Soviet-Japanese Relations, 1921–1930.* Tallahassee, Diplomatic Press, 1970.

——— *The Strange Neutrality: Soviet-Japanese Relations during the Second World War, 1941–1945.* Tallahassee, Diplomatic Press, 1972.

Louis, Wm. Roger. *British Strategy in the Far East, 1919–1939.* London, Oxford University Press, 1971.

Lowe, Peter. *Great Britain and Japan, 1911–1915.* New York, St. Martin's Press, 1969.

Manshūkokushi Hensan Kankōkai 満州国史編纂刊行会, ed. *Manshūkokushi* 満州国史 (A history of Manchukuo). 2 vols. Tokyo, Mammō Dōhō Engokai, 1971.

Martin, Bernd. *Deutschland und Japan im zweiten Weltkrieg.* Gottingen, Musterschmidt, 1969.

Masumi Junnosuke 升味準之輔. *Nihon seitō shiron* 日本政党史論 (A study of the history of political parties in Japan). 4 vols. Tokyo, Tōkyō Daigaku Shuppankai, 1965–68.

Matsumoto Shigeharu 松本重治, Oka Yoshitake 岡義武, Nishi Haruhiko 西春彦, Kawagoe Shigeru 川越茂, and Kase Toshikazu 加瀬俊一. *Kindai Nihon no gaikō* 近代日本の外交 (The diplomacy of modern Japan). Tokyo, Asahi Shimbunsha, 1962.

Meiji hyakunenshi sōsho 明治百年史叢書 (Historical materials of the century since the Meiji Restoration). Tokyo, Hara Shobō, 1965– . Volumes relating to Japan's foreign policy, 1868–1941:

Gaimushō Hyakunenshi Hensan Iinkai 外務省百年史編纂委員会, ed. *Gaimushō no hyakunen* 外務省の百年 (A century of the Japanese Foreign Ministry). 2 vols. (For a brief summary of the contents, see the review by Shumpei Okamoto in *Japan Institute of International Affairs Annual Review*, V (1969–70), 218–28.

Kurihara Ken 栗原健. *Tai-Mammō seisaku shi no ichimen* 対満蒙政策史の一面 (Studies of Japanese policies toward Manchuria and Mongolia).

Manshū Seinen Remmeishi Kankō Iinkai 満洲青年聯盟史刊行委員会, ed. *Manshū seinen remmeishi* 満洲青年聯盟史 (A history of the Manchurian Youth League). Originally published in 1933.

Manshū Teikoku Seifu 満洲帝国政府, comp. *Manshū kenkoku jūnenshi* 満洲建国十年史 (A ten-year history of Manchukuo). Edited by Etō Shinkichi 衛藤瀋吉.

Ogata Sadako 緒方貞子. *Manshū jihen to seisaku no keisei katei* 満洲事変と政策の形成過程 (The Manchurian Incident and the decision-making process in Japan).

Tani Toshio 谷寿夫. *Kimitsu Nichi-Ro senshi* 機密日露戦史 (A confidential history of the Russo-Japanese War).

Tsunoda Jun 角田順. *Manshū mondai to kokubō hōshin* 満洲問題と国防方針 (The Manchurian question and Japanese defense policy).

Mitani Taichirō 三谷太一郎. *Nihon seitōseiji no keisei: Hara Takashi no seiji shidō no tenkai* 日本政党政治の形成―原敬の政治指導の展開 (The establishment of party politics in Japan: The development of Hara Takashi's political leadership). Tokyo, Tōkyō Daigaku Shuppankai, 1967.

Morley, James William, ed. *Dilemmas of Growth in Prewar Japan*. Princeton, Princeton University Press, 1971.

Nakamura Kikuo 中村菊男. *Manshū jihen* 満洲事変 (The Manchurian Incident). Tokyo, Nihon Kyōbunsha, 1965.

—— ed. *Shōwa kaigun hishi* 昭和海軍秘史 (A confidential history of the navy in the Shōwa era). Tokyo, Banchō Shobō, 1969.

—— ed. *Shōwa rikugun hishi* 昭和陸軍秘史 (A confidential history of the army in the Shōwa era). Tokyo, Banchō Shobō, 1968.

—— *Tennōsei fashizumu ron* 天皇制ファシズム論(On emperor-system fascism). Tokyo, Hara Shobō, 1967.

Nakatsuka Akira 中塚明. *Nisshin sensō no kenkyū* 日清戦争の研究 (A study of the First Sino-Japanese War). Tokyo, Aoki Shoten, 1968.

Nihon kindaishi taikei 日本近代史大系 (Modern Japanese history series). 8 vols. Tokyo, Tōkyō Daigaku Shuppankai, 1968– . Volumes relating to Japan's foreign policy, 1868–1941:

Vol. I: Kamishima Jirō 神島二郎. *Kaikoku* 開国 (The opening of the country).

Vol. II: Masujima Hiroshi 増島宏. *Tennōsei to jiyūminken* 天皇制と自由民権 (The emperor system and popular rights).

Vol. III: Yasui Tatsuya 安井達彌. *Datsu A no michi* 脱亜の道 (Japan's road to casting off Asia).

Vol. IV: Matsumoto Sannosuke 松本三之助. *Meiji no shūen* 明治の終焉 (The end of the Meiji era).

Vol. V: Oka Yoshitake 岡義武. *Tenkanki no Taishō* 転換期の大正 (Taishō, an era of transition).

Vol. VI: Hayashi Shigeru 林茂. *Teikoku no kiro* 帝国の岐路 (Imperial Japan at the crossroads).

Vol. VII: Uchikawa Yoshimi 内川芳美. *Hijōji* 非常時 (The national emergency).

Nihon Kokusai Seiji Gakkai 日本国際政治学会, ed. *Kokusai seiji: kokusai seiji no riron to hōhō* 国際政治—国際政治の理論と方法 (International relations: Theories and methods in international politics). Tokyo, Yūhikaku, 1970.

—— ed. *Kokusai seiji: Manshū jihen* 国際政治—満洲事変 (International relations: The Manchurian Incident). Tokyo, Yūhikaku, 1970.

—— ed. *Kokusai seiji: Nichi-Bei kankei no imēji* 国際政治—日米関係のイメージ (International relations: Mutual images in Japanese-American relations). Tokyo, Yūhikaku, 1967.

—— ed. *Kokusai seiji: Nichi-Ro Nisso kankei no tenkai* 国際政治—日露日ソ関係の展開 (International relations: The development of Russo-Japanese and Soviet-Japanese relations). Tokyo, Yūhikaku, 1966.

—— ed. *Kokusai seiji: Nihon gaikōshi kenkyū—gaikō shidōsha ron* 国際政治—日本外交史研究—外交指導者論 (International relations: Studies in the diplomatic history of Japan—makers of Japanese foreign policy). Tokyo, Yūhikaku, 1967.

—— ed. *Kokusai seiji: Nihon gaikōshi kenkyū—gaikō to seron* 国際政治—日本外交史研究—外交と世論 (International relations: Studies in the diplomatic history of Japan—foreign policy and public opinion). Tokyo, Yūhikaku, 1970.

—— ed. *Kokusai seiji: Nihon gaikōshi no shomondai II* 国際政治—日本外交史の諸問題 II (International relations: Some problems in the history of Japanese foreign policy, II). Tokyo, Yūhikaku, 1965.

—— ed. *Kokusai seiji: Nihon gaikōshi no shomondai III* 国際政治—日本外交史の諸問題 III (International relations: Some problems in the history of Japanese foreign policy, III). Tokyo, Yūhikaku, 1968.

Nihon no rekishi 日本の歴史 (A history of Japan). 26 vols. Tokyo, Chūō Kōronsha, 1965–67. Volumes relating to Japan's foreign policy, 1868–1941:

Vol. XXII: Sumiya Mikio 隅谷三喜男. *Dai Nihon teikoku no shiren* 大日本帝国の試練 (The ordeal of Imperial Japan).

Vol. XXIII: Imai Seiichi 今井清一. *Taishō demokurashii* 大正デモクラシー (Taishō democracy).

Vol. XXIV: Ōuchi Tsutomu 大内力. *Fashizumu e no michi* ファシズムへの道 (The road to fascism).

Vol. XXV: Hayashi Shigeru 林茂. *Taiheiyō sensō* 太平洋戦争 (The Pacific War).

Nihon rekishi sōsho 日本歴史叢書 (Japanese history series). 16 vols. Tokyo, Iwanami Shoten, 1968. Volumes relating to Japan's foreign policy, 1868–1941:

Haraguchi Kiyoshi 原口清. *Nihon kindai kokka no keisei* 日本近代国家の形成 (The establishment of the modern Japanese state).

Ienaga Saburō 家永三郎. *Taiheiyō sensō* 太平洋戦争 (The Pacific War).

Inoue Kiyoshi 井上清. *Nihon teikokushugi no keisei* 日本帝国主義の形成 (The rise of Japanese imperialism).

Nihon Seiji Gakkai 日本政治学会, ed. *Nempō seijigaku 1969: kokusai kinchō kanwa no seiji katei* 年報政治学 1969—国際緊張緩和の政治過程 (The annals of the Japan Political Science Association, 1969: The political process in the reduction of international tensions). Tokyo, Iwanami Shoten, 1970.

Nihon zenshi 日本全史 (A complete history of Japan). 11 vols. Tokyo, Tōkyō Daigaku Shuppankai, 1962– . Volumes relating to Japan's foreign policy, 1868–1941:

Vol. VIII: Konishi Shirō 小西四郎. *Kindai I* 近代 I (Modern times, Part 1).

Vol. IX: Shimomura Fujio 下村冨士男. *Kindai II* 近代 II (Modern times, Part 2).

Vols. X-XI: Ōkubo Toshiaki 大久保利謙. *Kindai III* 近代 III (Modern times, Part 3) and *Kindai IV* 近代 IV (Modern times, Part 4).

Nish, I.H. *Alliance in Decline, 1908–1923*. London, Athlone Press, 1972.

Nishi Yoshiaki 西義顯. *Higeki no shōnin—Nikka wahei kōsaku hishi* 悲劇の証人—日華和平工作秘史 (Witness to tragedy: A secret history of the Sino-Japanese peace negotiations). Tokyo, Bunkensha, 1962.

Oka Yoshitake 岡義武. *Reimeiki no Meiji Nihon* 黎明期の明治日本 (Meiji Japan at dawn). Tokyo, Miraisha, 1964.

Okamoto, Shumpei. *The Japanese Oligarchy and the Russo-Japanese War*. New York, Columbia University Press, 1970.

Ōkochi Kazuo 大河内一男 and Ōya Sōichi 大宅壮一, eds. *Kindai Nihon o tsukutta hyakunin* 近代日本を創った 100 人 (One hundred builders of modern Japan). 2 vols. Tokyo, Mainichi Shimbunsha, 1966.

Okumura Fusao 奥村房夫. *Nichi-Bei kōshō to Taiheiyō sensō* 日米交渉と太平洋戦争 (The Japanese-American negotiations and the Pacific War). Tokyo, Maeno Shoten, 1970.

Presseisen, Ernst L. *Before Aggression: Europeans Prepare the Japanese Army*. Tucson, University of Arizona Press, 1965.

Rappaport, Armin. *Henry L. Stimson and Japan, 1931–33*. Chicago, University of Chicago Press, 1963.

Reischauer, Edwin O. *The United States and Japan*. 3d ed. New York, Viking Press, 1965.

Rekishigaku Kenkyūkai 歴史学研究会, ed. *Taiheiyō sensō shi* 太平洋戦争史 (History of the Pacific War). 6 vols. Tokyo, Aoki Shoten, 1971–73. A revised and enlarged edition of the work first published in 1954.

Seki Hiroharu 関寛治. *Gendai higashi Ajia kokusai kankyō no tanjō* 現代東アジア国際環境の誕生 (The emergence of the contemporary East Asian international setting). Tokyo, Fukumura Shuppan, 1966.

Shimada Toshihiko 島田俊彦. *Kantōgun* 関東軍 (The Kwantung army). Tokyo, Chūō Kōronsha, 1965.

Shin Kuk-ju 申国柱. *Kindai Chōsen gaikōshi kenkyū* 近代朝鮮交外史研究 (A study of the foreign relations of modern Korea). Tokyo, Yūshindō, 1966.

Shinobu Seizaburō 信夫清三郎. *Nisshin sensō* 日清戦争 (A study of the First Sino-Japanese War). Edited by Fujimura Michio 藤村道生. Tokyo, Nansōsha, 1970. First published in 1934.

Shōwa Dōjinkai 昭和同人会, ed. *Shōwa kenkyūkai* 昭和研究会 (The Shōwa Research Association). Tokyo, Keizai Ōraisha, 1968.

Takagi Sōkichi 高木惣吉. *Taiheiyō sensō to riku-kaigun no kōsō* 太平洋戦争と陸海軍の抗争 (The Pacific War and army-navy rivalry). Tokyo, Keizai Ōraisha, 1967.

Takagi Yasaka 高木八尺, ed. *Nichi-Bei kankei no kenkyū* 日米関係の研究 (Studies on Japanese-American relations), Vol. I. Tokyo, Tōkyō Daigaku Shuppankai, 1968.

—— *Takagi Yasaka chosakushū* 高木八尺著作集 (The collected works of Takagi Yasaka). 5 vols. Tokyo, Tōkyō Daigaku Shuppankai, 1970–71. (Particularly Vols. III and V.)

Taikei Nihonshi sōsho 体系日本史叢書 (A systematic anthology of Japanese history). 23 vols. Tokyo, Yamakawa Shuppansha, 1964– . The volume relating to Japan's foreign relations is Vol. V: Shimomura Fujio 下村冨士男, ed. *Taigai kankeishi* 対外関係史 (A history of Japan's foreign relations).

Tamura Kōsaku 田村幸策. *Taiheiyō sensō gaikōshi* 太平洋戦争外交史 (A diplomatic history of the Pacific War). Tokyo, Kajima Kenkyūjo Shuppankai, 1966.

Thorne, Christopher. *The Limits of Foreign Policy: The West, the League and the Far Eastern Crisis of 1931–1933*. London, Hamish Hamilton, 1972.

Toland, John. *The Rising Sun: The Decline and Fall of the Japanese Empire*. New York, Random House, 1970.

Ueda Toshio 植田捷雄. *Tōyō gaikōshi* 東洋外交史 (A diplomatic history of East Asia), Vol. I. Tokyo, Tōkyō Daigaku Shuppankai, 1969.

Usui Katsumi 臼井勝美. *Nitchū gaikōshi: hokubatsu no jidai* 日中外交史北伐の時代 (A history of Sino-Japanese diplomatic relations: The Northern Expedition period). Tokyo, Hanawa Shobō, 1971.

—— *Nitchū sensō* 日中戦争 (The Second Sino-Japanese War). Tokyo, Chūō Kōronsha, 1967.

Ward, Robert E., ed. *Political Development in Modern Japan*. Princeton, Princeton University Press, 1968.

Wilson, George M., ed. *Crisis Politics in Prewar Japan: Institutional and Ideological Problems of the 1930s*. Tokyo, Sophia University, 1970.

Yoshii Hiroshi 義井博. *Shōwa gaikōshi* 昭和外交史 (A diplomatic history of the Shōwa era). Tokyo, Nansōsha, 1971.

Yoshino Sakuzō 吉野作造. *Chūgoku Chōsen ron* 中国朝鮮論 (On China and Korea). Compiled by Matsuo Takayoshi 松尾尊兊. Tokyo, Heibonsha, 1970.

Young, L.K. *British Policies in China, 1895–1902*. London, Oxford University Press, 1970.

General Glossary

Advisory Council on Foreign Relations	臨時外交調査委員会	Rinji Gaikō Chōsa Iinkai
Agriculture and Commerce, Ministry of	農商務省	Nōshōmushō
Agriculture and Forestry, Ministry of	農林省	Nōrinshō
Agricultural Policy Bureau	農政局	Nōsei Kyoku
Alliance for Nonintervention in China	対支不干渉同盟	Tai-Shi Fukanshō Dōmei
America-Japan Society	日米協会	Nichi-Bei Kyōkai
Amur River Society	黒龍会	Kokuryūkai
Anglo-American faction	英米派	Ei-Beiha
Army Academy	陸軍士官学校	Rikugun Shikan Gakkō
Army Department (1871–85)	陸軍省	Rikugunshō
Army General Staff	参謀本部	Sambō Hombu
Intelligence Division	情報部	Jōhōbu
Operations Division	作戦部	Sakusembu
Operations Section	作戦課	Sakusenka
Army Ministry	陸軍省	Rikugunshō
Military Affairs Bureau	軍務局	Gummu Kyoku
Press Office	新聞班	Shimbunhan
Research Committee on Army Administration (1929)	軍制調査会	Gunsei Chōsakai
Taiwan Army Research Division (1941)	台湾軍研究部	Taiwangun Kenkyūbu
Army War College	陸軍大学校	Rikugun Daigakkō
Asahi shimbun	朝日新聞	
Asama Maru	浅間丸	
Asia Development Board	興亞院	Kōain
Axis faction	枢軸派	Sūjikuha

Bank of Korea	朝鮮銀行	Chōsen Ginkō
Bank of Taiwan	台湾銀行	Taiwan Ginkō
"Basic Principles for a Settlement of the Manchurian Problem" (August 1931)	満洲問題解決方策大綱	"Manshū mondai kaiketsu hōsaku taikō"
"Basic Principles of National Policy" (June 1936)	国策大綱	"Kokusaku taikō"
Cabinet Deliberative Council	内閣審議会	Naikaku Shingikai
Cabinet Planning Board	企画院	Kikakuin
Cabinet Research Bureau	内閣調査局	Naikaku Chōsa Kyoku
California Central Agricultural Association	加州中央農会	Kashū Chūō Nōkai
Central China Development Company	中支那振興会社	Naka Shina Shinkō Kaisha
chambers of commerce	商法会議所	shōhō kaigisho (1878)
	商工会	shōkōkai (1883)
	商業会議所	shōgyō kaigisho (1890)
chancellor	太政大臣	dajōdaijin
Changkufeng Incident (1938)	張鼓峯事件	Chōkohō jiken
Charter Oath (1868)	五箇條の御誓文	gokajō no goseimon
Cherry Blossom Society	櫻会	Sakurakai
Chiba Medical School	千葉医学専門学校	Chiba Igaku Semmon Gakkō
China Affairs League	支那問題連盟	Shina Mondai Remmei
China Incident (1937)	支那事変	Shina jihen
"China Policy of the Kwantung Army" (March 1935)	関東軍対支政策	"Kantōgun tai-Shi seisaku"
commander of all imperial military forces	帝国全軍参謀総長	teikoku zengun sambōsōchō
Commerce Control Office	商法司	Shōhōshi
commissioner of colonization	開拓使	kaitakushi
Committee on the Current Situation (1936)	時局委員会	Jikyoku Iinkai
Control faction	統制派	Tōseiha
Council of State	太政官	Dajōkan
Council on National Defense	防務会議	Bōmukaigi
daimyō	大名	
Dai Nihon Seisantō	大日本生産党	Great Japan Production Party

Dark Ocean Society	玄洋社	Genyōsha
defend the constitution movement	護憲運動	goken undō
dōgyō kumiai junsoku	同業組合準則	
Domestic Enterprise Encouragement Exposition (1872)	内国勧業博覧会	Naikoku Kangyō Hakurankai
East and West News Bureau	東西社	Tōzaisha
East Asia Common Culture Academy	東亜同文書院	Tōa Dōbun Shoin
East Asia Common Culture Association	東亜同文会	Tōa Dōbunkai
East Asia Cultural Council	東亜文化協議会	Tōa Bunka Kyōgikai
East Hopei Anti-Communist Autonomous Council	冀東防共自治委員会	Kitō Bōkyō Jichi Iinkai
Education, Ministry of	文部省	Mombushō
"ee ja nai ka"	ええじゃないか	
enlightenment movement	啓発運動 教化運動	keihatsu undō kyōka undō
"The Essence of National Defense and Proposals to Strengthen It" (October 1934)	国防の本義とその 強化の提唱	"Kokubō no hongi to sono kyōka no teishō"
"Essentials for Carrying Out the Policies of the Empire" (September 1941)	帝国国策遂行要領	"Teikoku kokusaku suikō yōryō"
Far Eastern Cultural Academy	東方文化学院	Tōhō Bunka Gakuin
Far Eastern Cultural Institute	東方文化研究所	Tōhō Bunka Kenkyūjo
February 26 Incident (1936)	二・二六事件	ni-ni-roku jiken
Federated Raw Silk Warehouse	聯合生糸荷預所	Rengō Kiito Niazukarijo
Finance Ministry Deposits Division	大蔵省 預金部	Ōkurashō Yokimbu
First Higher School	第一高等学校	Daiichi Kōtō Gakkō
Five Ministers Conference	五相会議	Goshō Kaigi
"Five Year Plan for Production of War Matériel" (June 1937)	軍需品製造工業 五ヶ年計画	"Gunjuhin seizōkōgyō gokanen keikaku"

"Five Year Program for the Development of Major Industries" (May 1937)	重要産業五ヶ年計画	"Jūyōsangyō gokanen keikaku"
Foreign Ministry	外務省	Gaimushō
America Bureau	アメリカ局	Amerika Kyoku
Asia Bureau	アジア局	Ajia Kyoku
Cultural Affairs Division	文化事業部	Bunka Jigyōbu
Europe-America Bureau	欧米局	Ō-Bei Kyoku
International Trade Bureau	通商局	Tsūshō Kyoku
Research Division	調査部	Chōsabu
Treaties Bureau	條約局	Jōyaku Kyoku
"The Foreign Policy of Imperial Japan" (August 1936)	帝国外交方針	"Teikoku gaikō hōshin"
Four Ministers Conference	四相会議	Yonshō Kaigi
Fukagawa Cement Factory	深川セメント製造所	Fukagawa Semento Seizōsho
Fukagawa White Brick Factory	深川白煉化製造所	Fukagawa Hakurenga Seizōsho
"Fundamental Policy for the Disposition of the China Incident" (January 1938)	支那事変処理根本方針	"Shina jihen shori kompon hōshin"
"Fundamentals of National Policy" (August 1936)	国策の基準	"Kokusaku no kijun"
gagaku	雅楽	
gekokujō	下剋上	
genrō	元老	
Greater East Asia Coprosperity Sphere	大東亜共栄圏	Dai Tōa Kyōeiken
Greater East Asia Ministry	大東亜省	Dai Tōashō
han	藩	
Han Yeh P'ing Company	漢冶萍公司	Kanyahyō Kōshi
Hibiya Riot	日比谷焼打事件	Hibiya yakiuchi jiken
Home Ministry	内務省	Naimushō
Trade Encouragement Bureau	勧商局	Kanshō Kyoku
Hopei-Chahar Political Council	冀察政務委員会	Ki-Satsu Seimu Iinkai
House of Peers	貴族院	Kizokuin
Hsueh-i	學藝	

Imperial Conference	御前会議	Gozen Kaigi
Imperial Council	朝議	Chōgi
Imperial Education Association	帝国教育会	Teikoku Kyōikukai
Imperial Guard Division	近衛師団	Konoe Shidan
Imperial Headquarters	大本営	Daihon'ei
Imperial Household	皇室	Kōshitsu
"Imperial National Defense Policy" (1907)	帝国国防方針	"Teikoku kokubō hōshin"
Imperial Reservists Association	帝国在郷軍人会	Teikoku Zaigō Gunjinkai
Imperial Rule Assistance Association	大政翼賛会	Taisei Yokusankai
Imperial Way	皇道	Kōdō
Imperial Way faction	皇道派	Kōdōha
Industrial Bank of Japan	日本興業銀行	Nihon Kōgyō Ginkō
Inner Council (1873)	内閣	Naikaku
"Instructions for the Employment of Foreigners" (1870)	外国人雇入方心得書	"Gaikokujin yatoiirekata kokoroesho"
International Student Institute	国際学友会	Kokusai Gakuyūkai
International Trade and Industry, Ministry of	通商産業省	Tsūshō Sangyōshō
Itō mission (1882–83)	伊藤使節	Itō shisetsu
Iwakura Embassy (1871–73)	岩倉遣外使節	Iwakura kengai shisetsu
Japanese-American Relations Committee	日米関係委員会	Nichi-Bei Kankei Iinkai
Japanese Association of America	在米日本人会	Zai-Bei Nihonjinkai
Japanese-German Association	日独協会	Nichi-Doku Kyōkai
jōi	攘夷	
junior councilor	参議	sangi
Justice Ministry	司法省	Shihōshō
kabuki	歌舞伎	
Kanshō shimpō	勧商新報	
kawase kaisha	爲替会社	
Kenseihontō	憲政本党	
kiito seizō torishimari kisoku	生糸製造取締規則	
kita	北	

Kogetsukai	湖月会	
koku	石	
Kokumin shimbun	国民新聞	
kokutai	国体	
Korea army	朝鮮軍	Chōsengun
Korean expedition (1873)	征韓	seikan
Kuomintang	国民党	
Kwantung army	関東軍	Kantōgun
Special Service Agency	特務機関	Tokumu Kikan
Kwantung Government-	関東総督府	Kantō Sōtokufu (1906–19)
General	関東庁	Kantōchō (1919–34)
	関東局	Kantōkyoku (1934–45)
Kwantung Leased Territory	関東州	Kantōshū
League of the Japanese	在華紡績同業会	Zai-Ka Bōseki Dōgyōkai
Textile Industry in		
China		
Liaison Conference	連絡会議	Renraku Kaigi
"Main Principles for Coping	世界情勢の推移に伴う	"Sekai jōsei no suii ni
with the Changing	時局処理要綱	tomonau jikyoku
World Situation"		shori yōkō"
(July 1940)		
Manchurian Incident (1931)	満州事変	Manshū jihen
Manshikai	満史会	Manchurian History
		Society
Man'yōshū	万葉集	
March Incident (1931)	三月事件	sangatsu jiken
Marco Polo Bridge Incident	蘆溝橋事件	Rokōkyō jiken
(1937)		
Maruzen Company	丸善	Maruzen
May 30 Incident (1925)	五・三〇事件	go-sanjū jiken
Meiji Restoration	明治維新	Meiji ishin
Minseitō (Rikken Minseitō)	立憲民政党	
Mita Agricultural Imple-	三田農具製造所	Mita Nōgu Seizōsho
ments Factory		
Mitsubishi Shōji	三菱商事	Mitsubishi Trading
		Company
Mitsubishi Steamship	三菱商会	Mitsubishi Shōkai
Company		
Mitsui Bussan	三井物産	Mitsui Trading Company
Mizunuma Silk Mill	水沼製糸所	Mizunuma Seishisho

National Alliance	国民同盟会	Kokumin Dōmeikai
National Defense Agency	防衛庁	Bōeichō
Military History Office	戦史室	Senshishitsu
national unity cabinet	挙国一致内閣	kyokoku itchi naikaku
Naval Academy	海軍兵学校	Kaigun Heigakkō
Naval Defense, Bureau of	海防局	Kaibō Kyoku
Navy Department (1872–85)	海軍省	Kaigunshō
Navy General Staff	軍令部	Gunreibu
Operations Section	作戦課	Sakusenka
Navy Ministry	海軍省	Kaigunshō
Navy War College	海軍大学校	Kaigun Daigakkō
New Order in East Asia	東亞新秩序	Tōa shinchitsujo
new political party movement	新党運動	shintō undō
Nihon Bōeki Shōkai	日本貿易商会	Japan Trade Firm
Nihongi	日本紀	
Nomonhan Incident (1939)	ノモンハン事件	Nomonhan jiken
North China Development	北支那開発株式会社	Kita Shina Kaihatsu Kabu-
Company		shiki Kaisha
North China Industrial	華北産業研究所	Kahoku Sangyō Kenkyūjo
Research Institute		
okage mairi	御蔭まいり	
oku	奥	
Ōkura Gumi	大倉組	Ōkura Combine
"One View of the China	対支所見	"Tai-Shi shoken"
Situation" (May 1935)		
"Order of Sending Japanese	魯國及朝鮮へ使節を派	"Rokoku oyobi Chōsen e
Delegates to Russia and	遣するの順序	shisetsu o haken suru
Korea" (February 1874)		no junjo"
Osaka Spinning Company	大阪紡績会社	Ōsaka Bōseki Kaisha
Ōtsu Incident (May 1891)	大津事件	Ōtsu jiken
"Outline for Negotiations	対獨伊蘇交渉案要綱	"Tai-Doku-I-So kōshōan
with Germany, Italy,		yōkō"
and the USSR"		
(February 1941)		
"Outline of Fundamental	基本国策要綱	"Kihon kokusaku yōkō"
National Policy"		
(July 1940)		
"Outline of National Policies	情勢の推移に伴う帝国	"Jōsei no suii ni tomonau
in View of the Changing	国策要綱	teikoku kokusaku
Situation" (July 1941)		yōkō"

"Outline of Overall National Policies" (January 1940)	綜合国策基本要綱	"Sōgō kokusaku kihon yōkō"
"Outline of Policy to Deal with North China" (January 1936)	北支那処理要綱	"Kita Shina shori yōkō"
"Outline of Policy to Deal with the Negotiations Concerning North China" (June 1935)	華北交渉問題処理要綱	"Kahoku kōshō mondai shori yōkō"
"Outline of Policy toward French Indochina and Thailand" (January 1941)	対佛印泰施策要綱	"Tai-Futsuin-Tai shisaku yōkō"
Pacific War	太平洋戦争	Taiheiyō sensō
parliamentary vice-minister of foreign affairs	外務政務次官	gaimu seimu jikan
Peiping Branch Military Council	北平軍事委員分会	Pei-p'ing Chün-shih Wei-yuan-fen-hui (Peipin Gunji Iinbun-kai)
Pekin Kaigi Jumbi Uchiawasekai	北京会議準備打合会	Preparatory Committee for the Peking Conference
Peking Humanities Research Institute	北京人文科学研究所	Pekin Jimbun Kagaku Kenkyūjo
pilgrimage to the Grand Shrine of Ise	伊勢参り	Ise mairi
popular rights movement	自由民権運動	jiyū minken undō
Privy Council	枢密院	Sūmitsuin
Proletarian Science Research Center	プロレタリア科学研究所	Puroretaria Kagaku Kenkyūjo
Raw Silk Improvement Company	生糸改会社	Kiito Aratame Kaisha
"Regulations Concerning Public and Private Schools Admitting Chinese Students" (November 1905)	清國人ヲ入學セシムル公私立學校ニ關スル規程	"Shinkokujin o nyūgaku seshimuru kō shiritsu gakkō ni kansuru kitei"
Returned Students Association	留徒学会	Liu-t'u Hsueh-hui (Ryūto Gakkai)
right of supreme command	統帥権	tōsuiken

rights recovery movement	国権回復運動	kokken kaifuku undō
Rikken Dōshikai	立憲同志会	
"Rules for Study Overseas" (1870)	海外留学規則	"Kaigai ryūgaku kisoku"
Russo-Japanese War (1904–5)	日露戦争	Nichi-Ro sensō
Sakhalin Colonization Agency	樺太開拓使	Karafuto Kaitakushi
sanshu seizō kisoku	蚕種製造規則	
sanshu seizō kumiai	蚕種製造組合	
Satsuma Rebellion (1877)	西南戦争	seinan sensō
School for Foreign Learning	開成学校	Kaisei Gakkō
	開成所	Kaiseijo
"Second Outline of Policy to Deal with North China" (August 1936)	第二次北支処理要綱	"Dainiji Hokushi shori yōkō"
Seiyūkai (Rikken Seiyūkai)	立憲政友会	
semmongunshugi	専門軍主義	
Senate	元老院	Genrōin
senior councilor	右大臣	udaijin
senior statesmen	重臣	jūshin
Senjū Woolen Factory	千住製絨所	Senjū Seijūsho
Shakai Minshūtō	社会民衆党	
Shanghai Science Institute	上海自然科学研究所	Shanhai Shizen Kagaku Kenkyūjo
Shih-hsueh-kuan	仕学館	
Shinagawa Glass Factory	品川硝子製造所	Shinagawa Garasu Seizōsho
shinaya	支那屋	
shōhō kaisho	商法会所	
shōsha	商社	
Sian Incident (1936)	西安事件	Seian jiken
Siberian Expedition	シベリヤ出兵	Shiberia shuppei
Sino-Japanese Association	日華学会	Nikka Gakkai
Sino-Japanese War (1894–95)	日清戦争	Nisshin sensō
Society for International Cultural Relations (K.B.S.)	国際文化振興会	Kokusai Bunka Shinkōkai
Society of Japanese Businessmen in China	日華実業協会	Nikka Jitsugyō Kyōkai
South Manchuria Railway Company	南満州鉄道株式会社	Minami Manshū Tetsudō Kabushiki Kaisha

superintendent of educational affairs	学監	gakkan
Supreme War Council	軍事参議官会議	Gunji Sangikan Kaigi
Takashima Coal Mine	高島炭坑	Takashima Tankō
Tientsin Residents Association	天津居留民団	Tenshin Kyoryū Mindan
Tokyo Higher Normal School	東京高等師範学校	Tōkyō Kōtō Shihan Gakkō
Tokyo Institute of Municipal Research	東京市政調査会	Tōkyō Shisei Chōsakai
Tonghak rebellion (1894)	東学党の乱	Tōgakutō no ran
Trade Control Office	通商司	Tsūshōshi
transcendental cabinet	超然内閣	chōzen naikaku
Triple Intervention (1895)	三國干渉	sangoku kanshō
Tsinan Incident (1928)	済南事件	Sainan jiken
tsūshō kaisha	通商会社	
Twenty-One Demands (1915)	二十一箇條要求	nijūikkajō yōkyū
United Formosans for Independence	台湾独立聯盟	Taigan Toklip Lianbeng (Taiwan Dokuritsu Remmei)
Universal Benevolence Association	同仁会	Dōjinkai
War Department (1869–71)	兵部省	Hyōbushō
Yokohama Specie Bank	横浜正金銀行	Yokohama Shōkin Ginkō
zaibatsu	財閥	

Glossary of
Personal Names

Abe Nobuyuki　阿部信行

Abo Kiyokazu　安保清種

Adachi Kenzō　安達謙蔵

Aizawa Seishisai　会沢正志斉

Aoki Norizumi　青木宣純

Aoki Shūzō　青木周蔵

Aoyama Kazuo　青山和夫 (黒田善治)
　(pen name of Kuroda Zenji)

Araki Sadao　荒木貞夫

Arao Okikatsu　荒尾興功

Arao Sei　荒尾精

Arisue Yadoru　有末次

Arita Hachirō　有田八郎

Asabuki Eiji　朝吹英二

Chang Hsueh-liang　張学良

Chang Tso-lin　張作霖

Chiang Kai-shek (Chieh-Shih)　蔣介石

Chiba Toyoji　千葉豊治

Chinda Sutemi　珍田捨巳

Chō Byong-sik　趙乗式

Doihara Kenji　土肥原賢二

Enomoto Takeaki　榎本武揚

Etō Shimpei　江藤新平

Fukudome Shigeru　福留繁

Fukushima Yasumasa　福島安正

Fukuzawa Yukichi　福沢諭吉

Funatsu Shin'ichirō　船津辰一郎

Gotō Shimpei　後藤新平

Gotō Shōjirō　後藤象二郎

Hamaguchi Osachi (Yūkō)　浜口雄幸

Hanaya Tadashi　花谷正

Hara Takashi (Kei)　原敬

Hara Yoshimichi　原嘉道

Harada Kumao　原田熊雄

Hata Shunroku　畑俊六

Hatoyama Kazuo　鳩山和夫

Hattori Unokichi　服部宇之吉

Hayashi Senjūrō　林銑十郎

Hayashi Tadasu　林董

Hioki Eki　日置益

Hiranuma Kiichirō　平沼騏一郎

Hirota Kōki　広田弘毅

Honjō Shigeru　本庄繁

Hori Teikichi　堀悌吉

Ichinomiya Reitarō　一宮鈴太郎

Ienaga Toyokichi　家永豊吉

Ijūin Hikokichi　伊集院彦吉

Ikawa Tadao　井川忠雄

Imamura Hitoshi　今村均

Inoue Junnosuke　井上準之助

Inoue Kaoru　井上馨

Inoue Katsunosuke　井上勝之助

Inui Kiyosue　乾清末

Inukai Tsuyoshi (Ki)　犬養毅

Ishii Kikujirō　石井菊次郎

Ishikawa Shingo　石川信吾

Ishimoto Shinroku　石本新六

Ishiwara Kanji　石原莞爾

Ishiwata Sōtarō　石渡荘太郎

Itagaki Seishirō　板垣征四郎

Itagaki Taisuke　板垣退助

Itō Hirobumi　伊藤博文

Itō Masanori　伊藤正徳
Itō Nobufumi　伊藤述史
Iwakura Tomomi　岩倉具視
Iwakuro Hideo　岩畔豪雄
Iwaya Magozō　巌谷孫蔵
Kabayama Aisuke　樺山愛輔
Kabayama Sukenori　樺山資紀
Kaji Wataru　鹿地亘 (瀬口貢)
　　(pen name of Seguchi Mitsugi)
Kanaya Hanzō　金谷範三
Kaneko Kentarō　金子堅太郎
Katō Kanji　加藤寛治
Katō Takaaki (Kōmei)　加藤高明
Katō Tomosaburō　加藤友三郎
Katsura Tarō　桂太郎
Kawakami Kiyoshi　河上清
　　(Karl K. Kawakami)
Kawakami Sōroku　川上操六
Kawakami Toshihiko　川上俊彦
Kazami Akira　風見章
Kido Kōichi　木戸孝一
Kido Takayoshi (Kōin)　木戸孝允
Kikuchi Teiji　菊地貞二
Kim Hong-jip　金弘集 (金宏集)
　　(adult name of Kim Koeng-jip)
Kishida Ginkō　岸田吟香
Kita Ikki　北一輝 (北輝次郎)
　　(pen name of Kita Terujirō)
Kodama Gentarō　児玉源太郎
Koiso Kuniaki　小磯国昭
Kojong, King of Korea　高宗
Kōmoto Daisaku　河本大作
Komura Jutarō　小村寿太郎
Kondō Nobutake　近藤信竹
Kōno Ichirō　河野一郎
Konoe Atsumaro　近衛篤麿
Konoe Fumimaro　近衛文麿
Kuki Ryūichi　久鬼隆一
Kume Kunitake　久米邦武
Kurino Shin'ichirō　栗野慎一郎

Kuroda Kiyotaka　黒田清隆
Kurusu Saburō　來栖三郎
Kushida Masao　櫛田正夫
Li Hung-chang　李鴻章
Machida Keiu　町田経宇
Maeda Masana　前田正名
Maeda Tamon　前田多門
Makino Nobuaki (Shinken)　牧野伸顕
Maruyama Sakura　丸山作楽
Matsuda Masahisa　松田正久
Matsudaira Tsuneo　松平恒雄
Matsui Iwane　松井石根
Matsui Keishirō　松井慶四郎
Matsukata Masayoshi　松方正義
Matsuoka Yōsuke　松岡洋右
Matsushita Hajime　松下元
Megata Tanetarō　目賀田種太郎
Minami Jirō　南次郎
Minobe Tatsukichi　美濃部達吉
Miura Horiyuki　三浦周行
Miura Takemi　三浦武美
Miyazaki Masayoshi　宮崎正義
Miyazaki Tōten　宮崎滔天 (宮崎寅蔵)
　　(pen name of Miyazaki Torazō)
Mori Arinori　森有礼
Mori Kaku (Tsutomu)　森恪
Motono Ichirō　本野一郎
Mushakōji Kintomo　武者小路公共
Mutō Akira　武藤章
Mutsu Munemitsu　陸奥宗光
Nagai Matsuzō　永井松三
Nagano Osami　永野修身
Nagata Tetsuzan　永田鉄山
Naitō Konan　内藤湖南 (内藤虎次郎)
　　(pen name of Naitō Torajirō)
Nakajima Tetsuzō　中島鉄蔵
Nakamura Shintarō　中村震太郎
Nakamuta Kuranosuke　中牟田倉之助
Nakano Buei　中野武営
Nakano Seigō　中野正剛

Nakayama Masao　中山正男

Natsume Sōseki　夏目漱石 (夏目金之助)
　(pen name of Natsume Kinnosuke)

Nezu Hajime　根津一

Niishima Jō　新島襄

Ninomiya Harushige　二宮治重

Nishi Amane　西周

Nishi Kanjirō　西寛二郎

Nishi Tokujirō　西徳二郎

Nishihara Kamezō　西原亀三

Nomura Kichisaburō　野村吉三郎

Numano Yasutarō　沼野安太郎

Obata Yūkichi　小幡酉吉

Ōhira Chūgo　大平忠吾

Oikawa Koshirō　及川古志郎

Okada Keisuke　岡田啓介

Okada Shigeichi　岡田重一

Okamoto Kansuke　岡本監輔

Okamura Yasuji　岡村寧次

Ōki Takatō　大木喬任

Ōkubo Toshimichi　大久保利通

Ōkuma Shigenobu　大隈重信

Ōkura Kishichirō　大倉喜七郎

Ōmura Masujirō　大村益次郎

Ono Eijirō　小野英二郎

Ōno Takeji　大野竹二

Ōshima Hiroshi　大島浩

Ōsumi Mineo　大角岑生

Ōta Tamekichi　太田爲吉

Ōyama Iwao　大山巌

Ōyama Ujirō　大山卯次郎

Ozaki Hotsumi　尾崎秀実

Ozaki Yukio　尾崎行雄

Saigō Takamori　西郷隆盛

Saigō Tsugumichi　西郷従道

Saionji Kimmochi　西園寺公望

Saitō Hiroshi　斉藤博

Saitō Makoto (Minoru)　斉藤実

Sakamoto Ryōma　坂本竜馬

Sakata Jūjirō　坂田重次郎

Sakatani Yoshirō　坂谷芳郎

Sanjō Sanetomi　三條実美

Sano Tsunetami　佐野常民

Sasaki Tōichi　佐々木到一

Satō Kenryō　佐藤賢了

Satō Naotake　佐藤尚武

Segawa Asanoshin　瀬川浅之進

Shibusawa Eiichi　澁沢栄一

Shidehara Kijūrō　幣原喜重郎

Shigemitsu Mamoru　重光葵

Shinagawa Yajirō　品川彌二郎

Shirai Shigeki　白井茂樹

Shiratori Toshio　白鳥敏夫

Soejima Taneomi　副島種臣

Suetsugu Nobumasa　末次信正

Sugiyama Gen　杉山元

Sun Yat-sen (I-hsien)　孫逸仙

Sung Che-yuan　宋哲元

Suzue Gen'ichi　鈴江言一

Suzuki Kantarō　鈴木貫太郎

Suzuki Sōroku　鈴木莊六

Suzuki Teiichi　鈴木貞一

Tada Shun　多田駿

Takahashi Korekiyo　高橋是清

Takahira Kogorō　高平小五郎

Takaishi Shingorō　高石眞五郎

Takamatsu no Miya Nobuhito
　(Prince Takamatsu Nobuhito)
　高松宮宣仁親王

Takamine Jōkichi　高峰譲吉

Takarabe Takeshi　財部彪

Takatsuki Tamotsu　高月保

Takeda Isao　武田功

Takezoe Shin'ichirō　竹添進一郎

Tanabe Sadayoshi　田辺定義

Tanaka Fujimaro　田中不二麿

Tanaka Giichi　田中義一

Tanaka Ryūkichi　田中隆吉

Tanaka Shin'ichi　田中新一

Taniguchi Naomi　谷口尚眞

Tatekawa Yoshitsugu　建川美次
Tejima Seiichi　手島精一
Terajima Munenori　寺島宗則
Terauchi Hisaichi　寺内寿一
Terauchi Masatake　寺内正毅
Tōgō Heihachirō　東郷平八郎
Tōgō Shigenori　東郷茂徳
Tōjō Hideki　東條英機
Tokugawa Akitake　徳川昭武
Tōmiya Kaneo　東宮鐵男
Toyoda Teijirō　豊田貞次郎
Tsuchihashi Yūitsu　土橋勇逸
Tsuji Masanobu　辻正信
Tsukada Osamu　塚田攻
Tuan Ch'i-jui　段祺瑞
Uchida Ryōhei　内田良平
Uchida Sadatsuchi　内田定槌
Uchida Yasuya (Kōsai)　内田康哉
Ueda Kenkichi　植田謙吉
Uehara Yūsaku　上原勇作
Ugaki Kazushige　宇垣一成
Usui Shigeki　臼井茂樹

Wakamatsu Tadaichi　若松只一
Wakatsuki Reijirō　若槻礼次郎
Wang Ching-wei　汪精衛
Yamada Akiyoshi　山田顯義
Yamagata Aritomo　山県有朋
Yamaguchi Iwao　山口厳
Yamamoto Gonnohyōe　山本権兵衛
　(Gombei)
Yamamoto Isoroku　山本五十六
Yamamoto Jōtarō　山本條太郎
Yamanashi Katsunoshin　山梨勝之進
Yamashita Tomoyuki　山下奉文
Yanagawa Heisuke　柳川平助
Yatabe Yasukichi　矢田部保吉
Yin Ju-ken　殷汝耕
Yonai Mitsumasa　米内光政
Yoshida Shigeru　吉田茂
Yoshida Zengo　吉田善吾
Yoshino Sakuzō　吉野作造
Yoshizawa Kenkichi　芳沢謙吉
Yuan Shih-k'ai　袁世凱
Yuri Kimimasa　由利公正

Index

❖

Abe Nobuyuki, 101; cabinet of (8/39–1/40), 226–27, 324–25, 402, 452–53

Abo Kiyokazu, navy minister under Wakatsuki (4/31–12/31), 51

Adachi Kenzō, home minister under Wakatsuki (4/31–12/31), 56

Advisory Council on Foreign Relations: established under Terauchi cabinet (1917), 30, 34; and Paris Peace Conference, 303; and Siberian Intervention, 36, 385–87 *passim*

Agriculture and Commerce, Ministry of, 250; and participation in international expositions, 161

Agriculture and Forestry, Ministry of, 250

Aizawa Seishisai, 88

Alexander, Wallace M., 172

Alliance for Nonintervention in China, 251

America-Japan Society, 180

Amō declaration, 221, 446

Amur River Society, 253

Anglo-German convention on China (1900), 286

Anglo-Japanese alliance: of 1902, 18–20, 193, 195, 196, 233, 285, 287–88, 360, 364; of 1905, 197–98, 199; of 1911, 23, 204–5, 378; bibliography on, 198–201, 218, 287–88, 361–63;

Chinese opposition to, 212; development of, 17–19, 191, 192–95, 234, 235, 283–86, 359–60; ending of, 37, 211–13, 216, 217, 233; and German-Japanese relations, 283–86; military agreement (1907), 24–25, 198; and Russo-Japanese relations, 19, 195–96, 197, 206, 241, 360–64 *passim*, 378, 379; and U.S.-Japanese relations, 204, 212, 213, 415, 429, 432; and World War I, 37, 206–8, 209, 234, 290–92, 296, 379

Anglo-Russian entente (1907), 203

Anti-Comintern Pact (November 1936), 180, 289, 334, 338; and Anglo-Japanese relations, 223–25, 229; development of, 222–23, 306–10; Italian adherence to (November 1937), 223, 315; Japan demands that China join, 313–14; public reaction in Japan to, 310–11; and Soviet-Japanese relations, 306, 309–10, 311, 383, 398–99

Aoki Norizumi, 258

Aoki Shūzō, as foreign minister (12/89–8/92, 11/98–10/1900), 195, 351, 358–59, 409; and Sino-Japanese War, 189, 274–77 *passim*, 281, 414; and treaty revision, 268, 269, 409

Aoyama Kazuo (Kuroda Zenji), 258

Araki Sadao, as army minister (12/31–1/34), 56, 62, 397, 398; and Shantung

Japan (*Continued*)

orientation in 1930s, 443–46, 447; gold embargo question in 1920s, 440–41; and Great Depression, 40, 111, 441; inflation in early Meiji, 131–37; military dominance in Far East, 39–40, 41, 43, 47, 198, 205, 234, 421; national character, 262–63; nationalism in, 15, 47, 115, 236–37, 264; participation in international expositions, 126, 160–64; policy aims in early Meiji, 3–4, 11, 118, 184–85, 236–37, 349 (*see also* Treaty revision); policy-making process in, 249–51; and railway issues in China and Manchuria, 202–3, 204, 206, 243, 376, 424, 426 (*see also* Chinese Eastern Railway); sanctions against (1938–41), 95, 229, 316, 321, 450–52, 459; specie policy in early Meiji, 121–22, 127–29, 131–40; structure of early Meiji government, 4–5; students sent abroad in early Meiji, 157–60; subordination of military to political leadership in early Meiji, 20–21, 22; and Washington Conference system, 30–31, 38–42, 54, 435–40 *passim; see also* Historiography; Treaty revision; U.S.-Japanese negotiations (1941)

—— *anti-communism and foreign policy:* China policy, 66; Siberian intervention, 389–91 *passim;* southern advance, 223–24; Soviet-Japanese relations, 389–91 *passim,* 393–96 *passim,* 399–400, 402; U.S.-Japanese relations, 430–31

—— *cultural foreign policies:* in early Meiji, 154; in 1930s, 178–82; since World War II, 182–83

—— *defense policies:* of 1907, 22–28 *passim,* 373, 375, 424; concepts of "national defense," 14, 39, 42, 62–63,

68–69, 72, 91–93; Yamagata proposal (1906), 22–23, 203; of 1922, 47, 49; after 1931, 54, 57, 68–69, 77–78, 83, 84–85, 87–88, 91–93

—— *and Nationalist government in China,* 39, 46, 59–60, 64–67, 216, 221, 245, 440, 446; during China War, 70–71, 73–78 *passim,* 87, 226–27, 248, 312–14 *passim,* 328; *see also* China: Japanese policies toward, Nationalist government in

—— *policy documents:* "Basic Principles for a Settlement of the Manchurian Problem" (August 1931), 53; "Basic Principles of National Policy" (June 1936), 68; "China Policy of the Kwantung Army" (March 1935), 65; "The Essence of National Defense and Proposals to Strengthen It" (October 1934), 62; "Essentials for Carrying Out the Policies of the Empire" (September 1941), 96; "Five-Year Plan for Production of War Matériel" (June 1937), 69; "Five-Year Program for the Development of Major Industries" (May 1937), 69; "The Foreign Policy of Imperial Japan" (August 1936), 69, 447; "Fundamental Policy for the Disposition of the China Incident" (January 1938), 76; "Fundamentals of National Policy" (August 1936), 60–61, 67, 68–69, 72, 78, 222–23, 447; "Imperial National Defense Policy" (1907), *see* Japan, defense policies; "Instructions for the Employment of Foreigners" (1870), 155; "Main Principles for Coping with the Changing World Situation" (July 1940), 84–85, 86; "One View of the China Situation" (May 1935), 65; "Order of Sending Japanese Delegates to Russia and Siberia" (February 1874), 343–44;

Tanaka Giichi: as army minister during Siberian intervention (9/18–6/21), 388, 430; cabinet of (4/27–7/29), 39, 44–46, 214–15, 244–46, 396, 438, 439; drafts defense policy (1907), 373; foreign policy of, 43–44, 436

Tanaka Ryūkichi, on army factionalism, 110

Tanaka Shin'ichi, 404; opposes southern advance policy, 89, 90, 93, 95

Tangku Truce (May 1933), 64, 65, 67

Taniguchi Naomi, as chief of Navy General Staff (1931), 51

Tatekawa Yoshitsugu: as ambassador to USSR (1940), 328, 403; and Manchurian Incident, 55

Tejima Seiichi, and Japanese participation in international expositions, 162

Terajima Munenori, concludes Washington treaty (1878), 186, 409

Terauchi Hisaichi, as army minister under Hirota (3/36–2/37), 309, 311

Terauchi Masatake: as army minister under Katsura and Saionji (3/02–8/11), 25, 26, 364, 372; cabinet of (10/16–9/18), 34–36, 244, 428–30; *see also* Lansing-Ishii agreement; Motono Ichirō; Siberian intervention

Tientsin, Treaty of (1885), 13, 15

Tientsin Residents Association, 255, 257

Tirpitz, Admiral Alfred von, 280

Tōgō Heihachirō, and naval building after World War I, 38

Tōgō Shigenori, 393; as ambassador to USSR (1939–40), 402–3; as foreign minister under Tōjō (November 1941), 333–34

Tōjō Hideki, 69, 400; as army minister under Konoe (7/40–10/41), 83, 89–90, 91, 95, 100–1, 326; cabinet of (1941), 81–82, 101–3, 229, 332, 456; *see also* Japan, decision for war (1941);

U.S.-Japanese negotiations (1941)

Tokugawa: overthrow of, 3; relations with Germany, 265–67; relations with Russia, 341–42; specie policy, 121

Tokugawa Akitake, 160, 162

Tokyo Institute of Municipal Research, 180

Tokyo Treaty Revision Conference (1882), 128

Tōmiya Kaneo, 253, 258

Tonghak rebellion (1894), 15

Toyoda Teijirō, as foreign minister under Konoe (7/41–10/41), 95, 100, 229, 330

Trade Control Office, 122

Trans-Siberian Railway, and Russo-Japanese relations, 19, 340, 350, 351, 353, 355

Trautmann, Oskar: mediation efforts in China War, 263, 313, 314; recalled, 316; *see also* China War, and German-Japanese relations

Treaty revision: bibliography on, 188, 268–69, 410–12, 425; and Britain, 127, 185–89, 200, 201, 233, 244, 268, 349, 409; as foreign policy goal of Meiji oligarchs, 3–4, 13–14, 15, 127–28, 185, 241, 267, 349; and Germany, 187, 265, 267–69; and Iwakura embassy, 156; and Japanese participation in international expositions, 161; and Russia, 187, 349, 350; and U.S., 186, 187, 268, 408–12

Tripartite Pact (1940), 180, 228, 338–39; German-Japanese relations under, 327–35; and issue of military assistance to Germany, 94; Japanese aims in, 80, 83, 88–89, 92; negotiations for (1938–39), 315–23, 450; negotiations for (1940), 83–88 *passim*, 289, 324, 325–27, 403, 455; and Soviet-Japanese relations, 327–28,

Studies of the
East Asian Institute

❖

The Ladder of Success in Imperial China, by Ping-ti Ho. New York, Columbia University Press, 1962.

The Chinese Inflation, 1937–1949, by Shun-hsin Chou. New York, Columbia University Press, 1963.

Reformer in Modern China: Chang Chien, 1853–1926, by Samuel Chu. New York, Columbia University Press, 1965.

Research in Japanese Sources: A Guide, by Herschel Webb with the assistance of Marleigh Ryan. New York, Columbia University Press, 1965.

Society and Education in Japan, by Herbert Passin. New York, Bureau of Publications, Teachers College, Columbia University, 1965.

Agricultural Production and Economic Development in Japan, 1873–1922, by James I. Nakamura. Princeton, Princeton University Press, 1966.

Japan's First Modern Novel: Ukigumo of Futabatei Shimei, by Marleigh Ryan. New York, Columbia University Press, 1967.

The Korean Communist Movement, 1918–1948, by Dae-Sook Suh. Princeton, Princeton University Press, 1967.

The First Vietnam Crisis, by Melvin Gurtov. New York, Columbia University Press, 1967.

Cadres, Bureaucracy, and Political Power in Communist China, by A. Doak Barnett. New York, Columbia University Press, 1967.

The Japanese Imperial Institution in the Tokugawa Period, by Herschel Webb. New York, Columbia University Press, 1968.

Higher Education and Business Recruitment in Japan, by Koya Azumi. New York, Teachers College Press, Columbia University, 1969.

The Communists and Chinese Peasant Rebellions: A Study in the Rewriting of Chinese History, by James P. Harrison, Jr. New York, Atheneum, 1969.

How the Conservatives Rule Japan, by Nathaniel B. Thayer. Princeton, Princeton University Press, 1969.

Aspects of Chinese Education, edited by C.T. Hu. New York, Teachers College Press, Columbia University, 1969.

Studies of the East Asian Institute

Documents of Korean Communism, 1918–1948, by Dae-Sook Suh. Princeton, Princeton University Press, 1970.

Japanese Education: A Bibliography of Materials in the English Language, by Herbert Passin. New York, Teachers College Press, Columbia University, 1970.

Economic Development and the Labor Market in Japan, by Koji Taira. New York, Columbia University Press, 1970.

The Japanese Oligarchy and the Russo-Japanese War, by Shumpei Okamoto. New York, Columbia University Press, 1970.

Imperial Restoration in Medieval Japan, by H. Paul Varley. New York, Columbia University Press, 1971.

Japan's Postwar Defense Policy, 1947–1968, by Martin E. Weinstein. New York, Columbia University Press, 1971.

Election Campaigning Japanese Style, by Gerald L. Curtis. New York, Columbia University Press, 1971.

China and Russia: The "Great Game," by O. Edmund Clubb. New York, Columbia University Press, 1971.

Money and Monetary Policy in Communist China, by Katharine Huang Hsiao. New York, Columbia University Press, 1971.

The District Magistrate in Late Imperial China, by John R. Watt. New York, Columbia University Press, 1972.

Law and Policy in China's Foreign Relations: A Study of Attitudes and Practice, by James C. Hsiung. New York, Columbia University Press, 1972.

Japan's Foreign Policy, 1868–1941: A Research Guide, edited by James William Morley. New York, Columbia University Press, 1974.

Japanese Culture: A Short History, by H. Paul Varley. New York, Praeger, 1973.

Doctors in Politics: The Political Life of the Japan Medical Association, by William E. Steslicke. New York, Praeger, 1973.

Teachers and Politics in Japan, by Donald Ray Thurston. Princeton, Princeton University Press, 1973.

Pearl Harbor as History: Japanese-American Relations, 1931–1941, edited by Dorothy Borg and Shumpei Okamoto, with the assistance of Dale K.A. Finlayson. New York, Columbia University Press, 1973.

Palace and Politics in Prewar Japan, by David Anson Titus. New York, Columbia University Press, 1973.

The Idea of China: Essays in Geographic Myth and Theory, by Andrew March. Devon, England, David & Charles, 1974.